America's National Wildlife Refuges

America's National Wildlife Refuges

A Complete Guide

Second Edition

RUSSELL D. BUTCHER

With contributions by
Stephen E. Adair and Lynn A. Greenwalt

Photographs by
JOHN AND KAREN HOLLINGSWORTH
(except as otherwise credited)

Foreword by
DAN ASHE
Former Chief, National Wildlife Refuge System
U.S. Fish and Wildlife Service

Taylor Trade Publishing
Lanham • New York • Boulder • Toronto • Plymouth, UK

Published by Taylor Trade Publishing
An imprint of The Rowman & Littlefield Publishing Group, Inc.
4501 Forbes Boulevard, Suite 200, Lanham, Maryland 20706
www.rlpgtrade.com

Estover Road, Plymouth PL6 7PY, United Kingdom

Distributed by NATIONAL BOOK NETWORK

Library of Congress Cataloging-in-Publication Data
Butcher, Russell D.
   America's national wildlife refuges : a complete guide / Butcher, Russell D. ; With contributions by
Stephen E. Adair and Lynn A. Greenwalt ; Photographs by John and Karen Hollingsworth ; foreword by
Dan Ashe. — 2nd ed.
      p. cm.
   Includes bibliographical references and index.
   ISBN-13: 978-1-58979-383-5 (pbk. : alk. paper)
   ISBN-10: 1-58979-383-8 (pbk. : alk. paper)
   ISBN-13: 978-1-58979-410-8 (electronic)
   ISBN-10: 1-58979-410-9 (electronic)
   1. Wildlife refuges—United States—Guidebooks. 2. United States—Guidebooks. I. Title.
QL84.2.B88 2008
333.95'4160973—dc22

                                                                                      2008032853

∞ ™ The paper used in this publication meets the minimum requirements of
American National Standard for Information Sciences—Permanence of
Paper for Printed Library Materials, ANSI/NISO Z39.48–1992.
Manufactured in the United States of America.

TO

All of the employees, researchers, interns, volunteers, and donors

who are helping to make the

National Wildlife Refuge System

a priceless American treasure.

Contents

Author's Note

Writing this book on all of the nearly 550 units of the National Wildlife Refuge System that totals more than 95 million acres has been an awesome but totally inspiring and fascinating endeavor. One of the special pleasures of the task was my conversations with literally hundreds of refuge system personnel. From all across America, I have sensed a tremendous depth of caring and commitment that these men and women bring to their tasks, as they strive to protect and enhance refuge habitats and wildlife populations. I have glimpsed how much they cherish a feeling of family with their dedicated colleagues throughout the refuge system. And I have heard again and again how much they value the generous assistance and hard work of numerous volunteers, interns, and partners, with whom so much is accomplished on the refuges that would otherwise be unattainable.

The National Wildlife Refuge System contains an almost mind-boggling diversity of wildlife and habitats. Each refuge, no matter how large or small, has an important role to play within America's overall program of wildlife conservation. Many refuges offer interpretive and educational programs, from which visitors can learn about and better appreciate the wildlife, habitats, ecological processes, and refuge management activities.

Each refuge, including the few that are closed to public visitation, is described in this volume. In the approximately 200 featured refuge texts, I have tried to provide at least some insight into what types of habitat-management activities are occurring and why. The more than 300 remaining refuges, including a few new ones established since this book's first edition, are described more briefly. To save a bit of space at the start of each text, only the refuge name is given without its National Wildlife Refuge designation, unless the designation differs from the norm. Not described in this revised edition are the more than 30 wetland management districts that are mostly in the northern Great Plains region—the majority of which are managed under perpetual conservation easement agreements with private landowners. Within these ease-ment districts, there are also more than 36,000 federally owned waterfowl production areas, ranging in size from 0.1 acre to 7,468 acres. Most of the WPAs are open to visitation.

To obtain more information on an individual refuge or other area, enter the name in your Internet provider's search window. To view a system-wide map, enter America's National Wildlife Refuge System, click on that heading, and click on <u>Map</u>.

The National Wildlife Refuge System offers valuable insight into what Native Americans have known for thousands of years: how critically important it is not to lose sight of the *inter-connectedness* of all life on Earth. It is especially important for us, as the world's most powerful and influential species, to view ourselves as not separate from but an integral part of the natu-ral environment and its long-evolved, life-supporting ecological processes. We are responsible for maintaining the health and wholeness of the life-sustaining environment around us. How well we are managing and protecting this heritage of America's National Wildlife Refuges is ul-timately an indication of how well we are protecting ourselves.

—*Russell D. Butcher*
Tucson, Arizona
January 2008

Acknowledgments

There is no way to adequately express my gratitude to all of the hundreds of national wildlife refuge personnel who provided research materials and who then reviewed each refuge description for accuracy. Without their enthusiastic assistance, I would not have even presumed to undertake the writing of this book. I am especially grateful to all those who provided quotable statements about some particular aspect of their refuges and to those who wrote the entire text for a refuge. My thanks as well to those who so generously contributed other parts of the book: Dan Ashe for his foreword; Lynn Greenwalt for his chapter on the history of the National Wildlife Refuge System; and Steve Adair for his chapter on America's vanishing wetlands. I am hugely grateful to Karen Hollingsworth for all of the many magnificent photographs that she and her late husband, John Hollingsworth, have taken over a period of many years, and to a number of U.S. Fish and Wildlife Service staff and others who provided photographs (these are credited to them throughout the book). I am extremely grateful for the cooperation of Ducks Unlimited, Inc. in the publication of this book. My thanks to Rick Rinehart and Dulcie Wilcox of Taylor Trade for publishing this book as well as two earlier volumes on the National Park System, and to Toni Knapp and Raven Amerman for their outstanding editing assistance. I would also like to thank Stephen Driver, Piper Furbush, Rebecca Olson, Dolly Eversole, Ollie Harmon-Gibbons, Jeremy Hite, Jason Rock, and Alden Perkins for their contributions.

These acknowledgments would not be complete without expressing gratitude to my parents, Mary and Devereux Butcher, for encouraging me to see and value the wonders and beauty of nature and for sharing with me some of their travels to and enthusiasm for the National Wildlife Refuge System many years ago as they were writing their book, *Exploring Our National Wildlife Refuges*. And I am lovingly grateful to my wife, Karen, for her supportive encouragement and help in this challenging book-writing endeavor.

—*Russ Butcher*

Foreword

We all like to be in on something secret. It's a privilege. Something special, held between people with a common interest or bond. In Russ Butcher's new book—*America's National Wildlife Refuges*—he shares some very special secrets with those of us who savor precious days afield in wild places and among wild things. As Chief of the National Wildlife Refuge System, I know the system is a treasure chest full of opportunity to get outdoors and experience the wonder, diversity, and beauty of our nation's wildlife heritage. But it remains one of the best-kept secrets among our nation's legacy of public lands. This book is your key to unlocking that treasure chest, and your gateway to some of the greatest spectacles that our nation has to offer.

Anyone who knows the secret of experiencing wildlife in wild places knows that timing is everything. Visiting one of our refuges at the wrong time of year might elicit a remark like "Nice house, but nobody was home." Being in the right place at the right time is an essential part of the secret shared in Russ Butcher's book. Take this book, mix with a pinch of that precious commodity that we call "time," and add some well-chosen and hopefully familiar gear like binoculars, good boots or waders, and perhaps a fishing rod or shotgun, and get outdoors! To really spice up the experience, add some family members or a good friend or two. This is a recipe guaranteed to reduce stress, strengthen families and friendships, and make great memories.

As I read through the entries in his book, my mind's eye focused on some of my most memorable days afield in the refuge system. Days in places like Blackbeard Island, Bosque del Apache, Kodiak, Tamarac, Monomoy, Klamath, and Bear River. I remember the solitude of an empty beach, the noise of thousands of geese and cranes, the grandeur of a bald eagle in flight, and the explosion of color from wild lupines blooming in the high desert. I remember days with my father, mother, and brothers; days with my wife and children; mornings and evenings with hunting buddies and a yellow Labrador retriever named Bo. This book holds promise and provides the information that we all can use to take advantage of the opportunity within our National Wildlife Refuge System.

Thanks to Russ Butcher and *America's National Wildlife Refuges*, you are now in on one of our nation's best-kept secrets. Use it to discover a refuge near you. With more than 530 "franchises," there is always one close by. If you like what you see, let other people know. Come back again and again, and consider becoming a refuge volunteer or joining a refuge Friends organization. There's lots more to discover.

—Dan Ashe, Former Chief
National Wildlife Refuge System

Prelude

President Theodore Roosevelt created our first National Wildlife Refuge in 1903. That was a time when thousands of herons, egrets, and other birds were being killed by market hunters who wanted their feathers to sell for women's hat decorations. Many kinds of birds were threatened with extinction because of a fashion trend. . . .

Today, Refuges are home to more than 700 species of birds and 800 species of mammals, reptiles, amphibians, and fish, including over 170 threatened or endangered species. More than 55 Refuges have been set aside specifically to protect species that are faced with extinction. Each Refuge is beautiful and vital in its own right. Each is a place where wildlife is protected. And many Refuges welcome people to enjoy the wonders and mysteries of nature. All it takes is one visit to understand why a Refuge is a place that matters—where wild things and their habitats are protected and preserved as part of our natural heritage.

People who work on Refuges are dedicated professionals who often work long hours in all kinds of weather performing a wide variety of tasks. A primary goal of Refuges is to provide the best possible habitat in order to fulfill the requirements of wildlife that live there. Employees actively manage Refuge lands, by changing water levels to improve wetland habitat, setting controlled fires or grazing livestock to improve pasture, farming with crops used by wildlife, and removing pest plants that out-compete desirable plants. Employees maintain facilities for the public, such as roads and historic structures, trail and observation facilities, and provide educational and interpretive information. Many employees have specialized education, training, and experience from many Refuges throughout the country, a background that is crucial when making improvements to the way Refuge lands are managed in order to increase wildlife populations. Life is not just out counting birds!

—Rich Guadagno
(Sept. 26, 1962–Sept. 11, 2001)

1

America's Vanishing Wetlands

Stephen E. Adair, Ph.D., Director, Great Plains Regional Office, Ducks Unlimited, Inc.

Today, wetlands are widely recognized as some of the most productive and valuable ecosystems on Earth. But that has not always been the case. Up until the 1960s, most Americans viewed wetlands as wastelands that were in the way of progress. The map on page 2, produced in 1919 and entitled "Wet Lands in Need of Drainage," is a vivid reminder of this historic perception.

When Europeans first arrived on America's shorelines, they found an abundance of wild lands and wildlife never before imagined in their homeland. Even discounting the astounding claims of early settlers—who perhaps embellished the abundance to encourage more immigration—ducks, geese, deer, turkeys, rabbits, pigeons, fish, and shellfish teemed in the wetlands and forests and were there for the taking.

As Captain John Smith wrote of Virginia:

The rivers became so covered with swans, geese, ducks, and cranes that we daily feasted with good bread, Virginia pease, pumpkins and putchamins [persimmons], fish, fowle and diverse sors of wild beasts, so fat as we could eate them (from *Eating in America: A History*, by W. L. and R. de Rochemont Root; New York: Ecco Press, 1976).

Although these abundant fish and wildlife populations provided important sustenance, most early settlers viewed these resources as unlimited and set out to change the landscape to support agriculture and accommodate a growing human population. Conquering the frontier also meant taming the land. The vast forests of New England and the Great Lakes region were cut down, and the lands converted for agriculture. Prairie grasslands were plowed under. Wetlands were drained and converted to farming lands. This wave of change marched westward, transforming the landscape into what were believed to be more beneficial uses.

While many early Americans were busy draining wetlands on their own initiative, the U.S. Department of Agriculture offered financial incentives to farmers to "reclaim" wetlands and convert them to productive farmland. Millions of acres of prairie potholes were tiled (a type of underground pipe that has small gaps in it) and drained to increase crop production. The U.S. Army Corps of Engineers drained and isolated many floodplains wetlands in their efforts to improve navigation, flood control, water supplies, and hydroelectric power on most of the nation's rivers. Coastal wetlands were dredged and filled for navigation, land development, and to control diseases carried by mosquitoes.

In 1849, Congress passed the Swamp Land Act, which granted the states control over swamplands to control flooding, thereby encouraging wetland elimination. Most Americans had little understanding of or concern for the inherent values that wetlands offered them. A small but significant conservation voice began to emerge from the woods of New England in Henry David Thoreau. But still, in the eyes of most, a good wetland was a drained wetland. These prevailing attitudes and programs led to the loss and degradation of nearly 50 percent of the original wetlands in the lower 48 states by the mid-1900s. The majority of these early wetland losses were for conversion to agricultural production, but urbanization in the form of industry, housing, and roads was also taking its toll.

The end of the Civil War began the transformation of America from a rural to an industrial nation, essentially marking the end of the American frontier. America's population was now clustered in the large urban areas of the Northeast and Midwest, far removed from the source of their food, water, and fiber, and largely employed in industry instead of agriculture. Growing markets for food and fiber accelerated the loss of America's wetlands, forests, and grasslands and of the fish and wildlife that depended on them for survival. Within states, drainage districts began to form, accelerating wetland drainage even further.

However, in the 1920s, public agencies and private organizations began to elevate the awareness of wetland loss and to take positive steps to slow it. The Migratory Bird Conservation Act of 1929 authorized the federal government to acquire wetlands and associated uplands and to preserve them as waterfowl habitat. The law also established a commission of federal and state officials to evaluate land for possible acquisition, and in so doing it established the National Wildlife Refuge System.

Although the Migratory Bird Conservation Act was an important step for wetland conservation, it provided no permanent source of funding to purchase wetlands. Largely due to the lobbying efforts of Jay N. Darling, a nationally known political cartoonist and the chief of the Bureau of Biological Survey, President Franklin Delano Roosevelt signed the Migratory Bird Hunting Stamp Act in 1934. All waterfowl hunters 16 years of age and older were required under the Act to buy a Migratory Bird Hunting Stamp. Funds from stamps would be used to pay for acquisition and protection of wetlands and other important waterfowl habitats. Some 635 thousand hunters paid $1.00 each for the first stamps, which went on sale August 22, 1934. Since then, the price has gradually risen to the current $15.00. Today, approximately 1.5 million stamps are sold each year. Federal Duck Stamps have generated close to $600 million, which has been used to preserve nearly 5 million acres of wetlands and associated uplands in the United States. Many of the more than 530 National Wildlife Refuges have been paid for either entirely or in part with federal Duck Stamp revenues.

Within the private sector, a small group of sportsmen, concerned with the decline of waterfowl populations along the Atlantic Coast, formed the More Game Birds in America Foundation in 1930. One of the most ambitious early efforts of the Foundation was the inaugural International Wild Duck Census in 1935 that covered most of Canada and the northern United States. Results of surveys such as this led the Foundation to conclude that, unless prompt action was taken to preserve breeding ground wetlands, the future of waterfowl and waterfowl hunting in the United States was in jeopardy. In light of these results, members of More Game Birds and its counterpart, American Wild Fowlers, rallied together to form Ducks Unlimited (DU), which was incorporated in Washington, D.C. on January 29, 1937. DU founders formed committees in each state to begin raising funds in the United States and send them to Canada to protect and restore large, permanent wetlands, nicknamed duck factories.

Despite the positive strides of these early conservation efforts, the magnitude of change that had been forced on the landscape was fully revealed during the Great Depression or "Dust Bowl" of the 1930s. For decades, homesteaders, farmers, ranchers, and entrepreneurs in the West and Midwest had unwittingly caused the erosion and instability of much of the nation's topsoil. Clear-cutting of forests, overgrazing of grasslands, draining and filling of wetlands, and poor cropping practices had exposed the soil to the powerful forces of wind and water. The drought that savaged the country in the 1930s forced the recognition that even with the conservation progress to date, America's lands and the wildlife that depended on them were threatened with destruction.

After a difficult legislative battle, the Federal Aid in Wildlife Restoration Act (Pittman–Robertson Act) was passed in 1937. The Act created an 11 percent excise tax on rifles, shotguns, and ammunition and a 10 percent tax on handguns. Revenues from the tax were collected in federal coffers and then passed through the U.S. Fish and Wildlife Service to state fish and wildlife agencies. Over the life of the program, 62 percent of federal aid grants have been used to protect and enhance nearly 20 million acres of state wildlife management areas, many of them wetlands. These state-owned lands add a critical component of biodiversity to America's landscape. In addition to acquisition of public lands, federal aid funds were also used to secure management agreements and leases to protect and enhance important wildlife habitats. There are now nearly 60 million acres, many of them wetlands, across the country that are managed for wildlife under agreements with private and corporate landowners.

The establishment of dedicated federal conservation funding and the advocacy and implementation of private organizations undoubtedly slowed wetland loss rates. But other programs, such as the U.S. Department of Agriculture's Agricultural Conservation Program and the Great Depression–era Works Progress Administration, continued to promote and fund wetland drainage. The first rigorous scientific studies of wetland losses conducted by the U.S. Fish and Wildlife Service revealed an alarming annual wetland loss rate of 458 thousand acres per year from the mid-1950s to the mid-1970s.

During the 1950s and 1960s, American concern for the environment was elevated to new levels. Aldo Leopold's *A Sand County Almanac* and Rachel Carson's *Silent Spring* urged Americans to think in terms of living with nature instead of conquering it. In the early 1970s, wetland scientists began to identify and quantify the many ecological values of wetland ecosystems. Evidence began to accumulate suggesting that wetlands were not only important as habitats for fish and wildlife populations, but they also stored and slowed floodwaters, thereby reducing property damage. In addition, evidence began to reveal that many wetlands discharge water into subsurface aquifers that support municipalities and agricultural operations; that wetlands stabilize shorelines and protect them from storm erosion; that wetlands purify water by removing sediments and nutrients; that many wetlands store large volumes of carbon and consequently help mitigate atmospheric concentrations of carbon dioxide; that wetlands provide economically important products like timber and commercial finfish and shellfish; and that wetlands are important venues for recreation and tourism, helping to generate millions of dollars in annual revenue. Increased understanding of these functions and values translated into more federal laws and policies to protect wetlands.

In 1972, the Federal Water Pollution Control Act (Clean Water Act) was passed by Congress, giving the U.S. Army Corps of Engineers, under Section 404 of the Act, the authority to establish a permitting process to regulate the dredging and filling of materials into waters of the United States. At first, the Corps applied this authority narrowly to include only navigable waters, but later court rulings extended this authority to almost all wetlands. Although the majority of wetland permits applied for have been approved by the Corps, perhaps the greatest value of Section 404 of the Clean Water Act has been as a deterrent to developers to avoid wetlands and the required mitigation process.

The Coastal Zone Management Act of 1972 provided funding to the states to develop coastal management plans that included wetland protection. President Jimmy Carter issued two executive orders in May 1977 that made the protection of wetlands, riparian areas, and floodplains a priority of each agency of the federal government. These orders were a landmark, because they established a review of wetland and floodplain policies by all federal agencies. Subsequent to federal wetland protection legislation, some states, primarily those with coastlines, enacted their own wetland protection laws. The USFWS found evidence of progress in reducing wetland loss in its updated wetland status report, which found an annual loss rate of 290 thousand acres from the mid-1970s to the mid-1980s—a decline of 37 percent from previous decades.

Conservationists increased their lobbying efforts for governmental programs that provided new funding to protect and restore large areas of wetlands and associated uplands. The Food Security Act of 1985 (Farm Bill) authorized 45 million acres of marginal cropland to be converted to grasslands and forests in order to slow soil erosion through the Conservation Reserve Program (CRP), but the impacts were much more far-reaching. Restored grasslands began to capture the sediments that were filling wetland basins and to reduce the runoff of nutrients, herbicides, and pesticides into wetlands. Populations of many wetland species, such as waterfowl, shorebirds, and some songbirds that nest in uplands adjacent to wetlands, began to improve.

The Swampbuster Provision of the 1985 Farm Bill provided increased federal protection of small wetlands in the predominantly agricultural Midwest, Northern Great Plains, and Southern High Plains. Although often incorrectly viewed as a regulatory program, Swampbuster actually offers a disincentive for wetland drainage by withholding USDA payments from farmers who destroy wetlands in order to grow a commodity crop. Farmers still have the option either to drain wetlands for commodity crops and forgo USDA payments or to drain wetlands for other uses. However, given the reliance of most farming operations on USDA subsidies, Swampbuster has been a very effective deterrent to wetland drainage.

During the 1980s, drought returned to the northern prairies, causing wetland numbers and waterfowl populations to plummet. As concern over depressed waterfowl populations grew, a consortium of public and private organizations, including the USFWS, state game and fish agencies, Ducks Unlimited, and university scientists, joined together in 1986 to formulate the North American Waterfowl Management Plan (NAWMP), a blueprint for recovery of waterfowl populations to 1970s levels. The 1986 Plan was signed by Canada and the United States and contained a Strategy for Cooperation, emphasizing the importance of a partnership approach to conserve habitats, improve scientific understanding, and periodically evaluate and update the Plan. Given the complex problems facing waterfowl and wetlands across the North American continent, the NAWMP partners concluded that the most effective means of securing the future of waterfowl populations was to improve land use practices on a landscape level. To achieve this objective, broad partnerships were formed between conservation organizations, private landowners, and state and federal wildlife agencies.

As public interest and funding grew for wetlands conservation, scientists began focusing more of their efforts on understanding the structure and function of habitats important to wildlife. Early works found that a diverse array of wetland types were necessary to meet waterfowl habitat requirements, both in breeding and wintering areas. Some of the most productive wetlands for wildlife were the shallowest basins, which went dry periodically and which supported rich plant communities. Unfortunately, these were the same sites that were the easiest to drain and were being lost disproportionately from the landscape.

Waterfowl biologists were becoming increasingly aware that waterfowl populations could not be maintained solely on public land, but that entire landscapes need to be preserved to meet all of the birds' habitat requirements. National Wildlife Refuges and State Wildlife Management Areas began to be viewed as core areas around which to secure wetlands and uplands, creating larger sustainable landscapes.

Wetland ecologists also began to gather evidence suggesting that wetlands could not be preserved just by protecting their boundaries. Adjacent lands must also be set aside to prevent sediments, human activity, pollutants, and nutrient-laden runoff from destroying important wetland functions. The source of water to many wetlands was found to exist beyond the wetland boundaries in shallow streams or aquifers that were recharged at upper reaches of watersheds. This understanding led to increased cooperation with farmers and ranchers to make their agricultural operations more environmentally friendly through practices such as no-till cropping, rotational grazing systems, watershed protection practices, and winter flooding of harvested agricultural fields. Long-term protection of the natural resources of private lands also began to increase through the use of conservation easements, leases, and management agreements.

In 1989, President George Bush introduced a policy of "no net loss," instructing federal agencies to achieve a zero wetland balance sheet. In that same year, the Congress and the Bush administration provided an incentive for NAWMP partners in the United States, Canada, and Mexico to accelerate efforts for conserving waterfowl and other migratory birds through passage of the North American Wetlands Conservation Act (NAWCA). NAWCA's grant program provided a funding mechanism for conservation partners throughout North America. Since 1989, NAWCA has provided $269 million in federal funds, which has been more than matched by $966 million from nonfederal partners, to conserve 2.8 million acres of wetlands and associated uplands.

The 1990 Farm Bill established the Wetlands Reserve Program (WRP), which authorized that nearly 1 million acres of marginal cropland be restored to wetlands. Farmers frustrated with chronic failures to grow crops on flood-prone land for low-priced commodities quickly filled this program. Wetlands across America have been restored under this program, many protected with permanent easements. The Farm Service Agency (FSA) and the Natural Resources Conservation Service (formerly the Soil Conservation Service), which had spent many years promoting wetland drainage and plowing of grasslands, suddenly became two of the strongest forces in the country for wetland and grassland conservation.

NAWMP partners also expanded from their traditional focus on public lands to outreach and incentives to private landowners. Rice growers across California, the Gulf Coast, and the Mississippi alluvial valley began flooding their harvested fields in winter and restoring wetlands in marginal cropland areas, to improve their farming operations and to enhance habitat for waterfowl and other wetland birds. Dedicated conservationists across the country began to voluntarily restrict the development rights on their private property in perpetuity, under the terms of donated conservation easements. According to the Land Trust Alliance, this movement has led to the voluntary protection of 6.2 million acres of land through the year 2000, with 2.6 million of these acres in permanent conservation easements. Wetlands were listed as the primary focus of the 1,263 land trusts currently in existence.

Expanding research and landscape modeling efforts through such tools as Geographic Information Systems (GIS) also began facilitating strategic placement of conservation projects in areas most limiting to wildlife populations and most threatened by habitat destruction. Beginning in 1994, wet weather finally returned to the drought-stricken Northern prairies, and the efforts of NAWMP partners to restore wetland basins and provide expansive upland nesting cover, through programs such as the Conservation Reserve Program, allowed waterfowl populations to rebound to new, record levels.

Also during that year, NAWMP was updated and became a truly continental effort when Mexico joined Canada and the United States as a signatory. In 1998, NAWMP was again updated under the theme of "Expanding the Vision." The revised plan recognized that waterfowl conservation was becoming more linked with and affected by a broad range of social and economic policies, as well as by a growing interest in conservation of other wildlife—all requiring international strategies. During the first 14 years of NAWMP, thousands of partners representing diverse interests invested more than $1.5 billion to conserve more than 5 million acres of wetlands and associated uplands, to improve habitats not only for waterfowl but also for other birds, mammals, fish, amphibians, and plants. These efforts have helped sustain this continent's rich biological diversity and have contributed to flood control, water purification, and atmospheric gas regulation.

Interest in wetland conservation has remained strong among sportsmen and sportswomen as well as among a growing number of wildlife watchers, which has boosted Ducks Unlimited's membership to more than 750 thousand, helped raise annual revenue to more than $150 million, and provided for the annual conservation of more than 500 thousand acres of wildlife habitat. Since its inception in 1937, DU has raised more than $1.2 billion, which has helped DU and its partners protect, restore, or enhance more than 10 million acres of wetlands and associated uplands across North America.

Many other public and private organizations now have some level of wetland conservation programs. The USDA Forest Service has increased its efforts in wetland conservation through its Taking Wings and Large Watershed initiatives. The Environmental Protection Agency has vigilantly guarded against wetland destruction and degradation through its authority to control water pollution. The Nature Conservancy has been especially successful in protecting many unique wetland types across the country, through its Last Great Places campaign. Many other nonprofit organizations, too numerous to list, have expended significant resources lobbying for legislation and entering into litigation to protect wetlands.

Because most of the early conservationists were sportsmen, waterfowl naturally served as the banner under which the majority of historic wetland conservation was accomplished. However, numerous other wildlife species have benefited both directly and indirectly from sportsmen-generated funding. Wildlife management areas purchased with federal aid funds and wetlands acquired through federal Duck Stamp funds support myriad fish and wildlife species. An estimated one-third of the nation's endangered and threatened species, for example, find food or shelter in National Wildlife Refuges acquired with Duck Stamp revenues. Swallow-tailed kites and Louisiana black bears, both endangered species, require large blocks of bottomland hardwood wetlands—exactly the kind of habitat that public and private conservation partners have been protecting and restoring in the Mississippi alluvial valley. Sharp-tailed and seaside sparrows nesting along the northeastern Atlantic coast require coastal marshes to successfully reproduce—exactly the same kind of habitat that NAWMP partners have been working to restore. Pacific salmon require floodplain wetlands as nursery grounds for juvenile fish to survive—exactly the same kind of habitats being restored for waterfowl in the Pacific Northwest. Increased recognition that wetland habitat is the common denominator for healthy populations of numerous fish and wildlife species has the potential to elevate conservation efforts by bringing new funds and expertise to on-the-ground efforts historically carried out by sportsmen and the public fish and wildlife agencies.

During the 1990s, multidisciplinary research teams began looking at wetlands not only for their ecological value, but also for their economic value. These efforts have led to increased documentation of the monetary significance of the functions provided by wetlands. A 9,000-acre wetland complex along the main stem of the Charles River in Massachusetts has been valued at $17 million per year, which is the estimated cost of flood damage that would occur if the wetlands were drained. A 550-thousand-acre freshwater wetland in Florida has been valued at $25 million per year for the water it recharges to an aquifer providing for municipal and agricultural needs. Wetland drainage and cultivation has released large quantities of carbon dioxide into the atmosphere, compounding the emissions from the burning of fossil fuels, and remedial actions to reduce carbon dioxide emissions could potentially cost the United States economy $10–$100 billion. New York City recently avoided spending $3–$8 billion on new water treatment plants by investing $1.5 billion to acquire and protect wetlands and associated uplands in their upstream watershed that naturally purify water sources.

Coastal wetlands provide critical nursery grounds for juvenile crabs, shrimp, and salmon, whose harvest value when they reach adulthood has been estimated at $15 million per year in the United States alone. Waterfowl hunters, wildlife watchers, and recreational fishers spend $60 billion annually in the United States pursuing their passions, often focusing their efforts on wetlands or associated habitats. Clearly, wetlands are vital not only to our recreational interests, but also to our economy and to the sustainability of America's resources.

Today, increased scientific understanding of wetlands, increased public and private conservation funding, and improved cooperation among diverse landowners and land use interests have resulted in the annual wetland loss rate slowing to 58,500 acres between 1986 and 1997. This is a reduction of 87 percent from losses during the 1950s to 1970s and 80 percent from losses during the 1970s and 1980s. However, this lower rate is a little misleading, as the vegetated wetlands that are the most important to fish and wildlife, water quality, and other valuable functions continue to be lost at a rate of 109 thousand acres per year. Open-water wetlands associated with agriculture, surface mining, and urban developments are increasing, but these fail to provide the full suite of ecological functions provided by large, diverse complexes of vegetated wetlands.

Despite progress in significantly slowing wetland loss in the United States over the past 50 years, our country has lost 115 million acres of the original 221 million acres that existed in the conterminous United States at the time of the country's settlement. Large-scale environmental problems, caused in part by historic wetland losses, persist and threaten the sustainability of our economy and our quality of life. Deterioration of water quality continues in many rivers and estuaries, affecting human drinking sources, recreational activities, and valuable commercial fisheries. In 2001, the hypoxic or low-oxygen zone in the Gulf of Mexico reached record size—8,006 square miles, which is the size of Massachusetts. (A hypoxic zone is an area of depleted oxygen in which organisms cannot survive.) Scientists have recommended that part of the solution to this nutrient loading (an overenrichment of nutrients that causes a large population explosion of plankton, which in turn results in the depletion of oxygen in the water) of nearshore Gulf waters is the restoration of 24 million acres of wetlands and riparian areas along the Mississippi River watershed, to filter nitrogen and phosphorus from agricultural and industrial runoff.

Although the arid West has been plagued with chronic water shortages, during the past several years, such normally wetter states as Illinois, Florida, Georgia, Texas, Kansas, and several New England states are confronted with projections of serious water shortages during the next decade. In many cases, wetland restorations to recharge groundwater aquifers will be an important part of the solution. Loss of wetlands, which function as sponges to absorb floodwaters, has caused increased flooding of valuable cropland and residential areas, causing billions of dollars in damage and affecting the lives of thousands of people. The 1993 floods along the Mississippi River, which have been linked to wetland loss, caused $12–16 billion in property damages. Conservationists continue to be faced with declines in populations of wetland-dependent species, such as northern pintails, lesser scaup, clapper rails, swallow-tailed kites, piping plovers, cerulean warblers, sharp-tailed sparrows, blue crabs, and Pacific salmon, just to name a few.

In addition to these issues of chronic water quality, catastrophic flooding, and declining biodiversity caused by past wetland losses, new threats have emerged. Recent studies by the USFWS show that, for the first time since surveys began, the majority of wetland loss is now due to urban and rural development. Given that the human population in the United States is expected to increase from 285 million to 413 million by the year 2050, pressures to convert wetlands to infrastructure to support this growing human population will certainly increase. There is growing international consensus suggesting that increased levels of greenhouse gases in the atmosphere caused by the burning of fossil fuels, clearing of forests, and draining of wetlands are contributing to global warming and rising of the sea level. Climate change models consistently predict accelerated sea level rise and increased frequency of midcontinent drought, which pose new threats to an already declining wetland base.

On January 9, 2001, the U.S. Supreme Court issued a decision in the case *Solid Waste Agency of Northern Cook County v. United States Army Corps of Engineers*. The Supreme Court ruled that the jurisdiction of the Corps included only "navigable waters, their tributaries, and wetlands that are adjacent to these navigable waterways and tributaries." From the Court's perspective, the Corps could not assert jurisdiction over isolated wetlands based on commerce related to migratory birds. This decision will likely increase the loss and degradation of isolated wetlands across the country. Lobbying efforts by many special interest groups continue to eliminate wetland regulations and policies, in order to streamline housing and industrial development. Obviously our work in wetland conservation is far from over. We must remain mindful that history has a way of repeating itself, with future generations sometimes having to relearn the lessons of the past. Aldo Leopold's guidance remains timeless:

Civilization is a state of mutual and interdependent cooperation between human animals, other animals, plants, and soils, which may be disrupted at any moment by the failure of any of them.

If we are going to make progress resolving these complex issues facing America during the new millennium, we must move into an era of not just slowing or eliminating net wetland loss, but of actually achieving a net gain. Achieving this progress requires us to think bigger and broader. Our National Wildlife Refuges have given us a critical foundation on which to build. These lands serve as cornerstones for conservation efforts, but by themselves they are not sufficient to sustain wildlife populations, water quality, and other valuable wetland functions at the levels expected by the majority of the American people. Without increased habitat conservation, especially on private lands, which contain 75 percent of our nation's remaining wetlands, the populations of fish and wildlife—and even humans—face a very uncertain future.

We must not only continue to provide funding for federal wetland acquisition and legislation, but must also seek new incentives for the private sector to contribute to larger conservation efforts. The most visionary and significant advances in wetland conservation will likely be achieved through legislation and private programs that provide landowners with increased options for voluntary, incentive-based conservation and allow them to stay on the land and work the land for both their benefit and that of society. Broader partnerships are needed with the growing number of wildlife watchers and nature-based tourists, to provide opportunities for increased financial contributions and political support for on-the-ground wetland conservation. Conservation efforts must continue to be based on the most recent scientific findings, so that efforts are strategically directed to the most critical habitats, to achieve population and biodiversity goals.

Finally, the National Wildlife Refuge System and many State Wildlife Management Areas have faced chronic shortages in funding for operations and maintenance. On a per-acre basis, National Wildlife Refuge System funding is far below that for the National Park System and other federal lands. Most refuges cannot provide for the complete suite of ecological functions for which they were purchased, because the hydrology, sediment process, exotic species abundance, and predator–prey relationships of surrounding landscapes have been so altered that natural processes do not occur without land management intervention. We as a nation have made a conscious decision that these wetlands and adjacent uplands are valuable enough to preserve; we must also provide the financial resources necessary for managing them to their full potential.

As you read Russ Butcher's marvelous accounts of our National Wildlife Refuges, notice how people, opportunity, and resources have come together in many unique ways to preserve and maintain some of America's richest treasures. Let us celebrate these accomplishments and the enduring legacy that the National Wildlife Refuge System has provided for ourselves and future generations. Let us honor the thousands of men and women who have dedicated their lives to these vital wild places—not by viewing the refuges as tokens of historic landscapes, but as foundations on which to rebuild larger ecological communities. Wetlands are critical to our nation's future, and we must protect and rebuild them. I am confident we can and will find common conservation ground among diverse landowners and organizational interests to accelerate wetlands conservation in this new millennium.

Stephen E. Adair is the Regional Director of the Great Plains office of Ducks Unlimited, Inc., a private, nonprofit, international conservation organization. Dr. Adair began his tenure with Ducks Unlimited, Inc. in 1997. Previously, he was employed as an ecologist for several private landowners in Georgetown, South Carolina, from 1994–1997.

Dr. Adair received his Ph.D. in wildlife ecology from Utah State University, his M.S. in wildlife management from Texas A&M University, and his B.S. in biology from the University of Texas. He has extensive experience in wetland protection, restoration, management, and research including program development, supervision, and evaluation. He has served on the National Riparian Roads Team, on the Society of Wetland Scientists Awards Committee, and as a member of the Citizens Ambassador Wetland Delegation to Australia and New Zealand. In 1996, Dr. Adair received the Outstanding Achievement for Stewardship Development Award from the South Carolina Department of Natural Resources. He helped to develop Ducks Unlimited's carbon sequestration, land protection, and Latin American conservation programs. Current responsibilities include supervision of Ducks Unlimited's biological, engineering, agronomy, and contract compliance programs across the northern Great Plains.

The views expressed herein are Dr. Adair's personal views and are not necessarily official positions of Ducks Unlimited, Inc.

A Brief History of the National Wildlife Refuge System

Lynn A. Greenwalt, Former Refuge Manager; Former Director of the U.S. Fish and Wildlife Service, 1973–1981

Readers of this book will learn about National Wildlife Refuges as they are today; this brief and simplified review of how they came to be cannot detail the effort expended to make these places attractive to wildlife and to keep them that way. The success of each refuge is a reflection of the people of the National Wildlife Refuge System, a dimension of refuge history that should not be overlooked. The rock-solid commitment of men and women, beginning almost a century ago, has made what the visitor sees today. These people and those who came before them guarantee that all of us are heirs to a priceless treasure.

I am fortunate to have been the beneficiary of life on a National Wildlife Refuge and, much later, to have been given responsibilities that included the Refuge System and later the entire U.S. Fish and Wildlife Service, the federal agency that has always been key to the study, understanding, protection, and management of wildlife and wild places in this country. I have had a rare opportunity to learn firsthand how important the people who have been a part of the evolution of the National Wildlife Refuge System are to what the refuge visitor enjoys today.

The men and women who manage these places are given responsibility to make sure this bit of America will serve the well-being of our fellow creatures, plant and animal, forever. This produces a sense of purpose that is unusual, and along with it a sense of personal accomplishment that I believe is rare in today's work world.

This pride in place and purpose is present in those who work in the National Park Service, in the U.S. Forest Service, and in the ranks of the Bureau of Land Management; it is in those managers of the wild lands of other landholding agencies; and it is prominent among state and local organizations with similar roles to play. I have heard it said that "It goes with the territory," especially when the territory is a place set aside for the purpose of providing a lasting benefit for future generations and for our fellow passengers on this small, vulnerable, and precious planet.

Of course, I know the people of the Fish and Wildlife Service and the Refuge System best, for I have been close to them all my life, 70 years. When I speak of the men and women involved, I do not refer only to the women who have lately—far too lately, in my view—come to be professional participants of the Refuge System. I include the wives who came with their husbands to assignments that even today may entail hardships and inconveniences few people would accept voluntarily. I know of husbands, too, who have made radical accommodations to their own lives so their wives can pursue opportunities in refuge work.

I think of my mother, who was the daughter of a university vice president, and who in 1928 left city life with her soon-to-be refuge manager husband to live in an 1890s rough-rock and lumber cabin in the wilds of northwestern Nevada, where there were no neighbors and where visitors were limited to the occasional cowboy and sheepherder. The land had been the "Last Chance Ranch," so named by an old rancher making his final try for success in this arid sagebrush country. The nearest town was about 40 miles away, and the trip down the face of an intervening lava bluff (and especially back up again) was an adventure in early-day automobiling.

My mother might go for a month or more without seeing another woman, and there was nothing in her home remotely resembling luxury. Winters were harsh, and her journal reveals that "Last Chance" was a name that fit the situation more often than not. She prevailed, of course, and she and my father went on to live on two other National Wildlife Refuges during his long career. Both of the other assignments were closer to towns and people and the ordinary things of life, but my mother was happiest, I am quite sure, when she and my father proved themselves in a distant wilderness, where life was difficult but full of adventure.

My own life has a parallel experience, though it took place a quarter century after the "Last Chance." My wife, Judy, and I were in our twenties when I was given an opportunity to take on my first job as a refuge manager. We two and our small child (and another on the way, about whom I did not tell my boss until we got relocated, lest he cancel the whole idea) moved to a wild and isolated place in western Utah, where our "Last Chance" was a small camping trailer and a front yard 15 miles deep and 40 miles wide—the distances we could see from our tiny residence. My wife learned to subdue the recalcitrant electric generator so she could have electricity briefly each day, and she endured the snakes (harmless), the distances (not harmless), and the fact that our nearest neighbor was 30 miles away. We lived in this place, albeit in steadily improving circumstances, for three years. As my mother did, my wife makes clear that those years in the faraway desert, where the view was always changing and the dust devils danced across the distant flats, are among her most cherished. These two women in my life revealed an inner toughness and strong self-confidence that must have been common among the women who were immigrant pioneers a century before.

They are by no means the only examples of women who have supported their husbands in ways most wives are never called upon to do. A wife at Cold Harbor, in the Aleutian Islands of southwestern Alaska, for example, faced immense problems of transport in case someone had a medical emergency. The weather there was calculated to test the will of even the most tenacious person, man or woman. Transportation is a little more convenient now, but the climate has not improved.

Winter in northern Michigan is a time during which the lowering clouds produce snow almost every day, and the gray envelopment can be devastating to the good humor of someone who may have been brought up in, say, Texas. Yet, Texans do accept—even seek—assignments in Michigan or Alaska or in urban San Francisco. It is because they care for the resources entrusted to them and because they know theirs is one of those rare callings that focus primarily on the future. What they do now will have a profound impact upon what the world may be like for their children and grandchildren—and yours.

As you read about or visit National Wildlife Refuges, recall that what you see got that way because of the people involved, then and now. As an old hand at the trade, I know they have had hard times—sometimes dangerous, usually a little uncomfortable, sometimes in the line of political fire, and occasionally subjected to the outright hatred of individuals or groups who do not agree with the idea that there is a place in the world for wildlife or who object to the occasional need to subordinate their own needs to those of wildlife and wild places. Yet, I know that if pressed, every refuge person—and the spouses who share their lives with them—will say they have the very best jobs in the world. And they mean it. They are what has made the National Wildlife Refuge System a success, a model for other nations to follow, and a source of great pride for all who have ever served in it.

The modern National Wildlife Refuge System, composed of more than 530 refuges, encompassing more than 93 million acres, and represented in every state in the nation, began on the east coast of Florida in 1903. A three-acre island, one of several in the Indian River south of Sebastian, was a famous pelican and heron rookery and had become the focus of feather hunters, who sold the plumes of herons and egrets to the makers of women's hats. A local concern was raised to the attention of President Theodore Roosevelt, who declared the tiny island a federal bird sanctuary in March 1903.

National Wildlife Refuges embrace islands smaller than an acre in size and Alaska's Arctic National Wildlife Refuge, larger than the state of Connecticut. The entire Refuge System is the size of Montana and is growing. It represents every kind of wildlife habitat found in the United States and its Territories. It is a remarkable assemblage of lands and waters and is managed to ensure the perpetuation of habitats necessary to the support of the Nation's wildlife resources.

In 1903, there were about 80.6 million people in the United States. It was a time when space for living and growing was abundant. It is remarkable that what was happening on three acres of truly isolated land in a remote part of Florida could be made to attract the attention of a president and inspire him to exercise the authority he used many times over the next few years to create National Parks and National Forests—and more National Wildlife Refuges. In hindsight, it seems almost miraculous that such action would be taken in a time when the popular view was that the nation's resources were limitless and would always be available.

The confident nation was poised to make the most of these natural resources. The continent had been explored and inventoried, and what were then termed "Indian problems" had been resolved, after a fashion. Plans were developing to "reclaim" the desert lands of the West with irrigation schemes taking advantage of water flowing out of the western mountains. Transportation was abundant, and resources from the West could be brought to the manufacturing centers of the East to develop an economy of immense potential. There was no question that a virtually unlimited opportunity for growth and economic progress was at hand.

A considerable, but not entirely obvious, price had already been paid for this opportunity, however. Millions of bison had been all but eliminated, and only a few specimens remained in zoos. Passenger pigeons, estimated to have existed in the billions in the woodlands of the eastern half of the country, were utterly extinguished by the end of the 19th century as a result of profligate overharvesting and habitat destruction. Wetlands and grasslands in the East and Midwest had given way to agriculture, and cattle grazing was to be a key economic activity of the West, along with timber harvesting and mining. Taken together, these were having a serious impact on wild habitats and the creatures depending on those places.

Grasslands and the variety of wildlife living in them were disappearing as cattle herds changed the nature of the vegetation in the West; large mammals were giving way to human activity; and predator populations were beginning to be a thorn in the side of those who grazed sheep and cattle, both easy prey for coyotes and wolves. Immediate control, if not outright elimination of pest species such as prairie dogs, rabbits, and bobcats, was demanded and undertaken.

Subtle changes were occurring in the biological processes that had supported a stunning variety of wild things, both plant and animal. Those changes were causing potentially serious problems for natural systems. A few people began to recognize that living natural resources were vulnerable to habitat destruction or overuse.

Not long after the creation of Pelican Island National Wildlife Refuge in 1903, the pace of refuge establishment increased and included seven more refuge areas in Florida by 1908, and eight in the Territory of Alaska by 1913. In 1909, elements of the Leeward Islands and the surrounding oceanic territory, far to the west of the main Hawaiian Islands, were added to the system. Each action was taken to prevent continuing harm to wildlife species or habitats suffering the effects of human activity.

It is ironic that some of the first refuges established were in parts of the nation that were then far from centers of human activity and where one would least expect wildlife to encounter problems. The creation of these refuges reflected an increasing understanding of how fragile the relationship between wildlife and habitat could be and how quickly permanent loss could occur.

A growing interest in the well-being of waterfowl inhabiting North America spurred an international agreement resulting in the Migratory Bird Treaty with Great Britain (representing Canada), which was signed in 1916. This measure set the stage for rapid progress in the development of means to protect migrating birds, largely waterfowl, the hunting of which was generally unregulated. In the absence of regulation, waterfowl hunting became a commercial activity in which hundreds of thousands of birds were killed each year for sale as food. The treaty, and the legislation passed by Congress in 1918 to carry out the treaty provisions, also protected migratory songbirds, but initially the most active concern was for waterfowl.

Ducks and geese nest in Canada or the northern United States, rest during their migrations on rivers and lakes and other wetland areas in the central United States, and winter in the southern states, or in Mexico and beyond. A similar treaty with Mexico was therefore executed in 1937, extending the provisions of the Canadian treaty to apply to the Republic of Mexico and helping ensure the protection of birds and their habitats throughout the birds' range.

Much of the early work done in identifying areas of potential value as refuges was accomplished by local citizens familiar with the needs of wildlife and the problems facing the resource. Hunters and anglers, who often noted changes in the presence of wildlife or the decline in habitat quality, reported what they saw and encouraged government action to protect localities critical for wildlife.

In the early decades of the 20th century, most refuge lands were simply set aside from the large inventory of public lands, located primarily in the western United States. This required no money for buying land, but did require funding to provide personnel to look after the new areas.

Not all of the areas were carved from free land, however. Some, like the important pronghorn and sage-grouse habitat in northwestern Nevada (now the Sheldon National Wildlife Refuge), involved private land, and national sportspersons' groups solicited private subscriptions to buy a ranch in the center of the area. The refuge was not created immediately; like many others, it required constant pressure to move it from planning to completion. Leaders of the National Audubon Society took an interest in the area, and in 1931, President Herbert Hoover made the refuge official. (This is the place of "Last Chance," which revealed my mother's indomitability.)

A powerful stimulus to refuge creation was a long and widespread drought that hovered over the central and western United States in the 1930s. This "Dust Bowl" created real problems for wildlife. There was little water for ducks and geese. Large areas of land were damaged by windstorms that sent dust clouds high into the skies, visible even in the East. Duck marshes were as vulnerable as wheat fields, and times were bleak for man and beast alike.

Once again, hunters and anglers agreed to help. In the early 1930s, a law was passed requiring waterfowl hunters to purchase a federal Duck Stamp in order to hunt waterfowl. The revenue from these stamps went into a fund to be used for the purchase of waterfowl habitat, with an emphasis on breeding grounds for ducks and geese. By 1940, 130 new refuges were bought, adding nearly 11 million acres to the system. Although most were relatively small units, some, such as the Okefenokee Swamp in Georgia, were extensive natural areas.

Even during the period of national preoccupation with the defense effort in World War II, 25 new refuges were added, including two large refuges for brown bears and other wildlife in Alaska, and several waterfowl areas in the upper Midwest. Wartime demands for military personnel and war industry support forced cutbacks in the staffs of almost every refuge in the system, and many managers found themselves assigned custodial responsibility for other areas in addition to their home stations.

In 1960, Interior Secretary Fred Seaton followed the example of Theodore Roosevelt more than a half century before: he established what is now the Arctic National Wildlife Refuge and some others in Alaska by employing at the last minute a secretarial authority that was about to expire. These refuges added nearly 12 million acres to the system. Refuges in Alaska were consolidated and expanded as a result of the far-reaching Alaska National Interest Lands Conservation Act (ANILCA) of 1980, which dealt with the future management of the public lands that make up virtually all of that resource-rich state. The Alaska refuges now embrace a total of about 77 million acres, from well above the Arctic Circle to the Aleutian Islands in far southwestern Alaska, and large tracts of interior wetlands, which are havens for an abundance of water birds as well as resident wildlife of many kinds.

The acquisition of land has been accomplished in a variety of ways over the years. Much of it has come from the public domain, land already owned by the federal government. Duck Stamp receipts have paid for more than 4.5 million acres of land, including small wetlands in the "Prairie Pothole" region of the upper Midwest, on which large numbers of waterfowl breed and raise their young each year.

On the Canadian side of the border, similar waterfowl habitat preservation has taken place, most notably by a private organization called Ducks Unlimited, Inc. (see chapter 1 for more on this organization). Using public or leased lands, DU raises money in the United States from hunters and others interested in the perpetuation of the North American waterfowl resource to create and manage hundreds of thousands of acres of wetland habitat in Canada. This is done in cooperation with the provinces and the national government. DU has been engaged in a somewhat similar program in Mexico for some years as well.

As a result of the Fish and Wildlife Coordination Act, passed shortly after World War II, federal agencies constructing major irrigation or flood control works have been required to assess the impacts those projects may have on fish and wildlife resources and to take action to diminish that impact. As a result, many National Wildlife Refuges have been created under this Act to offset losses to habitat for waterfowl and other migratory birds, and many state-managed refuges were created as replacement habitat for resident wildlife. About 2.7 million acres of National Wildlife Refuge lands have been acquired in this way. Included in this list is the very popular and decidedly atypical John Heinz National Wildlife Refuge at the southwestern edge of Philadelphia, which harbors large numbers of waterfowl during migration and is heavily used by school groups from the area. It originated as mitigation for habitat loss created by a major highway project in the vicinity. Habitat was created in a place that includes a closed landfill, hardly the sort of feature usually associated with a natural area. The refuge is now a riverside marsh between the Delaware River and Philadelphia's international airport. It is but one of several refuges successfully established within an urban setting, in which wildlife thrives close by the habitat of humans.

Some refuges have simply been gifts to the United States—often, but not always, stimulated by provisions of the tax laws that permit tax deductions for gifts. Among these is the nearly 250-thousand-acre Sevilleta National Wildlife Refuge in south-central New Mexico. This block of land was originally a Spanish land grant. The refuge is divided by the Rio Grande, and on either side is a remarkable example of desert grassland extending to the hills beyond. The entire grant was owned by one family, which conveyed it to the United States as a National Wildlife Refuge with the support of The Nature Conservancy, a national nonprofit organization that encouraged the donation and helped defray some of the legal and other costs.

Another gift stimulated by tax advantages was the Great Dismal Swamp National Wildlife Refuge in southern Virginia. Once owned by the Union Camp Paper Company, it was given to the United States, once again with the support and assistance of The Nature Conservancy. The refuge protects a rare eastern hardwood swamp rich in wildlife and history.

Wealthy individuals, small organizations, and local groups have worked to make land available to the refuge system at no cost or at sharply reduced prices. These generous actions have resulted in the addition of more than 664 thousand acres of often-unique habitat to the system.

Congress passed one of the most famous and powerful wildlife laws in the nation's history in 1973: the Endangered Species Act. This law pledged the country not to let any species of plant or animal pass into extinction if that can possibly be avoided. The legislation contained provisions that are often newsmakers, as when a species of butterfly or frog brings a major development program to a halt because the species may be put at risk by the project. These confrontations are inevitable when human activities come into conflict with the well-being of a species so vulnerable that its very existence may be in question if the activity is allowed to continue. These often-controversial dilemmas are a direct result of the fact that human population in this country has burgeoned, from the 80 million or so when Pelican Island Refuge was established, to now well over three times that number. More people demand more places to live, work, and recreate. Additional people require a steadily increasing support structure of highways, parking lots, port improvements, and flood protection. And there is a steady increase in the number of these things as our economy grows and our aspirations expand.

Humans displace wild living things by altering or destroying their habitats. Hunting may have depleted the bison and passenger pigeons a century or more ago, but now the steady removal or alteration of habitats exerts constant pressure on wildlife species, often to the point at which the most vulnerable and least numerous populations are in danger of disappearing.

The Endangered Species Act of 1973 and several subsequent amendments provided powerful legal protection, including additional authority to purchase habitats critical to the protection of endangered species in cases when land protection is key to the preservation of the species. This is not a new concept. The pronghorn refuges in Nevada and Oregon; the bison refuges in Montana and Oklahoma; and the extensive desert bighorn sheep ranges established in Arizona, New Mexico, and Nevada—all put in place in the first half of the 20th century—were intended to ensure the preservation of these and other species requiring specialized habitat.

The majestic whooping crane, never abundant, breeds in northern Manitoba and winters along the Gulf Coast of Texas, making the long trip twice each year. Pressure on its wintering habitat reduced the population to little more than a dozen birds in the late 1930s, when the Aransas National Wildlife Refuge in Texas was established to protect its winter range. These birds have since increased to a population of more than 150 migratory individuals and another 170 or so being bred in captivity—a minor miracle, given their original situation. The tiny Key deer, found only in the Florida Keys, had habitat set aside for them when a refuge was purchased shortly after World War II. Even so, the press of human activity in the realm of the Key deer is a serious problem, requiring constant attention to finding ways that humans and the deer can live together.

The Endangered Species Act made possible the use of money from the existing Land and Water Conservation Fund, as well as other sources, to purchase refuge lands for endangered species. As a result, refuges were created for the rare Attwater's prairie chicken in Texas, and for the masked bobwhite quail found only in limited numbers along the Mexico-Arizona border. Several refuges were established in Hawai'i, a state noted for having the greatest number of species on the endangered species list. This latter situation has been brought about by decades of intensive development, as well as a long history of introducing exotic species of plants and animals that have altered the habitat of the islands' native plants and animals.

The refuge system has developed in parallel with the problems faced by wildlife in this country. Initially, lands were set aside to deal with special situations, such as the overharvesting of birds in the rookeries of Pelican Island; or the pelicans on Anaho Island, Nevada; or the herd of bison reestablished in the Wichita Mountains of Oklahoma and at the National Bison Range in Montana after these animals were hunted almost to extinction in the 19th century. These refuges were put in place because of an obvious need that occurred in the first years of the 20th century. Later on, the drought and steadily declining habitats focused special effort on the establishment of refuges for migratory birds, especially waterfowl. That emphasis continues, especially through agreements with private landowners.

National Wildlife Refuges are not necessarily restricted to the wild and remote areas once associated with special places for wild animals. Some, such as the complex of refuges in the San Francisco area, lie within highly developed urban regions. A number of wetland tracts are preserved along the East Coast, from the tip of Florida to Maine, and many lie adjacent to heavily developed residential areas.

Cape Canaveral on the east coast of Florida, a site for rocket launches and space travel departures for many years, is located within a vast complex of coastal marshland. The Merritt Island National Wildlife Refuge was established to operate in association with the space program, to take advantage of the vast expanse of coastal marsh embraced by the space center. Regular launches of the space shuttle are made from there, with all the noise and light and dramatic activities we see on television. The many wildlife species using the area during these events seem to be unconcerned, and return to the coastal marshlands as they have for millennia.

A number of refuges have been created from military bases abandoned after World War II or identified as surplus during recent rounds of military base closure reviews. The Rocky Mountain Arsenal near Denver, once heavily contaminated with chemicals, has been designated as a refuge. Full control of the 17-thousand-acre area will be given to the Fish and Wildlife Service once contamination cleanup is completed under the direction of the U.S. Army. Eagles, other birds of all kinds, deer, and other wildlife typical of the Colorado high plains thrive there, within a few miles of metropolitan Denver.

Refuges are places where benefiting wildlife is the guiding purpose; however, these are not places where nature is left to its own devices. Habitats can be manipulated to improve conditions for wildlife; in many cases habitat is created and maintained where none existed before. Within National Wildlife Refuges, managers have the flexibility to make the areas as productive as possible for wildlife.

In the Florida panhandle, land that was farmed to exhaustion and abandoned as worthless in the 1930s was acquired as part of a government plan to recover and restore abandoned lands. Fish and Wildlife Service biologists believed that good wildlife habitat could be created on these worn and degraded lands. The construction of dikes and water controls helped re-create coastal marsh habitat, and forests were restored. This is now the St. Marks National Wildlife Refuge, a place rich in wildlife. It is just one example of active human intervention succeeding in re-creating a resource once thought to be beyond saving.

Many of the refuges established during the drought of the 1930s and early 1940s are the product of habitat improvement, often done by the Civilian Conservation Corps or the Work Projects Administration (federal programs established to help employ those hard-hit by the Great Depression). Refuges such as Bosque del Apache in New Mexico, Piedmont in Georgia, and Back Bay in Virginia are products of construction and management that have resulted in renewed wildlife use and fundamental environmental improvement.

Human intervention in the process of creating a successful wildlife refuge can be dramatic, as when a dike system is built and re-creates tens of thousands of acres of marsh at Bear River on the north side of Great Salt Lake in Utah, or when ditches and pumps provide water to a former great wetland, as at Stillwater in Nevada or Benton Lake in Montana. The intervention can be modest, as when planned and controlled fires improve range habitat for pronghorn at Sheldon in Nevada or Hart Mountain in Oregon, or when water levels are changed with the season to provide waterfowl nesting habitat, as at J. Clark Salyer in North Dakota and Fish Springs in Utah. Assisting natural processes through management is a never-ending requirement, if many of these remarkable places are to continue to make their contribution to the well-being of fish and wildlife resources for the nation and for the future.

It has been 20 years since I was director of the Fish and Wildlife Service. Since then, I have had the opportunity to work in a private conservation organization having an interest in the National Wildlife Refuge System; so, I know about its remarkable advances and improvements. Even so, when I contemplate the roster of National Wildlife Refuges as set forth in this book, I am pleased to find that there are a good many about which I know very little. This demonstrates the rapid progress made in the creation of new, valuable, and important refuges in the unending effort to make sure our wildlife heritage will thrive.

When I scan the descriptions of the new areas and review the material about the refuges I knew intimately from my childhood until I left the Service, I am struck by the contrasts between those times and the present day. I feel like a parent who reviews the progress of his own children and takes pride and pleasure in the fact that their lives are better in significant ways than his may have been.

Refuges today have larger staffs than was generally the case in my time. They do not have enough yet to realize the full potential of these places, to be sure, but specialists of many kinds have been made available. Biologists, key to the success of refuge management, are present in greater numbers and provide a wide range of skills. Range management specialists are assisted by men and women trained in the use of planned burning to improve habitat; there are foresters and wetland biologists and scientists who are expert in improving habitats vital to endangered species. Public-use specialists develop and carry out programs to make visitors' trips to the refuges more informative and safer and to ensure that public use does not interfere with the well-being of the creatures for whom the refuges were established.

When I visit a refuge today, I am drawn, invariably, to mundane things of the kind that were important to refuge managers 30 or 40 years ago. I am delighted to find equipment that is new: a bulldozer or road grader that is not secondhand; a dump truck actually designed to do the work the refuge needs; stockpiles of fresh materials and supplies.

These things stir me, because in the days when I was learning the refuge management trade, it was unlikely that we would ever see many items that were new. Much of what was available to us was gleaned from among items no longer needed by the military. From the end of World War II, the military has made available to qualifying federal and state agencies all manner of items—some new, some barely used, some barely functioning—from its changing inventory of construction equipment and supplies; motor vehicles; automotive repair items; countless kinds of pipe, lumber, and steel; and lesser items such as tools, tires, and assortments of nuts and bolts and nails. It was a kind of year-round Christmas for refuge folk, who were desperately short of these things.

It was quite possible for a refuge to be equipped with a bulldozer almost as old as the person who operated it. It might have only a few hundred hours of use on its clock, but may have been displaced by a more modern one, and a sharp-eyed refuge staff person, making the rounds of the military surplus depots, had put a tag on it. Refuges across the nation were maintained and construction work was undertaken with equipment that was still painted Army olive drab, Navy gray, or Air Force blue.

Some of us learned things the hard way during those times. One manager I knew failed to look carefully at the description of some steel chain he found on a surplus list, available at no cost except for the shipping. He was not as familiar with the nomenclature of chain as he should have been and was stunned to discover that he had become the proprietor of a few hundred feet of anchor chain, each link of which weighed a hundred pounds or more. One tries not to think about how he explained the freight charges to his supervisor.

Another manager found a gross or two of new and unused Quartermaster Corps padlocks, sturdy bronze things that would be ideal for the many gates and buildings on his place. Not until he got them home did he discover that no two were keyed alike: he would have needed a coaster wagon to carry all the keys he would need to make his rounds.

Word of these misadventures got around among refuge managers; so, people learned quickly to be very careful when getting something sight unseen, or at least to check locks and keys for variety. Some of us learned to cultivate friendships among the military managers of the surplus offices so we might get a little advance information about a near-pristine dump truck that might be coming up for disposal or a batch of lumber that was in the offing. These things could be shared with nearby refuges, and over the years, a lot of work got done at minimum cost, and managers learned things never taught in wildlife biology courses. The military is still a source of surplus items of value to refuge managers, though not on the scale that prevailed in the days when such things were rare delights.

Perhaps I can be forgiven for rhapsodizing over a two-year-old bulldozer or backhoe, yellow and gleaming, when I see one in a refuge maintenance yard. You can only imagine how I feel about seeing a communications network that really works in every corner of a 200-thousand-acre refuge, or the highly trained and well-equipped firefighting teams developed through cooperative ventures with neighboring landowners and other state and federal agencies.

I am pleased and proud that visitors to larger refuges today will find a visitor center, containing always-changing and improving information about the refuge, presided over by trained information and public-use specialists, themselves often assisted by a group of volunteers, prepared to make a visitor's stay a pleasant and rewarding one.

For many years, a "visitor center" usually consisted of a little shelf of brochures and a glass-topped display case in the outermost of a two-office headquarters. Visitors were welcome, to be sure, but sometimes tentatively so, simply because there was not enough money to prepare more than the most fundamental facilities for visitors.

Now visitor centers and facilities on many refuges are as modern and inclusive as on any public lands in the country. They are designed by architects who are guided by the specific needs of, and opportunities presented by, the refuge, and they are attractive structures of which refuge personnel and visitors alike can be proud.

As heartening as it may be to note how much the budgets for National Wildlife Refuges have improved over the decades since my last days in the Fish and Wildlife Service, there is still a need for increased funding. Over the years, routine maintenance has been given short shrift, and there is a growing urgency to provide funds so that facilities are kept fully functional. Only then will there be assurance that available water is used efficiently, roads and fences are kept up, and the routine of looking after the public's investment in these remarkable areas is provided.

There is another characteristic of the National Wildlife Refuge System that has emerged in recent times and that I find as encouraging as anything I have watched unfold. That is the powerful effort made by the Fish and Wildlife Service to engage private landowners in a variety of cooperative efforts that multiply and expand the effectiveness of the system of National Wildlife Refuges and other natural areas, upon which the perpetuation of the nation's wildlife resources will depend.

Wildlife refuges alone cannot guarantee that there will be fish and wildlife resources available for the enjoyment of future generations, even if one includes all similar public landholdings, such as forests, parks, and state areas, in the calculation. Most wildlife habitat in this country is on private land. Recognizing this, in recent years, the Service has set out to work with private landowners to engage them in the process of developing, enhancing, and maintaining wildlife habitat as a part of their own land management. This becomes a kind of extension of the National Wildlife Refuge System in that habitat otherwise vulnerable to conversion to another use is recognized as being valuable in and of itself.

Regardless of the process, there is an increasing involvement of the general public in wildlife protection and preservation. The National Wildlife Refuge System and the Fish and Wildlife Service are in the forefront of developing this new ethic, based on the fundamental idea that the living natural resources of the country are valuable assets. These wild creatures and the places they inhabit add to the quality of life and enjoyment of people here and in other countries, and, through tourism and wildlife-related outdoor recreation activities, they contribute significantly to the overall economy.

A few years ago, legislation was passed permitting the National Wildlife Refuge System to use volunteers to help with the day-to-day activities of refuge operation. Hundreds have joined the ranks of the volunteers and bring remarkable talents to bear on refuge problems. Volunteers help with public use and educational work, staffing visitor centers and tour routes. Others possess skills uniquely suited to meeting particular challenges. At a refuge in New Mexico, for example, a volunteer revealed that he was trained as an electrical engineer. With his help and the cooperation of the local electric power company, miles of overhead lines providing power to pumps, with which marsh areas were maintained, were expertly buried, removing an unsightly reminder of human presence—and a hazard to thousands of birds using the area in the winter. Volunteers help make the expanding system work, freeing full-time employees for other, less routine chores.

One of the greatest contributions volunteers make, however, is that they keep no secrets: They tell their friends—and anyone else who will listen—about the importance of wildlife and wild lands and create a general understanding that is vital if the Refuge System is to fulfill its promise in the long run. When enough people care in this way, we can be sure of having wildlife and their habitats recognized and protected, because we humans will have come to recognize and accommodate the value these treasures contribute to our lives.

As director of the Fish and Wildlife Service, working with the Congress to ensure funding for the Refuge System and other parts of the Service, I was often asked—as every director before and since has been—just how large the Refuge System should be. "How many more refuges do we need?" was a recurring question, sometimes asked out of curiosity and sometimes with an angry edge to the query. My response was, and is, that the system will always grow, though it may not expand at the rate it has in the past 30 years. As long as there are conflicts between the demands of increasing human population and the needs of wildlife and the places they inhabit, one solution will be to set aside land and water to ensure the continuation of other species in addition to our own.

I am honored to have been a part of the development, growth, and management of the National Wildlife Refuge System. I am doubly proud because my own father was one of the first refuge managers, beginning his long tour almost 75 years ago. I am fortunate because I married a woman whose father was also a refuge manager, one who in his time fought valiantly against long odds to make sure at least some water from the fast-draining Florida Everglades was devoted to wildlife. His daughter, therefore, understood the kind of life she was facing in my company and accepted it without reservation.

Those who use this volume as a guide to seeing the wildlife heritage of the United States will find it rewarding. Through its use, you will come to know the system of lands and waters identified by the Blue Goose signs, which symbolize National Wildlife Refuges across the country and give notice that something remarkable is at hand. The Blue Goose marks places intended for the continuing benefit of our fellow creatures, a place where human beings are welcome but on terms that are determined by the needs of those creatures.

You may come to know certain National Wildlife Refuges intimately and in detail; if so, you will always return. You will be drawn to these places because they are special; because they are places of re-creation; and because they constantly change and so are utterly unique. You will understand something of the feeling that all of us who ever worked on National Wildlife Refuges have for these treasures. A nation that for a hundred years has recognized and supported an obligation to the other beings on this planet is a nation that is truly enlightened—because its people understand.

3

Featured National Wildlife Refuges

(Descriptions Arranged Alphabetically by State)

Alabama

Bon Secour, containing more than 6,900 acres in five units, was established in 1980 to protect ecologically and scenically diverse parts of coastal barrier-island-type habitats on Fort Morgan Peninsula, between the Gulf of Mexico and Mobile Bay in southwestern Alabama. This refuge includes magnificent white sandy beaches; cypress swamps; salt marshes; gently rolling pine-and-oak woodlands; and coastal sand dunes, on and around which grow a beautiful variety of grass known as sea oats and some picturesque clumps of Spanish moss-draped, wind-sculpted live oaks. Among the wildlife at Bon Secour (a French name meaning "safe harbor") are alligators; sea turtles that lay their eggs in the refuge's beaches; the threatened gopher tortoise; birds such as brown pelicans, herons, and egrets; gulls and terns; black skimmers; ospreys; and numerous songbirds. This is one of the Gulf Coast refuges where the neotropical migratory songbird "fallout" phenomenon can occur in April (see the Aransas NWR text).

From east to west, Bon Secour refuge consists of the Sand Bayou Unit, bordering Oyster Bay, a segment of the Intracoastal Waterway, and Bon Secour Bay; the Perdue Unit, bordering Little Lagoon and the Gulf of Mexico and providing the refuge's visitor center and two trails; the Little Point Clear Unit; and the Fort Morgan Unit, near the tip of the peninsula. Little Dauphin Island, containing 280 acres, is located on the opposite side of the mouth of Mobile Bay.

The refuge is open daily during daylight hours and the visitor center is open on weekdays, except national holidays. There is no entrance fee.

Visitor activities include wildlife observation, hiking on two trails and the beaches, swimming, canoeing and boating (small boats with electric trolling motors), and fishing. Hunting and camping are not permitted. Campground facilities are available at nearby Gulf State Park. September through November and March through April are the best months for viewing migratory birds. More than 370 bird species have been recorded here. Although alligators are generally afraid of people, visitors are cautioned to stay a safe distance from them and to be alert for venomous snakes, fire ants, ticks, and chiggers. Insect repellent and sunscreen are advised.

Access to the refuge is from I-10 at Loxley, south on State Hwy. 59 to Gulf Shores, and west just over eight miles on State Hwy. 180 to the refuge headquarters.

Information: Bon Secour NWR, 12295 State Hwy. 180, Gulf Shores, AL 36542; tel.: (251) 540-7720.

Wheeler, consisting of 34,500 acres, was established in 1938 to manage and protect a variety of habitats for large concentrations of wintering waterfowl and other wildlife along the middle third of the Tennessee Valley Authority's Wheeler Reservoir, on the Tennessee River in northern Alabama.

Wheeler's ecological diversity includes upland pine plantations, southern bottomland hardwood and riparian woodlands, backwater embayments, expanses of open water, and cropland. In addition to tens of thousands of ducks, the refuge supports the southernmost significant concentration of wintering Canada geese. Water-control structures regulate the level of moist-soil impoundments, thereby promoting the growth of native plants that provide food for waterfowl. To benefit waterfowl and other wildlife, approximately 10 percent of the refuge is managed under cooperative agricultural crop production agreements, whereby local farmers leave unharvested a portion of crops of millet, corn, grain sorghum, and soybeans. In the autumn, the refuge produces wheat that provides green browse for wintering geese. Wood duck nesting boxes are provided, from which as many as 2,000 young are hatched annually. More than 280 bird species have been recorded here.

Ducks Unlimited, Inc. has provided financial assistance for important wetlands enhancement projects.

The refuge is open daily. There is no entrance fee. The visitor center is open daily from October 1 through February (except on Thanksgiving and Christmas) and on Tuesdays through Saturdays from March 1 through September.

Visitor activities include wildlife observation (including from an observation building), environmental education programs, driving and bicycling on unpaved refuge roads, hiking (including on five interpretive trails), horseback and mule riding on some of the roads, prearranged interpretive tours, canoeing and boating (boat-launching ramps are available), fishing (a wheelchair-accessible fishing pier is provided), and hunting on parts of the refuge during the designated seasons. Camping is not permitted on the refuge, but campground facilities are available at adjacent Point Mallard Park.

Although alligators (uncommon here) are generally afraid of people, visitors are cautioned to stay a safe distance from them and to be alert for venomous snakes, fire ants, ticks, and chiggers. Insect repellent is advised.

Access to the refuge's visitor center is east one mile from Decatur on State Hwy. 67, or west two miles from I-65 on Hwy. 67.

Information: Wheeler NWR, 2700 Refuge Headquarters Rd., Decatur, AL 35603; tel.: (256) 353-7243.

Alaska

Alaska Maritime, encompassing 4.5 million acres, was established in 1980 to protect more than 2,400 islands, islets, sea stacks, rocks, reefs, and headlands along the coastal waters of Alaska.

All but 460,000 acres of Alaska Maritime were previously within eleven separate national wildlife refuges, beginning with St. Lazaria and Bering Sea Refuges in 1909 and the 2.72-million-acre Aleutian Islands Refuge in 1913. The Alaska National Interest Lands Conservation Act of 1980 consolidated these refuges. The refuge's isolated habitats support enormous colonies of nesting seabirds and rookeries of sea lions and other marine mammals. Of the estimated 50 million seabirds that breed in Alaska, fully 80 percent nest in this five-unit refuge. More than 250 bird species have been recorded on this refuge.

The GULF OF ALASKA UNIT includes Forrester Island, Hazy Islands, and St. Lazaria Island in southeastern Alaska; the Chiswell Islands, Pye Islands, and Barren Islands along the southern shore of the Kenai Peninsula; Chisik and Duck islands in Cook Inlet; and scattered small islands around Kodiak and Afognak islands. Spectacular "bird cities" of colonial nesting seabirds and rookeries of sea lions are the major attractions of these wild, rugged places.

The 65-acre St. Lazaria Island is located 15 miles by boat from Sitka, in southeastern Alaska. It protects significant seabird nesting habitat, supporting roughly 500,000 birds of 15 species. Tufted puffins, rhinoceros auklets, ancient murrelets, and fork-tailed and Leach's storm petrels create nests by burrowing into the soil, and common and thick-billed murres, and pigeon guillemots lay their eggs on ledges and crevices along the sheer cliffs.

The Chiswell Islands are scattered at the mouth of Kenai Fjords National Park's Aialik and Harris bays. More than a dozen islands and sea stacks support great numbers of breeding kittiwakes, murres, guillemots, and puffins.

Visitor activities include wildlife observation, boat cruises, and boat charters.

The ALASKA PENINSULA UNIT, with more than 700 islands, islets, sea stacks, and rocks, includes Sutwik Island, the Semidi Islands, Shumagin Islands, and Sandman Islands along the southern shore of the Alaska Peninsula. Many of these small bits of land support tremendous concentrations of colonial nesting seabirds and sea lion rookeries. Many of this unit's species of birds and mammals are also found in the Gulf of Alaska Unit (see above). Visitor access to this unit is very difficult; some parts are closed to public visitation to avoid disturbing the sea lions.

The ALEUTIAN ISLANDS UNIT, with more than 2.7 million acres, takes in the 1,200-mile-long chain of approximately 200 treeless tundra islands. These mostly barren habitats support enormous concentrations of colonial nesting seabirds such as fulmars, storm petrels, kittiwakes, murres, murrelets, auklets, and puffins. Tiny Buldir Island, in the western Aleutians, supports more than 3.5 million birds in one colony. Sea lions, sea otters, and other marine mammals are also abundant here.

The archipelago actually consists of 57 spectacularly scenic, emergent volcanic summits of the Aleutian Ridge. Among several active volcanoes is the highest, Mt. Shishaldin on Unimak Island, a steaming, snow-covered cone that rises to 9,387 feet above sea level. Many of the islands rise dramatically from the ocean, with sheer, 2,000-foot-high cliffs and waterfalls that plunge into the sea. Island ponds attract loons and many species of ducks.

The primary reason for initially establishing a national wildlife refuge in the Aleutian Islands was to protect the sea otter, a species that was then on the brink of extinction. In the mid-1700s, Russian explorers discovered an abundance of this marine furbearer. By the end of that century, their merchants were demanding large quantities of the high-quality pelts from the Tlingit Indians of southeastern Alaska. This exploitation, which ran counter to the native people's ancient, conservative hunting traditions and practices, led to a sharp decline in the population of the sea otter. When Russia's economic incentive for controlling Alaska diminished, the United States acquired Russia's interests under the terms of the Treaty of Cession of 1867.

For several more decades, unregulated commercial exploitation continued to push the sea otter inexorably toward extinction. Finally, killing was banned in 1911, and in 1913, the Aleutian Islands National Wildlife Refuge was established to protect a major part of the animal's habitat, in the hope that just maybe it wasn't too late to save the species. That hope has become a dream fulfilled. Today, there are roughly 150,000 sea otters, and their numbers are continuing to rebound.

The Aleutians extend from the largest, Unimak Island, off the end of the Alaska Peninsula, westward to Attu Island. The latter is a special destination for birdwatchers eager to add a number of rare Asiatic species to their life list.

Seabirds are everywhere on the Aleutians. Their numbers are mind-boggling. Former director of the U.S. Fish and Wildlife Service Dr. Ira N. Gabrielson described an awesome flight of auklets on Kasatochi Island ("America's Greatest Bird Concentrations," *Audubon*, January-February 1941):

As the sun sank toward the horizon these birds began to leave their nests in increasing numbers and to fly out over the water in front of the great slides that harbored the colony. There were flocks of thousands . . . [that] played around and over each other until the air seemed awhirl with birds. . . . As it became a little darker, one after another of these great flocks came sweeping with a roar like a waterfall over the rock where I was sitting. The flocks passed overhead, but hundreds of individuals dropped like falling leaves to land all around me on the rocks.

Visitor activities include wildlife observation, hiking, cross-country skiing, wilderness camping in some places, fishing, and hunting. A visitor center with interpretive displays and programs is located on Adak Island.

Most of the islands are extremely difficult to reach. Fog, wind, and storms occur much of the year. When weather permits, scheduled flights go to Cold Bay, near the end of the Alaska Peninsula, and to Adak and Attu islands. Beyond Cold Bay, there are no lodgings. Some of the islands of the Aleutians have restricted entry to avoid disturbing the wildlife. Parts of several islands are owned by Native corporations, and permission to use these properties is required. Military permission is required to visit Adak, Shemya, Amchitka, and Attu islands.

Information: Aleutian Islands Unit, Alaska Maritime NWR, PSC 486, Box 5251, FPO-AP 96506; tel.: (907) 592-2406.

The BERING SEA UNIT includes the Pribilof Islands, Hagemeister Island, the wilderness of St. Matthew Island, and small capes and headlands along Norton Sound. The Pribilof Islands support one of North America's largest seabird colonies, totaling about three million birds—notably red-legged and black-legged kittiwakes; murres; auklets; and puffins. The Pribilofs also contain large rookeries of the northern fur seal. In the spring, approximately a million of these mammals migrate to these islands' rocky beaches to breed.

Visitor activities include wildlife observation package tours that can be arranged for guided visits to the Pribilof Islands.

The CHUKCHI SEA UNIT protects Chamisso and other islands in Kotzebue Sound; Little Diomede Island, just east of the International Date Line in Bering Strait; a number of sandy barrier islands along the Chukchi Sea; and Cape Thompson and Cape Lisburne on the mainland. The high coastal escarpments of Cape Lisburne support Alaska's northern coast's largest seabird nesting colony, including hundreds of thousands of murres and kittiwakes. Hundreds of walruses winter on the Bering Sea pack ice, summer at the ice's northward receding edge, and return southward ahead of the advancing ice to come ashore at this prominent cape. The highest point in the Cape Lisburne area is 2,034-foot Mount Hamlet, where the white Dall sheep and muskox inhabit this western end of the Brooks Range.

Although access is very difficult, visitor activities include wildlife observation and wilderness camping. The best months for wildlife observation on Alaska Maritime National Wildlife Refuge are June through mid-August, when seabirds are nesting and marine mammals are giving birth to and raising their pups. The Fish and Wildlife Service advises visitors to "Expect cold, wet, windy weather at any time and dress appropriately with rain gear and layers of warm clothing."

As for visiting the bird colonies and marine mammal rookeries of the Alaska Maritime NWR, all communities are served by scheduled flights; state ferries regularly serve Sitka, Seward, Homer, and Kodiak during the summer and stop once a month at Unalaska in the Aleutians. Scheduled boat tours and charter boat excursions operate out of Sitka, Seward, and Homer. In addition, charter boat trips are offered from such other coastal communities as Kodiak, Sand Point, Unalaska, and Nome. There are no camping facilities or trails on the refuge.

Visitor centers are located at the main refuge headquarters in Homer and at the Aleutian Islands Unit headquarters in Adak.

Information: Alaska Maritime NWR, 2355 Kachemak Bay Dr., Suite 101, Homer, AK 99603; tel.: (907) 235-6546.

Alaska Peninsula, comprising 3.5 million acres in two units, was established in 1980 by the Alaska National Interest Lands Conservation Act. This refuge protects spectacularly scenic wildlife habitats along much of the Alaska Peninsula's chain of volcanoes, glaciers, tundra, and rugged southern coast in southwestern Alaska.

The refuge's towering peaks include 8,225-foot Mt. Veniaminof—one of the world's largest volcanic cones. This smoldering giant has a base almost 30 miles wide, which is greater than any active volcano on record. The summit crater is more than 20 miles in circumference, and with a 25-square-mile ice field, it is the most extensive crater glacier in North America.

Other scenic and ecological highlights of Alaska Peninsula refuge include two long stretches of Pacific coastline containing sheer cliffs, rocky points and capes, strands of beach, and deep bays and fjords. There are numerous streams; glacial-fed Chignik and Black lakes, which support large salmon spawning runs; and the large Upper and Lower Ugashik lakes, known for salmon, grayling, and brown bears. In July and August, literally hundreds of these huge bears, which range extensively across the refuge's tundra lowlands, gather along the lakeshores to feast and fatten themselves on the abundance of fish.

Many thousands of caribou, comprising the northern Alaska Peninsula herd, annually migrate between King Salmon, near the refuge's northern boundary, and Port Moller, roughly 250 miles to the southwest. Other prominent species of terrestrial wildlife include moose, gray wolves, red foxes, and beavers. Inhabiting coastal waters are such marine mammals as Steller sea lions, harbor seals, sea otters, Dall and harbor porpoises, orcas (killer whales) of the family *Delphinidae*, and migratory humpback whales. Great numbers of seabirds, such as tufted and horned puffins, pigeon guillemots, and common murres, nest in colonies along the refuge's coastal cliffs. Migratory waterfowl and shorebirds pass through the refuge during their spring and autumn migrations.

Alaska Peninsula also serves as an invaluable salmon nursery. All five species of Pacific salmon—pink (humpy), king (chinook), sockeye (red), chum (dog), and coho (silver)—spawn in the streams and lakes of this refuge and adjacent Becharof NWR. These massive fish runs, from June into August and September, provide the majority of the world's most pristine and valuable salmon fishery located in the Bering Sea's Bristol Bay, to the north of the Alaska Peninsula.

Visitor activities include wildlife observation, hiking, boating, wilderness camping, flightseeing, fishing, and hunting. The best months for wildlife observation in this refuge are May to October. Information on hunting and fishing can be obtained from the refuge headquarters or the Alaska Department of Fish and Game, P.O. Box 37, King Salmon, AK 99613; tel.: (907) 246-3340. Extensive lands within the refuge are owned by Native corporations or individuals, and visitors are required to obtain permission to enter these private properties.

The Fish and Wildlife Service advises prospective visitors to plan far ahead. As the refuge is remote and difficult to visit, arrangements need to be carefully planned. The refuge's terrain is extremely rough, and the weather is often foggy, rainy, and windy. Severe storms with rain, snow, and cold wind can occur at any time of the year. A travel plan should be given to a relative, friend, or refuge headquarters.

Visitors are cautioned to avoid unwanted encounters with bears by making noise (talking, singing, whistling) while hiking; camping away from streams, wildlife trails, berry patches, and freshly killed game; maintaining a clean camp; cooking and storing food away from the campsite and where it is not accessible to wildlife; and packing out all garbage. As mosquitoes, gnats, and other pesky insects can be prolific during the warmer months, insect repellent and headnets are a must. Water should be micro-filtered, boiled, or chemically treated before drinking. Guides and air-taxi services are available at the small community of King Salmon.

Access to the refuge is by small aircraft; there are no roads to or within the area.

Information: Alaska Peninsula NWR, P.O. Box 277, King Salmon, AK 99613; tel.: (907) 246-3339; or the King Salmon Interagency Visitor Center, P.O. Box 298, King Salmon, AK 99613; tel.: (907) 246-4250.

Arctic, containing 19.65 million acres, was initially established in 1960 as the Arctic National Wildlife Range, and was renamed as a refuge and enlarged to more than twice its prior size in 1980 by the Alaska National Interest Lands Conservation Act (ANILCA). This magnificent and vast national wildlife refuge in the northeastern corner of Alaska protects one of America's most awesome wildlife and wilderness areas, reaching from the heights of the massive Brooks Range, down to the Beaufort Sea coast.

The Arctic refuge's scenic landscapes and fragile ecosystems are virtually unaltered by human impact, functioning naturally as they have for untold centuries. The arctic and subarctic habitats of this pristine wilderness include spectacularly massive mountains rising to 9,000 feet above sea level and glaciers slowly carving mountain valleys. To the north lies a vast expanse of treeless, tundra-covered foothills and flat coastal plain that is patterned by numerous braided rivers flowing northward to the Beaufort Sea, where lagoons and barrier islands extend along the coast. To the south of the Brooks Range, many rivers and streams wind through wide valleys of spruce-dominated boreal forest and a mosaic of lakes, ponds, sloughs, and marshy wetlands.

From April to early June, an estimated 130,000 barren ground caribou of the Porcupine herd annually migrate more than 900 miles, between wintering habitat south of the Brooks Range and their traditional summer calving grounds on the refuge's coastal plain.

In addition, polar, grizzly, and black bears; wolves; wolverines; arctic foxes; lemmings; resident herds of the reintroduced muskox inhabit the area. In summer, more than 65 species of birds nest and breed here, including many thousands of ducks, geese, swans, loons, and shorebirds. It is no wonder that this remarkable place has been referred to as the "Serengeti of North America."

Visitor activities include wildlife observation, hiking, wilderness camping, river rafting, kayaking, fishing, and hunting. A number of trek operators in Fairbanks provide guided tours and/or airdrops to certain places for unguided visits. The best months for wildlife observation on the refuge are June through August. Information on hunting and fishing can be obtained by contacting the refuge headquarters or the Alaska Department of Fish and Game, 1300 College Rd., Fairbanks, AK 99701; tel.: (907) 459-7200.

The Fish and Wildlife Service advises that prospective visitors plan far ahead. As the Arctic refuge is remote and very challenging to visit, arrangements need to be carefully planned. Weather can suddenly change, producing storms and strong winds. Strong, damp, cold winds and foggy or cloudy conditions often prevail along the coast. Freezing temperatures can occur even during the summer months, especially from the Brooks Range northward. A travel plan should be given to a relative, friend, or refuge headquarters.

Visitors are urged to take precautions against unwanted encounters with bears (see suggestions in the Alaska Peninsula NWR text, above). As mosquitoes, gnats, and other pesky insects can be prolific, especially during June and July, insect repellent and headnets are a must. Water should be micro-filtered, boiled, or chemically treated before drinking.

Access to the refuge is mostly by scheduled flights from Fairbanks to Fort Yukon, Kaktovik, or Deadhorse. Charter flights are available from there to sites within the refuge, although weather not infrequently delays flights into and out of the refuge.

Information: Arctic NWR, 101 Twelfth Ave., Room 236, Fairbanks, AK 99701; tel.: (907) 456-0250 or (800) 362-4546.

Izembek, comprising 417,533 acres, was established in 1960 to protect an "international cross-roads" for enormous numbers of migratory waterfowl and shorebirds at the tip of the Alaska Peninsula in southwestern Alaska. Autumn is especially awesome, when a quarter million migratory birds pour through Bristol Bay and across the peninsula from their arctic and subarctic Alaskan and Siberian breeding grounds.

The major ecological highlight of this refuge is the thirty-mile-long by five-mile-wide Izembek Lagoon, which is designated as a Wetland of International Importance, along the Bering Sea coast. In May and again in September and October, virtually the entire world population of Pacific black brant gathers here to rest and feed on one of the most extensive beds of eelgrass—a flowering plant of the pondweed family with grass-like leaves. This lagoon and other estuaries and bays also attract tens of thousands of Taverner's Canada geese and large concentrations of numerous other migratory waterfowl. Many thousands of emperor geese, most of the world population of this species, stop here on their spring and autumn migrations. Although a population of tundra swans inhabits the refuge most of the year, in winter these birds usually fly to nearby Unimak Island, where thermal springs keep the water ice-free.

The largest of Izembek refuge's prominent terrestrial mammals is the brown bear, which feasts on fish along the rivers. In autumn and winter, barren ground caribou of the southern Alaska Peninsula herd migrate through the refuge. Beginning in midsummer, hundreds of thousands of three species of Pacific salmon—pink (humpy), sockeye (red), and chum (dog)—swim from the sea to river and lake spawning grounds in the refuge.

Visitor activities include wildlife observation, hiking (no trails), wilderness camping, fishing, and hunting. Izembek refuge is renowned for waterfowl and brown bear observation and hunting. The best months for wildlife observation on Izembek refuge are September and October. Information on hunting and fishing is available by contacting the refuge headquarters or the Alaska Department of Fish and Game, P.O. Box 25526, Juneau, AK 99802; tel.: (907) 267-2137. Guiding services are available. Several thousand acres within the refuge consist of Native-owned inholdings, and visitors are urged to respect these properties.

The Fish and Wildlife Service warns that rainy, foggy, and windy weather is a common occurrence. "Fog, drizzle, and overcast skies are often succeeded by violent storms and bitter cold snaps that slow down all activity. It is not unusual for an entire year to go by with only a few days of mostly clear skies." A travel plan should be given to a relative, friend, or refuge headquarters.

Visitors are advised to take precautions to avoid unwanted encounters with bears (see suggestions in the Alaska Peninsula NWR text, above). As mosquitoes, gnats, and other pesky insects can be prolific during the warmer months, insect repellent and headnets are a must. Water should be micro-filtered, boiled, or chemically treated before drinking.

Lodgings, meals, and vehicle rentals are available in the small community of Cold Bay, which is located less than a mile from the refuge boundary.

Access to the refuge is by scheduled airline flights from Anchorage to Cold Bay.

Information: Izembek NWR, P.O. Box 127, Cold Bay, AK 99571; tel.: (907) 532-2445.

Kenai, containing 1.97 million acres, was established in 1941 as the Kenai National Moose Range, to protect the population of Kenai moose—the largest population of its species. In 1980, this vast area, encompassing much of the northern and western parts of the Kenai Peninsula in south-central Alaska, was expanded and re-designated by the Alaska National Interest Lands Conservation Act as the Kenai National Wildlife Refuge.

The spectacular Kenai Mountains, along the boundary with Kenai Fjords National Park, consist of jagged, snowy peaks that rise to more than 6,600 feet above sea level, the huge expanse of the Harding Icefield, and a multitude of glaciers. Lower elevations of the refuge contain rolling foothills; vast lowland forests of spruces, birches, and aspens; numerous rivers and streams; more than 1,200 lakes and ponds; and extensive wetland habitat. Kenai is one of only two refuges in Alaska that is accessible by road (Tetlin is the other).

The white Dall sheep and mountain goats live high in the rugged mountains. Moose are often seen in willow thickets and other marshy and swampy places. Kenai brown bears and the smaller black bears gather along salmon-spawning rivers and streams during the summer and early autumn months. Barren ground caribou have been successfully reestablished in two parts of the refuge.

Major Pacific salmon runs occur in the refuge's Kenai and Russian rivers. King (chinook) and sockeye (red) salmon runs are from late June through July, pink salmon (humpy) in August, and coho (silver) in August and September. Other Kenai fish include steelhead, rainbow trout, arctic grayling, lake trout, Dolly Varden, and arctic char.

The refuge is open daily. There is no entrance fee. The visitor center, which is open daily except some national holidays, is located just south of Soldotna (following directional signs, turn east immediately south of the Kenai River bridge). A visitor information station, open daily in summer, is located at the junction of State Hwy. 1 (the Sterling Highway) and the Skilak Lake Loop Road.

Visitor activities include wildlife observation, seasonal interpretive programs, hiking more than 200 miles of established trails and other routes, driving more than 100 miles of paved and unpaved roads—notably the nearly 20-mile unpaved Skilak Lake Loop Rd., camping at a half dozen campgrounds (campsite fee charged at Kenai–Russian River, Hidden Lake, and Upper Skilak), backcountry camping (numerous small, rustic overnight campsites are provided), canoeing (brochure/map is available), boating, whitewater rafting, horse pack excursions, cross-country skiing, snowshoeing, snowmobiling, fishing, and hunting on most of the refuge.

The best months for wildlife observation on the refuge are May to October. Information on hunting and fishing is available at the visitor center or by contacting the Alaska Department of Fish and Game, 333 Raspberry Ave., Anchorage, AK 99512; tel.: (907) 344-0541. Snowmobiling is permitted only in specifically designated areas outside the Kenai Wilderness from December through April, and then only when snow depth is sufficient to avoid damaging underlying vegetation.

One of this refuge's wilderness recreation highlights is the extensive network of canoeing routes through many of the beautiful lakes. The Fish and Wildlife Service requires that canoeists register at the trailhead and recommends giving a travel plan to family or a friend. As these routes are within a unit of the refuge's Kenai Wilderness, no motorized watercraft are permitted on the canoe system, nor are wheeled vehicles permitted on any of the canoe system's portages. Canoe rentals are available near the refuge.

Visitors should take precautions against unwanted encounters with bears (see suggestions in the Alaska Peninsula NWR text, above). As mosquitoes, gnats, and other pesky insects can be prolific during the warmer months, insect repellent and headnets are a must. Water should be micro-filtered, boiled, or chemically treated before drinking. Campers are urged to be very careful with fire. During periods of extreme fire danger, fires are prohibited.

Access to the refuge from Anchorage is approximately 110 miles on State Hwy. 1.

There are flights from Anchorage to airports at Kenai and Homer.

Information: Kenai NWR, P.O. Box 2139, Soldotna, AK 99669; tel.: (907) 262-7021.

Kodiak, encompassing 1.865 million acres, was established in 1941. The refuge protects roughly the southern two-thirds of ruggedly scenic Kodiak Island, adjacent Uganik Island, a small part of Afognak Island, and adjacent Ban Island, in the Kodiak Archipelago across Shelikof Strait from the Alaska Peninsula, in southwestern Alaska. This refuge provides habitat for a tremendous diversity of wildlife, notably the approximately 2,500 huge Kodiak brown bears—the world's largest carnivore.

Kodiak's stunning landscapes include rugged mountains, some of which rise 4,000 feet from the sea; hundreds of miles of coastline, including many fjord-like inlets and bays; hundreds of miles of salmon streams; 11 large lakes; abundant bogs, marshes, and sedge and grass meadows; extensive thickets of alders and willows; and wooded areas of Sitka spruce and black cottonwood.

Coastal cliffs, islets, and rocks support large colonies of seabirds, such as tufted and horned puffins, pigeon guillemots, three kinds of cormorants, glaucous-winged gulls, and black-legged kittiwakes. Common murres and marbled murrelets also nest here. Bays, fjord-like inlets, and tidal marshlands are a mecca for large concentrations of seabirds and waterfowl. In winter and spring, a few emperor geese and great numbers of another goose, the Pacific black brant, pause here on their migration north to breeding grounds along the coast of Alaska and Siberia. More than 235 bird species have been recorded on the refuge.

From late May to September, five species of Pacific salmon—pink (humpy), king (chinook), sockeye (red), chum (dog), and coho (silver)—leave the ocean to spawn by the hundreds of thousands in Kodiak's streams. The refuge's spawning streams supply well over half of the salmon commercially harvested in the vicinity of the Kodiak Archipelago. Other common Kodiak fishes include steelhead, rainbow trout, Dolly Varden, and arctic char.

The refuge is open daily. There is no entrance fee. A visitor center (open weekdays except national holidays and seasonally also on weekend afternoons) is located on Buskin River Rd., a mile north of the airport.

Visitor activities include wildlife observation, hiking (no maintained trails, and hiking in most areas is extremely difficult), interpretive programs, bear-viewing charter flights, sea kayaking, rafting, canoeing, wilderness camping, fishing, and hunting. The best months for observing bears on the refuge are July through September. Information on hunting and fishing is available at the visitor center or by contacting the Alaska Department of Fish and Game, 211 Mission Rd., Kodiak, AK 99615; tel.: (907) 486-1880. Several campgrounds are located outside the refuge on Kodiak Island; and guide services and charter flights and boats are available in the town of Kodiak. A variety of interpretive tours are provided by a number of commercial tour operators. The Fish and Wildlife Service recommends checking with refuge personnel while planning a visit, to be aware of what activities are permitted, what precautions to take, etc. Some lands within the refuge are Native-owned and permission to enter these properties is required.

Visitors are advised to take precautions to avoid unwanted encounters with bears (see suggestions in the Alaska Peninsula NWR text, above). As mosquitoes, gnats, and other pesky insects can be prolific during the warmer months, insect repellent and headnets are a must. Water should be micro-filtered, boiled, or chemically treated before drinking.

The weather on Kodiak Island is generally rainy or drizzly and cool, often with wind and sudden storms. Stormy weather can unexpectedly delay flights off the island for days at a time.

Native terrestrial mammals of the refuge include Kodiak brown bear, red fox, and river otter; and introduced species include mountain goat, Sitka black-tailed deer, and red and arctic foxes. Marine mammals in the waters around the refuge include sea otter, Steller sea lion, harbor seal, Dall and harbor porpoises, orca (killer whale) of the family *Delphinidae*, and minke and humpback whales.

Access to Kodiak Island is by scheduled daily flights from Anchorage, and by state ferry three times weekly from either Seward or Homer. Access to the refuge from the town of Kodiak is by charter flights and by charter or tour boats. There are no roads to or within the refuge. Seven cabins are available by reservation, for which a lottery is held four times annually.

Information: Kodiak NWR, 1390 Buskin River Rd., Kodiak, AK 99615, tel.: (907) 487-2600.

Tetlin, encompassing 730,000 acres, was established in 1980 by the Alaska National Interest Lands Conservation Act. The refuge protects an extensive wetland mosaic of marshes, hundreds of lakes, and mixed hardwood–spruce forest in the broad, level basins of the glacier-fed Chisana and Nabesna rivers; gently rolling hills that bisect these watersheds; and foothills of the Nutzotin and Mentasta mountains in east-central Alaska. Tetlin is one of only two refuges in Alaska that is accessible by road (Kenai is the other).

The refuge is located within a major corridor for numerous species of birds that migrate to and from nesting habitat in northern and western Alaska. The most prominent among these are large flocks of lesser sandhill cranes, whose impressive autumn migration peaks in September. Many tundra and trumpeter swans pause to rest and feed on the refuge, and increasing numbers of the latter nest here. Tetlin's wetlands provide important nesting habitat for exceptionally large concentrations of ducks. Arctic grayling, lake trout, northern pike, burbot, and whitefish inhabit Tetlin's waters.

The refuge is open daily. There is no entrance fee. The visitor center, providing interpretive exhibits and talks at the large viewing deck, is located at Milepost 1229 of the Alaska (Alcan) Hwy. and is open daily from Memorial Day to Labor Day. During the same period, evening programs are offered at 7:30 p.m. Monday through Friday at Deadman Campground.

Visitor activities include wildlife observation, hiking, camping at two campgrounds (at Mileposts 1249.3 and 1256.7), wilderness camping, rafting, canoeing, boating, fishing, and hunting. Boat-launching ramps are provided at several locations.

The best months for wildlife observation on Tetlin refuge are April to October. More than 180 bird species have been recorded here. Information about hunting and fishing can be obtained from the refuge headquarters or by contacting the Alaska Department of Fish and Game, P.O. Box 355, Tok, AK 99780; tel.: (907) 883-2971. No designated motorized-vehicle roads or trails exist on the refuge. Large parcels of the land within the refuge are owned by Native corporations and individuals. Permission is required to enter these properties.

Visitors who trek into the refuge's backcountry are advised to take precautions against unwanted encounters with bears (see suggestions in the Alaska Peninsula NWR text). As mosquitoes, gnats, and other pesky insects can be prolific during the warmer months, insect repellent and headnets are a must. Water should be micro-filtered, boiled, or chemically treated before drinking. Visitors in the backcountry should also be prepared for sudden weather changes. A backcountry travel plan should be given to a relative, friend, or the refuge headquarters.

Access to the refuge is by way of the Alaska Highway and charter flights from Tok.

Information: Tetlin NWR, P.O. Box 779, Tok, AK 99780; tel.: (907) 883-5312.

Yukon Delta, containing 19.624 million acres of federal lands, including a million acres on Nunivak Island in the Bering Sea, was established in 1980 by the Alaska National Interest Lands Conservation Act. The refuge protects the sprawling, treeless wetland plain of the Yukon and Kuskokwim rivers in western Alaska, consolidating three previously existing, smaller national wildlife refuges. This ecologically outstanding expanse of rivers, streams, sloughs, lakes, and ponds supports the single most productive nesting habitat in North America for waterfowl, other waterbirds, and shorebirds.

Roughly 750,000 geese and swans, as many as two million ducks, and more than five million shorebirds annually migrate to this refuge from all continents that border the Pacific Ocean. The refuge supports more than three-quarters of the world's population of the emperor goose, as well as major portions of North America's populations of the tundra swan, greater white-fronted goose, and the small "cackling" subspecies of Canada goose. Among the shorebirds, the refuge supports the entire world's population of adult and juvenile bristle-thighed curlews during migration each autumn, more than 80 percent of the world's breeding black turnstones, more than 60,000 bar-tailed godwits, and the majority of the Pacific Flyway populations of western sandpipers, dunlins, and rock sandpipers.

Although seabird rookeries dot the refuge coastline, the vast majority of colonies occur on Nunivak Island. Several hundred thousand seabirds nest on Nunivak's cliffs and offshore islets, including cormorants, kittiwakes, guillemots, murres, auklets, and puffins.

Prominent terrestrial mammals are muskox, barren ground caribou, moose, and grizzly and black bears. Marine mammals of the coastal waters include the walrus and four other species of seals, and beluga (belukha) whale.

Of the many fishes, five kinds of Pacific salmon—king (chinook), sockeye (red), coho (silver), pink (humpy), and chum (dog)—totaling about a million individuals, make their summer runs from the sea to spawning habitat on the refuge.

The refuge's visitor center, in the town of Bethel, is open on weekdays, except national holidays.

Visitor activities include wildlife observation, hiking, fishing, and hunting. The best months for wildlife observation on the refuge are June through September. Information on hunting and fishing can be obtained by contacting the refuge headquarters or the Alaska Department of Fish and Game, P.O. Box 1467, Bethel, AK 99559; tel.: (907) 543-2979.

The Fish and Wildlife Service advises that prospective visitors plan far ahead. As Yukon Delta refuge is remote and difficult to visit, arrangements need to be carefully planned. The weather is often windy and rainy, and sudden changes commonly occur. A travel plan should be given to a relative, friend, or the refuge headquarters.

In addition to the nearly twenty million acres of public land, the refuge boundaries encompass another seven million acres of private Native corporation lands.

Access to these lands is by permission only, and should be secured in writing well before visiting the refuge.

Visitors are advised to take precautions against unwanted encounters with bears (see suggestions in the Alaska Peninsula NWR text, above). As mosquitoes, gnats, and other pesky insects can be prolific during the warmer months, insect repellent and headnets are a must. Water should be micro-filtered, boiled, or chemically treated before drinking.

Lodgings, meals, camping supplies, guide services, and charter flights are available in Bethel.

Access to the refuge is by scheduled flights from Anchorage to Bethel. From Bethel, regularly scheduled flights go to many of the more remote villages. Charter flights provide access to and from additional sites on the refuge. There are no roads to the refuge.

Information: Yukon Delta NWR, P.O. Box 346, Bethel, AK 99559; tel.: (907) 543-3151.

Arizona

Bill Williams River, containing 6,105 acres, began in 1941 as a small part of the former 45,400-acre Havasu Lake National Wildlife Refuge. When some of that area was de-authorized in 1964, the Bill Williams River and Havasu refuges were established to continue the protection of especially important ecological values along the lower Colorado River. The Bill Williams River refuge encompasses an area of cattail marsh and one of the last remaining natural riparian stands of Fremont cottonwood/Goodding willow woodland along the lower Colorado River. Surrounded by the rugged Sonoran Desert, the refuge is located along the lowest stretch of the Bill Williams River, a tributary of the Colorado River in west-central Arizona.

The refuge's narrow strip of water-dependent habitat is an oasis for a large diversity of wildlife. More than 330 species of birds have been recorded here. A small population of the secretive and endangered Yuma clapper rail breeds in the river delta's dense cattail marsh, along with the Arizona state-listed endangered California black rail. Wintering waterfowl, such as Canada geese and numerous ducks come to the refuge's marsh and adjacent open water. A large variety of neotropical songbirds, such as summer and western tanagers, black-headed and blue grosbeaks, and hooded and Bullock's orioles, are attracted to the lush riparian habitat. Among the refuge's more than 50 species of mammals are desert bighorn sheep, mule deer, mountain lion, bobcat, coyote, gray fox, and collared peccary (javelina).

One of the refuge's important management activities is the reintroduction of two endangered species of native fish, razorback sucker and bonytail chub, in a cove impoundment near the mouth of the Bill Williams River. When the young reach about ten inches in length, they are released into Lake Havasu. The ultimate goal is to release these species into stretches of free-flowing river.

Establishment of this refuge was made possible partly with revenues from the sale of Migratory Bird Hunting and Conservation Stamps (Duck Stamps).

The refuge is open daily during daylight hours. There is no entrance fee. The refuge headquarters/visitor center is open on weekdays, except national holidays.

Visitor activities include wildlife observation (including from the visitor center's observation deck), driving the unpaved Planet Ranch Road about three miles east from State Hwy. 95 (and on another road several miles to the east by four-wheel-drive vehicle), hiking on the latter road, walking the 0.25-mile interpretive trail near the refuge office, canoeing and boating, fishing, and hunting on parts of the refuge during the designated seasons.

Hand carried boats and canoes can be launched adjacent to the refuge headquarters; and other boats can be launched from the end of Parker Dam Rd., a mile south of headquarters. Although camping is not permitted on the refuge, campground facilities are provided in the vicinity of Lake Havasu City to the north and Parker to the south.

Sunscreen and lots of water are advised, especially during the hotter months. Visitors are cautioned to be alert for the western diamondback and Mojave rattlesnakes. The best time to visit the refuge is from mid-autumn through mid-spring.

Access to the refuge from I-10 at Quartzsite is north about fifty miles (through Parker) on Arizona State Hwy. 95. Or from Exit 9 on I-40, it is south about forty miles (through Lake Havasu City) on State Hwy. 95. This highway crosses the refuge's delta marsh on the Bill Williams Bridge, and pull-offs are provided to the north and south of the bridge from which to view this part of the refuge. Planet Ranch Road branches east from Hwy. 95, 0.3 mile south of the bridge and just north of the refuge headquarters.

Information: Bill Williams River NWR, 60911 Hwy. 95, Parker, AZ 85344; tel.: (928) 667-4144.

Buenos Aires, comprising more than 117,000 acres, was established in 1985 to protect and restore an ecologically significant expanse of Sonoran Desert grassland for the masked bobwhite quail and a number of other threatened and endangered species, as well as a tremendous diversity of native fauna and flora. The refuge is located in the Altar Valley, near the base of the rugged Baboquivari Mountains, about 45 miles by highway southwest of Tucson in southern Arizona. The refuge's Spanish name, *Buenos Aires,* meaning "good winds," was derived from Buenos Ayres Ranch, founded by Pedro Aguirre, Jr., in 1864.

One of the refuge's primary objectives is to re-establish a self-sustaining breeding population of the federally listed endangered masked bobwhite. This subspecies, the male of which has a distinctive black facial mask and throat and rufous underparts, formerly ranged from the high desert grasslands of southeastern Arizona southward to central Sonora, Mexico. The last wild masked bobwhite populations occur on Mexican ranchlands.

Since 1985, the refuge has been expanded to give protection to ecologically significant wetland and riparian habitats along Arivaca Creek and Arivaca Cienega, and in Brown Canyon. As the Fish and Wildlife Service says, "This combination of grasslands, wetlands, cottonwood-lined streambeds, and sycamore and live oak mountain canyons preserves some of the Southwest's rarest habitats for seven endangered species, ten species of concern, and many other native plants and wildlife." In addition to the masked bobwhite, the endangered species are the cactus ferruginous pygmy-owl; peregrine falcon; southwestern willow flycatcher; razorback sucker; Kearney bluestar, a member of the dogbane family that is endemic to the Baboquivari Mountains; and Pima pineapple cactus. Over 320 bird species have been recorded here.

The refuge is open daily during daylight hours. There is no entrance fee, except in Brown Canyon, which is presently open by guided tour only. For information on the Brown Canyon tour schedule, group tours, and fees: tel.: (520) 823-4251, ext. 116. The refuge visitor center is open daily, and the headquarters is open on weekdays, except national holidays.

Visitor activities include wildlife and butterfly observation; driving the unpaved, 10-mile Antelope Drive; hiking; docent-led interpretive walks; environmental education programs; horseback riding on refuge roads to the north of Arivaca Rd.; camping at a number of primitive campsites along back roads (14-day limit); and hunting on most of the refuge during the designated seasons. Near the visitor center, there are pens that afford an opportunity to see the secretive masked bobwhite, bird feeders that attract numerous species of birds, a butterfly garden, and a grassland exhibit where more than twenty species of grasses can be identified.

Hiking opportunities include the 0.5-mile Arivaca Cienega boardwalk to Willow Pond or the entire two-mile loop trail; a one-mile trail at Arivaca Creek beneath giant cottonwood trees and other lush vegetation that contrasts with the surrounding high desert environment; and the more challenging five-mile round-trip Mustang Trail. Visitors are cautioned to be alert for rattlesnakes and be prepared for afternoon summer "monsoon" thunderstorm rains that can quickly flood normally dry washes.

Lodgings and meals are limited in the vicinity of the refuge, but (with advance reservations) are provided at Rancho de la Osa, tel.: (800) 872-6240, just north of Sasabe; Elkhorn Ranch, tel.: (520) 822-1040, in the Baboquivari Mountains' Sabino Canyon; and Casa Bella Bed and Breakfast, toll-free tel.: (877) 604-3385, just outside Arivaca. Lodgings and meals are also available in Tucson.

Access to the refuge visitor center from I-10 in Tucson is west 22 miles on State Hwy. 86 to Three Points, and south about 38 miles on State Hwy. 286.

Information: Buenos Aires NWR, P.O. Box 109, Sasabe, AZ 85633; tel.: (520) 823-4247.

Cabeza Prieta, consisting of 860,010 acres, was established in 1939 to protect desert bighorn sheep in a vast expanse of the Sonoran Desert. Eight serrated mountain ranges—Childs, Growler, Granite, Bryan, Agua Dulce, Sierra Pinta, Cabeza Prieta, and Tule—rise from broad desert valleys. A lava-capped granite peak in one of the remote ranges gave rise to the Spanish name *Cabeza Prieta*, meaning "dark head." The refuge is located along 56 miles of the U.S.-Mexico border, in southwestern Arizona.

From June through October, the daytime high temperature typically exceeds 100 degrees for roughly 100 consecutive days. Soaking winter rains and local midsummer "monsoon" thunderstorm showers annually average as much as nine inches of precipitation across the eastern end of the refuge, dropping to only about three inches on the western end. As author Bill Broyles explains, "The greater rainfall toward the east produces denser and more lush vegetation than occurs in the drier western end. Some plants, such as beavertail cactus, many-headed barrel cactus, and Bigelow nolina, prefer drier soil and are found mainly in the west. Large cacti, such as saguaro and organ pipe, require more precipitation, and are found mainly in the east."

Shrubby trees include honey and velvet mesquites, blue and foothill palo verdes, ironwood, desert-willow, smoke tree, and elephant tree. Other common plants include catclaw acacia, creosotebush, brittlebush, ocotillo, desert marigold, desert globemallow; sand verbena, primrose, and desert gold poppy.

The largest mammals on the refuge are the desert bighorn sheep and the rare and endangered Sonoran pronghorn. Past pronghorn management has included the protection of habitat, removal of grazing from the refuge, placement of experimental waters, fencing parts of the boundary to prevent trespass of cattle, and study of the pronghorn's movements and habitat use. Additional experimental waters and forage plots have been proposed.

The refuge is open daily. Visitors are required to obtain a free entry permit, which is available at the refuge office or from the office by mail. The refuge office/visitor center is open on weekdays, except national holidays. From November to March, the Cabeza Prieta Natural History Association presents biweekly programs on the natural history of the refuge. The refuge office can provide a schedule of free evening talks. Other special programs, events, and tours are scheduled throughout the year.

Visitor activities include wildlife observation, viewing interpretive displays in the visitor center, walking a self-guiding path near the visitor center and hiking anywhere on the refuge, driving on non-wilderness unpaved refuge roads, primitive camping, and a limited desert bighorn sheep hunt (the state issues from one to eight permits annually). Recommended campsites are located at Papago Well, Tule Well, and Christmas Pass.

Driving the refuge's roads, including Christmas Pass Rd. and the historic El Camino del Diablo, generally requires a four-wheel-drive vehicle, except on the Charlie Bell Trail, west from Ajo, on which a high-clearance, two-wheel-drive vehicle can generally be driven. Off-road driving is strictly prohibited. Sections of the refuge may also be closed during the endangered pronghorn fawning season (March 15 to July 15). Update: As of this writing, El Camino del Diablo is temporarily closed because of its impassable condition. Visitors are urged to contact the refuge office prior to arrival to obtain the latest information on road conditions.

Visitors are warned that driving and hiking excursions on the refuge are very challenging. Consequently, adequate preparations and provisions are essential (contact the refuge headquarters for suggestions and cautions). Visitors are urged to be alert for venomous rattlesnakes.

Lodgings and meals are available in Ajo.

Access to the refuge's visitor center from Exit 115 on I-8 at Gila Bend is south 42 miles on State Hwy. 85 to Ajo; or from Exit 99 on I-19 in Tucson, it is west 115 miles on State Hwy. 86 to Why and right 10 miles on State Hwy. 85 to Ajo.

Information: Cabeza Prieta NWR, 1611 North Second Ave., Ajo, AZ 85321; tel.: (520) 387-6483.

Cibola, encompassing 17,267 acres, was established in 1964 as mitigation for the loss of habitat and other environmental impacts of dams and flood-control facilities that were built on the Colorado River from the 1930s through the 1960s. The refuge protects important floodplain wetland habitat, including historic channels, backwaters, lakes, and ponds along a 12-mile stretch of the river. This oasis in the Sonoran Desert includes more than 16,000 acres of riparian habitat and attracts the largest concentrations of wintering Canada geese and greater sandhill cranes on the lower Colorado. The refuge is located in southeastern California and southwestern Arizona.

Common species of ducks that winter here include mallard, northern pintail, green-winged teal, gadwall, and American wigeon. The secretive Yuma clapper rail, a federally listed endangered subspecies, nests in the refuge's cattail-and-bulrush marsh habitat, along with the Arizona state-listed California black rail. More than 280 bird species have been recorded here.

Establishment of Cibola refuge was made possible partly with revenues from the sale of Migratory Bird Hunting and Conservation Stamps (Duck Stamps). The Fish and Wildlife Service's habitat management activities include the restoration and flooding of former river backwaters and meanders; control of the non-native, aggressively invasive tamarisk (salt cedar); and planting of native species such as Fremont cottonwood, willows, and mesquite. Under cooperative agreements with local farmers, approximately 1,600 acres of the refuge are planted with crops such as alfalfa, corn, milo, and millet that provide nutrient-rich food for wintering waterfowl and other wildlife.

As Refuge Manager Michael Hawkes explains:

Cibola is one of four national wildlife refuges on the lower Colorado River. . . . The Colorado River has historically been a key corridor for wildlife, especially neotropical migratory birds; and although the landscape, primarily vegetation and water flow, has been drastically altered over the last century, it remains a significant migration route. It is important to help preserve and restore the habitat components that numerous species of wildlife depend upon in this riparian system that lies within a harsh desert environment.

The refuge is open daily during daylight hours. There is no entrance fee. The refuge headquarters/visitor center is open on weekdays, except national holidays.

Visitor activities include wildlife observation; viewing displays at the visitor center; driving a 3-mile loop that offers views of flooded impoundments and farm fields, where large numbers of ducks, geese, and cranes can be seen during the winter; hiking; canoeing, kayaking, and boating; fishing; and hunting on parts of the refuge during the designated seasons. Camping is not permitted on the refuge.

Sunscreen and lots of water are advised; and visitors are cautioned to be alert for rattlesnakes. The best times to visit Cibola Refuge are from mid-autumn through mid-spring.

Lodgings and meals are available in Blythe, Calif.; and Ehrenberg and Yuma, Ariz.

Access to Cibola refuge from I-10 at Blythe, Calif., is south on Neighbor's Blvd., crossing the Colorado River on Cibola Bridge into Arizona, and continuing 3.5 miles (following directional signs) to the headquarters/visitor center.

Information: Cibola NWR, Route 2, Box 1, Cibola, AZ 85328; tel.: (928) 857-3253.

Havasu, containing 37,515 acres, began in 1941 as a small part of the former 45,400-acre Havasu Lake National Wildlife Refuge. When much of that refuge was de-authorized, the Havasu and Bill Williams River national wildlife refuges were designated in 1991 for migratory birds and other wildlife. Highlighted by the Topock Marsh and the ruggedly scenic Topock Gorge, this refuge is located on 85-mile-long Lake Havasu, a reservoir formed behind Parker Dam on the Colorado River, in west-central Arizona and southeastern California.

Topock Marsh, encompassing 4,000 acres in the northern end of the refuge, consists of large areas of emergent plants, such as cattails, bulrushes, rushes, and sedges. This ecologically significant wetland provides ideal habitat for numerous species of waterbirds, including the federally listed endangered Yuma clapper rail and the California black rail (listed by Arizona as endangered and by California as threatened). Other birds include great blue and green herons, great and snowy egrets, snow and Canada geese and numerous species of ducks that winter here. More than 300 bird species have been recorded here.

Much of the central area of the refuge contains both the Colorado River's spectacular Topock Gorge and adjacent designated wilderness, where the Sonoran Desert, to the south, and Mojave Desert, to the north, merge. This desert expanse comprises nearly a third of the refuge.

The contrast between the sparkling water of the lake; the green of small, scattered wetland and riparian habitats of cottonwoods and willows bordering the shore of sheltered coves; and the raw, jagged, multi-hued desert peaks, rock formations, and cliffs presents one of the most awesome scenes in the National Wildlife Refuge System.

Desert bighorn sheep inhabit sheer, rocky cliffs and mountains of the gorge. Other mammals include mule deer, mountain lion, coyote, and black-tailed jackrabbit. More than 300 species of birds, such as the roadrunner and phainopepla, have been recorded here. Four species of rattlesnakes have been identified—the western diamondback, speckled, Mojave green, and sidewinder. Shrubby desert trees include foothill and blue palo verdes, ironwood, and desert-willow. The smoketree grows in desert washes where little else survives. Cacti include beavertail prickly pear, several chollas, barrel, and hedgehog.

At the northern end of the refuge, the Fish and Wildlife Service provides an area of moist-soil impoundments and croplands, where wheat, millet, and various other crops provide an important source of food for wintering waterfowl. Establishment of the refuge was made possible partly with revenues from the sale of Migratory Bird Hunting and Conservation Stamps (Duck Stamps).

The refuge is open daily. There is no entrance fee. The refuge headquarters, located at 317 Mesquite Ave., Needles, Calif., is open on weekdays, except national holidays.

Visitor activities include wildlife observation; canoeing, boating, and rafting (there are several boat-launching sites); water skiing on designated areas of the lake; camping at RV and tent facilities located at Five Mile Landing; camping in the wilderness by permit only; fishing; and hunting in specified areas during the designated seasons.

Regarding the safe operation of watercraft, the Fish and Wildlife Service says, "To protect floating-nest birds, jet powered personal watercraft . . . are not allowed in backwaters off the main Colorado River channel for the 15-mile [Topock Gorge]. . . . Boating on refuge waters is extremely popular. Please stay out of restricted areas, which are marked by signs and buoys."

Hiking opportunities include a four-mile loop within the refuge's Topock Farm Unit on impoundment dikes; and within the wilderness areas. Wilderness hikers are cautioned to be well prepared before tackling the challenging conditions in these rugged and remote areas. Insect repellent, sunscreen, and lots of drinking water are advised, especially during hotter months. Visitors are cautioned to be alert for rattlesnakes. The most favorable times to visit the refuge are mid-autumn through mid-spring.

Lodgings and meals are available in Needles, Calif., and Lake Havasu City, Ariz.

Information: Havasu NWR, P.O. Box 3009, Needles, CA 92363; tel.: (760) 326-3853.

Kofa, consisting of 665,400 acres, was established in 1939 to protect and manage important Sonoran Desert habitat for desert bighorn sheep that live in and around the canyon-gashed Kofa and Castle Dome Mountains of western Arizona. The refuge supports roughly 800 of these mammals (their numbers fluctuate through time). As the Fish and Wildlife Service says, "Natural water sources are highly variable and may not last until seasonal changes can replenish the supply. By enlarging natural water holes, shading them to reduce evaporation, and blasting artificial basins in areas previously without a water supply, refuge managers have greatly increased the availability and reliability of water. . . . desert bighorn have responded to this assistance by producing a larger, healthier herd."

The name, *Kofa*, is derived from the former "King of Arizona" gold-mining operation that began in the late 19th century. More than a half-million acres were designated in 1990 by Congress as the Kofa Wilderness.

Probably the only native palm trees in Arizona grow in several of the refuge's hidden canyons. The California fan palm grows more abundantly along spring-fed streams within canyons and washes around the edge of California's Coachella Valley (see further information in the Coachella Valley NWR text). Here in the Kofa Mountains, there are small, scattered clusters of these picturesque palms—their lush green fronds providing a fascinating contrast to the raw, erosion-carved cliffs.

Among the refuge's trees are palo verde, ironwood, and mesquite. Shrubs and other plants include creosotebush, Kofa Mountain barberry, and a yucca-like plant known as nolina. Common birds include the verdin, canyon wren, black-tailed gnatcatcher, curve-billed thrasher, canyon towhee, black-throated sparrow, and phainopepla. The latter species feeds on the berries of mistletoe, and its fluttering flight pattern is suggestive of a butterfly. The male is jet black with white wing patches and the female is gray with wing patches, and both have a cardinal-like crest. More than 185 bird species have been recorded in this refuge.

The refuge is open daily. There is no entrance fee.

Visitor activities include wildlife observation, driving on unpaved refuge roads (many of which are passable only in a four-wheel-drive vehicle), hiking, and limited hunting during the designated seasons. Off-road vehicle travel is prohibited. Primitive camping on the refuge is limited to 14 days in any 12-month period, is not permitted within a quarter mile of a wildlife water hole, and vehicles are to remain within 100 feet of designated roads. Although campfires are allowed, wood is very scarce and the Fish and Wildlife Service emphasizes that only dead, down, and detached wood may be used.

Hiking opportunities include the Palm Canyon Trail—a 0.5-mile, 300-foot climb into this awesome, sheer-walled canyon for a view of fan palms growing in the narrow slot of a side canyon. This is also a place where desert bighorn sheep can sometimes be spotted. Other hiking options include challenging wilderness excursions, for which adequate preparations and provisions are essential (information is available at the refuge headquarters). Sunscreen and lots of drinking water are advised, especially during the hotter months. Visitors are cautioned to be alert for rattlesnakes. The most enjoyable time to visit the refuge is from late autumn through early spring.

Lodgings and meals are available in Yuma and Ehrenberg, Ariz., and Blythe, Calif.

Access to the refuge is east on several unpaved roads from U.S. Hwy. 95, between I-10 at Quartzsite and I-8 at Yuma. The 7-mile, signed road to Palm Canyon branches from Hwy. 95 just north of mile marker 85, about 18 miles south of Quartzsite and about 63 miles north of Yuma. The unpaved, county-maintained road into King Valley, between the Kofa and Castle Dome mountains, branches east from Hwy. 95 at mile marker 77; and the unpaved, county-maintained road to the Castle Dome Mountains branches from Hwy. 95 at mile marker 55.

Information: Kofa NWR, 356 West First St., Yuma, AZ 85364; tel.: (928) 783-7861.

Arkansas

Felsenthal, containing 65,000 acres, was established in 1975 to enhance and protect 10,000 acres of pine uplands, 40,000 acres of southern bottomland hardwood forest, and the 15,000-acre Felsenthal Pool, in southern Arkansas. This refuge is upstream from the U.S. Army Corps of Engineers' Felsenthal Dam, around the junction of the Ouachita and Saline rivers.

The Fish and Wildlife Service regulates the seasonal flooding of the refuge's bottomland forest habitat, known as green-tree reservoir management. Felsenthal Pool, the world's largest such impoundment, is flooded and expanded to more than twice its normal size for the benefit of herons, egrets, and large concentrations of at least twenty species of wintering ducks and other waterbirds.

During the summer, the water level in other impoundment areas, known as moist-soil units, is lowered to promote the growth of waterfowl plant foods. In the autumn, these areas are re-flooded to make this food readily available to the wintering waterfowl.

The refuge provides wood duck nesting boxes, supplementing the natural supply of nesting cavities. In the uplands, where the rare and endangered red-cockaded woodpecker drills nesting cavities in the boles of mature pine trees, the refuge practices selective cutting and periodic prescribed burning, to maintain open woodland with the mature pines required by this specialized species. To promote new woodpecker breeding colonies, artificial nest inserts are provided to supplement natural tree cavities.

Other wildlife inhabiting the refuge includes migratory shorebirds, wintering bald eagles, flocks of wild turkeys, numerous species of neotropical migratory songbirds, the rare Louisiana black bear, and the alligator, which is at the northern edge of its range here. Nearly 300 bird species have been recorded here.

The refuge is open daily. There is no entrance fee. The visitor center, which offers interpretive exhibits and programs, is open Sundays through Fridays and closed on Christmas.

Visitor activities include wildlife observation, interpretive programs, prearranged group tours, driving on 15 miles of unpaved roads, hiking on more than 60 miles of trails, high-flotation ATV use on designated ATV trails, canoeing and boating (a dozen boat ramps are available), camping (ten primitive campsites on the refuge, campground facilities at adjacent Moro Bay State Park, and two nearby privately run campgrounds), fishing (by boat and from a wheel-chair-accessible fishing area near the visitor center), and hunting during the designated seasons. November through April is the best time for birdwatching.

Although alligators are generally afraid of people, visitors are cautioned to stay a safe distance from them and to be alert for venomous snakes, fire ants, ticks, and chiggers. Insect repellent is advised.

Lodgings and meals are available in such communities as Crosset and El Dorado.

Access to the refuge's visitor center is west 5 miles on U.S. Hwy. 82 from Crossett, or east 45 miles on Hwy. 82 from El Dorado.

Information: Felsenthal NWR, 5531 Hwy. 82 West, Crossett, AR 71635; tel.: (870) 364-3167.

White River, containing 160,000 acres, was established in 1935 as a refuge for migratory birds and other wildlife along the White River of eastern Arkansas. The forest of oaks, bald cypress, and other tree species is one of the largest remaining seasonally flooded, hardwood-forested bottomland riparian areas in the lower Mississippi River Valley and the most extensive contiguous area of this habitat under a single ownership in the United States.

As Devereux Butcher wrote in his 1963 book, *Exploring Our National Wildlife Refuges,*

The outstanding feature of this refuge is its southern bottomland hardwood forest. . . . In places the effect is almost Amazonian, with vines clambering high among the trees. The White River winds a tortuous course through the refuge, forming oxbows, and branching with a number of equally twisting tributaries. Throughout the forest are innumerable crescent-shaped lakes, remnants of former river channels, many of them rimmed with cypress trees.

Highlighting the refuge's rich abundance and diversity of wildlife are several hundred thousand wintering ducks, earning the area's reputation as the duck capital of the United States. The mallard is by far the most abundant duck here, with more than a half million on refuge lakes in early January. Other species include nesting wood ducks, thousands of wintering Canada geese, migratory shorebirds, bald eagles, resident wild turkeys, huge influxes of neotropical migratory songbirds, and numerous black bears and whitetail deer.

The ivory-billed woodpecker, the largest woodpecker north of Mexico, once inhabited the virgin-growth bottomland forests of the Mississippi River Valley, including the refuge. Ornithologists are now virtually certain that this magnificent bird is extinct. (See further discussion of the species in the Tensas River NWR text.)

Establishment of the White River refuge was made possible mostly with revenues from the sale of Migratory Bird Hunting and Conservation Stamps (Duck Stamps).

The refuge is open daily. There is no entrance fee.

Visitor activities include wildlife observation, driving unpaved refuge roads and two-track trails during the drier seasons, hiking many miles of trails, camping during some of the year, canoeing and boating, fishing, and hunting on parts of the refuge during the designated seasons. During the winter and spring, parts of the refuge are often closed due to flooding, and other areas, which are designated as waterfowl sanctuaries, are closed to public access. November through June is the best time for birdwatching. Visitors are cautioned to be alert for venomous snakes, ticks, and chiggers. Insect repellent is advised.

Lodgings and meals are available in such communities as DeWitt, Helena, Stuttgart, and Clarendon.

Access to the refuge is south and east 27 miles on State Hwy. 30 from U.S. Hwy. 79 at Stuttgart to DeWitt; and 16 miles on State Hwy. 1 to St. Charles and the refuge entrance.

Information: White River NWR, P.O. Box 308, DeWitt, AR 72042; tel.: (870) 282-8200.

California

Don Edwards San Francisco Bay encompasses 25,902 acres and is working toward a goal of 43,000 acres. The refuge was established in 1974 to restore, enhance, and protect significant wetland habitat for the benefit of waterfowl and other waterbirds, shorebirds, a number of threatened and endangered species, and other wildlife. As America's largest urban national wildlife refuge, it offers a wide range of interpretive programs, and many opportunities for wildlife-oriented recreation. The refuge, which is one of seven in the San Francisco Bay NWR Complex, is located around the southern end of San Francisco Bay, in northern California. Over 290 bird species have been recorded here.

Among the refuge's habitats are about 12,000 acres of salt ponds, more than 3,600 acres of salt marsh, 1,200 acres of uplands, more than 1,000 acres of seasonal wetlands, and 4,400 acres of tidal mudflats/open water. Significant species include the federally listed endangered California brown pelican, California clapper rail, California least tern, and the threatened western snowy plover.

As described in the Fish and Wildlife Service's Autumn 2001 refuge newsletter, *Tideline*, by editor and refuge complex Outdoor Recreation Planner Carmen Leong, refuge complex Project Leader Marge Kolar, and Natalie Doerr:

In the mid-1960's, a group of local citizens decided too many wetlands had been lost, so they formed a grass-roots organization in hopes of creating a national wildlife refuge in south San Francisco Bay: the South San Francisco Baylands Planning, Conservation and National Wildlife Refuge Committee. At the time, the Fish and Wildlife Service was not interested in establishing a refuge in an urban area, so the Committee headed straight to Congress. . . . [legislation establishing] the refuge passed in 1972 with an approved boundary of 23,000 acres. On October 8, 1974, the San Francisco Bay National Wildlife Refuge became . . . the first urban refuge in the nation. In the mid 1980's, some of the same folks, involved with the earlier lobbying effort, resolved to protect all the remaining South Bay wetland areas. Through the Citizen's Committee to Complete the Refuge's efforts, Congress authorized the expansion of the refuge to 43,000 acres! Retired Congressman Don Edwards' name was added to the refuge title in 1995, as a tribute to the man who played a pivotal role in the establishment and expansion of the refuge.

In 1997, an opportunity to restore an area of salt marsh known as the "entry triangle marsh" arose when a salt company closed a rainwater-runoff culvert. Ducks Unlimited, Inc. contributed its expertise and time to design the restoration plan. Other contributors to this project were the San Francisco Bay Wildlife Society, National Fish and Wildlife Foundation, Wildlife Forever, the FWS Coastal Program, and the Oracle Corporation.

In 1999, following many decades of effort by local conservationists, the Fish and Wildlife Service acquired the largest privately owned parts of Bair Island from the Peninsula Open Space Trust (POST). This 3,200-acre area consists of three islands separated by tidal channels.

The refuge is open daily during daylight hours. There is no entrance fee. The refuge visitor center, in Fremont, is open on Tuesdays through Sundays, except national holidays. The Environmental Education Center, in Alviso (San Jose), is open during weekends to visitors. For information on the education center, tel.: (408) 262-5513.

Visitor activities include wildlife and butterfly observation; interpretive programs; hiking on more than thirty miles of trails; bicycling; canoeing, kayaking, and boating on the refuge's tidal sloughs and open bay waters; fishing from piers and shore; and hunting on parts of the refuge during the designated seasons. In late June, an annual butterfly count is held on the refuge by the North American Butterfly Association. For information, tel.: (510) 792-0222.

Access to the refuge's visitor center from State Route 84 (at the east end of Dumbarton Bridge) is by way of Thornton Ave. exit, south 0.8 mile, right into the refuge on Marshlands Rd., and left at the stop sign. Access to the refuge Environmental Education Center from State Hwy. 237 exit on U.S. Hwy. 101 is east on Hwy. 237 (toward Alviso) and left on Zanker Rd.; or from the State Hwy. 237 exit on I-880, it is west (toward Alviso) on Hwy. 237 and right on Zanker Rd.

Information: Don Edwards San Francisco Bay NWR, P.O. Box 524, Newark, CA 94560; tel.: (510) 792-0222.

Farallon, containing 211 acres, was established in 1909 by President Theodore Roosevelt to protect a cluster of surf-pounded islands that are located in the Pacific Ocean about 30 miles west of San Francisco, California.

The refuge contains the largest continental seabird breeding colony south of Alaska, with nearly 30 percent of California's breeding seabirds. Its islands support a dozen nesting seabird species, including the world's largest breeding colonies of ashy storm petrel, Brandt's cormorant, and western gull. Among other species that nest here are common murre, pigeon guillemot, Cassin's and rhinoceros auklets, and tufted puffin (the refuge is the letter's southernmost nesting colony). The islands also support six species of pinnipeds. After an absence of more than a century, northern elephant seals returned in 1959 and have been breeding on the South Farallon Islands for more than 25 years. Northern fur seals were extirpated in the 1800s and just recently (1996) began breeding here again.

Although the refuge is closed to visitation to avoid disturbing the wildlife, a Farallon natural history cruise from San Francisco provides a close-up view of the islands and their wildlife inhabitants as well as opportunities to see other marine mammals such as dolphins and whales. The Oceanic Society's all-day Farallon cruises depart from San Francisco's Marina District on Fridays, Saturdays, and Sundays from June through November. Information: tel.: (415) 474-3385. Other tour operators and boat charters that offer boat trips to the Farallons are based at Emeryville, Sausalito, and Half Moon Bay.

Information: Farallon NWR, c/o San Francisco Bay NWR Complex, P.O. Box 524, Newark, CA 94560; tel.: (510) 792-0222.

Guadalupe-Nipomo Dunes, encompassing 2,553 acres acquired toward a goal of approximately 8,900 acres, was established in 2000 to protect and restore an ecologically sensitive and significant stretch of Pacific coastal habitats. The refuge extends northward from the mouth of Santa Maria River, adjacent to the city of Guadalupe, in southern California.

Among the diverse habitats within the refuge boundary are fore-dunes, active sand dunes, an extensive area of coastal dune scrub, central coast sage scrub, arroyo willow riparian woodland, ephemeral dune swale, and open and deepwater wetlands. Establishment of the refuge was begun with The Nature Conservancy's donation of a 2,553-acre tract.

As explained by the Fish and Wildlife Service:

The . . . Refuge is located in a transition zone between Northern and Southern California plant communities, resulting in a high degree of habitat diversity, a high number of local endemics, and high susceptibility to disturbance. The . . . Refuge is located within the Dunes Complex which is a complex mosaic of terrestrial, semi-aquatic, and aquatic plant communities containing 18 species of rare, endangered, or sparsely distributed plants.

The fore-dunes along the strand of beach support sparse, low-growing plants such as crisp dune mint, beach bur, and beach saltbush. As the Fish and Wildlife Service says, "This is the habitat where the endangered least tern and threatened snowy plover nest, and management efforts will concentrate on providing an optimum nesting environment for these species."

The central coast dune scrub habitat, occurring farther inland, covers the majority of the stabilized sand dunes, with such low-growing shrubs as dune lupine and giant coreopsis. Areas of central coast sage scrub, occurring mostly on inland back-dunes, support such species as California sagebrush and pygmy coast live oak.

Arroyo willow riparian woodland, seasonal and permanent wetlands, and deepwater wetlands contain thickets of arroyo willow and wax myrtle. The threatened California red-legged frog inhabits wetland habitats within the authorized refuge boundary and will benefit from habitat enhancement. Migrating and resident waterfowl are also attracted to these wetlands.

The Guadalupe-Nipomo Dunes Center is an important nonprofit partner assisting the refuge with visitor orientation (Friday, Saturday, and Sunday afternoons), interpreter-guided walks, educational outreach, coordination of ecosystem-wide vegetation restoration efforts, and research facilitation to promote the protection of the Guadalupe-Nipomo Dunes.

Information: Guadalupe-Nipomo Dunes Center, P.O. Box 339, Guadalupe, CA 93434; tel.: (805) 343-2455; and Web site: www.dunescenter.org.

The refuge is open daily during daylight hours. There is no entrance fee.

Visitor activities include wildlife observation, hiking along the beach, and docent-led interpretive and environmental education programs by the Dunes Center. Sunscreen is especially advised during the warmer months.

Lodgings and meals are available in such communities as Santa Maria and Arroyo Grande.

Access to the Guadalupe-Nipomo Dunes Center is by way of State Hwy. 1 to Guadalupe; the Dunes Center is located at 1055 Guadalupe Street (State Hwy. 1). Access onto the refuge itself is provided through two access points. The northern access: through the Oso Flaco Natural Area, where visitors can walk along a (wheelchair-accessible) boardwalk through dune habitats and across a freshwater lake; upon reaching the beach, visitors can hike south to reach the refuge. The southern access: through the Rancho Guadalupe Dunes County Park, where visitors can drive along a scenic road to a parking area within the fore-dunes. From here visitors can hike north along the beach to reach the refuge.

Information: Guadalupe-Nipomo Dunes NWR, P.O. Box 9, Guadalupe, CA 93434; tel.: (805) 343-9151.

Hopper Mountain, comprising 2,471 acres, was established in 1974 primarily to protect habitat for the endangered California condor. The refuge contains a condor holding facility for captive-bred chicks and serves as a base of operations for Fish and Wildlife Service personnel involved with the condor recovery and reintroduction program. It is located adjacent to Los Padres National Forest, along the southern edge of the rugged Topatopa Mountains in Ventura

County, California. The majority of the refuge's habitats consist of grassland that is part of the condor's historic foraging habitat, chaparral and coastal sage scrub, and woodlands of California and canyon live oaks and California black walnut.

With a nine-foot wingspread, the California condor is North America's largest native land bird. As described in the mid-1960s by the National Audubon Society (NAS):

The California condor is an inspiring spectacle as it rides the currents of air above its wilderness home. . . . The condor's steady soaring may reach 30 to 40 miles per hour in a remarkable non-flapping flight pattern. . . .

The condor, like the turkey vulture, is primarily a carrion eater, feeding on the carcasses of cattle and sheep, deer and other wildlife which die of accident or disease or are killed by predators.

It is estimated that there were once thousands of these expert gliders, whose range extended south along the West Coast, from British Columbia to Baja California, east to Florida, and north along the East Coast to New York State.

By the late 19th century, the population had declined to around 600 birds. In 1939, with the condor population continuing its ominous decline, National Audubon researcher Carl B. Koford initiated intensive studies of the species, in which he estimated that between sixty and 100 condors then remained in the wild. In 1947, the Forest Service established the Sespe Wildlife Area (subsequently renamed the Sespe Condor Sanctuary) in Los Padres National Forest.

In 1965, with fewer than sixty birds remaining, the Fish and Wildlife Service began a full-time condor research program at its Patuxent Wildlife Research Center in Maryland (see the Patuxent NWR text). Two years later, the California condor was included on the first federal endangered species list. In 1975, the initial 1,800 acres of the Hopper Mountain refuge were acquired to provide "a protective buffer" for the Sespe sanctuary. In that same year, the California Condor Recovery Team was formed and a recovery plan was adopted.

In 1981, the California Department of Fish and Game gave permission to the San Diego Wild Animal Park (SDWAP) and Los Angeles Zoo to breed California condors in captivity and gave approval to the Fish and Wildlife Service to trap three condors for captive breeding and conduct a three-year research program. The first chick was captured in 1982 and delivered to SDWAP. By this time, only 21 to 24 birds remained in the wild. The following year, two chicks and four eggs were removed from the wild. The eggs were hatched under artificial incubation at the San Diego Zoo. In 1985, three more eggs were taken from the wild: one hatched at the San Diego Zoo and one of the others at SDWAP.

In 1987, the last free-flying California condor, an adult male, was brought into captivity. In 1988, the first successful captive condor breeding occurred at SDWAP. Four chicks were hatched in captivity in 1989; 8 in 1990; 12 in 1991 and 1992; 15 in 1993, 1994, and 1995; 18 in 1996; and 20 in 1997.

Meanwhile, condor releases were begun, some of which proved unsuccessful. In 1995, a rearing facility was constructed on Hopper Mountain refuge. Four parent-reared chicks, the first captive-bred condors reared by their parents while in captivity, were transferred to this new facility and were released the following year in the national forest.

At the same time, an additional release site was being planned for the U.S. Bureau of Land Management–administered Vermilion Cliffs Wilderness, to the northeast of the Grand Canyon in Arizona. The Peregrine Fund's World Center for Birds of Prey, in Boise, Idaho, was selected to manage this reintroduction project. In late 1996, six juvenile condors were released atop these spectacular cliffs—the first time in seventy years that condors were again flying over this region.

Many additional releases were carried out in the late 1990s, including within a mountain wilderness near the Big Sur Coast of central California. As of May 2002, there were 68 condors living in the wild (39 in central and southern California, plus 29 in northern Arizona), and 115 in captivity. Thanks to the coordinated teamwork and intense commitment of all the many partners, the California Condor Recovery Program is amazingly successful for a species that only a few years ago was sliding toward extinction.

Although Hopper Mountain and two other refuges were established to protect condor habitat (see Bitter Creek and Blue Ridge refuge texts) and are not open to visitation, there are a number places from which condors can sometimes be seen.

Information: Hopper Mountain NWR Complex, P.O. Box 5839, Ventura, CA 93005; tel.: (805) 644-5185.

Humboldt Bay, currently containing about 3,000 acres in seven units toward a goal of nearly 10,000 acres, was established in 1971 to restore, manage, and protect one of the most significant coastal wetland habitats for migratory birds along the Pacific Coast. The refuge's authorized boundary encompasses all of South Humboldt Bay and several parts of North Humboldt Bay, near the city of Eureka in northwestern California.

The refuge's diverse habitats include eelgrass beds and mudflats, salt marsh, brackish marsh, freshwater marsh, diked seasonal wetlands, sand spits, and uplands. Humboldt Bay ranks as one of the most important places in the United States for the black brant, a species of goose that thrives on eelgrass. More than 30,000 of these birds have been recorded at one time on the bay. Banding has revealed that some of those birds that are attracted to Humboldt Bay have been seen in Canada, Alaska, Siberia, and Mexico.

Refuge lands acquired since the first few acres in 1971 include the 1,100-acre Salmon Creek Unit, on which the refuge headquarters and visitor center are located; the adjacent Hookton Slough Unit; and South Spit, which lies between the South Bay and the Pacific Ocean.

Among the refuge's management goals for Humboldt Bay Refuge are to expand and enhance eelgrass habitat for the black brant, increase habitat diversity, enhance wintering and migratory waterbird use of diked seasonal wetlands, and restore the lower end of Salmon Creek for anadromous fish passage upstream. More than 250 bird species have been recorded here.

The refuge also includes the 473-acre Lanphere Dunes Unit, containing the most pristine remaining dune ecosystem in the Pacific Northwest. Beginning in the 1940s, protection efforts by two Humboldt State University biology professors and subsequently by The Nature Conservancy safeguarded these dunes, which contain one of only two remaining areas of the globally endangered native fore-dune grassland community.

Refuge partners include Ducks Unlimited, Inc. that has helped enhance more than 700 acres of the refuge's wetland habitat, the California Waterfowl Association, Redwood Audubon Society, The Conservation Fund and The Nature Conservancy, Humboldt State University, and the California Department of Fish and Game.

The refuge is open daily during daylight hours. There is no entrance fee. The refuge headquarters/visitor center is open on weekdays, except national holidays. The visitor center may also be open on weekends (contact the refuge for the latest updates).

Visitor activities include wildlife observation; viewing interpretive exhibits in the visitor center; hiking on several trails; interpreter-guided walks by the Friends of the Dunes (tel.: [707] 444-1397); canoeing, kayaking, and boating; fishing; and limited hunting on part of the refuge during the designated seasons. Camping is not permitted on the refuge, but campground facilities are located nearby. One non-motorized boat-launching site is located on the refuge, and several other boat-launching sites are available nearby.

Lodgings are available in such communities as Arcata, Eureka, Fortuna, and Ferndale.

Access to Humboldt Bay refuge's headquarters/visitor center from the U.S. Hwy. 101 free way northbound is by way of the Hookton Rd. exit, left at the end of the off-ramp, across the freeway overpass, and right onto Ranch Rd. From U.S. 101 freeway southbound, it is the Hookton Road exit, right at the end of the off-ramp, and immediately left onto Ranch Rd.

Information: Humboldt Bay NWR, P.O. Box 576, 1020 Ranch Rd., Loleta, CA 95551; tel.: (707) 733-5406.

Lower Klamath, comprising 46,900 acres, was established in 1908 by President Theodore Roosevelt as the first national wildlife refuge primarily for the benefit of waterfowl. It is located within the Klamath Basin of northern California and southern Oregon. The refuge's habitats include shallow cattail-and-bulrush marsh, open water, grassy uplands, and managed croplands that provide feeding, resting, and nesting habitat for awesome concentrations of migrating and wintering ducks, geese, swans, and other waterbirds.

Historically, the wetlands of the arid Klamath Basin of northern California and southern Oregon totaled roughly 185,000 acres of freshwater marshes and shallow lakes. This was a mecca for the more than five million waterfowl—the world's largest known concentration, as well as American white pelicans and other waterbirds that came here to rest and feed during the spring and autumn migrations or to breed and raise their young. In 1905, the U.S. Bureau of Reclamation undertook the Klamath Reclamation Project, by which a large proportion of the basin's marsh and lake habitats in the Lower Klamath and Tule Lake area were converted to agricultural development. Less than one-quarter of the basin's historic wetlands now exist as fragmented remnants.

To protect and manage much of the remaining wetlands, five refuges were established: Tule Lake and Clear Lake, in California; Lower Klamath, in California/Oregon; and Upper Klamath and Klamath Marsh, in Oregon. A sixth basin refuge, Bear Valley, in Oregon, was established to provide protection for a major night-roosting area of forest for large numbers of wintering bald eagles. (See texts on each of these refuges.)

Agricultural, wildlife refuge, and other uses of the available water supplies are coordinated under the terms of an agreement between the Bureau of Reclamation and the Fish and Wildlife Service. During periods of severe drought, as periodically occurs in this near-desert region, it becomes extremely difficult and controversial to determine just how to fairly allocate the vital but limited water resources. As *Ducks Unlimited* senior writer Matt Young explained in his January/February 2002 article, "Wetlands Under Siege":

Despite the tremendous importance of Klamath Basin wetlands to Pacific Flyway waterfowl populations, these habitats are currently threatened by severe water shortages. . . . In 2001, a severe drought forced federal authorities to divert water from the irrigation project to provide habitat for several endangered fish species, preventing farmers from irrigating their crops and restricting water deliveries to the refuges. This also resulted in a dramatic decrease in the habitat available to waterfowl last fall, as well as greatly diminished hunting opportunities for waterfowlers.

DU [Ducks Unlimited, Inc.] has joined the Wildlife Management Institute, National Audubon Society, Audubon Society of Portland, and National Wildlife Refuge Association in support of a series of measures to improve wetland management at both the Lower Klamath and Tule Lake national wildlife refuges. . . . To date, DU has helped to conserve, restore, and enhance more than 17,000 wetland acres in the Klamath Basin, with an additional 25,000 acres of wetlands to be restored in the near future.

From late February through early April, peak numbers of waterfowl, including tundra swans, pause to rest and feed on the five wetland refuges on their way to breeding grounds farther north. The influx of migrating shorebirds reaches its northbound climax between mid-April and mid-May and its southbound climax from late July through August. During October and November, between one and two million waterfowl are attracted to these refuges. At least 1,000 wintering bald eagles have been counted in mid-February. Among the more than 175 species of birds that have been recorded on the refuge are American white pelican, great and snowy egrets, white-faced ibis, geese (greater white-fronted, snow, Ross's, and Canada), and sandhill crane. Mammals include mule deer, bobcat, coyote, red fox, mink, and river otter.

This refuge is open daily during daylight hours. There is a tour-route fee and hunting and photo-blind fees. The Klamath Basin NWR's headquarters/visitor center, located five miles west of the community of Tulelake, Calif., on Hill Rd., is open weekdays, except Christmas and New Year's Day.

Visitor activities include wildlife observation (a number of photo blinds are available), driving and bicycling on the ten-mile auto tour loop road, viewing interpretive exhibits at the visitor center, and hunting on parts of the refuge during the designated seasons.

Lodgings and meals are available in such communities as Tule Lake, Calif., and Klamath Falls, Ore.

Access to the refuge from U.S. Hwy. 97 just south of the California-Oregon line is east through the refuge on California State Hwy. 161. To reach the Klamath Basin refuges visitor center, it is east about six miles beyond the refuge's east entrance on Hwy. 161 and right about four miles on Hill Rd.

Information: Lower Klamath NWR, c/o Klamath Basin NWRs, 4009 Hill Rd., Tulelake, CA 96143; tel.: (530) 667-2231.

Sacramento, comprising 10,783 acres, was established in 1937 to restore and manage seasonally flooded marsh, riparian, permanent pond, watergrass, and upland grass habitats. The refuge, which attracts more than 500,000 ducks and 300,000 geese during the autumn and winter months, is one of six national wildlife refuges in the Sacramento NWR Complex. It is located within the Sacramento Valley, in north-central California.

As the Fish and Wildlife Service describes the history of this part of California:

The Sacramento NWR Complex represents a small portion of the vast seasonal wetlands and grasslands that once existed in the Sacramento Valley. Millions of waterfowl migrated down the Pacific Flyway to winter in the valley. . . . With the development of agriculture, in the late 1800's and early 1900's, natural habitat was replaced with rice and other crops. Waterfowl substituted these farm crops for their original wetland foods, causing serious losses for farmers.

Today, 95% of California's wetlands are gone. . . . New wetlands cannot be created naturally, since levees have been constructed to confine the river for irrigation and flood control. . . .

The six Refuges of the Complex are almost entirely manmade. In 1937, with the establishment of Sacramento National Wildlife Refuge, managers and biologists worked to transform the Refuge's dry, al-kaline lands into productive marshes. The Civilian Conservation Corps (CCC) using bulldozers and trac-tors, began creating marshes and ponds.

From the 1950s through the 1980s, Delevan, Colusa, Sutter, and Butte Sink refuges were established principally to create and manage additional wetlands for wintering waterfowl, and the Sacramento River refuge was established primarily to restore and protect important stretches of the river's riparian habitat between Red Bluff and Princeton. More than 265 bird species have been recorded on these refuges. (See separate texts on each of the other refuges.)

The Fish and Wildlife Service's habitat management activities include irrigating the wet-lands to mimic the Sacramento River's historic cycle of flooding. These seasonally flooded marshes are drained during the late spring and summer months to promote the growth of nu-trient-rich plants and then re-flooded in the autumn, making the plants and their seeds avail-able for waterfowl and other water birds. Ducks Unlimited, Inc. has helped enhance more than 600 acres of the refuge's wetland habitat.

Sacramento refuge is open daily during daylight hours. A modest entrance fee is charged. The Sacramento NWR Complex's visitor center is open daily (except national holidays) from October 1 through March, and only on weekdays during the rest of the year.

Visitor activities on this refuge include wildlife observation (two photo blinds are available, by advance reservation and payment of a daily use fee), viewing interpretive exhibits at the vis-itor center, driving the six-mile auto tour route, hiking a two-mile interpretive trail, environ-mental education programs for school and other groups (by prior arrangement), and hunting on parts of the refuge during the designated seasons. Insect repellent and sunscreen are advised during the warmer months.

Lodgings and meals in the vicinity of Sacramento refuge are available in such communities as Willows, Williams, and Yuba City.

Access to the refuge, from I-5 northbound, is by way of the Road 68 exit (20 miles north of Williams), right at the end of the off-ramp, and left onto State Hwy. 99W to the refuge en-trance on the right. Or from I-5 southbound, it is by way of the Road 68 exit (about seven miles south of Willows), left at the end of the off-ramp, and left on State Hwy. 99W.

Information: Sacramento NWR, 752 County Rd. 99W , Willows, CA 95988; tel.: (530) 934-2801.

San Luis, consisting of 26,609 acres, was established in 1966. The refuge is restoring, manag-ing, and protecting extensive wetlands and riparian habitat, with numerous tree-lined oxbows and channels, for the benefit of large concentrations of migratory waterfowl and other wildlife. It is located within the floodplain of Bear Creek, Salt Slough, and the San Joaquin River, near the northern end of the San Joaquin Valley in central California.

As described by the Fish and Wildlife Service:

Thousands of acres of wetlands, fed by an intricate set of canals, are managed to produce natural food supplies for migratory waterfowl. San Luis also contains the most extensive network of pristine native grasslands, shrubs, and vernal pools that still remain with the Central Valley.

Hundreds of thousands of mallard, pintail, green-winged teal and ring-necked ducks flock into the managed wetlands, while colorful, yet secretive, wood ducks live throughout the tree-lined slough channels.

The refuge's most prominent mammal is the tule elk, a species (some authorities consider it a subspecies) that is smaller and paler in color than either the Rocky Mountain or Roosevelt elk. During the 20th century, the population of the tule (or dwarf) elk sharply declined through habitat loss and unregulated hunting, and the species was threatened with extinction. As Devereux Butcher wrote in his 1963 book, *Exploring Our National Wildlife Refuges*, "The tule elk, smallest elk on the continent, once ranged through the valleys of California west of the Sierra Nevada, particularly the lower San Joaquin and Sacramento valleys. By the early 1920's, the total population of the species . . . was confined to a herd of about 400 animals on a ranch . . . in the San Joaquin Valley."

In 1974, a herd of 18 tule elk was brought to the San Luis refuge. Since then, their fluctuating numbers have ranged between about 30 and 70 of these animals, living within a fenced enclosure that is encircled by one of the refuge's auto tour roads. As the population has periodically exceeded the carrying capacity of the 750-acre enclosure, some of the excess numbers have been relocated from the refuge to other suitable habitat. There are presently about 2,400 tule elk in more than two dozen locations in California.

Establishment of this refuge has been made possible partly with revenues from the sale of Migratory Bird Hunting and Conservation Stamps (Duck Stamps). Ducks Unlimited, Inc. has helped enhance more than 6,000 acres of the wetland habitat.

The refuge is open daily during daylight hours. There is no entrance fee. The San Luis NWR Complex headquarters, located at 947 West Pacheco Blvd., Suite C, Los Banos, is open on weekdays, except national holidays.

Visitor activities include wildlife observation, viewing spring wildflower displays in vernal pool areas (during March and April), driving the refuge's three unpaved auto tour routes, viewing wildlife from several observation platforms, hiking on several trails, canoeing and boating, fishing, and hunting on parts of the refuge during the designated seasons. Insect repellent and sunscreen are advised during the warmer months.

Lodgings and meals are available in such communities as Merced and Los Banos.

Access to this refuge from State Hwy. 152 at Los Banos is north eight miles on State Hwy. 165 (Mercy Springs Rd.) and right two miles on Wolfsen Rd.. The refuge's KESTERSON UNIT (the former 12,000-acre Kesterson National Wildlife Refuge) is east four miles from Gustine on State Hwy. 140.

Information: San Luis NWR, P.O. Box 2176, Los Banos, CA 93635; tel.: (209) 826-3508.

Sweetwater Marsh, containing 316 acres, was established in 1988 to restore, enhance, and protect an important remnant of tidal salt marsh and adjacent upland habitats, and a number of endangered and threatened species. This urban refuge is located on the eastern shore of South San Diego Bay, within the city of Chula Vista in southwestern California.

More than 90 percent of San Diego Bay's wetland habitat has been filled in, drained, or diked. Sweetwater Marsh refuge came into being as the result of a mitigation tradeoff for other San Diego Bay wetlands that have been eliminated for urban development. It protects a vital remnant of habitat for many species including large concentrations of migrating and wintering waterfowl and shorebirds.

According to the Fish and Wildlife Service, "San Diego County is now home to more federally listed threatened and endangered species than any other county in the continental United States." Among these are the endangered light-footed clapper rail (see the Seal Beach NWR text) and California least tern; the threatened western snowy plover; the state-listed endangered Belding's savannah sparrow; and two plants: the endangered four-inch-tall salt marsh bird's beak, which boasts fuzzy, white tubular flowers, and yerba reuma. The latter species, which is a member of the heath family that commonly grows in coastal wetlands along Mexico's Baja Peninsula, is at the northern end of its range on this refuge. More than 220 bird species have been recorded on Sweetwater Marsh refuge.

The educational highlight of the refuge is a nature center that is cooperatively operated by the refuge and the City of Chula Vista. As described by the Fish and Wildlife Service:

Surrounded by numerous gardens, the Chula Vista Nature Center soars like an ark above . . . Sweetwater Marsh. The Nature Center provides visitors with the opportunity to experience the marsh through interpretive and interactive exhibits, guided nature and bird walks, and a petting pool. Outdoor aviaries support burrowing owls, shorebirds, egrets, and herons. Aviary dwellers are all birds that have been injured or imprinted and cannot be released back into their native habitats. A full-time teacher leads groups of school children out on the refuge each week for outdoor classroom experiences.

The refuge and Chula Vista Nature Center are open daily, except Mondays. An admission fee is charged for the nature center, except for free entry on the first Tuesday of each month.

Visitor activities include wildlife observation, viewing interpretive exhibits at the nature center, viewing the refuge and its wildlife from the nature center's observation deck, interpreter-led walks, and walking on several short trails. Sunscreen is advised during the warmer months.

Lodgings and meals are available in Chula Vista and elsewhere throughout San Diego County.

Access to the refuge from the E Street exit on I-5 in Chula Vista is west to a parking area at the end of E St. Free shuttle-bus service, which operates every twenty minutes, takes visitors to the nature center.

Information: Sweetwater Marsh NWR, 1080 Gunpowder Point Dr., Chula Vista, CA 91910; tel.: (619) 409-5900.

Caribbean Islands: Puerto Rico

Culebra, comprising 1,568 acres, was established by President Theodore Roosevelt in 1909 to protect important seabird colonies on and around the island of Culebra, located about twenty miles east of Puerto Rico in the Greater Antilles of the West Indies. The refuge, which includes a number of units on Culebra and on more than twenty smaller islands, cays, and rocks, also offers protection for several species of sea turtles and various communities of native tropical vegetation.

Isla de Culebra's habitats include small areas of subtropical dry forest, brush, grasslands, and bordering mangroves and seagrass. The island's Monte Resaca supports the largest remaining mountainous forested area—an unusual "boulder forest" amid boulder-strewn terrain of canyons and ravines. Culebra's Punta Flamenco, a point which was part of a former U.S. Naval bombing range, supports the refuge's largest nesting colony of seabirds, notably 60,000 sooty terns, along with brown noddies; roseate and bridled terns; and brown, masked, and red-footed boobies. The exquisitely graceful red-billed and white-tailed tropicbirds, magnificent frigatebird, white-cheeked pintail, and American oystercatcher also inhabit the refuge. The endangered leatherback and hawksbill sea turtles haul themselves onto white coral sand beaches to lay their eggs, and the endangered green sea turtle finds food and shelter in beds of seagrass. The waters around the islands contain beautiful coral reefs that are inhabited by a myriad of colorful tropical fishes.

The Fish and Wildlife Service says, "Culebra may be the most precious jewel in the treasure chest of Caribbean refuges. More than 50,000 seabirds of 13 species find their way to this dot in the ocean every year to breed and nurture their young."

Cayo Luis Pena and Isla Culebrita are the only parts of the refuge that are open to visitation. There is no entrance fee. All other refuge lands, including Punta Flamenco, are closed because of unexploded military ordnance and/or to avoid disturbing wildlife. The refuge office, which is located in Lower Camp, a short drive from Culebra's airport, is open on weekdays, except national holidays.

Visitor activities include wildlife observation and hiking. Sunscreen is advised.

Access to the refuge is either by flights from Puerto Rico or by ferry service from Fajardo, at the eastern end of Puerto Rico.

Information: Culebra NWR, P.O. Box 190, Culebra, PR 00622; tel.: (787) 742-0115.

Caribbean Islands: U.S. Virgin Islands

Sandy Point, encompassing 423 acres, was established in 1984. The refuge is located at the southwestern tip of St. Croix Island, U.S. Virgin Islands, in the Lesser Antilles of the West Indies.

Sandy Point protects critical habitat for the largest nesting population of the federally listed endangered leatherback sea turtle in the United States and the northern Caribbean. This largest species of turtle in the world measures to more than six feet in length and weighs more than 1,000 pounds. The threatened green sea turtle, measuring up to four feet and weighing roughly 400 pounds, and the endangered hawksbill sea turtle, measuring an average of 2.5 feet long and weighing 95 to 165 pounds, also haul themselves onto the refuge's three-mile-long beach to lay their eggs.

The refuge's other habitats include permanent and ephemeral salt ponds, with fringing mangroves; and coastal woodland. Dry forest habitat includes pink cedar, water mampoo, and pigeon berry. Sea grape trees, with leaves that suggest the shape of a ping-pong paddle, border the beaches. St. Croix's only stand of a federally endangered species, Vahl boxwood, grows on the refuge.

More than 100 species of birds have been recorded on this refuge. Among them are brown pelican, brown booby, little blue heron, white-cheeked pintail, royal and least terns, white-crowned pigeon, zenaida and scaley-naped doves, common ground-dove, smooth-billed ani, Antillean crested hummingbird, bananaquit, and black-faced grassquit.

As evidence of early human occupation of St. Croix, the refuge contains ancient conch middens—piles of discarded, bleached conch shells—dating back thousands of years. The Aklis Site, dating from A.D. 600, was occupied for more than two centuries and is on the National Register of Historic Places. In the early 1980s, Sandy Point was rescued from plans to turn this ecologically fragile area into a commercial development. During the sea turtle nesting time, the refuge benefits greatly from assistance provided by volunteers, including community groups and local students.

The refuge is open from 10 a.m. to 4 p.m. on weekends, unless otherwise posted. There is no entrance fee. Visitor activities include wildlife observation, hiking, and swimming. Major stretches of the beach are seasonally closed to visitation to protect nesting activities of the sea turtles. Sunscreen is advised.

Lodgings and meals are available at a number of resorts and elsewhere on St. Croix.

Access to the refuge is west of Alexander Hamilton Airport on Hwy. 66 (Melvin Evans Hwy.).

Information: Sandy Point NWR, Federal Building, 3013 Estate Golden Rock, Suite 167, Christiansted, VI 00820-4355; tel.: (809) 773-4554.

Colorado

Alamosa, containing 11,169 acres, was established in 1962 to enhance and protect important river-bottom wetland habitat for migratory water birds and other wildlife in the 7,500-foot-elevation, mountain-framed San Luis Valley of south-central Colorado.

From mid-February to late March, some of the stately greater sandhill cranes pause at Alamosa on their way north from wintering areas, such as the Bosque del Apache NWR in southern New Mexico, to their breeding grounds, which are mainly in Montana, Wyoming, and Idaho. A few of these birds stop by here on their way south, from early September into mid-November, depending on weather and habitat conditions. Their numbers peak around mid-October. Regarding the annual springtime Monte Vista crane festival, see the text on nearby Monte Vista NWR, with which Alamosa is jointly managed.

As many as 15,000 ducks of numerous species occupy Alamosa during the peak of migrations, and many Canada geese, ducks, egrets, herons, and ibises nest in the refuge's wetlands. In early spring, Alamosa is a staging area for dozens of bald eagles that congregate here. More than 200 species of birds have been recorded on Alamosa and Monte Vista refuges.

The refuge's floodplain wetlands consist of river oxbows and sloughs, wet meadows, and cottonwood-and-willow riparian corridors, mostly to the east and along the winding course of the upper Rio Grande. In contrast to the arid valley's extensive surrounding expanses of irrigated potato, barley, wheat, and alfalfa fields, these ecologically rich habitats are a mecca for thousands of migratory and nesting geese and ducks, as well as numerous wading birds and neotropical migratory songbirds.

The Sangre de Cristo Mountains form a spectacularly scenic backdrop for the refuge. Their peaks rise more than 6,000 feet above the valley floor to more than 14,000 feet in elevation. To the west are the rugged San Juan Mountains.

Establishment of Alamosa was made possible partly with revenues from the sale of Migratory Bird Hunting and Conservation Stamps (Duck Stamps). Ducks Unlimited, Inc. and the San Luis Valley Wetlands Focus Group have assisted with important habitat enhancement projects.

The refuge is open daily during daylight hours. There is no entrance fee. The headquarters (serving both Alamosa and Monte Vista refuges) is open on weekdays, except national holidays.

Visitor activities include wildlife observation; driving the three-mile auto tour route beginning at headquarters and providing views of wetland, wet meadow, and upland habitats; hiking or bicycling a one-mile trail from the south end of the tour road; hiking, bicycling, horseback riding, or cross-country skiing the two-mile Rio Grande River Walk from refuge headquarters; and hunting on part of the refuge during the designated seasons. Although camping is not permitted on the refuge, campground facilities are available in the vicinity of Alamosa and Monte Vista, and in Rio Grande National Forest. Visitors are urged to be prepared for a variety of weather conditions, including springtime winds. Insect repellent is advised during the warmer months.

Lodgings and meals are available in such communities as Alamosa and Monte Vista.

Access to the refuge is east four miles on U.S. Hwy. 160 from the town of Alamosa, and right onto El Rancho Lane for two miles.

Information: Alamosa NWR, 9383 El Rancho Lane, Alamosa, CO 81101; tel.: (719) 589-4021.

Arapaho, containing 24,804 acres, was established in 1967 to create, enhance, and protect an ecologically significant area of wetlands in north-central Colorado. The wetlands are sustained by waters diverted from the north-flowing Illinois River, a tributary of the North Platte that flows through this refuge. It is located at 8,200 feet above sea level in the mountain-framed glacial basin known as North Park. Spectacular ranges of the Rocky Mountains form an encircling backdrop, with the Medicine Bows to the east; the Rabbit Ears to the south; and the Park Range to the west.

This refuge's numerous shallow ponds and irrigated marshy meadows are managed by regulating their water levels to provide breeding and feeding habitat for migratory waterfowl, shorebirds, and wading birds. Late May brings the peak of spring waterfowl migration, when at least

Western sandpipers and dunlins, Gray's Harbor NWR, Washington

Barn Owl, Don Edwards San Francisco Bay NWR. Mike Boylan photo

Gray wolf, Agassiz NWR, Minnesota

Cow moose and calves, Kenai NWR, Alaska. Mike Boylan photo

Mohawk Dunes, Cabeza Prieta NWR, Arizona. Jack Dykinga photo

Pronghorn, National Bison Range, Montana

Endangered Karner blue butterfly, Necedah NWR, Wisconsin

Blacktail jackrabbit, Modoc NWR, California

Great blue heron, Montezuma NWR, New York

Sandhill cranes at sunrise, Bosque del Apache NWR, New Mexico

A U.S. Fish and Wildlife Service outdoor class for school children, Minnesota Valley NWR

Yellow-headed blackbirds in marsh, Merced NWR, California

Wild turkey, Wichita Mountains NWR, Oklahoma

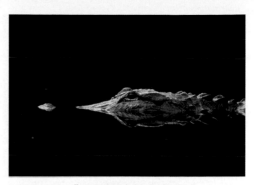

Alligator, Okefenokee NWR, Georgia

Public fishing, Choctaw NWR, Alabama

Horned Puffin, Alaska Maritime NWR

Fur seal, Alaska Maritime NWR

Tufted puffin, Alaska Maritime NWR. Mike Boylan photo

Arctic NWR, Alaska

Aerial view of the coastal plain, Arctic NWR

Arctic tern, Kenai NWR, Alaska. Mike Boylan photo

Kenai NWR

Kenai NWR

Bald Eagles, Kenai NWR, Mike Boylan photo

Caribou, Kenai NWR, Alaska. Mike Boylan photo

Kodiak NWR, Alaska

Alaskan brown bear dining on salmon, Kodiak NWR

Kodiak NWR

Dunlin in breeding plumage, Yukon Delta NWR, Alaska

Rabbit River, Selawik NWR. Leslie Kerr photo

Yukon Delta NWR, Alaska

Tundra swan nestlings, Yukon Delta NWR

Eskimo Fish Camp, Yukon Delta NWR

Storm clouds, Buenos Aires NWR

Masked bobwhite, Buenos Aires NWR, Arizona

Yucca, Buenos Aires NWR

Sunset and saguaro, Cabeza Prieta NWR

Cabeza Prieta NWR. Jack Dykinga photo

Cabeza Prieta NWR, Arizona

Red-tailed hawk nesting in saguaro, Cabeza Prieta NWR, Arizona

Greater roadrunner, Cibola NWR, Arizona

Colorado River at Topock Gorge, Havasu NWR. Russell D. Butcher photo

Kofa NWR. Russell D. Butcher photo

Desert bighorn sheep, Kofa NWR, Arizona

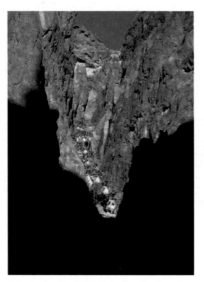
Palm Canyon, Kofa NWR. Russell D. Butcher photo

Leslie Canyon NWR, Arizona. William R. Radke photo

Blind cave crawfish, Logan Cave NWR, Arkansas

Wapanocca NWR, Arkansas

5,000 ducks arrive—either to merely pause in their northward flight or remain for nesting and rearing their young. Late September to early October is the peak of autumn migration, when as many as 8,000 waterfowl are attracted here. Prominent among the waterbirds are Canada goose, gadwall, lesser scaup, wigeon, mallard, shoveler, and cinnamon teal. More than 200 bird species have been recorded on this refuge.

The sage-grouse is a special attraction in Arapaho's sagebrush habitat, with large flocks wintering here. In the spring, visitors can watch and hear males inflating their bright orange throat sacs as they perform their remarkable courtship dances. Pronghorns also inhabit the sagebrush-covered flats and knolls.

Numerous neotropical migratory songbirds and such mammals as moose and mule deer seek out Arapaho's sheltered riparian areas. Elk are here, too, some residing year-round and others moving down from the mountains to winter on the refuge.

Establishment of this refuge was made possible partly with revenue from the sale of Migratory Bird Hunting and Conservation Stamps (Duck Stamps).

The refuge is open daily during daylight hours. There is no entrance fee. The refuge headquarters/visitor center is open on weekdays, except national holidays.

Visitor activities include wildlife observation, driving a six-mile tour route, hiking along the Illinois River on a 0.5-mile (wheelchair-accessible) interpretive trail and elsewhere on the refuge, prearranged guided group tours, fishing (on the Illinois River), and hunting on parts of the refuge during the designated seasons. Although camping is not permitted on the refuge, campground facilities are available at Lake John, Delaney Butte Lakes, and Seymour Reservoir state wildlife areas; and in the Routt National Forest. Visitors are advised to wear warm clothing, as it can be cold most of the year.

Lodgings and meals are available in Walden.

Access to the refuge headquarters is south eight miles of Walden on State Hwy. 125.

Information: Arapaho NWR, P.O. Box 457, Walden, CO 80480; tel.: (970) 723-8202.

Baca, authorized to ultimately contain 93,500 acres, was established in 2002 and is located in the eastern part of the San Luis Valley, near the base of the towering Sangre de Cristo Mountains of southern Colorado. Although this vast, high rift valley annually receives an average of only seven inches of precipitation, melting snows from surrounding mountains sustain a thriving agricultural economy and 230,000 acres of vital wetland habitat that supports large populations of breeding and migrating waterbirds. It is here in this rural western community that local citizens broke the stereotype and championed a federal land acquisition project.

In November 2000, Congress passed and President Bill Clinton signed into law the Great Sand Dunes National Park and Preserve Act of 2000. This legislation authorized the expansion and re-designation of Great Sand Dunes National Monument (established in 1932) as a national park and preserve, an addition to the Rio Grande National Forest, and the establishment of the new Baca National Wildlife Refuge.

The enabling legislation's key provision authorizes the Department of the Interior and the Department of Agriculture to purchase the Baca Ranch, which was in private ownership since 1860. When the Mexican-American War ended in 1848, the United States government agreed to honor all Spanish land grants that were lost during the conflict. In 1860, the heirs of Luis Maria de Baca were permitted to select five 100,000-acre grants of land. One of these was located on the eastern side of the San Luis Valley and became known as the Luis Baca No. 4. The ranch was owned by the Baca family for only two years before being sold to William Gilpin, the first territorial governor of the Colorado Territory.

Over the years, this ranch expanded its holdings but remained a site of regularly occurring speculation, starting with Gilpin and now ending after 15 years of water development proposals. Had those water developments been successful, they would have exported between 150,000 and 200,000 acre-feet of water from the valley—most likely to serve the rapidly growing Front Range cities along the eastern base of the Colorado Rockies. Few residents felt that the removal of such a large quantity of water from the San Luis Valley would be possible without seriously jeopardizing its agricultural economy and quality of life. Additionally, the exportation of this volume of water risked seriously damaging the ecological integrity and breeding bird habitat. Consequently, many agencies and organizations have been engaged in an almost continuous, expensive, and politically charged 15-year struggle with the water speculators, who were intent upon obtaining a behemoth water right on the Baca ranch.

During the summer of 1999, on the heels of a failed statewide ballot initiative that was meant to weaken the position of San Luis Valley's water defenders, the local community enlisted the assistance of U.S. Senators Wayne Allard and Ben Nighthorse Campbell and U.S. Representative Scott McIniss. This congressional delegation saw the environmental and economic wisdom of acquiring the Baca ranch and a small number of associated holdings in order to expand and re-designate the national monument as a national park and preserve, to acquire the mountainous holdings in the adjacent Rio Grande National Forest, and to establish the westernmost tract as the Baca National Wildlife Refuge. The Colorado governor's office and the Colorado Department of Natural Resources were also enthusiastic and supportive.

This is far from just another federal government effort toward land acquisition. The importance of the nonprofit organization The Nature Conservancy in this situation cannot be overstated. For years, TNC has been negotiating with the owners of the Baca Ranch, hoping for an opportunity to protect the property, not only for the good of San Luis Valley, but also to protect the adjoining 104,000-acre TNC-owned Medano/Zapata Ranch. The Conservancy obtained numerous loans and enlisted the financial help of the Colorado State Land Board and many others to make this $31.3 million acquisition happen expeditiously while giving the federal government the time needed to appropriate the funds to buy out TNC's interest in the property.

When completed, Baca National Wildlife Refuge will contain approximately 20,000 acres of wetland habitat, ranging from periodically flooded playas to more regularly but shallowly flooded wetlands dominated by short, emergent vegetation at the lower ends of several drainages. The wetlands are of great value to migrating birds, such as the sandhill crane, white-faced ibis, and some species of ducks and shorebirds. The Colorado National Heritage Program has identified many globally significant plant and animal communities within the boundaries of the refuge and the park/preserve. One of the most exciting elements of this project is the opportunity for the Fish and Wildlife Service, National Park Service, U.S. Forest Service, and The Nature Conservancy to manage roughly 350,000 acres of a unique landscape in a coordinated manner.

The Baca and adjoining ranches presently host a year-round population of about 4,500 Rocky Mountain elk. Their population has been growing because of a lack of hunting pressure and other predation and ample forage. Although these animals use almost all of the ranch's habitats, they are most frequently seen along some of the riparian areas.

Opportunities for visitor access and activities, including interpretive and environmental education programs, wildlife observation, hiking, and hunting, will be evaluated as part of the refuge's management planning process. Visitors will have the chance to learn about the history of this land and the interdependence of people, the land, water, and wildlife.

(With special thanks to Manager Michael Blenden of the Alamosa/Monte Vista/Baca NWR Complex for providing the above information.—RDB)

Information: Baca NWR, 9383 El Rancho Lane, Alamosa, CO 81101; tel.: (719) 589-4021.

Monte Vista, encompassing 14,800 acres, was established in 1953 to enhance and protect wetland habitat for migratory ducks and other waterbirds, at an elevation of 7,500 feet in the mountain-framed San Luis Valley of south-central Colorado.

The refuge consists of wetlands and numerous ponds that are maintained with a system of wells, canals, ditches, drains, and other water control structures for the benefit of many species of waterfowl and other wildlife. In addition, the Fish and Wildlife Service raises grain crops on fields that are feeding areas for sandhill cranes, ducks, and other wildlife.

The Sangre de Cristo Mountains form a spectacular scenic backdrop to the refuge. Their jagged peaks rise more than 6,000 feet above the valley floor to more than 14,000 feet in elevation. To the west are the rugged San Juan Mountains.

Monte Vista refuge, which is jointly managed with nearby Alamosa and Baca NWRs, is especially famous for its thousands of migratory sandhill cranes. From mid-February through late March, roughly 24,000 to 32,000 of these stately, red-crowned, gray birds pause here in the San Luis Valley on their northward migration from wintering areas, such as the Bosque del Apache NWR in southern New Mexico, to breeding areas mainly in Montana, Wyoming, and Idaho. Of this awesome number, 18,000 to 22,000 comprise about 95 percent of the total population of the Rocky Mountain greater sandhill subspecies. There are also from 3,000 to 5,000 each of the lesser and Canadian subspecies. Roughly 8,000 to 13,000 migrating cranes rest and feed on this refuge. During their southward autumn migration, somewhat smaller concentrations of these birds pause here from September into mid-November, depending on weather and habitat conditions. Their numbers generally peak around mid-October.

Since the early 1980s, the spring return of these birds has been celebrated by Monte Vista's Annual Crane Festival. This popular event is sponsored by the nonprofit Monte Vista Crane Committee and includes guided tours of the refuge, educational workshops, demonstrations, and lectures on a variety of environmental topics. Information and reservations: tel.: (719) 852-3552.

Monte Vista refuge is also a mecca for migratory waterfowl. As senior writer Matt Young explained in his article "High Country Ducks," in the March–April 2001 issue of *Ducks Unlimited*, "Believe it or not, some of the continent's most productive breeding habitat for ducks lies in a mountain valley in the heart of the southern Rockies. This remarkable place is Colorado's San Luis Valley, a broad expanse of high desert surrounded by majestic 14,000-foot mountains. Managed wetlands in the valley support an average of 200 to 300 duck nests per square mile, with some areas boasting as many as 1,000 nests per square mile."

But he also points out a potential threat:

As in many parts of the West, groundwater is the lifeblood of wetlands in the San Luis Valley. Beneath the valley floor lie two massive aquifers whose artesian springs, along with snowmelt from the surrounding mountains, historically supported a vast network of playa wetlands. However, people have increasingly tapped the valley's groundwater for a variety of purposes, depleting the underlying aquifer and, in effect, draining many crucial wetland systems from below. Stream runoff also has been largely diverted into ditches for human use, robbing many more wetlands of their supply.

Fortunately, state and federal agencies have established several large managed wetland complexes in the San Luis Valley that provide excellent habitat for breeding, migrating, and wintering waterbirds and a variety of other wildlife. The crown jewel of the valley's wildlife areas is . . . Monte Vista National Wildlife Refuge. Located nearby are several other highly productive managed wildlife areas, including the Alamosa National Wildlife Refuge, Blanca Waterfowl Management Area, and the Rio Grande State Wildlife Areas.

Establishment of this refuge was made possible partly with revenues from the sale of Migratory Bird Hunting and Conservation Stamps (Duck Stamps). Ducks Unlimited, Inc. (DU) and the San Luis Valley Wetlands Focus Group have assisted with extensive habitat enhancement projects. The latter group consists of a large partnership of federal and state governmental and nongovernmental agencies, organizations, and private citizens that have been working together for many years to accomplish numerous wetland restoration projects on the refuge complex and elsewhere within the San Luis Valley. A recent example of DU's assistance is the development of dikes and ditches and the installation of water control structures in the refuge's Unit 7. These improvements have created an extensive wetland impoundment, within which water levels are manipulated for the maximum benefit of waterfowl and other wildlife.

The refuge is open daily during daylight hours. There is no entrance fee. A visitor contact station is open daily in March and April, and only periodically the rest of the year.

Visitor activities include wildlife observation, driving the three-mile tour route and driving several county roads, and hunting on part of the refuge during the designated seasons. Although camping is not permitted on the refuge, campground facilities are available in the vicinity of Monte Vista and Alamosa, and in Rio Grande National Forest. Visitors are urged to be prepared for a variety of weather conditions, including springtime winds. Insect repellent is advised during the warmer months.

Lodgings and meals are available in the towns of Monte Vista and Alamosa.

Access to this refuge is six miles south on State Hwy. 15 from the town of Monte Vista.

Information: Monte Vista NWR, 9383 El Rancho Lane, Alamosa, CO 81101; tel.: (719) 589-4021.

Rocky Mountain Arsenal, comprising more than 16,000 acres, was established in 1992 to restore, protect, and interpret a remnant expanse of western Great Plains shortgrass prairie, scattered riparian woodland, marsh, intermittent streams, and more than a half dozen human-made lakes and ponds. It is located just ten miles northeast of downtown Denver, in Commerce City, Colorado. This is a unique paradox of a place: The area's ecologically important habitats surround a central area of former weapons and chemicals production and disposal facilities. More than 225 bird species have been recorded here.

Through a gradual transformation, the arsenal is becoming one of the largest urban wildlife sanctuaries and environmental education centers in the country. The great diversity of wildlife includes many species of migrating waterfowl; wintering bald eagles and other raptors, such as burrowing owls and ferruginous and Swainson's hawks; numerous neotropical migratory song-birds; prairie dogs; and herds of both white-tailed deer and mule deer.

By the late 1930s, most of the land that is now the arsenal had been cleared of its original shortgrass prairie and was devoted to farming. The U.S. Army purchased the land in 1942 to produce weapons, such as mustard gas and napalm, during World War II, and it subsequently manufactured incendiary weapons, nerve gas, and other chemical warfare munitions at the Rocky Mountain Arsenal until the 1960s.

Beginning in 1979, a number of interim cleanup actions on the property were undertaken; and from 1993 to 1994, the incineration of certain liquid wastes and a groundwater intercept-and-treatment program were undertaken. As of the beginning of the 21st century, this latter process continues to treat millions of gallons of groundwater annually, resulting in steadily de-creasing levels of contamination. In 1982, all military and commercial chemical production ac-tivities were terminated, and in 1983, the Environmental Protection Agency declared the Rocky Mountain Arsenal a Superfund cleanup site.

Both the production and subsequent disposal of these highly toxic military and commer-cial substances were limited to the arsenal's 3,840-acre core. Surrounding the central area was a 13,440-acre buffer zone. This relatively undisturbed open space was essentially a de facto wildlife refuge. The discovery in 1986 of a communal roost of wintering bald eagles, a species that symbolizes this nation's pride, inspired the goal of establishing a national wildlife refuge here. Intense local public support spurred national commitment to both a refuge and appro-priately high standards for a hazardous-waste cleanup program.

The enormous, $2-billion challenge of tearing down munitions and pesticide factories and cleaning up the contaminated central core was finally begun in 1996 and is expected to be com-pleted by around 2011. Once the Superfund cleanup program is completed, the area will offi-cially become the Rocky Mountain Arsenal National Wildlife Refuge.

Beginning in 1987, the Fish and Wildlife Service started managing the arsenal's wildlife, and since 1992, when Congress passed the Rocky Mountain Arsenal National Wildlife Refuge Act, the Fish and Wildlife personnel have been engaged in a number of habitat restoration proj-ects. These include re-vegetating parts of the area with native grasses and other plants and en-hancing and maintaining riparian corridors, wetlands, and lakes for the benefit of wildlife. Other objectives include managing the deer population so that its genetic diversity is maintained and so that the herds do not exceed the area's carrying capacity; reintroducing such native prairie fauna as the American bison (buffalo), pronghorn, sharp-tailed grouse, and greater prairie chickens; and begin planning for visitor access and environmental education programs.

The plans for visitor use intended to include a visitor center with interpretive exhibits and an auditorium for interpretive programs; an environmental education center and laboratory; a picnic area; a trail network winding through the southern part of the refuge to offer views of marsh, wooded riparian, and lake habitats and their wildlife; and a tram route through the northern part of the area for viewing prairie habitat and its wildlife. The refuge is currently closed to visitation. Potential visitors should call the number below for details on visitor access and programs.

Visitor activities are expected to include wildlife observation; tours by tram (fee) and interpretive walks led by staff and trained volunteers; school and other youth-group environmental education programs; hiking; bicycling; fishing; and a wide variety of programs (a calendar of events will be available). November to March will be the best time to see bald eagles. Although their numbers fluctuate over the winter, twenty to fifty of these birds spend part of the winter. Visitors will be cautioned to be alert for rattlesnakes during the warmer months.

Lodgings and meals are available throughout the Denver metropolitan area.

Access to the refuge will be north on Quebec St. from either I-70 or I-270, right onto Seventy-Second Ave., and east into the main entrance. Plans call for eventually shifting the entrance to the southwest corner of the property, to be accessed from Sixty-Fourth Ave. and Quebec St.

Information: Rocky Mountain Arsenal NWR, Building III, Commerce City, CO 80022; tel.: (303) 289-0930.

Connecticut

Stewart B. McKinney consists of 825 acres in eight units scattered along sixty miles of the Long Island Sound coastline of southern Connecticut. The refuge was established in 1971 and developed as the Connecticut Coastal NWR. In 1987, it was renamed for the late Rep. Stewart B. McKinney, in honor of his efforts that succeeded in winning congressional approval for the refuge's first five units. Four of the units are described below.

The nine-acre MILFORD POINT UNIT, which was one of the initial parts of the refuge, encompasses part of a narrow barrier peninsula at the mouth of the Housatonic River. The point of land contains a sandy barrier beach, where piping plovers and least terns nest during spring and summer. Low sand dunes rise just inland from the beach, and salt marsh and mudflats are sheltered behind the peninsula.

Although this unit is closed to visitation, the Connecticut Audubon Coastal Center, which is located almost adjacent to the refuge unit, offers interpretive exhibits, programs, walks, and wildlife viewing opportunities from an observation tower. The center is open daily, except on Mondays and national holidays. Information: (203) 878-7440.

The 247-acre SALT MEADOW UNIT was donated to the Fish and Wildlife Service in 1971. This property was formerly owned by Esther Lape, who was a medical advisor to President Franklin D. Roosevelt and a good friend of the president's wife, Eleanor. The fieldstone house that dates from 1929 has been converted to the Stewart B. McKinney refuge headquarters. The unit's habitats include mixed hardwood forest and an area of tidally influenced salt marsh. Ducks Unlimited, Inc. has helped enhance about twenty acres of Salt Meadow's wetland habitat.

This unit is open to visitation daily during daylight hours. There is no entrance fee. The refuge headquarters is open on weekdays, except national holidays. Hiking opportunities here include 2.5 miles of trails.

The 450-acre GREAT MEADOWS UNIT, which protects an area of salt marsh near the Housatonic River, has not been opened to visitation, except by prearrangement for school and other groups.

The 67-acre SHEFFIELD ISLAND UNIT provides a 2,000-foot-long (wheelchair-accessible) nature trail that was recently created with the help of volunteers.

Refuge land acquisition was made possible partly with revenues from the sale of Migratory Bird Hunting and Conservation Stamps (Duck Stamps).

Visitor activities include wildlife observation, viewing the Milford Point Unit from an observation platform, and walking designated trails. Although camping is not permitted on the refuge, campground facilities are available at Hammonasset Beach State Park, located near the Salt Meadow Unit. Over 310 bird species have been seen on the refuge.

Visitors are cautioned to be alert for ticks, which may carry Lyme disease.

Lodgings and meals are available in such communities as Milford, Stratford, and Bridgeport (near the Milford Point Unit); and Clinton, Westbrook, and Old Saybrook (near the Salt Meadow Unit).

Access to the Milford Point Unit from Exit 34 on I-95 is right 0.5 mile, left 0.8 mile on Naugatuck Rd., right 0.5 mile on Milford Point Rd., and right 0.3 mile on Sea View Ave., then right at a fork that ends at the Hubbell Wildlife Sanctuary and the Connecticut Audubon Coastal Center. Access to the Salt Meadow Unit from Exit 64 on I-95 is south to a stop at a blinking red light, and left 1.1 mile on Old Clinton Rd. (the refuge parking area is on the right).

Information: Stewart B. McKinney NWR, P.O. Box 1030, Westbrook, CT 06460; tel.: (860) 399-2513.

Delaware

Bombay Hook, comprising 15,978 acres, was established in 1937 to manage and protect a significant area of coastal wetlands for spectacular concentrations of migrating, wintering, and nesting waterfowl and shorebirds as well as other wildlife. The refuge is located along the bay shore, in northeastern Delaware.

Approximately three-quarters of the refuge contains extensive, tidally influenced salt marsh; more than 1,000 acres consist of impounded freshwater pools, as well as brushy and wooded swamp habitat; and more than 1,000 acres include mixed pine and deciduous woodland, grassland, and agricultural fields. The latter are managed under cooperative agreements with local farmers, who plant such crops as winter wheat, buckwheat, and millet for the benefit of waterfowl and other wildlife.

Water levels of the impounded pools are seasonally raised and lowered with a system of dikes and water control structures. This management promotes the growth of emergent and underwater plants for waterfowl. While pools are drawn down, their mudflats attract great numbers of shorebirds and wading birds. When water levels are raised, the impoundments provide habitat for large concentrations of waterfowl that either winter on the refuge or pause here on their flights farther south.

October and November are usually the best months for observing impressive concentrations of migrating waterfowl. More than 150,000 ducks and geese are commonly attracted to Bombay Hook during the autumn. The other peak of waterfowl generally comes in March. Although early migrating shorebirds from South America normally arrive in April, the peak numbers of these birds are present in May. Large influxes of neotropical migratory songbirds, including numerous species of warblers, arrive in late April and early May. The greatest numbers of herons, egrets, and glossy ibis are on the refuge during the summer.

The refuge's salt marsh habitat, with its mosaic of intersecting tidal streams and rivers, not only provides habitat for many species of birds and mammals, but also serves as an ecologically rich nursery and spawning area for finfish and shellfish and numerous other marine organisms.

As *Ducks Unlimited* senior writer Matt Young wrote in the September–October 2001 issue of the magazine, "Acre for acre, coastal wetlands are among the most productive ecosystems on the planet. Their bountiful waters, rich in plant and animal life, support a remarkable diversity of waterfowl. . . . Sadly, thousands of acres of coastal wetlands continue to be lost each year. Protection is clearly the best line of defense against these losses, because once these fragile habitats disappear, they are gone forever."

The architectural highlight of the refuge is the two-story, Queen Anne–style Allee House that dates from around 1753 and is one of the best preserved examples of an early red-brick farmhouse in the state of Delaware. Tours of the house are offered during spring and autumn weekend afternoons.

Establishment of Bombay Hook was made possible partly with revenues from the sale of Migratory Bird Hunting and Conservation Stamps (Duck Stamps). Ducks Unlimited, Inc. has helped enhance approximately 800 acres of the refuge's wetland habitat.

The refuge is open daily during daylight hours. An entrance fee is charged. The visitor center is open daily during spring and autumn and on weekdays, except national holidays, during the rest of the year.

Visitor activities include wildlife observation, driving the 12-mile auto tour route, hiking on several trails, viewing interpretive displays and programs at the visitor center, and hunting on parts of the refuge during the designated seasons. More than 265 bird species have been recorded on the refuge. Visitors are cautioned to be alert for ticks; insect repellent is advised during the warmer months.

Lodgings and meals are available in such communities as Dover and Smyrna.

Access to Bombay Hook NWR from Dover is north on U.S. Hwy. 13 to Bishops Corner, right onto State Hwy. 42 to Leipsic, left two miles on State Hwy. 9, and right just over two miles on Whitehall Neck Rd. Or from Smyrna, it is southeast five miles on Smyrna-Leipsic Rd. (State Hwy. 12) to its junction with Hwy. 9, right 0.25 mile on Hwy. 9, and left just over two miles on Whitehall Neck Rd.

Information: Bombay Hook NWR, 2591 Whitehall Neck Rd., Smyrna, DE 19977; tel.: (302) 653-9345.

Prime Hook, containing 9,722 acres, was established in 1963 to manage and protect a significant area of coastal wetlands for spectacular concentrations of migrating, wintering, and nesting waterfowl and shorebirds, as well as other wildlife. The refuge is located along the western shore of Delaware Bay, in southeastern Delaware.

Roughly three-quarters of the refuge consists of tidally influenced salt marsh, open water, and managed freshwater impoundments, one of which covers 2,500 acres. As the Fish and Wildlife Service describes the impounded wetlands, "Water levels on more than 4,200 acres of marsh are raised or lowered at different times of the year through a system of low dikes and water control structures. This management stimulates the growth of emergent aquatic plant species for wildlife use."

The best times to observe large numbers of waterfowl and shorebirds on the refuge are during their migrations. Concentrations of Canada and snow geese and such ducks as American black, mallard, northern pintail, and teal are especially impressive during the autumn. The Fish and Wildlife Service has provided nesting boxes for wood ducks and nesting platforms for ospreys.

In addition to the wetlands, the refuge also includes about 2,300 acres of upland habitat and areas that include mixed woodland of pines and deciduous trees, grasslands, and agricultural fields. These habitats are managed for the benefit of many species of neotropical migratory songbirds and for resident wildlife, including the Delmarva Peninsula fox squirrel, an endangered subspecies that was reintroduced to this refuge in 1986. (A description of this squirrel is included in Maryland's Blackwater NWR text.) As refuge manager Barron Crawford explained, "Through a cooperative effort between the U.S. Fish and Wildlife Service; the nonprofit organization, American Forests; the Delaware Department of Agriculture's Forest Service; and the Delaware Department of Natural Resources and Environmental Control, the refuge was able to reforest 100 acres with 47,000 hardwood seedlings. Refuge staff hope to continue creating and managing more forested habitat for . . . the Delmarva Peninsula fox squirrel and forest-dwelling birds."

The refuge also contains about 1,300 acres of grassland and agricultural fields. The latter are managed under cooperative agreements with local farmers, who leave unharvested a portion of crops such as corn and wheat to provide an important supplemental source of food for waterfowl and other wildlife.

Establishment of Prime Hook Refuge was made possible partly with revenues from the sale of Migratory Bird Hunting and Conservation Stamps (Duck Stamps). Ducks Unlimited, Inc. and a variety of private contributions have provided major assistance for the refuge's wetland habitat enhancement efforts.

The refuge is open daily during daylight hours. There is no entrance fee. The visitor center is open daily from April 1 to Thanksgiving and on weekdays, except national holidays, from November 1 through March.

Visitor activities include wildlife and butterfly observation, viewing interpretive displays and programs at the visitor center, driving on the entrance road and several state highways that run through the refuge, hiking on several trails, canoeing on more than 15 miles of streams and ditches, boating on ponds and tidal waters (several boat-launching ramps are provided), fishing, and hunting on parts of the refuge during the designated seasons. A 7-mile, self-guiding canoe trail follows Prime Hook Creek (an interpretive pamphlet is available). Although camping is not permitted on the refuge, campground facilities are available at Cape Henlopen State Park.

Visitors are cautioned to be alert for ticks. Insect repellent is advised during the warmer months.

Lodgings and meals are available in such communities as Milford, Lewes, Rehoboth Beach, and Dewey Beach.

Access to Prime Hook NWR from the junction of U.S. Hwy. 113 and State Hwy. 1 (near Milford) is south 15 miles on Hwy. 1, left onto Broadkill Beach Rd. (State Hwy. 16) for one mile, and left onto the refuge entrance road to the visitor center. Or from Dewey Beach, it is north 14 miles on State Hwy. 1, right onto Broadkill Beach Rd. (State Hwy. 16), and left onto the refuge entrance road.

Information: Prime Hook NWR, 11978 Turkle Pond Rd., Milton, DE 19968; tel.: (302) 684-8419.

Florida

Archie Carr was established in 1991 to protect the most important nesting habitat for the loggerhead sea turtle in the Western Hemisphere and its second most important nesting habitat in the world. It is here that 25 percent of all loggerhead sea turtle nesting and 35 percent of all green sea turtle nesting occur in the United States.

The refuge is located along a 20.5-mile stretch of seashore between Melbourne Beach and Wabasso Beach, on the central Atlantic Coast of Florida. The core acreage being acquired comprises nearly 10 miles of this coastal strip in four separate tracts. When land acquisition is completed, it is expected that the refuge will contain approximately 900 acres.

The primary management activity at the Archie Carr refuge is "protecting critical nesting sites from human activity and development." This challenging mission is being coordinated with the state and local governments for jointly managing the beaches, conducting sea-turtle nesting surveys, offering public education programs, and providing environmentally compatible visitor use facilities.

The refuge is named in honor of naturalist Dr. Archie F. Carr (1909–1987), who, at the time of his death, was the world's foremost authority on sea turtles. As a highly esteemed research biologist, he traveled and worked extensively throughout the Gulf of Mexico, the Caribbean Sea, the Pacific Coast of Costa Rica, and such other places as Australia, the east coast of Africa, and Papua New Guinea. Dr. Carr served for two decades as chairman of the Marine Turtle Specialist Group of the International Union for the Conservation of Nature's Survival Service Commission; and he was the founding director of the Caribbean Conservation Corporation, an international leader in the protection of sea turtles.

Information: Caribbean Conservation Corporation, 4424 NW Thirteenth Street, Suite A1, Gainesville, FL 32609; tel.: (352) 373-6441; e-mail: ccc@cccturtle.org.

The refuge is open daily during daylight hours. There is no entrance fee. Visitor activities include wildlife observation, hiking, and swimming.

Lodgings and meals are available in such communities as Melbourne and Melbourne Beach.

Access to the northern units of the refuge from U.S. Hwy. 1 at Melbourne is east on U.S. Hwy. 192 (across the Intracoastal Waterway) to Indialantic and right onto State Hwy. A1A. Access to the southernmost unit from U.S. Hwy. 1 at Wabasso is east on County Hwy. 510 (across the Intracoastal Waterway) and left onto State Route A1A.

Information: Archie Carr NWR, 1339 Twentieth St., Vero Beach, FL 32960; tel.: (772) 562-3909.

Arthur R. Marshall Loxahatchee, containing 147,392 acres, was established in 1951 to protect the last remaining pristine expanse of the northernmost part of the "River of Grass," known as the Everglades, in south Florida. The refuge consists of extensive wet prairies and sawgrass marshes; numerous tree islands; and smaller areas of sloughs, cattails, a number of managed wetland impoundments, and a 400-acre bald-cypress swamp.

Loxahatchee is the southernmost significant wintering area for ducks in the Atlantic Flyway and is also visited by many species of shorebirds and neotropical songbirds during spring and autumn migrations. The refuge provides important nesting, roosting, and foraging habitat for egrets, herons, white ibis, anhinga, Florida sandhill crane, Everglades snail kite, and limpkin.

As Devereux Butcher wrote in his 1963 book, *Exploring Our National Wildlife Refuges*,

One of the most characteristic birds of Loxahatchee is the limpkin, a brown wading bird . . . [larger than] a bittern, with long, downward-curving bill. On one of those brilliant days typical of winter in Florida, we visited Loxahatchee. At nearly every turn among the islands a limpkin flew from a thicket. The weird cries of this bird carried across the vast solitudes of the marshes. Long lines of white ibises flew across or soared against the blue sky adding a touch of indescribable beauty; while occasionally the clear, gleaming white of an American egret or a flock of little snowy egrets flew overhead. . . . but the bird which many hope will benefit from protection in this area is the Everglade [snail] kite. . . . this handsome species is now close to extinction.

By the end of the 20th century, the Fish and Wildlife Service reported that "The Everglades snail kite has had poor nesting success on the refuge with a total of only seven nests observed from 1976 to 1997. With the change in the water regulation schedule in 1995 providing better habitat for its primary prey, the apple snail, it is hoped the nomadic Everglades snail kite will increase its nesting activities at the refuge. In 1998, 18 Everglades snail kite nests were found and approximately one-third of the nests were thought to be successful."

In 1986, the refuge's name was changed to honor Arthur Raymond Marshall, a prominent local wildlife conservationist and former employee of the Fish and Wildlife Service.

The refuge is open daily during daylight hours. An entrance fee is charged. The visitor center is open daily from mid-October through April, except on Christmas, and is closed on Mondays and Tuesdays during the rest of the year.

Visitor activities include wildlife observation, viewing wildlife from an observation platform (wheelchair-accessible) and from an observation tower, viewing butterflies at the visitor center's butterfly garden, interpretive programs, interpreter-guided walks, interpreter-guided canoe excursions, walking and hiking on several trails including a (wheelchair-accessible) boardwalk, bicycling (mountain bikes on the perimeter levee, from the headquarters area south to the Hillsboro Recreation Area), canoeing on the 5.5-mile Everglades Canoe Trail, boating on the 57-mile perimeter canal (three boat-launching ramps are provided), fishing (a wheelchair-accessible fishing pier is provided; bank fishing in the Hillsboro Recreation Area), and waterfowl hunting in a designated hunt area at the south end of the refuge during the designated season. Over 250 bird species have been recorded on the refuge.

Although camping is not permitted on the refuge, campground facilities are available at Jonathan Dickinson State Park (about an hour away) and elsewhere in the general area. Swimming, personal motorized watercraft, airboats, and hovercraft are not permitted on the refuge.

Even though alligators, which are abundant on the refuge, are generally afraid of people, visitors are cautioned to stay a safe distance from them and to be alert for venomous snakes and fire ants. Insect repellent and sunscreen are advised.

Lodgings and meals are available in such nearby communities as West Palm Beach, Boynton Beach, Delray Beach, Boca Raton, and Fort Lauderdale.

Access to the A.R.M. Loxahatchee NWR, from either Exit 86 on Florida's Turnpike or from Exit 44 on I-95, is west on Boynton Beach Blvd. (State Hwy. 804), left onto State Hwy. 441/U.S. Hwy. 7, and right onto Lee Rd. into the refuge. Access to the refuge's Hillsboro Recreation Area, at the southern end of the refuge, is by continuing south on State Hwy. 441 and west on County Hwy. 827 from Deerfield Beach.

Information: Arthur R. Marshall Loxahatchee NWR, 10216 Lee Rd., Boynton Beach, FL 33437; tel.: (561) 734-8303.

Chassahowitzka, comprising more than 31,000 acres, was established in 1943 to protect a magnificent expanse of pristine estuaries, bays, brackish marshland, and some bottomland hardwood swamps extending for 12 miles along and adjacent to the lower Chassahowitzka River, on the northwest Gulf Coast of Florida. Approximately three-quarters of the refuge is designated as a unit of the National Wilderness Preservation System.

Although this area formerly attracted great numbers of wintering ducks and coots, their numbers have declined in recent years. However, the refuge has become an increasingly important haven of bays and tidal rivers and streams for the federally listed endangered West Indian manatee (see description of this species in the Crystal River Refuge text).

There are also numerous species of birds, notably cormorants, herons, egrets, white ibis, anhinga, wood stork, brown pelican, osprey, bald eagle, swallow-tailed kite (in the spring), and wood duck. Great numbers of warblers and other species of neotropical migratory songbirds pass through the refuge during spring and autumn migrations. Reptiles include an abundance of alligators (visitors are urged to stay a safe distance from these reptiles) and several species of sea turtles.

As the Fish and Wildlife Service says, "Chassahowitzka is unspoiled habitat . . . that serves as important breeding and feeding ground for marine life. Shallow bays support an abundant growth of muskgrass which provides food for various birds and the endangered manatee. Inland from the bays are the brackish creeks and ponds where widgeongrass, watermilfoil and other foods grow in abundance. The eastern boundary provides a few thousand acres of swamp habitat, where oaks, cypress and red cedar grow. The outer islands consist mainly of red and black mangrove which provides habitat for colonial [nesting] birds."

An especially exciting wildlife management program at Chassahowitzka refuge is the reintroduction of the endangered whooping crane (see the Aransas NWR text for a description of this species). In the summer of 2001, chicks that were hatched in the captive breeding program at the Patuxent Wildlife Research Center in Maryland were taken to the Necedah National Wildlife Refuge in Wisconsin. There the birds underwent training with small ultralight aircraft (with crane-costumed pilots) that prepared them for an amazing migration. In October 2001, the cranes flew more than 1,200 miles with several ultralights from Necedah to Chassahowitzka, pausing more than thirty times along the route. (See further discussion of the crane recovery program in the Necedah NWR text.)

Although the refuge is open daily, accessible only by boat, visitation is subject to special regulations. To provide protection for the manatee, slow speed limits are posted for boats on parts of the Chassahowitzka River from April 1 through August 31. The use of airboats is restricted to the southern end of the refuge (in Hernando County) and to two posted airboat routes (in Citrus County). There is no entrance fee. The refuge headquarters, in the town of Crystal River, is open on weekdays, except national holidays.

Visitor activities include wildlife observation, boating, fishing, and hunting (designated hunts) on part of the refuge during the designated seasons. Camping is not permitted on the refuge, but campground facilities are available in Homosassa and Crystal River. Insect repellent and sunscreen are advised.

Lodgings and meals are available in such communities as Homosassa, Crystal River, Weeki Wachee, and Brooksville.

Access to the Chassahowitzka refuge from U.S. Hwy. 19/98 at Homosassa Springs is southwest about two miles on County Road 490 to a boat-launching ramp at Homosassa onto the Homosassa River; or, from the intersection of U.S. Highways 19 and 98 it is west just over a mile on County Rd. 480 to a boat-launching ramp onto the Chassahowitzka River.

Information: Chassahowitzka NWR, 1502 Southeast Kings Bay Dr., Crystal River, FL 34429; tel.: (352) 563-2088.

Crocodile Lake, encompassing 6,700 acres, was established in 1980 to protect critical habitat for the federally listed endangered American crocodile. The refuge is located on North Key Largo in south Florida.

Key Largo and the extreme southern tip of Florida are within the northern end of the crocodile's range, which extends southward through the coastal waters of the Caribbean islands and Central and South America. This large reptile, measuring as much as 15 feet in length, is similar to the American alligator, but is distinguished from the alligator by its long, tapered, much more slender snout. As the Fish and Wildlife Service explains, "The southeastern United States hosts two of the world's 22 crocodile species. Many Americans are quite familiar with the American alligator. . . . Few are aware of the American crocodile. . . . our crocodiles are shy, solitary creatures who would rather run and hide than have anything to do with humans." As for their habitat, "Crocodiles prefer mangrove-lined saltwater bays, creeks, and mangrove swamps; alligators primarily reside in inland freshwater glades, sloughs, bayous, cypress swamps, marshes, ponds, and canals. Both may be found in brackish water (water near the coast that has some salt content).

The refuge's habitat, which had been threatened with real estate development, consists of mangrove wetlands and wooded hammocks of slightly higher terrain. As the Fish and Wildlife Service says, "An abandoned subdivision development on the Refuge with miles of canals and exposed canal banks provides the only known nesting area for crocodiles on Key Largo. Although crocodile numbers are difficult to estimate, there may be somewhere between 600 and 800 of them in south Florida and around 100 on the refuge. The population is reportedly doing well, but the Service emphasizes, "Their future is in the hands of factors such as hurricanes, cold spells, poaching, road kills, continued habitat degradation, and disturbances by humans to them and their nests."

Crocodile Lake refuge and the adjacent Dagny Johnson Key Largo Hammock Botanical State Park contain the largest continuous tract of tropical hardwood forest remaining in the Florida Keys. Eighty percent of the diverse plant species are of West Indian origin. These wooded hammocks contain close to 100 species of native trees and shrubs, including such species as gumbo limbo, *lignumvitae*, and paradise tree. This forested habitat attracts numerous species of neotropical migratory songbirds. Common breeding birds on the refuge and park include the mangrove cuckoo and black-whiskered vireo. These areas are also inhabited by tree snails and butterflies.

An interpretive butterfly garden (with a wheelchair-accessible path) has been created adjacent to the refuge headquarters, which is located at 10750 County Rd. 905, Key Largo. However, to avoid human disturbance of sensitive habitat and wildlife, the remainder of the refuge is presently closed to visitation, except by special use permit. The adjacent Dagny Johnson Key Largo Hammock Botanical State Park provides a self-guiding nature trail into an area that is similar to Crocodile Lake refuge. The cooler winter months are the most comfortable season for visiting this area. Summers are typically hot and humid, with lots of biting insects.

One of the annual avian highlights of the Florida Keys is the spectacular autumn concentration of migrating raptors. Casey Lott, project director for the Florida Keys Raptor Migration Project, says that "the largest-known concentration of migrating peregrine falcons in the world" occurs along the Florida Keys. The biggest concentration of hawks can be seen from within Curry Hammock State Park, at mile marker 56 on Little Crawl Key (just south of Grassy Key). The Florida Keys Raptor Migration Project is sponsored and funded by the Florida Fish and Wildlife Conservation Commission and is run by HawkWatch International and the Audubon of Florida. For information on the Project's research and environmental education programs: e-mail: caseylott@hotmail.com or telephone: (305) 852-5318 or 5092.

Lodgings and meals are available in such communities as Key Largo, Islamorada, Long Key, Marathon, Florida City, and Homestead.

Information: Crocodile Lake NWR, P.O. Box 370, Key Largo, FL 33037; tel.: (305) 451-4223.

Florida Panther, containing nearly 30,000 acres, was established in 1989 to help promote the recovery of the federally listed endangered Florida panther. The refuge encompasses the northern part of the Fakahatchee Strand—a forested swamp that lies along the main drainage slough of the Big Cypress Swamp. This area is located about 20 miles east of Naples, bordered on the east by State Hwy. 29 and on the south by I-75 (Alligator Alley), in southwestern Florida. The refuge adjoins the National Park Service-administered Big Cypress National Preserve/ Everglades National Park and the Fakahatchee Strand State Preserve. All these public lands total more than one million acres that are offering protected panther habitat.

The Florida panther, a subspecies of the cougar (mountain lion), has adapted to south Florida's subtropical environment but is ranked as one of the world's rarest and most endangered mammals. The most common morphologic characteristic that distinguishes this sub-species from other cougars is its skull, which has been described as having higher-arched nasal bones than other cougars. This gives the panther the appearance of having a prominent or "Roman" nose. Other differences are so subtle that most experts would have a difficult time distinguishing one subspecies from another. Florida panthers are large, long-tailed, tawny-colored cats. The males weigh between 100 and 150 pounds and the females between 65 and 100 pounds. A mere 60 to 70 of these secretive, mostly nocturnal cats remain in the mixed forest swampland and pineland habitat, where they stalk and ambush such prey as deer, wild hogs, raccoons, and nine-banded armadillos.

This cat needs large areas of wilderness with little human intervention or disturbance. A single male panther in South Florida maintains at least 200 square miles of territory. As Refuge Manager Jim Krakowski states, "Because of the panther's widespread use of undisturbed forested habitats, it truly could be labeled as a 'barometer' of healthy swamps and forests of south Florida. These same forests provide habitat to a myriad of other animal and plant species, many of which are also threatened. In addition, these forests and wetlands safely soak up and store the heavy summer/fall rains."

Unfortunately, a long history of hunting (a bounty was once offered) and dwindling habitat have caused the Florida panther's alarming decline. Of major concern to wildlife biologists is the evidence among a high percentage of panthers of harmful impacts that are believed caused by isolation and inbreeding.

In an attempt to restore genetic diversity within the Florida panther population, a number of females of a closely related subspecies, the Texas cougar, were brought to Florida in 1995. This crossbreeding effort received the endorsement of federal and state wildlife agencies, environmental groups, and independent biologists.

The refuge includes lakes and ponds that are surrounded by swamps, grassy prairies, cypress domes, hardwood hammocks, and pine forests. Rising slightly higher than the grassy prairies and swamps are island-like areas known as hammocks. They support the growth of such species as cabbage palmetto, saw palmetto, live and laurel oaks, gumbo limbo, and holly.

The Fakahatchee Strand area also boasts North America's greatest numbers and density of native species of orchids (at least 46 species recorded). But according to the refuge's *Comprehensive Conservation Plan*, "Many of these orchids have been pilfered by humans and are now rare. Through a combination of agency and organization partnership . . . [the Rare Orchid Restoration] project would restore rare orchid species to suitable, historic habitats in southwest Florida."

The refuge is presently not open to public visitation, except for limited, small-group tours, to avoid disturbance of endangered species and their habitat. Refuge staff members offer environmental education programs at schools and elsewhere. A mile-long self-guiding foot trail with interpretive exhibits is proposed for construction in the southeast corner of the refuge.

Information: Florida Panther NWR, 3860 Tollgate Blvd., Suite 300, Naples, FL 34114; tel.: (239) 353-8442.

Hobe Sound, consisting of 967 acres, was established in 1969 and is located about twenty miles north of West Palm Beach on the Atlantic Coast of South Florida. The refuge protects coastal barrier island beach, sand dune, and mangrove swamp habitats on its 735-acre Jupiter

Island tract and a remnant of sand pine/scrub oak/saw palmetto forest on its 232-acre mainland tract. Among the birds of Hobe Sound Refuge are the brown pelican, herons, egrets, terns, shorebirds, osprey, and numerous species of neotropical songbirds during the spring and autumn migrations.

One of the major purposes of the refuge is to protect a 3.5-mile beach where the threatened loggerhead sea turtles and the endangered green and leatherback sea turtles deposit their eggs during the summer. Each egg-laden female hauls herself ashore, scoops out a nest with her rear flippers, lays about a hundred eggs, covers them with sand, and returns to the sea. For about two months, if undisturbed by predators or humans, the eggs are incubated within the sun warmed sand. Under the cover of darkness, the hatchlings, as a group, finally burst from their eggshells, scramble out of their nest, and dash into the ocean. Public use of the beach is limited, to avoid disturbing the sea turtles.

Another goal of the refuge is to help protect the endangered West Indian manatee, a marine mammal that inhabits the Intracoastal Waterway in Hobe Sound. Bobcats, gray foxes, raccoons, and eastern gray squirrels are among the terrestrial mammals that visitors may see.

As the Fish and Wildlife Service explains, fire management, with periodic low-intensity burning, is ecologically important:

The mainland unit of sand pine-scrub forest requires fire for its regeneration. Without fire, sand pine becomes too dense and tall, over-shadowing the scrub oak and rosemary, as well as covering open sand with needles. The numerous endemic plants and animals that have adapted to the open oak-scrub, including the Florida scrub-jay, cannot survive. Although the tract is small, its value is magnified by the fact that over 90 percent of this community type in South Florida has been lost to development.

Establishment of this refuge was made possible when local landowners generously donated their properties to The Nature Conservancy, which then transferred them to the Fish and Wildlife Service. In addition, a 173-acre parcel, which is listed as a National Natural Landmark, was donated by the Reed family as the Reed Wilderness Seashore Sanctuary.

The refuge is named for the Jobe (pronounced HO-bay) Indians, who lived in this area when Jonathan Dickinson and his party were shipwrecked at Jupiter Inlet during a hurricane in 1696. On lands now within the refuge, settlers constructed dwellings of palmetto fronds, called chickee huts.

The refuge is open daily during daylight hours. An entrance fee is charged at the beach parking area. The refuge headquarters is open on weekdays, except national holidays. Public entry onto the refuge is permitted at only three places: the headquarters area on the mainland unit, the beach on Jupiter Island unit, and the Peck Lake stretch of the Intracoastal Waterway.

Visitor activities include wildlife observation; hiking along the beach and on an interpretive trail); interpreter-guided sea turtle watches; swimming; canoeing, kayaking, and boating on the Intracoastal Waterway; and saltwater fishing along the beach and Intracoastal Waterway. Camping is not permitted on the refuge, but campground facilities are available across the highway at Jonathan Dickinson State Park and elsewhere in the vicinity.

A special environmental education program is provided at the refuge by the nonprofit Hobe Sound Nature Center, Inc. This organization operates the refuge's interpretive museum, which is open only on weekdays until 3 p.m., presents a lecture series during the spring and autumn, runs a summer camp for youth, and offers outreach programs for schools and other groups in the area.

Visitors are cautioned to be alert for venomous snakes. Insect repellent and sunscreen are advised.

Lodgings and meals are available in Stuart, Jensen Beach, Tequesta, and Jupiter.

Access to the refuge headquarters from Exit 60 on I-95 is east on State Hwy. 708/Bridge Rd., and right two miles on U.S. Hwy. I. To access the beach tract, go east on State Hwy. 708/Bridge Rd. to its end and left to the refuge parking area.

Information: Hobe Sound NWR, P.O. Box 645, Hobe Sound, FL 33475; tel.: (561) 546-6141.

J. N. "Ding" Darling, containing 6,400 acres, was established in 1945 to protect a magnificent area of important subtropical wildlife habitats on part of Sanibel Island, a barrier island on the southwestern Gulf Coast of Florida. Roughly 2,800 acres have been designated as a unit of the National Wilderness Preservation System.

The refuge consists of a variety of brackish estuarine and interior freshwater wetlands, including cordgrass marshes, dense stands of mangrove swamp, and West Indian hardwood hammocks. About half of the refuge supports mangrove estuary habitat, which is dominated by three species of mangrove. The red mangrove, growing partially or entirely in the water, is the most common, its tangle of twisted roots suggestive of the name "the tree that walks." Large seedlings, known as propagules, commonly hang from the branches of these trees. The black mangrove "breathes" through pneumatophores—specially developed roots that grow upward through the marshy soil. The white mangrove, growing the farthest from the water, excretes salt through the nodes at the base of its leaves.

As the Fish and Wildlife Service explains:

Mangroves play a vital role in the food chain of this marine environment. Microorganisms thriving on the decaying leaves of mangroves become food for animals such as shrimp, crabs, snails and worms. Rich in marine life these shallow waters attract thousands of small fish which are preyed upon by the numerous wading birds of the refuge.

The distinctive roots of the mangrove tree serve as nursery areas for many fish species such as mullet, snook, and snapper, and provide shelter for numerous marine organisms. The roots also serve to stabilize sediments and to provide coastal protection against erosion and storm damage.

The refuge's slightly higher ground consists of sand-and-shell ridges, on which grow such species as cabbage palmetto, saw palmetto, sea grape, wild coffee, and Jamaica caper. Hardwood hammocks include gumbo limbo, strangler fig, and mastic.

The refuge, which extends along the Pine Island Sound (inland) side of Sanibel Island and parts of Buck Key adjacent to Captiva Island, attracts large numbers of such birds as the roseate spoonbill, anhinga, brown pelican, white ibis, wood stork, great and snowy egrets, little blue and tricolored herons, mottled duck, osprey, and bald eagle. Over 240 species of birds have been recorded here. The largest of the refuge's reptiles is the abundant American alligator, the federally listed endangered American crocodile, and several species of endangered sea turtles that haul themselves onto island beaches to deposit their eggs.

The refuge was initially known as the Sanibel National Wildlife Refuge but was renamed in 1967 to honor the nationally syndicated, twice Pulitzer Prize–winning editorial cartoonist and pioneer wildlife conservationist, Jay Norwood "Ding" Darling (1876–1962).

As described by the Fish and Wildlife Service:

An avid hunter and fisherman, Mr. Darling became alarmed at the loss of wildlife habitat and the possible extinction of many species. Concerned about wildlife conservation, he worked this theme into his cartoons.

In July 1934, President Franklin D. Roosevelt appointed "Ding" Darling as the Director of the U.S. Biological Survey, the forerunner of the U.S. Fish and Wildlife Service. While Director, Darling initiated the Federal Duck Stamp Program, designed the first duck stamp, and vastly increased the acreage of the National Wildlife Refuge System.

Director Darling also designed the Blue Goose logo, the national symbol of the refuge system.

Habitat management activities on the refuge include periodic, low-intensity, prescribed burning to reduce fuel overloads and dense undergrowth that can cause destructive wildfires, cycle nutrients and maintain a diversity of important plant communities for the benefit of wildlife, control invasive non-native species of plants, and approximate ecologically natural fire cycles. Hundreds of acres of the refuge are also chemically treated to control such invasive non-native plants as the Brazilian pepper and Australian pine, species that rapidly impair the quality of natural wildlife habitat.

The refuge is open daily, except Fridays, during daylight hours. There is an entrance fee to the Wildlife Drive. The Center for Education is open daily. This visitor center was constructed entirely with private donations raised by the nonprofit organization "Ding" Darling Wildlife Society, which assists the refuge in many ways.

Visitor activities include wildlife observation, interpretive and environmental education programs at the visitor center, driving and bicycling the four-mile Wildlife Drive auto tour route, viewing wildlife from an observation tower, observing wildlife from several (wheelchair-accessible) observation platforms, hiking on several trails, joining guided walks and tours by refuge rangers and trained volunteer interpreters (reservations are requested for some outings: [239] 472-1100, ext. 222), canoeing and kayaking (two launch sites are provided), boating (a launch site is provided), fishing, and crabbing. Tram tours of Wildlife Drive, tours of Commodore Creek Canoe Trail, and other interpretive tours and programs are offered by Tarpon Bay Recreation, Inc., 900 Tarpon Bay Rd. Information and reservations: (239) 472-8900.

All refuge waters, including Tarpon Bay, are zoned slow speed/minimum wake; and the Fish and Wildlife Service urges extreme caution, to avoid disturbing or harming manatees.

Even though alligators and crocodiles are usually afraid of people, visitors are cautioned to stay a safe distance from them and to be alert for venomous snakes. Insect repellent and sunscreen are advised.

Although camping is not permitted on the refuge, campground facilities are provided on Sanibel, at Fort Myers Beach, and elsewhere in the Fort Myers vicinity. Swimming is not permitted on the refuge, but there are ample opportunities on the outer beaches of Sanibel and Captiva islands, where shelling has also long been popular.

Lodgings and meals are available in Sanibel, Captiva, Fort Myers Beach, and Fort Myers.

Access to the refuge from U.S. Hwy. 41 in Fort Myers is southwest 17 miles on State Hwy. 867 (MacGregor Blvd., Sanibel Bridge [toll], and Periwinkle Way) to the community of Sanibel; right on Palm Ridge Road, which becomes Sanibel-Captiva Rd.; and just over two miles to the refuge entrance on the right.

Information: J. N. "Ding" Darling NWR, 1 Wildlife Dr., Sanibel, FL 33957; tel.: (239) 472-1100.

Lower Suwannee, containing 52,935 acres and working toward a goal of nearly 63,000 acres, was established in 1979 to enhance and protect an ecologically rich diversity of wildlife habitats in one of the most extensive undeveloped estuarine river deltas in the United States. The two-unit refuge is located along the lower 20 miles of this river, made famous by Stephen Foster's song, "The Old Folks at Home," and stretches along 26 miles of the Gulf Coast of Florida.

The wetlands of the river's floodplain consist of bald-cypress swamps, tidally flooded bottomland hardwood forests, and freshwater marshes. Some of the river's tributaries are freshwater creeks, and others are tidal saltwater streams. The refuge's uplands support areas of scrub oak habitat and pine plantations. Along the coast, extensive salt marshes, numerous tidal creeks, and scattered islands comprise a magnificent, pristine coastal ecosystem.

As the Fish and Wildlife Service explains:

A constant influx of nutrients from the river system coupled with numerous offshore islands and tidal creeks create excellent wildlife habitat. Marine mammals such as bottlenose dolphin and the endangered West Indian Manatee, along with several species of marine turtles, utilize the coastal waters of the Suwannee Sound. Natural salt marshes and tidal flats attract thousands of shorebirds and diving ducks while acting as a valuable nursery area for fish, shrimp and shellfish. . . .

Floodplain wetlands . . . support nesting wood ducks, black bear, otter, alligator, wading birds, raccoons and . . . wintering waterfowl. Mixed hardwood-pine forests and uplands offer cover to turkey and white-tailed deer.

The refuge's habitat management activities include seasonally managed wetlands that provide supplemental habitat for egrets, herons, ibises, wood storks, and other water birds. Nesting boxes are provided for wood ducks, and nesting platforms offer extra sites for ospreys.

Forest habitats are being enhanced and maintained by the restoring of woodland communities that were previously altered by commercial timber harvesting; by selective thinning; and with periodic, low-intensity prescribed burning that promotes nutrient cycling, triggers the growth of understory vegetation that is of value to wildlife, creates or maintains habitat diversity, and reduces fuel overloads of organic debris that poses the risk of high-intensity wildfires.

The refuge is open daily during daylight hours. There is no entrance fee. Refuge headquarters is open on weekdays, except national holidays.

Visitor activities include wildlife observation, driving fifty miles of designated roads, hiking on trails and roads, bicycling on refuge roads, canoeing (canoe rentals available in the town of Suwannee), boating (boat-launching ramps onto the Suwannee River are provided at Fowler's Bluff and in the town of Suwannee), fishing (piers/observation decks at Salt Creek and Shell Mound are wheelchair-accessible), and hunting on parts of the refuge during the designated seasons. Camping is not permitted on the refuge, but county campground facilities (and boat-launching sites) are available at the end of Dixie County Rd. 357 and adjacent to the refuge's Shell Mound Unit, at the end of Levy County Rd. 326.

Even though alligators are usually afraid of people, visitors are cautioned to stay a safe distance from them and to be alert for venomous snakes and ticks. Insect repellent and sunscreen are advised.

Lodgings and meals are available in such communities as Cross City, Old Town, Chiefland, and Cedar Key.

Access to the refuge headquarters from U.S. Hwy. 19/98 at Chiefland is west and then south 6 miles on County Rd. 345, right 12 miles on County Road 347, and right onto the refuge. The Shell Mound Unit is reached by continuing south on County Rd. 347 and right onto County Rd. 326. To the west of the Suwannee River, there are two other access routes: from U.S. Hwy. 19/98 at Old Town, it is south 23 miles to the town of Suwannee on County Rd. 349 (the refuge borders much of this route to the east); and from U.S. Hwy. 19/98 at Cross City, it is south about 17 miles to the refuge on County Rd. 357.

Information: Lower Suwannee NWR, 16450 Northwest 31st Place, Chiefland, FL 32626; tel.: (352) 493-0238.

Merritt Island, containing 140,000 acres, overlays the NASA John F. Kennedy Space Center, at Cape Canaveral, on Florida's central Atlantic Coast. The refuge was established in 1963 to protect the diverse habitats of this barrier island, including extensive saltwater estuaries, brackish marshes, freshwater impoundments, coastal sand dunes, scrub oaks, cabbage palmetto-and-oak hammocks, and pine forests and flatwoods. The refuge lies between the Kennedy Space Center to the south and the National Park Service–managed Canaveral National Seashore to the north.

This refuge provides important habitat for numerous federally and state-listed endangered and threatened species. Among these are an aquatic mammal, the manatee; reptiles such as sea turtles (loggerhead, green, and leatherback), gopher tortoise, eastern indigo and Atlantic salt marsh snakes, and an estimated 5,000 alligators; and birds such as wood stork, roseate and least terns, piping plover, southern bald eagle, and Florida scrub-jay.

Of the more than 330 species of birds that have been recorded here, more than 23 are migratory waterfowl that winter by the thousands on the refuge's areas of open water. Resident waterbirds include herons, egrets, and brown and white pelicans.

To enhance the wetland habitat, a program of marsh restoration was begun in 1993 that has reconnected many of the refuge's impoundments with either the Indian River or Banana River. Ducks Unlimited, Inc. has assisted by enhancing approximately 5,000 acres of the refuge's wetlands.

The palm-and-oak hammocks are especially fascinating areas, supporting a mixture of tropical, subtropical, and temperate trees and other plants, including epiphytes (airplants). Numerous species of neotropical migratory songbirds pass through the wooded hammocks and pine forest during their spring and autumn migrations.

The refuge's habitat management activities include the seasonal management of water levels within 76 impoundments for the benefit of migratory waterfowl, wading birds, shorebirds, and other wildlife. Low-intensity prescribed burning is periodically implemented to enhance and maintain vegetative communities that are dependent upon or positively influenced by fire. Pine woodlands are thinned to enhance nesting habitat for bald eagles.

The refuge is open daily during daylight hours. From time to time, part or all of the refuge is temporarily closed during NASA's space launches or for other national security reasons. There is no entrance fee. The visitor center is open daily, except on national holidays, and on Sundays from April through October.

Visitor activities include wildlife observation, driving the seven-mile Black Point Wildlife Drive (an interpretive leaflet is available), hiking on several trails, canoeing on the estuaries and lagoon, boating (boat-launching ramps are provided, speed limits are posted in some areas to protect manatees), fishing, and hunting on parts of the refuge during the designated season. Although camping is not permitted on the refuge, campground facilities are provided at a number of nearby places, including on a first-come, first-served basis at Canaveral National Seashore.

Even though alligators are usually afraid of people, visitors are cautioned to stay a safe distance from them and to be alert for venomous snakes and ticks. Insect repellent and sunscreen are advised. The best seasons for visiting the refuge are spring, autumn, and winter.

Lodgings and meals are available in such communities as Titusville, Cape Canaveral, Merritt Island, Cocoa Beach, Melbourne, New Smyrna Beach, and Orlando.

Access to the refuge from Exit 80 on I-95 is east two miles on State Hwy. 406 to Titusville, east five miles across the Intracoastal Waterway, and right onto State Hwy. 402 to the visitor center.

Information: Merritt Island NWR, P.O. Box 6504, Titusville, FL 32782; tel.: (321) 861-0667.

National Key Deer Refuge, containing 8,381 acres, was established in 1957 to protect the critically endangered Key deer, the smallest of all the subspecies of white-tailed deer, which lives in the Lower Keys, northeast of Key West, Florida. The refuge consists of scattered tracts of land on two islands, with about three-quarters of the deer population inhabiting Big Pine Key and No Name Key. At shoulder height, adult bucks measure only 24 to 32 inches tall and average 85 pounds.

As a direct result of the destruction of the natural habitat and unregulated hunting, the numbers of Key deer sharply declined for many years; by the 1940s there were estimated to be fewer than fifty individuals. After the refuge was established and a law enforcement program was implemented, their numbers gradually increased and now appear to have stabilized between 700 and 800 animals.

It is believed that these deer originally migrated from the mainland thousands of years ago, following a land bridge that existed when the sea level was lower during the most recent period of continental glaciation. Over the subsequent centuries, these deer, living on what became a series of small islands, gradually evolved into a diminutive form of the mainland deer.

Habitats of this refuge include slash pine-and-thatch palm rocklands; freshwater and brackish wetlands; hardwood hammock; and dense areas of mangroves. Among the numerous species of birds that breed and forage on the refuge are the white-crowned pigeon, mangrove cuckoo, and black-whiskered vireo. More than 280 species of birds have been recorded here.

The refuge is open daily during daylight hours. There is no entrance fee. The refuge headquarters is open on weekdays, except national holidays.

Visitor activities include wildlife observation, driving roads within and adjacent to the refuge, and hiking on three short trails. Visitors are urged to drive cautiously to avoid hitting a deer. Camping is not permitted on the refuge.

Even though alligators are usually afraid of people, visitors are cautioned to stay a safe distance from them and to be alert for venomous snakes. Insect repellent and sunscreen are advised.

Lodgings and meals are available in such communities as Key West, Summerland Key, Little Torch Key, and Marathon.

Access to the refuge is southwest on U.S. Hwy. I (Overseas Highway) from the mainland to Big Pine Key, and right at the traffic light onto Key Deer Blvd. for 0.25 mile. The refuge visitor center is on the right, in the Big Pine Key Plaza.

Information: National Key Deer Refuge, P.O. Box 430510, Big Pine Key, FL 33043; tel.: (305) 872-2239.

Pelican Island, located in the Indian River Lagoon stretch of the Intracoastal Waterway on the central Atlantic Coast of Florida, was established on March 14, 1903, as the first national wildlife refuge in the United States. Under the terms of an Executive Order issued by President Theodore Roosevelt, 5.5-acre Pelican Island was "reserved and set aside . . . as a preserve and breeding ground for native birds." In 1970, Pelican Island became the smallest unit of the National Wilderness Preservation System, and in 1993, the refuge was designated as a Wetland of International Importance.

As the Fish and Wildlife Service describes the island's landmark history:

Pelican Island has long been home to many kinds of birds. In 1859, Dr. Henry Bryant reported seeing thousands of herons, egrets, pelicans, ibises, and spoonbills, all nesting in harmony among the tree tops of black and red mangroves. However, plume hunters had already arrived to begin their relentless slaughter of countless egrets, herons, spoonbills, and even pelicans. The annihilation was so complete that by 1903 only brown pelicans were left. And Pelican Island was the last breeding ground for brown pelicans along the entire east coast of Florida.

The pelicans might not be here today . . . [had it not been] for a man by the name of Paul Kroegel . . . a German immigrant who homesteaded in Sebastian . . . , partly because of the proximity to Pelican Island.

Paul Kroegel took a special interest in the pelicans as he watched them from his home. In 1883, he became Game Warden for the American Ornithologist's Union, began lobbying for the birds, and initiated a campaign to protect the birds from plume hunters . . . and invited influential visitors to go with him and witness the carnage. . . .

In 1900, a federal law, the Lacey Act, was passed by Congress to make the interstate transport of birds illegal. It was at the urging of both the Florida Audubon Society and the American Ornithologist's Union, that President Theodore "Teddy" Roosevelt issued the Executive Order on March 14, 1903. . . . Two weeks later, . . . Kroegel was appointed warden by the federal government for a salary of $1 per month. . . .

The threat from plume hunters diminished, but a new threat was looming. In the Spring of 1918, a group of young commercial fishermen set out for Pelican Island at night and killed hundreds of defenseless pelican chicks. They claimed that the pelicans were taking too many fish. This controversy was spreading until a Florida Audubon Society study showed that the bulk of the pelican's diet consisted of commercially unimportant baitfish.

In 1918, the Migratory Bird Treaty Act, passed by Congress, made hunting of nongame birds and taking of eggs illegal. The threat of a $500 fine or six months in prison halted plume hunting.

Paul Kroegel protected and managed Pelican Island NWR until 1926 after the island became flooded and the pelicans abandoned Pelican Island for several years. . . .

After years of decimation at the hands of plume hunters and the ravishing effects of DDT, the birds have begun to make a comeback. The diversity of bird species as seen in 1859 can be seen again. However, the total number of birds that once were counted in the thousands, are now counted in the hundreds. . . .

Increasing human population growth and land development around Indian River Lagoon and increasing recreational watercraft traffic are posing challenges to the welfare of Pelican Island. Since 1943, the island has diminished in size by more than 50 percent. In 2000, to curtail erosion, the Fish and Wildlife Service began a shoreline restoration project, which consisted of planting smooth cordgrass and red mangroves along the eroding northern and western edges of the island and installing a natural wave break of an oyster bar that reduces and deflects wave energy from the island, provides habitat for shorebirds, and reestablishes mangroves for nesting habitat.

The refuge is open daily during daylight hours. There is no entrance fee. Facilities include various walking trails, a "Centennial Trail" boardwalk, and an observation tower from which to view Pelican Island. A wildlife drive is planned for the future. Insect repellent and sunscreen are advised.

Lodgings and meals are available in such communities as Sebastian, Vero Beach, and Melbourne.

Access to the refuge from Exit 69 on I-95 is east on State Hwy. 512 to Sebastian; from Exit 69 on I-95 go east on State Highways 512 and 510, across Wabasso Island, left 3.7 miles on State Hwy. A1A, and left onto Jungle Trail. Or the refuge can be accessed by boat from boat-launching sites at Sebastian, at the east end of State Hwy. 512, or on Wabasso Island. Commercial boat-tour operators are located in Sebastian.

Information: Pelican Island NWR, 1339 Twentieth St., Vero Beach, FL 32960; tel.: (772) 562-3909.

St. Marks, comprising more than 68,000 acres in three contiguous units, was established in 1931 with acquisition of the St. Marks Unit. The Wakulla and Panacea units were added in the late 1930s. This ecologically spectacular refuge is located along the shores of Apalachee Bay, in the Big Bend region of Florida's Gulf Coast.

The refuge manages and protects a wide diversity of habitats that attract tens of thousands of wintering waterfowl as well as numerous other birds such as anhingas, brown pelicans, egrets, herons, ibises, swallow-tailed and Mississippi kites, nesting bald eagles and ospreys, wood ducks, bluebirds, red-cockaded woodpeckers and multitudes of migrating shorebirds and neotropical songbirds. Over 300 bird species have been recorded here.

Major habitats include extensive needlerush salt marshes; freshwater marshes; meandering rivers, streams, and tidal creeks; bald-cypress swamps; bogs; hardwood hammocks; picturesque cabbage pine-and-palm hammocks; forests of longleaf pine, slash pine, and loblolly/mixed hardwoods; several freshwater lakes and ponds (notably cypress-framed Otter Lake); and nearly 2,000 acres of levee-contained pools.

The refuge's forest management activities include periodic, low-intensity prescribed burning of the pine woodlands to promote nutrient cycling, spur the growth of new plants of value to wildlife, and reduce dangerous fuel overloads that risk destructive wildfires. Other activities include selective thinning of pine woodlands to promote the growth of understory vegetation, and the restoration of the native longleaf pine forests. Much of this woodland management is carried out for the benefit of the federally listed red-cockaded woodpecker, which requires an open-grown forest with nesting cavities in older growth pines.

The refuge's ecologically rich tidal salt marshes are invaluable as vital spawning and nursery habitat for many species of marine organisms. As the Fish and Wildlife Service explains, "The food and cover available in these wetlands are used by a variety of juvenile estuarine fish and shellfish .... For this reason, salt marshes are considered to be an important nursery ground for much of the Florida Gulf Coast's commercial seafood harvest." Salt marshes such as these also act as buffers that "can absorb most of the impact associated with storm surges" such as occur during hurricanes.

The refuge's most dramatic insect event is the southward annual migration of great numbers of monarch butterflies, which climaxes during October. Other colorful butterflies include the tiger swallowtail, zebra, viceroy, queen, sulfurs, fritillaries, and the American painted beauty.

Establishment of the refuge was made possible partly with revenues from the sale of Migratory Bird Hunting and Conservation Stamps (Duck Stamps). In the 1930s, the Civilian Conservation Corps built levees and other structures for the benefit of wintering waterfowl. In 1975, approximately 17,546 acres of the refuge were designated as a unit of the National Wilderness Preservation System. Ducks Unlimited, Inc. has helped enhance about 350 acres of the refuge's wetland habitat.

The refuge is open daily during daylight hours. An entrance fee is charged at the St. Marks Unit of the refuge. The visitor center is open daily, except on national holidays. A fee is charged for the use of the Aucilla Boat Ramp, at the eastern end of the refuge.

Visitor activities include wildlife observation, driving the 6.8-mile interpretive Lighthouse Road Wildlife Drive, viewing the refuge from an observation deck that overlooks an expanse of salt marsh and a managed pool, hiking on many trails (including 43 miles of the Florida National Scenic Trail that runs through the refuge), bicycling, viewing interpretive exhibits and programs at the visitor center, environmental education programs for school and other groups, guided migratory bird tours, and viewing the historic St. Marks Lighthouse, which dates from 1831 (at the south end of Lighthouse Rd.).

Other activities include picnicking (two picnic areas are provided), canoeing (rentals are available near the refuge), boating (not more than 10 HP motors on refuge pools from March 15 to October 15; four launching ramps onto Apalachee Bay are provided), fishing, crabbing, and hunting on parts of the refuge during the designated seasons. A two-day hunt is held for mobility-challenged visitors in early December.

Although camping is not permitted on the refuge, campground facilities are available nearby.

The most favorable seasons for hiking or biking on the refuge trails are late autumn through early spring.

Mid-November through January is the best time to see the large concentrations of wintering waterfowl; and March through early April brings the peak influx of large numbers of warblers and other neotropical migratory songbirds. One aspect of this huge influx is referred to as "fallout," a frenzied phenomenon that occasionally occurs in the spring when unfavorable headwinds from the north slow down and make even more difficult the birds' energy-depleting nonstop flight across the Gulf of Mexico. Coming from such launching places as Mexico's Yucatan Peninsula, the exhausted birds drop into coastal wooded areas from the Florida Panhandle to Texas (see the Aransas NWR text for a further description of this event).

Even though alligators are usually afraid of people, visitors are cautioned to stay a safe distance from them and to be alert for venomous snakes and ticks. Insect repellent and sunscreen are advised.

Lodgings and meals are available in St. Marks, Wakulla Springs, and Tallahassee.

Access to the refuge's visitor center from U.S. Hwy. 98 at Newport is south three miles on County Hwy. 59.

Information: St. Marks NWR, P.O. Box 68, St. Marks, FL 32355; tel.: (850) 925-6121.

St. Vincent, containing 12,358 acres, was established in 1968 to protect an undeveloped coastal barrier island located at the western end of Apalachicola Bay, on the central Gulf Coast of the Florida Panhandle. The Fish and Wildlife Service acquired St. Vincent Island from The Nature Conservancy with revenues from the sale of Migratory Bird Hunting and Conservation Stamps (Duck Stamps).

Roughly triangular in shape, St. Vincent Island measures about nine miles long and four miles wide, and contains ten types of habitat. Among this subtropical diversity are Spanish "moss"–festooned live oaks and/or scrub oaks that grow on a series of east-west trending dune ridges, slash pine woodlands, magnolia-and-cabbage palmetto hammocks, lakes and streams, sloughs and salt marshes, sand dunes, and broad, sandy beaches along the south and east shores. Ducks Unlimited, Inc. has helped enhance wetland habitat on more than 100 acres of the refuge.

In addition to attracting concentrations of waterfowl, St. Vincent refuge is a haven for a number of endangered and threatened species of wildlife. These include loggerhead sea turtles, which come ashore to lay their eggs on the beaches.

In 1990, St. Vincent became one of several coastal islands in the southeastern United States on which the endangered red wolf was reintroduced and is being bred. This species, which has mostly brown and buff fur with some black color along the back, is between the size of the larger gray wolf and the smaller coyote. As the Fish and Wildlife Service explains:

The red wolf is one of the most endangered animals in the world. It is a shy species that once roamed throughout the Southeast as a top predator. Aggressive predator control programs and clearing of its forested habitat combined to cause impacts that brought the red wolf to the brink of extinction. By 1970, the entire population of red wolves was believed to be less than 100 animals confined to a small area of coastal Texas and Louisiana.

To save the species from extinction, the Service captured as many as possible of the few remaining animals from 1974 through 1980. Only 14 captured animals met the criteria established to define the species and stood between existence and extinction. These animals formed the nucleus of a captive-breeding program established at the Point Defiance Zoo and Aquarium in Tacoma, Wash., with the final goal of reestablishing the species in portions of its original southeastern range. Thirty-three zoos and nature centers in 21 states and the District of Columbia now cooperate in a national breeding program and are valuable partners in efforts to restore red wolves.

The red wolf is now back in the wild, hunting, rearing young, and communicating by its characteristic howl, in several locations. . . . Since 1987, red wolves have been released into northeastern North Carolina and now roam over more than 560,000 acres that includes three national wildlife refuges. . . . Other red wolves have been released on coastal islands in Florida, Mississippi, and South Carolina as a steppingstone between captivity and the wild.

By 2001, the total population of red wolves in the wild was estimated at approximately 100 individuals. Of this number, two were living on St. Vincent refuge. (For a further discussion of the red wolf recovery program and the Red Wolf Coalition, see the Pocosin Lakes NWR text.)

Among the more prominent species of birds are nesting bald eagles and ospreys, wood storks, anhingas, great and snowy egrets, wood ducks (for which the refuge provides nesting boxes), swallow-tailed kites, wild turkeys, and brown pelicans.

The refuge is open daily during daylight hours. The refuge is reached by boat. There is no access fee. The refuge's visitor center/headquarters, located in the Harbor Master Building, Market Street, Apalachicola, is open on weekdays, except national holidays.

Visitor activities include wildlife observation, hiking on 80 miles of sand roadways and 14 miles of beaches, boating (a public boat-launching ramp is provided in Indian Pass, at the end of State Hwy. C30B), fishing on refuge lakes (except when seasonally closed to protect nesting bald eagles), and hunting during the designated seasons. Camping is not permitted on the refuge (except for primitive camping associated with designated annual hunts for deer and feral hogs), but campground facilities are provided at St. George Island State Park and other nearby places.

Late November through December is the best time to see the peak concentrations of wintering waterfowl. March through early April brings the peak numbers of warblers and other neotropical migratory songbirds. One aspect of this impressive influx is referred to as "fallout," a frenzied phenomenon that occasionally occurs in the spring, when unfavorable headwinds from the north slow down and make even more challenging the birds' energy-depleting nonstop flight across the Gulf of Mexico. From such launching places as Mexico's Yucatan Peninsula, the exhausted birds drop into coastal wooded areas, from the Florida Panhandle to Texas (see the Aransas text for a further description of this migration event).

Even though alligators are usually afraid of people, visitors are cautioned to stay a safe distance from them and to be alert for venomous snakes and ticks. Insect repellent and sunscreen are advised. As there is no drinking water available on the island, visitors should bring an adequate supply.

Lodgings and meals are available in Apalachicola.

Access to the boat ramp at Indian Pass from Apalachicola is west about seven miles on U.S. Hwy. 98, left ten miles on State Hwy. 30, and left three miles to the end of State Hwy. C30B.

Information: St. Vincent NWR, P.O. Box 447, Apalachicola, FL 32329; tel.: (850) 653-8808.

Ten Thousand Islands, containing about 35,000 acres, was established in 1996, with the transfer of private lands to the Fish and Wildlife Service, under authority of the Arizona-Florida Land Exchange Act of 1988. The refuge protects a large part of the vast Ten Thousand Islands estuary, on the southern Gulf Coast of Florida. This ecologically rich area lies down the watershed from the Florida Panther NWR and Big Cypress National Preserve, about 20 miles southeast of Naples.

The northern part of the refuge contains an extensive freshwater marsh system, with scattered freshwater ponds and small island-like hammocks of slightly higher terrain. The hammocks support such species as live and laurel oaks, cabbage palmetto, saw palmetto, and gumbo limbo. Along some areas where freshwater mixes with saltwater, there are expanses of salt marsh. The southern part of the refuge encompasses an estuarine ecosystem of coastal lagoons, embayments, brackish streams, and a multitude of coastal saline islands. Dense stands of mangroves are the dominant vegetation of these islands and mainland tidal edges. The most coastal of the islands have sand or shell beaches, some of which contain ancient Indian shell middens that have raised the elevation of the islands by several feet (Dismal Key rises 13 feet). Here thrive such subtropical plant species as stopper, gumbo limbo, bay trees, cabbage palm, and sea grape.

As the Fish and Wildlife Service explains in the refuge's November 2000 *Comprehensive Conservation Plan*, "The refuge . . . represents a nearly pristine mangrove estuary system. [It] . . . is part of the larger Ten Thousand Islands system, one of the largest mangrove-forested regions in the New World."

Several significant threatened and endangered species of wildlife inhabit the refuge, including loggerhead, green, and Kemp's ridley sea turtles; wood stork, and West Indian manatee. Regarding the latter, the Fish and Wildlife Service says, "West Indian manatees use refuge waters throughout the year. Collier County is the third highest area of watercraft-related manatee mortality in the state. With the predicted boat traffic increase in county waters, it will be important for the refuge to monitor the impacts of this traffic and enforce manatee protection areas."

As described by Refuge Manager Jim Krakowski:

As one quietly paddles through the backcountry maze of mangrove islands, the peace and solitude are broken by surprising views of wildlife: manatees and dolphins surface near your boat to loudly suck air; giant sea turtles bob up for a look; a huge 100-pound tarpon may roll on the water surface showing a big eye and dorsal fin; spoonbills, storks, and ibis squawk and feed on an exposed oyster bar; and bald eagles, swallow-tailed kites, and ospreys soar overhead; while raccoons and river otters scour the shoreline.

The refuge is open daily, with visitation preferably only during daylight hours in the northern marshes. There is no entrance fee.

Visitor activities include wildlife observation, canoeing and kayaking float trips, motorized boating during winter months, fishing, and hunting on part of the refuge during the designated season. Camping on the refuge is mostly restricted to coastal beaches of Panther, Hog, and Round keys during the winter. This activity does not conflict with loggerhead and green sea turtles, as they deposit their eggs on beaches during the summer.

Even though alligators and crocodiles are usually afraid of people, visitors are urged to stay a safe distance from them and to be alert for venomous snakes. Insect repellent is advised.

Lodgings and meals are available in such communities as Naples and Everglades City.

The refuge lies just east of the Collier-Seminole State Park, extending south from the Tamiami Trail (U.S. Hwy. 41). Although there is presently no access into the refuge's northern freshwater-marsh habitat from the Tamiami Trail, the Fish and Wildlife Service is evaluating proposals to establish a one-mile interpretive hiking trail and an observation tower along an abandoned oil pad road; and a canoe and non-motorized boat loop trail that could be used during periods of high water.

Although motorboat access into the southern part of the refuge is presently largely unrestricted, the Fish and Wildlife Service and the Rookery Bay National Estuarine Research Reserve are planning to assess the impacts on wildlife and submerged land resources from powered watercraft operating in shallow water environments within the Ten Thousand Islands region.

Information: Ten Thousand Islands NWR, 3860 Tollgate Blvd., Suite 300, Naples, FL 34114; tel.: (239) 353-8442.

Georgia

Blackbeard Island, encompassing 5,618 acres, was established in 1940 to protect this barrier island's ecologically rich habitats of maritime forest, salt marsh, man-made freshwater pools, and sandy beach, on the central coast of Georgia. In 1975, more than half of the refuge (the southwestern part) was designated as a unit of the National Wilderness Preservation System, and within the wilderness lies a 450-acre research natural area, about one-quarter of which contains an area of virgin-growth slash pines.

Brown pelicans, black skimmers, ospreys, and many species of wading birds, shorebirds, and wintering ducks, shorebirds, gulls, terns, and painted buntings are just a few of the more common birds that use Blackbeard Island. A large wading bird rookery is located at Flag Pond. White-tailed deer and raccoons are abundant. In summer, loggerhead sea turtles haul themselves onto the seven-mile ocean beach to lay their eggs. Alligators are numerous.

The island is named for Edward Teach, known as Blackbeard the Pirate. According to legend, he sailed up and down the coast, plundering and murdering, and making occasional stops on this island to bury his stolen fortunes. Although rumors still abound as to the whereabouts of Blackbeard's buried treasure, nothing has ever been discovered.

Blackbeard Island has actually been in federal ownership since 1800, when the U.S. Navy Department acquired it at public auction as a source of live oak lumber for shipbuilding. A limited amount of timber harvesting occurred.

In 1924, Blackbeard Island was transferred to the Bureau of Biological Survey, to be managed as a breeding ground for migratory birds and other wildlife. Under the terms of a Presidential Proclamation signed in 1940 by President Franklin D. Roosevelt, the island became a national wildlife refuge.

As described by the Fish and Wildlife Service:

The island comprises interconnecting linear dunes thickly covered by oak/palmetto vegetation. Between these ridges are numerous ponds and savannas. . . . Protected from tides by dikes and dunes, these savannas are filled by seasonal rains and are utilized by waterfowl and wading birds. . . . The island's forests range from maritime live oak forest on the north end, mixed live oak/pine forests in the middle of the island, to predominantly slash pine on the south end. These forests are used by numerous species of resident and migrant songbirds, hawks, and owls.

The refuge is open daily. There is no entrance fee. A visitor information kiosk is located near Blackbeard Creek.

Visitor activities include wildlife observation, hiking and bicycling on a network of trails, boating (a dock is provided on Blackbeard Creek), saltwater fishing, and archery deer hunting during the designated season. Camping is not permitted on the refuge, except during managed deer hunts. More than 230 bird species have been recorded here.

Even though alligators are generally afraid of people, visitors are cautioned to stay a safe distance from them and to be alert for venomous snakes and for ticks, chiggers, and fire ants. Insect repellent and sunscreen are advised.

Lodgings and meals are available in such communities as Darien, Brunswick, St. Simons Island, and Richmond Hill.

Access to Blackbeard Island Refuge can be by chartered boat from Shellman Bluff (reached from U.S. Hwy. 17 on Shellman Bluff Rd.) or by boat from Barbour River Landing—a public boat-launching ramp on Harris Neck NWR that is open all day.

Information: Blackbeard Island NWR, c/o Savannah Coastal Refuges, Parkway Business Center, Suite 10, 1000 Business Center Dr., Savannah, GA 31405; tel.: (912) 652-4415.

Okefenokee, containing 395,080 acres, was established in 1937 to protect migratory birds and their habitat within one of the world's most extensive, intact freshwater ecosystems. The refuge is located almost entirely in the southeastern corner of Georgia, with several thousand acres in northeastern Florida. The Okefenokee, which has been designated as a Wetland of International Importance, consists of a mosaic of bog habitats that includes forested cypress swamps, open wet "prairies," natural lakes, islands, shrub-scrub thickets, and upland pine forests. More than 353,000 acres have been designated as a unit of the National Wilderness Preservation System. More than 230 bird species have been recorded here.

The refuge's habitats are a haven for a rich variety of wildlife—from egrets, herons, ibises, wood storks, anhingas, wood ducks, sandhill cranes, red-cockaded and pileated woodpeckers, and numerous species of neotropical migratory songbirds; to black bears, white-tailed deer, bobcats, gopher tortoises, a multitude of snakes and turtles, and one of America's largest populations of the American alligator.

The word Okefenokee is derived from a Choctaw Indian expression meaning "land of the trembling earth." Much of the swamp contains 10- to 15-foot-thick deposits of peat. In some places, it is possible to walk on these thick deposits and cause nearby trees and other vegetation to shake.

A description of the Okefenokee Swamp during the heat, humidity, and green of springtime is provided by Delos E. Culver, writing in the January–March 1947 issue of *National Parks*:

The swamp lay shimmering in the midday heat enveloped in a silence unbelievable in this day and age. Its appearance seemed to carry us back to the pre-dawn of man. Our tiny boat turned its prow from the deep waters of a canal . . . as we obtained our first view. Before us spread the forest primeval. . . . Stretching off to the horizon lay mile upon mile of shallow open swamp—a vast plain of clear amber water, dotted with islands near and far. . . . Perhaps the magnificent beauty is due in part to the uniform uncrowded distribution of plant life over the surface of the water that reflects the towering moss-draped pine and cypress. . . .

An occasional egret or great blue heron . . . could be seen. Vultures . . . perched motionless on dead cypresses. . . .

. . . the dim hours following dawn were sonorous with amphibian thunder [of chorusing frogs]. Rolling across the miles of swamp land . . . was . . . occasionally . . . the growl of an old bull alligator exhibiting his vocal powers in mighty tones that echoed and re-echoed.

In 1891, a canal company acquired 234,000 acres of the Okefenokee from the state of Georgia, with the intention of draining the swamp, logging its cypress forests, and planting crops. . . . In 1899, the land was sold to a lumber company. Between 1910 and 1927, more than 400 million board-feet of timber—three-quarters of which was cypress—were harvested from the Okefenokee Swamp.

Cornell University biologists, who had been researching the swamp since 1909, initiated a proposal to protect the Okefenokee. With the backing of a number of conservation organizations, the Georgia state legislature passed a resolution in 1919 that asked the federal government to purchase the swamp. Federal acquisition finally began in 1936, followed by an Executive Order signed by President Franklin D. Roosevelt establishing the Okefenokee NWR.

The refuge is open daily, except on Christmas. Entry fees are charged at each of the three manned entrances: the East Entrance at Suwannee Canal Recreation Area, near Folkston—the refuge's Richard S. Bolt Visitor Center, located just west of State Hwy. 121/23, is at this entrance and is open daily, except Christmas; the West Entrance (known as the Stephen C. Foster State Park, which is under a concession contract with the Fish and Wildlife Service) near Fargo; and the North Entrance (known as Okefenokee Swamp Park, which is also under a concession contract with the Service) near Waycross. There are also two unmanned entrances: Kingfisher Landing, 15 miles north of Folkston; and Suwannee River Recreation Area, 6 miles west of Stephen C. Foster State Park.

Visitor activities include wildlife observation, visitor center interpretive programs, driving and bicycling on Swamp Island Drive and the refuge's entrance roads, walking (wheelchair-accessible) boardwalks, hiking on several trails, viewing the refuge and wildlife from observation towers, canoeing on an extensive network of canoe trails (rentals are offered at the East and West entrances; and a canoeing brochure is available), motor-boating on boat trails, guided boat tours, camping (at a number of sites for which a permit is required and a fee is charged), and fishing.

Even though alligators are generally afraid of people, visitors are cautioned to stay a safe distance from them and to be alert for venomous snakes, ticks, chiggers, and fire ants. Insect repellent is advised to ward off mosquitoes and biting flies.

Lodgings and meals are available in such communities as Waycross and Folkston.

Access from Exit 3 on I-95 to the refuge's visitor center is west, through Kingsland, 22 miles to Folkston, left 8 miles on State Hwy. 121/23, and right 3 miles on the refuge's East Entrance Rd. From U.S. Hwy. 84 at Waycross, it is southeast 34 miles on U.S. Hwy. 1 to Folkston, right on State Hwy. 121/23, and right 3 miles on the refuge's East Entrance Rd.

Information: Okefenokee NWR, Route 2, Box 3330, Folkston, GA 31537; tel.: (912) 496-7836.

Piedmont, comprising 34,967 acres, was established in 1939 to restore an area of gently rolling hills and bottomland that had previously been denuded, and the soil severely eroded and depleted from past farming practices. The refuge, located in central Georgia, is an example of how an utterly devastated ecosystem can be successfully restored to fertility with a rich diversity of habitats and wildlife. More than 200 species of birds have been recorded here.

As described by the Fish and Wildlife Service:

When Franklin D. Roosevelt signed the Executive Order establishing Piedmont National Wildlife Refuge . . . , the land's fertility and abundant wildlife populations had been ravaged. The vast forest, which had reigned supreme for eons, had been cleared by European settlers in the early 1800's. Cotton became king and farming soon robbed the soil of its natural fertility. The loss of forest, with its soil stabilizing root system, led to massive erosion problems. The Civil War, the boll weevil, and the Great Depression [of the 1930s] combined to cause large scale land abandonment. . . .

Today, through the efforts of the Fish and Wildlife Service, the . . . refuge is once again a forest. It hosts loblolly pines on the ridges with hardwoods found along creek bottoms and in scattered upland coves. Clear streams and beaver ponds provide ideal wetlands for migrating waterfowl. Wildlife populations have been restored.

One of the primary resource management activities in this mosaic of habitats is periodic prescribed burning. Relatively low-burning fires promote nutrient cycling that spurs the growth of plants valued by many species of wildlife. Other forest management activities include timber thinning to promote wildlife habitat diversity in both loblolly pine woodlands and hardwood forests, for the benefit of such species as the endangered red-cockaded woodpecker and wild turkeys. Eleven ponds are managed for the benefit of fish and wildlife, and nesting boxes are located around the ponds for wood ducks.

Piedmont Refuge is open daily during daylight hours. There is no entrance fee. The visitor center is open daily, except on national holidays.

Visitor activities include wildlife observation; viewing interpretive exhibits at the visitor center; group interpretive programs and tours (by advance reservation); driving the six-mile interpretive Little Rock Wildlife Drive; hiking numerous trails; fishing by boat (electric motors only) on Allison Lake and Pond 2A from May through September; bank fishing on some ponds from May through September; fishing from piers at Pond 2A and the Children's pond; and hunting on part of the refuge during the designated seasons. In mid-October, a two-day deer hunt for mobility-challenged hunters is offered. Camping is not permitted on the refuge, except during big game hunts, at which times Pippen Lake Campground in Compartment 19 is available for hunters with a refuge special use permit.

Visitors are cautioned to be alert for venomous snakes, ticks, and chiggers. Insect repellent is advised during the warmer months.

Lodgings and meals are available in such communities as Macon, Forsyth, and Gray.

Access to refuge's visitor center from Exit 186 on I-75 in Forsyth is northeast 18 miles on Juliette Rd.

Information: Piedmont NWR, 718 Juliette Rd., Round Oak, GA 31038; tel.: (478) 986-5441.

Hawai'i and Pacific Remote Islands Complex: Hawai'i

Hakalau Forest, consisting of 32,733 acres, was established in 1985 to enhance and protect an outstanding area of the often-misty, mid-elevation, montane rainforest that is vital habitat for a number of endangered species of forest birds along the windward slope of Mauna Kea, on the

Big Island of Hawai'i. Of the 14 kinds of native birds inhabiting this refuge, 8 are listed as endangered.

One of the most interesting of the latter species is the rare 'akiapola'au, a member of the Hawaiian Honeycreeper family. It has an unusual-shaped beak—a short, stout, lower mandible and a long, down-curving, upper bill, uniquely adapted to peck holes into and pull off tree bark in search of insect larvae and other prey. The male has a yellow head and breast and olive-green back, and the female has dull greenish plumage. Another endangered honeycreeper is the Hawai'i 'akepa, which feeds on insects with its slightly crossed bill and which nests in tree cavities. The male is bright orange, and the female is greenish-gray.

The Hawai'i creeper is an endangered, small, olive-green bird with habits similar to North America's nuthatches—creeping up and down tree trunks and along the underside of branches in search of insects.

The endangered 'io, the Hawaiian hawk, is often seen soaring over the forest. This species, whose numbers have been increasing in recent years, is revered by many Polynesian-Hawaiians as their guardian spirit, or 'aumakua. The state-listed, endangered pueo, the Hawaiian short-eared owl is sometimes seen gliding across open habitat seeking rodents, small birds, and other prey.

The endangered nene, known as the Hawaiian goose, has recently been reintroduced to Hakalau Forest refuge. This official state bird of Hawai'i also inhabits nearby Hawai'i Volcanoes National Park and Maui's Haleakala National Park. It has a black head and nape, buff-yellow cheek and neck, and heavily barred brownish-gray plumage on the back.

Common native birds of the refuge include the i'iwi, a striking bright red bird with black wings and a long, orange, down-curved bill; the 'apapane, a bright scarlet little bird that flies in flocks through the forest; the 'amakihi, a yellowish honeycreeper; and the 'oma'o, also known as the Hawai'i thrush, which forages for fruits in understory vegetation and which is recognized by its whistled, slurred, flute-like musical trills.

In addition, a dozen of the Hakalau Forest refuge's 29 rare plants are listed or proposed for listing as endangered. Over the decades, the decline of these and related fauna and flora has resulted from the destruction and impairment of this habitat.

Elevations within the refuge extend from 2,500 to over 6,600 feet above sea level, with rainfall dramatically decreasing upward. Below 4,000 feet elevation, slopes and deep gulches, which annually receive from 250 to 300 inches of rainfall, contain dense forest vegetation, areas of tree ferns, and bogs.

From around 4,500 to near 6,000 feet elevation, annual precipitation averages around 150 inches. Here grows a beautiful, closed-canopy forest that is dominated by the 'ohi'a, a tree bearing distinctive, brush-like flowers without petals and with clusters of long, bright-red stamens; and the majestic acacia, koa, the massive trunks of which the Polynesian-Hawaiians once carved their great ocean canoes (wa'a opela). Understory trees, shrubs, and the Hawaiian tree fern also grow here.

The Fish and Wildlife Service has been implementing a number of habitat restoration management projects at the refuge. These include the elimination of livestock grazing; fencing of some key units, from 500 to 2,000 acres, to keep out wild pigs and cattle; the removal of feral and exotic animals, such as pigs, mongooses, cats, and rats; control of non-native plants with hand grubbing, fire, and herbicides; and the propagation in the refuge's nursery of thousands of seedlings and cuttings of native trees, shrubs, and ferns for planting to restore native habitat that was previously impaired by cattle grazing and the invasion of exotic plants. This refuge is an outstanding example of major ecological restoration in Hawai'i. The Nature Conservancy of Hawai'i has purchased lands to expand the refuge.

Visitor activities include wildlife observation and hiking. Visitors are permitted onto the refuge's Maulua Tract on Saturdays, Sundays, and holidays, with prior permission from the refuge headquarters. There is no entrance fee. Twice-monthly refuge ecotours are offered by Hawai'i Forest and Trail; tel.: (800) 464-1993.

Lodgings and meals are available in Hilo, Mountain View, and Hawai'i Volcanoes National Park.

Access to the refuge is west by way of Saddle Rd. (State Hwy. 200) from Hilo, right onto Mauna Kea Summit Rd. for 2 miles, and right onto Keanakolu Rd. for about 14 miles—a 40-mile drive, requiring nearly two hours each way and only accessible by four-wheel-drive vehicle (rentals available in Hilo).

Information: Hakalau Forest NWR, 60 Nowelo St., Suite 100, Hilo, HI 96720; tel.: (808) 443-2300.

Kilauea Point, consisting of 203 acres, was established in 1985 to enhance and protect an ecologically outstanding seabird nesting colony on the ruggedly scenic north coast of the Island of Kaua'i, Hawai'i. Because of predator-proof fencing and a program of trapping feral animals, this vital habitat is one of the few places on the main islands of Hawai'i where colonial seabirds, such as the Laysan albatross, red-footed booby, red-tailed and white-tailed tropicbirds, wedge-tailed shearwater, and great frigatebird are able to breed. In 1988, the refuge was expanded to provide protection for the endangered nene, the Hawaiian goose.

At the northernmost point on Kaua'i, the spectacular, surf-pounded sheer cliffs provide a breathtaking backdrop to the refuge's incredible wealth of wildlife. The albatrosses (moli, in Hawaiian), navigate annually across thousands of miles of the open Pacific Ocean. They appear to fly without effort, held aloft on their seven-foot wingspread. Returning each spring to breed and raise their young, these amazing birds perform elaborate courtship rituals of bowing, "sky-pointing," and bill-clapping, accompanied by an array of strange whistling and moaning sounds.

More than a thousand nests of the red-footed booby ('a) are crowded together across a steep hillside's windswept trees and shrubs. These predominantly white birds, with black wing tips and large, pale-bluish beaks, build crude nests of sticks and breed here from March through May.

Among the most graceful birds in the world are the red-tailed tropicbirds (koa'e 'ula), which perform elaborate, paired aerial courtship displays during their March–October breeding season. This red-billed species nests beneath sheltering rock ledges and shrubs. The smaller white-tailed tropicbird (koa'e kea) nests along stretches of sheer, inaccessible cliffs.

The gracefully soaring, brownish-gray, wedge-tailed shearwaters ('ua'u kani) return in March, after wintering in the Gulf of Panama. As many as 1,000 nests occupy crevices and burrows, the latter scraped out with their beaks and feet. These birds' nocturnal courtship activities are accompanied by weird wailing and moaning sounds. In June, when a pair's single egg hatches, the adults fly off during the day to gather food for their chick.

The great frigatebird ('iwa) is another graceful soaring bird. Cruising effortlessly on oceanic trade winds, it has a wingspan of 7.5 feet; slender, angular-shaped wings; and a long, deeply forked tail. During courtship, the predominantly black males boast an inflated, bright red throat pouch.

The goose known as the nene, the official state bird of Hawai'i, has a distinctive black head and nape, pale yellowish-buff cheek and neck, and barred brownish-gray plumage on the upper body. It came perilously close to extinction, but thanks to successful captive propagation and reintroduction programs in recent decades, it now inhabits this refuge after vanishing from Kaua'i hundreds of years ago. It is also found in Haleakala National Park on the island of Maui, and in Hawai'i Volcanoes National Park on the Big Island.

In addition to the birds described above, there are such others as ruddy turnstone, wandering tattler, Pacific golden plover, lesser yellowlegs, and several non-native species: cattle egret, spotted and zebra doves, common myna, and northern and red-crested cardinals.

From December through April, the North Pacific humpback whale (kohola, in Polynesian-Hawaiian) can often be seen in the waters around Kilauea Point. In the autumn, this endangered species migrates 3,500 miles from Alaska to the warm tropical waters around Hawai'i, where it mates and gives birth to its young. Adults weigh more than 40 tons (80,000 to 90,000 pounds), females average 45 feet in length, and males are slightly smaller. Newborn calves weigh as much as two tons (4,000 pounds) and are 10 to 15 feet in length.

Spinner dolphins can sometimes be spotted cavorting offshore. They are named for their remarkable spinning leaps out of the ocean. The Hawaiian monk seal, an endangered marine mammal, can sometimes be seen hauled out on the rocks below the cliffs.

A prominent historical feature of this refuge is Kilauea Lighthouse. It was built in 1913 as an aid to ships sailing between Hawai'i and the Orient. In 1979, it was placed on the National Register of Historic Places.

The refuge and its visitor center are open daily from 10 a.m. to 4 p.m. Trained volunteers provide interpretive services for visitors. There is a refuge entrance fee.

Visitor activities include wildlife observation (binoculars may be borrowed at the visitor center) and walking the 0.2-mile path from the parking area to the point. Picnicking is not permitted, as crumbs of food attract rodents that are harmful to the ground-nesting seabirds. As part of an annual whale festival in March, the refuge hosts a Hawaiian Islands Humpback Whale National Marine Sanctuary whale count by volunteers and an ocean fair that includes interpretive displays and lectures about whales, children's activities, and cultural presentations.

Lodgings and meals are available in such communities as Princeville, Kapa'a, Wailua, and Lihu'e.

Access to the refuge from State Hwy. 56 at Kilauea is north two miles on a paved spur road. Information: Kilauea Point NWR, P.O. Box 87, Kilauea, HI 96754; tel.: (808) 828-1413.

O'ahu Forest, consisting of 4,525 acres, was established in the year 2000 to protect some of the last remaining native forest habitats in the Waipio area on the Island of O'ahu, Hawai'i. According to the Fish and Wildlife Service, the mission of this refuge is "to conserve the structure and function of the native ecosystem and the natural diversity of flora and fauna, and to assist in the recovery of native plants and animals that are federally listed as threatened or endangered in the northern Ko'olau Mountains."

The Hawai'i Chapter of The Nature Conservancy helped to conduct biological surveys of this property, obtained funding, and negotiated the acquisition with the private landowner, Castle & Cooke, Inc. The Fish and Wildlife Service anticipates "working with the U.S. Army and the State of Hawaii's Department of Land and Natural Resources to protect a larger area of the northern Koolaus through the Koolau Forest Watershed Partnership."

The refuge contains at least nine natural habitat communities. These include the dense, 'ohi'a-dominated rainforest on leeward upper mountain slopes; wind-gnarled 'ohi'a-and 'olapa-dominated cloud forest on windward upper slopes and ridge crests; scattered groves of loulu hiwa fan palms in the upper reaches of valleys and on steep windward slopes; 'uluhe-dominated wet shrubland on lower slopes; and koa-dominated mesic (moderately moist) forest at the refuge's lowest elevations. Numerous native species of plants are found on the refuge, including 17 that are listed as endangered, one that is a candidate for listing, and two others that are species of concern. In addition, there are four species of endangered endemic O'ahu tree snails.

Among the greatest threats to the refuge's ecosystem are a number of non-native animals including feral pigs; rats; mongooses; a predatory land snail; mosquitoes that transmit deadly avian malaria and pox diseases to birds; and insect pests, such as the two-spotted leafhopper and the black twig borer, that are harmful to native plants. The Fish and Wildlife Service considers the feral pig to be "one of the most pervasive and disruptive non-native animals in Hawaiian forests." A number of invasive non-native plant species also pose a serious ecological challenge. The Fish and Wildlife Service is planning "to implement long-term management efforts to address the most critical threats and to promote rehabilitation of the natural ecosystem."

Visitor activities, such as wildlife observation and environmental education programs, are expected to eventually be offered to small groups of visitors, consistent with the refuge's management goals. Fees may be charged to help cover costs. Research projects that relate to management goals will likely be encouraged and allowed under the terms of special use permits.

Information: O'ahu Forest National Wildlife Refuge, c/o O'ahu NWR Complex, 66-590 Kamehameha Highway, Room 2C-D, Haleiwa, HI 96712; tel.: (808) 637-6330.

Hawai'i and Pacific Remote Islands Complex: Pacific Remote Islands Complex

Guam, containing 23,228 acres, was established in 1993 to enhance and protect ecologically significant marine and terrestrial habitats for native fauna and flora on the Island of Guam, a U.S. territory in the southwestern Pacific Ocean. The refuge's stated goals are "to manage and conserve coral reef resources, restore native forest for the reintroduction of Guam's native birds, and protect the area's rich cultural heritage."

In 1993, the U.S. Navy's 371-acre Ritidian property, at the northern tip of the island, was transferred to the Fish and Wildlife Service. In 1994, cooperative agreements were signed with the U.S. Navy and Air Force, establishing overlay units of the refuge on 22,456 acres of Department of Defense property. The latter lands are not open to visitors.

In the 1970s, conservationists began to be aware of and became alarmed by the rapidly dwindling numbers of many native bird species. A major culprit was the non-native brown tree snake, which was accidentally introduced onto Guam soon after the end of World War II.

According to the U.S. Department of Agriculture's Animal and Plant Health Inspection Service, "Brown tree snakes are excellent climbers. The fact that they can support their weight with their tail enables them to stretch both upward and sideways." Large adults can grow to as much as 10 feet in length. With no natural predators to control this nocturnal snake, its population rapidly increased over the past half century, as it aggressively preyed upon vulnerable small mammals and many native birds and their eggs. In the late 1990s, estimates ran as high as 15,000 of these mildly venomous snakes per square mile on Guam.

The young of an endangered mammal, the Mariana fruit bat, are a favored prey of the snake. The last remaining colony of these bats is located on one of the refuge's overlay units, on the Andersen Air Force Base.

At least eight species of native forest birds, several of which formerly lived only on Guam, have been eliminated. The Guam rail, Mariana moorhen, Mariana crow, and Mariana gray swiftlet, which are federally listed as endangered or threatened, are presently at risk. According to the Fish and Wildlife Service, however, "multi-agency recovery efforts are underway" for the swiftlet and moorhen, "and both species' prospects for future recovery are good."

Guam's native terrestrial fauna and flora have also been seriously impacted by habitat destruction, over-hunting, and the introduction of three other non-native species—the feral pig, water buffalo, and deer. These three species, in particular, are major factors in the continuing decline of Guam's native forest.

As in many places around the world, the island's magnificent but fragile coral reef ecosystems have been impaired by soil erosion, pollution, and over-fishing. And the vital nesting and foraging habitat of the threatened green sea turtle (haggan) continues to be severely impacted by human activities. A small part of this habitat is being given special protection along the three-mile beach in the RITIDIAN UNIT and elsewhere on overlay refuge lands.

The refuge's Ritidian Unit is open daily during daylight hours, Except on Christmas, New Year's Day, and Thanksgiving. There is no entrance fee. Refuge headquarters, located here, is open on weekdays, except national holidays.

Visitor activities include hiking on a forest road that loops back along the beach; guided interpretive programs on the natural resources and cultural history for families, teachers, and youth groups (by prior arrangement); picnicking; fishing in certain areas; and swimming, snorkeling, and scuba diving. Visitors are cautioned that ocean currents can be "very strong and hazardous," there are no lifeguards on duty, and visitors swim at their own risk. Coconuts, lemai (breadfruits), and plants containing medicinal properties may be collected by obtaining a free permit from the refuge headquarters. Collecting coral is prohibited. Camping is not allowed on the refuge.

Lodgings and meals are available elsewhere on the island.

Access to Guam Refuge's Ritidian Unit from Agana is north 5.5 miles on Marine Dr. (Hwy. 1), left 6 miles on Hwy. 3, and left 6 miles on Hwy. 3a.

Information: Guam NWR, P.O. Box 8134, MOU-3, Dededo, GU 96912; tel.: (671) 355-5096.

Midway Atoll, encompassing 298,369 acres, was established in 1988 to restore and protect vital habitats for a remarkable variety of birds and marine life. This ecologically rich atoll, which consists of a coral-reef-encircled lagoon and three islands, is located about 1,250 nautical miles west-northwest of Honolulu, Hawai'i, near the west end of the Hawaiian archipelago in the mid-Pacific Ocean. Sand Island consists of about 1,200 acres, Eastern Island 334 acres, and Spit Island six acres. The entire atoll measures approximately five miles in diameter.

The refuge is an astounding mecca for nearly two million birds, highlighted by 15 species of colonial nesting seabirds. From late October or early November through July, Midway supports the world's largest nesting colony of the Laysan albatross ("white gooney"), totaling close to 400,000 pairs. These graceful gliders are held aloft on slender wings that span about 6.5 feet. They appear to fly without effort, annually navigating across thousands of miles of open Pacific Ocean and feeding mostly on squid. On Midway, these birds choose nesting sites that are densely scattered across grassy and other open areas. Here they perform elaborate courtship rituals of bill-clapping, bowing, head-wagging, and "sky pointing," accompanied by an array of whistling and moaning sounds. The female usually lays the pair's single egg by mid-December, and the fuzzy chick hatches in late January or early February, fledges in July, and remains at sea for several years before returning to breed on Midway.

The world's second largest nesting colony of the darker and slightly larger black-footed albatross ("black gooney"), with a seven-foot wingspan, numbers about 18,000 pairs. It is typically seen along the atoll's sandy shorelines, feeding mostly on the eggs of flying fish. A few of the rare short-tailed albatross, with a 7.5-foot wingspread, also nest on Midway.

From February to August, Midway hosts about 5,000 pairs of the ground-nesting red-tailed tropicbird. These stunningly beautiful and graceful birds have mostly pure white plumage, red bills, and long red tail streamers. There are also just a few breeding pairs of the smaller and more slender white-tailed tropicbird.

A few hundred red-footed boobies build their nesting platforms of sticks on Eastern Island's shrubby tree heliotropes and beach naupakas. A few of the ground-nesting masked boobies also breed on Eastern Island. Roughly 100 pairs of the great frigatebird nest among the red-footed boobies. Riding the air currents on their 7.5-foot wingspan and long, forked tail, they easily circle and glide long distances without flapping their wings. These "pirates" have a habit of ganging up on a tropicbird or booby that is bringing food to a hungry chick, and forcing it to disgorge its catch of squid or fish. During courtship, the male frigatebird inflates its bright-red throat pouch to attract a mate.

Five species of terns nest on Midway. From March through August, roughly 50,000 pairs of ground-nesting sooty terns breed and raise their young on Eastern and Spit islands. Gray-backed terns also nest on these two islands. About 6,000 pairs of black noddies, occupying Sand Island from November through August, build their nests in ironwood trees, and roughly 1,000 brown noddies may be seen between May and November. More than 7,000 pairs of the common fairy-tern (also known as the white tern) breed and raise their young on Midway. These graceful birds simply lay their single egg—often precariously, with no semblance of a nest—on the branch of an ironwood tree or other handy surface.

Three species of nocturnal seabirds come to Midway. Up to 50,000 pairs of the burrow-nesting Bonin petrel return in August to breed. In March, about a thousand pairs of the wedge-tailed shearwater return to nest in shallow burrows, and a few of the smaller, ground-nesting Christmas shearwater occupy Eastern Island.

Wintering shorebirds that nest in Alaska include the Pacific golden plover, wandering tattler, bristle-thighed curlew, and ruddy turnstone.

Most endangered of Midway's marine fauna is the Hawaiian monk seal. The world's total population of this species in the wild is fewer than 1,500. Approximately sixty of them inhabit the waters around the atoll and haul themselves up on island beaches to rest. About 250 spinner dolphins regularly seek the shelter of the atoll's lagoon during the day to rest, play, or mate after feeding in the open ocean at night. Threatened green sea turtles frequent Sand Island's harbor and sometimes haul themselves onto the atoll's beaches. Spotted eagle rays are often seen swimming in the lagoon. Tiger sharks enter the lagoon when vulnerable albatross chicks offer tempting prey; and Galapagos sharks inhabit the waters outside the reef. The more than 250 kinds of tropical reef fishes include such species as convict and other surgeonfishes, angelfishes, butterflyfishes, damselfishes, regal and other parrot fishes, reef triggerfish, yellow and other tangs, Hawaiian squirrelfish, Hawaiian morwong, sunrise and other wrasses, and the dragon moray. Marlin and tuna inhabit the ocean waters outside the atoll.

In 1988, the U.S. Navy agreed to the establishment of an "overlay" national wildlife refuge at Midway, so that threatened and endangered species of seabirds and other wildlife could be given urgently needed enhanced protection. Closure of the naval air facility was announced in 1993, and the atoll was transferred to the Fish and Wildlife Service in 1996. Before departing, the Navy spent nearly $100 million in a major cleanup and restoration program. More than 100 dilapidated buildings and other structures were demolished. Many above-ground and underground fuel storage tanks were also removed, and environmentally harmful contaminants were cleaned up.

Habitat restoration programs have continued in earnest. Rats, which had preyed upon the eggs and chicks of petrels and other seabirds since being introduced to Midway, have been eradicated. With the assistance of refuge volunteers, some of the Australian ironwood trees, golden crown-beard, and other non-native plants are being removed, and grasses and native shrubs, such as beach naupaka, are being planted to reestablish and enhance habitat for the nesting seabirds and other wildlife.

Weeklong birdwatching and snorkeling tours of Midway Atoll for up to 16 visitors are offered by the Oceanic Society, a nonprofit marine protection organization. For information: www.oceanic-society.org.

Information: Midway Atoll NWR, P.O. Box 29460, Honolulu, HI 96820; tel.: (808) 792-9540 or 9530.

Palmyra Atoll, containing more than 515,200 acres, was established in 2001. This refuge consists of a wet tropical atoll in the Line Islands, just over a thousand miles south of Hawai'i and about 300 miles north of the Equator, in the central Pacific Ocean.

As the Fish and Wildlife Service explains:

The islets at Palmyra Atoll are densely vegetated with native coastal strand flora and an outstanding natural Pisonia grandis rainforest community. The islets and surrounding waters of the atoll support endangered and threatened sea turtles and a large and diverse seabird community. Large areas of tidal sand-flats are exposed at low tide and serve as important foraging grounds for migratory shorebirds. The lagoon, reefs, and open waters of the atoll support a diversity of coral reef and other marine species, including giant clams, pearl oysters, and reports of endangered Hawaiian monk seals.

As described by regional director Anne Badgley of the Fish and Wildlife Service's Pacific Islands Ecoregion, "Palmyra hosts the second-largest nesting colony of red-footed boobies in the world and large colonies of other seabirds, including 750,000 sooty terns. These birds rely on the surrounding waters to provide the food they and their chicks need, and it's critical that the entire atoll ecosystem be protected."

In addition to the forests of *Pisonia* trees that grow up to eighty feet tall; other native flora include several species of ferns, such as bird's-nest and lau'ae; and two plants of the coastal strand, beach naupaka and tree heliotrope. The coconut palm is the most prominent non-native species.

The nearly thirty varieties of birds that have been recorded here include nesting red-footed, brown, and masked boobies; black and brown noddies; sooty and white terns; white-tailed and red-tailed tropicbirds; and great frigatebird. Wintering species include Pacific golden plover, ruddy turnstone, bristle-thighed curlew, and wandering tattler.

Land crabs are abundant—notably two kinds of land hermit crabs, a native land crab, and the coconut crab. The latter species is recognized as the largest terrestrial invertebrate in the world.

According to the Fish and Wildlife Service's Jim Maragos, a preliminary survey of coral fauna has revealed many genera: "Of particular interest at Palmyra is the spectacular development of table and staghorn Acropora species on the shallow western reefs outside the lagoon. The southern reefs and eastern pools provide an amazing display of coral diversity, abundance, and high underwater visibility. Additionally, the coral reefs on the western portion of the atoll were less affected by past Navy dredging activities. Despite major dredging impacts to the three lagoon areas, the outer reefs remain healthy and vibrant and support approximately 36 genera and 150 species of stony corals. This is more than double the coral species diversity of that in the main Hawaiian Islands or Johnston Atoll; nearly double that of Howland and Baker islands; and five times that of Jarvis Island. This unusually diverse coral community may be the result of Palmyra Atoll's proximity to the equatorial countercurrent, which brings coral larvae from the diversity-rich western Pacific, and the atoll's great variety of habitats favorable for coral development."

The endangered Hawaiian monk seal has twice been seen at Palmyra Atoll, and the pilot whale and bottlenose dolphin have been spotted in the lagoon. Both the endangered hawksbill sea turtle and the threatened green sea turtle are known to nest on the atoll. About 200 fish species have already been identified in the waters around the reefs and in the lagoon, including bonefish, milkfish, mullet, and blacktip reef sharks. More thorough surveys in deeper water and in the lagoon would yield numerous additional species.

The atoll was named for a vessel, the *Palmyra*, which came ashore during a storm in 1802. In 1922, the Fullard-Leo family of Honolulu purchased the atoll. Starting in 1938, in spite of strong opposition from the owners, the U.S. Navy constructed an airstrip and then used the atoll as a strategic military base during World War II. Following the war, the owners successfully defeated the federal government's attempt to retain ownership, in a lawsuit that was appealed to the U. S. Supreme Court.

At the time the refuge was added to the National Wildlife Refuge System, the atoll's 680 acres of emergent lands had been acquired from the surviving Fullard-Leo family members and were owned by a private conservation organization, The Nature Conservancy (TNC). According to the Fish and Wildlife Service, the agency "is negotiating with TNC to purchase a major part of the atoll, and both entities would work together to conserve the atoll's rich biological diversity. The submerged lands and waters at Palmyra were [previously] administered by the Office of Insular Affairs and . . . were transferred to the Fish and Wildlife Service. . . ."

A few visitor activities, compatible with the needs of protecting the atoll's natural ecosystems, are anticipated by the Fish and Wildlife Service, in partnership with TNC. It is expected that guided and unguided activities will include wildlife observation, hiking on designated trails, snorkeling and scuba diving in certain areas, limited recreational fishing, and possibly kayaking tours on the lagoon. "Visiting boats would be allowed to come to Palmyra on a 'prior permission required' basis." An entrance fee is likely to be charged, to cover costs of managing the visitor use program. It is also expected that lodging and dining facilities will be provided.

Information: Palmyra Atoll NWR, 300 Ala Moana Blvd., Room 5-231, Box 50167, Honolulu, HI 96850; tel.: (808) 792-9550.

Idaho

Deer Flat encompasses 11,427 acres in two separate sectors. The refuge's 10,587-acre LAKE LOWELL SECTOR, which was established in 1909 by President Theodore Roosevelt, is located between the Boise and Snake rivers in southwestern Idaho and eastern Oregon. It overlays a U.S. Bureau of Reclamation reservoir that is managed to supply irrigation water for agricultural production in the surrounding area. During normal years, water management also sustains a variety of aquatic habitats that benefit a diversity of wildlife.

As the Fish and Wildlife Service says, "The refuge is a significant waterfowl wintering area in the Pacific Flyway. The slow summer draw-down of the lake exposes mud flats which produce bumper crops of aquatic vegetation, particularly smartweed. The refuge cooperatively farms 250 acres of land for wildlife. . . . Crops are manipulated to 'set the table' for the arrival of migratory waterfowl. . . . Current populations are 150,000 ducks and 15,000 geese."

The refuge's SNAKE RIVER SECTOR consists of 840 acres on 94 islands scattered along a 113-mile stretch of the Snake River, between Melba, Ida., and Huntington, Ore. Acquisition of these islands began in 1937. They are particularly important for waterfowl and other migratory birds and provide a vital riparian corridor through the surrounding arid, high-desert region. The islands range in size from less than 1 acre to 58 acres. In the upstream section, they mostly contain grass-sagebrush habitat; and in the lower stretch they are generally covered with such trees as cottonwoods and boxelders.

The Lake Lowell Sector is open daily, and the Snake River Sector is open daily from June 1 through January, during daylight hours. There is no entrance fee. The refuge headquarters is open on weekdays, except national holidays.

Visitor activities on the Lake Lowell Sector include wildlife observation, driving the 29.5-mile Bird Watching Tour loop, hiking, mountain biking on all maintained roads and trails (within all recreation areas), horseback riding on maintained roads and trails (within the north, south, and east side recreation areas), cross-country skiing and ice skating (within all recreation areas), swimming at designated places on the Upper and Lower Embankments (no lifeguards), boating (motor and sail, from April 15 through September), fishing from upper and lower embankments, and hunting during the designated seasons. Camping is not permitted, but campground facilities are available in the general vicinity.

On the Snake River Sector, bank fishing is permitted from June 1 through January and hunting is permitted during the designated seasons.

Lodgings and meals are available in such communities as Nampa, Meridian, Caldwell, Marsing, and Weiser, Ida., and Ontario, Ore.

Access to the Lake Lowell Sector from Twelfth Avenue in Nampa is west on Lake Lowell Rd. to Upper Embankment Road, and west one mile across the upper embankment to the end of the road and refuge headquarters.

Information: Deer Flat NWR, 13751 Upper Embankment Rd., Nampa, ID 83686; tel.: (208) 467-9278.

Grays Lake, containing approximately 19,000 acres and working toward a goal of more than 32,000 acres, was established in 1965 primarily to restore and protect important wetland habitat for migrating and nesting geese and ducks. The refuge is scenically located just west of, and 3,400 feet below, the 9,803-foot summit of Caribou Mountain, in southeastern Idaho. Grays Lake itself is actually an extensive, shallow cattail and bulrush marsh—the largest wetland of hardstem bulrush in the world, the majority of which lies within the refuge.

Among the most common of the refuge's nesting waterfowl are Canada geese, mallards, cinnamon teal, canvasbacks, redheads, and lesser scaup. Grays Lake is also one of this region's most important breeding places for the trumpeter swan—a rare species that has reestablished itself here in recent years. According to the Fish and Wildlife Service, "In a typical breeding season, the refuge may produce up to 5,000 ducks, 2,000 geese, and over 20 swans." In addition, "Franklin's gulls nest in large colonies in bulrush habitat, along with a lesser number of white-faced ibis."

One of the most prominent and exciting birds of this refuge is the sandhill crane. The Fish and Wildlife Service says that the refuge "hosts the largest nesting population of greater sandhill cranes in the world. Over 200 nesting pairs have been counted in some years.

Sandhills begin arriving in early April. In the fall, the refuge serves as a staging area, a place where cranes gather before migrating south to New Mexico, Arizona and Mexico for the winter.

During the staging period in late September and early October, as many as 3,000 cranes have been observed in the valley at one time.

On refuge lands surrounding the lake, vegetation is managed by hay cutting, limited livestock grazing, and prescribed burning. The controlled use of fire promotes nutrient cycling and spurs the growth of new vegetation that is of value to wildlife. The refuge also plants fields in barley and other grain crops that provide a supplemental, nutrient-rich source of food for the cranes and geese before their southward migration.

Grays Lake refuge also includes several hundred acres of arid sagebrush-and-grass habitat and barely extends into Douglas-fir forest at the base of the mountains. Establishment of the refuge was made possible partly with revenues from the sale of Migratory Bird Hunting and Conservation Stamps (Duck Stamps).

The refuge is open daily during daylight hours. There is no entrance fee. The refuge headquarters is open daily, from April 1 to November 15.

Visitor activities include wildlife observation; driving the roads that encircle the refuge; viewing the refuge and wildlife from the headquarters overlook (open from May 1 to November 15) at Beavertail Point next to State Hwy. 34 (at the southern end of Grays Lake) and from a roadside overlook adjacent to unpaved Westside Rd.; cross-country skiing and snowshoeing; canoeing and boating (with non-motorized, car-top watercraft only); and hunting on part of the refuge during the designated season. Camping is not permitted on the refuge, but campground facilities are provided in the adjacent Caribou National Forest. Although opportunities are limited, hiking is permitted on the northern half of the refuge from September 20 through March. Insect repellent is advised during the warmer months. Visitors are cautioned to be prepared for cold weather at this refuge's 6,400-foot elevation.

Lodgings and meals are available in such communities as Idaho Falls, Pocatello, and Soda Springs.

Access to the refuge from U.S. Hwy. 30 at Soda Springs is north 33 miles on State Hwy. 34, and turning onto the entrance road, two miles to the northwest of Wayan.

Information: Grays Lake NWR, 74 Grays Lake Rd., Wayan, ID 83285; tel.: (208) 574-2755.

Kootenai, comprising 2,774 acres, was established in 1964 to restore and manage an important area of valley-bottom wetlands along the Kootenai River. The refuge is located in Kootenai Valley, which is bounded on the west by the spectacular Selkirk Mountains and on the east by the Purcell Range, less than twenty miles south of the border with Canada, in northern Idaho.

Regarding the history of this part of the state, the Fish and Wildlife Service says that

In the 1920s, humans began to tame the wild Kootenai River. Dikes were built to contain spring floods within the river channel. Once the river bottom lands were protected from flooding, the [riparian] cottonwood forests were removed and the wetlands were drained or leveled. The rich soils were planted with crops.

The construction of Libby Dam in Montana in 1975, to provide flood control and power generation, completed the taming of the river. Today, the Kootenai River meanders through fields of wheat and barley. The Kootenai National Wildlife Refuge was established . . . to reclaim some of the Idaho Panhandle wetlands lost to development.

The centerpiece of the refuge's diverse habitats is the more than 800 acres of impounded wetland habitat, in which water levels are managed to maintain a series of permanent ponds and to flood moist-soil food plots for concentrations of migrating waterfowl in the autumn. Water for these wetlands is mainly derived from Myrtle Creek, which flows northward through the western part of the refuge on its way to the Kootenai River. Some additional water is pumped from Deep Creek and the river, which flow northward along the refuge's eastern boundary.

Canada geese, wood ducks, mallards, cinnamon and blue-winged teal, and common goldeneyes are prominent among the waterfowl that migrate to the refuge in the spring and nest here. Other migrants that pause on the refuge's wetlands during migration include tundra swans, American wigeons, northern pintails, and redhead ducks. During the autumn, there may be as many as 3,500 geese. Other wetland inhabitants include moose, river otters, beavers, and muskrats.

More than 300 acres of the refuge are devoted to the planting of wheat and barley by refuge personnel. These crops are left unharvested to provide a supplemental food source for waterfowl and other wildlife. Additional habitats include riparian woodlands of cottonwoods and willows, shrubby areas, and a narrow strip of Douglas fir and Engelmann spruce forest where the western edge of the valley and refuge meet the base of the Selkirk Mountains. Among the wildlife inhabiting this coniferous forest are Rocky Mountain elk, white-tailed and mule deer, moose, black bear, and ruffed grouse.

Establishment of Kootenai Refuge was made possible with revenues from the sale of Migratory Bird Hunting and Conservation Stamps (Duck Stamps).

The refuge is open daily during daylight hours. There is no entrance fee. The refuge headquarters is open on weekdays, except national holidays.

Visitor activities include wildlife observation, driving the 4.5-mile auto tour route, hiking on a number of trails, canoeing and boating on the Kootenai River (launching sites are available near the refuge), cross-country skiing, fishing along Myrtle Creek, and hunting on parts of the refuge during the designated seasons (hunting blinds are scattered throughout the part of the refuge that is open to waterfowl hunting). Although camping is not permitted on the refuge, campground facilities are available in the Panhandle National Forest. Over 220 bird species have been recorded on the refuge.

Lodgings and meals are available in Bonners Ferry.

Access to Kootenai Refuge from U.S. Hwy. 95 at Bonners Ferry is five miles west on Riverside Rd. to the refuge office.

Information: Kootenai NWR, HCR 60, Box 283, Bonners Ferry, ID 83805; tel.: (208) 267-3888.

Minidoka, containing 20,699 acres, was established in 1909 by President Theodore Roosevelt for the protection of native birds. The refuge, which overlays lands withdrawn by the Bureau of Reclamation (BOR) for the construction of Minidoka Dam in 1906, is on the Snake River in southeastern Idaho. The refuge's central feature is the reservoir known as Lake Walcott, the water level of which is regulated by the BOR. Slightly more than half of the refuge consists of open water, several islands, small areas of bulrush and cattail marsh that are located in shallow coves and inlets, and a stretch of the Snake River upstream from the reservoir. Along the shorelines are willows, cottonwoods, and other trees and shrubs.

The most numerous birds attracted to Minidoka Refuge include American white pelicans, many species of migrating and nesting waterfowl, wading birds, shorebirds, gulls, and terns. The refuge contains the only consistent pelican nesting colony in Idaho, and it is a major waterfowl molting area, annually attracting as many as 100,000 ducks. Unlike most birds, waterfowl molt their wing and tail feathers at the same time and are flightless for about a month while their feathers grow back. During this month, they need good habitat that is free of human disturbance. During spring and autumn migrations, more than 500 tundra swans come here. A number of bald eagles winter on the refuge. Because of the nesting colonies and concentrations of water-fowl, the refuge has been designated by the American Bird Conservancy as an Important Bird Area of Global Importance. More than 230 species have been recorded here.

Most of the rest of the refuge contains semiarid uplands of predominantly sagebrush-and-grass and grassland, a gently rolling landscape that is frequently punctuated with outcroppings of volcanic basalt.

The refuge is open daily during daylight hours. There is no entrance fee. The refuge head-quarters is open on weekdays, except national holidays

Visitor activities include wildlife observation, driving on unpaved and unimproved roads, hiking, boating on the western one-third of the lake, fishing within the designated boat fishing area, and hunting on two parts of the refuge during the designated seasons. Camping is not per-mitted on the main part of the refuge. Campground and picnic facilities and a boat-launching ramp are available at the 30-acre Lake Walcott State Park (entrance fee is charged), which over-lays part of the refuge's west end. Information on the state park: tel.: (208) 436-1258.

Parts of the refuge are seasonally closed to visitors, to avoid disturbing colonial bird nest-ing activities. Visitors are cautioned to be alert for rattlesnakes.

Lodgings and meals are available in such communities as Chubbuck/Pocatello Rupert, and Burley.

Access to Minidoka Refuge from Exit 211 on I-84 at Heyburn is northeast 5.9 miles on State Hwy. 24: through Rupert (after crossing the railroad tracks, bear right and continue northeast on Route 24), and right onto Minidoka Dam Rd. Or from Exit 216 on I-84, it is north about three miles on State Hwy. 25, left onto Baseline Rd. about two miles to Rupert, right onto State Hwy. 24 (after crossing the railroad tracks, bear right and continue northeast on Route 24), and right onto Minidoka Dam Rd.

Information: Minidoka NWR, 961 E. Minidoka Dam Rd., Rupert, ID 83350; tel.: (208) 436-3589.

Illinois

Chautauqua, containing 4,488 acres, was established in 1936 to protect Illinois River flood-plain and bordering upland habitats in west-central Illinois. The refuge's major feature is 3,200-acre Lake Chautauqua, comprising two shallow, impounded pools along a stretch of the river where water levels are seasonally regulated. In addition, the refuge consists of adjacent, season-ally flooded wooded bottomland, backwater lakes, a small area of upland forest, and two rem-nants of prairie grassland. More than 250 bird species have been recorded here.

Adjacent to the impounded Illinois River that borders the refuge to the west, habitats in-clude mixed bottomland and hardwood forests; buttonwood-willow swamps; and sedge marshes. Forty-foot-high sandy bluffs rise along the east side of the refuge, on the crests of which are oak-hickory upland hardwoods, which grade down-slope to the floodplain which supports such trees as sycamore, maple, and cottonwood. A number of springs seeping out from below the bluffs keep stretches of the lake near the shore open during the winter.

This refuge attracts enormous concentrations of waterfowl and shorebirds. As many as 10,000 to 20,000 migrating shorebirds pour onto the refuge's mudflats, as they stop on their southward migration in late summer and early autumn. During the autumn months, as many as 150,000 to 250,000 waterfowl pause to rest and feed before continuing to wintering grounds farther south. Anywhere from 50 to 80 bald eagles also often winter here, preying upon fish and weakened waterfowl. May brings the peak influx of numerous warblers and other neotropical migratory songbirds. Many wood ducks nest in tree cavities and in nest boxes that are provided by the refuge.

The refuge is open daily during daylight hours. There is no entrance fee. The refuge office is open on weekdays, except national holidays.

Visitor activities include wildlife observation; driving the road along the east edge of the refuge; viewing the refuge and wildlife from four observation decks; hiking on the 0.5-mile (wheelchair-accessible) Chautauqua Nature Trail and on refuge dikes from mid-January through mid-October; fishing from the bank or by boat (a boat-launching ramp is provided at the Eagle Bluff Access Area); and waterfowl hunting on the Liverpool Lake part of the refuge during the designated seasons. Camping is not permitted on the refuge, but campground facilities are available at Sand Ridge State Forest and other nearby places. Insect repellent is advised during the warmer months.

Chautauqua is one of three national wildlife refuges comprising the Illinois River National Wildlife and Fish Refuges Complex, located along a 125-mile stretch of the river. Meredosia and Emiquon refuges and the Cameron/Billsbach units are the others.

The CAMERON UNIT, containing 636 acres, was established in 1958, when the area was donated to the Fish and Wildlife Service by the late Judge Glen J. Cameron, of Pekin, Ill. The unit, located 65 miles upriver from Chautauqua Refuge along the west side of the Illinois River, contains bottomland forest, backwater habitat, and old fields along the west side of the Illinois River's Weis and Meridian lakes.

The BILLSBACH UNIT, consisting of 1,072 acres, was established in 1981. The unit, located across the river from the Cameron Unit, contains wetland habitats and part of Billsbach Lake. The Illinois Chapter of The Nature Conservancy purchased this land from the Armour Club (a private hunting club) and sold it to the Fish and Wildlife Service.

Lodgings and meals are available in such communities as Havana and Peoria.

Access to the refuge from U.S. Hwy. 136 at Havana is north on Promenade St., which turns into Manito Blacktop. Proceed northeast eight miles on Manito Blacktop, left onto County Rd. 1950E, and left at the refuge headquarters entrance sign.

Information: Chautauqua NWR, c/o Illinois River National Wildlife and Fish Refuges, 19031 E. County Rd. 2110N, Havana, IL 62644; tel.:(309) 535-2290.

Crab Orchard, consisting of 43,890 acres, was established in 1947 to enhance, protect, and manage a variety of habitats for the benefit of migratory waterfowl and other wildlife in southern Illinois. The refuge contains 8,810 acres in three man-made lakes—Crab Orchard Lake, Devil's Kitchen Lake, and Little Grassy Lake. Roughly 21,000 acres of the refuge are densely forested, and scattered here and there are marshes and other wetland habitat and about 1,500 acres of grasslands. More than 220 bird species have been recorded here.

In addition, there are about 5,000 acres of cropland, where a portion of the corn, soybeans, and other crops cultivated by local farmers, is left unharvested for the benefit of Canada geese and other wildlife. Just over 4,000 acres of Crab Orchard Refuge is designated as a unit of the National Wilderness Preservation System.

From November to March, anywhere from 67,000 to 275,000 Canada geese and 30,000 to 40,000 ducks of many species are attracted to the lakes of the refuge. During the spring, the forests are filled with great numbers of warblers and other neotropical migratory songbirds. More than 250 bluebird nesting houses have been erected.

The Fish and Wildlife Service's management activities include the regulation of water levels for the benefit of waterfowl and other wildlife, and prescribed burning, limited grazing, and haying to help maintain areas of prairie and other grasslands within the refuge.

The refuge's vision statement says, "Crab Orchard National Wildlife Refuge is recognized as an outstanding example of enlightened resource management and use. Refuge resources are managed so that agricultural, industrial, recreational and wildlife conservation purposes of the Refuge are accomplished in concert with each other and in full compliance with a long-term natural resource stewardship responsibility."

The refuge is open daily, with some parts open 24 hours. Fees are charged for motor vehicles and boats. The visitor center is open daily.

Visitor activities include wildlife observation; driving (more than thirty miles of public roads provide access to and through the refuge); hiking on several trails (including the paved 0.5-mile Visitor Center Trail; picnicking; camping (campgrounds are provided—one on the shore of each lake); swimming (a designated swimming area is provided on Crab Orchard Lake); canoeing, kayaking, and boating (one or more boat-launching ramps are provided on each lake; power boats and water skiing are permitted only on Crab Orchard Lake); fishing; horseback riding; bicycling; and hunting on parts of the refuge during the designated seasons.

Visitors are urged to be alert for the venomous copperhead snake, especially in rocky areas. Insect repellent is advised during the warmer months.

Lodgings and meals are available in such communities as Marion and Carbondale.

Access to the refuge's visitor center is west three miles from I-57 at Marion on State Hwy. 13; and left 1.75 miles on State Hwy. 148.

Information: Crab Orchard NWR, 8588 Route 148, Marion, IL 62959; tel.: (618) 997-3344.

Cypress Creek, containing more than 14,000 acres and working toward a goal of 35,200 acres, was established in 1990 to restore and protect an ecologically significant corridor of wetlands along the Cache River, at the southwestern tip of Illinois. The Cache River Wetlands, also referred to as the "Illinois bayou," consists of the largest remaining area of wetland habitat in the state, attracting large numbers of migratory waterfowl, wading birds, neotropical migratory songbirds, and other wildlife. The refuge includes bald-cypress and tupelo swamps, bottomland forest, and gently rolling upland. Notable among the area's natural assets are numerous thousand-year-old cypress trees. More than 250 bird species have been recorded here.

This refuge is part of the cooperative ecosystem restoration and protection effort along fifty miles of the river, known as the Cache River Wetlands Joint Venture. In addition to the Fish and Wildlife Service, there are a number of key project partners. The Illinois Department of Natural Resources manages its three-unit Cache River State Natural Area, located just up-stream from the refuge. The Illinois Chapter of The Nature Conservancy (TNC), which has been involved with land protection along the river since 1970, made possible a 2,000-acre expansion of the refuge (formerly TNC's Limekiln Springs Preserve) and owns the nearby Grassy Slough Preserve. Ducks Unlimited, Inc. formerly owned and created shallow-water habitat on the 1,000-acre Frank Bellrose Waterfowl Reserve, which is now part of this refuge.

The refuge is open daily during daylight hours. There is no entrance fee. The refuge head-quarters is open on weekdays, except national holidays. The Cache River Wetlands Center of-fers environmental education programs.

Visitor activities include wildlife observation from observation sites, hiking on a number of trails, canoeing and boating (several launching sites are available), fishing, and hunting during the designated seasons. Although camping is not permitted on the refuge and the state natural area, campground facilities are provided at nearby Ferne Clyffe State Park and Horseshoe Lake Conservation Area. Visitors are urged to be alert for the several species of venomous snakes here, and for poison ivy. Insect repellent is advised during the warmer months.

Lodgings and meals are available in the communities of Ullin, Vienna, Anna, and Cairo.

Access to the refuge from I-57 is by way of Exit 18 and east onto Shawnee College Rd. The refuge headquarters is located near the junction of Shawnee College Rd. and State Hwy. 37.

Information: Cypress Creek NWR, 0137 Rustic Campus Dr., Ullin, IL 62992; tel.: (618) 634-2231.

Indiana

Big Oaks, consisting of approximately 50,000 acres, was established in 2000 under a joint agreement with the U.S. Army and U.S. Air Force, "to preserve, conserve, and restore biodiver-sity and biological integrity for the benefit of present and future generations of Americans." The refuge is located on the U.S. Army's now-closed Jefferson Proving Ground, which extends across parts of Jefferson, Ripley, and Jennings counties, in southeastern Indiana.

Several large blocks of habitat types that are rare in the surrounding landscape are present within the boundaries of this refuge. It contains the largest forested expanse in southeastern In-diana and some of the region's largest areas of grassland. The refuge provides managed habitat for at least 120 species of breeding birds and more than 40 species of fish and is also home to white-tailed deer, wild turkey, river otter, bobcat, coyote and the federally endangered Indiana bat. More than 25 state-listed animal species and 46 state-listed plant species have so far been discovered here.

Most notable of the many species of management concern is the large population of Henslow's sparrows, of which more than 1,000 singing males have been estimated during the

Fish and Wildlife Service's annual surveys in the large grasslands. Breeding bird surveys have also revealed such species as yellow-crowned night-herons, sharp-shinned and red-shouldered hawks, and such warblers as cerulean, Swainson's, worm-eating, and hooded. Big Oaks refuge has been designated as a Globally Important Bird Area because of its value to Henslow's sparrows and other migratory birds.

The refuge's habitat management activities include enhancing and maintaining a variety of ecosystems—grasslands, early successional shrublands, and forest. Grasslands, for example, are being maintained with an extensive prescribed burning program that annually encompasses approximately 5,000 acres. Wetlands also constitute a large proportion (more than 30 percent) of the refuge. Beavers are constantly reworking their shallow ponds throughout the refuge's drainages. New beaver impoundments are rapidly and naturally increasing the area of permanent water and the diversity of wetland habitat.

The northeast corner of the refuge is presently open to visitors during daylight hours on Mondays and Fridays and on the second and fourth Saturdays of each month, from April through November. A small entrance fee is charged.

Visitor activities include wildlife observation, walking on gravel roads, interpretative tours (by prior arrangement), fishing (excellent opportunities on Old Timbers Lake), and hunting in designated areas and seasons. As this refuge is a former U.S. Army test site, visitors are required to attend a safety briefing and sign an acknowledgment-of-danger agreement. Insect repellent is advised during the warmer months.

(With special thanks to the Refuge Operations Specialist Joe Robb for providing the above information.—RDB)

Lodgings and meals are available in such communities as Madison, Versailles, and North Vernon.

The entrance to the refuge is located on U.S. Hwy. 421, approximately five miles north of Madison. The refuge office is located in Building 125, in the cantonment area of the former Jefferson Proving Ground. From Madison, drive north on U.S. Hwy. 421 through the Main Entrance onto the Jefferson Proving Ground, proceed west on Ordnance Dr., right onto Shun Pike, and left onto Niblo Rd.

Information: Big Oaks NWR, 1661 West JPG Niblo Rd., Madison, IN 47250; tel.: (812) 273-0783.

Muscatatuck, comprising 7,802 acres in two units, was established in 1966 to restore, enhance, and protect wetland, forest, and grassland habitats for the benefit of waterfowl, neotropical migratory songbirds, and other wildlife, in southeastern Indiana. The refuge is named for the Muscatatuck River, which meanders from east to west along the southern boundary of the refuge's main unit. The name, *Muscatatuck*, is derived from a Native American word meaning "the land of winding waters."

As the Fish and Wildlife Service describes the refuge's water-management program:

Muscatatuck's moist soil units, low open areas surrounded by dikes, are drained of water in the spring to promote plant growth and filled with water in the fall to provide feeding and resting areas for waterfowl and shorebirds. Similarly, green tree units, diked lowland forests, are flooded with water in the fall for waterfowl and drained in the spring to keep the trees healthy. These units provide feeding and nesting areas for the wood duck, a bird that naturally nests in tree cavities in wetland areas.

One result of this water manipulation is the creation of permanent marshes—swampy areas of lush vegetation interspersed with pockets of shallow open water, which are ideal homes for ducks and geese to raise their young.

In 1995, this refuge became the first place in Indiana where the river otter was reintroduced. This formerly abundant species was previously extirpated from the state by over-trapping and loss of habitat. The copper-bellied water snake, a federally listed threatened/state-listed endangered subspecies of the plain-bellied water snake, also inhabits the refuge. Land acquisition, which was primarily to provide nesting habitat for wood ducks, was made possible with revenues from the sale of Migratory Bird Hunting and Conservation Stamps (Duck Stamps). Ducks Unlimited, Inc. has helped enhance part of the refuge's wetland habitat.

The refuge's main unit is open daily from sunrise to sunset. There is no entrance fee. The visitor center is open during all refuge hours.

Visitor activities include wildlife observation, interpretive programs, interpreter-guided walks, driving nine miles of refuge roads including an auto tour route, hiking, horseback riding, bicycling, fishing, and hunting on parts of the refuge during the designated seasons. Although camping is not permitted on the refuge, campground facilities are available at Muscatatuck County Park, Jackson Washington State Forest, and Hardy Lake State Recreation Area.

Hiking opportunities include eight designated trails, including the (wheelchair-accessible) Chestnut Ridge Interpretive Trail and the Richart Lake Hiking Trail, which offers an excellent view of Richart Lake from Hackman Overlook.

The refuge's RESTLE UNIT, containing 78 acres, is located several miles northwest of Bloomington, in south-central Indiana. In 1990, this tract was donated to the Fish and Wildlife Service by Mrs. Barbara Restle. Although the unit is not open to visitors, an observation deck overlooks the unit, which adjoins two protected areas owned by the Sycamore Land Trust.

Lodgings and meals are available near the refuge's main unit in such communities as Seymour, Scottsburg, North Vernon, and Columbus, Indiana.

Access to the refuge from Exit 50 from I-65 is east three miles on U.S. Hwy. 50 and right onto the entrance road.

Information: Muscatatuck NWR, 12985 East U.S. Highway 50, Seymour, IN 47274; tel.: (812) 522-4352.

Patoka River National Wildlife Refuge and Management Area was established in 1994 to protect, restore, and manage 22,083 acres of bottomland hardwood forest wetlands and adjacent upland slopes in the Southern Bottomlands Natural Region of southwestern Indiana.

Stretching for 20 miles (as the crow flies) in an east-west direction along the lower third reach of the 162-mile Patoka River, the acquisition area includes 30 miles of river channel, 19 miles of cut-off river oxbows, and 12,700 acres of existing wetland habitat. Primary resource management efforts are directed toward restoring more than 5,000 acres of bottomland hardwood forest on prior wetlands that were converted to farmland.

In the late 1700s, European settlers entering southwestern Indiana heard the resident Piankashaw Indians refer to one of the rivers as Pah-tah-ka-tah. This translated as either "crooked river filled with logs" or "logs on the bottom." Eventually shortened to Patoka, the name was and is a very appropriate one.

This area represents one of the most significant bottomland hardwood forests remaining in the Midwest. This portion of the Patoka River bottoms is often referred to as a "biodiversity factory," with a new species of mud darter and burrowing crayfish discovered in 2001 in addition to 380 recorded species of wildlife, including a pair of nesting bald eagles and the endangered Indiana bat. At least 20 plant species and 62 animal species that inhabit the river valley are considered as threatened, endangered, or of special concern by the State of Indiana. The refuge provides habitat for 21 species on National Audubon's Watchlist. The refuge is the result of persistent, informed citizens' support that entailed eight years of planning and public involvement.

Patoka River has the distinction of being the only refuge project in the country with surface coal mines operating within the acquisition area. This apparent enigma was the result of a compromise worked out to avoid conflict with the Surface Mining Control and Reclamation Act of 1977 (SMCRA).

A provision of SMCRA states that any lands within the boundary of a national wildlife refuge are off-limits to surface coal mining. A Department of the Interior (DOI) solicitor advised that establishment of the refuge acquisition boundary could result in the prohibition of surface coal mining on both public and private lands within the defined boundary area. This could, in turn, result in "takings" claims (taking a property right without just compensation) being filed by landowners not permitted to sell or lease their coal rights for surface mining.

Consequently, the Patoka River National Wildlife Refuge and Management Area was approved as a 6,800-acre national wildlife refuge adjacent to a 15,283-acre wildlife management selection area. Lands within the selection area are not off-limits to surface coal mining until owned by the Fish and Wildlife Service. The DOI solicitor advised that establishing a wildlife management selection area would be similar to establishing a waterfowl production area. Although an acreage acquisition goal is identified, there is no implicit understanding that all lands within a wildlife management selection area will be purchased, as there is when a refuge boundary is established. To avoid potential costly "takings" claims, the refuge acquisition boundary was defined based on the absence of surface-minable coal deposits.

By January 2002, more than 5,100 acres, including surface and mineral rights, had been purchased from 38 landowners, with no added value paid for surface-minable coal. Since 1994, four mining companies have operated five surface mines within the wildlife management selection area. Most of the area being mined consists of row-crop farmland on north and south upland slopes above the Patoka River bottoms. The total amount of land likely to be mined within the wildlife management selection area will probably not exceed 2,500 acres. Much of this land has already been mined and is in various stages of reclamation. After final reclamation and bond release, efforts will be made to purchase these areas to be managed for upland wildlife habitat.

Recent refuge-funded studies by Indiana State University have shown that similar reclaimed mine lands managed as grasslands in southwestern Indiana are now providing critical habitat for the reproduction of grassland-nesting birds, such as Henslow's sparrow and eastern meadowlark. The management personnel of the refuge cite the presence of surface coal mining activity as an opportunity to provide important grassland habitat that might not otherwise be provided.

(With special thanks to Refuge and Management Area Manager Bill McCoy for providing the above description.—RDB)

Information: Patoka River NWR & Management Area, P.O. Box 217 (510 West Morton), Oakland City, IN 47660; tel.: (812) 749-3199.

Iowa

DeSoto, comprising 7,823 acres, was established in 1959 to enhance and protect ecologically important wetland habitat of a former Missouri River bend. The 750-acre, seven-mile-long De-Soto Lake, in southwestern Iowa, was created when the U.S. Army Corps of Engineers straightened and channelized the river.

More than one-half million lesser snow geese of both the white and blue morphs (color phases), numerous greater white-fronted and Canada geese, and as many as 50,000 mallards and other ducks typically pause on this refuge to rest and feed during their autumn migration from Arctic breeding grounds. Bald eagles often accompany these concentrations of migratory waterfowl, preying upon weak individuals. Well over 100 eagles have been seen at a time here.

One of the most prominent breeding waterfowl on this refuge is the wood duck. Beavers and muskrats inhabit the lake's backwaters and other wetland habitat. Wild turkeys, northern bobwhite, the non-native ring-necked pheasant, and numerous songbirds can often be seen and heard in areas of woodland, prairie grassland, and hedgerows.

Refuge management activities include prescribed burning to help maintain areas of native-grass habitat (1,100 acres of the refuge have been restored to grassland); installing nesting boxes for wood ducks; and managing expanses of sandbar, especially for the benefit of two rare nesting species—the piping plover and least tern. In addition, a few hundred acres of the refuge are cooperatively cultivated by local farmers, providing a portion of grain crops for deer, pheasants, and other wildlife.

Establishment of DeSoto refuge was made possible partly with revenues from the sale of Migratory Bird Hunting and Conservation Stamps (Duck Stamps).

The refuge is open daily during daylight hours. An entrance fee is charged. The visitor center is open daily, except Thanksgiving, Christmas and New Year's Day.

Visitor activities include wildlife observation (peaks of migrating waterfowl are around mid-October through November; and early March to mid-April); environmental education programs; driving 12 miles of paved and gravel refuge roads; hiking on several trails (including a wheelchair-accessible paved path); bicycling on refuge roads; boating and fishing from April 15 to October 14 (a boat-launching ramp, no-wake speeds up to five mph, and wheelchair-accessible fishing piers); and hunting on parts of the refuge during the designated seasons. Although camping is not permitted on the refuge, campground facilities are available at the adjacent Wilson Island State Recreation Area. Insect repellent is advised during the warmer months.

Lodgings and meals are available in Missouri Valley and Council Bluffs, Iowa and in Blair and Omaha, Nebraska.

Access to this refuge from Interstate-80 in Council Bluffs, Ia., is north 25 miles on I-29 to the Missouri Valley exit, and west about 5 miles on U.S. Hwy. 30; or from I-680 in Omaha, Neb., north 18 miles on U.S. Hwy. 75 to Blair, and right about 7 miles on U.S. Hwy. 30.

Information: DeSoto NWR, 1434-316th Lane, Missouri Valley, IA 51555; tel.: (712) 642-4121.

Neal Smith, containing more than 5,000 acres and working toward a goal of 8,654 acres, was established in 1990 to restore, protect, and interpret an ecologically significant area of native tallgrass prairie in the Walnut Creek watershed, twenty miles east of Des Moines in central Iowa. A key part of this national wildlife refuge is its Prairie Learning Center, where interpretive exhibits and programs are presented and where ecologically important prairie research is being carried out.

The refuge was initially known as the Walnut Creek NWR. It was re-named in honor of former Rep. Neal Smith, who was instrumental in Congress for obtaining federal funding for the refuge's biodiversity and habitat restoration program and for construction of its major environmental education center.

As the Fish and Wildlife Service's Master Plan (1992) for the refuge and learning center stated, this national wildlife refuge " . . . is unlike any existing refuge in that it has been established by Congress to restore a major expanse of tallgrass prairie. The Refuge is the largest prairie reconstruction effort in the country and is symbolic of a growing national and international interest in healing the environment."

The refuge boundary initially encompassed a mixture of cropland, pasture, and remnant native plant communities. Privately owned lands have gradually been acquired from willing sellers and, as the refuge's bird checklist says, "Over the past several years, much of the Neal Smith National Wildlife Refuge landscape has been transformed from cropland to tallgrass prairie. The reconstructed and restored prairies and savannas are providing food, cover, and breeding habitat for local and migratory birds. Each year, ornithologists conduct singing bird surveys and the results have shown that more and more grassland-dependent bird species are using the refuge." More than 250 bird species have been recorded here.

A major goal of the Neal Smith refuge is the reestablishment and protection of biological diversity. The Fish and Wildlife Service's stated management objectives include "reconstructing native tallgrass prairie, oak savanna, and riparian woodlands for the benefit of migratory and resident wildlife." To achieve this habitat diversity, native seed stock is being used to restore and maintain native grassland prairie; areas of bur oak savanna are being restored and maintained "to achieve a biologically rich transition between riparian woodlands and open prairie"; existing riparian woodlands along the floodplain of Walnut Creek and its major tributaries are being enhanced; and new wetland habitat is being created "to contribute to a national net gain of migratory bird habitat."

Although an autonomous entity, the refuge lies within the more extensive Des Moines Recreational River and Greenbelt—a regional open-space corridor extending along more than fifty miles of the Des Moines River and a number of its tributaries.

The refuge is open daily during daylight hours. The Prairie Learning Center is open Mondays through Saturdays, and Sunday afternoons.

Visitor activities include wildlife observation, viewing interpretive exhibits and attending interpretive programs at the Prairie Learning Center, driving the auto tour route, hiking on a number of trails (including the two-mile interpretive, paved Tallgrass Trail), bicycling on the refuge's entrance road, and picnicking in the Center's lunchroom and at picnic tables outside the lunchroom.

Lodgings and meals are available in Prairie City and Des Moines.

Access to the refuge entrance is just west of Prairie City, on State Hwy. 163, following refuge signs to the south.

Information: Neal Smith NWR, P.O. Box 399, Prairie City, IA 50228; tel.: (515) 994-3400.

Kansas

Flint Hills, comprising 18,500 acres, was established in 1966 to enhance and protect an area of important wildlife habitats along the Neosho River and the upstream end of the U.S. Army Corps of Engineers' John Redmond Reservoir, in east-central Kansas. The refuge, which is managed under an agreement with the Corps of Engineers, consists of marsh, sloughs, wooded bottomland, grassland, and gently rolling uplands. In addition, some agricultural lands on the refuge are sharecropped with local farmers, with the refuge's share of the grain crop usually left unharvested to provide food for migrating waterfowl.

Tens of thousands of migratory waterfowl, notably snow and Canada geese and many species of ducks, and thousands of white pelicans and numerous bald eagles pause here during the spring and autumn migration. As many as 100,000 mallards spend the winter on the refuge. In spring, greater prairie chickens perform their courtship displays. Numerous neotropical migratory songbirds also migrate through this area.

Ducks Unlimited, Inc. has provided funds for the engineering and construction of the refuge's moist-soil management units. These wetlands are mowed and disced in the summer to promote the growth of natural food plants. In the autumn, the wetlands are flooded, which produces feeding habitat for migrating waterfowl. The Wild Turkey Federation has also contributed funding to help with the planting of trees to restore the refuge's riparian habitat.

The refuge is open daily during daylight hours, although there are times when seasonal flooding inundates much of the refuge, including its roads and trails. Parts of the refuge are closed to public use from November 1 through February. There is no entrance fee. The refuge headquarters, in Hartford, is open weekdays, except on national holidays.

Visitor activities include wildlife observation, driving on refuge roads, hiking on three interpretive trails and elsewhere, picnicking, camping, canoeing and boating, fishing, and hunting on parts of the refuge during the designated seasons. November brings the peak of the autumn waterfowl migration; and April and May are the best months to see neotropical migratory songbirds. More than 290 bird species have been recorded here.

Visitors are cautioned to be alert for ticks, venomous snakes, and poison ivy. Insect repellent is advised during the warmer months.

Lodgings and meals are available in Emporia.

Access to the refuge headquarters is east of Emporia on I-35 North, south from Exit 141 on State Hwy. 130 to Hartford, west on Maple Ave. (Hartford High School is on the southeast corner) three blocks, and right one block.

Information: Flint Hills NWR, P.O. Box 128, Hartford, KS 66854; tel.: (620) 392-5553.

Kirwin, containing 10,778 acres, was established in 1954 as an overlay refuge on and surrounding a Bureau of Reclamation irrigation and flood control reservoir, in north-central Kansas. The refuge supports diverse wildlife habitats, including wooded riparian areas, marsh, open water, grasslands, and croplands.

The reservoir is fed by the North Fork of the Solomon River and Bow Creek. Its level fluctuates widely from year to year, depending upon runoff from rain and snow. Although the BOR owns the land and controls the level of the reservoir, the Fish and Wildlife Service manages all other activities on the refuge.

Thousands of Canada and white-fronted geese, many species of ducks and shorebirds, sandhill cranes, and white pelicans pause at this refuge during their spring and autumn migrations. As many as 20,000 Canada geese and 10,000 mallards spend the winter here. Waterfowl that nest on the refuge include Canada geese, wood ducks, and mallards.

Kirwin refuge is located within the transition zone between the tallgrass prairie of the eastern Great Plains and arid shortgrass plains of farther west. Management practices that are used to provide optimum habitat for wildlife include controlled burning, grazing, farming, mowing, and haying. Crops such as wheat, milo, and corn are grown under a cooperative farming program. A portion of the crop is left unharvested to provide food for the thousands of ducks and geese that use the area during migration. More than 200 bird species have been recorded here.

The refuge is open daily. There is no entrance fee.

Visitor activities include wildlife observation, driving the refuge's auto tour route, hiking on two interpretive trails, bicycling on roads open to vehicular travel, picnicking, camping (four campsites are available), canoeing and boating (two boat ramps are provided), fishing, and hunting on parts of the refuge during the designated seasons. The Solomon River Arm of the reservoir is closed to motor-boating, to avoid disturbance of wildlife. Non-motorized boating is permitted on Solomon Arm from August 1 through October.

Visitors are cautioned to be alert for ticks. Insect repellent is advised during the warmer months.

Lodgings and meals are available in Kirwin and Phillipsburg.

Access to the refuge is south five miles from Phillipsburg on State Hwy. 183, east six miles from Glade on State Hwy. 9, and south one mile on a county road, following the refuge directional signs.

Information: Kirwin NWR, R.R. 1, Box 103, Kirwin, KS 67644; tel.: (785) 543-6673.

Quivira, comprising 22,135 acres, was established in 1955 to enhance and protect an area of cattail marsh, salt flats, cropland, prairie grassland, gently rolling sandhills, and a bit of woodland, in south-central Kansas. These ecologically significant habitats are a mecca for vast numbers of migratory waterfowl and shorebirds, white pelicans, sandhill cranes, wintering bald and golden eagles, resident turkeys and bobwhite, briefly a few of the endangered whooping cranes, yellow-headed blackbirds, and numerous other species of wildlife. Even the refuge's salt flats have special significance, as this is favored nesting habitat for the endangered interior least tern.

From mid-September through November, as many as 500,000 Canada geese and ducks and nearly 200,000 sandhill cranes pause here on their way south to wintering habitats along the Gulf of Mexico. From mid-February into April, as many as 200,000 geese and ducks stop on their way north to breeding areas in the north-central United States and Canada. Tens of thousands of shorebirds of many species pause at Quivira refuge, with the spectacular peak of their migrations occurring from late April through early May and again from mid- to late October, depending upon the weather. Some of the plovers and sandpipers that use this refuge as a resting and feeding place spend the winter as far south as Tierra del Fuego, at the southern tip of South America, and nest in the far north of Canada, Alaska, and Siberia.

The refuge is named for the Quiviran Indians, a tribe of Native Americans who were living in this area when Spanish explorer Coronado led his exploration through this region in 1541, searching in vain for gold.

The largest part of the refuge is its 13,000 acres of grassland. Quivira is situated within the transition zone of the vast Great Plains, where the lush tallgrass prairie to the east merges with the arid shortgrass prairie to the west. Fires and short-term grazing by huge herds of bison (buffalo) occurred naturally before the arrival of European settlers. The Fish and Wildlife Service's grassland management practices on refuges, such as Quivira, are designed to reestablish this ecologically important pattern, by implementing periodic prescription burns and short-term livestock grazing to help enhance and maintain the ecological health of the refuge's prairie grassland habitat for wildlife.

The environmental centerpiece of Quivira Refuge is its wetland habitat—notably the 1,500-acre Big Salt Marsh and 900-acre Little Salt Marsh. Many years prior to the refuge's establishment, populations of geese, ducks, and shorebirds were decimated by profit-driven market hunting in the marshlands. Then more than a dozen private hunting clubs, each with exclusive membership hunting rights, acquired parts of the wetland. They improved some of the vital habitat, initially creating a channel to bring water from Rattlesnake Creek directly into Little Salt Marsh. More than eighty water control structures, 15 miles of additional canals, and flood spillways were subsequently built, ensuring a more dependable water supply. The Conservation Fund recently assisted with acquisition of an ecologically significant wet-meadow habitat containing the only known bobolink nesting colony in Kansas.

Under cooperative agreements with farmers, a portion of crops cultivated on 1,300 acres of the refuge, such as winter wheat and milo, are left unharvested for the benefit of wildlife.

The refuge is open daily during daylight hours. There is no entrance fee. The visitor center, featuring interpretive exhibits and programs, is open weekdays, except national holidays. Over 310 bird species have been recorded here.

Visitor activities include wildlife observation, driving twenty miles of refuge roads, hiking on trails (including sections of wheelchair-accessible paths), prearranged interpretive group tours and educational gatherings, fishing (a wheelchair-accessible fishing pier is provided at a children's fishing pond), and hunting on parts of the refuge during the designated seasons. Boating and camping are not permitted.

Visitors are cautioned to be alert for rattlesnakes and ticks. Insect repellent is advised during the warmer months.

Lodgings and meals are available in Stafford, Hutchinson, and Great Bend.

Access to the refuge is west from Hutchinson approximately 30 miles on Fourth Ave.; or west from Hutchinson on U.S. Hwy. 50 to Zenith, right onto State Hwy. 14 for 5 miles, and left onto Seventieth St. for 17 miles.

Information: Quivira NWR, Route 3, Box 48A, Stafford, KS 67578; tel.: (620) 486-2393,

Kentucky

Clarks River, currently containing more than 7,000 acres toward a goal of around 18,000 acres, was established in 1997. The refuge's mission is to protect and manage a diversity of floodplain habitats for migratory waterfowl, neotropical songbirds, and other wildlife along the Clarks River in western Kentucky.

As Refuge Manager Rick Huffines has described the history of this refuge:

In the 1960s, Kentucky lost the only jewel it had in the crown of the National Wildlife Refuge System, when most of the Kentucky Woodlands NWR was flooded by the reservoir impoundment, Kentucky Lake. Sometime around 1969, the Kentucky Department of Fish and Wildlife Service, and other conservation organizations, contacted the U.S. Fish and Wildlife Service and began a mission to . . . [replace the refuge].

Together, these trailblazers, as I like to call them, identified an area on the east fork of the Clarks River as high priority for protection. It was a rare complete river system that remained unchannelized and free from dams: a bottomland hardwood forest, with cherrybark oaks, towering sycamore trees, and natural ponds and sloughs; a place teeming with migratory songbirds, waterfowl and a wide array of other wildlife all dependent on this wetland; a place worthy of inclusion in the crown [of the refuge system]. For the next 28 years, those trailblazers fought head-on to protect this place and make it part of the refuge system.

In December 1997, I was asked to go to Benton, Kentucky, to start up a new refuge—the newly authorized Clarks River National Wildlife Refuge. Well, they gave me an acquisition map, an environmental assessment, and told me there were 18,000 acres identified in the proposed boundary, and to go and get them. So, I arranged for a temporary apartment, packed a bedroll, a beanbag chair and a cardboard box of cooking utensils, dumped all of the heavy responsibility of the move on my wife and son, and I headed for Kentucky.

The next morning, I thought to myself "What in the heck have I gotten myself into?" Surely there was a manual lying around here somewhere on how to start a National Wildlife Refuge. But there wasn't and I began to panic. So, I sat down in my beanbag chair and pulled my cardboard box beside me to make a desk and a place to think. It was there that I thought about my responsibility to all of those dedicated individuals who had blazed the path to this very room; and I realized that I had no reason to panic, because I wasn't truly alone. I had an army of trailblazers, past and present, in that room. I knew that if all

I had was a beanbag chair and a cardboard box, with the help of those trailblazers and the backing of my family we would make a place called the Clarks River National Wildlife Refuge.

This ecologically rich refuge-in-the-making already consists of about a dozen tracts of land along roughly twenty miles of the Clarks River Valley, in the vicinity of Benton and Sharpe-Elva. The refuge continues to grow through land purchases from willing sellers.

Two neotropical migratory birds for which the refuge's protected bottomland forest is especially important are the cerulean and Swainson's warblers. Among the many other birds attracted to this habitat are prothonotary and Kentucky warblers; vireos; thrushes; and scarlet tanager. Mammals include white-tailed deer, bobcat, mink, river otter, and raccoon. Of the reptiles, there are eastern box turtle and ringneck snake.

The refuge is open daily during daylight hours. There is no entrance fee. The refuge headquarters, at 91 U.S. Highway 641N in Benton, is open on weekdays, except national holidays.

Visitor activities include wildlife observation, hiking, horseback riding, bicycling on the refuge's gravel roads that are open to visitors, interpretive programs, fishing, and hunting on parts of the refuge during the designated seasons. Although camping is not permitted on the refuge, campground facilities are provided at Land Between the Lakes Recreation Area and Kenlake State Recreational Park.

Lodgings and meals are available in such communities as Benton and Paducah.

For information on how to reach the various parcels of refuge land, prospective visitors are urged to contact the headquarters.

Information: Clarks River NWR, P.O. Box 89, Benton, KY 42025; tel.: (270) 527-5770.

Louisiana

Atchafalaya, containing 15,000 acres, was established in 1984 to protect and enhance a portion of the nation's most extensive bottomland hardwood swamp habitat, located just north of I-10, between Baton Rouge and Lafayette, in southeastern Louisiana. Public use of this refuge is managed, in conjunction with the Sherburne Wildlife Management Area, by the Louisiana State Department of Wildlife and Fisheries.

More than 150 species of birds have been recorded here. Reptiles include turtles (musk, mud, red-eared slider, and yellow-bellied), snakes (rat, mud, king, and several species of water snakes), and the American alligator.

Establishment of the refuge was made possible partly with revenues from the sale of Migratory Bird Hunting and Conservation Stamps (Duck Stamps).

The refuge is open daily. There is no entrance fee.

Visitor activities include wildlife observation (the best months for birdwatching are March through May and August through October), hiking along ridges and on many unimproved paths, boating (shallow-draft boats), primitive camping, fishing, and hunting during the designated season. Because of the area's numerous waterways, public access is limited.

Visitors are cautioned to be alert for venomous snakes, to stay a safe distance from alligators, and to be aware of the possibility of encountering black bears. Insect repellent is advised.

Lodgings and meals are available in Baton Rouge, Breaux Bridge, and Lafayette.

Access to the refuge is by State Hwy. 975 and by way of the Whiskey Bay exit from I-10.

Information: Atchafalaya National Wildlife Refuge, c/o Sherburne Wildlife Management Area, 61389 Hwy. 434, Lacombe, LA 70445; tel.: (985) 882-2000.

Cameron Prairie, comprising 24,548 acres, was established in 1988 to protect and enhance important wildlife habitats on two units, in southwestern Louisiana. The 9,621-acre GIBBSTOWN UNIT contains freshwater marsh, coastal prairie, and former rice fields and provides feeding and resting areas for tremendous concentrations of wintering waterfowl and other water birds. More than a thousand acres of former rice-farming lands are being restored, with the help of discing, mowing, and occasional burning, to promote the growth of moist-soil plants that benefit wildlife.

This unit's freshwater marshes are managed with water control structures and levees. Some of these wetlands are drained and periodically burned in the autumn to help promote a healthy ecosystem. In early winter, these areas are re-flooded with water to benefit waterfowl.

The EAST COVE UNIT, which was formerly part of Sabine National Wildlife Refuge until 1992, contains 14,927 acres of brackish and saltwater marsh that is an important nursery for shrimp, crabs, and many species of finfish. Water-control structures, located along a 19-mile levee bordering Calcasieu Lake, regulate an essential, delicate balance between fresh and salt water in the marshes, to restore important wildlife habitat that was historically impaired or destroyed by the intrusion of saltwater.

Establishment of Cameron Prairie was made possible partly with revenues from the sale of Migratory Bird Hunting and Conservation Stamps (Duck Stamps). Ducks Unlimited, Inc. has assisted with important habitat enhancement projects.

The refuge's Gibbstown Unit is open daily during daylight hours. The visitor center, located on the this unit, is open on weekdays, except national holidays, and Saturdays. The East Cove Unit is open daily during daylight hours to general visitation, except during the Louisiana waterfowl hunting season and when the Grand Bayou Boat Bay is closed to public access. There is no entrance fee to either unit.

Visitor activities at the Gibbstown Unit include wildlife observation, driving refuge roads—notably Pintail Wildlife Drive, hiking on levees and dikes, boating (non-motorized boats in the bank fishing area and motorized boats in the outfall canal, from March 15 to October 15), fishing (from March 15 to October 15), and bow hunting for white-tailed deer during the designated season. Although camping is not permitted on the refuge, a campground is provided at Sam Houston Jones State Park, to the north of Lake Charles.

At the East Cove Unit, visitor activities (access by boat only) include wildlife observation, boating (motorized boats on canals, bayous, and lakes; only electric trolling motors in marshes), and fishing (except during the Louisiana waterfowl hunting season and when Grand Bayou Boat Bay is closed). November through February is the best time for birdwatching. More than 200 species of birds have been recorded on Cameron Prairie refuge.

Even though alligators are generally afraid of people, visitors are cautioned to stay a safe distance from them and to be alert for venomous snakes, including the cottonmouth, whose bite can be fatal. Insect repellent is advised.

Lodgings and meals are available in the towns of Lake Charles, Sulphur, and Jennings. Access to the refuge's visitor center from Holmwood is south 11 miles on State Hwy. 27. Information: Cameron Prairie NWR, 1428 Highway 27, Bell City, LA 70630: tel.: (337) 598-2216.

Catahoula, consisting of 25,162 acres in two units, was established in 1958, initially to protect and enhance an area of annually inundated floodplain, lying along the northeast shore of Catahoula Lake, and recently expanded to protect a forested area along the Ouachita, Black, and Red rivers. Habitats include marsh, bottomland hardwood forest, cypress-bordered Cowpen Bayou, and the 1,200-acre Duck Lake impoundment, which is managed to promote the growth of moist-soil plants for the benefit of wintering waterfowl. Tens of thousands of ducks spend part or all of the winter on and near the refuge, wood ducks nest here, and a nearby wading bird rookery is used by a large concentration of herons and egrets.

Many species of neotropical birds return to the refuge in the spring to nest and rear their young. Special acreage is set aside for some declining neotropical and other species, including the dickcissel in the spring and LeConte's and Henslow's sparrows in the autumn. The American alligator also inhabits the refuge.

Catahoula refuge was acquired to preserve bottomland hardwood forest. New additions to the refuge are being restored by planting oak, bald-cypress, water and black tupelos, and pecan trees on the land that was previously cleared for agriculture.

Usually in March and April, this refuge becomes flooded by backwater from the rising level of adjacent Catahoula Lake. During the summer, the lake is partially drained to promote the growth of an important source of food for waterfowl—a member of the sedge family known as chufa.

The refuge manages the water level under a cooperative agreement with the Louisiana Department of Wildlife and Fisheries and the U.S. Army Corps of Engineers, which built the structure that regulates the water level. Because of the lake's value to more than 350,000 wintering waterfowl, this 26,000-acre State of Louisiana–owned expanse of water is designated as a Wetland of International Importance.

Establishment of the refuge was made possible partly with revenues from the sale of Migratory Bird Hunting and Conservation Stamps (Duck Stamps). Because the U.S. Fish and Wildlife Service could not acquire the subsurface mineral rights when the refuge was established, limited oil drilling by the owner of those rights occurs here.

The refuge is open daily during daylight hours. There is no entrance fee.

Visitor activities include wildlife observation, environmental education programs, interpretive tours, viewing wildlife from an observation tower, driving the nine-mile Wildlife Drive around Duck Lake and along Cowpen Bayou, hiking a one-mile interpretive trail and other trails; canoeing and boating (two boat-launching ramps are provided); fishing on both Duck Lake and Cowpen Bayou (a wheelchair-accessible fishing pier is located on the bayou), and firearm and archery hunting on most of the refuge during the designated seasons. Camping is not permitted on the refuge, but campgrounds are available nearby.

Even though alligators are generally afraid of people, visitors are cautioned to stay a safe distance from them and to be alert for venomous snakes. Insect repellent is advised.

Lodgings and meals are available in Jena, Jonesville, Ferriday, and Alexandria.

Access to Catahoula is about 1.5 miles west on U.S. Hwy. 84 from the junction of Hwy. 84 and State Hwy. 28; or approximately 12 miles east of Jena on Hwy. 84.

Information: Catahoula NWR, P.O. Drawer Z, Rhinehart, LA 71363; tel.: (318) 992-5261.

Delta, encompassing 49,000 acres, was established in 1935 to protect and enhance part of the ecologically significant Mississippi River Delta, in southeastern Louisiana. The refuge mostly contains extensive marshes, bayous, and ponds. These habitats provide sources of food and resting places for an enormous variety of wintering waterfowl, including both the white and "blue" morphs (phases) of snow geese and more than a dozen species of ducks. Brown pelicans and wading birds, such as several species of herons and egrets, live here.

This is also one of the Gulf Coast refuges where the neotropical migratory songbird "fallout" occurs in April (see the Aransas NWR text). Great concentrations of warblers, buntings, tanagers, grosbeaks, and other birds land here after their exhausting nonstop flight across the Gulf of Mexico. Among the mammals inhabiting this refuge are river otters, mink, raccoons, and muskrats. Reptiles include turtles, snakes, and alligators.

The Fish and Wildlife Service is working to divert some of the flow of the Mississippi and its load of silt into the coastal marshes to replenish and enhance this vital habitat. Coastal wetlands are of enormous value not only to wildlife, but as nurseries for shrimp and many species of finfish. As *Ducks Unlimited* senior writer Matt Young wrote in the September–October 2001 issue of the magazine, "Acre for acre, coastal wetlands are among the most productive ecosystems on the planet. Their bountiful waters, rich in plant and animal life, support a remarkable diversity of waterfowl. . . . Sadly, thousands of acres of coastal wetlands continue to be lost each year. Protection is clearly the best line of defense against these losses, because once these fragile habitats disappear, they are gone forever."

Establishment of this refuge was made possible partly with revenues from the sale of Migratory Bird Hunting and Conservation Stamps (Duck Stamps).

Because the Fish and Wildlife Service could not acquire the subsurface mineral rights when the refuge was established, oil-and-gas development activities by the owner of those rights occur on Delta refuge. As reported by Douglas Jehl, in *The New York Times* (February 20, 2001):

Jetta [Production Company] and Texaco operate some 78 oil and gas wells in the refuge, making the operation the largest at any wildlife refuge in the lower 48 states.

Under these companies and Jetta's predecessor, the Chevron Corporation, there have been a number of small oil and gas spills here in the last 10 years, during which a concerted effort at environmental record-keeping began. Wildlife service officials describe several as having been significant, killing vegetation and affecting 40 to 80 acres of marsh. But the agency says there was no indication of harm to wildlife.

That record is roughly comparable with those of other refuges where oil and gas activity is under way, with no major spills or widespread death of wildlife in recent memory, wildlife officials say. . . .

At the D'Arbonne refuge and others in the South, environmental problems arise when drilling brings to the surface saltwater that is not part of the natural habitat. And in the Delta refuge and others along the Gulf Coast, the dredging of canals has contributed to the loss of wetlands. . . .

At the refuge[s] in Louisiana, wildlife managers say, oil companies have been quick to report even the smallest spill and willing to shift pipelines and even drilling sites to meet environmental concerns.

In the last 10 years, said James O. Harris, supervisory biologist for the federal refuges in southeast Louisiana, the wildlife service has collected about $1 million in fees from the oil companies to mitigate damage in the Delta refuge. That, Mr. Harris said, has been enough to help the agency recover more than 1,000 acres of wetlands, or 10 times the amount lost to energy operations in the period [the last decade]. . . .

In 2005, this refuge took a direct hit from Hurricane Katrina. As the Fish and Wildlife Service says, "The refuge . . . was . . . changed in many ways, as it has over the years when hurricanes and tropical storms have hit the area. Marsh and beach areas were eroded, trees were blown down or damaged, debris was washed onto the refuge and vegetation was stressed by saltwater intrusion. Several oil spills . . . impacted the refuge. We expect the refuge to slowly adjust and recover from the hurricane."

The refuge is open daily. There is no entrance fee.

Visitor activities include wildlife observation, boating, canoeing the refuge's waterways and bayous, primitive camping, fishing, and hunting during the designated season.

Visitors are cautioned to be alert for venomous snakes. Insect repellent and sunscreen are advised.

Lodgings and meals are available in and around New Orleans.

Access to this refuge is by way of State Hwy. 23 and from there only by a seaworthy boat.

Information: Delta NWR, c/o Southeast Louisiana Refuges, 1010 Gause Blvd., Slidell, LA 70458; tel.: (504) 646-7555.

Lacassine, encompassing 34,878 acres, was established in 1937 partly to protect and enhance 16,000-acre Lacassine Pool—an extensive levee-contained impoundment of open water and freshwater marsh of great benefit to an enormous concentration of wintering waterfowl, including the white and "blue" morphs (phases) of lesser snow goose, numerous species of ducks, and other water birds. The refuge staff continually manages the pool's habitat to maintain beneficial ecological conditions for waterfowl. In past years, as many as 800,000 ducks and geese have been seen here, where the Central and Mississippi Flyways converge.

Approximately 1,500 acres of the refuge are managed to produce grain crops and moist-soil plants for waterfowl. An ecologically important area of sawgrass marsh borders the circuitous course of Lacassine Bayou, and 3,345 acres of Lacassine have been designated as wilderness. Outside this relatively pristine area of the refuge, oil and gas development occurs. The Intracoastal Waterway slices through the southern part of the refuge.

Virtually the only trees on the refuge are bald-cypresses that grow in two groves along the edge of Mud Lake. During the breeding season, these small groves are filled with nests—a veritable bird city of herons, egrets, cormorants, and anhingas.

The refuge's 345-acre VIDRINE UNIT (Duralde Prairie), to the north of Eunice, Louisiana, was added to Lacassine in 1993. Since 1994, it has been the focus of a prairie-restoration project—converting former agricultural land to coastal prairie that consists of native grasses and forbs. Few remnants remain of this natural ecosystem that once covered more than two million acres of southwestern Louisiana.

Establishment of Lacassine was made possible partly with revenues from the sale of Migratory Bird Hunting and Conservation Stamps (Duck Stamps).

The refuge is open daily during daylight hours, and the headquarters is open on weekdays, except for national holidays. There is no entrance fee.

Visitor activities include wildlife observation; driving four miles of refuge roads; hiking on about thirty miles of levees and service roads; boating during most of the year on canals, bayous, and other waterways (two boat-launching sites are provided at Lacassine Pool, from March 15 to October 15; commercial launching sites provide access to other parts of the refuge); recreational fishing on both the pool and bayou; and archery deer hunting and waterfowl hunting on part of the refuge during the designated seasons. November through April is the best time for birdwatching. Although camping is not permitted on the refuge, campgrounds are provided nearby.

Even though alligators are generally afraid of people, visitors are cautioned to stay a safe distance from them and to be alert for venomous snakes. Insect repellent is advised.

Lodgings and meals are available in such towns as Lake Charles, Sulphur, and Jennings.

Access to Lacassine's visitor contact station is south from westbound I-10 at Jennings on State Hwy. 26 to Lake Arthur, right onto State Hwy. 14 for seven miles, and left onto State Hwy. 3056 for 4.5 miles to the refuge entrance; or south from eastbound I-10 at Welsh on State Hwy. 99, left onto Hwy. 14 for three miles, and right onto Hwy. 3056 for 4.5 miles to the refuge. Access to Lacassine Pool is west from Lake Arthur on State Hwy. 14 for 15 miles or east from Hayes on Hwy. 14 for 3 miles, and south 4.5 miles on Illinois Plant Rd.

Information: Lacassine NWR, 209 Nature Rd., Lake Arthur, LA 70549; tel.: (337) 774-5923.

Tensas River, containing roughly 66,000 acres (with additional tracts of land still planned for purchase), was established in 1980 to protect and enhance ecologically rich, seasonally flooded bottomland cypress-and-hardwood forest and oxbow lakes along the winding course of the Tensas River, in northeastern Louisiana. This remnant of pristine forest had been targeted for timber harvesting and agricultural development, but a coalition of conservationists was instrumental in mounting a campaign that rescued the area in the nick of time.

More than 400 species of birds, mammals, reptiles, amphibians, and fish inhabit the refuge, including the American alligator, wood duck, wild turkey, pileated woodpecker, numerous songbirds, and a remnant population of the rare and threatened Louisiana black bear. Unfortunately, the ivory-billed woodpecker, apparently last recorded in the 1940s on what is now the Tensas River refuge, is generally believed to be extinct. This woodpecker measured to about 20 inches in length, compared to another red-crested species, the pileated woodpecker, which measures to around 16 inches.

The Fish and Wildlife Service is managing this refuge to protect, enhance, and restore its bottomland hardwood forest habitat. Other parts of the refuge are devoted to moist-soil management (seasonally raising and lowering water levels) and crop cultivation that benefit thousands of wintering waterfowl. Ducks Unlimited, Inc. has assisted with important habitat enhancement projects.

The refuge is open daily during daylight hours. There is no entrance fee. The visitor center is open daily, except on national holidays.

Visitor activities include wildlife observation, environmental education programs, driving and bicycling on refuge roads, hiking on several trails, canoeing (a primitive canoe-launching site is available), ATVs (only on ATV trails during the designated period), fishing on two refuge lakes, and hunting during the designated seasons.

Even though alligators are usually afraid of people, visitors are cautioned to stay a safe distance from them and to be alert for venomous snakes. Insect repellent is advised.

Lodgings and meals are available in such communities as Tallulah and Winnsboro.

Access to the refuge from the Waverly exit on I-20 is north 1.5 miles on State Hwy. 577, east 4 miles on U.S. Hwy. 80, right at the refuge sign, and south 10 miles to the visitor center.

Information: Tensas River NWR, 2312 Quebec Rd., Tallulah, LA 71282; tel.: (318) 726-4400.

Maine

Maine Coastal Islands encompasses roughly 7,400 acres consisting of a 5,500-acre mainland unit that was established in 1972 as the Petit Manan NWR, and forty coastal islands along 200 miles of the coast of Maine, including former separate refuges: 1,355-acre Cross Island, 65-acre Seal Island, 20-acre Franklin Island, and 10-acre Pond Island.

As explained by the Fish and Wildlife Service:

The Service's primary focus . . . is colonial seabird restoration and management. Refuge islands provide nesting habitat for common, arctic, and endangered roseate terns, Atlantic puffins, razorbills, black guillemots, Leach's storm-petrels, laughing gulls, and common eiders. Over the last 25 years, the Service has worked to reverse the decline in these birds' populations. As a result, many species have returned to islands where they nested historically. . . .

Seabirds have always relied on Maine's offshore islands as havens for raising their young. Small unforested, rocky islands provide a setting free of mammalian predators such as foxes, coyotes, and raccoons.

In the 17th century, Euro-Americans started to settle on many coastal islands, farming and raising sheep and other livestock. Carl W. Buchheister, former president of the National Audubon Society, wrote in his preface for the book *Maine Paradise* (Russell D. Butcher, 1973):

Not long after the European immigrants settled along America's East Coast, the rape of Maine's island seabird colonies began. The eggs of gulls and other species were gathered for food—at first, here and there, but then with increasing fervor and thoroughness. Egging was carried on as if the supply were inexhaustible; no one gave thought to the welfare of the species. Consequently, under the impact of egging and related disturbances, the bird populations began to decline.

Then a still more devastating practice descended upon the island bird colonies. Fashion, the most powerful of dictators, demanded more and more plumage for the millinery trade, and the gulls and terns of Maine were among its principal victims. Both the native Indians and white man invaded the island nurseries during the summer months, killing the parent birds and leaving their eggs and young to perish. . . .

As great barrels filled with the bodies of dead birds were brought to the villages of the inhabited islands and mainland, scores of women were employed to prepare the skins, keeping their feathers intact. After being treated with alum, salt, and preservatives, the skins were packed in cases and shipped aboard coastal sailing vessels to New York City, the major center of the booming, multimillion-dollar millinery industry.

For many years thousands upon thousands of these birds were slaughtered. . . .

. . . following three hundred years of egging and slaughter, the summer islands of Maine that had once been so crowded with avian life had virtually become biological deserts.

Around the end of the 19th century and start of the 20th century, the American Ornithologists' Union's Committee on Bird Protection engaged the services of several outer-island light-station personnel, such as those on Matinicus Rock, now a refuge island, to help protect the seabird colonies. Public concern for the welfare of birds in general resulted in the passage by Congress of the Migratory Bird Treaty Act in 1918. This landmark legislation was enacted into law to protect migratory birds, their eggs, and their nests. As a result of these and other wildlife conservation efforts, the populations of arctic and common terns rebounded, increasing to more than 15,000 pairs along the coast of Maine.

But as described by the Fish and Wildlife Service:

The recovery was short-lived, however. During the mid-1900s, the spread of open landfills along the coast and an increase in fishery waste provided easy pickings for herring and great black-backed gulls. These birds nest earlier than terns, claiming prime habitat and relegating terns to inferior nest sites. Some gulls also prey on tern eggs and chicks. The artificial food sources led to an explosion in gull populations. By 1977, the tern population in the Gulf of Maine had declined to roughly 5,000 nesting pairs.

Between 1972 and 1980, this refuge complex was established mainly to provide the management necessary to restore breeding populations of terns. According to the Fish and Wildlife Service, "To restore terns to an island, it must first be made suitable for the birds again. This requires [discouraging the] . . . gulls."

Large nesting colonies of arctic and common terns are now supported on Petit Manan, Matinicus Rock, and Seal Islands, the latter comprising the largest tern colony in the Gulf of Maine; and the federally listed endangered roseate tern is also now nesting on Petit Manan Island. Similar tern restorations have also occurred on other islands. Other colonial nesting seabirds have benefited from these successes. Among them are the Leach's storm petrel and three alcids—Atlantic puffin, black guillemot, and razorbill.

The mainland properties of the refuge consist of the 628-acre Sawyer's Marsh Division, at the head of an expanse of salt marsh in Milbridge; the 572-acre Gouldsboro Bay Division, containing mixed upland hardwood forest; and the 2,166-acre Petit Manan Point Division in Steuben. This latter contains a remarkable diversity of habitats on a narrow peninsula that juts into the Atlantic Ocean, including the intertidal zone, cobble beaches, granite shoreline ledges with visually contrasting bands of basaltic dikes, salt marsh, tidal mudflats, cedar swamps, freshwater marsh, sphagnum-and-heath bogs, spruce forest, open stands of jack pines, blueberry barrens, and old hay pastures.

Concentrations of migrating waterfowl, wading birds, and shorebirds are attracted to the refuge's salt marsh and tidal mudflat habitats. During the autumn, Petit Manan Point's eighty-acre Cranberry Flowage draws more than 4,000 ducks, many of which are black ducks. During the winter, large numbers of common eiders; surf, black, and white-winged scoters; common goldeneyes; and long-tailed ducks (oldsquaws) are abundant offshore.

Blueberry barrens and open grassy areas, which are maintained by periodic mowing and pre-scribed burning, offer nesting habitat for bobolink and other grassland species. During the spring, woodcock make use of these open places to perform their aerial courtship displays (see discussion of this species in the Moosehorn NWR text).

One successful refuge partnership has been with the National Audubon Society, which has worked with the Fish and Wildlife Service since the early 1980s to restore colonial nesting seabirds to Seal Island, located about twenty miles southeast of Rockland. As described by the Service, "Through its Project Puffin, the Society successfully reintroduced Atlantic puffins to the island by transplanting chicks from Newfoundland, Canada, and hand-raising them. Puffins now nest on the island, after a 150-year absence."

Some parts of the refuge complex, including Petit Manan Point, are open daily, during day-light hours. There is no entrance fee. Scotch, Cross, Halifax, and Bois Bubert islands are open all year. Seal Island is not open to visitation, because of the risk of harm from unexploded ord-nance that results from previous U.S. military shelling and bombing activities. All other islands are closed from April 1 through August, to avoid disturbing the nesting seabird activities.

Visitor activities include wildlife observation, hiking, commercial boat tours (as from Bar Harbor) that offer views of nesting seabirds on Petit Manan and Machias Seal islands, and hunting on parts of the refuge during the designated seasons.

Hiking opportunities on the Petit Manan Point Division include two trails: The Birch Point Trail is a two-mile route from a parking area through mixed coniferous-and-deciduous forest to Birch Point and the interpretive John Hollingsworth Memorial Trail, which is a 1.5-mile loop that winds from the parking area and an expanse of blueberry barrens, across granite ledges where jack pines grow, through shaded stands of spruces and miniature cedar swamps, and emerges on the shore of cobble beaches and rocky ledges that shelve into the sea. This trail is named in honor of the memory of the late John Walker Hollingsworth, Jr. (1942–1995), who beautifully and tirelessly photographed a great many of the national wildlife refuges throughout the United States. As former Secretary of the Interior Bruce Babbitt said, in a Citation for Conservation Ser-vices (Nov. 7, 1995), "Mr. Hollingsworth was a man of patience, vision and fortitude and one of those remarkable individuals whose achievements have left a profound and indelible mark on others. . . . It is reassuring to know that his images will continue to capture the hearts, souls, and support of future generations." Most of the photographs in this book were taken by John or his wife, Karen. She continues to be actively photographing the refuges.

Insect repellent is advised during the warmer months.

Lodgings and meals near Petit Manan Point Division are available in such communities as Milbridge, Ellsworth, and Machias.

Access to the Petit Manan Point Division is west from Milbridge 2 miles on U.S. Hwy. 1, and left 5.8 miles on Pigeon Hill Rd. to the Birch Point Trail parking area or 6.2 miles to the Hollingsworth Trail parking area; or from Steuben, it is east 2.5 miles on U.S. Hwy. 1 and right onto Pigeon Hill Rd., and as above.

Information: Maine Coastal Islands NWR, P.O. Box 279, Milbridge, ME 04658; tel.: (207) 546-2124.

Moosehorn, comprising 27,616 acres in two divisions, was established in 1937 to protect and manage a diversity of ecologically significant wetland and forest habitats in eastern Maine. The 7,577-acre Edmunds Division borders the tidal waters of Cobscook Bay, along U.S. Hwy. 1 between Whiting and Pembroke. The 20,039-acre Baring Division includes an extensive inland area of mixed coniferous-and-deciduous forest and freshwater wetlands, near Calais. Roughly one-quarter of the refuge has been designated as two units of the National Wilderness Preservation System. More than 225 bird species have been recorded on the refuge.

The refuge provides important feeding, resting, and nesting habitat for waterfowl, wading birds, shorebirds, upland game birds, raptors, and numerous neotropical migratory songbirds. Moosehorn's habitat diversity includes northern forests, freshwater marshes and bogs, lakes and ponds, and more than fifty managed freshwater impoundments. There are numerous streams and beaver flowages. Stretches of rocky shore and salt marsh are tidally influenced by twice-daily twenty-foot fluctuations. Areas of blueberry barrens and grasslands are scattered here and there within the expanses of forest.

The Fish and Wildlife Service carries out a number of important management activities. To help create and maintain habitat diversity, selected areas of forest are harvested and/or enhanced with prescribed burning. The Service explains that "Woodcock, ruffed grouse, moose, deer, and a variety of songbirds prosper in a young forest. In the past, fires revitalized areas of the forest, while farming maintained open areas." However, fires are a rare event today and farmland acreage has substantially decreased. Habitat management programs, including timber harvesting and controlled burning, mimic the natural processes of fire, blow-downs, and insect damage by providing clearings and areas of early growth woodlands.

The American woodcock is one of this refuge's avian species that most benefits from woodland habitat management activities. It has steadily declined throughout much of its range because of the loss of its natural habitats. Woodcock need clearings for roosting and their aerial spring courtship displays, shrubby alder thickets for foraging with their long beaks for earthworms, and young deciduous woodlands for nesting. Moosehorn refuge has pioneered efforts to understand woodcock biology and develop management strategies.

As described by the Fish and Wildlife Service:

Woodcock are best known for their spectacular courtship flights. At dusk and dawn from early April to mid-May, the males fly to their territories in open areas. Each bird begins this mating ritual with a series of nasal "peents." He then takes wing in a spiral flight that carries him several hundred feet into the air while he warbles a plaintive song to waiting females. He returns to the same spot after each flight and repeats his performance several times over the next half hour.

Refuge Manager Tim Cooper says:

The refuge is famed for its involvement in research on the American Woodcock. Intensive management for this species has been a hallmark of the refuge since the 1940's. Management practices primarily targeted for the woodcock have provided ideal habitats for other species. . . . Early successional forest management creates a rolling mosaic of habitat types. Everything from clear openings to old-growth forest can be found on the refuge. Research indicates that Moosehorn's innovative management practices have resulted in more quality habitats for a greater variety of species than in unmanaged areas.

Management of the refuge's freshwater wetlands is carried out with water-control structures that enable the raising and lowering of water levels within pond and wetland impoundments. Three of these structures, which have been designed and installed by Ducks Unlimited, Inc., provide for the annual migration of the alewife. This silvery gray species of anadromous fish, a member of the herring family, is a living link between the sea and freshwater lakes and ponds. In May, large numbers of these 10- to 12-inch-long alewives migrate from coastal waters up the streams that lead them back to their ancestral spawning places. They swim upstream—mysteriously and relentlessly driven against great odds, fighting the current, and battering themselves against rocks and each other. Finally they reach the tranquil waters where they once again ensure the continuation of their species. The young spend the summer growing to a size of three or four inches before dashing down to the sea in early autumn. Wetland management has also greatly increased the numbers of waterfowl, notably black and wood ducks.

To enhance nesting opportunities for bald eagles and ospreys, the refuge has erected nesting platforms on both divisions of Moosehorn. Common loons nest on Bearce Lake and Vose and Cranberry ponds, where their activities are monitored and protected.

Establishment of this refuge was made possible partly with revenues from the sale of Migratory Bird Hunting and Conservation Stamps (Duck Stamps). In addition to assistance provided by Ducks Unlimited, other nonprofit organizations that have helped include the Ruffed Grouse Society, The Nature Conservancy, and the Quoddy Regional Land Trust.

The refuge is open daily during daylight hours. There is no entrance fee. The refuge headquarters, located on the Baring Division, is open on weekdays, except national holidays.

Visitor activities include wildlife observation, driving on public highways that run through both divisions, hiking on several trails, bicycling, cross-country skiing, snowshoeing, canoeing (especially enjoyable on Bearce Lake), fishing (a wheelchair-accessible pier is provided), and deer hunting on parts of the refuge during the designated season.

More than fifty miles of roads that are closed to motor vehicles are also available for hiking, bicycling, cross-country skiing, and snowshoeing. The refuge offers a limited environmental education program that is focused mainly on the woodcock and bald eagle. A viewing platform on the west side of U.S. Hwy. I, in the Baring Division, provides opportunities to see nesting bald eagles and ospreys. Although camping is not permitted on the refuge, campground facilities are available at Cobscook Bay State Park, located within the Edmunds Division.

Insect repellent is advised during the warmer months.

Lodgings and meals are available in such communities as Calais and Robbinston.

Access to the refuge headquarters, on the Baring Division, is about three miles from Calais on U.S. Hwy. I (to the southwest of Calais), left onto Calais-Charlotte Rd. for three miles, and right onto the headquarters entrance road; or from the junction of U.S. Hwy. I and State Hwy. 214 in Pembroke, it is northwest six miles on Hwy. 214, right onto Calais-Charlotte Rd. for 8.3 miles, and left onto the refuge.

Information: Moosehorn NWR, 103 Headquarters Rd., Suite 1, Baring, ME 04694; tel.: (207) 454-7161.

Rachel Carson, presently containing over 5,000 acres toward a goal of more than 7,600 acres, was established in 1966 as the Coastal Maine National Wildlife Refuge. The refuge's ten divisions are scattered along a nearly fifty-mile coastal stretch between Kittery Point and Cape Elizabeth, in southwestern Maine.

In 1970, the refuge was renamed to honor the memory of the late environmental author Rachel Carson (1907–1964), who wrote the landmark book, *Silent Spring*. Published in 1962, it described the post-World War II unrestricted use and widespread, harmful impacts of highly toxic chemical pesticides and herbicides upon humans and wildlife. She also wrote *The Sea Around Us* (1951) and *The Edge of the Sea* (1955) and was employed by the Fish and Wildlife Service from 1936 to 1952 as an aquatic biologist and editor-in-chief.

The refuge consists of strategic places along this part of the Maine coast that are important feeding, resting, and nesting areas for migratory waterfowl, colonial seabirds, wading birds, shorebirds, raptors, and songbirds. As the Fish and Wildlife Service explains, "The unique mixture of over 5,000 acres of salt marsh estuary/barrier beach habitat, rocky shore, forests, scrub/shrub and grassland supports nearly 400 species of birds, mammals, fish, reptiles and amphibians."

The refuge's marsh habitat offers vital food and cover for nesting waterfowl such as American black and wood ducks, mallards, green-winged and blue-winged teal, common eiders, and Canada geese. Of the wintering waterfowl, black ducks are the most abundant. The bald eagle, piping plover, and roseate and least terns are among the many other avian species attracted to the refuge.

Habitat management activities on the refuge include restoring tidal wetland areas that were previously drained and ditched, to reestablish the natural tidal flow for the benefit of waterfowl and shorebirds, and to provide vital nursery habitat for various species of finfish and shellfish. As *Ducks Unlimited* senior writer Matt Young wrote in the September–October 2001 issue of the magazine, "Acre for acre, coastal wetlands are among the most productive ecosystems on the planet. Their bountiful waters, rich in plant and animal life, support a remarkable diversity of waterfowl. . . . Sadly, thousands of acres of coastal wetlands continue to be lost each year. Protection is clearly the best line of defense against these losses. . . ."

Prescribed burning and mowing are implemented to maintain existing refuge grasslands and to convert some areas of shrub-invaded habitat back to productive warm-season grasses for the benefit of nesting waterfowl and grassland songbirds. To protect the endangered piping plover, refuge beaches are protectively managed and monitored during the spring and summer nesting period. The refuge staff report that "Least tern populations have dramatically increased due to their proximity to protected plover habitat."

The refuge is open daily during daylight hours. There is no entrance fee. The refuge headquarters and visitor contact station, located on the Upper Wells Division near the intersection of U.S. Hwy. 1 and State Hwy. 9, is open on weekdays, except national holidays, and open during limited weekend hours in the summer.

Visitor activities include wildlife observation, hiking on the one-mile interpretive Carson Trail, cross-country skiing, environmental education programs, limited fishing, and hunting on some of the refuge's divisions during the designated seasons. Although camping is not permitted on the refuge, a number of private campground facilities are provided in the vicinity. More than 245 species of birds have been recorded on this refuge.

Insect repellent is advised during the warmer months.

Lodgings and meals are available in Kittery, Cape Elizabeth, and elsewhere.

Access to the refuge headquarters and the Upper Wells Division from the intersection of U.S. Hwy. I and State Hwy. 9 in Wells is east 0.7 mile on Hwy. 9 and right onto Port Rd.

Information: Rachel Carson NWR, 321 Port Rd., Wells, ME 04090; tel.: (207) 646-9226.

Sunkhaze Meadows, consisting of 10,190 acres in three units, was established in 1988 to protect the second most extensive peat bog in the state of Maine, as well as adjacent forested wetland and upland habitats. The refuge's main unit is located in the town of Milford, about 15 miles north of Bangor, in central Maine.

As explained by the Fish and Wildlife Service:

The bogs and stream wetlands, along with the adjacent uplands and associated transition zones, provide important habitat for many wildlife species. The wetland complex consists primarily of wet meadows, shrub thickets, cedar swamps, extensive red and silver maple floodplain forests and open freshwater stream habitats, along with those plant communities associated with peatlands such as shrub heaths and cedar and spruce bogs.

Ducks Unlimited, Inc. has helped enhance more than 1,000 acres of the refuge's wetland habitat.

In the early 1980s, the peat mining industry proposed to extract commercial quality peat from this area for use as a heating fuel. These plans were not carried out and, as the result of increased public support, the area was acquired by The Nature Conservancy and subsequently purchased by the federal government for the national wildlife refuge.

The two smaller refuge units are located in the towns of Unity and Benton. The American woodcock is one of the common inhabitants of the Unity unit. When the sedge wren, a state-listed endangered species, was discovered in the Benton vicinity, that refuge unit was established.

The refuge is open daily during daylight hours. There is no entrance fee. The refuge headquarters is open on weekdays, except national holidays.

Visitor activities include wildlife observation, environmental education programs, hiking on several trails, bicycling (on certain roads), cross-country skiing and snowshoeing, canoeing, snowmobiling (on the Interconnected Trail System 84, where it crosses the southwestern part of the refuge), fishing, and hunting during the designated seasons. More than 180 bird species have been recorded here.

Canoeing opportunities, which offer the best way to see the refuge, include Sunkhaze Stream (accessed by way of the 250-yard portage on Ash Landing Trail); and Baker Brook, accessed from a point on County Road (no parking area) located 4.2 miles east of U.S. Route 2.

Insect repellent is advised during the warmer months.

Lodgings and meals are available in Milford, Orono, and Bangor.

Access to the refuge from Exit 51 on I-95 at Orono is northeast four miles on U.S. Hwy. 2 to Old Town and across the Penobscot River bridge to Milford, right (after the stoplight) onto County Rd. for just over four miles.

Information: Sunkhaze Meadows NWR, 1033 South Main St., Old Town, ME 04468; tel.: (207) 827-6138.

Maryland

Blackwater, containing more than 26,000 acres, was established in 1933 and is located in Dorchester County, on the Eastern Shore of Maryland. It was the first and is the largest refuge in the Chesapeake Marshlands National Wildlife Refuge Complex.

The refuge consists of extensive brackish tidal marshes; seasonally regulated, freshwater moist-soil impoundments; and a variety of cultivated croplands. This trio of habitats attracts large numbers of migrating and wintering waterfowl and is one of the major wintering places for Canada geese in the Atlantic Flyway. During the peak of the autumn concentrations in early November, the wetlands and fields of crops support as many as 35,000 Canada geese and more than 20 species of ducks, many of which winter here. The best time for observing waterfowl, including several hundred tundra swans, is from mid-October to mid-March. Waterfowl that nest on the refuge include Canada geese, American black and wood ducks, mallards, and blue-winged teal.

This is also a haven for the bald eagle. The refuge is the center of the greatest nesting density of these majestic birds on the Atlantic Coast. About a dozen pairs nest and as many as 150 winter on the refuge. Ospreys, which are here from March to September, build their nests on platforms that are placed throughout the wetlands by the refuge staff. During spring and autumn migrations, the refuge also hosts large influxes of many species of warblers and other neotropical migratory songbirds. More than 300 bird species are attracted to the refuge.

Prior to the refuge's establishment, the Blackwater River marshes were used as a fur farm, largely for the trapping of muskrats. Most of the area's forest had been harvested, and some of the land was drained and farmed. Today, muskrats are common residents, along with the non-native nutria. The population of the latter South American rodent has unfortunately greatly increased, causing significant impairment of the marsh habitat. As on many national wildlife refuges where this invasive species has proliferated, the Fish and Wildlife Service is attempting to control its numbers.

Other mammals include the white-tailed deer; the much smaller Asian elk, known as sika; and the Delmarva Peninsula fox squirrel. The latter large squirrel, with steel gray fur (lacking the yellowish, orange, tawny, or black phases of fox squirrels elsewhere), formerly ranged throughout open woodlands, primarily on the Delmarva Peninsula of Delaware and the Eastern Shore of Maryland and Virginia. As the Fish and Wildlife Service explains, "The loss of suitable woodland habitat (due primarily to land clearing) is the major factor in the squirrel's decline. Forest management programs at Blackwater are designed to restore and protect forest habitats that are essential for the long-term viability of this endangered species."

Establishment of the refuge was made possible partly with revenues from the sale of Migratory Bird Hunting and Conservation Stamps (Duck Stamps). Ducks Unlimited, Inc. has helped enhance more than 350 acres of the refuge's wetland habitat. Another national nonprofit organization, the National Park Trust, is currently working with the Fish and Wildlife Service to help coordinate the purchase of private lands by conservation groups within and around the refuge.

The refuge is open daily during daylight hours. There is an entrance fee. The visitor center is open daily, except on Thanksgiving and Christmas.

Visitor activities include wildlife observation; driving the 3.5-mile interpretive, paved Wildlife Drive that offers views of ponds, brackish and freshwater marshes, woodland, and fields; hiking on two interpretive loop trails (one is a wheelchair-accessible boardwalk); bicycling on 5 miles of the Wildlife Drive and bike trail; canoeing and boating (from April 1 through September); fishing and crabbing (from April 1 through September; but not shore fishing); trapping; and white-tailed deer and sika hunting during the designated season. A boat-launching site is available at Shorter's Wharf (just outside the refuge). Camping is not permitted on the refuge.

Visitors are cautioned to be alert for ticks and chiggers. Insect repellent is advised during the warmer months.

Lodgings and meals are available in such communities as Cambridge and Salisbury.

Access to the refuge from U.S. Hwy. 50 at Cambridge is southwest six miles on State Hwy. 16 to Church Creek, left onto State Hwy. 335 for four miles, and left onto Key Wallace Dr.

Information: Blackwater NWR, c/o Chesapeake Marshlands NWR Complex, 2145 Key Wallace Dr., Cambridge, MD 21613; tel.: (410) 228-2677.

Eastern Neck, encompassing 2,286-acre Eastern Neck Island, was established in 1962 to protect important habitat for wintering migratory waterfowl, the endangered Delmarva fox squirrel, and other wildlife. The refuge is located at the confluence of the Chester River and Chesapeake Bay, near the Chesapeake Bay Bridge and toward the northern end of the Eastern Shore of Maryland.

Among Eastern Neck Refuge's spectacular concentrations of wintering waterfowl, the Fish and Wildlife Service has recorded more than 7,000 tundra swans (the refuge is a major staging area for these migrating swans), 20,000 Canada geese, and 15,000 canvasbacks, their peak numbers generally occurring in mid-November through January.

Nesting birds include wood ducks, eastern bluebirds, ospreys, and bald eagles. The eagles rebuild their nests in late December and in January and lay their eggs in February, and their eaglets start to hatch in late April and fledge in July. Woodcocks perform their unusual courtship activity in February, and their chicks are hatched in May. Neotropical migratory songbirds, including many species of warblers, reach their peak influxes from late April to early May and from late September to October. More than 240 species of birds have been recorded here.

Of the resident mammals, white-tailed deer are commonly seen, and less obvious is the federally listed endangered Delmarva Peninsula fox squirrel (see discussion of this species in the Blackwater NWR text).

The National Tree Trust has assisted the refuge by donating hundreds of tree seedlings for an upland reforestation program on some of the former agricultural land. This program is partly to provide future habitat for the fox squirrel.

In addition to nearly 1,000 acres of brackish, tidally influenced wetlands containing salt marsh and salt meadow cordgrasses and bulrushes, the island refuge consists of 40 acres of open-water impoundments, more than 500 acres of woodland containing a mixture of loblolly pines and various deciduous trees, 50 acres of grassland, and more than 600 acres of cultivated cropland. Under a cooperative agreement with a local farmer, a portion of crops, such as corn, winter wheat, sunflowers, soybeans, and clover, is left unharvested, to provide supplemental food and cover for waterfowl and other wildlife.

The refuge's wetland habitats are managed for the benefit of waterfowl and other wildlife. Lowering the water levels within moist-soil impoundments promotes the growth of nutrient-rich plants and also provides favorable habitat for wading birds and shorebirds. Raising the water levels during the winter provides habitat for migrating and wintering waterfowl.

Water levels of the refuge's five winter-flooded green-tree reservoirs, dominated mostly by such trees as swamp chestnut and willow oaks, sweetgum, and black tupelo, are managed to provide food for such wintering waterfowl as wood and American black ducks.

The southeastern end of Eastern Neck Island contains brackish marsh surrounding an area of loblolly pine and American holly. In 1975, this wild area was designated as the Hail Point Research Natural Area. In a cooperative effort with other federal and state agencies to protect the refuge's marshland and halt shoreline erosion, the Fish and Wildlife Service is using sandy dredge material from shipping channels to restore eroded marshland.

Establishment of the refuge was made possible partly with revenues from the sale of Migratory Bird Hunting and Conservation Stamps (Duck Stamps). Ducks Unlimited, Inc. has assisted with a wetland restoration project here.

The refuge is open daily during daylight hours. There is no entrance fee. The refuge office is open on weekdays and most weekends, except national holidays.

Visitor activities include wildlife and butterfly observation, driving and bicycling on unpaved refuge roads that are not closed to visitation and on a number of paved county roads, hiking on several trails (including a wheelchair-accessible boardwalk), picnicking (at the county's Ingleside Recreation Area, from April 1 through September), canoeing and boating (hand-carried boat launching is at the Ingleside area, from April 1 through September; trailered boat launching is at Bogle's Wharf landing), fishing, crabbing, and deer hunting (including non-ambulatory and youth hunts) on parts of the refuge during the designated season.

Visitors are cautioned to be alert for ticks and chiggers. Insect repellent is advised during the warmer months.

Lodgings and meals are available in Rock Hall, Grasonville, Chestertown, and Annapolis.

Access to the refuge from State Hwy. 213 at Chestertown is southwest 13 miles on State Hwy. 20 to Rock Hall, and left onto State Hwy. 445 for 7 miles, which crosses Eastern Neck Narrows onto the island.

Information: Eastern Neck NWR, 1730 Eastern Neck Rd., Rock Hall, MD 21661; tel.: (410) 639-7056.

Patuxent Research Refuge, comprising 12,750 acres, was established in 1936 specifically to support wildlife research. It is located adjacent to the Baltimore-Washington Parkway, roughly midway between Baltimore and Washington, D.C., in central Maryland. The Patuxent and Little Patuxent rivers wind through the refuge. A great diversity of resident and migratory wildlife inhabits the refuge's ecologically rich forests, meadows, and wetlands, which include forty managed impoundments. As urban development has fragmented and destroyed large areas of forest, this refuge has continued to protect one of the largest forested areas in the mid-Atlantic region. The name *Patuxent* is derived from an Algonquin Indian name meaning "where the water falls."

Cottonmouth snake, White River NWR, Arkansas

Endangered Lange's metalmark butterfly on naked buckwheat, Antioch Dunes NWR, California

Endangered fringe-toed lizard, Coachella Valley NWR, California

California condor, Hopper Mountain NWR. U.S. Fish and Wildlife Service photo

Don Edwards San Francisco Bay NWR

American avocet, Don Edwards San Francisco Bay NWR. Mike Boylan photo

White pelicans, Don Edwards San Francisco Bay NWR

Long-billed dowitcher, Don Edwards San Francisco Bay NWR. Mike Boylan photo

Shorebirds in salt water marsh, Humboldt Bay NWR, California

American coot feeding young, Kern NWR, California

Lower Klamath NWR, California

Lower Klamath NWR

Male buffleheads, Lower Klamath NWR

Canada goose with brood, Modoc NWR, California

Dowitchers feeding in wetland, Sacramento NWR, California

Light-footed clapper rail, Tijuana Slough NWR, California

Alamosa NWR, Colorado

Displaying sage grouse, Arapaho NWR, Colorado

Arapaho NWR, Colorado

Greater sandhill cranes in flight, Monte Vista NWR, Colorado

Outdoor classroom, Rocky Mountain Arsenal NWR, Colorado

Brown pelican silhouette, Cedar Key NWR, Florida

Endangered Florida panther, Florida Panther NWR

Florida panther research, Florida Panther NWR

Snowy egret in breeding plumage, J.N. "Ding" Darling NWR, Florida

Roseate spoonbills, J.N. "Ding" Darling NWR

White ibis, J.N. "Ding" Darling NWR

Children exploring a wetland at Lake Woodruff NWR

Prescribed burn, Lake Woodruff NWR, Florida

White ibis, Merritt Island NWR, Florida

Courting common moorhens, Merritt Island NWR, Florida

Endangered Key deer buck, Key Deer NWR

Pelican Island NWR, Florida

Brown pelicans and great blue herons, Pelican Island NWR

Ghost crab, St. Vincent NWR, Florida

St. Marks NWR, Florida

Bond Swamp NWR, Georgia

Okefenokee NWR

White ibis, Okefenokee NWR, Georgia

Wood stork young, Harris Neck NWR, Georgia

Okefenokee NWR

Okefenokee NWR

U.S. Fish and Wildlife personnel installing a nest box for red-cockaded woodpeckers in Piedmont NWR

Red-cockaded woodpecker at nest cavity, Piedmont NWR, Georgia

Red-footed boobies courtship, Kilauea Point NWR, Kauai, Hawai'i

Endangered nene, Kilauea Point NWR

Kilauea Point NWR

Patuxent has been at the forefront of world-renowned endangered species research, pioneering captive breeding and release technologies in support of the recovery of many species. For example, during the 1950s and 1960s, scientists at Patuxent (as well as elsewhere) documented irrefutable evidence of the harmful impacts upon bald eagles, ospreys, and other wildlife of a chlorinated hydrocarbon, DDT, and other highly toxic chemical insecticides and herbicides. Widespread publicity of these findings, notably by Rachel Carson in her landmark 1962 book, *Silent Spring*, eventually led to the banning or curtailed use of DDT and certain other of these chemical poisons in the United States. This has allowed the gradual recovery of the eagles, ospreys, and other species and to the recent delisting of the bald eagle from the federal endangered species list. Today, bald eagles are frequently observed on Patuxent, as well as numerous other refuges and elsewhere.

Among other endangered avian species that have been the focus of Patuxent's research are the California condor, Aleutian Canada goose, masked bobwhite, Mississippi sandhill crane, and the whooping crane. (Recent reorganization at Patuxent shifted whooping crane research from the Fish and Wildlife Service to the U.S. Geological Survey's Biological Resources Division.)

The refuge's Central Tract, which is not open to visitation, contains the Patuxent Wildlife Research Center, where the offices and study sites of the many research biologists are located. The Center's mission is "To excel in wildlife and natural resource science, providing information needed by federal, state and other agencies to better manage the Nation's biological resources."

Patuxent is divided into two other parts, both of which are open to visitation. The South Tract contains the National Wildlife Visitor Center—one of the Department of the Interior's largest science and educational centers. As described by the Fish and Wildlife Service:

The National Wildlife Visitor Center features interactive exhibits which focus on global environmental issues, migratory bird studies, habitats, endangered species, and the tools and techniques used by scientists. The visitor center also offers hiking trails, tram tours, a seasonal fishing program, wildlife management demonstration areas, and an outdoor education site for school classes. A large auditorium and meeting rooms can accommodate scientific conferences, meetings, teacher workshops, lectures, and traveling displays. A bookstore, Wildlife Images, operated by the Friends of Patuxent Wildlife Research Center, Inc., a non-profit cooperating association, offers a variety of conservation books and other educational materials.

The visitor center is open daily, except on Thanksgiving, Christmas, and New Year's Day. There is no fee. Tram tours (fee) are operated seasonally. A variety of trails offer about five miles of hiking opportunities on this part of the refuge.

The 8,100-acre North Tract, which was formerly a military training facility and was transferred from the Department of Defense in 1991, is open for wildlife observation, driving on the nine-mile Wildlife Loop, hiking and horseback riding on twenty miles of trail, viewing wildlife from an observation tower, interpreter-led walks, educational programs, fishing, and hunting on parts of the tract during the designated seasons. Although camping is not permitted on the refuge, several campground facilities are available nearby. Visitors are required to check in at the North Tract's visitor contact station and receive an access pass. This tract is open daily during daylight hours, except on Thanksgiving, Christmas, and New Year's Day.

Lodgings and meals are available in Laurel, Beltsville, Greenbelt, College Park, Bowie, Jessup, Baltimore, and Washington, D.C.

Access to the refuge's South Tract and its visitor center from Washington, D.C. is north on the Baltimore-Washington Parkway to the Powder Mill Rd. exit, and right two miles on Powder Mill Rd. From Baltimore, it is south on the B-W Parkway to the Powder Mill Rd. exit, left onto Powder Mill Rd. for two miles, and following directional signs to the visitor center.

Access to the refuge's North Tract from Washington, DC. is north on the B-W Parkway to the State Hwy. 198 exit, and right onto Hwy. 198 for 1.4 miles. From Baltimore, it is south on the B-W Parkway to the Hwy. 198 exit, and left onto Hwy. 198 for 1.4 miles.

Information: Patuxent Research Refuge, 10901 Scarlet Tanager Loop, Laurel, MD 20708; tel.: (301) 497-5580.

Massachusetts

Great Meadows, comprising more than 3,700 acres in two units, was established in 1944 "for use as an inviolate sanctuary, or for any other management purpose, for migratory birds." The refuge protects important freshwater floodplain wetlands and bordering woodlands along 12 miles of the Concord and Sudbury rivers, about 20 miles west of Boston in eastern Massachusetts. The rivers have been federally designated as Wild and Scenic Rivers.

The CONCORD UNIT includes a number of impoundments, the water levels of which are seasonally managed for the benefit of migrating waterfowl, wading and shorebirds.

A large part of this refuge contains expanses of marsh that are mostly dominated by cattails, along with other emergent plants such as sedges, arrowhead, pickerelweed, bladderwort, American lotus, wild iris, and the non-native purple loosestrife. One of the Fish and Wildlife Service's management goals is the control of the latter aggressive, invasive European species (see further explanation in the Montezuma NWR text).

Other refuge habitats include areas of swamp containing red maples and willows; and woodland with such trees as white pine, eastern hemlock, white and red oaks, and hickories. A number of ponds and diked impoundments provide important habitat for waterfowl and other waterbirds. Water levels within the impoundments are seasonally regulated to promote the growth of plants that provide habitat and food for fish and wildlife. Nesting boxes are provided for wood ducks and bluebirds. More than 220 species of birds have been recorded on the refuge.

Expansion of the refuge has been made possible partly with revenues from the sale of Migratory Bird Hunting and Conservation Stamps (Duck Stamps).

The refuge is open daily during daylight hours. There is no entrance fee. The refuge headquarters and visitor center, located on the SUDBURY UNIT, are open daily, except on winter weekends and national holidays.

Visitor activities include wildlife observation; interpretive programs and exhibits at the visitor center; hiking on a number of trails; cross-country skiing and snowshoeing; and canoeing, boating, and fishing on the rivers (canoe- and boat-launching sites onto the Concord River are adjacent to the State Hwy. 225 bridge; and onto the Sudbury River adjacent to the U.S. Hwy. 20 bridge). A canoe-landing (but not launching) site is provided near the visitor center. Although camping is not permitted on the refuge, campground facilities are provided at Harold Parker State Forest. Hunting is not permitted on this refuge, but opportunities are available on the state's adjacent Pantry Brook Wildlife Management Area.

Visitors are cautioned to be alert for ticks, which may carry Lyme disease. Insect repellent is advised during the warmer months.

Lodgings and meals are available in such communities as Concord and Sudbury.

Access to the refuge's visitor center in the Sudbury Unit from U.S. Hwy. 20 at Wayland is northwest 1.7 miles on State Hwy. 27, right onto Water Row Rd. for 1.2 miles, right onto Lincoln Rd. for 0.5 mile, and left onto Weir Hill Rd.

Information: Great Meadows NWR, 73 Weir Hill Rd., Sudbury, MA 01776; tel.: (978) 443-4661.

Monomoy, containing 7,604 acres, was established in 1944 to protect barrier island habitats extending about ten miles southward from the southeastern end of Cape Cod, Massachusetts. The refuge, which lies between Nantucket Sound and the Atlantic Ocean, contains beaches, sand dunes, intertidal mudflats, salt and freshwater marshes, and freshwater ponds. It is a major stopping place for large numbers of migratory birds. In 1970, most of the refuge was designated as a unit of the National Wilderness Preservation System—the only one in southern New England. More than 300 bird species have been recorded on the refuge.

Although North and South Monomoy islands can be reached only by boat, the refuge's forty-acre parcel on Morris Island is accessed by road. As the Fish and Wildlife Service explains,

Monomoy has evolved from a series of small, sand-spit barrier islands in the 1800s to an arm of land connected to the mainland in the 20th century. In 1958, a spring storm tore the sand spit from the mainland, creating a single island separated from Morris Island, Chatham. Twenty years later, the island split in two during a turbulent blizzard. Left in its wake was the present-day 2.5-mile stretch of North Monomoy and the six mile arm of South Monomoy.

Shorebird migrations through the refuge are spectacular, and during the autumn and winter months, large concentrations of eiders, scoters, mergansers, brant, and other waterfowl gather offshore. Parts of the refuge are closed to visitation, to avoid disturbing the nesting activities of such birds as the federally listed threatened piping plover, several species of terns, and a large colony of gulls. The gull colony grew from a single nesting pair in 1961 to as many as 20,000 in the 1990s.

One of the refuge's most successful management activities is occurring on a small part of the refuge. This area is being kept free of the omnivorous and aggressive great black-backed and herring gulls that typically monopolize nesting habitat. This gull-free area has provided vital habitat for nesting common and roseate terns, black skimmers, and other species.

Establishment of this refuge was made possible partly with revenues from the sale of Migratory Bird Hunting and Conservation Stamps (Duck Stamps).

The refuge is open daily during daylight hours. There is no entrance fee. The refuge headquarters is open on weekdays, except national holidays, and is also open on summer weekends.

Visitor activities include wildlife observation, hiking on the 0.75-mile Morris Island Trail, and surf-fishing on Morris Island. Camping is not permitted on the refuge, but facilities are provided elsewhere on Cape Cod.

Visitors are cautioned to be alert for poison ivy and ticks. The latter may carry Lyme disease. Insect repellent and sunscreen are advised during the warmer months.

Lodgings and meals are available in such communities as Chatham, East Harwich, Harwich Port, and Orleans.

Access to the refuge from Exit 11 on U.S. Hwy. 6 is south 3 miles on State Hwy. 137, left onto State Hwy. 28 for 3.5 miles through Chatham to the Chatham Lighthouse and Coast Guard Station, the first left turn after the lighthouse, and then the first right onto Morris Island Rd.

Information: Monomoy NWR, Wikis Way, Morris Island, Chatham, MA 02633; tel.: (508) 945-0594; or c/o Eastern Massachusetts NWR Complex, 73 Weir Hill Rd., Sudbury, MA 01776; tel.: (978) 443-4661.

Parker River, containing 4,662 acres, was established in 1942 to protect important feeding, resting, and nesting habitat for migratory birds and other wildlife. The refuge is located near Newburyport, much of it on Plum Island, along the northeastern coast of Massachusetts. The ecologically rich diversity of habitats includes sandy ocean beaches, sand dunes, shrub thickets, woodlands, bog, swamp, freshwater and salt marshes, salt pannes (shallow tidal pools), tidal creeks and river, and estuary.

The Fish and Wildlife Service says, "Parker River Refuge is noted as one of the finest birding areas in the nation with more than 300 species recorded. While any season can produce a memorable visit, spring, summer, and fall offer the best birdwatching opportunities."

Plum Island gets its name from the beach plum. Within sheltered places among the sand dunes, it forms shrubby thickets, along with northern bayberry, shadbush, poison ivy, and other shrubs and vines. Growing on the dunes closest to the beach and the most exposed to wind and salt spray are beach pea and American beach grass.

Plum Island's 6.3-mile ocean beach provides vital nesting habitat for the federally listed threatened piping plover and least tern. Although this beach is closed to visitation from April 1 through mid- or late August to avoid disturbing the birds' sensitive nesting activities, parts of the beach not being used for nesting may be reopened to visitor use on July 1.

The refuge's nesting waterfowl include Canada geese, American black ducks, mallards, gadwalls, and green-winged and blue-winged teal. American woodcocks begin their aerial courtship displays in March. The peak influxes of northbound neotropical songbird migration occurs during May; and the largest numbers of southbound shorebirds and tree swallows come through the refuge in August.

Among the Fish and Wildlife Service's habitat management activities are seasonally regulating water levels within impoundments: lowering them to provide mudflat feeding and resting areas for concentrations of migrating shorebirds and to promote the growth of nutrient-rich plants that provide food and cover for waterfowl and other water birds in the autumn and winter, when water levels are raised. Parts of the refuge are mowed to maintain open areas, providing food and cover for such species as the bobolink and woodcock. Periodic prescribed burning of freshwater marsh and other grasslands is implemented to promote nutrient cycling and spur new growth. Non-native plants, such as the purple loosestrife that crowds out native species, are controlled (see further discussion in the Montezuma Refuge text). Nesting boxes are provided for purple martins and other cavity-nesting birds; and nesting platforms are placed near open water for ospreys. Ducks Unlimited, Inc. has helped enhance several hundred acres of the refuge's wetland habitat.

The refuge is open daily during daylight hours. The visitor center is open daily, except on national holidays. The Fish and Wildlife Service alerts prospective visitors to the possibility that the Plum Island section (entrance fee) often fills to capacity during the warmer months.

Visitor activities include wildlife and butterfly observation, interpretive exhibits and programs at the visitor center, driving the 6.5-mile road on Plum Island, hiking several trails (including the wheelchair-accessible Pines Trail), bicycling on the road, swimming, surf-fishing, shell-fishing, and hunting on part of the refuge during the designated times. Camping is not permitted on the refuge, but facilities are available at Salisbury Beach State Reservation.

Visitors are cautioned to be alert for poison ivy and ticks. The latter may carry Lyme disease. Insect repellent and sunscreen are advised during the warmer months.

Lodgings and meals are available in Newburyport.

Access to the refuge's Plum Island section from Exit 57 on I-95 is east 3.5 miles on State Hwy. 113 and U.S. Hwy. 1A South, at a stoplight turn left onto Rolfe's Lane, right onto Plum Island Turnpike for two miles, and right onto the refuge. The visitor center is at 6 Plum Island Turnpike.

Information: Parker River NWR, 6 Plum Island Turnpike, Newburyport, MA 01950; tel.: (978) 465-5753.

Silvio O. Conte National Fish & Wildlife Refuge was established in 1991. The refuge's partnership mission is to help restore, enhance, and protect the diversity and abundance of native fish and wildlife species and the health of the ecosystems on which they depend, within the 7.2-million-acre Connecticut River watershed, in eastern Vermont, western New Hampshire, and central Massachusetts and Connecticut. The refuge is named in honor of the late Congressman Silvio O. Conte, from Massachusetts, who had "a dream that includes a Connecticut River, cleaned, fishable, swimmable, and with salmon restored to abundant numbers. And a dream that someday my children and grandchildren will continue to enjoy the outdoors as I have."

The main emphasis of this watershed-oriented refuge is achieving and maintaining a constructive and positive working partnership among many stakeholders. These partners include private landowners, land trusts, nonprofit environmental organizations, water supply districts, municipalities, state agencies, and the Fish and Wildlife Service and other federal agencies. The refuge acts through these partnerships in three main areas: environmental education; performing research, inventories, and habitat-management assistance; and land acquisition.

As a summary of the refuge's activities explains:

The Refuge provides financial and technical support to improve stewardship and habitat management on lands throughout the watershed. Research, inventory and management projects assist a variety of landowners . . . and help accomplish Refuge purposes. Notable projects have included the songbird stopover habitat survey, the invasive plant control initiative, cooperating with the U.S. Department of Agriculture to target their Wildlife Habitat Incentives Program to important habitats within the watershed, and providing fish passage facilities at small mill dams on tributaries in Connecticut.

Environmental education is another key component of the mission. The refuge's Great Falls Discovery Center, in Turners Falls, Mass., provides educational information and programs on the refuge; and the Colebrook Interpretive Center, on U.S. Hwy. 3 in Colebrook, N.H., provides exhibits and information on the refuge. Information on these centers: tel.: (413) 863-0209.

The Montshire Museum of Science in Norwich, Vt., provides educational exhibits and programs on habitats and species of the Connecticut River watershed. It is reached from Exit 13 on I-91 in Vermont, and following directional signs. Information: tel.: (802) 649-2200.

The Springfield Science Museum's River Education and Awareness Program (REAP) in Springfield, Mass., which is partially supported with a Conte Refuge Challenge Cost-Share Grant, has involved thousands of middle school students, their teachers, and some parents in an interdisciplinary watershed-based science program.

Another important part of the refuge's partnership program is the protection of specific areas of land. Most of these land protection projects are accomplished in partnership with non-profit conservation organizations or state agencies that end up owning adjacent parcels. As of 2001, the largest tract owned by the Fish and Wildlife Service was a 26,000-acre tract within the 71,000-acre Nulhegan Basin, in northeastern Vermont. The latter encompasses part of the basin's cold microclimate and acidic and nutrient-poor peat soils that combine to produce an ecologically outstanding environment, which is typical of places at least 200 miles farther north. This part of the refuge includes such habitats as black spruce swamp, spruce-balsam fir-tamarack swamp, northern white cedar swamp, dwarf shrub bog, and sedge meadow.

One of Vermont's most outstanding areas of black spruce bog is located at the refuge's 76-acre Mollie Beattie Bog, where a boardwalk and viewing platform offer visitors an easy (wheelchair-accessible) opportunity to see this scenic area. Information on access: tel.: (802) 723-4398.

Nulhegan Basin was long owned by the Champion International Corporation, as part of its extensive timber holdings in northern New England and New York State. In 1999, negotiations between Champion and The Conservation Fund resulted in a landmark transaction by which the timber company sold nearly 330,000 acres of its land in New Hampshire, Vermont, and New York State to The Conservation Fund. The Fund, in turn, transferred some acreage to public ownership and sold other lands to timber companies after placing conservation easement restrictions on them. The transaction has been described as the most extensive land conservation project ever implemented east of the Mississippi.

In Vermont, the 133,000 acres of former Champion lands were divided three ways: 22,000 acres donated to the state as the West Mountain Wildlife Management Area; 85,000 acres, with state-acquired conservation and public access easements, sold to Essex Timber; and 26,000 acres acquired by the Fish and Wildlife Service as the Nulhegan Basin Division of the Silvio O. Conte National Fish & Wildlife Refuge.

Lodgings and meals are available in Turners Falls, Greenfield, and many other communities throughout the Connecticut River watershed.

Access to the refuge headquarters and Great Falls Discovery Center from Exit 27 on I-91 in Massachusetts is east a few miles on State Hwy. 2 and right at the second traffic light.

Information: Silvio O. Conte National Fish & Wildlife Refuge, 52 Avenue A, Turners Falls, MA 01376; tel.: (413) 863-0209.

Michigan

Detroit River International Wildlife Refuge was established in December 2001 as the first international refuge in North America. Its boundaries include the former 322-acre Wyandotte National Wildlife Refuge and encompass more than 5,000 acres along the Lower Detroit River, in southeastern Michigan and adjacent Ontario, Canada.

The Lower Detroit River is located at the intersection of the Atlantic and Mississippi migratory bird flyways. According to the Fish and Wildlife Service, "an estimated three million ducks, geese, swans, and coots migrate annually through the region. More than 300,000 diving ducks stop each year to feed on wild celery beds in the river. The Canada-United States North American Waterfowl Management Plan has identified the Detroit River as part of one of 34 waterfowl habitat areas of major concern in the U.S. and Canada (Lower Great Lakes-St. Lawrence Basin)."

The refuge's authorized boundaries include islands, coastal marshes and other wetlands, shoals, and riverfront lands along 18 miles of the river and northwestern shore of Lake Erie, stretching from Zug Island south to the southern boundary of Sterling State Park. When Antoine de la Mothe Cadillac founded Detroit in 1701, the river contained extensive marshes and other wetlands and adjacent uplands that were inhabited by a great diversity of wildlife. It is estimated that more than 95 percent of the river's coastal wetlands that once existed have been eliminated by development. The U.S. and Canadian governments have designated the river as a Waterfowl Habitat Area of Concern. The goal of this refuge is, therefore, to protect, manage, and restore the most important remaining habitat for the benefit of 65 species of fish and more than 300 species of birds, including approximately 30 species of waterfowl.

As the Fish and Wildlife Service further explains:

The refuge is a result of an unprecedented partnership of government agencies, business, conservation groups, landowners and private citizens on both sides of the border who came together to improve the quality of life on the Lower Detroit River. The refuge is also a key component of the Downriver Linked Greenways Initiative, a community-based program that seeks to build "green" infrastructure and create outdoor recreational opportunities in Wayne County, Mich. The public-private partnership gained momentum . . . through a series of intricate cooperative agreements, land exchanges and acquisitions involving governments, private businesses, citizens and conservation groups.

The former Wyandotte refuge was established in 1961 to restore and protect Grassy and Mamajuda islands, "as a refuge and breeding place for migratory birds and other wildlife." In 2001, 18-acre Mud Island, located northeast of Grassy Island, was added to the refuge through a donation from the National Steel Corporation. These islands are now part of the international refuge.

Canada's Canard River Marsh Complex, located across the river from Grassy Island, is a major waterfowl staging area. Its wetland habitat is an especially significant resting and feeding area for canvasbacks, as they migrate from their nesting grounds in the Canada's prairie provinces to wetlands along the East Coast. As of this writing (early 2002), members of the

Canadian parliament are working toward enactment of Canada's component of the international refuge, including the Canard River Marsh area.

The Detroit River refuge's U.S. Refuge Manager Doug Spencer explains that "As managers of the refuge, one of our first initiatives will be to reach out and engage partners and citizens and involve them in the planning process, to help us plot conservation and recreation decisions for the future of the refuge. . . . it is our policy to make areas of this refuge open to hunting, fishing, wildlife observation, wildlife photography, environmental education and environmental interpretation."

Information: Detroit River International Wildlife Refuge, 9311 Groh Rd., Large Lakes Research Station, Grosse Ile, MI 48138; tel.: (734) 692-7608.

Kirtland's Warbler Wildlife Management Area, containing more than 6,600 acres in 118 units, was established in 1980 to protect nesting habitat that is vital to one of North America's rarest birds, the Kirtland's warbler. The management area's units are located within eight counties in the northern part of Michigan's Lower Peninsula. Breeding "colonies" of this federally listed endangered species are scattered primarily throughout the Au Sable River watershed, especially within Crawford, Oscoda, and Ogemaw counties.

As the U.S. Fish and Wildlife Service says, "The Kirtland warbler nests primarily in young jack pine forest growing on Grayling sand. This soil type is found only in a few counties in northern lower Michigan. The warblers prefer to nest in forests that are about 80 acres or larger with numerous small, grassy openings. Kirtland's warblers prefer to nest in groups. They build their nests only on the ground among grass or other plants like blueberries. Jack pine trees . . . must be about 5 to 16 feet tall and spaced to let sunlight reach the ground. The sunlight keeps the lower branches alive and bushy, hiding the . . . nest beneath them. When the trees grow larger, their upper branches block the sun and the lower branches die. Grasses and other plants become less dense. The warblers then cease use of the area."

Prior to 1973, the U.S. Forest Service and Michigan Conservation Department (now the Michigan Department of Natural Resources) had set aside certain areas of public forest specifically for management as warbler habitat. To meet the warbler's exacting environmental needs for successful breeding, there would always have to be sufficient stands of jack pines containing trees of the appropriate age and size.

In 1973, Congress passed the Endangered Species Act. Under its provisions, the Kirtland's warbler was among the first species to be listed as endangered. A recovery plan that was completed in 1976 and revised nine years later provided for intensive habitat management activities on state and federal forestlands to maintain a self-sustaining population of 1,000 pairs. As described by the Fish and Wildlife Service, "Management consists of commercial logging of 50 year old jack pine stands followed by planting or seeding to regenerate the stand. . . . The objective is to manage a minimum of 127,600 acres of habitat for the Kirtland's warbler."

Annual population censuses of Kirtland's warblers have shown that there were about 200 singing males recorded during the 1970s and 1980s, dropping to a low of only 167 in 1974 and 1987. Beginning in 1990, however, their research has shown an encouraging climb: to 766 singing males in 1995, 905 in 1999, and about 1,700 in 2007. Other encouraging news is that this species has also recently been reported from Michigan's Upper Peninsula and Wisconsin.

The warbler's breeding areas are posted, and visitors are not permitted onto these lands during the nesting season, except on guided tours that are provided by the Fish and Wildlife Service (FWS) and U.S. Forest Service. The best time for hearing and perhaps seeing these birds is from late May through June. For information on daily FWS-escorted tours (free, as of this writing) from mid-May to early July, departing at 7 a.m. and 11 a.m. from the Holiday Inn in Grayling, Michigan: Fish and Wildlife Service, 2651 Coolidge Road, East Lansing, MI 48823; tel.: (517) 351-2555.

Information: Kirtland's Warbler Wildlife Management Area, c/o Seney National Wildlife Refuge, HCR #2, Box 1, Seney, MI 49883; tel.: (906) 586-9851.

Seney, encompassing 95,212 acres, was established in 1935 to enhance and protect an extensive mosaic of marsh, bog, and swamp habitats interspersed with scattered areas of northern woodlands, for the benefit of migratory birds and other wildlife. The refuge is located in the central Upper Peninsula of Michigan.

As described by Refuge Manager Tracy Casselman:

Within its boundaries is a 25,000-acre designated wilderness area and tens of thousands of acres of roadless areas. Vast expanses are dominated by knee-high sedge grass, with scattered red and jack pine islands. One can almost see and feel the power of the glaciers that created the sedge meadow complexes. In the drier uplands, beautiful stands of red, white, and jack pine are dominant, with aspen and paper birch scattered throughout. Pockets of northern hardwoods of sugar maple, beech, yellow birch, and northern hemlock add diversity. Black spruce, tamarack, and other lowland trees occupy habitats between the open sedge meadows and the uplands. Three rivers and several streams wind their way through the refuge.

Water levels of impounded pools are seasonally manipulated to regulate the growth of aquatic vegetation. High water helps protect nesting water birds from predation and protect populations of fish during the winter months. Low water exposes mudflats that offer feeding habitat for cranes, shorebirds, and waterfowl and makes feeding on fish easier for bald eagles and ospreys.

Other activities that are designed to maintain healthy and diverse habitats include periodic prescribed burning to promote nutrient cycling; wetland and river restoration; mowing; and forest management.

A particularly exciting Seney success story is the reintroduction of the trumpeter swan, the largest species of North American waterfowl. In the early 1990s, the Fish and Wildlife Service released 42 captive-reared swans as part of a program to increase North America's interior population, which had been extirpated during the late 19th century. Seney refuge was selected because of its extensive, ideal swan habitat of actively managed, open, shallow water; the abundance of submergent vegetation that is an important source of food; and the absence of power lines and toxic lead shot. More than 200 bird species are attracted to the refuge.

As shown by the refuge's monitoring, "In 2001, the refuge contained an adult flock of 151 swans, with 76 hatched and 29 fledged." "The flock continues to expand off the refuge. The reintroduction has been the most successful in Michigan, and prospects appear favorable for continued growth of the Seney flock."

The refuge is open daily during daylight hours. There is no entrance fee. The visitor center is open daily from May 15 to October 15.

Visitor activities include wildlife observation; driving the seven-mile Marshland Wildlife Drive, along which are three wildlife observation decks; hiking on many miles of backcountry gravel roads and the 1.4-mile Pine Ridge Nature Trail near the visitor center; bicycling the refuge roads, except where posted; canoeing on a stretch of the Manistique River (canoe rentals at outfitters in the nearby town of Germfask); interpretive programs at the visitor center and interpreter-led field programs; cross-country skiing on nine miles of groomed trails; snowshoeing anywhere except the groomed ski trails; fishing along a three-mile Fishing Loop or at the (wheelchair-accessible) fishing pier; and hunting on parts of the refuge during the designated seasons. Boats and other flotation devices are not permitted on refuge pools. Camping is not permitted on the refuge, but facilities are available nearby.

The best time to see migratory birds is from late March through early April, when Canada geese usually arrive, soon followed by sandhill cranes; late May through early June, for the influx of neotropical songbirds, such as warblers and thrushes; and late September through October, for the peak of the autumn waterfowl migration. The height of the autumn foliage color of aspens, birches, and maples is usually during the first half of October.

Insect repellent is advised during the warmer months, and visitors should be alert for the possibility of ticks.

Lodgings and meals are available in such communities as Manistique and Newberry.

Access to the refuge from U.S. Hwy. 2 near the town of Blaney Park is north 12 miles on State Hwy. 77; or from State Hwy. 28 at the town of Seney, south 5 miles on Hwy. 77.

Information: Seney NWR, 1674 Refuge Entrance Rd., Seney, MI 49883; tel.: (906) 586-9851.

Shiawassee, containing more than 9,700 acres with plans to expand to about 16,000 acres, was established in 1953. The refuge protects part of the extensive Shiawassee Flats, within the Saginaw River floodplain, in the central Lower Peninsula of Michigan.

The Shiawassee, Flint, Cass, and Tittabawassee rivers converge here, forming the Saginaw River near the refuge's northern boundary. Roughly three-quarters of the refuge consists of marsh and seasonally flooded bottomland hardwood forest. Much of the remaining land is devoted to impounded moist-soil units, within which water levels are seasonally managed for many species of waterfowl and shorebirds. Part of the refuge contains cultivated croplands, where cooperative agreements with local farmers provide for a portion of such crops as corn, barley, soybeans, and winter wheat to be left unharvested for the benefit of migrating waterfowl and other wildlife.

During the most recent period of continental glaciation, between 5,000 and 15,000 B.C., much of what is now east-central Michigan lay beneath the waters of vast Glacial Lake Saginaw. The former lakebed formed the basis of today's level landscape, known as "The Flats."

Beginning in the late 19th century, human impacts upon the area and its resources sharply increased. Lumber companies logged off the swampland's virgin-growth trees. In the early 20th century, farmers started draining the wetlands, and by mid-century, extensive agricultural production was made possible with elaborate networks of dikes, ditches, and other water control facilities. Coal mining also occurred in part of the area during the early 20th century.

The primary goal of the refuge is to restore, enhance, and manage part of these historically significant wetlands for the benefit of migrating waterfowl and other wildlife. Shallow marshes are drained and flooded periodically to provide productive feeding habitat for migrating birds. During the peak of spring and autumn migrations, more than 20,000 Canada geese are attracted to the refuge; and during autumn migration as many as 35,000 ducks of many species, including up to 4,000 black ducks, pause here. The best months for viewing these concentrations of waterfowl are March-April and September-November. The refuge supports a large nesting colony of great blue herons. Other commonly seen birds include tundra swans, bald eagles, wading birds, and shorebirds. May is the best month to see and hear influxes of warblers and other neotropical migratory songbirds.

Establishment of Shiawassee Refuge was made possible partly with revenues from the sale of Migratory Bird Hunting and Conservation Stamps (Duck Stamps).

Regarding partners that provide generous assistance to Shiawassee Refuge, the assistant refuge manager, Edward P. DeVries, explains:

Our partnerships include the Saginaw Bay Watershed Initiative Network, which is a group of local, state, and federal agencies and private organizations teamed up with funding sources to improve the quality of life in this part of Michigan. This group has funded a wheelchair-accessible wildlife watching platform at our Curtis Road parking lot. The Shiawassee Flats Citizens and Hunters Association has provided funding and manpower to improve some of our dikes, and the Shiawassee Flats Advisory Council (SFAC) has funded some of our special public events. . . . The Friends of the Shiawassee NWR was started in 1998 for the purpose of providing the Refuge with additional support through funding, grant-writing, and volunteerism. Their main focus has been on generating public support and funding for the construction of a state-of-the-art refuge visitor center, the Great Lakes Discovery Center, at Exit 144 on I-75. . . . Ducks Unlimited, Inc. continues to be an active partner with the Refuge through funding sources such as the North American Wetlands Conservation Act.

DU has also helped enhance several hundred acres of the refuge's wetland habitat.

The refuge is open daily during daylight hours. There is no entrance fee. The refuge headquarters is open on weekdays, except national holidays.

Visitor activities include wildlife observation, hiking on two interpretive trails, bicycling, cross-country skiing (on ungroomed trails), and hunting on parts of the refuge during the designated seasons. Camping is not permitted on the refuge. More than 265 bird species have been recorded on the refuge.

Interpretive and educational exhibits and programs for youth groups, families, and other visitors are provided at the Green Point Environmental Learning Center, operated by the Fish and Wildlife Service; it is located near the northern end of the refuge at 3010 Maple Street, Saginaw, MI 48602; telephone: (517) 759-1669. The center consists of the interpretive building and 76 acres of bottomland habitats, with 2.5 miles of interpretive trails.

Insect repellent is advised during the warmer months.

Lodgings and meals are available in Saginaw.

Access to the refuge headquarters from Saginaw is south about 5 miles on State Hwy. 13 and right about 0.5 mile on Curtis Rd.

Information: Shiawassee NWR, 6975 Mower Rd., Saginaw, MI 48601; tel.: (989) 777-5930.

Minnesota

Agassiz, comprising 61,500 acres, was established in 1937 to restore and manage a diversity of ecologically important wildlife habitats, in northwestern Minnesota. This refuge lies within the aspen-parkland transition zone between the coniferous forest, tallgrass prairie, and prairie pot-hole regions of the Red River watershed. The refuge was originally named the Mud Lake Migratory Waterfowl Refuge and was changed to Agassiz National Wildlife Refuge in 1961.

There are 40,100 acres of open water and marshes that attract large concentrations of breeding and migrating waterfowl; about 10,000 acres of willow and alder thickets and other shrubby habitat; 7,000 acres of scattered stands of predominantly aspen woodland; over 4,000 acres of grassland; and 150 acres of cultivated cropland for the benefit of wildlife. The refuge protects two black spruce-and-tamarack bogs and related bog lakes, Kuriko and Whiskey, that are located within a 4,000-acre unit of the National Wilderness Preservation System.

During an average year, this refuge attracts roughly 250 nesting pairs of Canada geese, and 7,500 nesting pairs of ducks (especially blue-winged teal, mallard, gadwall, and ring-necked ducks) that produce an average of 12,000 juveniles. The largest nesting colony of Franklin's gulls in North America—20,000 to 40,000 pairs—is found on the refuge. Other colonial nest-ing birds include 1,000 black terns, 300 to 900 pairs of black-crowned night-herons, eared and western grebes, Forster's terns, and double-crested cormorants. There are also four pairs of nest-ing bald eagles. More than 285 bird species have been recorded on the refuge.

The refuge supports a long-term average of approximately 1,700 white-tailed deer. Moose populations have varied from a high of 450 animals during the 1980s to a low of fifty during the late 1990s. Other noteworthy mammals are black bear, eastern gray wolf, fisher, and river otter.

Agassiz refuge occupies a small part of an enormous glacial lake that was created some 10,000 years ago, by the melting and receding continental glacial ice. The lake covered an area larger than the present five Great Lakes combined. The refuge is named in honor of the Swiss-American glacial geologist and Harvard professor, John Louis Rodolphe Agassiz.

Prior to Euro-American settlement of this part of Minnesota, extensive lakes and marshes attracted enormous concentrations of waterfowl, shorebirds, and other wildlife. As described by the U.S. Fish and Wildlife Service:

In 1909, the first drainage district was organized in the area to convert the marshes to arable land. The drainage system earned the distinction of being the largest single public drainage project in the United States.

By 1933, approximately one million dollars had been expended on the drainage system without suc-cess. . . . To save the County from bankruptcy, the State legislature passed an act absorbing the drainage taxes and authorized the lands to be purchased for the development of Mud Lake Migratory Waterfowl Refuge.

The Fish and Wildlife Service's primary habitat management activity on Agassiz refuge is the regulation of water levels to create a diversity of emergent and submergent wetland plant communities. Twenty pools, ranging from 100 to 10,000 acres, the largest of which is Agassiz Pool, are manipulated with a system of dikes and water control structures. Although cattails are the dominant emergent variety of plant, wetland management also promotes the growth of bul-rushes, spike rushes, and sedges. Submergent species include sago pondweed, water milfoil, and muskgrass. In addition, there are free-floating aquatic plants, such as bladderwort and duckweed.

Other management activities include prescribed burning and brush mowing, to maintain grass and shrub habitats for the benefit of deer, moose, nesting waterfowl, and other wildlife. Crops of barley, oats, and winter wheat are planted to provide supplemental food for waterfowl during autumn migration.

Establishment of Agassiz Refuge was made possible partly with revenues from the sale of Migratory Bird Hunting and Conservation Stamps (Duck Stamps). Ducks Unlimited, Inc. helped enhance 2,400 acres of wetland habitat at Farmes Pool, constructing seven miles of dike and a water-control structure.

The refuge is open daily during daylight hours. There is no entrance fee. The refuge office, which includes wildlife displays and a bookshop, is open on weekdays (except national holidays) and Sunday afternoons in June, July, and August.

Visitor activities include wildlife observation; observing the refuge from a 14-foot obser-vation platform; driving the 4-mile Lost Bay Habitat Drive—open May through October; hik-ing on two designated trails (including a 0.5-mile wheelchair accessible path near headquarters); group tours (by prior arrangement); and deer hunting on most of the refuge during the desig-nated season. Although camping is not permitted on the refuge, campground facilities are avail-able at such places as Old Mill State Park.

The best months for observing concentrations of migratory waterfowl are May to mid-June and late September through October. In the autumn, as many as 25,000 Canada geese, 500 snow geese, 100,000 ducks (especially mallards and gadwall), and up to 6,000 sandhill cranes can be seen on the refuge. The peak of the spring influx of warblers and other neotropical migratory birds occurs from around May 15–25. The best months to see moose are September and October.

Lodgings and meals are available in such communities as Thief River Falls, Roseau, and Grygla.

Access to the refuge headquarters from State Hwy. 32 at Holt is east 11 miles on Marshall County Hwy. 7.

Information: Agassiz NWR, 22996-290th St., NE, Middle River, MN 56737; tel.: (218) 449-4115.

Minnesota Valley presently encompasses 11,500 acres in eight separate units, within and up-river from Minneapolis, along 34 miles of the Lower Minnesota River Valley, in southeastern Minnesota. The refuge was established in 1976 to restore and protect riverine wetlands, flood-plain and hillside forest, oak savanna, and remnant prairie habitats. The valley's bluffs rise about 150 feet above the floodplain. More than 225 bird species have been recorded here.

As refuge interpreter Ed Moyer explains:

This Refuge is an urban green belt consisting mostly of marsh areas, bordered by grain terminals, highways, residential areas, office buildings, and in some places farmland. It is probably the largest natural corridor within an urban setting in America today. Bald eagles soar over rush-hour traffic and nest in cottonwood trees below office towers. Foxes and mink snatch prey outside the visitor center door; and wild turkeys and an occasional coyote visit the courtyard.

The wetland habitat includes fens, seeps, and marshy lakes along the cottonwood-lined Minnesota River. The wetlands contain sedge meadow, cattail, and river bulrush. . . .

Floodplain forest is dominated by silver maple, black willow, eastern cottonwood, and elm. . . . Remnant prairies and savannas provide nesting habitat for dabbling ducks, wild turkeys, and a variety of songbirds. . . .

The Visitor Center is a focal point of the Refuge. It features an 8,000 square-foot exhibit space, a 125-seat auditorium, two multi-purpose classrooms, a bookstore, an observation deck, and an adjacent, half-mile, loop hiking trail. Environmental education and interpretive programs are conducted in and from this facility.

Among the refuge's nine units are the following:

The LONG MEADOW LAKE UNIT is a 2,400-acre area of lakes, ponds, marshes, spring-fed streams, floodplain woodlands, and historic sites. The Minnesota Valley Refuge Visitor Center is located here.

The BLACK DOG PRESERVE is a 1,400-acre area containing tallgrass prairie and a variety of wetland habitats. Two miles of trail pass a variety of wetland habitats and remnants of tallgrass prairie.

The WILKIE UNIT is a 2,100-acre area of marshes and bottomland hardwood forest. Five miles of former farm roads and dirt trails offer opportunities for hiking and cross-country skiing to wetland and floodplain forest habitats. A major wildlife attraction of this unit is the large colony of great blue herons, containing more than 600 nests in the tops of cottonwoods and other trees (this area is closed to visitation from March 1 through August, to avoid disturbing the nesting birds).

The LOUISVILLE SWAMP UNIT is a 2,600-acre area containing remnants of tallgrass prairie, old fields, oak savanna, riparian forest, and historic stone farmsteads. Prominent among the wildlife of this unit are busy beavers that build dams that alter habitat by flooding parts of the refuge and creating new wetlands. Four established trails offer opportunities for hiking and cross-country skiing.

The Fish and Wildlife Service's habitat management activities include prescribed burning to maintain areas of grassland. Water level manipulation promotes productive wetland habitats.

The refuge is open daily during daylight hours. There is no entrance fee.

Insect repellent is advised during the warmer seasons, and visitors are cautioned to be alert for ticks.

Lodgings and meals are available throughout the Minneapolis-St. Paul area.

To reach the refuge's visitor center, at the northern end of the Long Meadow Lake Unit, exit from Interstate 494 onto Thirty-Fourth Avenue southbound, left onto East Eightieth Street for 0.25 mile, and then right (opposite the Airport Hilton Hotel). Directions to other units can be obtained by contacting the visitor center.

Information: Minnesota Valley NWR, 3815 American Blvd. E, Bloomington, MN 55425; tel.: (952) 854-5900.

Northern Tallgrass Prairie presently contains more than 2,000 acres toward a multi-unit goal of 77,000 acres within 48 counties, in western Minnesota, and within 37 counties, in northwestern Iowa. The refuge was established in 1998 to protect, restore, enhance, and manage areas of the fragmented northern tallgrass prairie and aspen parkland ecosystems.

A significant refuge objective is to encourage and develop partnerships with landowners, communities, educational institutions, local and state governments, and nonprofit organizations that will assist in permanently protecting the biological and cultural prairie heritage. An integral part of this objective, as explained by the Fish and Wildlife Service, is "To foster an awareness of the tallgrass prairie ecosystem as a unique and important part of the American landscape, and to publicize the . . . Service's efforts to preserve and restore the few remaining parcels." Acquisition of native prairie lands from willing sellers is being accomplished by purchasing either permanent easements or fee-title acquisition. Habitat management activities will include prescribed burns, prescribed grazing, native prairie reconstruction, and wetland restoration.

At the August 9, 2001, dedication of the first prairie tract purchased in fee title for the refuge, Don Hultman, the Service's Region 3 refuge supervisor, said,

I have been thinking of this thing called prairie and wondering why it has caught the imagination and the caring of so many. What is it about the tallgrass prairie that draws us like a moth to light?

Perhaps it is its rarity. We seem drawn to the underdog, whether it is in sports, politics, or everyday life. We value those things that are uncommon, unusual, and unique.

Perhaps it is the landscape itself, the Big Sky as they say in Montana, which allows the eye and the spirit to travel unimpeded, and to dream dreams as small, as large, and as diverse as the clouds that race across the prairie sky.

Perhaps it is the plants. The names of prairie plants ring out with excitement and possibility. They seem more verb than noun: big bluestem, Indian grass, prairie cord grass, switch grass, sideoats grama, needle and thread, porcupine grass, blazing star, purple coneflower, black-eyed Susan, prairie smoke, and hundreds more.

Perhaps it is the wildlife. Badgers, coyotes, red fox, jumping mice, meadow voles, deer mice, snakes and skinks, a bunch of sparrows hard to identify, bobolinks and meadowlarks that perch and sing with pure optimism, and butterflies and bugs that bite. Yet with wildlife, it is the possibilities and "what was" that is the biggest draw. Wolves, bison, elk, and grizzlies may never come back to these fragments we save, but it is here we can look and dream and remember.

But perhaps what really draws us to the tallgrass prairie is us. A brochure we did to help kick off the prairie initiative years ago said in the beginning that prairies are "places where men and women can seek to understand the hardships, challenges, and triumphs of the native and immigrant people who came before them."

We are forever part of those who came before. Prairie helps keep that link alive and, perhaps as much as any of our conservation efforts, is a shining example of our love for ourselves and for those who will follow.

The poet, Carl Sandburg, wrote, "The prairie sings to me in the forenoon and I know in the night I rest easy in the prairie arms, on the prairie heart."

In addition to the private landowners, two of the key partners in the Northern Tallgrass Prairie refuge are the Brandenburg Prairie Foundation and the Friends of the Prairie.

Visitor use activities on federally owned parts of the refuge will include wildlife observation, photography, environmental education and interpretation, fishing, and hunting.

Information: Northern Tallgrass Prairie NWR, 44843 County Rd. 19, Odessa, MN 56276; tel.: (320) 273-2191.

Rydell, consisting of 2,120 acres, was established in 1992 to protect marshes, deciduous wood-lands, and grassland for the benefit of wood ducks, migratory waterfowl, neotropical migratory songbirds, and other wildlife. The refuge is located within Polk County, in northwestern Minnesota. The Mellon Foundation acquired the land from the Leonard Rydell family and then donated it to the federal government as a national wildlife refuge. Among the more prominent species of wildlife are trumpeter swans, Canada geese, wood ducks, white-tailed deer, and beavers. Nearly 200 bird species have been recorded here.

As the U.S. Fish and Wildlife Service says, "Prior to settlement, the land which now lies within the boundaries of the Refuge was a mosaic of wetlands, bog, Maple/basswood forest and scattered grasslands—a transition zone between the tallgrass prairie zone to the west and the forest to our east. As the land was cleared and plowed for agriculture, wetlands were drained. Today, in addition to ten natural large wetlands, the Refuge has restored 5 small wetlands with 8 additional restorations planned. Plans also call for the restoration of several hundred acres of hardwood forest habitats for neotropical bird habitat."

In 1994 and 1995, a team of biologists from the University of Minnesota-Crookston conducted a baseline inventory of plants, with emphasis on native remnant communities. The biologists concluded, " . . . the Refuge is in a uniquely positioned ecotonal setting on the borders of major North American biomes." The biologists further identified Sundew Bog as the most unusual remnant community on Rydell Refuge. Numerous species of bog plants may be observed from the 400-foot elevated bog walk.

The refuge is open daily during daylight hours. There is no entrance fee. The visitor center is open on Sunday afternoons only.

Visitor activities include wildlife observation, hiking nine miles of trails (four miles are paved and wheelchair-accessible), and hunting on part of the refuge during the designated season (including a two-day wheelchair deer hunt). The best months for observing wildlife are May through June and August through October. In the winter, the trails are groomed for cross-country skiing.

Insect repellent is advised during the warmer months.

Lodgings and meals are available in such communities as Fosston, Crookston, Mahnomen, and Thief River Falls.

Access to the refuge's visitor center from U.S. Hwy. Route 2 (about three miles east of Mentor or three miles west of Erskine) is south about 2.5 miles on Polk County Rd. 210. If arriving from the south, turn north from Polk County Rd. 41 onto County Rd. 210, and north about 3.5 miles.

Information: Rydell NWR, 17788 349th St. SE, Erskine, MN 56535; tel.: (218) 687-2229.

Sherburne, consisting of 30,665 acres, was established in 1965 to restore and protect a stretch of the ecologically rich St. Francis River Valley in east-central Minnesota. The refuge is located within the biologically diverse transition zone between tallgrass prairie and eastern deciduous forest. Its wetland, oak savanna, and woodland are being restored and managed for the benefit of a great diversity of wildlife. More than 230 bird species have been recorded here.

Regarding the history of this area, the Fish and Wildlife Service says that, "Historically, the St. Francis River Basin was known as one of the finest wildlife areas in the state. Tremendous numbers of ducks, muskrats, beaver and mink were supported on small lakes and marshes near the river, which were abundant with wild rice and other wetland plants. The surrounding upland was primarily oak savanna, which provided habitat for elk, bison, and timber wolves.

"By the early 1940s, several developments had severely reduced the value of wildlife habitat in the basin. A ditch system, built in the 1920s, enhanced drainage to increase agricultural acreage. This resulted in fewer wetlands holding water throughout the year. . . . In addition, the native oak savanna upland habitat was converted to agriculture or home sites, through logging and/or plowing. In other areas, protection from fire converted the oak savanna to dense woodlands."

At the urging of local conservationists, the State of Minnesota undertook studies to determine how the river basin's once-rich wildlife habitat could be restored. But by the 1960s, it became clear that the task of acquiring and enhancing more than 30,000 acres, stretching across several hundred private properties, far exceeded the state's financial capability. Consequently, the state requested that the federal government take over the project as a national wildlife refuge.

All of Sherburne refuge's lands were acquired with revenues from the sale of Migratory Bird Hunting and Conservation Stamps (Duck Stamps). Since then, the refuge's management has included a variety of activities to restore, enhance, and maintain its three basic habitat types: wetlands, oak savanna, and deciduous-forested "big woods."

Approximately one-third of Sherburne Refuge consists of wetlands. Twenty-three of these low-lying areas are managed impoundments, which are regulated at various fluctuating levels, to promote a diversity of habitats for waterfowl and other wildlife.

The oak-savanna plant community consists of scattered individual oaks or clumps of oaks, growing amid openings and expanses of understory native prairie forbs (wildflowers) and tall grasses, such as big and little bluestems, Indiangrass, and switchgrass. The Fish and Wildlife Service carries out periodic prescribed burns as an ecologically natural and essential method of helping to restore and maintain this fire-dependent plant ecosystem.

Among the refuge's more prominent nesting birds are common loon, Canada goose, wood duck, hooded merganser, sandhill crane, bald eagle, and black tern.

The refuge is open daily during daylight hours. There is no entrance fee. The refuge headquarters is open on weekdays, except national holidays.

Visitor activities include wildlife observation (four observation decks are provided); driving the 7.3-mile Prairie's Edge Wildlife Drive (open from late April through late October); hiking on several trails (including a wheelchair-accessible path); cross-country skiing and snowshoeing; canoeing (four canoe-launching sites are available); fishing (limited to four access sites along the St. Francis River); and hunting on parts of the refuge during the designated seasons. Although camping is not permitted on the refuge, campground facilities and a picnic area are available on adjacent Sand Dunes State Forest.

Insect repellent is advised during the warmer months.

Lodgings and meals are available in Princeton, Elk River, Becker, and St. Cloud.

Access to the refuge headquarters is north four miles from Zimmerman on U.S. Hwy. 169; then, at a refuge directional sign, left four miles on County Road 9, which runs east-west through the refuge. An informational kiosk is located at the refuge entrance. From Princeton, it is south five miles on U.S. Hwy. 169 and right four miles on County Road 9.   Access to the refuge's Prairie's Edge Wildlife Drive from U.S. Hwy. 10 at Big Lake is north about eight miles on County Road 5 to Orrock (where a refuge informational kiosk is located at the junction of County Roads 5 and 4), continuing north 1.2 miles from Orrock on County Road 5, and right onto the entrance road.

Information: Sherburne NWR, 17076-293rd Ave., Zimmerman, MN 55398; tel.: (763) 389-3323.

Tamarac, containing 42,724 acres, was established in 1938 to protect ecologically important wetlands for large concentrations of migratory waterfowl and other wildlife within an area of glacial lakes, in northwestern Minnesota. This refuge lies within a transition zone of the boreal forest to the north, northern deciduous forest to the south, and tallgrass prairie to the west. Tamarac's diverse habitats include forest-covered, gently rolling hills; marshes, bogs, and shrubby swamps; rivers and streams; and 21 lakes.

For many centuries, Native Americans treasured this area for hunting, fishing, maple-sugaring, and harvesting the nutrient-rich wild rice that grows extensively in marshes and along the edges of lakes and rivers. The Dakota Sioux Indians formerly occupied the area, followed by the Chippewa. The northern half of the refuge is located within the White Earth Indian Reservation, which was established in 1867.

In the late 1930s and 1940s, initial development of the refuge was carried out by the Civilian Conservation Corps. In the 1960s, assistance was provided by a Job Corps Conservation Center, and in the 1970s and 1980s, further help was provided by the Young Adult Conservation Corps.

The Fish and Wildlife Service carries out a number of important habitat management activities. Prominent among these is the regulation of water levels on seven of the refuge's lakes, to promote the growth of wild rice for the benefit of migratory waterfowl and the Chippewas (see the Rice Lake NWR text for description of traditional Native American ricing, which occurs on Tamarac refuge for about a month, beginning in mid-August).

Other management activities include prescribed burning of forested habitat to reduce unnatural and hazardous fuel overloads, and selective cutting and follow-up prescribed burning to maintain woodland diversity. Efforts are also being made to increase age diversity of aspen stands. Grassland habitat is also enhanced and maintained with the aid of prescribed burns, as well as haying in some circumstances; and efforts are being made to reseed areas with native grass species.

Among Tamarac's great diversity of wildlife are large concentrations of ducks during the autumn migration; a nesting population of the trumpeter swan, a species that was successfully reintroduced in 1987; many pairs of nesting bald eagles; spectacular numbers of warblers and other neotropical migratory songbirds that reach peak concentrations around the middle of May; and a resident pack of the eastern gray wolf, which has annually produced young in recent years.

Establishment of the refuge was made possible with revenues from the sale of Migratory Bird Hunting and Conservation Stamps (Duck Stamps). Several private organizations have assisted in the refuge's efforts to enhance habitats, including the Ruffed Grouse Society, Minnesota Deer Hunters Association, Ducks Unlimited, Inc., and the Minnesota Waterfowlers Association. The Tamarac Interpretive Association is a nonprofit educational support group that is providing assistance to the refuge.

Refuge Manager Jay Johnson says, "I believe Tamarac to be one of the National Wildlife Refuge System's 'crown jewels' and as ecologically diverse as any areas in the Upper Midwest. It contains an unusual mix of woodland/prairie flora and fauna, and remains as near pristine as any refuge in the lower 48 states." More than 250 bird species have been recorded here. The height of the usually spectacular autumn foliage color occurs during the latter part of September.

The refuge is open daily during daylight hours. There is no entrance fee. The visitor center, which features interpretive exhibits, interpretive programs in its auditorium, a bookshop, and an observation deck, is open on weekdays, except national holidays, and is also open on Saturday and Sunday afternoons during the summer months.

Visitor activities include wildlife observation, interpretive programs, driving the five-mile Blackbird Auto Tour Route (open from May through October, as road conditions allow), hiking on several trails, cross-country skiing on the ungroomed Pine Lake Ski Trail, snowshoeing, picnicking (a picnic area is provided), boating (boat-launching sites are provided at lakes that are open to summer fishing), fishing (under state and/or tribal regulations), and hunting on parts of the refuge during the designated seasons. Bicycling and horseback riding are permitted on the auto tour and refuge service roads. ATVs, snowmobiles, personal watercraft, waterskiing, and swimming are not permitted on the refuge. In 1992, a Challenge Grant project with the White Earth Indian Reservation led to the installation of a (wheelchair-accessible) fishing pier on the shore of Many Point Lake, at the northeast corner of the refuge. Although camping is not permitted on the refuge, campground facilities are available at many nearby locations.

Insect repellent is advised during the warmer months.

Lodgings and meals are available in such communities as Detroit Lakes, Park Rapids, and Mahnomen.

Access to the Tamarac NWR visitor center from Detroit Lakes on U.S. Hwy. 10 is east eight miles on State Hwy. 34, and left onto County Hwy. 29 for ten miles.

Information: Tamarac NWR, 35704 County Hwy. 26, Rochert, MN 56578; tel.: (218) 847-2641.

Upper Mississippi River National Wildlife and Fish Refuge comprises roughly 230,000 acres in four districts along more than 260 miles of the Mississippi River, from just upriver from Wabasha, Minn., southward to just upriver from Rock Island, Ill. This refuge was established in 1924 for the benefit of migratory birds, game animals, furbearers, wildflowers, aquatic plants, fish, and other aquatic life. It manages ecologically vital components of the river floodplain, including wooded islands, open water, river channels, meandering sloughs, marshes and other wetlands, bottomland forest, and remnants of sand prairie.

In 1930, the U.S. Army Corps of Engineers was directed by Congress to construct a series of 26 locks and dams between Minneapolis, Minn., and St. Louis, Mo. The reservoir-like "pools" that were created behind these structures provided a nine-foot-deep navigation channel to accommodate commercial barge traffic. These pools also greatly altered much of the refuge's habitats, forming three basic ecological zones. Immediately upriver from each lock and dam, there are open and deep expanses of water, attracting large concentrations of diving ducks. The central zone of each pool consists of shallow water with extensive marsh habitat that attracts large concentrations of dabbling ducks. The upper stretch of each pool consists of the braided-stream zone, in which river channels, narrow cuts, and meandering sloughs wind between bottomland forested islands—resembling conditions prior to the construction of the locks and dams.

The refuge's units, in downriver sequence, are the WINONA DISTRICT, including pools 4, 5, 5A, and 6, extending along the river in southeastern Minnesota and western Wisconsin; LACROSSE DISTRICT, including pools 7 and 8, along the river in southeastern Minnesota and western Wisconsin; MCGREGOR DISTRICT, including pools 9, 10, and 11, along the river in the southeastern tip of Minnesota, western Wisconsin, and northeastern Iowa; and SAVANNA DISTRICT, including pools 12, 13, and 14, along the river in the southwestern tip of Wisconsin, northwestern Illinois, and eastern Iowa. Ten detailed pool maps are available at the refuge headquarters.

Since creation of the locks, dams, and pools, the quality of many wildlife habitats has been gradually declining. As the Fish and Wildlife Service explains, "Sediment is filling valuable backwaters, islands are eroding, and vegetation is disappearing from the river." In an effort to restore these degraded habitats, Congress funded the Corps of Engineers' Environmental Management Program in 1986, to be jointly implemented by the Fish and Wildlife Service and the natural resources agencies of the four adjoining states. Dikes and other water-control structures have been installed, by which water levels are regulated for the benefit of waterfowl and other wildlife; islands have been restored and protected from erosion; and water flows have been enhanced. As a result, thousands of acres of habitat have been restored.

Why is the word *fish* included in the name of this refuge? According to the Fish and Wildlife Service,

. . . this refuge was established . . . as the result of a victorious battle to save critical Mississippi River bass spawning areas from destruction, so the name makes sense.

The richness and diversity of the refuge's water areas are unequaled in the Midwest. The main channel, with its navigation dams and wing dams, side channels, sloughs, chutes, backwater lakes and ponds, marsh areas, flooded bottomland forest and tributaries make this a complex and magnificent home for at least 118 species of fish.

The refuge is accessed primarily by water and is open daily. There is no entrance fee. There are two refuge visitor centers: in McGregor, Ia., and Thompson, Ill. The LaCrosse District office, in Onalaska, Wis., includes exhibits in the Resource Center. The refuge headquarters and Winona District office are located in downtown Winona, Minn.

Visitor activities include wildlife observation; interpretive and environmental education programs; driving an interconnected series of bordering highways known as the Great River Road (offering numerous overlooks); hiking trails that are located at various places along the river; picnicking, primitive camping; canoeing, kayaking, and boating (numerous boat-launching ramps are provided); cross-country skiing and snowshoeing; fishing and ice-fishing; trapping; and hunting on parts of the refuge during the designated seasons.

More than 300 species of birds have been recorded on the refuge, which has been designated as a Globally Important Bird Area. Prominent among them are tundra swans, as many as 25,000 of which pause on the refuge to rest and feed during their spring and autumn migrations—notably in an area about 15 miles north of Winona, Minn.; numerous species of ducks, including up to 400,000 canvasbacks; hundreds of bald eagles; 16 rookeries of nesting great blue herons and great egrets; and multitudes of warblers and other neotropical migratory songbirds that funnel through the river corridor's bottomland forests during April and May.

Insect repellent is advised during the warmer months. Visitors are urged to be alert for ticks.

Lodgings and meals are available in numerous communities along the river corridor.

Access into the refuge is from numerous boat-launching sites; and there are many roadside turnouts from which to view the refuge and its wildlife.

Information: Upper Mississippi River National Wildlife and Fish Refuge, 51 East Fourth St., Room 101, Winona, MN 55987; tel.: (507) 452-4232.

Mississippi

Hillside, encompassing 15,572 acres, is located in west-central Mississippi. The refuge was established in 1975 to restore, enhance, and protect an ecologically important area of bottomland hardwood forest, cypress-tupelo brakes, buttonbush and swamp privet thickets, and areas of cultivated crops that are partly unharvested for the benefit of wildlife. These habitats attract large concentrations of wintering waterfowl, nesting wood ducks, wild turkeys, numerous species of neotropical migratory songbirds, white-tailed deer, bobcats, river otters, beavers, alligators, and other wildlife.

Establishment of this refuge was made possible partly with revenues from the sale of Migratory Bird Hunting and Conservation Stamps (Duck Stamps). Ducks Unlimited, Inc. has helped enhance more than 400 acres of the refuge's wetland habitat.

Matt Young, senior writer for *Ducks Unlimited*, cherishes his memories of many visits to this refuge: "My father and I hunted ducks several times a year at Hillside throughout the 1980s. Two things stand out in my recollection of this watery wilderness. First was its unique location nestled against the loess bluffs on the very edge of the Mississippi Delta. From parts of the refuge, you can gaze up into the forested hills rising to the east—quite a view for Mississippi. The other thing I remember was the vastness of its flooded bottomlands. We would launch our canoe from the levee and then paddle seemingly for miles through expanses of flooded cypress, tupelo, buttonbush, and cane to inaccessible areas that were rarely hunted. I have especially fond memories of gliding silently through the flooded woods just before dawn and listening to hundreds of mallards, gadwalls, wigeons, green-winged teal, and wood ducks calling all around us in the darkness. When Hillside is flooded and full of ducks, it is truly a magical place."

The refuge is open daily during daylight hours. There is no entrance fee.

Visitor activities include wildlife observation, hiking on the 0.6-mile Alligator Slough Nature Trail and on refuge roads and levees, and hunting during the designated seasons. Camping is not permitted on the refuge, but facilities are available nearby. November through April is the best time for birdwatching.

Even though alligators are generally afraid of people, visitors are cautioned to stay a safe distance from them and to be alert for venomous snakes, fire ants, chiggers, and ticks. Insect repellent is advised.

Lodgings and meals are available in such communities as Yazoo City and Greenwood.

Access to the refuge is north 13 miles from Yazoo City on U.S. Hwy. 49E, turning right at Thornton and continuing for 5 miles.

Information: Hillside NWR, c/o Yazoo National Wildlife Refuges Complex, 1562 Providence Rd., Cruger, MS 38924; tel.: (662) 839-2638.

Mississippi Sandhill Crane, containing more than 19,000 acres in four units, was established in 1975. The refuge provides protection for the critically endangered Mississippi sandhill crane and for vital remnants of the bird's wet-pine savanna habitat, in southeastern Mississippi. This bird is a non-migratory subspecies whose original range extended along the Gulf Coast plain, from the western Florida panhandle westward through Alabama and Mississippi to Louisiana. As the wet-pine savanna was degraded or destroyed during the latter half of the 20th century, the crane's numbers dwindled to thirty or forty individuals by the 1970s. Today's population of about 100 to 120 individuals is limited to a relatively small area on and adjacent to this refuge.

Research has revealed that this sandhill crane, although similar to the two other non-migratory and three migratory subspecies, has certain physiological, morphological, and behavioral differences from the others. For instance, they have noticeably darker gray plumage that gives greater emphasis to their white cheek patch. These red-crowned birds stand three to four feet tall and have a wingspread of roughly six feet. Their call is a rolling, trumpeting sound that can be heard for at least a mile.

The refuge's savanna habitat consists of extensive wet prairies with many grasses and sedges, and a tremendously rich variety of low-growing herbaceous species, including native orchids and an array of carnivorous plants. Scattered across these open expanses are occasional longleaf pines and pond cypresses (a variant of the bald-cypress). One of the major management programs of this refuge is the restoration and maintenance of its savanna habitat, with periodic prescription burns, timber sales, and selective thinning. To restore the savanna ecosystem, which has been unnaturally invaded by dense growths of trees and shrubs as the result of fire suppression, planting, and ditching for pulpwood, some ecologists are urging that as much as 90 percent of the slash pines be removed.

The list of other bird attracted to the savannas includes such species as Bachman's sparrow, red-headed woodpecker, brown-headed nuthatch, American kestrel, and many wintering sparrows, including Henslow's and LeConte's. The refuge has been designated as a Globally Important Bird Area by the American Bird Conservancy.

A significant aspect of this refuge is that its establishment was the first legal use of Section 7 of the Endangered Species Act of 1973. This section provides for "taking such action necessary to ensure that actions authorized, funded, or carried out . . . [by the federal government] . . . do not jeopardize the continued existence of such endangered species and threatened species or result in the destruction or modification of habitat of such species. . . ."

In 1975, the National Wildlife Federation filed a lawsuit that succeeded in blocking construction of federally funded Interstate 10 through critical Mississippi sandhill crane habitat, until steps were taken to provide for the continued existence of the cranes. The Nature Conservancy assisted by acquiring much of the refuge's initial acreage.

The refuge is open on weekdays during daylight hours, except national holidays. There is no entrance fee.

Visitor activities include wildlife observation, environmental education programs at the visitor center, hiking on two trails, and picnicking (near the visitor center). During the annual

Crane Festival (contact the refuge for the date), visitors may participate in prescribed-fire and other management demonstrations.

To avoid disturbing the cranes, most of the refuge is not open to visitation. However, refuge staff and trained volunteers lead groups (with reservations) on tours that may include a visit to an elevated viewing blind. Camping is not permitted on the refuge, but campground facilities are available at a number of nearby locations, including Gulf Islands National Seashore and Shepard State Park. Fishing, trapping, and hunting are not permitted on the refuge.

Visitors are cautioned to be alert for venomous snakes, fire ants, chiggers, and ticks.

Lodgings and meals are available in Ocean Springs, Biloxi, Moss Point, Pascagoula, and Gautier.

Access to the refuge from Exit 61 on I-10 is 0.5 mile north on the Gautier-Vancleave Rd. and right onto the refuge.

Information: Mississippi Sandhill Crane NWR, 7200 Crane Lane, Gautier, MS 39553; tel. (228) 497-6322.

Noxubee, encompassing 48,026 acres, was established in 1940 to restore and protect an area that had previously been seriously degraded by overgrazing, intensive agricultural development, and soil erosion along the Noxubee River (pronounced NOX-u-bee), in east-central Mississippi. Following decades of conservation enhancement, this refuge has become a model of forest and wildlife-habitat restoration.

More than three-quarters of the refuge consists of upland pine woodland, bottomland hardwood forest, and seasonally flooded cypress swamp. Among the numerous species of wildlife inhabiting these forested lands are wild turkey, northern bobwhite, and the federally listed endangered red-cockaded woodpecker. In its program to enhance populations of this habitat-specific woodpecker, the Fish and Wildlife Service manages areas of pine woodland, using prescription burning and selective thinning, to maintain open stands with mature trees, in which the bird creates nesting cavities. Some man-made cavities are also provided. (See further description of this species in the Carolina Sandhills NWR text).

Noxubee Refuge contains 1,200-acre Bluff Lake and 600-acre Loakfoma Lake, plus 16 smaller impoundments, beaver ponds, and streams. These wetlands provide important resting and feeding habitat for wintering waterfowl; resident and migratory Canada geese; wading birds including the wood stork, hundreds of which visit the refuge in late summer; and bald eagles that prey upon fish and weakened ducks. More than 250 species of birds have been recorded on the refuge. Alligators are near the northern edge of their range here.

As part of the refuge's waterfowl habitat management, several low levees have been built, allowing for periodic winter flooding of some bottomland hardwood forest—a practice known as "green-timber reservoir management." The refuge is also taking steps to restore part of the vanishing "Alabama Black Belt Prairie." Morgan Hill Overlook Trail offers visitors an opportunity to hike through this ecologically important habitat.

Establishment of the refuge was made possible partly with revenues from the sale of Migratory Bird Hunting and Conservation Stamps (Duck Stamps). Ducks Unlimited, Inc. has assisted with important habitat enhancement projects.

The refuge is open daily during daylight hours. Its office, overlooking Bluff Lake, is open on weekdays, except for national holidays. There is no entrance fee.

Visitor activities include wildlife observation, environmental education programs (by pre-arrangement), driving some of the refuge roads, hiking on a number of trails, watching wildlife from (wheelchair-accessible) viewing platforms, canoeing and boating, fishing, and hunting during the designated seasons. Although camping is not permitted on the refuge, campground facilities are available nearby.

Even though alligators are generally afraid of people, visitors are cautioned to stay a safe distance from them and to be alert for venomous snakes, fire ants, chiggers, and ticks. Insect repellent is advised.

Lodgings and meals are available in Starkville.

Access to the refuge from Starkville is south 12 miles from State Highways 12/25 (at Hampton Inn) on Oktoc Road and right about 6 miles on the dirt road to the refuge office; or south 15 miles on State Hwy. 25 and left 10 miles on a dirt road.

Information: Noxubee NWR, 2970 Bluff Lake Rd., Brooksville, MS 39739; tel.: (662) 323-5548.

Missouri

Mingo, comprising 21,676 acres, was established in 1945 to restore and protect Mingo Swamp, in southeastern Missouri. More than 7,700 acres of the refuge have been designated as a unit of the National Wilderness Preservation System. In the early part of the 20th century, largely unsuccessful efforts were made to drain this ecologically rich swamp, log off the timber, and convert the land to agricultural production.

As the Fish and Wildlife Service says,

The condition of the land was deplorable. In the previous fifty years, man had reduced a beautiful swamp, lush with the growth of plants and alive with animals, into a burnt and eroded wasteland.

Through careful management, most of the natural plants and animals were restored. Native trees have replaced much of the brush and briers, and a canoe trip down the Mingo River will now reveal little to the casual observer of the abuses to this land in years past. Deer, wild turkey, bobcat, and beaver have returned and are plentiful. The . . . refuge is now able to accomplish its primary objective; providing food and shelter for migratory waterfowl.

This refuge encompasses the only remaining large tract of the linear basin that was formed when the Mississippi River abandoned its former channel roughly 18,000 years ago. In addition to its swamp and bottomland-forest habitat, the refuge also contains upland forests and fields, and rocky bluffs.

Establishment of the refuge was made possible partly with revenues from the sale of Migratory Bird Hunting and Conservation Stamps (Duck Stamps).

The refuge is open daily during daylight hours. An entrance fee is charged. The visitor center is open on weekdays, except national holidays, and is also open on weekends from March 1 through June 15 and from September 1 through November.

Visitor activities include wildlife observation; driving a seasonal auto tour route; hiking on several trails, including a (wheelchair-accessible) boardwalk nature trail; picnicking; canoeing; fishing; and hunting during the designated season. Another fifty miles of refuge roads, dikes, and levees that are closed to motor vehicles are available for hiking from March 15 through September.

Visitors are cautioned to be alert for venomous snakes. Insect repellent is advised during the warmer months.

Lodgings and meals are available in Puxico, Wappapello, Poplar Bluff, and Dexter.

Access to the refuge from Poplar Bluff is east 14 miles on U.S. Hwy. 60 and left onto State Hwy. 51 for 11 miles; or from Dexter it is west 13 miles on U.S. Hwy. 60 and right onto State Hwy. 51 for 11 miles.

Information: Mingo NWR, 24279 State Hwy. 51, Puxico, MO 63960; tel.: (573) 222-3589.

Squaw Creek, encompassing 7,350 acres, was established in 1935 to restore, enhance, and protect more than 3,000 acres of ecologically important wetland habitat for the benefit of migratory waterfowl and other wildlife. Initially called a "migratory waterfowl refuge," it is located along the bluffs-bordered eastern edge of the Missouri River floodplain, in the northwest corner of Missouri. Other habitats include 350 acres of moist-soil units; more than 1,500 acres of woodland; 2,000 acres of upland grassland, including small remnants of native tallgrass prairie; and more than 500 acres of cultivated cropland. More than 300 bird species have been recorded on the refuge.

The refuge attracts large concentrations of lesser snow geese—sometimes as many as 300,000 of them stopping to rest and feed during the autumn migration. Both the white and blue morphs (phases) make up this spectacular show, which peaks in November. Up to 100,000 migrating ducks of numerous species also pause at the refuge, along with 1,000 or more American white pelicans. From mid-November into January, approximately 200 to 250 bald eagles commonly gather here, preying upon fish and weakened waterfowl and roosting in the large cottonwood trees. This is one of the largest wintering eagle concentrations in the lower 48 states.

Management of this refuge's wetlands is accomplished by a system of dikes, dams, and other water-control structures—a few of which were built by the Civilian Conservation Corps in the mid-1930s. A dozen separately regulated areas of marsh habitat contain ten designated pools. Two of the refuge's impoundments are permanent pools, with such marsh vegetation as cattails, bulrushes, arrowhead, and American lotus that provide important habitat for waterfowl, and marsh and other waterbirds. Another impoundment consists of a moist-soil green-tree reservoir, an area of woodland that is seasonally flooded for the benefit of such species as wood ducks.

The refuge's other habitat management activities include periodic prescribed burning, mowing, and haying, to maintain the health of grasslands and control the growth of invasive woody plants. Under cooperative agreements with local farmers, a portion of cultivated crops of corn, soybeans, and wheat are left unharvested for the benefit of wildlife.

Establishment of the Squaw Creek refuge was made possible partly with revenues from the sale of Migratory Bird Hunting and Conservation Stamps (Duck Stamps).

The refuge is open daily during daylight hours. There is no entrance fee. The refuge head-quarters/visitor contact station is open on weekdays, except national holidays. Open house weekends are held during spring and autumn migrations.

Visitor activities include wildlife observation—notably from a (wheelchair-accessible) observation tower overlooking 900-acre Eagle Pool, viewing interpretive exhibits in the visitor contact station, environmental education programs for teachers and student groups, driving the ten-mile Wild Goose Interpretive Auto Tour Loop (periods of rain can make refuge roads impassable), hiking on several trails (including a wheelchair-accessible path), fishing, and hunting (managed deer hunts to reduce an overpopulation) on part of the refuge during the designated seasons. Although camping is not permitted on the refuge, campground facilities are available at nearby Big Lake State Park.

In early December, the refuge and the Missouri Department of Conservation co-sponsor "Squaw Creek Eagle Days," a weekend event featuring special educational programs, displays, and eagle viewing opportunities.

Insect repellent is advised during the warmer months. Visitors are cautioned to be alert for rattlesnakes. The Fish and Wildlife Service also asks that special care be taken while driving on refuge roads, to avoid running over the state-listed endangered eastern massasauga or swamp rattlesnake (that commonly measures about two feet long). This species is described as "a small, timid rattlesnake that lives in the big river floodplains of northern Missouri. . . . Massasaugas are primarily encountered by visitors during the spring and fall."

Lodgings and meals are available in such communities as Mound City and St. Joseph.

Access to the refuge from Exit 79 on I-29 is west 2.5 miles on U.S. Hwy. 159.

Information: Squaw Creek NWR, P.O. Box 158, Mound City, MO 64470; tel.: (660) 442-3187.

Montana

Benton Lake, comprising 12,383 acres, was established in 1929 to enhance and protect a 5,000-acre, closed-basin, cattail-and-bulrush marsh that is surrounded by a mountain-framed expanse of gently rolling, shortgrass prairie. The refuge, which is just north of Great Falls, in north-central Montana, is a mecca for large concentrations of migratory and nesting waterfowl, shore-birds, and other waterbirds. More than 200 bird species have been recorded here.

During the spring and autumn migrations, as many as 5,000 tundra swans, 100,000 snow and Ross's geese, 20,000 Canada geese, 100,000 ducks, 50,000 shorebirds, and some bald eagles and peregrine falcons pause at Benton Lake's marsh. As early as mid-March, large concentrations of tundra swans, pintails, and mallards arrive as the lake's ice is melting. During the summer months, roughly 20,000 ducklings of a dozen species are hatched—twice that number in especially favorable years. Species that nest in colonies, such as Franklin's gulls and eared grebes, raise their young here.

The star attraction of the grassland habitat is the sharp-tailed grouse. Males perform their incredible courtship displays in the spring (described in the Medicine Lake NWR text). Observation blinds are available in April and May for viewing and photographing the grouse (reservations required). Other common grassland wildlife includes pronghorn, badgers, burrowing owls, horned larks, and chestnut-collared longspurs.

During the first 28 years of the refuge's existence, this priceless wetland habitat was unfortunately dry more often than it contained water. In 1957, thanks largely to the urging of the Cascade County Wildlife Association, congressional funding was obtained, by which the marsh became a more consistently wet habitat. A pump and pipeline were constructed that brought Muddy Creek water to the refuge, and dikes were built, dividing the marsh into sections for easier water-level management.

Subsequently, the Fish and Wildlife Service has divided the marsh still further, into eight diked units, and has installed an interior pumping system. These improvements have resulted in enhanced water management that promotes the growth of submergent and emergent aquatic plants for the benefit of waterbirds and other wildlife. This enhanced water management flexibility also enables the refuge to control outbreaks of botulism—an often fatal poisoning of water birds caused by a toxin that is produced by the bacterium, *Clostridium botulinum*.

Areas of former farmlands have been restored to a mixture of grasses and forbs, providing nesting habitat for waterfowl and other species. Roughly once every decade, these areas are revitalized by such management tools as haying, prescription burning, grazing, and reseeding.

Four mountain ranges provide a distant scenic backdrop for this refuge. To the west are the Rocky Mountains, to the east the Highwoods, to the southeast the Little Belts, and to the south the Big Belts.

Establishment of this refuge was made possible partly with revenues from the sale of Migratory Bird Hunting and Conservation Stamps (Duck Stamps). Ducks Unlimited, Inc. has helped with a number of important habitat enhancement projects, including the construction of several water-control structures.

The refuge is open daily during daylight hours. There is no entrance fee.

Visitor activities include wildlife observation, photography, driving the refuge's nine-mile Prairie Marsh Wildlife Drive and Lower Marsh Road (the latter rough is open from July 15 through September), hiking on a short trail and elsewhere, and limited hunting on part of the refuge during the designated seasons. Although camping is not permitted on the refuge, campground facilities are available in Great Falls and in the Lewis and Clark National Forest.

Visitors are cautioned to be alert for prairie rattlesnakes, and for the possibility of sudden weather changes and extremely strong Chinook winds that frequently blow across from the Rocky Mountains in spring and autumn. Insect repellent is advised during the warmer months.

Lodgings and meals are available in Great Falls.

Access to the refuge from Great Falls is north about a mile on U.S. Hwy. 87, and left at the directional sign onto Bootlegger Trail.

Information: Benton Lake NWR, 922 Bootlegger Trail, Great Falls, MT 59404; tel,: (406) 727-7400.

Charles M. Russell, containing 1.1 million acres, was established in 1936 as the Fort Peck National Game Range and re-designated in 1976 as the Charles M. Russell (CMR) National Wildlife Refuge. It encompasses a 125-mile stretch of Fort Peck Lake and the Missouri River, upstream from Fort Peck Dam in north-central Montana. From 1933 to 1939, this earth-filled dam was constructed by the U.S. Army Corps of Engineers and the Public Works Administration to serve as a flood control and navigation enhancement project. Its waters inundated about 245,000 acres of river, riparian habitat, and lower tributary valleys.

The refuge is named for the cowboy artist Charles Russell (1864-1926), who arrived in Montana at the age of 16, was employed as a range rider and herder, and lived with and deeply respected the Native Americans. In numerous watercolor and oil paintings, as well as bronze sculptures, he dramatically portrayed the wildlife, Indians, cowboys, and magnificent landscapes of this region.

The refuge overlays the huge Fort Peck reservoir and protects a variety of adjacent ecologically significant habitats: prairie grassland, wooded coulees, river bottom (riparian) woodlands, and colorful and scenically spectacular eroded breaks, mesas, and badlands. The steep-sided Missouri River Breaks were created over a long period of geologic time by the river as it cut a deep, winding channel into a relatively flat plain and by side drainages dropping down to meet the river and eroding steep ravines and gullies, known as coulees.

Upstream from the reservoir, the western end of the refuge contains an inspiringly beautiful, 35-mile, free-flowing stretch of the Missouri. The upper dozen miles of this part of the river (upstream from the U.S. Route 191 bridge) are within the lower end of the 149-mile Upper Missouri National Wild and Scenic River. This area provides outstanding opportunities for float trips by canoe and raft. For information on the latter, visitors are urged to contact the U.S. Bureau of Land Management, P.O. Box 1160, Lewistown, MT 59457; tel.: (406) 538-7461.

From 1804 to 1806, the 29-man Corps of Discovery, under the leadership of Meriwether Lewis and George Rogers Clark, carried out the instructions of President Thomas Jefferson, "to explore the Missouri river, & such principal stream of it, as, by its course & communication with the waters of the Pacific Ocean, may offer the most direct & practicable water communication across this continent, for the purposes of commerce." The Lewis and Clark Expedition journeyed up the Missouri on a 55-foot-long keelboat with a large square sail and 22 oars, and on two smaller, canoe-like pirogues, with sails and 7 oars. In the stretch of river that is within today's CMR refuge, the explorers camped at 16 sites on the nights of May 9 through 24, 1805.

Today, upriver from the reservoir, the refuge contains much the same landscapes as seen and described by the Lewis and Clark Expedition. The area is dominated by four main vegetative types. Nearly two-thirds of the refuge land consists of sagebrush-greasewood-grassland. About one-third is the ponderosa pine-juniper. Less than a mere 2 percent is grassland-deciduous shrub. And less than 1 percent of the land consists of the ecologically rich, riparian-deciduous habitat of cottonwoods and willows, along the river and in the coulees.

Although grizzly bears and bison (buffalo) no longer inhabit this part of Montana, visitors can still see elk (reintroduced from Yellowstone National Park in the early 1950s), deer, pronghorn, Rocky Mountain bighorn sheep (introduced in 1980; the original Audubon bighorn became extinct), beavers, and prairie dogs. Large numbers of sharp-tailed grouse and greater sage-grouse perform their amazing courtship rituals in the spring (see expanded description of sharp-tail grouse courtship in the Bowdoin NWR text and of sage-grouse in the Seedskadee NWR text).

The refuge is open daily. There is no entrance fee. Refuge headquarters, located on Airport Rd. in Lewistown, is open on weekdays, except national holidays. Some of the land along the north shore of the reservoir, including the peninsula within the lake's large U-turn, lies within the UL Bend National Wildlife Refuge. Much of this area has been established as a unit of the National Wilderness Preservation System. This area is often one of the best places to see sage-grouse.

Visitor activities include wildlife observation; driving the twenty-mile, gravel, interpretive tour drive and numerous dirt roads (many of the latter require a high-clearance four-wheel-drive vehicle); hiking (no established trails); horseback riding; camping (throughout the refuge, at James Kipp Recreation Area, and at a number of Corps of Engineers recreation area campgrounds); boating (boat-launching ramps are provided); river rafting and canoeing; fishing; and hunting (on parts of the refuge during the designated seasons). More than 235 bird species have been recorded on the refuge.

Visitors are cautioned to be alert for western (prairie) rattlesnakes and for the possibility of rapid weather changes and very strong Chinook winds in the spring and autumn. Visitors should carry sufficient water, especially when backpacking in the remote backcountry.

Lodgings and meals are available in Lewistown, Malta, Glasgow, and Jordan.

Access to the entrance of the refuge's auto tour road from Lewistown is north 67 miles on U.S. Hwy. 191; or from Malta it is south 66 miles on Hwy. 191. To reach Fort Peck Dam, it is south 15 miles from U.S. Hwy. 2 at Glasgow on State Hwy. 24; or from State Hwy. 200, it is north 60 miles on Hwy. 24.

Information: Charles M. Russell NWR, P.O. Box 110, Lewistown, MT 59457; tel.: (406) 538-8706.

Lee Metcalf, containing 2,800 acres, was established in 1963 to enhance and protect an ecologically important area of Bitterroot River bottomland, nestled within the spectacularly scenic, mountain-framed Bitterroot Valley of western Montana. This refuge includes ponds, sloughs, meadows, marsh, and woodlands of pine and riparian cottonwoods. These habitats attract a great diversity of wildlife, including numerous migratory birds and a nesting pair of bald eagles. To the west, the rugged, snow-capped Bitterroot Mountains rise dramatically from this long, narrow valley; and along the east are the Sapphire Mountains.

The refuge is named for former U.S. Congressman and Senator Lee Metcalf, who for many years was an outstanding legislative leader in promoting wildlife conservation. In the words of author James B. Trefethen in his book, *An American Crusade for Wildlife*, published in 1975 by the Boone and Crockett Club, Missoula,

The [Eisenhower Administration's] Republican choice for Secretary of the Interior was Douglas McKay, a wealthy automobile dealer . . . whose sole qualification for office was a substantial contribution to the Republican war chest. One of McKay's first steps was to introduce the spoils system to the U.S. Fish and Wildlife Service. . . .

As a result of the Administration's threats to dedicated wildlife lands, Congressman Lee Metcalf of Montana introduced a bill early in 1956 to exempt the national wildlife refuges from oil and gas exploration. Metcalf was joined by Congressman Henry S. Reuss of Wisconsin and Senator Hubert Humphrey of Minnesota, who introduced identical bills to stay McKay's open-handed generosity. These three congressional leaders became the nucleus of a conservation bloc that thwarted the virtual dismantling of the American conservation system under McKay's leadership.

Seven years later, the then United States senator was instrumental in the establishment of the Ravalli National Wildlife Refuge. In 1978, this refuge was renamed to honor the late senator for his many years of conservation accomplishments.

Among the more prominent wildlife of the refuge are waterfowl such as Canada geese and twenty species of ducks. Ospreys, wintering bald eagles, magpies, white-tailed deer, and moose also inhabit the refuge. Ospreys and Canada geese may be seen nesting atop dead pine and cottonwood trees. More than 230 birds species have been recorded here.

Managing the refuge's fishery resources is another priority for the benefit of many fish-eating birds, such as the osprey, bald eagle, and great blue heron. Other management programs include controlling a number of non-native plant species such as hound's tongue, with periodic prescription burns, mowing, reseeding, and grazing.

One of the refuge's native wildflowers is the attractive but rarely seen bitterroot. This low-growing little plant, with bright rose, pink, or white blossoms, is the official Montana state flower. Its generic Latin name, *Lewisia*, honors the Lewis and Clark Expedition's Captain Meriwether Lewis, who collected samples of the plant as he journeyed down the Bitterroot Valley on September 9–11, 1805. Its species Latin name, *rediviva*, means "revived" or "brought to life." This plant was once gathered for its edible, starchy root by the Salish-speaking Native Americans who formerly lived in this valley.

Of historical interest is the Whaley Homestead, a white clapboard house built here by early settlers in 1885. This unusual house is a hand-hewn log structure that is sided over to give the appearance of a more expensive frame home.

Establishment of this refuge was made possible partly with revenues from the sale of Migratory Bird Hunting and Conservation Stamps (Duck Stamps). Ducks Unlimited, Inc. has assisted with important habitat enhancement projects.

The refuge is open daily during daylight hours. There is no entrance fee.

Visitor activities include wildlife observation, educational programs at a teaching pavilion, driving the refuge road to the Whaley Homestead historic site and to the 160-acre Bitterroot River Recreation Area, hiking on two miles of trails in the latter area and a (wheelchair-accessible) path along the river, picnicking at a picnic area by the river, fishing along the river and within the sloughs (a wheelchair-accessible observation and fishing deck overlooks one of the sloughs), and hunting of deer (bow-and-arrow) and waterfowl on parts of the refuge during the designated seasons (two wheelchair-accessible blinds are available). Camping is not permitted on the refuge, but campground facilities are available in the nearby Bitterroot National Forest.

Visitors are cautioned to stay an especially safe distance from the high, fast-moving flood-waters of the river during springtime.

Lodgings and meals are available in Stevensville, Hamilton, Darby, and Missoula.

Access to the refuge from Missoula is south about 25 miles on U.S. Hwy. 93, left onto the road across the river to Stevensville, left onto East Side Hwy. (State Hwy. 203), and left at the refuge sign onto Wildfowl Lane; or north from Salmon, Ida., 114 miles on U.S. Hwy. 93, over 6,995-foot Lost Trail Pass, to the Stevensville turnoff. Refuge headquarters is located at 115 West Third St., Stevensville.

Information: Lee Metcalf NWR, 4567 Wildfowl Lane, Stevensville, MT 59870; tel.: (406) 777-5552.

Medicine Lake, encompassing 31,660 acres in two units, was established in 1935 to enhance and protect an ecologically important prairie pothole area of lakes and ponds, impoundments, marshes, brush-covered coulees (ravines), cultivated lands, and gently rolling prairie grasslands, in the northeastern corner of Montana. The refuge provides vital resting and nesting habitats for a great diversity of waterfowl and other wildlife.

The Northern Unit consists of 8,200-acre Medicine Lake, a number of smaller lakes and ponds, and numerous potholes. In 1976, the 11,360-acre Medicine Lake Wilderness was established, providing additional protection for the lake, its islands, and an adjacent 2,320-acre area of gently rolling sandhills. The latter support a diversity of prairie flora: native grasses, cacti, chokecherry, buffaloberry, snowberry, and various wildflowers. The Southern Unit contains a 1,280-acre impoundment known as Homestead Lake, and surrounding upland prairie.

This refuge's marsh and open-water habitats are a mecca for thousands of waterfowl during spring and autumn migrations. Mallards, blue-winged teal, gadwalls, shovelers, lesser scaup, and ruddy ducks are generally in greatest abundance. Some of the ducks nest on the refuge, annually raising as many as 30,000 ducklings. More than 1,000 Canada geese reside here, annually raising around 900 goslings. Medicine Lake's Big Island supports one of the nation's largest American white pelican rookeries, with more than 10,000 birds. Over 2,000 young are raised here annually. Refuge islands offer nesting habitat for other species, including herons, gulls, shorebirds, and cormorants. As many as 30 pairs of the endangered piping plover breed on the refuge. And in October, thousands of sandhill cranes pause in the refuge vicinity on their southward migration.

Prominent among the prairie grasslands wildlife is the sharp-tailed grouse. In early spring, they perform elaborate courtship displays on the refuge's numerous dance grounds, known as leks. They begin at the first light of day and increase in tempo with sunrise. The cocks fan their tails, vibrate their outstretched wings, rattle the quills of their wing feathers, and rapidly shuffle and stamp their feet. As if possessed, these pale, brown-speckled birds rush about, leaping wildly over each other and fighting. They make cackling sounds and repeatedly inflate a pair of lavender air sacs on their necks. Lowering their heads and forcing the air out of the sacs, they create a low coo-oo-ing sound that can be heard across the prairie. The refuge provides a viewing blind (reservations advised) so that visitors can see and photograph these birds' incredible ritual.

From 1937 to 1941, the Civilian Conservation Corps completed a number of refuge enhancement projects such as dams, dikes, roads, buildings, fences, and shelterbelts. Today, the Fish and Wildlife Service manages a series of impoundments, canals, and other water control structures that help maintain and enhance water quality and water bird habitat. The refuge has created wildlife nesting cover on nearly 3,000 acres of former agricultural lands. And under cooperative agreements, a portion of cultivated grain crops, planted on certain refuge lands by nearby farmers, is left unharvested for the benefit of waterfowl and other wildlife.

During periods of drought, the refuge waters and concentrations of waterbirds are greatly diminished. According to the Fish and Wildlife Service, "Though large-scale drought can be devastating to waterfowl populations, this drying of wetland basins [potholes] is very important to maintain the productivity of the wetlands. Nutrients that are accumulated in dead plant matter decompose in the presence of oxygen and return to the soil. With the return of the wet cycle comes an increased growth of aquatic vegetation and invertebrates—both a prime food source for waterfowl.

Establishment of the refuge was made possible partly with revenues from the sale of Migratory Bird Hunting and Conservation Stamps (Duck Stamps). Ducks Unlimited, Inc. has contributed funds and staff efforts toward the restoration and enhancement of the refuge's wildlife habitats. Because the Fish and Wildlife Service could not acquire the subsurface mineral rights when the refuge was established, oil and gas development by the owner of those rights occurs here.

The refuge is open daily during daylight hours. There is no entrance fee. The headquarters is open on weekdays, except national holidays.

Visitor activities include wildlife observation, driving an auto tour route, viewing the refuge and wildlife from an observation platform, hiking, picnicking (a picnic area is available), boating (motors not permitted on Medicine Lake, and landing on the lake's islands is prohibited) and canoeing, fishing, trapping, and hunting on parts of the refuge during the designated seasons. Camping is not permitted on the refuge. May to October is usually the best time for seeing wildlife. More than 225 bird species have been recorded here.

Visitors are cautioned to be alert for the possibility of rapid weather changes and strong Chinook winds in the spring and autumn. Insect repellent is advised during the warmer months.

Lodgings and meals are available in Culbertson and Plentywood, and meals are available in the town of Medicine Lake.

Access to the refuge is north from U.S. Hwy. 2 at Culbertson on State Hwy. 16 for 25 miles, right at a refuge directional sign, and east 2 miles to headquarters.

Information: Medicine Lake NWR, 223 North Shore Road, Medicine Lake, MT 59247; tel.: (406) 789-2305.

National Bison Range, consisting of 18,560 acres, was established in 1908 to help save the American bison (buffalo) from extinction. Located in northwestern Montana, this refuge consists of steeply rolling hills that are predominantly covered with prairie grasslands, scattered areas of ponderosa pines and Douglas-firs on some of the higher slopes, occasional groves of quaking aspens, several ponds, and a number of streams. Some streams flow intermittently, but others—notably Mission Creek—are permanent and are bordered by lush riparian wetlands, thickets, and woodlands. These habitats support a great diversity of wildlife, including more than 210 species of birds that have been recorded here.

The bison was once one of the world's most abundant large mammals. Population "guesstimates" range from 30 to 70 million, or even as many as 100 million, of them inhabiting the vast prairie grasslands of the Great Plains and ranging far to the east of the Mississippi River and west of the Rocky Mountains. As Euro-American civilization pushed westward across the continent, the vast and seemingly endless herds were slaughtered.

As Victor H. Cahalane wrote in his 1947 book, *Mammals of North America,*

By 1820 not a bison was left east of the Mississippi River. Through the fifties and sixties the slaughter went on. With the Civil War out of the way, the nation turned to the West. Like slender steel tentacles, the transcontinental railroads stretched toward the Rockies and out through the buffalo range. They brought men to slaughter buffalo. . . .

Buffalo Bill Cody contracted to supply the Kansas Pacific construction crews. . . . In eighteen months Cody killed four thousand two hundred and eighty animals and earned the nickname which became world famous. Railroads advertised special excursions, "with refreshments," and practically guaranteed a kill from the [railroad] car windows. . . . By 1889 [William T.] Hornaday was able to account for only five hundred and forty-one buffaloes remaining alive in the United States.

. . . these millions of slaughtered buffaloes were wasted. Many were killed merely for their hides, or for their tongues alone. Thousands were shot for sport and never touched. Buffaloes in the northern plains region were killed for the express purpose of destroying the principal food supply of the Sioux, the Crows, and other tribes, in order to starve them off the warpath. Soon the grasslands were empty. The hordes of big game had vanished, and only their bones lay bleaching in the sunshine.

Responding to this dramatic decline in the latter half of the 19th century, Congress passed legislation in 1893 that banned the hunting of a remnant wild band of bison still surviving in Yellowstone National Park. Toward the end of the century, a number of fenced, zoo-like wildlife parks were created in the eastern United States for captive herds.

During the first several years of the 20th century, concerned individuals and groups began advocating a bison protection program. Prominent among the organizations were the New York Zoological Society and the Boone and Crockett Club, which joined to advocate setting aside a bison reserve in the Wichita Mountains of Oklahoma. In 1905, President Theodore Roosevelt signed into law a measure authorizing this area within the Wichita National Forest Reserve "for the protection of game animals and birds and be recognized as a breeding place thereof." Later that year, the president signed an executive order re-designating the area as the Wichita National Game Reserve (see the Wichita Mountains Wildlife Refuge text). After the area was fenced, the New York Zoological Society donated 15 purebred Great Plains bison as the nucleus of the reserve's breeding stock. Still later that same year, the American Bison Society was founded to help promote the bison restoration program. Its president was Dr. William T. Hornaday, who was also the director of the New York Zoological Society.

Three years later, only about 20 free-roaming bison and a few hundred others in captivity remained in the United States. At that time, the American Bison Society succeeded in obtaining congressional authorization, signed by President Theodore Roosevelt, to purchase land from the "Confederated Tribes of the Flathead, Kootenai and Pend d'Oreille" (Flathead Indian Reservation), in Montana, to establish a national refuge specifically for the bison—"a permanent national bison range."

The American Bison Society then sponsored a fund-raising campaign, which raised $10,000, including nickels and dimes from schoolchildren, for the purchase of a nucleus breeding herd.

The following year, Dr. Hornaday enthusiastically wrote in a report for the American Bison Society: "The American people have thus become owners in perpetuity of what we believe to be the richest and the most beautiful grazing grounds ever trodden by bison hoofs."

Today, there are more than 250,000 bison in North America. Between 350 and 500 of them range across the hills of the National Bison Range. The Fish and Wildlife Service carries out a program of rotational grazing, so that no part of the range becomes overgrazed. To keep the population from exceeding the habitat's carrying capacity, surplus animals are rounded up annually and sold or donated, to provide breeding stock for other public and private herds. In addition, animals are donated to the Inter-Tribal Bison Cooperative, to help promote the restoration of bison herds on Native American lands.

Other ungulates inhabiting this refuge are about 130 elk; 40 to 50 bighorn sheep; 150 to 200 white-tailed deer; 200 to 300 mule deer; 100 pronghorns; and a few mountain goats. Like the bison, the numbers of these species are managed to maintain an ecologically sound balance between all these grazers and the forage of native bunchgrasses and forbs. Excess animals are transplanted to other places.

The National Bison Range is open daily during daylight hours. There is an entrance fee during the summer season. The visitor center is open daily from mid-May through September and on weekdays during the rest of the year, except for national holidays.

Visitor activities include wildlife observation, viewing interpretive exhibits in the visitor center, student environmental educational programs, driving the range's gravel roads (open all year, winter weather permitting), hiking several designated trails (including a wheelchair-accessible path around a pond), picnicking (a day use area is provided a short distance from the visitor center), and fishing (along certain stretches of Mission Creek and Jocko River, with a joint State of Montana-Flathead Reservation Use and Conservation Permit and joint Fishing Stamp). Hunting and camping are not permitted on the range, but campground facilities are available nearby.

Visitors are warned: "Bison can be very dangerous. Keep your distance." Consequently, among the regulations: "Remain at your car and on the road. If you are near bison, do not get out of your vehicle. Hiking is permitted only on designated footpaths." Visitors are also cautioned to be alert for western (prairie) rattlesnakes.

Lodgings and meals are available in St. Ignatius, Polson, Missoula, and Kalispell.

Access to the National Bison Range is 8 miles west on I-90 from Missoula to Exit 96, north 27 miles on U.S. Hwy. 93 to Ravalli, left 6 miles on State Hwy. 200 to Dixon, right 4 miles on Flathead Indian Reservation Hwy. 212 to Moiese, and right at the refuge sign.

Information: National Bison Range, 58355 Bison Range Road, Moiese, MT 59824; tel.: (406) 644-2211.

Red Rock Lakes presently contains 47,756 acres toward a goal of more than 53,000 acres and manages another 20,281 acres under conservation easement agreements with landowners, in the upper Centennial Valley of southwestern Montana. The refuge was established in 1935 to help rescue from extinction the then-vanishing and nearly extinct trumpeter swan—America's largest waterfowl.

With white plumage and a black beak, it measures as much as five feet long and has an eight-foot wingspread. The bird is named for its clear, resonant, French horn-like trumpeting note that carries great distances. In addition, trumpeter swans are attracted to two impounded warm-water springs that remain partially open during the winter, at which time visitor access to these ponds is not permitted to avoid disturbing the swans.

This remote, mountain-framed refuge enhances and protects a great diversity of ecologically significant marsh-prairie-alpine habitats near the headwaters of the Missouri River, below the Continental Divide. Upper and Lower Red Rock lakes, marshy Swan Lake, and a number of smaller ponds provide major waterfowl habitats. There are also many dashing streams, riparian and sub-irrigated meadows, as well as sagebrush- and grassland-covered foothills, numerous stands of quaking aspens, and conifer forests on the lower mountain slopes of the rugged Centennial Mountains. With elevations ranging from 6,600 to just under 10,000 feet, the area also extends well up the north slope of the mountains, where wind-sculpted clumps of firs are scattered across the open expanses of alpine meadows.

During the 19th century, commercial harvesting, subsistence hunting, and loss of habitat devastated the swan populations in the United States and Canada. Wildlife experts warned that this species was on the brink of extinction and would likely soon disappear. Small flocks of Rocky Mountain trumpeters remained only in remote places of the northern Rockies region, notably in the vicinity of Yellowstone National Park, including Red Rock Lakes. (Subsequently, an Alaskan swan population was discovered, most of which inhabited wilderness lakes in what is now the Kenai National Wildlife Refuge.) The Rocky Mountain birds, some of which breed in Canada, dwindled to around 200 swans. In 1932, a survey of breeding trumpeters within the Greater Yellowstone Ecosystem in Montana, Wyoming, and Idaho, tallied only 69. When the refuge was established, there were fewer than 50 swans inhabiting the Red Rock Lakes.

As the result of successful conservation efforts spanning many subsequent decades, trumpeter swans breeding in the Greater Yellowstone region now total nearly 500 birds, with an average of 100 on and in the vicinity of this refuge. Nesting begins in May, with muskrat houses frequently used as nest sites. About a month after incubation begins, the eggs hatch, and the cygnets soon leave the nest to swim. Four months later, they are able to fly. In the autumn, around 2,000 swans migrate south from Canadian breeding grounds, joining the resident birds in and around Yellowstone for the winter.

Wildlife experts believe, however, that expanding the swans' wintering range from the relatively small, high-elevation Yellowstone region is essential to the long-term survival of this species. Consequently, in recent years, a joint federal-state-private Rocky Mountain Trumpeter Swan Expansion Program relocated more than 1,000 trumpeters from Red Rock Lakes and elsewhere in the hope that these efforts will restore the swans' historic, expanded migration patterns to warmer wintering habitat. Their range formerly reached from interior Canada to the Mississippi Delta, and from the northwestern United States to the Gulf Coast of Texas and Mexico.

Other prominent wildlife on the refuge are moose, elk, pronghorn, white-tailed and mule deer, American white pelicans, numerous species of ducks, and sandhill cranes. The male cranes perform their remarkable, high-stepping courtship rituals here during the spring.

A wide variety of habitat management programs are carried out on the refuge. The Fish and Wildlife Service carefully manages the refuge's water, to ensure favorable nesting habitat for the trumpeter swans and other waterfowl. Periodic prescribed burns help maintain the health of forage for elk, mule deer, and other grazers and to provide favorable habitat of mixed shrubs and grasses for numerous nesting birds and other wildlife. Extensive, dense willow thickets are maintained to provide moose forage and habitat for many other species.

Ducks Unlimited, Inc. has assisted with important habitat enhancement projects on more than 1,500 acres of the refuge. Another nonprofit organization, the National Park Trust, saved from residential development an ecologically important 40 acres of wetland along Red Rock River and near Shambow Lake. This parcel, which has been added to the refuge, is rated as one of the most significant natural landscapes in Montana because of its intact ecosystems, expansive wetlands, and diversity of native fauna and flora, including a concentration of rare species.

The refuge is open on weekdays, except national holidays. There is no entrance fee. Much of the refuge has been established as a unit of the National Wilderness Preservation System—one of the system's very few marshland wilderness areas.

Visitor activities include wildlife observation; driving refuge roads; hiking (two former roads are designated for short hikes; but no trails within the wilderness area); bicycling; canoeing, kayaking, and non-motorized boating in designated areas (launching sites are provided on

Upper and Lower Red Rock lakes); picnicking; camping at two primitive campgrounds on a first-come, first-served basis (wheelchair-accessible facilities at Upper Lake Campground); fishing; and hunting on Lower Red Rock Lake during the designated season. The best months to view swans and other wildlife are June through September. Over 230 bird species have been recorded here.

Visitors are urged to be prepared for cold and wet weather at this high altitude, boaters are cautioned to be alert for sudden storms and strong winds, and hikers are advised to stay clear of sinkholes and other potentially hazardous boggy areas. Insect repellent is recommended during the warmer months.

Lodgings and meals are available in such communities as West Yellowstone, Dillon, and Ennis, Mont., and St. Anthony, Ida.

Access to the refuge from I-15 at Monida, Mont., is east 28 miles on a partially graveled dirt road; or from West Yellowstone west for about 12 miles on U.S. Hwy. 20, right for about 5 miles on Idaho State Hwy. 87, left at the Sawtell historical marker onto a paved road (passing Henry's Lake State Park) for about 5 miles, and right onto Red Rock Pass Rd. (an improved dirt road that crosses over this 7000-foot-elevation pass into Montana) for about 25 miles to the refuge entrance. Access to Red Rock Lakes is seasonal, and roads are open as weather allows. The road across Red Rock Pass is generally open from around mid-May to November. Visitors are advised to check on road conditions and to fill up the fuel tank before heading for the refuge.

Information: Red Rock Lakes NWR, 27820 Southside Centennial Rd., Lima, MT 59739; tel.: (406) 276-3536.

Nebraska

Fort Niobrara encompasses 19,131 acres of gently rolling sandhills and wooded breaks along the Niobrara River in north-central Nebraska. Six important natural ecosystems converge here—sandhills prairie, mixed prairie, tallgrass prairie, eastern deciduous forest, Rocky Mountain coniferous forest, and northern boreal forest, as they occur in few other parts of North America.

Although this refuge consequently supports a great diversity of wildlife, it was initially established in 1912 as a sanctuary to manage breeding habitat for native birds. Later that year, the refuge's wildlife management mission was expanded to protect remnant herds of the then-dwindling bison, elk, and deer that formerly inhabited the Great Plains in great numbers. J. W. Gilbert, of the community of Friend, Neb., offered to give the federal government six bison, seventeen elk, and a few deer if a suitable area of land could be found for these animals. The U.S. Government's Fort Niobrara had helped maintain the peace, from 1879 to 1906, between the Sioux Indians and the influx of Euro-American settlers. Soldiers stationed here never fought any battles, and the facility was abandoned soon after the beginning of the 20th century. Property associated with this old fort was chosen to become the Fort Niobrara National Wildlife Refuge.

Today, this refuge's grasslands habitat supports approximately 350 bison and between 70 and 100 elk. In the spring, the refuge's staff, riding on horseback, drive the bison herd south across the Niobrara River to summering grasslands, where the calves are born. In July and August, the 2,000-pound bulls battle furiously with each other as they compete for females during the rutting season. In autumn, most of the herd is driven back north across the river, where the animals spend the winter on the grasslands and timbered breaks. In September, the bull elk begin their rutting, and refuge visitors can hear the piercing, musical whistles that carry far across the prairie. As with bison, the elk calves are born in the spring.

Maintaining an appropriate carrying capacity of bison and elk is a guiding management priority here. So that their numbers are in balance with an ecologically healthy habitat, the Fish and Wildlife Service donates or auctions off excess animals.

Many other species of native wildlife inhabit the refuge. Wild turkeys and many species of songbirds live among the river-bordering oaks and pines; and mule deer, prairie dogs, burrowing owls, greater prairie chickens, and sharp-tailed grouse favor the open sandhill prairie.

In April, the prairie chickens and sharp-tails congregate on their dancing grounds, known as leks. The cocks perform elaborate, frenzied courtship rituals. The prairie chickens repeatedly inflate and deflate their golden neck sacs, emitting eerie, hollow, oo-loo-woo moaning sounds that sound like air being blown across the top of an empty bottle. The sharp-tails' foot-stomping, shuffling, and wing-vibrating are accompanied by coo-oo-ing and cackling sounds as they deflate their purplish neck sacs. More than 230 species of birds have been recorded here.

The refuge is open daily during daylight hours. There is no entrance fee. The visitor center is open daily from Memorial Day to Labor Day, and on weekdays, except national holidays, during the remainder of the year.

Visitor activities include wildlife observation (including seeing the autumn bison roundup and auction); driving the 3.5-mile interpretive Wildlife Drive; hiking the 0.6-mile Fort Falls Nature Trail and trails into the 4,635-acre Fort Niobrara Wilderness; canoeing, kayaking, and float-tubing downstream from Cornell Bridge on the refuge's stretch of the 76-mile Niobrara National Scenic River (a small user fee to float the river through the refuge is charged, a canoe-launching site is located near Cornell Bridge, and canoe rentals are available in Valentine); fishing; and picnicking (facilities are provided at the Bur Oak Wildlife Viewing Area, near Cornell Bridge). Although camping is not permitted on the refuge, facilities are available nearby.

Visitors are cautioned to stay in their vehicles on the Wildlife Drive, as bison and elk are unpredictable and potentially dangerous; and to be alert for rattlesnakes while hiking.

Access to the refuge from Valentine is east four miles on State Hwy. 12.

Information: Fort Niobrara NWR, HC 14, Box 67, Valentine, NE 69201; tel.: (402) 376-3789.

John W. and Louise Seier was established in 1999 and is located in the Sandhills of north-central Nebraska. This state's sandhills region is the largest remaining tract of mid- and tallgrass prairie in North America, encompassing 19,000 square miles. It is also the most extensive sand dune area in the Western Hemisphere. The 2,400-acre refuge was donated to the Fish and Wildlife Service by John W. and Louise Seier. As the refuge is still in the planning stage, it is presently closed to visitation.

The purpose of the refuge is to preserve, restore, and enhance the ecological diversity and abundance of migratory and resident wildlife. Management of the refuge will provide the opportunity for wildlife observation, and seasonal hunting. Environmental education and interpretation programs will be offered so that visitors may learn about the refuge's resources. In 2001, the American Bird Conservancy designated this refuge as a Globally Important Bird Area in recognition of its value to the conservation of birds and their habitats.

The mid-continental position of the John W. and Louise Seier refuge; the large groundwater reservoir beneath the Sandhills, known as the Ogallala Aquifer; and the highly varied topography of the Sandhills are partly responsible for the unique mix of the refuge's plant and animal species. The refuge grassland is composed of plants from the tallgrass prairie, shortgrass prairie, and plants unique to sandy soils. Species such as big bluestem, switchgrass, blue and hairy grama, sandy muhly, and sand lovegrass grow in association with each other; and a few trees and shrubs, such as eastern cottonwood, peachleaf willow, American plum, snowberry, and Arkansas rose, add to this diversity. Bloody Creek and Skull Creek and their adjacent rich wetland communities cut through the refuge.

The refuge is located 26 miles south of Bassett and is managed through the Fort Niobrara-Valentine National Wildlife Refuge Complex.

(With special thanks to Refuge Manager Royce Huber for providing the above information.—RDB)

Information: John W. and Louise Seier National Wildlife Refuge, c/o Fort Niobrara-Valentine NWR Complex, HC 14, Box 67, Valentine, NE 69201; tel.: (402) 376 3789.

Valentine, containing 71,516 acres, was established in 1935 as a breeding ground for migratory birds and other wildlife. The refuge protects an ecologically significant area of numerous lakes, marshes, small patches of woods, tallgrass-covered meadows, and extensive, gently rolling sandhills prairie, in north-central Nebraska. The lakes, pothole ponds, and wetlands attract thousands of migratory and breeding waterfowl and shorebirds. May and October are the peak months, when as many as 150,000 ducks are present on this refuge.

In April, greater prairie chickens and sharp-tailed grouse congregate on their dancing grounds—the cocks performing elaborate, frenzied courtship rituals. The prairie chickens' performance is accompanied by eerie, hollow, oo-loo-woo moaning sounds that resemble air being blown across the top of an empty bottle. The sharp-tails' foot-stamping, shuffling, and wing-vibrating are accompanied by coo-oo-ing and cackling sounds.

Although few sandhill cranes stop, large numbers of them fly over the refuge on their spring and autumn migrations. Several thousand white pelicans summer here. Many Canada geese build their nests on top of muskrat houses. Numerous neotropical migratory songbirds come through Valentine in the spring. More than 260 bird species have been recorded here.

Although most of Valentine Refuge's lakes and marshes are natural, the Fish and Wildlife Service has created a few additional ponds, and the water levels on some of the latter are regulated for the benefit of waterfowl. Marsh and prairie grassland habitats are enhanced with springtime livestock grazing and prescribed burns. These management activities spur the release and recycling of plant nutrients, help control non-native species of grasses, and stimulate regrowth. Large areas of the refuge, which are given a rest from grazing and prescribed fire, offer tall, dense cover that is preferred by ground-nesting birds.

Establishment of this refuge was made possible partly with revenues from the sale of Migratory Bird Hunting and Conservation Stamps (Duck Stamps). In 1976, Valentine was designated as a national natural landmark, in recognition of this ecologically outstanding part of the vast sandhills prairie region.

The refuge is open daily during daylight hours. There is no entrance fee. The headquarters is open on weekdays, except on national holidays.

Visitor activities include wildlife observation, driving designated roads, hiking refuge trails and roads, viewing elaborate prairie chicken and sharp-tailed grouse courtship displays in April from blinds (reservations advised), fishing, and hunting on parts of the refuge during the designated seasons. Although camping is not permitted on the refuge, campground facilities are available at Ballards Marsh Wildlife Management Area and at Merritt Reservoir.

Lodgings and meals are available in the community of Valentine.

Access to the refuge from the town of Valentine is south 16 miles State Hwy. 83, and west 13 miles on Spur Road 16B to the refuge's Hackberry Headquarters.

Information: Valentine NWR, HC 14, Box 67, Valentine, NE 69201; tel.: (402) 376-3789.

Nevada

Ash Meadows, encompassing 23,000 acres, was established in 1984. The refuge protects and manages a desert oasis ecosystem of spring-fed wetlands, located within an area of alkaline desert uplands of the Mojave Desert, in southwestern Nevada.

The refuge's habitats support at least 24 species of endemic plants and animals, including four species of endangered fish that are found nowhere else in the world. As the Fish and Wildlife Service says, "This concentration of indigenous life distinguishes Ash Meadows NWR as having a greater concentration of endemic life than any other local area in the United States. . . . Ash Meadows provides a valuable and unprecedented example of desert oases that are now extremely uncommon in the southwestern United States."

The wetlands habitat is fed by more than thirty seeps and springs. At least 10,000 gallons of water per minute are discharged year-round from an enormous subsurface aquifer system. Most of this water emerges from seven major springs. According to the Fish and Wildlife Service,

The reason for this abundance of water in an otherwise dry and desolate region is the presence of a geological fault. The movement of this particular fault acts as an "underground dam," blocking the flow of water and forcing it to the surface. The water arriving at Ash Meadows is called "fossil" water, because it is believed to have entered the ground water system thousands of years ago.

In addition to the refuge's colorful spring pools, spring-brook channels, and wetlands that are scattered across the refuge, there are groves of mesquite and ash trees in the vicinity of the wetlands and stream channels, and sand dunes rising as much as fifty feet in the central part of the refuge. Drier areas are dominated by four-winged saltbush, creosotebush, a number of species of cacti, and other high-desert vegetation.

Regarding the history of this area, the Fish and Wildlife Service explains:

Ash Meadows was intensively farmed prior to its establishment as a National Wildlife Refuge. During the 1960's and early 1970's in particular, irrigated row crops, grazing, and development took a heavy toll on the area's natural resources. Plants, fish, and wildlife declined as pumping and diversion of spring channels, development of roads, large scale earth moving, and introduction of over 100 non-native plants and animals occurred in a "blink" of evolutionary time. The Carson Slough, an area in the northwestern portion of the refuge, which was historically the largest wetland in southern Nevada, was drained and mined for its peat in the 1960's.

In the early 1980s, the area's fragile habitat was further impaired by speculative land developers as they began preparing for an extensive residential development. The Nature Conservancy acted in the nick of time by acquiring 12,654 acres in 1984 and selling it to the Fish and Wildlife Service later that year. The agency says, "The refuge is currently in the habitat restoration stage and will likely remain so for years to come. The overall goal of the refuge and its Recovery Plan for threatened and endangered species is to restore the area to its natural historic condition. This will involve re-directing spring outflows back into former natural channels, restoring wetlands, removing non-native species (particularly saltcedar, bass, tropical fish, and crayfish), restoring native riparian and upland vegetation, and removing unnecessary structures such as roads, fences, and power lines."

Four endemic endangered species of fish of the minnow family inhabit the refuge: Devil's Hole pupfish, Ash Meadows pupfish, Warm Springs pupfish, and Ash Meadows speckled dace. There are also a number of endangered or threatened plant species at Ash Meadows, including the Amargosa niterwort, Ash Meadows gumplant, Ash Meadows ivesia, spring-loving centaury, Ash Meadows milk vetch, Ash Meadows sunray, and Ash Meadows blazing star. More than 210 bird species have been recorded on the refuge.

Within the Ash Meadows Refuge's authorized boundary, the Fish and Wildlife Service manages more than 22,600 acres, the Bureau of Land Management cooperatively manages 9,460 acres, and the National Park Service cooperatively manages the forty-acre Devil's Hole Unit of Death Valley National Park.

The refuge is open daily (including holidays) during daylight hours. There is no entrance fee. A refuge leaflet can be obtained from an information box at each of the three main refuge entrances. The refuge office is often open for additional information, but hours vary depending on staffing.

Visitor activities include wildlife observation, driving refuge roads, walking the 0.3-mile (wheelchair-accessible) Crystal Springs Interpretive Boardwalk Trail (adjacent to the refuge office) and elsewhere on the refuge, swimming only in Crystal Reservoir (but the water there may be infested with dermatitis-causing larvae), swimming is prohibited in the spring pools, canoeing and non-motorized boating only on Crystal and Peterson reservoirs, horseback riding in designated areas, picnicking, and hunting on parts of the refuge during the designated seasons.

Camping is not permitted on the refuge, but facilities are offered in the main unit of Death Valley National Park.

Sunscreen and lots of drinking water are advised. Visitors are asked to respect private properties within the refuge boundaries.

Lodgings and meals are available in Amargosa Valley, Pahrump, Las Vegas, and Beatty, Nev.; and Death Valley National Park, Calif.

Access to the refuge from Exit 33 on I-15 is west/northwest 56 miles on State Hwy. 160 (through Pahrump), left about 20 miles on the Bell Vista Rd.-Bob Rudd Memorial Hwy., and right onto an unpaved road onto the refuge.

Information: Ash Meadows NWR, HC 70, Box 610-Z, Amargosa Valley, NV 89020; tel.: (775) 372-5435.

Desert National Wildlife Range, comprising 1.588 million acres, was established in 1936. The refuge protects a diversity of habitats for the desert bighorn sheep and other wildlife, in the Mojave Desert of southern Nevada.

Within this largest unit of the National Wildlife Refuge System in the lower 48 states, there are six major mountain ranges, the highest of which rises from around 2,500 feet elevation in desert valleys to 9,920 feet atop the Sheep Range's Hayford Peak. The ranges and valleys, which run mostly north and south through this region, are geologically part of the vast basin-and-range province that sprawls across nearly all of Nevada and parts of several adjacent states.

As explained by refuge manager Amy Sprunger-Allworth:

The name, "Desert National Wildlife Range," does not provide an adequate overall description of the refuge. One might envision sand and cactus. However, most visitors begin their visit to the refuge by stopping at Corn Creek. They are awed by the beauty and solitude of the natural springs that have existed here for centuries, providing a desert oasis for Native Americans and European settlers. As visitors continue towards the interior of the refuge, they experience extreme elevational changes offering unexpected expansive vistas. Pinyon and juniper dominate the landscape above 6,000 feet, affording quiet respites for travelers who have bounced in their vehicles up the rugged roads.

The refuge's single most important mission is the protection of the Nelson's desert bighorn sheep and the natural environment that supports this species. Because of the low-elevation rainfall that annually averages a mere 4.5 inches, the Fish and Wildlife Service has developed a number of springs and rainwater catchments to ensure adequate supplies of water during periods of drought and heat. The desert bighorn belongs to the same species as the Rocky Mountain bighorn sheep, but the desert environment has brought about certain basic differences. The desert subspecies is smaller and of a lighter grayish-buff, and its horns are thinner and more outward spreading.

Bighorns occur on all six of the refuge's mountain ranges, but nowhere are they densely populated. Use of different elevations varies with season, food availability, and reproductive cycle. Sheep are generally below timberline on desert-shrub and grass-covered slopes. Because they blend extremely well with their surroundings and tend to remain widely scattered in small groups during most of the year, the best opportunity to observe them occurs during the summer, when they tend to concentrate at or within a two-mile radius of a water course. As of late

2001, the Fish and Wildlife Service estimates that there are between 700 and 750 desert bighorn sheep on the refuge.

Numerous species of birds are attracted to the oasis at Corn Creek—especially migratory songbirds, during spring and autumn. More than 320 bird species have been recorded on the Desert refuge. Many species of desert wildflowers bloom with spectacular abundance, spreading their bright colors across the landscape following periodic winters of generous rainfall. Among them are the yellow desert marigold, orange globemallow, pink penstemon, sand verbena, red paintbrush, blue desert larkspur, and lavender Mojave aster.

More than 500 species of plants have been identified on this refuge. Vegetative types include the saltbush community in a number of high-salinity valley basins; creosotebush community (roughly between 2,600 and 4,200 feet elevation), with Mojave yucca, Mormon tea (*Ephedra*), and several species of cacti; blackbrush community (between 4,200 and 6,000 feet), with scattered, open-grown stands of Joshua trees (a species of tree-sized yucca); singleleaf pinyon-Utah juniper woodland (between 6,000 and 7,400 feet); ponderosa pine-white fir forest (from 7,500 to over 9,000 feet); and small areas of bristlecone pines, the world's oldest-known living tree species (above 8,500 feet).

The refuge is open daily. There is no entrance fee. The refuge office is open on weekdays, except national holidays.

Visitor activities include wildlife observation, driving, hiking trails in the immediate vicinity of Corn Creek Field Station, hiking anywhere else on the refuge (no designated trails), horseback riding, picnicking, camping, and hunting (bighorn ram only) on parts of the refuge during the designated seasons. Although camping is permitted, all camps, except backpack camps, are required to be within 100 feet of designated roads. Except for the four-mile main entrance road, the refuge's other unpaved, rough, unimproved roads (including the 47-mile Mormon Well Rd., the 16-mile Gass Peak Rd., and the 70-mile Alamo Rd.) are best negotiated with a four-wheel-drive, high-clearance vehicle. Off-road driving is not permitted.

Visitors are advised to bring an adequate supply of drinking water on backcountry excursions, especially during the intense dry heat of summer; and to plan backcountry excursions with great care and to let a friend or relative know your travel plans. The U.S. Air Force's Nevada Test and Training Range, where bombing, gunnery, and aerial warfare training activities occur, overlays the western half of the Desert National Wildlife Range (to the west of Alamo Rd.). All public access into that area of the range is strictly prohibited.

Lodgings and meals are available in Las Vegas.

Access from Las Vegas to the Desert National Wildlife Range is northwest about 25 miles on U.S. Hwy. 95 and right 4 miles on the gravel entrance road to Corn Creek Field Station.

Information: Desert National Wildlife Range, HCR 38, Box 700, Las Vegas, NV 89124; tel.: (702) 879-6110.

Ruby Lake, comprising 37,632 acres, was established in 1938 to protect an extensive area of marshes, ponds, islands, bordering wet meadows, and sagebrush-and-grass uplands. The bulrush wetlands attract large concentrations of nesting and migrating waterfowl and other water birds, with as many as 25,000 ducks in September and October. The refuge is scenically located at the 6,000-foot elevation of Ruby Valley, nestled along the eastern base of the rugged Ruby Mountains, which rise to more than 11,000 feet on the highest peaks, in northeastern Nevada.

The juxtaposition of rugged, up-thrusted mountain ranges, such as the Ruby Mountains, and intervening valleys or basins, such as Ruby Valley, is typical of the vast "washboard" topography of this region's basin-and-range province, which extends throughout nearly all of Nevada and parts of several neighboring states. The oasis of the Ruby Marshes is a fascinating and wonderful contrast to the surrounding high-desert Great Basin landscape.

Water from more than 160 springs along the base of the mountains either surfaces within various marsh units or flows into the Collection Ditch and is then directed by a network of dikes into the 3,000 acre central area of marsh habitat. Water that reaches the southern end of the ditch flows into the 7,300-acre South Marsh, which is situated in a natural depression, and water that is sometimes allowed to flow from the ditch's northern end helps to maintain the shallower 6,800-acre North Marsh. In 1972, the South Marsh was designated by the National Park Service as a National Natural Landmark, because of its biological diversity and its pristine habitat condition. The North Marsh is an especially important wetland habitat for puddle ducks and shorebirds. More than 220 species of birds have been recorded on the refuge.

As the Fish and Wildlife Service explains:

Water is managed to provide optimum nesting and feeding habitat for migratory waterfowl and water-dependent birds. By careful manipulation of water levels and flows, 12,000 acres of marshlands can be maintained. Periodically, individual habitat units are rejuvenated by drying them up. As a result, the food resources and productivity of the aquatic environment are greatly enhanced. Management tries to imitate the processes of naturally occurring wetland ecosystems as much as possible to maintain the vitality and productivity of the marshes. . . .

Waterfowl are the most conspicuous and most important to the primary objectives of the refuge. Nesting canvasbacks and redhead ducks are particularly important. The South Marsh supports the largest nesting population of canvasback ducks west of the Mississippi River and holds the highest concentration of this species in North America. In good years, the refuge has produced 3,500 canvasbacks and 2,500 redheads.

The trumpeter swan, originally a transplant from the Red Rock Lakes National Wildlife Refuge in Montana, is also found on the refuge. Several pairs nest each year. [Both the trumpeter and tundra swans may winter on the refuge.] In all, 15 . . . species of waterfowl nest on the refuge, as well as a variety of other water-dependent birds, such as coots, grebes, sandhill cranes, great blue herons, black-crowned night-herons, white-faced ibis, and snowy egrets.

Although most of the marsh habitat contains dense stands of bulrush that provide nesting sites for waterfowl, marsh birds, and other birds, transition areas around the edge of the wetland support rushes, sedges, grasses, and various forbs. Wet meadows and drier grasslands are important feeding and nesting habitats for many migratory birds. Haying, limited grazing, and periodic prescribed burning are implemented to help revitalize and maintain the health of meadows and grassland areas.

Establishment of the refuge was made possible partly with revenues from the sale of Migratory Bird Hunting and Conservation Stamps (Duck Stamps). Ducks Unlimited, Inc. has helped enhance more than 2,600 acres of Ruby Lake's wetland habitat.

The refuge is open daily during daylight hours. There is no entrance fee. The refuge headquarters/visitor center is open on weekdays, except national holidays.

Visitor activities include wildlife observation (two photo blinds are available; permit required), driving the 7.5-mile unpaved auto tour route and the Ruby Valley Rd., interpretive programs and environmental education, hiking on the 0.5-mile Cave Creek Trail near the visitor center and on refuge roads, bicycling on the tour route, canoeing and boating (from June 15 through December, but under specific restrictions to avoid disturbing nesting waterfowl), fishing, and hunting on parts of the refuge during the designated seasons (to protect the trumpeter swans, Ruby Valley is closed to the hunting of all white waterfowl). Although camping is not permitted on the refuge, the South Ruby Campground (1.5 miles south of refuge headquarters) is available in the Humboldt-Toiyabe National Forest (reservations: tel.: (877) 444-6777). Primitive camping is also allowed on the national forest (300 feet west of County Rd. 767) and on Bureau of Land Management lands to the east of the refuge.

Insect repellent is recommended during the warmer months. Visitors are advised to be alert for rattlesnakes, especially in the drier parts of the refuge, and to be prepared for cold weather at this elevation. Canoeists and boaters are cautioned that it is easy to become disoriented and lost in the South Marsh's maze of waterways.

Lodgings and meals are available on a seasonal basis in Ruby Valley at the Ruby Lake Resort: tel.: (775) 779-2242. Otherwise, the nearest accommodations are in Wells, Elko, and Ely.

Access from Exit 352 on I-80 at Wells to the refuge's headquarters/visitor center is south 28 miles on U.S. Hwy. 93, right onto State Hwy. 229 for 15 miles, and left onto unpaved Ruby Valley Rd.for 35 miles; or from Ely, it is west 32 miles on U.S. Hwy. 50, right onto unpaved Long Valley Rd. (recommended only in good weather) for 35 miles, and continuing north 32 miles on Ruby Valley Rd.. Prospective visitors are encouraged to contact the refuge to ask about road conditions, especially from November to May.

Information: Ruby Lake NWR, HC 60, Box 860, Ruby Valley, NV 89833; tel.: (775) 779-2237.

Sheldon, containing more than 573,503 acres, was initially established in 1931. The refuge protects a vast expanse of high-desert habitat for the benefit of the pronghorn (antelope), California bighorn sheep, mule deer, greater sage-grouse (see Hart Mountain and Seedskadee NWR texts for discussions of the latter), and many other species of wildlife. It is located mostly in northwestern Nevada, with a few hundred acres in Oregon.

In the 1870s, livestock ranching began in the Great Basin Desert of northern Nevada and parts of neighboring states. These operations grew and prospered, soon developing into extensive empires. Where previously there had only been such native animals as the pronghorn, mule deer, and bighorn sheep using the arid land, there were now huge numbers of cattle, sheep, and horses. As the Fish and Wildlife Service explains:

Range deterioration resulted from excessive use. Soon, both wildlife and the ranching industry were in trouble. Native wildlife had been exploited for food and was unable to compete with domestic livestock on the deteriorating rangelands. California bighorn sheep disappeared, mule deer became rare, antelope numbers were drastically reduced, and sage grouse, once numerous, became hard to find. Overgrazing changed plant types and led to erosion; economic hardships caused livestock empires to sell out to small family owned ranches. By the . . . [start of the 20th] century, only a few small ranches remained in existence on the Sheldon.

In the late 1800's and early 1900's, the decreasing antelope populations of northwestern Nevada began to concern both residents and conservation groups.

In 1920, E. R. Sans, a biologist with the U.S. Biological Survey, saw his first pronghorn—an event that inspired a vision in his mind of establishing an antelope refuge and seeking the enactment of hunting regulations including a closed season on this species. As a result of his efforts, both Washoe and Humboldt counties set closed seasons, soon followed by a statewide seasonal closure established by the Nevada State Fish and Game Commission. As described by Sheldon refuge volunteer history recorder/compiler Ralph Murphy (*Sheldon National Wildlife Refuge: A Collection of Historical Vignettes*, 1984):

Sans, and others concerned about the pronghorn and other threatened species, had meanwhile been . . . [urging enactment of] a law authorizing the Governor to set aside certain state controlled lands for recreation and game refuges. This was signed into law by Governor James C. Scrugham on March 5, 1923. Washoe County Commissioners also designated 400 square miles in northern Washoe County as an antelope refuge.

In spite of the county and state actions, these lands remained seriously overgrazed, and their widely scattered springs, creeks, lakes, and other aquatic habitats continued to be severely degraded. There was no funding for habitat management or enforcement of hunting regulations.

In 1927, Sans took Gilbert Pearson, the president of the National Association of Audubon Societies (subsequently the National Audubon Society), on a tour of the 30,000-acre Last Chance Ranch, on which Sans envisioned the headquarters for a national antelope range. Pearson was so impressed with the proposal that he returned to New York City, met with the association's board of directors, and secured a commitment of $10,000. He then contacted the Boone and Crockett Club, which provided an equal sum, with the suggestion that the refuge be named in memory of Charles Sheldon, who was an avid sportsman, conservationist, and the organization's long-time member and chairman of its Game Preservation Committee. The ranch was acquired in 1928. In 1931, the Charles Sheldon Wildlife Refuge was established by executive order; and the following year, Audubon transferred its ranch property to the federal government. In 1936, another area, encompassing more than 500,000 acres, was established as the Charles Sheldon Antelope Range. Finally, in 1976, both areas were combined and renamed the Sheldon National Wildlife Refuge.

The refuge's habitat management activities include a program of prescribed burning. Fire is mostly used to create and maintain patches of grassland within the predominant high-desert sagebrush, thereby providing habitat diversity that benefits many species of wildlife. Fire also promotes nutrient cycling that in turn spurs new growth of grasses and forbs. Another primary management activity is the enhancement of stream flow by rehabilitating riparian habitat throughout the refuge.

As for the pronghorn, current estimates range between 1,200 and 1,500 of these fleet-footed animals that summer on the refuge. During hard winters, their numbers may increase to 3,000 or more as animals migrate down from such areas as the Hart Mountain National Antelope Refuge, in southern Oregon.

The refuge is open daily. There is no entrance fee. The refuge's administrative headquarters, located in the Post Office building in Lakeview, Ore., is open on weekdays, except national holidays.

Visitor activities include wildlife observation, driving paved State Hwy. 140 and the refuge's graded roads and backcountry jeep routes, hiking, camping at more than a dozen primitive campgrounds, fishing at the Dufurrena Ponds that are near the refuge field office, and hunting during the designated seasons. The Fish and Wildlife Service advises visitors to inquire about road conditions, especially in winter and spring, before venturing into the remote backcountry of the refuge. Visitors are cautioned to be alert for rattlesnakes. More than 200 species of birds have been recorded on the refuge.

Lodgings and meals are available in such communities as Winnemucca, Nev.; Lakeview, Oregon; and Cedarville, California.

Access from I-80 at Winnemucca to the Sheldon refuge's Dufurrena Ponds/field office is north 31 miles on U.S. Hwy. 95 and left onto State Hwy. 140 for 99 miles; or from Lakeview, Ore., it is north 5 miles on U.S. Hwy. 395, and right onto State Hwy. 140 for 73 miles.

Information: Sheldon National Wildlife Refuge, P.O. Box 111, Lakeview, OR 97630; tel.: (541) 947-3315.

Stillwater, encompassing 79,600 acres in two units, was originally established in 1948. The refuge protects and manages an extensive area of the Stillwater Marsh, an oasis for large concentrations of waterfowl, shorebirds, and other wildlife at the end of the Carson River, within the Great Basin Desert of west-central Nevada.

When the first Euro-American explorers discovered this marshland, it was filled with an abundance of fish and wildlife, and the native "Cattail-Eater" Paiute people had long been deriving sustenance from the wealth of resources. As for subsequent human history of this area, the Fish and Wildlife Service explains:

In 1898, one visitor described the wetland as a "half shallow lake, half tule swamp which extends for 20 miles along the valley bottom . . . a breeding ground for great numbers of water and shore birds."

Then, in the early 1900s, the Newlands Irrigation Project was developed by the Bureau of Reclamation to supply Lahontan Valley farmers with an abundant and reliable water source. The Carson River was dammed, creating the Lahontan Reservoir. This reduced water flowing into the marsh to a trickle. . . . The great flights of birds that Pony Express riders saw darkening the skies in the 1860s dwindled to a remnant.

In 1948, action was taken to prevent complete loss of the Stillwater marshes. The U.S. Fish and Wildlife Service and the Nevada Fish and Game Commission entered into an agreement with the Truckee-Carson Irrigation District to develop and manage . . . lands for wildlife and grazing. These were designated as the 140,000-acre Stillwater Wildlife Management Area and 24,200-acre Stillwater National Wildlife Refuge. Although at that time Carson River flows sustained only a fraction of the original marsh, this action prevented the loss of the Pacific Flyway in western Nevada. In 1990, 55,000 acres of the management area were added to the Stillwater National Wildlife Refuge.

As *Ducks Unlimited* senior writer Matt Young explained in his January/February 2002 article, "Wetlands Under Siege":

In partnership with the USFWS and U.S. Bureau of Reclamation (BOR), DU [Ducks Unlimited, Inc.] has completed several wetland conservation projects on the refuge. DU currently is participating in a project to refurbish the refuge's water-delivery system by constructing new canals, installing water-control structures, and repairing levees. These improvements will enable managers to more efficiently use limited water supplies and provide better habitat for waterfowl and other wildlife.

The refuge's STILLWATER UNIT is today a vast stretch of diked ponds and bulrush- and cattail-dominated marshland—an oasis, surrounded by greasewood-and-saltbush desert and pickleweed-bordered salt flats. In years of adequate water (there are periodic cycles of drought, as between 1986 and 1992, when there was virtually none), several thousand ducks pause here in March and April, on their way to breeding grounds farther north.

Other concentrations of ducks, such as redheads, cinnamon teal, and gadwalls, along with grebes, herons, ibises, Canada geese, plovers, sandpipers, stilts, avocets, and phalaropes, raise their young on the refuge during the summer. Flotillas of American white pelicans swim about on the ponds, grabbing fish with their large orange beaks; flocks circle overhead in V forma- tions, flapping and gliding in sequence or unison, and fly to Anaho Island National Wildlife Refuge, where they nest and raise their young (see the Anaho refuge text for more information on these pelicans).

The major migration influx of waterfowl, however, occurs from August to November, when as many as a quarter million ducks, including redheads, canvasbacks, pintails, shovelers, and green-winged teal, gather here on their southward migration. The Stillwater wetlands also provide vital resting and feeding habitat for enormous numbers of migrating shorebirds— sometimes totaling more than 300,000 individuals. In 1988, Stillwater was recognized as a key area in the Western Hemisphere Shorebird Reserve Network. In winter, 1,000 or more tundra swans may be attracted to the refuge. Lahontan Valley also brings the largest concentration of bald eagles in Nevada. More than 280 bird species have been recorded here.

A proposal is pending to change the status of the nearby 17,902-acre Fallon National Wildlife Refuge to a unit of Stillwater Refuge (see the Fallon refuge text).

Stillwater refuge is open daily during daylight hours. There is no entrance fee. The refuge headquarters, located at 1000 Auction Rd. in Fallon, is open on weekdays, except national hol- idays.

Visitor activities include wildlife observation, driving the 15-mile auto tour route and other refuge roads, hiking on refuge roads, canoeing and boating (more than a dozen boat-launching sites are available), camping (eight-day limit), fishing, and hunting on the refuge's public use ar- eas during the designated seasons.

Insect repellent and sunscreen are advised during the warmer months.

Lodgings and meals are available in Fallon.

Access to the refuge from Fallon is east five miles on U.S. Hwy. 50, east/northeast about ten miles on State Hwy. 116, and on unpaved Stillwater Rd. within the refuge.

Information: Stillwater NWR, 1000 Auction Rd., Fallon, NV 89406; tel.: (775) 423- 6452.

New Hampshire

Great Bay, containing 1,083 acres in two units, was established in 1992 to restore and manage a diversity of wildlife habitats, including wooded and shrub uplands, fields, vernal and beaver ponds, intertidal mudflat, and open bay. The main part of the refuge, containing 1,057 acres, is located along the eastern shore of Great Bay, in southeastern New Hampshire.

The bay and mudflats attract concentrations of waterfowl, wading birds, shorebirds, gulls, and terns. Among the waterfowl, there are large numbers of wintering American black ducks, as well as Canada geese, wood ducks, mallards, green-winged teal, ring-necked ducks, greater scaup, common goldeneyes, buffleheads, and mergansers. Wading birds include great blue and green herons, snowy egrets, and glossy ibis. Nesting ospreys and wintering bald eagles are among the refuge's raptors.

Upland areas support ruffed grouse, wild turkey, and American woodcock. In May, peak influxes of neotropical migratory songbirds come here to nest or pause on their way to breeding areas farther north.

The lands in and around what is now the refuge used for many years for farming and harvesting of hay. Most of the area was grassland. Then the U.S. Government purchased the area and established the Pease Air Force Base. In 1990, the base was closed, and two years later, Great Bay refuge was established. The Fish and Wildlife Service is beginning to restore and manage the refuge to enhance the quality and diversity of its habitats. One major goal is to restore areas of grassland for the benefit of such species as bobolink, woodcock, and upland sandpiper. Ducks Unlimited, Inc. has helped enhance about fifty acres of the refuge's wetland habitat.

The refuge's smaller unit is the 26-acre Karner Blue Butterfly Easement in Concord, located in pine-barrens habitat. In 1991, the Fish and Wildlife Service acquired a conservation easement (mostly from the city), with the goal of reestablishing the federally listed endangered Karner blue butterfly to the area. This northeastern subspecies of the orange-bordered blue butterfly is named for Karner, N.Y., where it was initially described more than a century ago. As described by the Fish and Wildlife Service, "The male is distinctively silvery or dark blue with narrow black margins on the back of his wings." The Karner blue butterfly depends upon the wild lupine plant: caterpillars feed only on its leaves, adults consume the nectar of its flowers and lay their eggs on or near the plant.

In the past, this butterfly ranged across the pine barrens and oak savannas from Minnesota, Wisconsin, and Michigan to New York and New Hampshire. In 1983, researchers discovered roughly 5,000 Karner blues in the Concord Pine Barrens. But by 1998, a mere thirty individuals could be found. Why the sharp decline?

According to the Fish and Wildlife Service, "Suppressed wildfires, forest succession, and urbanization are the greatest threats to the Karner blue's continued existence in New England and elsewhere. . . . The fragmentation that results from these factors, combined with the extremely small size of the remaining population, prevents movement and dispersal of butterflies, resulting in small isolated populations. The Karner blue's habitat is very specific and the butterfly is unable to adapt to the swift changes in its environment."

In an effort to enhance the easement property's habitat toward the hoped-for repopulating of the area with the butterfly, The Nature Conservancy and the Fish and Wildlife Service have been planting lupine, New Jersey tea, spreading dogbane, common milkweed, and meadowsweet (all crucial sources of nectar) since 1991. Exclosure fences erected within the easement keep woodchucks and white-tailed deer from eating new plants. The Nature Conservancy also manages a crucial Karner blue captive breeding program.

Historically, wildfires maintained Concord's Karner blue habitat by curtailing plant succession and creating a matrix of open habitat. Annual prescribed burning and mowing attempt to duplicate the favorable effects of these natural disturbances. Active management may be the only means of protecting this species and its dwindling habitat. (See the Necedah refuge text for further information on this butterfly.)

The refuge units are open daily during daylight hours. There is no entrance fee.

Visitor activities include wildlife and butterfly observation, hiking on several trails, and cross-country skiing and snowshoeing.

Visitors are cautioned to be alert for ticks, which may carry Lyme disease. Insect repellent is advised during the warmer months.

Lodgings and meals are available in such communities as Newington and Portsmouth.

Access to the refuge from Exit 4 on I-95 is north about 5 miles to Exit I on U.S. Hwy. 4, left at the stoplight at the bottom of the exit ramp, proceeding straight about 0.5 mile to a T junction in the Peas Tradeport, and right onto Arboretum Drive for a couple of miles.

Information: Great Bay NWR, 100 Merrimac Dr., Newington, NH 03801; tel.: (978) 465-5753.

Lake Umbagog, comprising 14,640 acres, was established in 1992 to protect ecologically important lands around Lake Umbagog (pronounced um-BAY-gog) in northeastern New Hampshire and western Maine. The name, *Umbagog*, is derived from a Native American word, meaning "clear water." The refuge is a partnership involving the Fish and Wildlife Service, the states of New Hampshire and Maine, the Society for the Protection of New Hampshire Forests, and other landowners. Under a combination of ownerships and conservation easements, much of the lakeshore in both states and long stretches of the shoreline of the Androscoggin and Magalloway rivers is under protective management.

As the Fish and Wildlife explains:

The lake itself—more than 10 miles in length and covering more than 8,500 acres—is one of the largest lakes along the New Hampshire/Maine border. It has an average depth of only 15 feet. . . . More than 50 miles of shoreline, many islands, and extensive wetlands and marshes along the rivers all provide ideal habitat for waterfowl pairing, nesting and brood rearing during the summer. The forested swamplands and upland areas are important habitat for many species of passerines, including 24 varieties of warblers. . . .

Lake Umbagog hosts the largest nesting concentration of common loons in New Hampshire. Abundant fish populations and wetland habitat support one of the highest concentrations of nesting osprey in New Hampshire. The area's forested wetlands support good numbers of black ducks, hooded and common mergansers and mallards also nest in the area. The lake provides habitat for migrating scaup, three varieties of scoters and Canada geese.

. . . Also found around the lake are gray jay, spruce grouse, black-backed and northern three-toed woodpeckers and palm warblers, all northern species considered rare in New Hampshire.

The lake area also supports a variety of mammals, including white-tailed deer, a high density of moose, black bear, beaver, fisher, coyote and bobcat.

The Fish and Wildlife Service's habitat management activities include forest enhancement for the benefit of wildlife diversity, through a cooperative forest management plan; monitoring common loon nesting activities (more than twenty nesting pairs) and the effects of dam-controlled water levels on nesting birds; and monitoring and protecting the habitat and nesting activities of bald eagles.

The refuge is open daily. There is no entrance fee. The refuge headquarters is open on weekdays, except national holidays.

Visitor activities include wildlife observation; hiking; boating, kayaking, and canoeing (a canoe-trips leaflet is available at refuge headquarters); camping; fishing; and hunting on parts of the refuge during the designated seasons. The refuge's campground facilities are managed by the State of New Hampshire's Division of Parks and Recreation. To call for camping reservations: tel.: (603) 271-3628.

Insect repellent is advised during the warmer months.

Lodgings and meals are available in Berlin and Gorham, N.H., and Bethel and Rangeley, Me.

Access to the refuge's headquarters from State Route 26 at Errol, N.H. is northeast 4.5 miles on State Hwy. 16.

Information: Umbagog NWR, P.O. Box 240, Errol, NH 03579; tel.: (603) 482-3415.

New Jersey

Cape May, containing more than 10,000 acres in three parts toward an anticipated goal of 21,000 acres, was established in 1989, when the Fish and Wildlife Service acquired the initial 90-acre tract from The Nature Conservancy. The refuge manages and protects vital habitat for spectacular concentrations of migrating birds on Cape May Peninsula, in southeastern New Jersey. More than 315 bird species have been recorded here.

Nearly 100 species of neotropical migratory songbirds traveling between Central or South America and the northern United States or Canada, and at least 17 species of raptors, notably sharp-shinned, Cooper's, broad-winged, red-tailed, and red-shouldered hawks, northern harriers, and merlin, pause to rest and feed on the peninsula. Large numbers of the American woodcock congregate here in autumn. The vicinity of Cape Charles, at the southern end of the Delmarva Peninsula on Virginia's Eastern Shore, is the only other major "funneling" place along the Atlantic coast where woodcock gather in such numbers (see the Eastern Shore of Virginia refuge text for further discussion of the woodcock).

As the Fish and Wildlife Service explains,

Cape May Peninsula's unique configuration and location concentrate songbirds, raptors and woodcock as they funnel south to Cape May Point during their fall migration. Faced with 12 miles of water to cross at . . . [the mouth of] Delaware Bay, [many of the] migrants linger in the area to rest and feed until favorable winds allow them to cross the Bay. . . .

The Refuge's five-mile stretch along . . . Delaware Bay is a major resting and feeding area for migrating shorebirds and wading birds each spring. The Delaware Bay shoreline has gained international recognition as a major shorebird staging area in North America, second only to the Copper River Delta in [southern]

Alaska. Each year, hundreds of thousands of shorebirds—nearly 80 percent of some populations—stop to rest and feed here [on Cape May Peninsula] during their spring migration from Central and South America to their Arctic breeding grounds.

The arrival at Cape May of more than twenty shorebird species—primarily red knots, ruddy turnstones, sanderlings and semipalmated sandpipers—coincides with the horseshoe crab spawning season, which occurs in May/early June. The crab eggs provide an abundant food supply which these long-distance flyers use to replenish their energy reserves before moving on. (In May, virtually the entire North American red knot population gathers along Delaware Bay beaches!)

The refuge's diverse habitats include expanses of tidally influenced salt marsh and salt meadow that are interspersed with a mosaic of meandering tidal creeks and inlets; freshwater ponds, creeks, marshes, and shrub/scrub wetlands and bogs; seasonally flooded lowland swamp; upland forest; fields; and a stretch of ocean beach. Nearly half of the refuge consists of upland habitat, dominated by such species of trees as pitch pine and oaks (white, chestnut, black, and scarlet). The other half of the refuge is wetland, with the majority of this area consisting of ecologically rich deciduous-forest swamp.

The refuge's Great Cedar Swamp Division, in Dennis and Upper townships, is named for its once-abundant Atlantic white cedar tree, which now generally occurs only in small patches. Several miles to the southwest, the Delaware Bay Division stretches along five miles of the eastern shore of Delaware Bay. And the nearly 500-acre Two-Mile Beach Unit, containing a stretch of Atlantic Ocean beach, sand dunes, and salt marsh, is about five miles to the southeast of the Delaware Bay Division, near the southern tip of the peninsula. There are some interior trails on the latter unit, but the beach may continue to be seasonally closed (from April 1 through September) to avoid disturbing the beach-nesting piping plovers, least terns, and black skimmers.

Following decades of ecologically unnatural fire suppression, the Fish and Wildlife Service's planned habitat management activities include periodic prescribed burning: in upland forests to "reduce hazardous fuel, reduce overstory stand density, reduce understory density, increase heath or grass/forb density, [and] control invasive species"; in upland brush habitat to "reduce hazardous fuel, set back succession, [and] control invasive species"; and in grassland to "reduce hazardous fuel, set back succession (woody growth), [and] control invasive species."

Establishment of the refuge is being made possible partly with revenues from the sale of Migratory Bird Hunting and Conservation Stamps (Duck Stamps).

The refuge is open daily during daylight hours. There is no entrance fee. The refuge headquarters, at 24 Kimbles Beach Rd. in the town of Cape May Court House, is open on weekdays, except national holidays.

Visitor activities include wildlife and butterfly observation (including migrating monarchs), hiking, fishing, crabbing, and hunting on parts of the refuge during the designated seasons. Although camping is not permitted on the refuge, campground facilities are available at several nearby locations. Swimming, sunbathing, and surfing are not permitted on the Two-Mile Beach Unit. Hiking opportunities on trails and woodland roads include the Woodcock Trail—a 1.5-mile path, located a short distance south of the refuge headquarters.

Visitors are cautioned to be alert for ticks, which may carry Lyme disease. Insect repellent is advised during the warmer months.

Lodgings and meals are available in such communities as Cape May Court House and Cape May.

Access to the refuge headquarters from Exit 10 on the Garden State Parkway is west about 0.2 mile on Stone Harbor Blvd. (Route 657), left at the stoplight onto U.S. Hwy. 9 for about 0.5 mile, right onto Hand Ave. for 2.8 miles, left onto State Hwy. 47 for 0.1 mile, and right onto Kimbles Beach Rd. to the refuge headquarters on the right.

Information: Cape May NWR, 24 Kimbles Beach Rd., Cape May Court House, NJ 08210; tel.: (609) 463-0994.

Edwin B. Forsythe, comprising more than 43,000 acres, protects and manages coastal habitat for migratory water birds, in southern New Jersey. The refuge's first segment was established in 1939 as the Brigantine National Wildlife Refuge. In 1984, Brigantine was combined with Barnagat National Wildlife Refuge (which had been established in 1967), and the complex was renamed in honor of the conservation achievements in Congress of the late Rep. Edwin B. Forsythe.

More than 80 percent of the refuge consists of ecologically important tidal salt marsh and salt meadow habitat, interspersed with bays and coves. Approximately 5,000 acres of the refuge contain woodlands with such trees as pitch pine, white cedar, and oaks.

Refuge wetlands have long attracted large concentrations of migratory waterfowl—notably the Atlantic brant and American black duck, the populations of which have significantly declined in recent decades. In spring, peak concentrations of migrants generally occur from late March into early April. During the spectacular autumn migration, the refuge can attract more than 100,000 ducks and geese. The greatest numbers of brant and snow geese are here from mid-November through December. The peak of the spring influx of neotropical migratory songbirds, including many species of warblers, occurs in early May. When horseshoe crabs spawn in May and June at such places as Turtle Cove, large numbers of shorebirds gather to feast on crab eggs.

Regarding habitat management activities, the Fish and Wildlife Service explains:

On the Brigantine Division, refuge staff have used the management technique of "diking" to create 1,415 acres of impounded fresh- and brackish-water marsh habitat in the heart of naturally occurring tidal salt marsh. We created these wetlands to support a wider variety of wildlife than could native salt marsh alone. Water levels in the impoundments are managed to enhance the resources on which wildlife depend[s]. In spring, refuge staff draw the water down to maximize growth of plants beneficial to waterfowl. The drawdown also provides mud flat feeding habitat for shorebirds and wading birds. We reflood the impoundments just in time for the arrival of fall migrants.

Each spring and fall, tens of thousands of migrating ducks and geese, wading birds and shorebirds concentrate here. They linger to rest and feed on the rich resources provided by our managed impoundments. . . . Several migratory species, including the black duck, remain at the refuge through summer to nest and raise their young. Atlantic brant and black ducks also overwinter here.

More than 290 species of birds have been recorded on the refuge.

The refuge also includes the Holgate Unit, which protects an ecologically important area of wild barrier island beach and sand dunes at the southern end of Long Beach Island. Piping plovers, least terns, and black skimmers nest here, in one of the very few remaining places along the New Jersey coast where these and other beach-nesting species can find suitable nesting habitat. All three of these birds are state-listed endangered species, and the plover is also a federally listed endangered species.

Consequently, during the nesting season, which runs approximately from April 1 through August, the Holgate Unit is closed to all public entry to avoid disturbing the birds' nesting activities. Another stretch of protected barrier island beach and sand dunes, which is closed all year to general visitation, is located on Little Beach Island. In 1975, both of these ecologically sensitive areas, along with about 6,000 acres of the refuge's previously unditched salt marsh, were designated as the 6,600-acre unit of the National Wilderness Preservation System.

Habitat-management activities include the use of prescribed burning. (For a discussion of the reasons for using fire in the same habitat types, see the Cape May Refuge text.)

Establishment of the refuge was made possible partly with revenues from the sale of Migratory Bird Hunting and Conservation Stamps (Duck Stamps). Ducks Unlimited, Inc. has helped enhance nearly 1,000 acres of the refuge's wetland habitat.

The refuge is open daily during daylight hours. An entrance fee is charged. The refuge headquarters is open on weekdays, except national holidays. Most of the refuge's visitor use facilities are located at the Brigantine Division's headquarters area.

Visitor activities include wildlife observation, viewing wildlife displays at refuge headquarters, environmental education programs, driving the eight-mile Wildlife Drive that loops around freshwater pools and the brackish East Pool and offers views of wetlands and uplands, and viewing the refuge and wildlife from two observation towers along the drive. Elsewhere on the refuge, visitor activities include interpretive walks, canoeing and boating (a launching ramp at Scotts Landing), fishing, and hunting during the designated seasons. Swimming and camping are not permitted on the refuge, but campground facilities are provided at Wharton State Forest.

Hiking opportunities on the Brigantine Division include two short trails, one of which includes a boardwalk across salt marsh. The Barnegat Division offers a woodland trail (reached from the junction of Mantoloking and Adamston roads in Brick Township); and (wheelchair-accessible) observation platform offering a view of 600-acre Barnegat impoundment (adjacent to Bay Shore Drive, east of State Hwy. 9).

Visitors are cautioned to be alert for ticks, some of which may carry Lyme disease. Insect repellent is advised during the warmer months.

Lodgings and meals are available in Smithville, Absecon, and Atlantic City.

Access to the refuge headquarters on the Brigantine Division is east from U.S. Hwy. 9 at Oceanville, by way of Great Creek Road.

Information: Edwin B. Forsythe NWR, Box 72, Great Creek Rd., Oceanville, NJ 08231; tel.: (609) 652-1665.

Great Swamp, encompassing 7,530 acres, was established in 1960 to protect a miraculously surviving, ecologically rich area of swamp woodland, cattail marsh, grassland, and wooded upland ridges. The refuge, which lies a mere 26 miles to the west of New York City's skyscrapers, is surrounded by the sprawling suburban, urban, and industrial development of northern New Jersey. More than 240 bird species have been recorded here.

Historically, parts of the Great Swamp were logged for its virgin-growth timber, and other parts were drained and converted to agriculture. But then, in 1959, the Port Authority of New

York and New Jersey proposed construction of a huge jetport to occupy 10,000 acres, including the Great Swamp. An outpouring of public opposition succeeded in defeating the proposed destruction of the swamp's irreplaceable ecological values. The Great Swamp Committee of the North American Wildlife Foundation, with the assistance of numerous volunteers, spearheaded a fund-raising campaign that raised more than $1 million to acquire 3,000 acres of the swamp's core. This success quickly led to saving the Great Swamp when the acreage was donated to the Fish and Wildlife Service as a national wildlife refuge. In 1966, the area was honored when it was designated as a National Natural Landmark, and two years later, roughly 3,600 acres became the refuge system's first unit of the National Wilderness Preservation System.

The Great Swamp's diverse habitats contain more than 600 documented species of trees and other plants. Among the most spectacular of these are some huge, virgin-growth beech and oak trees, the trunks of which measure as much as 10 to 12 feet in circumference at breast height. Lowland swamp habitat consists primarily of such species as American sycamore, sweetgum, swamp white oak, river birch, black willow, black tupelo, and red maple. Areas of marsh support such aquatic plants as cattails, sedges, blue flag (wild iris), marsh marigold, white water lily, spatterdock (yellow pond lily), arrowhead, and pickerelweed.

Refuge habitat-management activities include the seasonal raising and lowering of water levels within a number of shallow, diked pools, known as moist-soil impoundments. Water levels are lowered part of the year to promote the growth of submergent and emergent vegetation that later in the year provides nutrient-rich food and shelter for migratory waterfowl. Previously drained wetlands are restored. The refuge's several hundred acres of grassland and shrubby habitats are maintained with periodic mowing to prevent woody plants from taking over this important wildlife area. Young to old-age forests are maintained to provide a diversity of habitats. Nesting boxes are placed on the refuge for wood ducks and bluebirds, to supplement the limited number of natural nesting cavities.

The refuge is open daily during daylight hours. There is no entrance fee. The refuge headquarters is open on weekdays, except national holidays, and on Sundays.

Visitor activities include wildlife observation; hiking; prearranged group tours; limited deer hunting; and driving Pleasant Plains Road, which leads to the refuge headquarters, and Long Hill Road, which leads to the refuge's Wildlife Observation Center. Boating, fishing, and camping are not permitted on the refuge. Campground facilities are available on Mahlon Dickerson and Lewis Morris county parks. Hiking opportunities include two (wheelchair-accessible) boardwalks in the vicinity of the Wildlife Observation Center. There are also about eight miles of hiking trails within the refuge's wilderness area (waterproof footgear recommended).

Visitors are cautioned to be alert for poison ivy and ticks. The latter may carry Lyme disease. Insect repellent is advised during the warmer months.

Lodgings and meals are available in Summit, Chatham, Madison, Basking Ridge, Morristown, Whippany, and Parsippany.

Access to the Great Swamp Refuge's Wildlife Observation Center (WOC) from Exit 30A on I-287 is south on North Maple Ave. to a stoplight; left onto Madisonville Rd. (which becomes Lee's Hill Rd.) for 2.7 miles; and right onto Long Hill Rd. for 2.2 miles to the WOC. To reach the refuge headquarters, continue south on Long Hill Rd., right onto White Bridge Rd., and right onto Pleasant Plains Rd.

Information: Great Swamp NWR, 241 Pleasant Plains Rd., Basking Ridge, NJ 07920; tel.: (973) 425-1222.

Wallkill River, containing more than 5,100 acres toward an anticipated goal of about 8,200 acres, was established in 1990. The refuge's mission is to enhance and protect a diversity of ecologically important habitats along a nine-mile stretch of the north-flowing Wallkill River and a number of its tributaries, in northwestern New Jersey and southern New York State. More than 220 bird species have been recorded here.

Forested wetlands and wet meadows border the Wallkill River. This rich bottomland provides valuable habitat for migrating and nesting waterfowl, such as American black and wood ducks, mallards, green-winged teal, common mergansers, and Canada geese. Among the swamp and floodplain trees are American sycamore, river birch, and red maple. Hardwood forest at high elevations contains such species as white oak, shagbark hickory, and sugar maple; and limestone outcroppings support "islands" of eastern hemlocks.

Much of the refuge's upland terrain consists of grasslands. Under cooperative agreements with local farmers, former farm fields are being restored and maintained with native warm-season grasses that are harvested as hay crops late in the summer.

One of this refuge's biologically outstanding aspects is the large number of butterflies and dragonflies. According to the Fish and Wildlife Service, more than fifty species of butterflies and approximately sixty species of dragonflies and damselflies have been identified here.

Regarding the refuge's management, the Fish and Wildlife Service explains, "Many of the historic wetland areas along the river were drained in the past. Management activities include restoring some areas to their natural wetland condition, creating "potholes" which hold spring and fall floodwaters in areas where the original hydrology cannot be restored, and managing some areas as moist-soil units for waterfowl and wading birds."

Other activities include the "management of early successional growth to benefit breeding woodcock and songbirds such as the golden-winged warbler"; the "protection and management of upland forests in large unfragmented blocks to benefit songbirds such as the cerulean warbler and worm-eating warbler"; and the "management of non-native invasive species, such as purple loosestrife." (See further discussion of loosestrife in the Montezuma NWR text.)

Establishment of this refuge has been made possible partly with revenues from the sale of Migratory Bird Hunting and Conservation Stamps (Duck Stamps). Among the refuge's non-profit partners are a number of chapters of the National Audubon Society, The Nature Conservancy, Trust for Public Land, The Conservation Fund, National Fish and Wildlife Foundation, Orange County Land Trust, Wallkill River Task Force, and Ducks Unlimited, Inc.

The refuge is open daily during daylight hours. There is no entrance fee. The refuge headquarters is open on weekdays, except national holidays.

Visitor activities include wildlife and butterfly observation, hiking on several trails, canoeing and kayaking, fishing, and hunting on parts of the refuge during the designated seasons. Although camping is not permitted on the refuge, facilities are available nearby. Canoeing and small-boating access to the Wallkill River is provided at County Hwy. 565 in Vernon, N.J.; at Bassetts Bridge Rd. in Wantage, N.J.; and at Oil City Rd. in Pine Island (Warwick), N.Y. The refuge is planning for canoeing and fishing access and a Wood Duck Nature Trail parking area near the south end of the refuge, adjacent to Scenic Lakes Rd., about 200 yards north of that road's junction with State Hwy. 23 in Hardyston.

As described by Refuge Manager Libby Herland:

Your impression of the refuge is greatly influenced by your mode of transportation. Driving along the edge of the refuge, one gets a sense of broad, open expanses with wonderful Appalachian Mountain views and valleys. From the trails, one experiences the intimacy of singing songbirds right above your head, bobolinks perched on the tip of a grass blade, and wood ducks flying through the trees. From the river, the quiet stillness reflected in the great blue heron, the forest canopy reaching over the river, and the moss-covered limestone provide a completely different experience.

Visitors are cautioned to be alert for poison ivy and ticks. The latter may carry Lyme disease. Insect repellent is advised during the warmer months.

Lodgings and meals are available in Hamburg, Colesville, and Vernon, N.J., and Warwick, N.Y.

Access to the refuge from State Hwy. 23, about midway between Hamburg and Sussex, is north 1.5 miles on County Hwy. 565.

Information: Wallkill River NWR, 1547 County Hwy. 565, Sussex, NJ 07461; tel.: (973) 702-7266.

New Mexico

Bosque del Apache, comprising 57,331 acres, was established in 1939 to enhance and protect an ecologically diverse and scenically spectacular area at the northern end of the Chihuahuan Desert, in the middle Rio Grande Valley of south-central New Mexico. This magnificent refuge reaches across the valley, between the Chupadera Mountains on the west and the San Pascual Mountains on the east. The 7,000-acre central core of the area consists of riparian floodplain habitat, onto which Rio Grande waters are diverted to maintain wetlands and croplands for the benefit of large concentrations of wintering geese, ducks, sandhill cranes, and other wildlife. Over 375 bird species have been recorded here.

The Spanish name *Bosque del Apache* means "woods of the Apache," derived from the time when Apache Indians occupied encampments in the sheltered riparian woodlands of willows and great cottonwood trees bordering the Rio Grande. In 1845, the land within today's refuge was designated by the Mexican government as the Bosque del Apache land grant.

From mid-November through mid-February, this is an especially magical place, where visitors may enjoy watching huge clouds of snow geese against the distant mountains: flock after flock, wave upon wave of undulating lines and Vs, circling, gliding, and calling as they come, then landing and covering the ground like snow, to feed for a while, only to erupt en masse into the air once more amid a great chorus of their honking calls. Up to 50,000 of these Arctic-nesting geese spend the winter here.

This, too, is the time to observe sandhill cranes, groups of these stately, red-crowned, gray birds stalking slowly across cornfields in search of food, their guttural, deep-rolling, honking calls heard for miles. When this refuge was established, there were fewer than 1,000 of this species remaining in the Central Flyway—and a mere 17 of them wintering here. Today, thanks to theFish and Wildlife Service's management programs, this refuge hosts roughly 18,000 of them.

Huge undulating flocks of red-winged and yellow-headed blackbirds fill the air above the wetlands. Wintering mallards, shovelers, pintails, and other ducks find areas of open water on ponds often partially frozen over and bordered by frost-highlighted cattails. Flocks of wild turkeys strut across fields and within the bosque woodlands.

The refuge implements a number of habitat-management programs. Water-control structures, including fifty miles of irrigation canals, divert and contain some of the waters of the Rio Grande to maintain marshes, rotational moist-soil units, and cropland. Grain crops are produced, some under cooperative agreements with farmers, for the benefit of the geese, cranes, and other wildlife. Marshy, moist-soil impoundments are drained, burned or disced, and refilled to promote the growth of marsh plants such as smartweed, chufa, bulrushes, sedges, and wild millet for the benefit of ducks and other water birds. Areas of tamarisk, an aggressive, non-native shrubby tree, are eradicated to allow the reestablishment of cottonwoods, willows, and other native species.

Roughly 30,000 acres of the refuge's Chihuahuan Desert uplands and foothills have been designated as the Chupadera, Indian Well, and Little San Pascual Wilderness—units of the National Wilderness Preservation System.

Adjacent to the refuge's visitor center, volunteers and refuge staff have created a native plant garden with an extensive area of cacti, many flowering plants that attract more than sixty species of butterflies, native desert shrubs, and a tiny cienega where seeping water creates a pond attracting quail and other wildlife.

Establishment of this refuge was made possible partly with funding from the sale of Migratory Bird Hunting and Conservation Stamps (Duck Stamps). Ducks Unlimited, Inc. has assisted with important habitat-enhancement projects.

The refuge is open daily during daylight hours. The visitor center, which is open daily, presents interpretive displays and programs.

Visitor activities include wildlife observation; driving the 12-mile tour loop road (access fee); viewing the wetland habitats and wildlife from seven (wheelchair-accessible) observation platforms along the tour road; hiking a number of trails (including several offering views of wetland and bosque habitats; and a challenging climb to the 6,272-foot summit of Chupadera Peak); bicycling on roads open to motor vehicles and on designated bike trails; picnicking (a picnic pavilion is available adjacent to the visitor center); interpretive group tours (reservations required); primitive group camping for educational and volunteer groups only (reservations required); fishing; and limited hunting on part of the refuge during the designated season. Although there are no camping facilities provided on the refuge, campgrounds are located near the refuge.

Visitors are cautioned to be alert for rattlesnakes. Insect repellent is advised during the warmer months. Hikers are urged to carry a generous supply of water, especially on the longer excursions.

In late November, the Bosque del Apache Festival of the Cranes features guided refuge tours, study groups, demonstrations, workshops, exhibits, and other environmental education programs for adults and children. For a copy of the festival brochure: tel.: (505) 835-0424.

Lodgings and meals are available in Socorro; and two B&Bs are located in San Antonio.

Access to the refuge is south 9 miles from Socorro to Exit 139 on I-25 at San Antonio, east 0.25 mile on State Hwy. 380, and right (at the flashing signal light) south 9 miles on Old State Hwy. 1 to the visitor center.

Information: Bosque del Apache NWR, P.O. Box 1246, Socorro, NM 87801; tel.: (575) 835-1828.

Las Vegas, containing 8,672 acres, was established in 1965 as a sanctuary for the conservation of migratory birds. The refuge protects a scenically beautiful, canyon-bordered plateau in the 6,000- to 6,500-foot elevation foothills of the rugged Sangre de Cristo Mountains, in northern New Mexico.

Here at the merging of the western edge of the Great Plains with the southern end of the Rocky Mountains, habitats atop the plateau include broad expanses of shortgrass prairie; scattered marshes, ponds, and impoundments where water levels are regulated for the benefit of waterbirds; groves of cottonwood trees; and croplands that are planted with wheat, barley, corn, and peas for the benefit of waterfowl and other wildlife. Gambel oak and pinyon pine-juniper woodlands grow on canyon slopes; tall ponderosa pines rise along canyon rims.

Raptors, such as bald and golden eagles and numerous hawks, are prominent among the migratory and nesting birds of this refuge. When there is sufficient water, thousands of geese and ducks, hundreds of sandhill cranes, and many shorebirds pause on their southward autumn migration or spend the winter on the refuge. Numerous neotropical migratory songbirds also pass through here during spring and autumn. More than 270 bird species have been recorded here.

Establishment of the refuge was made possible partly with revenues from the sale of Migratory Bird Hunting and Conservation Stamps (Duck Stamps).

The refuge is open daily during daylight hours. There is no entrance fee. The refuge office is open on weekdays, except national holidays.

Visitor activities include wildlife observation; driving the eight-mile tour road (also, on Sunday afternoons in November, driving a 4.5-mile autumn-wildlife route through part of the refuge that is otherwise closed to visitors); hiking the scenic but fairly steep 0.5-mile Gallinas Nature Trail (open by permit only on weekdays) that descends into scenic Gallinas Canyon; fishing (only at Lake McAllister—a state-owned waterfowl area within the refuge); and limited hunting on part of the refuge during the designated seasons. Although camping is not permitted on the refuge, primitive camping is allowed at Lake McAllister. Camping facilities are available in Storrie Lake State Park. Visitors are cautioned to be alert for rattlesnakes.

Lodgings and meals are available in Las Vegas, N.M..

Access to the refuge from Exit 345 on I-25 at Las Vegas is east 1.5 miles on State Hwy. 104 and south about four miles on State Hwy. 281.

Information: Las Vegas NWR, Route 1, Box 339, Las Vegas, NM 87701; tel.: (505) 425-3581.

Sevilleta, consisting of 229,673 acres, was established in 1973 to restore and protect a vast, ecologically outstanding area of diverse wildlife habitats at the northern end of the Chihuahuan Desert, in central New Mexico's Rio Grande Valley. The refuge extends across the valley from the Ladrone Mountains on the west to the Los Pinos Mountains on the east. Although there are extensive expanses of semiarid and arid upland and foothills, a relatively small but significant portion of Sevilleta contains riparian wetland.

Most of this refuge was formerly part of a Spanish land grant established in 1819 and known as the Sevilleta de la Joya ("the Jewel"). After New Mexico became a United States territory, the former grant was bought by businessman General Thomas Campbell who grazed cattle on the land. Following prolonged drought, the Campbell Family Foundation decided to make the Sevilleta available for environmental research and protective management. In 1973, at far below market value, the Foundation conveyed the land to The Nature Conservancy, which then donated it to the Fish and Wildlife Service.

The major focus of this refuge is long-term ecological research, combined with ecologically sensitive restoration and protective management of land that was previously impaired by many years of livestock grazing, aggressive invasion of non-native vegetation, ecologically disruptive fire suppression, and other harmful human impacts. A number of habitat-restoration programs have been and continue to be implemented. Among them are the reintroduction of fire by means of periodic prescribed burning; removal and control of non-native plant species, such as tamarisk and Russian olive; replanting with native cottonwoods and willows; and restoration of natural wetland areas with construction of water control structures and impoundments.

Among the refuge's habitat-enhancement partners are Ducks Unlimited, Inc., Bosque Improvement Group, New Mexico State Game & Fish, and the Intermountain West Joint Venture.

Geese, ducks, sandhill cranes, shorebirds, and neotropical migratory songbirds pause on the refuge during their spring and autumn migrations. Rocky Mountain bighorn sheep, pronghorn, and mule deer are among the roughly ninety species of mammals. In 1995, Sevilleta was chosen to help implement the Mexican Gray Wolf Reintroduction Program. The Mexican wolf is genetically the most distinct, rarest, and southernmost subspecies of the North American gray wolf.

The refuge is open daily during daylight hours. There is no entrance fee. The visitor center, where information on the wolf program is offered, is open on weekdays, except national holidays.

Visitor activities include wildlife observation on the refuge's Unit A, Cornerstone Marsh, and Unit B; hiking in scenic San Lorenzo Canyon and on a one-mile interpretive trail with four "biome" loops featuring Great Plains prairie grassland, Rocky Mountain pinyon-juniper woodland, Great Basin steppe-shrubland, and Chihuahuan Desert; and hunting on Unit A during the designated seasons. Educational programs and interpretive tours may be scheduled with the refuge staff.

Visitors are cautioned to be alert for rattlesnakes. More than 200 species of birds have been recorded on the refuge.

Lodgings and meals are available in Socorro.

Access to the refuge headquarters is a short drive west from Exit 169 on I-25.

Information: Sevilleta NWR, P.O. Box 1248, Socorro, NM 87801; tel.: (575) 864-4021.

New York

Iroquois, consisting of 10,818 acres, was established in 1958 to manage and protect an area of hardwood swamps, woodlands, freshwater marshes, wet meadows, pastures, and croplands for the benefit of migratory waterfowl and other wildlife. The refuge is located midway between Rochester and Buffalo, in northwestern New York.

A primary purpose of this refuge is to offer migratory birds a resting and feeding area on their flights between breeding and wintering grounds. The largest influx of migrating waterfowl occurs from mid-March through early April, with totals averaging from 40,000 to 80,000 Canada geese and more than 4,000 ducks of two dozen species. According to the Fish and Wildlife Service, only a few hundred of these birds remain each year to nest on the refuge. The less spectacular peak of autumn waterfowl migration generally occurs from mid-September through early October. Migrating shorebirds reach the peak of their northbound numbers in May and southbound numbers in July and August. Large influxes of neotropical migratory songbirds, including many species of warblers, pass through the refuge from late April to mid-May. More than 265 species of birds have been recorded here.

A number of habitat management activities occur on the refuge. Water levels are managed within each of 16 diked shallow impoundments. Draw downs for each impoundment occur on a five-year cycle, so that several of these areas are drained down each year, providing habitat for migrating shorebirds and to promote the growth of nutrient-rich submergent and emergent plants. These aquatic plants provide food and shelter for migratory waterfowl when water levels are subsequently raised.

Woodland areas are managed with selective cutting and mowing "woodcock strips" with a brush hog. Grassland habitat is maintained by mowing and periodic prescribed burning to prevent the invasion of woody plants and to promote nutrient cycling. The refuge also controls certain pest plants, notably the non-native, invasive purple loosestrife (see discussion of this species in the Montezuma Refuge text).

Establishment of this refuge was made possible partly with revenues from the sale of Migratory Bird Hunting and Conservation Stamps (Duck Stamps). Ducks Unlimited, Inc. has helped enhance more than 300 acres of the refuge's wetland habitat.

The refuge is open daily during daylight hours. There is no entrance fee. The visitor center is open on weekdays, except national holidays, and is also open on weekends during the spring migration.

Visitor activities include wildlife observation, viewing interpretive exhibits at the visitor center, driving on a number of public highways and roads that run through or adjacent to the refuge, viewing refuge wetlands from four observation overlooks, hiking on several trails, cross-country skiing and snowshoeing, bicycling (only on Feeder Road and public roads), canoeing and non-motorized boating only on Oak Orchard Creek, fishing, trapping, and hunting on parts of the refuge during the designated seasons. Although camping is not permitted on the refuge, facilities are available at a number of nearby places.

Visitors are cautioned to be alert for ticks, which may carry Lyme disease. Insect repellent is advised during the warmer months.

Lodgings and meals are available in such communities as Batavia, Medina, and Corfu.

Access to the refuge from Exit 48A on the New York State Thruway (I-90) is north and northwest eight miles on State Hwy. 77 and right on Casey Rd. to the visitor center.

Information: Iroquois NWR, 1101 Casey Rd., Basom, NY 14013; tel.: (585) 948-5445.

Montezuma, comprising 7,889 acres, was established in 1938 to restore and protect part of the once-vast Montezuma Marsh for the benefit of large concentrations of migratory waterfowl and other wildlife. The refuge is located at the northern end of Cayuga Lake, in the Finger Lakes Region of north-central New York.

For thousands of years, this marsh, which measured roughly 12 miles in length by 8 miles at its widest, was among North America's most important freshwater wetlands. Native Americans, first the Algonquin Indians and then the Cayugas of the Iroquois Nation, obtained some of their food and other needs from the marsh while leaving the habitat intact. As Euro-American settlers moved into the region in the 19th century, small areas around the edge of the wetlands were drained for agriculture. But the Fish and Wildlife Service explains:

There were no dramatic changes in the marsh until the development of the Erie Canal . . . [constructed from 1817 to 1825], when it became apparent that feeder canals from Seneca and Cayuga Lakes would in time link these lakes with the main line. . . .

In 1910, construction of the Seneca and Cayuga extension of the New York State Barge Canal altered the marshes. A lock was built at the north end of Cayuga Lake and a dam was constructed at the outlet of the lake. This effectively lowered the level of the river by eight to ten feet . . . and the waters drained from the marshes. The meandering rivers were straightened and deepened, thereby creating additional drainage-ways.

In 1937, after the Bureau of Biological Survey (which later became the Fish and Wildlife Service) acquired 6,432 acres of the former marshland, the Civilian Conservation Corps started to create a network of low dikes within which water could be held and regulated to begin the task of marsh restoration. The following year, the Montezuma Migratory Bird Refuge (subsequently renamed as a national wildlife refuge) was established. By the early 1940s, the refuge's wetlands were gradually restored.

Under a cooperative conservation program, known as the Montezuma Wetlands Complex Initiative, 30,000 acres of other lands are now being enhanced and managed for the benefit of the wetland-dependent wildlife and compatible public recreational uses. These lands are a mixture of marsh habitat, grasslands, farm fields, and small patches of woodland.

Montezuma refuge contains about 3,500 acres of diked shallow pools, known as moist-soil impoundments, within which water levels are seasonally regulated. During part of the year, the water is lowered to provide shallow water and mudflats for shorebirds and wading birds and to promote the growth of submergent and emergent plants that will later provide food for the influx of migrating waterfowl. During the remainder of the year, water levels are raised to provide resting and feeding habitat for the large concentrations of waterfowl. Submergent plants include sago pondweed, water milfoil, and bladderwort; and emergent species consist mostly of cattails and purple loosestrife.

This refuge has focused on researching ways to control and manage the purple loosestrife— a non-native, invasive wetland pest plant. Although it is visually attractive with its tall, slender spikes of brilliant purplish-pink flowers that bloom from June to September, it aggressively competes with and overwhelms native wetland plants. The Fish and Wildlife Service explains:

Purple loosestrife appeared along the New England seaboard in the early 1800's. A native of Eurasia, it probably arrived with the early maritime traffic. . . . By the late 1800's, . . . [it] had spread throughout the northeastern United States and southeastern Canada. . . .

After the [beginning of the 20th] century, when purple loosestrife began its westward expansion . . . , the plant became a serious threat to wetland communities throughout the northeastern and north central regions of the country. . . .

The impact of this weed on North American wetlands has been disastrous. Native wetland plants have been crowded out by purple loosestrife. The loss of these [native] plants has led to a reduction in suitable habitat for wildlife. . . .

Montezuma National Wildlife Refuge has been, and will remain, a key area for research into management and control of purple loosestrife [because] the refuge has suffered one of the nation's worst infestations [of the plant].

A 1998 Cornell University pamphlet, *Biocontrol Insects Feast on Purple Loosestrife*, states that, "biological control, the use of natural enemies to control a pest, shows real promise. . . . Since 1992, a nationally coordinated program has introduced four species of European insects (one root-mining weevil, one flowering-feeding weevil and two leaf-feeding beetles) in North America." In 1993, the two species of beetles were released at a site in southern Ontario where there was a solid stand of loosestrife. By 1996, "the purple loosestrife biomass was reduced by over 90 percent," while native species such as cattails were flourishing. "The results observed in Ontario are expected to be repeated at many purple loosestrife infestations where insects are introduced. . . ."

Establishment of Montezuma Refuge was made possible partly with revenues from the sale of Migratory Bird Hunting and Conservation Stamps (Duck Stamps). Ducks Unlimited, Inc. has helped enhance more than 3,700 acres of the refuge's wetland habitat.

The refuge is open daily during daylight hours. There is no entrance fee. The visitor center is open daily from March to November and on weekdays during the rest of the year, except Christmas and New Year's Day.

Visitor activities include wildlife observation, viewing interpretive exhibits and programs at the visitor center, viewing the Main Pool and Tschache Pool from observation towers, driving the 3.5-mile Wildlife Drive (an interpretive brochure is available), hiking on the Esker Brook Nature Trail and other trails, guided tours in the spring and autumn, picnicking (at a wheelchair-accessible picnic area), and hunting on parts of the refuge during the designated seasons. Educational programs are offered to organized groups by prearrangement. Camping is not permitted on the refuge, but facilities are available at a number of nearby places, including Cayuga Lake State Park.

Visitors are cautioned to be alert for ticks, which may carry Lyme disease. Insect repellent is advised during the warmer months.

Lodgings and meals are available in Seneca Falls, Waterloo, Auburn, Weedsport, Ithaca, and Syracuse.

Access to the refuge from Exit 41 on I-90 (the New York State Thruway) is south on State Hwy. 414, left at the traffic light and proceeding about five miles on State Hwy. 318 (to the end of the latter route, where it meets U.S. Hwy. 20), left onto Hwy. 20 for 1.25 miles, and left onto the refuge entrance road.

Information: Montezuma NWR, 3395 Route 5 & 20 East, Seneca Falls, NY 13148; tel.: (315) 568-5987.

Oyster Bay, encompassing 3,209 acres, was established in 1968 to protect salt marsh and tidal-bottom bay habitats and a small freshwater wetland. The refuge is located along Oyster Bay, about twenty miles east of New York City, on the north shore of Long Island, N.Y. It is adjacent to Sagamore Hill National Historic Site—a National Park Service–administered area that protects the home of former President Theodore Roosevelt, who established Pelican Island, Florida, as the first national wildlife refuge in 1903.

During the winter, large concentrations of waterfowl are attracted to the refuge, with peak numbers sometimes reaching as many as 24,000 birds. Generally the most common species are greater scaup, American black duck, bufflehead, canvasback, mallard, long-tailed (oldsquaw), common goldeneye, red-breasted merganser, and Canada goose. Frost and Mill Neck creeks provide nesting habitat for black ducks, clapper rails, and ospreys. More than 125 species of birds have been recorded on the refuge.

The bay waters and wetlands attract a number of marine fauna, including harbor and gray seals, Kemp's ridley and loggerhead sea turtles, and an exceptionally large number of the northern diamondback terrapin.

The refuge is open daily during daylight hours. There is no entrance fee.

Visitor activities include wildlife observation, environmental education and interpretive programs, boating, and fishing. The Fish and Wildlife Service says that, "The Refuge receives heavy use from recreational boaters from May through September, numbering three thousand boats on peak weekends and a thousand boats a day during the week. . . . The only remaining commercial oyster farm/aquaculture operation on Long Island operates on the Refuge. It provides 90 percent of New York State's oysters. In addition, fifty independent commercial shellfishers (mainly clammers) are active at the Refuge."

Lodgings and meals are available in Oyster Bay, East Norwich, Huntington Station, and Glen Cove.

Access to the refuge is by boat, public beach, and private docks.

Information: Oyster Bay NWR, c/o The Long Island NWR Complex, P.O. Box 21, Shirley, NY 11967; tel.: (631) 286-0485.

Shawangunk Grasslands, containing 566 acres, was established in 1999 to manage and protect one of the most extensive, intact, and ecologically significant wet grasslands remaining in the northeastern United States. The refuge is located near the village of Wallkill, at the southern edge of Ulster County in southeastern New York. It encompasses most of the former U.S. Army's Galeville Training Site, a West Point Military Academy facility that most recently was being leased to the FBI. When neither the U.S. Army nor the FBI had any further use for the area, it was transferred to the Fish and Wildlife Service. The name *Shawangunk* is pronounced SHAWN-gum.

As the Fish and Wildlife Service explains, "The primary habitat-enhancement activity on the refuge is grassland management to increase the productivity of nesting grassland birds. This includes the management of non-native invasive species, such as purple loosestrife, *Phragmites* [common reed], and Canada thistle." (See further discussion of this species and its control in the Montezuma NWR text.)

Among the many breeding species of grassland birds that are attracted to the refuge are bobolink, upland sandpiper, eastern meadowlark, and a number of sparrows including savannah, vesper, and grasshopper. The grasslands also offer the opportunity of planting grassland wildflowers that attract many species of butterflies. Wintering raptors include short-eared owl and northern harrier.

In addition to the 400 acres of grassland, the refuge includes about 160 acres of mixed hardwood forest of predominantly oak and beech trees; and two small ponds.

The Trust for Public Land has assisted with land acquisition and Ducks Unlimited, Inc. has helped enhance approximately 150 acres of the refuge's wetland habitat.

The refuge is open daily during daylight hours. There is no entrance fee. The headquarters is open on weekdays, except national holidays.

Visitor activities presently include wildlife and butterfly observation, and hiking on the interpretive Dagmar Dale Trail. Future refuge plans include offering interpretive programs, developing an environmental-education program, and providing for limited hunting. More than 150 bird species have already been recorded here.

Visitors are cautioned to be alert for ticks, especially as some of them may carry Lyme disease. Insect repellent is advised during the warmer months.

Lodgings and meals are available in New Paltz, Highland, Poughkeepsie, Milton, Newburgh, and Middletown.

Access to the refuge from Exit 5 on I-84 is north about five miles on County Hwy. 208 into the village of Wallkill, then left one block and left onto Bruyn Turnpike for two miles, and right onto Hoagerburg Rd. for one mile.

Information: Shawangunk Grasslands NWR, c/o Wallkill River NWR, 1547 County Hwy. 565, Sussex, NJ 07461; tel.: (973) 702-7266.

North Carolina

Alligator River, containing 152,195 acres, was established in 1984 to enhance and protect an expanse of diverse wetland habitats, in northeast coastal North Carolina. The Alligator River/Intracoastal Waterway borders the refuge to the west, Albemarle Sound lies to the north, Croatan Sound is to the east, and Pamlico Sound extends to the southeast.

The refuge contains hardwood and Atlantic white cedar swamps, freshwater and brackish marshes, bogs, and areas of pocosin. The latter, also known as "southeast scrub bog," consists of very thick growths of largely evergreen shrubs and scattered pond pines. It is characterized by poorly drained peat soils that are rich in organic matter. Pocosin is derived from a Native American word that means "swamp-on-a-hill."

Large concentrations of migratory waterfowl, wading birds, shorebirds, and neotropical migratory songbirds are attracted to the refuge's diverse habitats. Prominent among these are wintering tundra swans, greater snow and Canada geese, and numerous species of ducks, such as mallards, green-winged teal, northern pintails, ring-necked, and hooded mergansers. As the refuge name implies, a few American alligators inhabit this area, near the northern end of their range.

One of the management highlights of this refuge has been the reintroduction of the red wolf to this area in 1987, as part of the Fish and Wildlife Service's red wolf recovery program. This endangered species historically ranged widely throughout the southeastern United States.

Its population declined nearly to extinction. Today, Alligator River NWR is among a few key places where this species is gradually rebuilding its numbers. (See further discussion of this recovery program in the Cape Romain, Pocosin Lakes, and St. Vincent NWR texts.)

Another endangered species inhabiting Alligator River refuge is the red-cockaded woodpecker. Areas of pine woodlands are being managed to enhance its nesting success. (For further description of this species, see further discussion of this species in the Carolina Sandhills NWR text.)

With assistance of The Nature Conservancy, a substantial portion of this refuge was donated by the Prudential Life Insurance Company. This area had previously been targeted for drainage of its wetlands and mining of peat deposits. Since the refuge was established, Ducks Unlimited, Inc. has helped enhance more than 400 acres of wetland.

The refuge is open daily during daylight hours. There is no entrance fee. The refuge office, in Manteo, is open on weekdays, except national holidays.

Visitor activities include wildlife observation; driving the Wildlife Drive and other refuge roads; hiking on two (wheelchair-accessible) trails; red wolf howling and other interpretive and environmental education programs; canoeing and guided canoe excursions (fee), kayaking, and boating (several boat-launching sites are provided); fishing (a wheelchair-accessible fishing dock is available); and limited hunting on most of the refuge during the designated seasons. Camping is not permitted on the refuge, but facilities are available at Cape Hatteras National Seashore and elsewhere.

Even though alligators are generally afraid of people, visitors are cautioned to stay a safe distance from these sluggish-looking but potentially fast-moving reptiles and to be alert for venomous snakes, ticks, and chiggers. Insect repellent is advised during the warmer months.

Lodgings and meals are available in such communities as Manteo, Wanchese, and Nags Head.

Access to the refuge from U.S. Route 17 at Williamston is east about 75 miles on U.S. Hwy. 64, which runs through the northern part of the refuge; or from U.S. Hwy. 17 at Washington, it is about 85 miles on U.S. Hwy. 264, which runs through the eastern part of the refuge.

Information: Alligator River NWR, P.O. Box 1969, Manteo, NC 27954; tel.: (252) 473-1131.

Mackay Island, containing more than 8,150 acres, was established in 1961 to protect an area of extensive coastal wetlands, known as the Great Marsh, located between Currituck Sound and Back Bay, in the northeast corner of North Carolina and the southeast corner of Virginia. The refuge attracts large concentrations of waterfowl—notably the greater snow goose, as well as numerous wading birds, shorebirds, and neotropical migratory songbirds.

Nearly three-quarters of this refuge consists of slightly brackish to freshwater marsh that is dominated by cattails, black needlerush, and giant cordgrass. Approximately 1,500 acres support upland forest habitat of loblolly pine and hardwoods; and there is a small area of cropland.

The Fish and Wildlife Service is implementing a number of habitat-management activities. Seasonal manipulation of water levels within a number of marsh impoundments (pools) promotes the growth of aquatic plants containing high food value for waterfowl. Nest structures are provided and maintained for breeding wood ducks and ospreys. To prevent an overpopulation of white-tailed deer, the refuge administers an annual hunt. Under cooperative agreements with local farmers, a portion of such cultivated crops as corn, wheat, and soybeans is left unharvested for the benefit of waterfowl and other wildlife.

Periodic prescribed burning helps manage habitats. As explained by the Fish and Wildlife Service, "Fire can provide many benefits to the natural ecosystem. . . . Goose browse is improved by removing old, rank vegetation and enabling the fresh green growth to be accessed by the birds. Fire helps to recycle nutrients that add to the productivity of the marsh. Fire also helps set back the successional stage and prevents the growth of woody vegetation. In addition, these fires are used to help reduce the buildup of wildfire fuels."

A major mission of Mackay Island refuge is to provide vital wintering habitat for the greater snow goose. During the spring and summer, this subspecies nests and raises its young on the Arctic tundra of Canada's Ellesmere and northern Baffin islands. In November, thousands of them arrive on their wintering grounds along the Atlantic Coast—principally from Delaware and Chesapeake bays south to the coastal sounds of North Carolina. Concentrations of 10,000 or more are occasionally seen on the Great Marsh.

Other waterfowl include large numbers of Canada geese, tundra swans, wood and black ducks, mallards, green-winged and blue-winged teal, pintails, northern shovelers, wigeons, and gadwalls. More than 200 bird species have been recorded here.

In 1918, printing magnate and philanthropist Joseph Palmer Knapp acquired the property and built a private resort. He raised waterfowl and experimented with various pioneering wetland-management strategies. In 1937, he was one of the founders of Ducks Unlimited, Inc., a nonprofit conservation organization dedicated to restoring, enhancing, and protecting wetland habitats for North America's waterfowl populations. As *Ducks Unlimited* senior writer, Matt Young, explained in a conservation article in the March–April 1997 magazine:

Knapp is regarded as the father of Ducks Unlimited. His greatest passion in life was waterfowling at his club on North Carolina's Currituck Sound. Dismayed by the decline of waterfowl populations there, Knapp dedicated his energy and much of his vast fortune toward conservation. . . .

DU's revolutionary conservation strategy was to restore extensive permanent wetlands—nicknamed "duck factories"—using modern engineering and construction methods.

Ducks Unlimited has subsequently helped enhance wetland habitats on more than 150 national wildlife refuges across the country. Since its founding, this volunteer-based, grassroots organization has helped restore and conserve more than ten million acres of wetlands on both public and private lands throughout the United States and Canada. In focusing on its "singleness of purpose," DU has formed countless successful partnerships with federal, state, and county governmental agencies; corporations, foundations, private landowners, and other individuals. Information: Ducks Unlimited, Inc., National Headquarters, One Waterfowl Way, Memphis, TN 38120; tel.: (901) 758-3825; Internet: www.ducks.org.

The refuge is open daily during daylight hours. There is no entrance fee. The refuge office is open on weekdays, except national holidays.

Visitor activities include wildlife observation; hiking on two trails (one of which offers views of Great Marsh from an observation platform); bicycling; canoeing, kayaking, and boating (from March 15 to October 15; an unimproved boat-launching ramp is provided at the dike gate); fishing; crabbing; and deer hunting on part of the refuge during the designated season. By prearrangement, the refuge offers opportunities for mobility-challenged hunters. Waterfowl hunting is not permitted on Mackay Island refuge, but it is permitted on nearby Currituck NWR. Camping is not permitted on Mackay Island refuge.

Visitors are cautioned to be alert for venomous snakes, ticks, and chiggers. Insect repellent is advised.

More than 200 species of birds have been recorded here.

Lodgings and meals are available in Currituck and Elizabeth City, N.C.; and Virginia City, Va.

Access to the refuge office from the town of Currituck, N.C., is on the Currituck Sound Ferry and then north just over eight miles on N.C. State Hwy. 615. From the Virginia-North Carolina state line, at the southern edge of Virginia Beach, Va., it is south one mile on Hwy. 615.

Information: Mackay Island NWR, P.O. Box 39, Knotts Island, NC 27950; tel.: (252) 429-3100.

Mattamuskeet, consisting of 50,180 acres, was established in 1934 to protect outstanding wintering waterfowl habitat on Lake Mattamuskeet—North Carolina's largest natural lake—and related wetland habitats. The refuge is located just inland from Pamlico Sound, on the central coast of North Carolina.

From November to March, 20,000 to 35,000 tundra swans, which breed and raise their young in the Arctic habitat of Canada and Alaska, come to this migratory bird mecca. Also during the winter, thousands of snow and Canada geese and tens of thousands of ducks, along with shorebirds and bald eagles, are also attracted to this shallow body of water.

The Fish and Wildlife Service provides nesting boxes for wood ducks, to help increase successful breeding. Bald-cypress trees around the edge of the lake offer nest sites for ospreys. Influxes of neotropical songbirds come through the refuge during their spring and autumn migrations. Over 240 bird species have been recorded here. The American alligator, close to the northern end of its range, occasionally inhabits the refuge's wetlands.

In addition to the lake's 40,000 acres of open water, adjacent wetland habitats comprise just over 3,100 acres of freshwater marsh, 3,500 acres of hardwood swamp, and 2,600 acres of moist-soil impoundments. The water levels within these managed wetlands are drawn down in the spring, providing habitat for egrets, herons, and other wildlife, while at the same time promoting the growth of nutrient-rich plants for waterfowl. Water levels are raised later in the year, offering habitat where wintering waterfowl can rest and feed.

The refuge includes a few hundred acres of cultivated croplands on which local farmers, under cooperative agreements with the Fish and Wildlife Service, leave a portion of crops such as corn, winter wheat, and soybeans unharvested, to provide supplemental food for waterfowl and other wildlife. The refuge also contains a small area of mature loblolly woodland.

Of historic interest is the Mattamuskeet Lodge, near the lakeshore at New Holland. This structure initially housed pumps that drained the lake, and it was subsequently used as a hunting lodge. It is now open for touring, offers space for educational programs, meetings, and other functions. The lodge is open during certain hours on Tuesdays through Saturdays. Information: (252) 926-1422.

Establishment of this refuge was made possible partly with revenues from the sale of Migratory Bird Hunting and Conservation Stamps (Duck Stamps). Ducks Unlimited, Inc. has helped enhance 1,900 acres of the refuge's wetland habitat.

The refuge is open daily during daylight hours. There is no entrance fee. The refuge headquarters is open on weekdays, except national holidays.

Visitor activities include wildlife observation; driving the three-mile refuge entrance road and the five-mile Wildlife Drive—a gravel road that borders the lake's southern shore; hiking on a short interpretive trail near the refuge headquarters and on miles of grass-covered dikes; viewing the refuge and wildlife from two observation decks; canoeing, kayaking, and boating (from March 1 to November 1; three boat-launching ramps into the lake are provided); fishing; crabbing; and hunting (including special youth hunts) on part of the refuge during the designated seasons. Camping is not permitted on the refuge, but facilities are available nearby.

Visitors are cautioned to be alert for venomous snakes, ticks, chiggers. Insect repellent is advised during the warmer months.

Lodgings and meals are available in Belhaven, Fairfield, Engelhard, Swan Quarter, and Washington.

Access to the refuge from U.S. Route 17 at Washington is east 63 miles on U.S. Hwy. 264, and left onto State Hwy. 94 for 1.5 miles to the refuge entrance road. Hwy. 94 continues on north, cutting across Mattamuskeet Lake.

Information: Mattamuskeet NWR, 38 Mattamuskeet Rd., Swan Quarter, NC 27885; tel.: (252) 926-4021.

Pea Island, consisting of 5,834 acres, was established in 1938 to protect a stretch of Outer Banks coastal barrier island habitat along the northern end of Hatteras Island, in northeastern North Carolina. The refuge is about 13 miles long from north to south. It varies from one-quarter mile to one mile in width, between the Atlantic Ocean on the east and Pamlico Sound on the west. An adjacent 25,700 acres of Pamlico Sound are also federally protected. More than 300 bird species have been recorded on the refuge.

The refuge's habitats include sandy ocean beaches, coastal sand dunes, freshwater and brackish ponds and managed impoundments, saltwater marsh, and salt flats.

A major mission of this refuge is to provide vital wintering habitat for migratory waterfowl, including the greater snow goose. During spring and summer, this subspecies nests and raises its young on the Arctic tundra of Canada's Ellesmere and northern Baffin islands. In November, thousands of these magnificent birds arrive on their wintering grounds along the Atlantic Coast—principally from Delaware and Chesapeake bays south to the coastal sounds of North Carolina.

In addition to the geese, the refuge provides wintering, nesting, and resting habitat for other migratory waterfowl, wading birds, shorebirds, raptors, and neotropical songbirds. Several wading bird rookeries and shorebird nesting areas are also located here. The Fish and Wildlife Service manages the water levels on 1,000 acres of impoundments, to promote the growth of plant foods for the benefit of waterfowl and other wildlife. The federally listed threatened piping plover and loggerhead sea turtle nest on the refuge's strand of beach.

The refuge is open daily during daylight hours. There is no entrance fee. The visitor center is open daily from April 1 through November, and at least on weekends from December 1 through March.

Visitor activities include wildlife observation; interpretive programs; hiking on 0.5-mile North Pond Wildlife Trail (which includes four observation platforms), a 4-mile service road around North Pond, and 12 miles of ocean beach; bicycling (on refuge roads); canoeing, kayaking, and boating (a Pamlico Sound boat-launching site is provided); beachcombing; and surf- and sound-fishing. Camping is not permitted on the refuge, but campgrounds are available on the adjacent Cape Hatteras National Seashore and elsewhere.

Visitors are cautioned to be alert for ticks and chiggers. Insect repellent during the warmer months and sunscreen are advised.

Lodgings and meals are available in Manteo, Wanchese, Kitty Hawk, Kill Devil Hills, Nags Head, Buxton, and Hatteras.

Access to the refuge is on State Hwy. 12, which runs through the refuge at the northern end of Hatteras Island, ten miles south of Nags Head.

Information: Pea Island NWR, P.O. Box 1969, Manteo, NC 27954; tel.: (252) 473-1131.

Pee Dee, containing 8,443 acres, was established in 1963 to manage river bottomland and gently rolling hills in the Piedmont region of south-central North Carolina. The refuge's diverse habitats include hardwood and mixed pine-and-hardwood forests, pine plantations, fallow and cultivated fields, lakes and pools, seasonally flooded moist-soil impoundments, numerous creeks, and the Pee Dee River.

During the 1960s, concentrations of ducks and Canada geese started to decline in this part of North Carolina. As explained by the U.S. Fish and Wildlife Service:

Fortunately, lands adjacent to the Pee Dee River and Brown Creek offered excellent potential for waterfowl habitat development. With local and state support, Pee Dee National Wildlife Refuge was established . . . to provide wintering habitat for migratory waterfowl. . . .

The refuge contains 3,000 acres of contiguous bottomland hardwood forest along Brown Creek. This area forms the core of the largest bottomland hardwood tract left in the Piedmont of North Carolina, and has been placed on the registry of State Natural Heritage Areas.

Peak numbers of wintering waterfowl on the refuge can exceed 10,000 ducks, the largest numbers of which are mallards and wood ducks. Several hundred migrating Canada geese pause on the refuge; and there is an increasing flock of around 200 resident Canada geese.

The Fish and Wildlife Service carries out a number of habitat-management activities on the refuge:

Moist soil impoundments are managed by lowering and raising water levels, and discing, mowing, or burning every few years to maintain plants in an early successional stage. These shallowly flooded areas are drained over a period of weeks beginning in late March. This regime creates the proper germination conditions for many favorable moist soil plants, such as smartweed, and produces mudflats needed by migrating shorebirds moving through in April.

Selected impoundments are drained, disked, and shallowly flooded to create mudflats again for shorebirds during their critical August migration. All impoundments, whether they be moist soil plant areas, mudflats, or crops left in the fields by refuge farmers, are flooded in early fall to "set the table" for arriving waterfowl.

In the refuge's upland pine woodlands, prescribed burning helps to curtail dense growths of oaks and other hardwoods that would otherwise eventually become the dominant trees of the forest. Relatively low-burning fires promote nutrient cycling and maintain an open pine woodland ecosystem that is preferred by many species of flora and fauna, including the federally listed endangered red-cockaded woodpecker (see a description of this species in the Carolina Sandhills NWR text). These fires also reduce hazardous accumulations of dead wood, needles, leaves, and other organic debris—fuel overloading—that can contribute to uncontrolled and destructive stand-replacing wildfires. Upland pine stands are selectively thinned "to achieve the tree density required by the red-cockaded woodpecker."

Ducks Unlimited, Inc. has enhanced several hundred acres of the refuge's wetland habitat.

The refuge is open daily during daylight hours. There is no entrance fee. The refuge headquarters is open on weekdays, except national holidays. A refuge environmental education and visitor center is anticipated, as funding becomes available.

Visitor activities include wildlife observation; environmental education events; driving the refuge's 2.5-mile interpretive drive, other refuge roads, and several state roads that run through or border the refuge; hiking on a number of trails (one is wheelchair-accessible); bicycling; canoeing and kayaking (on Brown Creek and Pee Dee River); boating on Ross and Andrews ponds, Beaver Ponds, and Arrowhead Lake (electric motors only); fishing on six ponds, Brown Creek, and Pee Dee River; and hunting on parts of the refuge during the designated seasons (a youth hunt is held in mid-October). Camping is not permitted on the refuge, but facilities are available in Uwharrie National Forest.

The best time to observe concentrations of wintering waterfowl is from November through February. The spring influx of neotropical migratory songbirds reaches its peak during April. More than 200 bird species have been recorded here.

Visitors are cautioned to be alert for ticks and chiggers.

Lodgings and meals are available in Wadesboro, Mount Gilead, and Albemarle.

Access to the refuge from Wadesboro is north seven miles on U.S. Hwy. 52.

Information: Pee Dee NWR, 5770 U.S. Hwy. 52 N, Wadesboro, NC 28170; tel.: (704) 694-4424.

Pocosin Lakes, encompassing 113,674 acres, was established in 1990 to enhance and protect a variety of wetlands, located between Pamlico and Albemarle Sounds in northeastern North Carolina. The refuge includes the 12,000-acre PUNGO LAKE UNIT, which was formerly the Pungo National Wildlife Refuge, established in 1963.

Prominent among the refuge's habitats are the more than 50,000 acres of pocosin wetlands, also known as "southeastern shrub bog." The name *pocosin* is derived from a Native American word meaning "swamp-on-a-hill." This ecologically rich ecosystem contains very thick growths of largely broadleaf-evergreen shrubs, such as sweetbay, loblolly bay, and blueberry, along with scattered pond pines. It is characterized by poorly drained, organically rich, usually waterlogged peat soils that range from four to eight or more feet in depth. As the Fish and Wildlife Service explains:

A significant percentage of the soil volume consists of buried roots, stumps, and logs that persisted as the organic soil accumulated. Most of these organic soils have been subjected to some degree of drainage and will burn when dry.

Due to the volatility of the natural vegetation, the organic soils, the drained condition of the land, and the limited accessibility, the area is one of the most hazardous areas for destructive wildfires in the eastern United States. The most recent large wildfires occurred in 1981 and 1985. Surface elevations were reduced by as much as three feet in parts of the area due to combustion of the peat.

Other refuge habitats include lakes and ponds, managed moist-soil impoundments, riverine swamp, bottomland hardwood forest, farm fields, and agricultural lands. Under cooperative agreements, local farmers who plant crops such as corn and soybeans leave a portion unharvested, providing supplemental food for waterfowl and other wildlife.

The refuge attracts large concentrations of wintering tundra swans, greater snow and Canada geese, numerous species of ducks, and a multitude of neotropical songbirds during the spring and autumn migrations. Resident wildlife includes the black bear, red wolf, and the American alligator, the latter being near the northern end of its range.

The red wolf is a federally listed endangered species that historically ranged widely throughout the southeastern United States. Its population declined nearly to extinction. Today, Pocosin Lakes NWR is among a few key places where this species is gradually rebuilding its numbers, under the Fish and Wildlife Service's red wolf recovery program. In 1987, a number of these animals were introduced onto Alligator River refuge. Since then, a few of them have been brought to Pocosin Lakes, and others have arrived on their own. (See further discussion of the red wolf recovery program in the Alligator River, Cape Romain, and St. Vincent NWR texts.)

Since 1997, an important partner in the red wolf recovery program has been a nonprofit organization known as the Red Wolf Coalition. As the Fish and Wildlife Service explains, "The founding concepts of the Coalition were to serve as the hub of private support for the red wolf, giving the public the first real opportunity to become involved in the Fish and Wildlife Service's Red Wolf Recovery program." Pocosin Lakes refuge is presently working with the coalition toward the goal of developing a Red Wolf Lookout and Education Center. The Coalition has been receiving the support of such organizations as Defenders of Wildlife, the Turner Foundation, Rhode Island Zoological Society, and Roger Williams Park Zoo. Further information about the coalition and its efforts: Red Wolf Coalition, P.O. Box 2318, Kill Devil Hills, NC 27948; tel.: (252) 441-3946.

Habitat management activities include extensive restoration of wetlands on 19,000 acres of this refuge, with installation of water control structures. In the 1990s, a cooperative reforestation project with North Carolina State University was undertaken in an attempt to restore a severely impaired 640-acre pocosin tract. Thousands of Atlantic white cedars and smaller numbers of bald cypress, pond pine, tupelo, ash, and several species of oaks were planted. Prescribed burning within the Pungo Unit's moist-soil impoundments promotes nutrient cycling, enhances habitat and spurs the growth of plant foods for the benefit of waterfowl. In addition, nesting boxes have been provided for wood ducks.

In 1989, The Conservation Fund, with the assistance of the Richard King Mellon Foundation, acquired more than 104,000 acres of wetlands. Donation of these lands the following year to the Fish and Wildlife Service made possible the establishment of Pocosin Lakes NWR.

Since then, Ducks Unlimited, Inc. has helped enhance several hundred acres of the refuge's wetlands habitat.

The refuge is open daily during daylight hours. There is no entrance fee. The refuge headquarters/visitor center—the Walter B. Jones, Sr. Center for the Sounds, located next to the Scuppernong River, in the town of Columbia—is open on weekdays, except national holidays. The center is named in honor of the former congressman, who was an ardent supporter of protecting the wetlands and water resources of northeastern North Carolina during his more than 25 years in Congress.

Visitor activities include wildlife observation; interpretive exhibits and environmental education programs at the visitor center; walking the 2,300-foot (wheelchair-accessible) Scuppernong Boardwalk near the visitor center; hiking the refuge's dikes and lakeshore roads; bicycling on dikes and roads; driving on unpaved roads (muddy in wet weather); canoeing and kayaking on creeks and canals; canoeing on Phelps, New, and Frying Pan lakes (but not on Pungo Lake, to avoid disturbing waterfowl); fishing; and hunting on parts of the refuge during the designated seasons. Camping is not permitted on the refuge, but facilities are available on nearby Pettigrew State Park.

Even though alligators are generally afraid of people, visitors are cautioned to stay a safe distance from them and to be alert for venomous snakes, ticks, and chiggers. Insect repellent is advised during the warmer months.

More than 200 species of birds have been recorded on this refuge.

Lodgings and meals are available in Williamston, Plymouth, Columbia, Manteo, Belhaven, and Washington.

Access to the visitor center from U.S. Hwy. 17 at Washington is east 57 miles on U.S. Hwy. 64—on the right, immediately east of the highway bridge across the Scuppernong River; or from State Hwy. 12 at Whalebone, it is west 42 miles—on the left, just before the bridge.

Information: Pocosin Lakes NWR, P.O. Box 329, Columbia, NC 27925; tel.: (252) 796-3004.

Roanoke River, containing more than 20,000 acres toward a goal of 33,000 acres, was established in 1989 to enhance and protect ecologically significant areas of forested floodplain wetlands along the lower reaches of the Roanoke River, in northeastern North Carolina. The five units of the refuge along the north bank of the river encompass part of what is viewed as "the largest intact and least disturbed bottomland forest ecosystem remaining in the Mid-Atlantic Region." The North Carolina Wildlife Resources Commission and The Nature Conservancy manage other parts of this vital wildlife habitat, bringing the total area presently under protection to nearly 50,000 acres.

The refuge's 8,000 acres of bald-cypress/tupelo swamps and 9,500 acres of bottomland hardwood forests support a tremendous diversity of wildlife. Biologists believe that the Roanoke River's wooded floodplain supports the greatest density of nesting birds—notably neotropical migratory songbirds—of any place in North Carolina. The peak months for exceptional birdwatching are March through June. Several heron rookeries are located on the refuge, one of which is located on Conine Island and is the largest inland rookery in the state. Wood ducks, green-winged and blue-winged teal, mallards, black ducks, wigeon, and hooded mergansers are prominent among the concentrations of waterfowl that are attracted to the river and its wet-

White terns, Midway Atoll NWR. Robert Shallenberger photo

Spinner dolphin, Midway Atoll NWR. Robert Shallenberger photo

Kayaking, Midway Atoll NWR. Robert Shallenberger photo

Albatross display, Midway Atoll NWR. Robert Shallenberger photo

Eastern monk seal, Midway Atoll NWR. Robert Shallenberger photo

Great frigatebird, Midway Atoll NWR. Robert Shallenberger photo

Albatross, Hawaiian Islands NWR. Robert Shallenberger photo

Palmyra Atoll NWR. Robert Shallenberger photo

Palmyra Atoll NWR. Robert Shallenberger photo

Rose Atoll NWR. Robert Shallenberger photo

Canada goose in nest basket, Kootenai NWR, Idaho

Cypress trees and "knees," Cypress Creek NWR, Illinios

Wood ducks, Muscatatuck NWR, Indiana

Snow geese at sunset, DeSoto NWR, Iowa

Ring-necked pheasant, Quivara NWR, Kansas

American bittern swallowing a snake, Rachel Carson NWR, Maine

Bayou Sauvage NWR, Louisiana

Lacassine NWR, Louisiana

Vose Pond beaver lodge, Moosehorn NWR, Maine.
Tim Cooper photo

Water control structure at Moosehorn NWR, Maine.
U.S. Fish and Wildlife Service photo

Maine Coastal Islands NWR, Maine

Observation Deck, Rachel Carson NWR, Maine

Rachel Carson NWR

Sunkhaze Meadows NWR, Maine

Bald eagles at sunset, Blackwater NWR, Maryland

Delmarva Fox Squirrel, Eastern Neck NWR, Maryland

National Wildlife Visitor Center, Patuxent NWR, Maryland

Gray Seals, Monomoy NWR, Massachusetts

Seney NWR, Michigan

Common Loon, Seney NWR

Spruce Grouse, Seney NWR, Michigan

Red fox pups, Agassiz NWR, Minnesota

Agassiz NWR, Minnesota

Rice Lake NWR, Minnesota

Beaver activity, Rice Lake NWR

Mingo NWR, Missouri

Mingo NWR

Bald eagle, Squaw Creek NWR

Bald eagle viewing, Squaw Creek NWR, Missouri

Charles M. Russell NWR, Montana

Lee Metcalf NWR, Montana

Elk in silhouette, National Bison Range, Montana

National Bison Range

Yellow-headed blackbirds, Red Rock Lakes NWR, Montana

Red Rock Lakes NWR

lands. Wild turkeys feed and nest on the floodplain's terraces and ridges. Bald eagles winter and nest along the river. More than 200 species of birds have been recorded on this refuge.

In addition to such mammals as white-tailed deer, mink, and river otter, the lower Roanoke River bottomlands offer one of the very few remaining areas in the state for a remnant black bear population. And the refuge supports a large diversity of turtles, frogs, and snakes.

Fishes are also an important part of the ecosystem here. The Fish and Wildlife Service points out that "The Roanoke River and the associated refuge floodplain wetlands are especially important to anadromous fish—marine species that ascend rivers to spawn." Among these are hickory shad, striped bass, blueback herring, and alewife. By contrast, the American eel, a catadromous species, descends the river when it reaches reproductive age. In addition, there are resident species, such as catfish, crappie, longnose gar, carp, largemouth bass, bluegill, darters, and white perch.

As described by the Fish and Wildlife Service:

Water is the driving force of bottomland hardwood communities. Annual floods over the centuries have overtopped the riverbanks, dropping the coarser, heavier sediments from upriver to form the levees and ridges of the floodplain, resulting in forested communities characterized by sugar berry, sycamore, green ash, beech, cottonwood, elm, sweetgum, loblolly pine, and mesic oak and hickory species. The finer, light sediments (silts and clays) gradually settle in the slack water areas ponded behind the levees supporting stands of bald cypress and tupelo gum.

This natural pattern of river floods and deposition of sediments, however, has been substantially altered by man. The lower stretch of the Roanoke River, where the refuge is situated, is downriver from a series of hydroelectric dams and their reservoirs and a large U.S. Army Corps of Engineers flood control project. To satisfy power generation, flood control, and recreational goals, these facilities control the river's flow of water. As refuge biologist Jean Richter says:

As a result, the flows for the past 50-plus years are, for the most part, not ecologically compatible. Sometimes there isn't enough water coming our way because they hold it in the reservoirs for recreational needs; while at other times, they will flood the bottomland forests for weeks on end during the growing season. This is an extremely unnatural situation. The bottomland forests didn't evolve under this type of managed flow regime and we are beginning to see significant shifts in the types of forest communities. We are in the long and tedious process of documenting changes in the Roanoke River's wildlife populations and floodplain geomorphology.

Adding to the problems caused by the regulation of the river's flow is the loss of a substantial proportion of the sediment load that was formerly carried by the river. With those nutrient- and mineral-rich materials now largely trapped behind the dams, the bottomland ecosystem is consequently deprived of this source of enrichment and renewal.

Acquisition of this refuge's lands was made possible partly with revenues from the sale of Migratory Bird Hunting and Conservation Stamps (Duck Stamps). Establishment of the refuge occurred with the cooperative efforts of the North Carolina Wildlife Resources Commission, Bertie and Halifax counties, and such private organizations as The Nature Conservancy, the North Carolina Wildlife Federation, and Sierra Club.

The refuge is open daily during daylight hours. There is no entrance fee. The refuge head-quarters, at 114 W. Water St., Windsor, is open on weekdays, except national holidays.

Visitor activities include wildlife observation, hiking, canoeing and boating, fishing, and hunting during the designated seasons. Camping is not permitted on the refuge, except primi-tive camping in conjunction with hunts. Campgrounds facilities are provided at Pettigrew State Park.

Visitors are cautioned to be alert for venomous snakes, ticks, chiggers. Insect repellent is advised during the warmer months.

Lodgings and meals are available in such communities as Williamston, Windsor, Edenton, and Scotland Neck.

Access to the refuge by canoe or boat is from public boat-launching ramps at the town of Hamilton; from U.S. Hwy. 13/17, adjacent to the refuge's Conine Island tract; and at Ply-mouth, near the Great and Goodman Islands tract. U.S. Hwy. 13/17 runs through the Conine Island tract, and State Hwy. 45 cuts across the Great and Goodman Islands tract.

Information: Roanoke River NWR, P.O. Box 430, Windsor, NC 27983; tel.: (252) 794-3808.

North Dakota

Arrowwood, containing 15,934 acres, was established in 1935 to enhance and protect more than 3,500 acres in three impounded riverine lakes and an area of marsh that attract large con-centrations of migratory waterfowl. This refuge is located along a 14-mile stretch of the James River, in Foster and Stutsman counties of east-central North Dakota. During spring and au-tumn migrations, tundra swans, Canada and snow geese, and numerous kinds of ducks pause at this refuge to rest and feed. American white pelicans sometimes fly the thirty miles from their summer breeding colony on Chase Lake National Wildlife Refuge to feed at Arrowwood. More than 260 bird species have been recorded here.

Nesting water birds include such ducks as mallard, blue-winged teal, gadwall, wood duck, and hooded merganser, and the giant Canada goose. The latter subspecies was brought to the brink of extinction by habitat loss and over-hunting, but has been successfully restored to the northern Great Plains. Artificial nesting structures have been placed on the refuge's wetlands to provide secure sites for Canada geese and other waterfowl. In addition, because of the scarcity of natural nesting cavities in wooded habitat, the refuge has installed roughly 250 artificial cav-ities to enhance the nesting productivity of wood ducks and hooded mergansers.

Managed water levels of the refuge's wetlands vary seasonally, to provide a mix of habitats for nesting and migrating waterfowl. Runoff from winter snow and spring rainfall fills the im-pounded lakes. In late spring, open-water stands of sago pondweed provide favorable habitat for a variety of aquatic invertebrates that are an important source of food for duck broods. As care-fully managed water levels gradually recede during late spring and summer, seasonally flooded mudflats are exposed around the edges of the impoundments, attracting shorebirds and promoting the growth of emergent marsh vegetation. Once this vegetation is well developed, the impoundments can be re-flooded, so that this vital vegetative cover is available for the broods of ducks and other waterbirds. The refuge's moist-soil areas, which are managed during the summer to promote the growth of seed-producing plants, are re-flooded in the autumn in time to be used by migrating waterfowl. At least, that's the way these wetlands are supposed to work.

However, water management in Arrowwood refuge has been significantly compromised since Jamestown Dam was built in the mid-1960s by the U.S. Army Corps of Engineers, downstream from the refuge. As the Fish and Wildlife Service explains:

During flood years, water from Jamestown reservoir backs into the Refuge and eliminates or severely reduces water management capability. After water in the reservoir recedes, excess water often remains in the refuge because of poor pool drainage and channel obstructions between the lowermost Refuge pool (DePuy Marsh) and the reservoir. During normal years, the difference in elevation between Jamestown Reservoir and the Refuge pools is too small to allow the Refuge to draw down pools in a timely manner.

By the late 1990s, an environmental plan was chosen for mitigating the harmful impacts of the reservoir upon the refuge. It calls for lowering the Jamestown Reservoir's joint-use pool, constructing bypass channels around Mud and Jim lakes, thereby permitting independent management of these two major impoundments, and making several other impoundment and channel improvements. As of this writing, the outcome of implementing these mitigation measures to help resolve the challenging environmental impacts is still uncertain.

This refuge's other habitats include more than 100 acres of wooded riparian habitat in coulees (narrow ravines), more than 8,200 acres of native prairie grasslands, more than 3,200 acres of seeded grasslands, and 780 acres in cultivated crops for the benefit of wildlife. Prominent among the nesting grassland birds are upland sandpiper, marbled godwit, bobolink, LeConte's and grasshopper sparrows, the non-native gray partridge and ring-necked pheasant, the reintroduced greater prairie chicken, and sharp-tailed grouse.

To view and photograph the grouse's impressive courtship displays, an observation blind is available (by reservation) during April and May. The male spreads his wings, raises his pointed tail, lowers his head, and rapidly stomps his feet. At the same time, he inflates and deflates purplish neck sacs, and makes a *coo-oo* sound that is accompanied by the rattling of wing quills.

Both the sharp-tailed grouse and prairie chicken are birds of the prairie. The sharp-tails have thrived in areas where the ecologically unnatural exclusion of periodic fire has allowed an invasion of brush and other woody vegetation. But, as the Fish and Wildlife Service explains,

Prairie-chickens failed to adapt to the changes in the prairie. Fire exclusion and intensive use of the prairie for agricultural purposes probably led to its demise in this area. No prairie-chickens were seen in the refuge after the late 1960s. Today, prescribed burns are used as a management tool by the refuge and have created conditions where prairie-chickens may once again live. A reintroduction program is underway to return the prairie-chicken to Arrowwood.

Establishment of the refuge was made possible partly with revenues from the sale of Migratory Bird Hunting and Conservation Stamps (Duck Stamps). Nearly one-sixth of this refuge's acreage is being protectively managed under the terms of perpetual conservation easement agreements with local landowners.

In cooperation with farmers, roughly 1,000 acres of Arrowwood's uplands are devoted to a crop-rotation program that offers cover and food for wildlife. During some years, alfalfa is produced, providing important nesting cover and soil-enhancing nitrogen. In other years, crops such as wheat, millet, barley, oats, and sunflowers are cultivated, with part of the crop left in the fields to provide important supplemental food for many species of wildlife.

Generally poor duck breeding occurs on the refuge's prairie habitat. Consequently, a 38-acre fenced exclosure of grassland has been created, with the assistance of Ducks Unlimited, Inc, to provide a predator-free nesting area for waterfowl and upland birds.

This refuge is open daily during daylight hours. There is no entrance fee. The refuge head-quarters is open on weekdays, except national holidays.

Visitor activities include wildlife observation; driving the 5.5-mile interpretive auto tour route that leads through marsh and grassland habitats; hiking (a short loop trail is provided near the picnic area); canoeing (a canoe trail is available on a stretch of river between Arrowwood and Mud lakes); picnicking (a picnic area is provided near the southeastern shore of Arrow-wood Lake); cross-country skiing and snowshoeing; and hunting on parts of the refuge during the designated seasons. The best time for seeing waterfowl and other waterbirds is from April through October, with the latter offering the best opportunities to view tundra swans and geese.

Insect repellent is advised during the warmer months.

Lodgings and meals are available in such communities as Jamestown and Carrington.

Access to the refuge from I-94 at Jamestown is north 35 miles on U.S. Hwy. 281/52 and right onto State Hwy. 9 for 7.5 miles; or from Carrington, south 9 miles on U.S. Highways 281/52 and left onto Hwy. 9 for 7.5 miles.

Information: Arrowwood NWR, 7745 Eleventh St., SE, Pingree, ND 58476; tel.: (701) 285-3341.

Audubon, consisting of 14,739 acres, is located 65 miles north of Bismarck, in west-central North Dakota. The refuge was established in 1955 as the Snake Creek National Wildlife Refuge. It was renamed in 1967, in honor of the famous nineteenth-century wildlife artist and naturalist John James Audubon, who traveled up the Missouri River in 1843. The mission of this refuge is to manage habitat that replaces extensive Missouri River bottomland that was in-undated when the U.S. Army Corps of Engineers built the Garrison Dam.

More than 10,000 acres of the refuge consist of the southern and eastern part of Lake Audubon, the shoreline wetlands, and roughly 100 islands, which are a mecca for large concen-trations of nesting and migrating waterfowl, gulls, terns, and cormorants.

Prominent among the refuge's waterfowl is the giant Canada goose. As many as 500 pairs nest on Lake Audubon's islands. This subspecies, which formerly inhabited the Great Plains in abundance, was reduced to the brink of extinction by the mid-1930s, as the result of extensive market hunting and egg collecting. Audubon refuge is one of several places in North Dakota where a successful program of reintroducing, captive rearing, releasing, and transplanting the gi-ant Canada geese to numerous parts of this state has been carried out. Many private organiza-tions and individuals have assisted the federal and state agencies in bringing this species back to the northern Great Plains.

The refuge's wetlands also support many species of nesting ducks—notably blue-winged teal, mallards, pintails, gadwalls, canvasbacks, redheads, lesser scaups, and ruddy ducks. Other nesting water birds include pied-billed and eared grebes, American white pelican, gulls, and terns. Of the nesting shorebirds, there are American avocets, willets, piping plovers, spotted sandpipers, and Wilson's phalaropes. During the spring and autumn, large numbers of snow geese, Canada geese, ducks, and shorebirds, as well as many tundra swans and sandhill cranes, migrate through the refuge. Whooping cranes pause here each autumn, on the refuge or nearby private lands. Other birds associated with the wetlands include yellow-headed blackbirds, sora and Virginia rails, and bald eagles that are common during the winter and spring.

Another 3,000 acres of this refuge consist of grassland habitat (both native prairie and introduced tame grasses) that supports many species of upland grassland birds. Among these are sharp-tailed grouse, short-eared owls, northern harriers, upland sandpipers, marbled godwits, the non-native ring-necked pheasants and gray partridges, bobolinks, meadowlarks, lark buntings, clay-colored and Baird's sparrows, and chestnut-collared longspurs.

Several hundred acres of refuge land are also planted annually with grains. Under sharecrop agreements with local farmers, part of the crop is left standing for the benefit of wildlife—especially for waterfowl, and secondarily for pheasants and deer.

Establishment of Audubon refuge was by perpetual, but revocable, agreement with the U.S. Army Corps of Engineers, which owns Lake Audubon. Water level management is by long-term agreement with the U.S. Bureau of Reclamation, which pumps Lake Audubon full each spring and lowers it two feet each autumn. Ducks Unlimited, Inc. has helped enhance some of the refuge's wetland habitat.

The refuge is open daily during daylight hours. There is no entrance fee. The refuge headquarters is open on weekdays, except national holidays.

Visitor activities include wildlife observation; driving the 7.5-mile interpretive auto tour road along the south shore of Lake Audubon; riding a barge (pontoon) to a Lake Audubon bird nesting island; walking the one-mile prairie trail; bird identification classes in May for beginners; group field trips (prior scheduling required); ice fishing; and hunting on part of the refuge during the designated seasons. Although camping is not permitted on the refuge, facilities are available at such places as Lake Sakakawea and Fort Stevenson state parks. More than 235 bird species have been recorded on the refuge.

Lodgings and meals are available in Garrison, Underwood, and Minot.

Access to the refuge from Minot is south 46 miles on U.S. Hwy. 83, left at the refuge sign for just under a mile to the refuge headquarters; or from Coleharbor, it is north two miles on U.S. Hwy. 83 and right to the refuge headquarters.

Information: Audubon NWR, 3275 Eleventh St. NW, Coleharbor, ND 58531; tel.: (701) 442-5474.

Des Lacs, consisting of 19,547 acres, was established in 1935 to enhance and protect an ecologically rich stretch of the Des Lacs River (River of the Lakes), extending 26 miles southward from the Canadian border, in northwestern North Dakota. The refuge contains three natural lakes and eight areas of managed marsh habitat totaling 5,000 acres. The marshland between the lakes is a mecca for vast numbers of migrating and nesting waterfowl and other water birds.

During spring and autumn migrations, many thousands of ducks and geese pause here to rest and feed. The peak months are typically April through May and September through October, with as many as one-half million snow geese in the fall. Nesting ducks, such as mallards, pintails, blue-winged teal, gadwalls, canvasbacks, redheads, and ruddy ducks, annually raise as many as 7,000 ducklings! Five species of grebes are among other water birds that nest on the refuge. Horned, eared, and western grebes are especially numerous. The latter are entertaining as they perform their elaborate and spectacular spring courtship displays. During these displays, a male and female rise to a vertical position and dash side-by-side with their feet splashing the surface of the water, before diving underwater.

Initially called the Des Lacs Migratory Waterfowl Refuge, the Des Lacs NWR, is one of many refuges in this part of the country that were specifically set aside in response to the devastating impact of the severe drought of the 1930s' Dust Bowl upon migratory waterfowl. To enhance the refuge's lake and marsh habitats, the Civilian Conservation Corps built facilities such as a series of eight low dikes and other water-control structures.

As described by the Fish and Wildlife Service:

The purpose was to allow the manipulation of water levels, which is important in maintaining optimum nesting conditions and food production for waterfowl. The marshes and lakes are managed to provide emergent vegetation such as cattail and bulrush for nesting habitat and the submergent plant, sago pondweed, that is critically important to provide food and habitat to raise ducklings and other waterbirds.

The Des Lacs River is not a permanent flowing stream and therefore the water cycle fluctuates wildly with boom and bust years. The majority of water runoff comes in the spring during snowmelt and then sporadically during summer from thunderstorms. As recently as the early 1990s a prolonged drought dried up the middle Des Lacs Lake at Kenmare, but the refuge was completely flooded again in 3-4 days from a heavy July thunderstorm. The past few years have seen abundant water similar to the flood years of 1969, 1970, and 1979. The drought cycle will no doubt return and we'll again see low water levels in the area lakes.

Adjacent to the lakes and marshes is a mixture of other habitats. There are wooded coulees and draws, where white-tailed deer and other wildlife find shelter. Remnants of once-extensive native prairie grassland cover the 50- to 125-foot-high hillsides and the gently rolling Drift Plain above. Areas of native prairie provide critical habitat for such species as Sprague's pipit, chestnut-collared longspur, Baird's and LeConte's sparrows, short-eared owl, and sharp-tailed grouse. Some of the refuge's grasslands were previously farmed and are now maintained as a mixture of cultivated grasses and alfalfa, to provide protective habitat for upland nesting ducks.

An observation blind is available (by reservation) for viewing and photographing the sharp-tailed grouse's spring courtship displays from April through June. The male spreads his wings, raises his pointed tail, lowers his head, and rapidly stomps his feet. At the same time, he inflates and deflates purplish neck sacs, and makes a coo-oo sound that is accompanied by the rattling of wing quills.

Enhancement of these grasslands is accomplished by short periods of carefully managed grazing and the haying of grasses on lands previously cultivated with crops. Periodic prescribed burning helps to curtail the spread of woody plants that results from unnatural fire suppression.

Establishment of Des Lacs Refuge was made possible partly with revenues from the sale of Migratory Bird Hunting and Conservation Stamps (Duck Stamps).

Des Lacs Refuge is open daily during daylight hours. There is no entrance fee. The refuge headquarters/visitor center is open on weekdays, except national holidays.

Visitor activities include wildlife observation; viewing interpretive exhibits in the visitor center; driving the 11-mile interpretive auto tour route along the shores of Lower, Middle, and the southern end of Upper Des Lacs lakes and the wetlands between them; hiking several trails that lead through woodland and grassland habitats; picnicking (two picnic areas—notably at Tasker's Coulee); canoeing on Upper Des Lacs Lake (a launching site is provided); cross-country skiing and snowshoeing; and hunting. Fishing is not permitted. Although camping is not permitted on the refuge, facilities are available in the adjacent town of Kenmare. The best times for birdwatching are May through July and late September through October.

Insect repellent is advised during the warmer months.

Lodgings and meals are available in Kenmare, Minot, and Stanley.

Access to the refuge from Minot is northwest 52 miles on U.S. Hwy. 52 to Kenmare, west 0.5 mile on County Road 1A, and following the refuge's directional sign.

Information: Des Lacs NWR, P.O. Box 578, Kenmare, ND 58746; tel.: (701) 385-4046.

J. Clark Salyer, containing 59,383 acres, was established in 1935, extending southward from the U.S.-Canada border, in north-central North Dakota. The refuge manages a diversity of habitats, including riparian woodland, aspen parkland, various wetland types, mixed-grass prairie, and sandhills, which occur along the lower stretch of the Souris (Mouse) River. Initially the Lower Souris National Wildlife Refuge, it was renamed in 1967 to honor J. Clark Salyer, the chief of the Fish and Wildlife Service's Division of Wildlife Refuges from 1934 to 1961. More than 260 bird species have been recorded on Salyer, Des Lacs, and Upper Souris refuges.

During the early decades of the 20th century, riparian wetlands of the Dakotas were drained for the production of cash crops, resulting in the extensive destruction of waterfowl habitat. Because at that time many of these former wetlands proved unsuitable for agriculture, numerous crop failures resulted. Then in the 1930s, a severe drought greatly reduced the productivity of wetlands that were available for waterfowl populations. At that time, the federal government began establishing many national wildlife refuges in this region, launching a major program to restore these vital marshes.

The construction of five levees within J. Clark Salyer refuge created a series of pools, to increase the availability of waterbird habitat along 75 miles of meandering river. The pools' fluctuating water levels, regulated by water control structures, enhance nutrient cycling and promote the production of aquatic plants used by breeding water birds.

During spring and autumn migrations, waterbird concentrations on the refuge are spectacular—now numbering as many as 400,000 to 500,000 birds of numerous species. Approximately fifty man-made and natural islands, which are relatively secure from predators, offer summer nesting areas, especially for mallards, blue-winged teal, gadwalls, and the giant Canada goose. This Canada goose subspecies, which had previously been eliminated by habitat loss and over-hunting, was successfully reintroduced when a small captive flock was brought onto the refuge in 1937. Several hundred goslings are now hatched here annually.

The refuge provides nesting boxes for wood ducks and hooded mergansers. Other birds attracted to the wetlands include summering American white pelicans, five species of grebes, sandhill cranes, herons, cormorants, terns, and large numbers of shorebirds.

The upland habitats, specifically the prairie grasslands, are managed for the benefit of nesting waterfowl, sharp-tailed and ruffed grouse, wild turkeys, the non-native gray partridges and ring-necked pheasants, upland sandpipers, chestnut-collared longspurs, bobolinks, and Baird's and LeConte's sparrows.

In the spring, sharp-tailed grouse perform their impressive courtship displays on a number of dancing grounds, known as leks. The male spreads his wings, raises his pointed tail, lowers his head, and rapidly stomps his feet. At the same time, he inflates and deflates purplish neck sacs, and makes a hollow *coo-oo* sound that is accompanied by the rattling of vibrating wing quills.

To enhance and maintain the quality of native prairie grasses and forbs, the refuge implements short-term livestock grazing and periodic prescribed burning. These management activities promote nutrient cycling and help curtail woody plant expansion.

Establishment of this refuge was made possible partly with revenues from the sale of Migratory Bird Hunting and Conservation Stamps (Duck Stamps). Ducks Unlimited, Inc. has helped enhance some of the refuge's wetland habitat.

The refuge is open daily during daylight hours. There is no entrance fee. The refuge headquarters is open on weekdays, except national holidays.

Visitor activities include wildlife observation, hiking two trails, driving the refuge's two auto tour routes, canoeing and boating, picnicking (three picnic areas are provided), fishing (at 13 sites), and hunting on parts of the refuge during the designated seasons. Although camping is not permitted on the refuge, facilities are available at Lake Metigoshe State Park and elsewhere nearby. A scenic stretch of the river bottom woodland and marsh is accessible by way of the J. Clark Salyer NWR Canoe Trail—on either the entire 13-mile meandering route or a 5.5-mile segment (an interpretive brochure is available). The best times for birdwatching are May through July and late September through October. More than 300 species of birds have been recorded here.

Insect repellent is advised during the warmer months.

Lodgings and meals are available in Bottineau, Westhope, and Minot.

Access to the refuge from U.S. Hwy. 2 at Towner is north 26 miles on State Hwy. 14. The refuge headquarters is located on Salyer Rd., three miles north of Upham, just east of State Hwy. 14.

Information: J. Clark Salyer NWR, P.O. Box 66, Upham, ND 58789; tel.: (701) 768-2548.

Lostwood, consisting of 26,904 acres, was established in 1935 to manage and protect an outstanding part of the northern Missouri Coteau. The refuge contains a mixed-grass landscape of gently rolling hills with scattered copses of quaking aspens, and more than 4,000 shallow lakes, ponds, sloughs, and marshes, in the prairie pothole region of northwestern North Dakota.

The refuge's topography is actually a small part of an extensive line of hills made up of gravel and rocks that were deposited as a vast moraine along the edge of the slowly melting continental glacier, toward the end of North America's most recent ice age. This band of hills, ranging from 12 to nearly 20 miles in width, extends from northwestern Iowa northwestward across the Dakotas and into Alberta, Canada. The refuge contains the largest contiguous, federally owned tract of this northern Great Plains "knob-and-kettle" (hill-and-pothole) physiographic region.

In 1975, Congress designated 5,577 acres in the northwestern part of the refuge as a unit of the National Wilderness Preservation System. The enabling legislation declared that this area is "a unique example of the Coteau du Missouri of the Northern Great Plains . . . that constitutes the last sizeable tract of this interesting formation."

Lostwood refuge provides valuable habitat for large concentrations of nesting waterfowl, such as mallards, blue-winged teal, wigeons, gadwalls, and lesser scaup. The giant Canada goose also nests here. This subspecies, which formerly inhabited the Great Plains in great abundance, was reduced to the brink of extinction in the mid-1930s by extensive market hunting and egg collecting. It was successfully reintroduced on this refuge in 1964. Other nesting species attracted in substantial numbers to these pothole wetlands include eared grebes, Virginia rails, Wilson's phalaropes, American avocets, willets, and marbled godwits. Prominent among the birds that pause here during spring and autumn migrations are tundra swans, greater white-fronted and lesser snow geese, and sandhill cranes.

Among prairie grassland birds are upland sandpipers, chestnut-collared longspurs, Sprague's pipits, bobolinks, Baird's and LeConte's sparrows, and an extraordinary concentration of the sharp-tailed grouse. From April through June, a blind is available (by reservation) for viewing and photographing the grouse's courtship displays. Roughly 600 males perform on the refuge's many dancing grounds, known as leks. The male spreads his wings, raises his pointed tail, lowers his head, and rapidly stomps his feet. At the same time, he inflates and deflates purplish neck sacs, and makes a hollow *coo-oo* sound that is accompanied by the rattling of vibrating wing quills. More than 225 species of birds have been recorded here.

Historically, profound changes were caused by the elimination of short-duration grazing of the once-vast herds of American bison (buffalo) prior to the mid-1880s, and by the subsequent introduction of long-duration domestic livestock grazing. In addition, ecologically unnatural suppression of fire from the early 20th century to the mid-1980s and the invasion of non-native plants, such as the aggressive smooth brome grass and leafy spurge, further contributed to the decline in the quality of the prairie grasslands. As the Fish and Wildlife Service explains, "Native uplands, once dominated with waving seas of grass, were replaced in many areas with dense shrub stands."

To restore and maintain the health of this grassland habitat, the refuge carries out periodic prescribed burning and carefully managed short-duration livestock grazing. These management practices help control an unnatural invasion of woody plants, release vital plant nutrients, and promote new growth of native grasses and forbs. These management activities are designed to benefit numerous species of wildlife that are dependent upon the mixed-grass prairie habitat.

Establishment of this refuge was made possible partly with revenues from the sale of Migratory Bird Hunting and Conservation Stamps (Duck Stamps).

The refuge is open daily during daylight hours. There is no entrance fee. The refuge headquarters is open on weekdays, except national holidays.

Visitor activities include wildlife observation, driving the seven-mile interpretive auto tour route, hiking two trails, cross-country skiing and snowshoeing, and hunting on parts of the refuge during the designated seasons. The best times for birdwatching are May to July and late September through October.

Insect repellent is advised during the warmer months.

Lodgings and meals are available in Kenmare, Stanley, and Minot.

Access to the refuge from U.S. Hwy. 52 at Kenmare and from Des Lacs NWR is west 12 miles on County Hwy. 2 and south 4 miles on State Hwy. 8; or from U.S. Hwy. 2 at Stanley, it is north 21 miles on State Hwy. 8.

Information: Lostwood NWR, 8315 Hwy. 8, Kenmare, ND 58746; tel.: (701) 848-2722.

Sullys Hill National Game Preserve, containing 1,674 acres, was initially set aside in 1904 by President Theodore Roosevelt as "Sullys Hill Park." Located on the south shore of Devils Lake, in east-central North Dakota, it manages herds of American bison (buffalo), Rocky Mountain elk, and white-tailed deer.

The park's mission was part of an early 20th-century national effort to help save from extinction the remnant population of once-vast numbers of bison and elk. In North Dakota, the bison had been wiped out by 1884, and elk were gone by the end of the century. In 1914, Congress appropriated funds to provide for the construction of game preserve facilities (corrals, sheds, etc.), within a fenced enclosure. In 1917, fifteen elk were brought to Sullys Hill from Yellowstone National Park; and in 1918, six bison arrived from Oregon.

In 1931, the park's name was changed to Sullys Hill National Game Preserve, and the responsibility for administering the area was transferred from the National Park Service to the Fish and Wildlife Service.

Sullys Hill is named for a 19th-century U.S. general, Alfred Sully, who had been expected to join a cavalry unit from Illinois. When he failed to arrive, the troops named the highest hill in this vicinity after him. Nearby resident Dakota Sioux refer to the hill by its traditional name, Paha Tanka, which means Big Hill. Most of the preserve consists of woodland- and grassland-covered glacial-moraine hills. Wetland habitats border the preserve's 12-acre Sweetwater Lake and the shore of Devils Lake.

The preserve's bison herd is maintained at between twenty and thirty animals, the elk number at between twenty-five and forty, and the white-tailed deer at between twenty and thirty. In addition to the three large mammal species, there are red and gray foxes, mink, beaver, woodchuck, raccoon, striped skunk, eastern cottontail, eastern fox squirrel, and a colony of introduced black-tailed prairie dog.

Prominent among the more than 260 species of birds that have been recorded on the preserve are wild turkeys; American white pelicans; snow (both white and blue morphs) and Canada geese; ducks of many species; several species of grebes; great blue herons; various shorebirds; and numerous neotropical migratory songbirds, including flycatchers, vireos, and warblers.

The preserve is open daily during daylight hours. A fee is charged to drive the four-mile tour road (normally open from May through October). The visitor center is open daily during the summer months.

Visitor activities include wildlife observation; viewing interpretive displays in the visitor center; summer interpretive programs in the amphitheater; guided interpretive walks; driving the tour road, hiking a 1-mile interpretive trail (part of which is wheelchair-accessible) along a stream and through a wooded area; and cross-country skiing on a 1.5-mile trail. The preserve also provides conservation education programs for school and other groups. The best times for peak bird influxes are late April to early June and late August to mid-October.

Lodgings and meals are available at such communities as New Rockford and Devils Lake.

Access to the preserve from U.S. Hwy. 2 at the town of Devils Lake is south 13 miles on State Hwy. 57, and left onto BIA Route 6, following signs to the preserve.

Information: Sullys Hill National Game Preserve, c/o Devils Lake Wetland Management District, P.O. Box 908, Devils Lake, ND 58301; tel.: (701) 662-8612.

Tewaukon, comprising 8,363 acres in two units, restores, enhances, and protects important wetland and prairie grassland habitats for the benefit of migratory birds and other wildlife. In 1934, a non-federally owned easement refuge was initially established, with authority to acquire perpetual easements from landowners for flowage and refuge purposes. Refuge easements reserved the right to impound water and maintain it during periods of drought.

In 1945, Tewaukon National Wildlife Refuge was authorized and federal land acquisition began the following year, with the purchase of 512 acres around Lake Tewaukon. Named for an ancient legendary Native American leader, Te Wau Kon, meaning "Son of Heaven," this refuge is located along Wild Rice River, in southeastern North Dakota.

The Tewaukon area is located within what was once a vast expanse of nearly 200 million acres of tallgrass prairie extending along the eastern part of the Great Plains, from Manitoba, Canada, south to Texas. As described by the Fish and Wildlife Service in its September 2000 *Comprehensive Conservation Plan* for the refuge:

Prior to settlement by Europeans, this area was inhabited by several plains nomadic tribes that were primarily hunter-gatherers. . . .

Very little farming took place, and the majority of the grassland remained intact. As European settlers moved into southeastern North Dakota, farming was introduced and the highly productive cropping potential of the soils was discovered. . . . Currently, the majority of the land . . . capable of producing a crop is farmed. . . . A few areas of native prairie still remain primarily due to poorer soil quality and cattle or buffalo are raised on these sites.

The refuge's many prairie pothole wetlands and marshes, which are scattered across a gently rolling glacial till plain, are a mecca for as many as tens of thousands of geese and ducks during the spring and autumn migrations. Especially from mid-October to mid-November, large concentrations of snow, greater white-fronted, and Canada geese pause here to rest and feed. Bald eagles also pass through here during migrations.

In the 1960s, four large concrete dams were built on the river, creating hundreds of acres of lakes and wetlands, the largest of which is 1,057-acre Lake Tewaukon. On the refuge's dozen primary impoundments and nearly forty other ponds, water levels are carefully regulated to promote high-quality waterbird nesting and feeding habitat. In addition, numerous natural prairie potholes, scattered across the refuge's uplands, provide more than 100 acres of additional wetland habitat.

Shelterbelt trees and shrubs have been planted on Tewaukon Refuge, offering valuable cover and food for many species of wildlife, including white-tailed deer and numerous songbirds. More than 4,000 acres of the refuge consist of grasslands, of which only 616 acres of native prairie remain. Some tallgrass habitat has been restored from former cropland. Grassland birds include the upland sandpiper, chestnut-collared longspur, grasshopper sparrow, and bobolink. More than 240 bird species have been recorded here.

The health of the refuge's grassland ecosystems is maintained with the help of grazing, mowing, haying, and periodic prescribed burning. The refuge carries out prescription burning to mimic historic fire occurrence and promote nutrient cycling. As the refuge's *Comprehensive Conservation Plan* further states, "Since the 1960s, . . . managers have used prescribed fire to restore, change, and maintain the diversity in plant communities. Prescribed fire is also used to reduce hazardous fuels. . . . Reducing these high amounts of litter can reduce fire intensity and make wildfires easier and more cost effective to control."

Approximately 500 acres of the refuge are devoted to a cooperative program of sharecropping, by which local farmers leave unharvested a portion of cultivated grain crops of corn, millet, winter rye, and winter wheat, to provide a supplemental food source for migrating waterfowl, wintering deer, and other wildlife.

More than one-sixth of the refuge's acreage is being protectively managed under the terms of perpetual conservation easement agreements with local landowners. Such organizations as Ducks Unlimited, Inc., the North Dakota Wetlands Trust, and the Delta Waterfowl Foundation, have helped enhance some of Tewaukon's wetland habitat.

The refuge is open daily during daylight hours. There is no entrance fee. The refuge headquarters/visitor center is open on weekdays, except national holidays.

Visitor activities include wildlife observation; viewing interpretive exhibits in the visitor center; driving the unpaved 8.5-mile Prairie Lake Auto Tour route (open from May 1 through September); walking a short interpretive (wheelchair-accessible) trail through a section of native prairie; hiking (east of County Road 12 only) in the vicinity of Lake Tewaukon; picnicking (two picnic areas are provided on the shore of Lake Tewaukon); boating on Lake Tewaukon and Sprague Lake (May 1 through September—boat ramps are available, no power boating, jet skiing, or water skiing); fishing (year-round from the banks of Tewaukon and Sprague lakes); and hunting on parts of the refuge during the designated seasons. Although camping is not permitted on the refuge, facilities are available at nearby Silver Lake County Park.

Lodgings and meals are available in Lidgerwood, Milner, Forman, Lisbon, Wahpeton, and Fargo.

Access to the refuge from Exit 8 on I-29 is west 28 miles on State Hwy. 11 to Cayuga, and left onto County Rd. 12 for five miles.

Information: Tewaukon NWR, Cayuga, ND 58013; tel.: (701) 724-3598.

Upper Souris, containing 32,311 acres, was established in 1935 to restore and manage ecologically important wetland and grassland habitats for migrating and nesting waterfowl and other wildlife, in northwestern North Dakota. The refuge extends for more than 35 miles along the Souris River Valley, with lakes and ponds, marshes, meandering river, and shrubby habitat of coulees and draws.

As Refuge Manager Dean F. Knauer describes the Upper Souris Refuge:

The backbone of this unique refuge, one of the most scenically beautiful in North Dakota, is the Souris River and its striking, deeply incised drainages called coulees that flow into it. These narrow, shortgrass-prairie-covered ridges quickly transition to steep sides covered with tallgrass-prairie species where snowdrifts have been the heaviest. The coulee bottoms are intermittently wet, with nearly impenetrable patches of thorny wild plum, hawthorn, chokecherry, and Juneberry, the latter laden with blueberry-like fruit in

July. Solitary green ash trees and/or stands of American elms are interspersed here and there. The river bottoms are covered with mature elms, boxelders, and ashes. The large number of habitats within a short distance helps give the refuge a surprising and fascinating diversity of plant and animal species. While much of the area is not easily accessible from public roads, thus making it a challenge for visitors, the remoteness also leaves many ecologically rich places undisturbed throughout the year.

The primary focus of the Upper Souris Refuge is 9,900-acre Lake Darling. This impoundment, occupying about one-third of the refuge, was created in 1936 by a dam on the Souris River. As explained by the Fish and Wildlife Service, "Lake Darling was named in honor of Jay N. 'Ding' Darling, a flamboyant political cartoonist from Iowa, who became the director of the newly formed Bureau of Biological Survey in 1934, the precursor of the Fish and Wildlife Service. [See the Jay N. 'Ding' Darling NWR text.] The primary purpose of the lake is to furnish a regulated supply of water to marshes downstream on Upper Souris and J. Clark Salyer Refuges."

The refuge attracts roughly 350,000 waterfowl during the spring and autumn migrations, including as many as 300,000 lesser snow geese, 50,000 ducks of many species, and 5,000 Canada geese. Tundra swans; ducks such as mallards, pintails, blue-winged teal, shovelers, gadwalls, canvasbacks, redheads, and ruddies; and five species of grebes are among the nesting waterbirds. In 1940, the Canada goose was reintroduced, and as the result of a successful management program, the refuge's resident flock now numbers roughly 250 birds. Canada geese, American white pelicans, and white-tailed deer are among the wildlife frequently seen in the vicinity of the spillway from "A" Pool.

The refuge's prairie habitat is managed for the benefit of many species, such as Sprague's pipit, Baird's and LeConte's sparrows, upland sandpiper, the non-native gray partridge, and sharp-tailed grouse. During April and May, blinds are available (by reservation) for observing the grouse's fascinating spring courtship displays. The male spreads his wings, raises his pointed tail, lowers his head, and rapidly stomps his feet. At the same time, he inflates and deflates purplish neck sacs and makes a *coo-oo* sound that is accompanied by the rattling of wing quills.

In addition to mixed-grass native prairie, some areas of the refuge are planted with a mixture of grasses, alfalfa, and clover to provide important protective habitat for upland nesting ducks such as mallards, pintails, and shovelers. More than 300 species of birds have been recorded on this refuge.

Upper Souris is one of many refuges in this part of the country that was established in response to the devastating impact of the severe drought of the Dust Bowl era of the 1930s upon migratory waterfowl. To enhance the wetland habitats of this and other nearby refuges, more than 250 men were hired under the Civilian Conservation Corps and the Work Projects Administration to build such habitat improvement facilities as dikes, water control structures, and nesting islands. Water levels are regulated to prevent flooding of nest sites and to promote the growth of emergent and other aquatic plants. Mudflats can also be "produced" to benefit shorebirds.

Establishment of this refuge was made possible partly with revenues from the sale of Migratory Bird Hunting and Conservation Stamps (Duck Stamps). "Ding" Darling was instrumental in advocating congressional enactment of the Duck Stamp Act in 1934, which required waterfowl hunters 16 years of age and older to purchase an annual Duck Stamp. Funds from the sale of these stamps are earmarked for the federal acquisition of waterfowl habitat.

The refuge is open daily during daylight hours. There is no entrance fee. The refuge office and visitor center are open on weekdays, except national holidays.

Visitor activities include wildlife observation; viewing interpretive exhibits at the visitor center; educational programs; driving the 3.5-mile interpretive Prairie-Marsh Scenic Drive; hiking five trails (one of which is wheelchair-accessible); cross-country skiing; picnicking (facilities are provided at four sites); canoeing two canoe trails (May 1 through September); boating for fishing or wildlife observation only (five boat-launching sites are provided); fishing (the Outlet Fishing Area pier is wheelchair-accessible); and hunting on parts of the refuge during the designated season. Although camping is not permitted on the refuge, facilities are available at Mouse River Park. The best times for birdwatching are April to June and late September through October.

Insect repellent is advised during the warmer months.

Lodgings and meals are available in Minot and Mohall.

Access to the refuge's visitor center from Minot is northwest about 19 miles on U.S. Hwy. 52 to Foxholm, and right onto County Road 11 for 7 miles; or from Minot, north 18 miles on U.S. Hwy. 83, and left onto County Road 6 for 12 miles to the refuge visitor center.

Information: Upper Souris NWR, 17705-212th Ave. NW, Berthold, ND 58718; tel.: (701) 468-5467.

Ohio

Ottawa, containing more than 5,500 acres in three units, was established in 1961 to restore, enhance, and manage a diversity of habitats along the southwestern shore of Lake Erie, in northwestern Ohio. The refuge includes part of the once-extensive, heavily wooded Great Black Swamp, expanses of coastal marshland, and small areas of hardwood forest, scrub/shrub habitat, grassland, and cultivated cropland.

The refuge, which lies within a major migration corridor, at the crossroads of the Mississippi and Atlantic flyways, attracts large concentrations of migrating waterfowl, shorebirds, raptors, and neotropical songbirds. Its wetland and other habitats provide significant resting, feeding and staging areas, before these migrants cross Lake Erie in the spring and after crossing the lake in the autumn. Concentrations of at least 15,000 geese and 30,000 ducks are attracted to the refuge. During autumn migration, roughly 70 percent of the Mississippi Flyway's black ducks use Lake Erie marshes. Canada geese, wood ducks, mallards, and blue-winged teal are the most common nesting waterfowl. Bald eagles are frequently observed during migrations, and a number of active nests are located on the refuge.

The best months for concentrations of birds are March and April for migrating waterfowl; April for migrating shorebirds; May for the peak of warblers and other neotropical songbirds; July and August for herons, egrets, geese, and shorebirds; September for bald eagles; and October for the peak of migrating waterfowl. More than 300 species of birds have been recorded on the refuge. Mammals include white-tailed deer, coyote, red and gray foxes, mink, muskrat, raccoon, and striped skunk.

As the Fish and Wildlife Service explains the history of this area, "In the 1794 Battle of Fallen Timbers, the Ottawa Indians were defeated and forced out. . . . Their departure opened up the area to white settlers. Soon, 'progress' prevailed: the formidable Black Swamp was drained; farmers and farm fields replaced Indians and forests; eagles and panthers were supplanted by the blackbird. The Great Black Swamp was reduced from 300,000 to 15,000 acres."

The refuge's habitat-management activities include the manipulation of water levels within moist-soil and marsh impoundments with dikes, ditches, and water-control structures. These wetland units are drained in the late spring or early summer to promote the growth of plants, and are re-flooded in the autumn to provide food and habitat for migrating waterfowl and other wildlife. As the Fish and Wildlife Service states in the refuge's *Comprehensive Conservation Plan* (*CCP*) document (2000):

Seasonal manipulation of water levels simulates the natural fluctuations that occur in wetlands connected to Lake Erie. The majority of the wetlands at Ottawa National Wildlife Refuge are diked wetlands with no direct connection to the lake. Diking . . . is done in an effort to protect wetlands from the rapid water level changes and wave action associated with Lake Erie. However, the dikes prohibit the entry of fish into the marshes for spawning and reduce the exchange of nutrients between a marsh and the lake, two important functions of coastal wetlands. . . .

In the 1990s, a decision was made . . . to build a dike to protect Metzger Marsh and reestablish vegetation and management capabilities. With the help of many partners, and a permit from the Army Corps of Engineers, a 7,700-foot dike was constructed across the mouth of Metzger Marsh. This dike was different from others in the area because it was built with a connection to Lake Erie.

Conditions of the Corps . . . permit required a fish passage structure to be installed in the dike to allow Lake Erie fish to enter and exit the marsh for feeding, spawning and protection. . . . In March 1999, the gates were opened to Lake Erie and [were] left open for four years. . . . Water levels [rose and fell] with Lake Erie. . . . Fish passage and nutrient flow [resumed].

Establishment of this refuge was made possible with revenues from the sale of Migratory Bird Hunting and Conservation Stamps (Duck Stamps). Ducks Unlimited, Inc. has helped enhance several hundred acres of the refuge's wetland habitat.

The refuge's MAIN UNIT contains about 4,400 acres along the Lake Erie shore. The 520-acre DARBY MARSH UNIT is located about 12 miles to the southeast of the main unit. Even though the 591-acre NAVARRE MARSH UNIT, which is located about 6 miles to the southeast of the main unit, is owned by two power companies, the Fish and Wildlife Service manages the wetland habitat. Visitor entry onto Darby Marsh and Navarre Marsh units is allowed only by special permit.

The refuge's main unit is open daily during daylight hours. There is no entrance fee. The refuge headquarters is open on weekdays, except national holidays.

Visitor activities on the refuge's main unit include wildlife observation, hiking on seven miles of trails (part of which is wheelchair-accessible), cross-country skiing, interpretive and environmental education programs, fishing, and hunting on parts of the refuge during the designated seasons. Although camping is not permitted on the refuge, facilities are available at Maumee State Park and elsewhere nearby.

Lodgings and meals are available in such communities as Oregon, Port Clinton, and Toledo.

Access to Ottawa Refuge's main unit is east approximately 15 miles from Toledo on State Hwy. 2; or about 90 miles west of Cleveland on State Hwy.2.

Information: Ottawa NWR, 14000 West State Route 2, Oak Harbor, OH 43449; tel.: (419) 898-0014.

Oklahoma

Salt Plains, containing 32,000 acres, was established in 1930 to enhance and protect important resting and feeding habitats for migratory waterfowl and other wildlife on the Salt Fork of the Arkansas River, in north-central Oklahoma. This refuge features 12,000 acres of salt flats that are famous for their unique, hourglass-shaped selenite gypsum crystal formations; 10,000 acres of the Great Salt Plains Reservoir behind the U.S. Army Corps of Engineers' Great Salt Plains Dam; and a network of freshwater ponds and marshes.

The water level of the ponds and marshes fluctuates seasonally—either from rainfall or regulated as necessary with the use of water control structures. This provides for the growth of waterfowl plant foods, such as millet and grasses, during the dry summer months, and re-flooding of these areas to accommodate the autumn and winter influx of ducks. The Fish and Wildlife Service also provides wood duck nesting boxes.

The refuge includes roughly 10,000 acres of gently rolling upland, of which most is native grassland, with some areas of brush and woodland habitats. Periodic prescribed fires help to maintain the ecological health of certain habitats, such as the grasslands. For the benefit of waterfowl and other wildlife, more than 1,000 acres of cropland are planted in wheat, milo, and cowpeas.

Acquisition of lands for the Salt Plains Refuge was made possible with revenues from the sale of Migratory Bird Hunting and Conservation Stamps (Duck Stamps).

The refuge is open daily. There is no entrance fee. The visitor center is open daily from April 1 to October 15 and on weekdays the rest of the year, except national holidays.

Visitor activities include wildlife observation; interpretive programs and tours; driving the 2.5-mile Harold F. Miller Auto Tour Route that affords views of the refuge's diverse habitats of woods, ponds, marsh, and fields; hiking on a number of trails; viewing the refuge and wildlife from Casey Marsh Tower, from another tower at the entrance to the Selenite Crystal Area, and from several overlooks; picnicking; swimming; canoeing and boating on some parts of the refuge from April to mid-October; fishing; and hunting on parts of the refuge during the designated seasons. Camping is permitted on the refuge at the Jet Recreation Area, from April 1 to October 15 and all year on the adjacent Great Salt Plains State Park.

Among the birds attracted to this refuge are migratory and wintering ducks and geese, nesting wood ducks, herons and egrets, many kinds of migratory shorebirds, American white pelicans, sandhill cranes, and even a few whooping cranes. Some of the latter pause here in the autumn on their 2,400-mile flight from breeding grounds in northern Canada's Wood Buffalo National Park to their wintering habitat on Aransas National Wildlife Refuge, on the Texas

Gulf coast. Among the birds that inhabit and nest on the salt flats are the endangered least tern, the threatened snowy plover, and avocet. November through May is the best time for bird-watching. More than 300 bird species have been recorded here.

Between April 1 and October 15, visitors are allowed to collect selenite gypsum crystals within a number of digging areas, which are annually rotated to allow sufficient time for crystal growth replacement. A refuge brochure on the crystals explains that, "Only in certain places on the Salt Plains, gypsum and saline solutions in the soil are sufficiently concentrated to promote crystal growth. When temperature and brine conditions are ideal, the crystals may form very rapidly." The brochure tells how to carefully collect them to observe the beauty of their fascinating shapes, which vary from single crystals to twins and clusters.

Visitors are cautioned to be alert for rattlesnakes, ticks, chiggers, and poison ivy. Insect repellent and sunscreen are advised, the latter especially on the glary salt flats of the Selenite Crystals Area.

Lodgings and meals are available in Cherokee, Alva, and Enid.

Access to this refuge from U.S. Hwy. 64 at Jet is north 14 miles on State Hwy. 38 and left at the refuge sign, continuing a mile to headquarters. The entrance to the Selenite Crystal Area is six miles west of Jet on U.S. Hwy. 64, right onto an unpaved road for three miles, and right onto a paved road for a mile. From Cherokee, the crystal area entrance is south approximately three miles on U.S. Hwy. 64, and left five miles on a paved road.

Information: Salt Plains NWR, Route 1, Box 76, Jet, OK 73749; tel.: (580) 626-4794.

Sequoyah, comprising 20,800 acres, was established in 1970 upon completion of the U.S. Army Corps of Engineers' Robert S. Kerr Reservoir. This refuge enhances and protects a variety of habitats including woodlands, wetlands, flooded fields, and cropland of winter wheat and soybeans, at the junction of the Arkansas and Canadian rivers in eastern Oklahoma. Cradled in a river valley in the gently rolling Ozark Mountain foothills, Sequoyah attracts large concentrations of wintering mallards, many thousands of snow geese, nesting wood ducks, herons and egrets, American white pelicans, migratory shorebirds, nesting bald eagles, scissor-tailed flycatchers, and numerous species of neotropical migratory songbirds. More than 250 species of birds have been recorded here.

An oxbow lake restoration project was recently completed with the assistance of the Oklahoma Department of Wildlife Conservation, the U.S. Army Corps of Engineers, Ducks Unlimited, Inc., and Tulsa-based Natureworks. The project now enables the Fish and Wildlife Service to manage approximately 700 acres of previously unmanageable wetlands in a manner that is hydrologically similar to the lake's natural conditions. Other ongoing habitat improvement actions include the restoration of bottomland hardwoods, native grassland savannah, and other plant communities. Periodic prescription burns are used to enhance the health of certain native plant ecosystems.

This refuge is named in honor of Sequoyah, the Cherokee Indian who created his tribe's alphabet that was instrumental in preserving his Native American people's customs and history in writing. By the 19th century, the Cherokees lived to the north of the Arkansas and Canadian rivers, and the Chickasaw and Choctaws lived to the south. Several sites of the much earlier pre-Columbian Caddoan Indian culture's encampments, dating from A.D. 1100 to 1400, are protected within the refuge.

The refuge is open daily during daylight hours. There is no entrance fee.

Visitor activities include wildlife observation, driving and bicycling on unpaved refuge tour roads, hiking on trails and other areas such as Girty Bottom, viewing wildlife from observation platforms, prearranged interpretive programs and tours for groups, canoeing and boating (five launching ramps are available), fishing, and hunting on parts of the refuge during the designated seasons. Camping is not permitted, but facilities are available at three nearby state parks. November through April is the best time for birdwatching. Part of the refuge is closed to entry from September 1 through the end of the waterfowl season, except on designated trails.

Visitors are cautioned to be alert for venomous snakes, ticks, chiggers, wasps, and poison ivy. Insect repellent is advised.

Lodgings and meals are available in Vian, Gore, Sallisaw, and Webbers Falls.

Access to the refuge from Exit 297 on I-40 at Vian is south three miles on a county road. Information: Sequoyah NWR, Route 1, Box 18A, Vian, OK 74962; tel.: (918) 773-5252.

Wichita Mountains Wildlife Refuge, containing 59,020 acres in southwestern Oklahoma, is one of the magnificent showplaces of the National Wildlife Refuge System, and is the oldest managed wildlife preserve in the United States. This ecologically rich and scenically beautiful area was initially set aside in 1901 as a forest reserve. It was re-designated as a game preserve by President Theodore Roosevelt in 1905, partly to help rescue from extinction the American bison (buffalo), and was established as the Wichita Mountains Wildlife Refuge in 1935. The mountains and refuge are named for the tribe of Native Americans who were living here when 17th-century Spanish explorers traveled through this region.

The refuge's rugged, uplifted range of geologically ancient granite peaks, hills, and ridges is adorned with weather-sculpted rock outcrops and rises from surrounding gently undulating grassy valleys, meadows, and plains. Some of the narrower mountain valleys are densely wooded, with groves of trees extending up their slopes. The endlessly fascinating, lichen-covered rock formations are fractured and eroded into extensive jumbles of huge, rounded boulders. Exposed rocky slopes, ridges, peaks, gorges, crevices, and ledges are picturesquely interspersed with groves and clumps of oaks, cedars, and other trees and shrubs.

More than twenty lakes and ponds scattered throughout the refuge add tremendously to the refuge's scenic charm and ecological diversity. These man-made impoundments, totaling 673 acres, were created or enlarged in the 1930s, when small dams were built by the Civilian Conservation Corps to conserve water runoff.

The refuge contains an unusually rich diversity of flora and fauna. Situated in the middle of the southern Great Plains region, the Wichita Mountains are an outstanding biotic crossroad of numerous species of plants and animals that are representative of both the lush eastern and arid southwestern United States. An ecologically significant aspect of this refuge's east-west meeting and overlapping is its protected remnant of the once-vast natural merging of eastern woodland and western Great Plains grassland—known as cross timbers biota. This term refers specifically to the "fingers" of oak woods that extend into the grasslands from the east.

The flora of the refuge contains a mixture of grasses representative of both the lush eastern Great Plains tallgrass prairie, such as the big and little bluestems, Indiangrass, and switch grass; and shortgrass species of the arid western plains, such as buffalograss and the sideoats and blue gramas.

Seedlings are constantly attempting to expand the groves of post and blackjack oaks into the grassland habitat. At the same time, the aggressive and fast-growing eastern redcedar continually tries to crowd out the oaks and ultimately become the dominant species. Bordering the refuge's intermittently flowing streams are such other trees as black walnut, ash, pecan, flowering dogwood, redbud, cottonwood, black willow, and elm.

Among the Wichita Mountains' eastern and western birds are the ruby-throated and black-chinned hummingbirds, eastern and western kingbirds, yellow-shafted and red-shafted phases of northern flicker, broad-winged and Swainson's hawks, eastern and mountain bluebirds, Baltimore and Bullock's orioles, Carolina and canyon wrens, summer and western tanagers, painted and lazuli buntings, and the chuck-wills-widow and poor-will. Two of North America's most beautiful birds are the graceful scissor-tailed flycatcher and Mississippi kite, both of which breed on the refuge. A prominent resident species is the wild turkey, numbering several hundred individuals that are descendants of a male and two females that survived from a disease-plagued reintroduction program in 1912.

In 1907, two years after the area was designated as a game preserve, the New York Zoological Society and American Bison Society donated 15 bison (6 bulls and 9 cows) to reestablish this magnificent Great Plains mammal to the Wichitas. Today, the refuge's population totals approximately 570 animals, and visitors can usually enjoy seeing scattered herds of them on the refuge's grasslands.

Although the original native Merriam's elk that once inhabited these mountains had become extinct, a number of the Rocky Mountain elk were introduced from Jackson Hole, Wyo., in 1912. They have subsequently become well established here, with annual autumn elk hunts to maintain the population within the carrying capacity of the refuge's habitat. In addition, the white-tailed deer, which in 1907 was estimated at a mere 15 in the game preserve, now numbers more than 1,000 individuals.

Another ungulate inhabiting the refuge is the non-native but historically significant Texas longhorn. This visually impressive animal was the first kind of cattle to be introduced to North America, arriving in 1521 with the Spanish explorers. During the last several decades of the 19th century, an estimated ten million longhorns were raised on the southern Great Plains of Texas and Oklahoma Territory. By the early years of the 20th century, as short-horned cattle became more popular, the longhorn population sharply declined. In 1927, when this form of cattle was nearing extinction, Congress authorized the maintenance of a remnant herd in the Wichita Mountains. The herd is now maintained at about 300 individuals, with an annual autumn public auction of excess animals.

The Fish and Wildlife Service is carrying out a variety of management programs. One bird that is receiving special attention is the black-capped vireo, a rare and endangered neotropical migratory songbird that breeds in oak-woodland habitat from central Oklahoma, southward through the Edwards Plateau of Texas, to Coahuila in northern Mexico (see the Balcones Canyonlands NWR text). The predatory brown-headed cowbird lays its eggs in the vireo's nest. The vireo incubates the cowbird's egg, and then raises the cowbird while neglecting its own young. To reduce this harmful impact of nest parasitism, the refuge has implemented a live-trapping program to reduce the cowbirds. The refuge's estimated vireo breeding population is presently around 600 individuals, having roughly tripled its numbers in the last few years.

The refuge is also carrying out an ecologically important program of carefully reintroducing fire with periodic prescribed burns. These fires are vital in helping to maintain the natural health of the grasslands, control the invasion of the aggressive redcedar into grassland habitat, and encourage a diversity of wildflowers and other forbs and legumes.

In 1970, Congress added 8,570 acres of the refuge to the National Wilderness Preservation System. The 5,723-acre Charons Garden Unit is open to hiking (a backcountry camping permit is required), and the 2,847-acre North Mountain Unit, which is managed as a Research Natural Area, is closed to public access except for approved scientific and educational purposes.

Nearly 280 species of birds, more than 50 species of mammals, 60 species of reptiles and amphibians, 35 species of fish, and more than 800 kinds of trees and other plants have been recorded in the Wichita Mountains. Spring and autumn are the best months for bird-watching.

The refuge is open daily. There is no entrance fee. The visitor center, at the junction of State Highways 115 and 49, is open daily, except on Tuesdays and major national holidays.

Visitor activities include wildlife observation; driving 35 miles of roads in the public use area, including a road to the summit of 2,464-foot Mt. Scott; interpretive programs; guided walks and tours (such as Saturday wildflower walks in May, elk-bugling tours in September/October, and weekend autumn foliage walks in November); hiking on 15 miles of trails in the refuge's 22,400-acre public use area (including a short wheelchair-accessible nature trail); bicycling on some refuge roads; rock climbing; picnicking (four picnic areas); camping at Doris Campground (on a first-come, first-served basis; fee charged) and at a youth group campground (by prearrangement); canoeing and boating; fishing (a wheelchair-accessible fishing pier at 360-acre Elmer Thomas Lake); and hunting (elk and deer, only by lottery).

Visitors are cautioned to be alert for rattlesnakes and ticks and to stay a safe distance from bison and elk, which can become aggressive.

Lodgings and meals are available in Lawton.

Access to the refuge from Cache is north six miles on State Hwy. 115; or from I-44 just north of Lawton, it is west eight miles on State Hwy. 49.

Information: Wichita Mountains Wildlife Refuge, Route 1, Box 448, Indiahoma, OK 73552; tel.: (580) 429-3221 or 3222.

Oregon

Cape Meares, comprising 138 acres in two separate tracts, was established in 1938 by a land transfer from the U.S. Coast Guard. The refuge, which protects one of the few remnants of magnificent coastal old-growth forest in Oregon, is located just north of Oceanside. In 1987, the refuge was designated as a Research Natural Area.

Some of the refuge's large Sitka spruces and western hemlocks rise more than 200 feet tall and are hundreds of years old. Among the many species of birds that are attracted to this ecologically rich habitat are the marbled murrelets, bald eagles, peregrine falcons, northern spotted owls, varied thrushes, Steller's and gray jays, chestnut-backed chickadees, and winter wrens. The sea cliffs support nesting common murres, tufted puffins, Brandt's and pelagic cormorants, pigeon guillemots, western gulls, and black oystercatchers.

The refuge is open daily during daylight hours. There is no entrance fee. Interpretive overlooks are provided at the adjacent Cape Meares State Park, where the 38-foot Cape Meares Lighthouse, dating from 1890, is located. From these scenic points, visitors can observe a variety of migrating seabirds and waterbirds, as well as occasional bald eagles, peregrine falcons, and marine mammals. From December through May, migrating gray whales can sometimes be spotted from here. The Oregon Coast NWR Complex's Project Leader Roy W. Lowe says that, "Cape Meares provides one of the most stunning coastal views along the entire U.S. West Coast, from a magnificent ancient forest to vertical sea cliffs with waterfalls. It also provides the unusual opportunity to stand in one location and view three national wildlife refuges—Cape Meares, Oregon Islands, and Three Arch Rocks."

The state park's entrance road runs through part of the refuge, and a stretch of the Oregon Coast Trail offers an excellent hiking opportunity. A cooperative interpretive project at the park includes a large kiosk, interpretive panels, viewing overlooks, and improved trails. These facilities were provided through the joint efforts of the Friends of Cape Meares Lighthouse and Wildlife Refuge, the Native Plant Society of Oregon, the Tillamook Utilities District, Oregon State Parks, the U.S. Forest Service, and the Fish and Wildlife Service. Additional improvements, including two wheelchair-accessible viewing decks, have recently been completed.

Lodgings and meals are available in Netarts, Oceanside, and Tillamook.

Access to the refuge and state park from Tillamook is west of U.S. 101 on Three Capes Scenic Loop Road.

Information: Cape Meares NWR, c/o Oregon Coast NWR Complex, 2127 SE OSU Dr., Newport, OR 97365; tel.: (541) 867-4550.

Hart Mountain National Antelope Refuge, consisting of 268,997 acres, was established in 1936 to provide habitat and protection for remnant bands of pronghorn (antelope). Located in the Great Basin Desert's vastness of southeastern Oregon, the refuge encompasses what was then one of the last places in North America where this fleet-footed mammal still survived. Over 260 bird species have been recorded here.

The scenic centerpiece of this refuge is 12-mile-long Hart Mountain, which rises from Warner Valley more than 3,500 feet to its crest at 8,065 feet elevation. As this writer described in the 1976 book *The Desert*, "Hart Mountain is actually a giant fault-block range, steeply uplifted along the western escarpment and gently sloping downward for many miles to the east. In this lonely sagebrush country, one of the largest pronghorn herds in the country spends the spring, summer, and autumn. Only a few winter at this higher elevation, many of them migrating southward into the Sheldon refuge."

Other species of wildlife include the majestic California bighorn sheep that skillfully scale the mountain's sheer cliffs. By 1915, this species was eliminated from Hart Mountain by diseases transmitted from livestock and by over-hunting. As the result of a successful program of reintroduction and management that began in 1954, several hundred of these agile mammals now inhabit the refuge. Mule deer live in higher areas of bitterbrush, mountain mahogany, junipers, and ponderosa pines. Prominent among the refuge's many avian species is the greater sage-grouse, the largest grouse in North America (see description in the Seedskadee NWR text). As the Fish and Wildlife Service describes the latter:

The drumming chest and elaborate strut of the male sage grouse is a renowned spectacle of the high desert. This early morning courtship dance occurs on numerous refuge strutting grounds (leks) in late March and April. Once bred, hens build a nest, generally under a sagebrush bush, and lay about 9 eggs. Grouse were once so plentiful that settlers gathered buckets of eggs for camp fare. Through careful research and management, it is hoped that sage grouse will recover some of their former abundance.

A major management mission at Hart Mountain Refuge is the restoration and management of natural ecological processes and conditions that were previously altered by human activities. Until the early 1990s, the mountain had long been heavily grazed by sheep and cattle. As the Fish and Wildlife Service says, "Releasing habitat from the pressures of livestock grazing is an important component of current refuge restoration." In addition, carefully prescribed burning that mimics natural ecological processes is the refuge's single most significant management strategy to revitalize wildlife habitat. Fire promotes nutrient cycling, spurs the growth of forbs and grasses, and creates habitat diversity in a mosaic of successional stages that benefits numerous species of wildlife.

The refuge is open daily. There is no entrance fee. The refuge's administrative headquarters, located in the Post Office building in Lakeview, is open on weekdays, except national holidays. The small visitor center on the refuge is open 24 hours daily but is generally not staffed.

Visitor activities include wildlife observation, viewing Warner Valley from a spectacular overlook, driving refuge roads that range from graded roads to jeep trails, hiking, mountain biking on roads open to motor vehicles, horseback riding, backpacking (a free backcountry permit is required), camping, fishing at Warner Pond and on Rock and Guano creeks, and hunting (a limited number of tags are offered for deer, antelope, and bighorn sheep hunts) on parts of the refuge during the designated seasons. Primitive camping is permitted year-round at Hotsprings Campground (14-day limit) and at seasonal campsites along Guano Creek, during special authorized hunts, from August 1 to November 1. Potable water is available at refuge headquarters. Campfires are permitted only during periods of low fire hazard.

Visitors are cautioned to be alert for rattlesnakes, especially in rocky terrain. Since the nearest gas stations and grocery stores are many miles from the refuge, visitors should be sure to have a full fuel tank, a spare tire and emergency tools, and adequate first-aid and food supplies before venturing toward the refuge. Insect repellent, sunscreen, warm clothing for cool nights, and a generous supply of drinking water are recommended during the warmer months. Most of the refuge's unpaved roads are not suitable for regular passenger cars; high-clearance vehicles are definitely required when traveling roads other than those leading from Frenchglen, Blue Sky, and Hotsprings. In late autumn, winter, and early spring, visitors should be especially alert for sudden changes in the weather that can bring plunging temperatures and snow to the higher elevations.

Lodgings and meals are available in Lakeview and Burns. A gas station and small convenience store are located at Plush, about 25 miles from the refuge's visitor center.

Access to the refuge from Lakeview is north 5 miles on U.S. Hwy. 395, right 16 miles on State Hwy. 140, left 19 miles to Plush, left 1 mile, and right to the visitor center (the road is paved only to the top of the west-facing escarpment). From U.S. Hwy. 20 at Burns, it is south

71 miles on State Hwy. 205 (through Malheur NWR and Frenchglen) and right onto a graded road for 52 miles to the visitor center.

Information: Hart Mountain National Antelope Refuge, P.O. Box 111, Lakeview, OR 97630; tel.: (541) 947-3315.

Klamath Marsh, comprising 40,646 acres, was established in 1958 to protect and manage a large cattail-and-bulrush marsh and surrounding meadows and pine forest. The refuge is located within the northern end of the Klamath Basin, in south-central Oregon.

The refuge's wetland habitat attracts impressive concentrations of ducks, geese, swans, and shorebirds; the grasslands provide feeding and nesting habitat for sandhill cranes; and the forest of ponderosa and lodgepole pines is inhabited by numerous species of wildlife, including the Rocky Mountain elk and great gray owl. More than 160 bird species have been recorded here.

This refuge, which was initially established as the 16,400-acre Klamath Forest National Wildlife Refuge, was purchased from the Klamath Indians with revenues from the sale of Duck Stamps. It was expanded in 1990 and again 1998, to include virtually all of the historic wetland in this area, and it was subsequently renamed Klamath Marsh NWR. It is one of six national wildlife refuges in the Klamath Basin. The others are Upper Klamath and Bear Valley, Ore.; Lower Klamath, Ore./Calif.; and Tule Lake and Clear Lake, Calif. (see texts on each). A discussion of the history of the Klamath Basin's wetlands and peak influxes of migratory waterfowl and other water birds is presented in the Lower Klamath refuge text.

Klamath Marsh refuge is open daily during daylight hours. There is no entrance fee. The refuge headquarters is open daily, except on national holidays. The Klamath Basin NWR Complex headquarters/visitor center, located five miles west of the California community of Tulelake on Hill Road, is open daily, except on Christmas and New Year's Day.

Visitor activities on Klamath Marsh include wildlife observation, driving a gravel loop road, hiking and cross-country skiing on a ten-mile loop trail that offers views of marsh and forest habitats, canoeing, fishing, and hunting on the area to the south of Silver Lake Hwy., during the designated seasons. Only motorless boats are permitted within this hunting area. Roughly 700 acres at the southern end of the marsh (where motorized watercraft and fishing are not permitted) are available for canoeing a canoe trail that is usually open from July 1 through September (closures may occur to avoid disturbing wildlife or because of fluctuating water levels). Camping is not permitted on the refuge, but facilities are provided on the adjacent national forest.

Insect repellent and sunscreen are advised during the warmer months.

Lodgings and meals are available in Klamath Falls.

Access from Klamath Falls to the refuge's hiking trail and canoe launch is north 45 miles on U.S. Hwy. 97, right on Silver Lake Rd., and right 4 miles on Forest Service rd. 690.

Information: Klamath Marsh NWR, c/o Klamath Basin NWRs, 4009 Hill Rd., Tulelake, CA 96143; tel.: (530) 667-2231.

Malheur, containing more than 186,500 acres, was initially established in 1908 by President Theodore Roosevelt as a wetland bird refuge for herons, egrets, and ibis, in the Harney Basin of southeastern Oregon. The refuge's diversity of habitats in and adjacent to the Blitzen Valley include lakes and ponds, extensive areas of marsh and lush meadows, stark expanses of playa, and bordering high-desert, sagebrush uplands and rimrock cliffs of dark basaltic lava rock. More than 320 bird species have been recorded here.

The most spectacular concentrations of birds come to this refuge during the spring. As early as February, tundra swans and pintails start arriving. Soon there are large flocks of greater and lesser sandhill cranes. Peak influxes of waterfowl occur during March. In March and April, there can be more than 200,000 and sometimes more than 300,000 snow and Ross's geese, the latter migrating toward their Arctic breeding grounds in northern Canada. Migrating shorebirds are most numerous in April, and neotropical migratory songbirds reach their peak numbers in May.

Some species of waterfowl, including trumpeter swans and many ducks, come to Malheur to nest and raise their young from May through July. And in early July, many shorebirds begin their return southward, pausing in great numbers on the refuge's mudflats and playas.

The autumn migration brings heightened activity at Malheur, as described by the Fish and Wildlife Service, "One of the refuge's greatest attractions occurs in September and October, when greater sandhill cranes 'stage,' or gather, in the southern Blitzen Valley before migrating to wintering grounds in California's Central Valley. Look for large flocks of ducks and Canada geese during these months. In November, tundra swans can be seen in abundance."

Winter provides the quietest season, and many of the ponds freeze over. Yet, bald and golden eagles, northern harriers, rough-legged hawks, mallards, and common goldeneyes are common wintering species.

The refuge carries out a number of habitat management activities. A system of dams, levees, canals, ditches, and water control structures is used to regulate water supplies for the ponds, marshes, and meadows. For example, water levels are raised to provide favorable habitat for waterbirds while they raise their broods; and they are lowered to promote the growth of desirable plant foods for waterfowl. Willows, which are planted along the refuge's riparian border of the Donner und Blitzen River, provide shelter, food, and nest sites for many species of wildlife.

Other management activities include mowing, grazing, and prescribed burning of meadows to maintain feeding habitat for Canada geese and sandhill cranes and nesting habitat for many waterfowl. Fire is especially important in promoting nutrient cycling and triggering new growth of grasses and forbs valued by wildlife.

Fire is also carefully applied to the refuge's upland areas of sagebrush and greasewood to stimulate the growth of such native grasses as Great Basin wild-rye and to create diversity within the sagebrush-steppe habitat that benefits such species as the pronghorn, mule deer, quail, and greater sage-grouse (see discussions of the latter in the Hart Mountain and Seedskadee texts).

During the first several decades of the 20th century, increasing quantities of water were being diverted from the Donner und Blitzen River for agricultural irrigation, thereby reducing the water available for maintaining the wetlands. A series of dry years in the early 1930s finally prompted the acquisition of 64,000 acres in 1935, so that the refuge could maintain water in Malheur Lake. In 1941, nearly 15,000 acres to the northwest of Harney Lake were added, and the refuge was officially named as a national wildlife refuge.

For the benefit of the redband trout and other native fishes, the Fish and Wildlife Service has carried out a 3.5-mile riparian and fish-habitat improvement project on the Donner und Blitzen River near P-Ranch. Three new fish ladders have been installed within existing water-control structures to improve fish passage, and state-of-the-art fish screens have been constructed. Consequently, the historic trout migration has been reestablished and enhanced to more than sixty miles of headwater spawning areas in the Steens Mountain/Blitzen River watershed. Ducks Unlimited, Inc. has helped enhance more than 29,000 acres of the refuge's wetland habitat.

The refuge is open daily during daylight hours. There is no entrance fee. The refuge headquarters, visitor center, and George Benson Memorial Museum are open on weekdays, except national holidays. The visitor center and museum are also open on most weekends during the spring and summer. Of historic interest are the P-Ranch's Long Barn, beef wheel, and willow corrals, located at the southern end of the refuge and dating from the 1880s. A walk on a nearby dike offers an opportunity to view wildlife inhabiting riparian willow habitat.

Visitor activities include wildlife observation; viewing interpretive exhibits at the museum; driving the gravel Center Patrol Rd., other refuge roads that are open to visitors, and paved State Hwy. 205; bicycling and horseback riding on roads open to motor vehicles; hiking on several paths and the 13-mile public fishing-loop trail near near P-Ranch; canoeing and boating (electric motors only) on Krumbo Reservoir (a dock and ramp are provided) during the fishing season, and on the north side of Malheur Lake during the waterfowl hunting season; fishing (a fishing platform is provided at Krumbo Reservoir); and hunting on parts of the refuge during the designated seasons. Swimming is not permitted.

Although camping is not permitted on the refuge, facilities are provided at nearby Bureau of Land Management and national forest sites.

Insect repellent and sunscreen are recommended during the warmer months. Visitors are cautioned to be alert for sudden weather and temperature changes and to be alert for rattlesnakes.

Lodgings and meals are available in Burns; meals and groceries are available at the Narrows; and fuel and limited groceries are available in Crane, Frenchglen, and Diamond.

Access to the refuge visitor center from Burns is east about 2 miles on State Hwy. 78, right onto State Hwy. 205 for 26 miles, and left onto Sodhouse Lane (County Rd. 405) for 6 miles; or from Hart Mountain refuge's visitor center, it is northeast 36 miles on the graded road and left onto State Hwy. 205 for 10 miles to Frenchglen, at the southern end of the refuge.

Information: Malheur NWR, 36391 Sodhouse Lane, Princeton, OR 97721; tel.: (541) 493-2612.

Oregon Islands, consisting of approximately 900 acres, was initially established as the Goat Island Reservation in 1935 and was renamed as a national wildlife refuge in 1940. The refuge contains more than 1,400 offshore rocks, sea stacks, reefs, and islands scattered along virtually the entire length of the scenic coast of Oregon. There are also two mainland units: Coquille Point near Bandon and Crook Point between Gold Beach and Brookings.

More than a dozen species of nesting seabirds are attracted to the array of rocky, surf-pounded habitats that jut out of the Pacific Ocean. They include Leach's and fork-tailed storm petrels, Brandt's and pelagic cormorants, common murres, pigeon guillemots, rhinoceros auklets, and tufted puffins. An estimated 1.2 million seabirds nest along the Oregon coast, which is apparently more than nest along the Washington and California coasts combined. According to the Fish and Wildlife Service, more than 700,000 common murres nest here, which is approximately two-thirds of the total nesting population south of Alaska. The Oregon Coast NWR Complex's Project Leader Roy W. Lowe says, "Most of the nesting seabirds in Oregon use this refuge because of the abundance and diversity of nesting habitat managed as sanctuary for wildlife and the location of the refuge with a productive marine ecosystem."

Great numbers of pinnipeds use the refuge for haulout and/or pupping. These marine mammals include more than 5,000 harbor seals, 100 northern elephant seals, 1,000 California sea lions, and 4,000 Steller sea lions. The latter is a federally listed threatened species.

Many of the refuge can be viewed from mainland sites, such as state parks and other scenic overlooks along the coast. Among the best of these locations (from north to south) are Ecola State Park, just north of Cannon Beach; Haystack Rock, in Cannon Beach; Yaquina Head Outstanding Natural Area, near Newport; Heceta Head Lighthouse/Devils Elbow State Park/Sea Lion Caves, between Yachats (pronounced YAH-hahts) and Florence; Cape Arago State Park, southwest of Coos Bay; Coquille Point, in Bandon; Cape Blanco, south of Bandon; and Boardman State Park, north of Brookings.

To avoid disturbing the extremely sensitive seabird colonies and marine mammals, all of the refuge's offshore islands, rocks, and reefs are closed to public visitation. In addition, all watercraft are requested to remain at least 500 feet away. Most of the refuge has also been designated as the Oregon Islands Wilderness, a unit of the National Wilderness Preservation System.

One of the largest sea stacks is 235-foot Haystack Rock, in Cannon Beach. Depending on the twice-daily tidal fluctuations, this huge rock is either surrounded by the ocean or is connected to the beach. To avoid disturbing the seabird colonies, climbing Haystack Rock is not permitted. To help the Fish and Wildlife Service promote the protection of the rock's sensitive ecosystem and provide educational information, the Haystack Rock Awareness Program was established by the local Puffin Club. Assistance was provided by the City of Cannon Beach, Seaside School District 10, the Oregon Department of Fish and Wildlife, the Governor's Watershed Enhancement Board, and the Seaside Aquarium.

Two other nonprofit organizations are assisting by offering interpretive services and brochures on the Oregon south coast: Shoreline Education for Awareness, Inc. provides docent-led, on-site interpretative programs, campfire talks, and intertidal guided walks for visitors and school groups from Memorial Day to Labor Day, and by appointment as docents are available during the rest of the year. Information: P.O. Box 957, Bandon, OR 97411; tel.: (541) 347-3683. Friends of Shore Acres, Inc. offers interpretive services at Shore Acres State Park and other parks in the Sunset Bay State Park District. Information: P.O. Box 1172, Coos Bay, OR 97420; tel.: (541) 888-4902 or 888-3732.

In 1991–1992, five parcels totaling 36 acres were acquired at Coquille Point, in Bandon, making this the first mainland addition to the Oregon Islands NWR. A popular visitor use area, Coquille Point, is open daily to visitors. As Roy Lowe explains:

The purpose of this mainland addition to the refuge was to protect adjacent seabird nesting colonies from encroaching development, provide a highly visible public use area for environmental education and interpretation, and restore native habitat on the headland. I'm proud to say that we have been successful in all three areas. Fully accessible paved trails and a parking area were constructed and stairways to the beach, at the north and south ends of the headland, were added. Native grassland habitat has been restored and interpretive panels have been installed throughout the area. As a result, the headland is protected in perpetuity and educational efforts have all but eliminated trespass on the adjacent rocks.

Crook Point, the second mainland addition to the refuge, was acquired in May 2000. This site (located between Gold Beach and Brookings) contains numerous rare plant species, undisturbed cultural resource sites, and a mile of pristine beach and intertidal rocky habitat. This area is managed as a biological reserve and is not yet open to visitors.

Lodgings and meals are available in numerous communities along the Oregon coast.

Access to most of the viewing places of the refuge is along or just off of U.S. Hwy. 101. Access to the Coquille Point unit in Bandon is west on Eleventh St. to the end of the road.

Information: Oregon Islands NWR, c/o Oregon Coast NWR Complex, 2127 SE OSU Drive, Newport, OR 97365; tel. (541) 867-4550.

Three Arch Rocks, encompassing 15 acres, was established in 1907 by President Theodore Roosevelt and became the first national wildlife refuge west of the Mississippi River. It has also been designated as the Three Arch Rocks Wilderness, one of the smallest units in the National Wilderness Preservation System. It is located a half-mile offshore from the community of Oceanside, toward the northern end of the coast of Oregon.

The refuge features three gigantic, surf-pounded rocks that rise dramatically from the Pacific Ocean. All three contain a large arch, hence the name. These barren habitats support Oregon's largest colony of nesting seabirds, which is estimated at more than 230,000 individuals of a dozen species. The state's largest nesting colony of tufted puffins, which is located on Finley Rock, is estimated at between 2,000 and 4,000 of these alcids. The refuge supports more than 200,000 nesting common murres—the largest colony south of Alaska. Other breeding birds are pigeon guillemot, rhinoceros auklet, three species of cormorants, and glaucous-winged and western gulls. The refuge's Seal Rock is the only breeding place for the threatened Steller sea lion on the state's northern coast. Other pinnipeds include California sea lions.

As the Fish and Wildlife Service explains the early history:

By the early 1900s, many seabird colonies on the West Coast were in danger of being wiped out. During the California Gold Rush, egg hunters harvested millions of eggs annually to supply restaurants in San Francisco and the gold fields. Adult birds were slaughtered for target practice as weekend sport. Unfortunately, most people were unaware of the problem.

In the early 1900s, naturalist and photographer William Finley and his partner Herman Bohlman visited the Oregon Coast and documented the devastation. They launched open boats through heavy surf and then literally risked life and limb to haul heavy photographic equipment up and down steep, treacherous cliffs. Finley informed President Theodore Roosevelt of the national importance of this seabird nesting area, convincing him to issue an Executive Order designating Three Arch Rocks the first National Wildlife Refuge on the west coast.

The refuge can be viewed from Oceanside Beach and Cape Meares.

To avoid disturbing the extremely sensitive seabirds and marine mammals, the refuge is closed to visitation. In addition, the waters within at least 500 feet of the rocks are closed to all watercraft from May 1 through September 15.

Lodgings and meals are available in Netarts, Oceanside, and Tillamook.

Access to Oceanside and Cape Meares from U.S. Hwy. 101 at Tillamook is west on Three Capes Scenic Loop Rd.

Information: Three Arch Rocks NWR, c/o Oregon Coast NWR Complex, 2127 SE OSU Dr., Newport, OR 97365; tel.: (541) 867-4550.

William L. Finley, encompassing 5,325 acres, was established in 1964 as the first of three national wildlife refuges in the Willamette Valley NWR Complex. The primary purpose of the refuge is to provide wintering habitat for dusky Canada geese and other waterfowl. It is located between Corvallis and Eugene, in the Willamette Valley of west-central Oregon.

The refuge was named in honor of early photographer-naturalist William L. Finley, who convinced President Theodore Roosevelt to designate national wildlife refuges in the West. As a result of his efforts, Malheur, Klamath, and Three Arch Rocks were established as refuges.

The refuge's diverse habitats include areas of Oregon white oak savanna; old-growth bigleaf maples; bottomland Oregon ash, black cottonwood, and willows along meandering Muddy Creek; native wet prairie; and fields of food crops that are planted for the benefit of wildlife. The refuge contains one of the largest remaining native wet-prairie habitats in the Willamette Valley—a 450-acre remnant at the northeast entrance. Refuge staff and volunteers are working to restore native plant communities, including oak savanna and wet prairie, through control of non-native species, planting of native species, and fire management.

During the fall, winter, and spring, Canada geese can be seen here in large numbers as they feed and rest on the refuge's rich farmed grasslands on their migratory journey south. Dusky Canada geese make the refuge their winter home, then return to the Copper River Delta in southern Alaska in the spring (see also the Ankeny, Baskett Slough, and Ridgefield NWR texts). Many ducks, geese, swans, and shorebirds can also be observed here in the fall and winter.

Mallards, wood ducks, hooded mergansers, and coots nest on the refuge. A visit to Cabell Marsh and Beaver Pond in June or July offers opportunities to see these birds with their young feeding and swimming. Ospreys, bald eagles, peregrine falcons, and white-tailed kites are attracted here, and kites are occasionally seen flying over native prairie habitat near the refuge's northern entrance. More than 235 bird species have been recorded on the refuge.

Prominent among the mammals are the stately Roosevelt elk and black-tailed deer, the latter a Pacific Northwest subspecies of the mule deer.

Of historic interest is the Fiechter House, completed in 1857. This two-story, wood-frame structure, of the Classical Revival style of architecture, is believed to be the oldest house in Benton County. It is listed on the National Register of Historic Places and is periodically open to visitors by the Benton County Historical Society.

The refuge is open daily during daylight hours. Portions of the refuge are closed from November 1 through March 31, to provide a sanctuary for wintering waterfowl. There is no entrance fee. The refuge headquarters is open on weekdays, except national holidays.

Visitor activities include wildlife observation, driving the auto tour route, hiking on a half-dozen trails (four of which are open from April 1 through October), and deer hunting on parts of the refuge during the designated season. A wildlife viewing kiosk is located just behind the refuge headquarters, which overlooks Cabell Marsh. A short trail leads to a wildlife-viewing blind on McFadden Marsh, at the south end of the refuge just off Bruce Rd. An observation platform overlooking the wet prairie is provided near the refuge's northeast entrance. Interpretive signs are placed at various turnouts along both the refuge road and Bruce Rd. Although camping is not permitted on the refuge, facilities are available in the vicinity of Corvallis and Alsea.

Visitors are cautioned to be alert for poison oak. Insect repellent is advised during the warmer months.

Lodgings and meals are available in Corvallis and Eugene.

Access to the refuge from Exit 228 on I-5 is west nine miles on State Hwy. 34 to Corvallis, left onto State Hwy. 99W for ten miles, and right onto Finley Refuge Rd. for two miles.

Information: William L. Finley NWR, c/o Willamette Valley NWR Complex, 26208 Finley Refuge Rd., Corvallis, OR 97333; tel.: (541) 757-7236.

Pennsylvania

Erie, containing 8,780 acres in two divisions, was established in 1959 to enhance, manage, and protect significant wetland habitats for migratory waterfowl and other wildlife. The refuge is located a few miles south of Lake Erie, in northwestern Pennsylvania.

The 5,205-acre SUGAR LAKE DIVISION, near the village of Guys Mills, is an intensively managed area that lies in a long, narrow valley that runs from north to south. Along north-flowing Woodcock Creek and south-flowing Lake Creek are many beaver ponds, pools, managed impoundments, and areas of marsh and swamp. The riparian wetlands are bordered by forested valley slopes with scattered agricultural lands, grassland, and wet meadows. The 3,571-acre SENECA DIVISION, located ten miles to the north, consists of another forested valley with swamps, bogs, and other wetland habitat, mostly along Muddy and Dead creeks.

As the Fish and Wildlife Service explains its management activities on the refuge:

Water control structures on refuge impoundments permit the [seasonal] manipulation of water levels to encourage the growth of waterfowl food and cover plants such as smartweeds and bulrushes. Future plans call for more than doubling the amount of manageable habitat now available.

Grasslands are being developed near wetlands to provide dense nesting cover for ground-nesting waterfowl and other birds. . . .

A cooperative farming program permits farmers to cultivate crops on refuge lands. Farmers agree to raise certain crops such as oats, grass, clover and corn. In return for using the land, farmers leave the refuge a share of the crops. These refuge shares are usually left in the field as supplemental food for wildlife.

The best times to see large concentrations of waterfowl are March and early April and September into November. As many as 4,500 Canada geese and 2,500 ducks are attracted to the refuge during the peak days of migration. Wood ducks are the most common nesting waterfowl, for which the Fish and Wildlife Service has placed nesting boxes to supplement tree cavities and enhance successful breeding. Other ducks that nest on the refuge include mallards, blue-winged teal, and hooded mergansers. Bald eagles and great blue herons also nest here, the latter in rookeries. More than 235 bird species have been recorded.

Establishment of this refuge was made possible partly with revenues from the sale of Migratory Bird Hunting and Conservation Stamps (Duck Stamps). Ducks Unlimited, Inc. has helped enhance a few acres of the refuge's wetland habitat.

The refuge is open daily during daylight hours. There is no entrance fee. The refuge visitor center/headquarters, located on the Sugar Lake Division, is open on weekdays, except national holidays.

Visitor activities include wildlife observation, driving a number of township roads through the refuge, hiking on several trails, cross-country skiing, fishing (a wheelchair-accessible fishing pier is provided at Pool K), and hunting on parts of the refuge during the designated seasons. By prearrangement, the refuge also provides programs and tours for school groups and teacher workshops. Deer Run Overlook, off of Allen Road, offers a view of 130-acre Pool 9, where bald eagles can sometimes be seen. The Seneca Division provides a one-mile (wheelchair-accessible) boardwalk, located off of Johnstown Road.

Insect repellent is advised during the warmer months.

Lodgings and meals are available in Meadville, Edinboro, and Erie.

Access to the refuge's visitor center from Exit 36 on I-79 is northeast 2 miles to Meadville, southeast 7 miles on State Hwy. 27, left onto State Hwy. 3032 for 3.5 miles to Guys Mills, east about 0.75-mile on State Hwy. 198, and right onto Wood Duck Lane.

Information: Erie NWR, 11296 Wood Duck Lane, Guys Mills, PA 16327; tel.: (814) 789-3585.

John Heinz National Wildlife Refuge at Tinicum, comprising 1,200 acres, was established in 1972 to restore and protect Tinicum Marsh for the benefit of waterfowl and other wildlife. The refuge is located in the City of Philadelphia and adjacent Delaware County, in southeastern Pennsylvania. The area was initially called the Tinicum National Environmental Center, but in 1991, the name was changed to honor U. S. Senator John Heinz, who was instrumental in helping protect the marsh. More than 300 bird species have been recorded here.

Tinicum was formerly a 5,700-acre, tidally influenced, freshwater marsh along Darby Creek, on the west bank of the Delaware River. For many years, this ecologically rich habitat was viewed as a "wasteland" to be drained, diked, and filled with sediments dredged from the Delaware and Schuylkill rivers. By the mid-20th century, only about 200 acres of wetland remained undisturbed. Then in 1969, highway engineers announced their intention to obtain sand and gravel from the marsh for use in constructing Interstate Highway 95. Conservationists mounted a legal challenge that delayed the sand and gravel extraction proposal and succeeded in having part of the freeway route shifted and obtaining congressional authorization for the restoration and protection of the area as a national wildlife refuge.

Restoring the marsh was one of the legislatively mandated goals of the refuge. As the Spring 1994 *Refuge Reporter* explained:

Little did anyone know that another major highway project would help serve that objective. Completion of I-476, around the west side of Philadelphia, took 18 acres of wetland that had to be replaced [as a "mitigation" project elsewhere]. Highway engineers turned again to Tinicum Marsh, but this time to create rather than destroy.

After nearly a year of dredging and planting and expending some $2 million, an 18-acre area on the refuge was transformed during 1991-92 from an old spoils deposition site into a replicated tidal marsh.

Several years later, another wetlands mitigation project occurred on the refuge. Because marsh habitat had to be filled in for construction of a new runway at nearby Philadelphia International Airport, it was agreed that a 26-acre part of the refuge that had previously been used for river-dredged silt would be restored as wetland at a cost of about $3 million.

In January 2000, a major milestone for this refuge was achieved with the opening of the 14,000-square-foot Cusano Environmental Education Center. The initial phase of this energy-efficient facility contains an exhibit and interactive display area, a multipurpose meeting room, classrooms, resource library, and a gift shop that is operated by the nonprofit Friends of the Heinz Refuge at Tinicum. Two outstanding exhibits are the life-sized, free-standing, 100-foot-long cross section of the Tinicum Marsh and a state-of-the-art greenhouse wastewater treatment plant. Other phases of the center are the construction of an administrative wing and an enclosed 100-foot-high (wheelchair-accessible) viewing platform.

The education center is named in memory of the late Antonio Cusano, whose generous bequest provided about half of the center's $5-million construction cost. The balance of the funding was raised by the National Fish and Wildlife Foundation and the Friends organization.

As Refuge Manager Dick Nugent says,

Some folks still debate the issue of having an urbanized national wildlife refuge, with its inherent "problems" of air, ground, and water pollution; expensive land acquisition; security concerns; and public apathy. I side with the many counterpoints and opportunities presented by each "problem" and redefine them as "challenges."

The National Wildlife Refuge System is a spectacular network of "dirt" and water oases for wildlife and humankind. The "human" aspect has only recently been highlighted—much of that via the landmark Refuge System Improvement Act of 1997, which emphasizes that the refuge system "shine bright" for wildlife, habitat, and people.

The refuge and the environmental education center are open daily during daylight hours. There is no entrance fee.

Visitor activities include wildlife observation; viewing interpretive exhibits and programs at the education center; interpreter-led walks; hiking on more than ten miles of trails; canoeing, kayaking, and non-motorized boating on Darby Creek (a hand-carried boat-launching site is provided near the education center); and fishing.

Insect repellent is advised during the warmer months.

Lodgings and meals are available in Philadelphia and Essington.

Access to the from I-95 northbound is by way of the State Hwy. 291/Philadelphia International Airport exit, left at the first light onto Bartram Ave., left at the third light onto Eighty-Fourth St., and left at the second light onto Lindbergh Blvd. From I-95 southbound, it is by way of the Hwy. 291/airport exit (taking the right fork and exiting for Hwy. 291-Lester), right at the first light onto Bartram Ave., left at the second light onto Eighty-Fourth St., and left at the second light onto Lindbergh Blvd.

Information: John Heinz NWR at Tinicum, 8601 Lindbergh Blvd., Philadelphia, PA 19153; tel.: (215) 365-3118.

Rhode Island

John H. Chafee, consisting of 727 acres, was originally established in 1988 as the Pettaquam-scutt Cove National Wildlife Refuge and was renamed in 1999 in honor of U.S. Senator John H. Chafee for his contributions to natural resource conservation. The refuge is located around the shore of tidally influenced Pettaquamscutt Cove, which is part of the Narrow (Pettaquam-scutt) River estuary, near the mouth of Narragansett Bay in southern Rhode Island.

Refuge habitats include areas of salt marsh, containing salt marsh and salt meadow cord-grass, spikegrass, saltwort, and sea lavender. Several islands within the tidal wetlands support oaks and an understory of poison ivy. Black oaks and red maples are the dominant trees on the gently sloping uplands around the western side of the cove; woodlands along the eastern side consist mostly of maples.

The refuge was established mainly to provide important wintering habitat for concentra-tions of American black ducks, along with Canada geese, mallards, canvasbacks, buffleheads, red-breasted mergansers, and the non-native mute swan.

Other birds of this refuge include great blue and green herons, snowy egrets, ospreys, salt-marsh sharp-tailed sparrows, and numerous neotropical migratory songbirds such as thrushes and warblers. More than 215 species of birds have been recorded here.

Water pollution is unfortunately a cause of concern in Pettaquamscutt Cove. As the U.S. Fish and Wildlife Service says, "Failing septic systems have been implicated as one of the most significant contributions to water quality problems. . . ." Another harmful environmental impact is the aggressive, invasive common reed (*Phragmites*), which forms "virtually impenetrable stands" that choke out native emergent freshwater plants, such as cattails, sedges, and rushes, offering "little suitable food or cover for wildlife."

The refuge is open daily during daylight hours. There is no entrance fee. The Rhode Island NWR Complex headquarters, located at U.S. Route 1A, Shoreline Plaza, in Charlestown, is open on weekdays, except national holidays.

Visitor activities include wildlife observation; limited hiking on unmaintained trails; ca-noeing, kayaking, and boating on state waters within the cove; and fishing. Although there are presently no visitor facilities on the refuge and few places from which to view the cove, the Fish and Wildlife Service plans to provide a (wheelchair-accessible) trail and observation platforms at Middle Bridge and Bridgeport Commons and to designate an interpretive canoe/kayak trail.

Visitors are cautioned to be alert for ticks, which may carry Lyme disease. Insect repellent is advised during the warmer months.

Lodgings and meals are available in Narragansett, Wakefield, and Charlestown.

Information: John H. Chafee NWR, c/o Rhode Island NWR Complex, P.O. Box 307, Charlestown, RI 02813; tel.: (401) 364-9124.

Ninigret, comprising 409 acres in two units, was established in 1970 to restore and manage wetland, grassland, woodland, and barrier beach habitats for a diversity of migrating and breeding birds. The refuge is located near Charlestown, along the shore of 1,711-acre Ninigret Pond, about three miles west of Trustom Pond Refuge, on the south shore of Rhode Island.

Approximately 16 percent of this refuge contains wetland habitats. These are salt marsh, most of which is on the refuge's small barrier beach unit; scrub-shrub and wooded wetlands; a number of man-made freshwater ponds; and areas of natural freshwater wetlands. Most of the latter are located in *kettles*, which are small basins created roughly 10,000 years ago by melting blocks of glacial ice. Such blocks were left behind by the main mass of the continental glacier, as its terminal zone was thinning and withdrawing northward from southern New England.

According to the Fish and Wildlife Service, "Unfortunately, most of the wetlands have diminished wildlife value because of the presence of Phragmites [common reed]. . . . The monotypic, virtually impenetrable stands of Phragmites choke out native plants, and provide little suitable food or cover for wildlife." Other emergent, freshwater-wetland plants include cattails, sedges, and rushes. Scattered areas of "scrub-shrub" wetland contain speckled alder, buttonbush, swamp rose, and swamp loosestrife (the latter not to be confused with the invasive, non-native purple loosestrife). An area of red maple swamp extends along the western edge of the refuge.

A major goal of the refuge is to restore and maintain more than 200 acres of grassland habitat, thereby attracting wildlife that is associated with it, such as upland sandpipers, bobolinks, eastern meadowlarks, and grasshopper sparrows. These grasslands also attract numerous species of butterflies, including large concentrations of the monarch butterfly during their autumn migration.

About a quarter of the refuge consists of upland shrub habitat that is typically dominated by northern arrowwood, northern bayberry, sumacs, shadbush, and highbush blueberry. And about a third of the refuge is wooded, with such trees as red maple; white, northern red, and black oaks; quaking aspen; gray birch; eastern redcedar; and a few eastern white and pitch pines.

The refuge's main unit, along the northern shore of the Ninigret Pond, occupies the U.S. Navy's former Charlestown Naval Auxiliary Land Facility (naval air station). Removal of the facility's aircraft runways and taxiways has been accomplished with the assistance of U.S. Army and U.S. Navy Seabee reserve units. Areas of wetland and other habitats are being restored.

The open expanse of Ninigret Pond, which is outside the refuge, is a major attraction for many species of migratory waterfowl, notably Canada geese, American black ducks, mallards, greater scaup, common goldeneyes, buffleheads, and red-breasted mergansers. However, as explained by the Fish and Wildlife Service, "The construction of a permanent breach-way in 1962 to stabilize the pond radically changed its ecology of the formerly productive estuarine fisheries. Habitat degradation includes the loss of 40 percent of its eelgrass beds over the last 32 years due to sedimentation and nutrient loading. . . . Water quality in Ninigret Pond is poor."

In addition to waterfowl, wildlife of the refuge include raptors, such as bald eagles and sharp-shinned and other hawks that migrate through the area during the autumn and ospreys that nest around Ninigret Pond. Enormous concentrations of tree swallows pass through here on their autumn migration. Large influxes of warblers and other neotropical migratory songbirds arrive in late April and early May. A few of these birds remain to nest here, but the majority of them continue to breeding grounds farther north. Woodcocks nest on the refuge from March to June, during which they perform their courtship flight displays at dusk, accompanied by nasal "peent" calls and the vibrating sound of their fast-beating wings. The federally listed threatened piping plover nests from April to August on the refuge's barrier beach unit and/or on the state's adjacent Ninigret Conservation Area. More than 250 bird species have been recorded on the refuge.

The refuge's main unit is open daily during daylight hours. The barrier beach unit is closed to motor vehicles from April 1 through August, to avoid disturbing the nesting piping plovers. There is no entrance fee. The Rhode Island NWR Complex headquarters, at U.S. Route 1A, Shoreline Plaza, in Charlestown, is open on weekdays, except national holidays.

Visitor activities include wildlife and butterfly observation, hiking on two (wheelchair-accessible) trails (one of which ends at an observation platform overlooking Ninigret Pond), and surf fishing on the barrier beach. Although camping is not permitted on the refuge, facilities are available at the state's Ninigret Conservation Area and elsewhere nearby.

On the adjacent town of Charlestown's Ninigret Park, the Frosty Drew Nature Center provides a variety of interpretive programs and outings—some of which are held on the refuge. The nature center is open and staffed on weekdays from July 1 through August, and on Tuesdays through Fridays during the rest of the year. It may also be open on weekends, depending upon the availability of volunteers. Nature center information: tel.: (401) 364-9508.

Visitors are cautioned to be alert for ticks, especially as the refuge is a known "hot spot" for deer ticks carrying Lyme disease. Insect repellent is advised during the warmer months.

Access to the refuge from Charlestown is just west on U.S. Hwy. 1A and left into Ninigret Park, to the parking area adjacent to the refuge's east entrance. The refuge's west entrance road is a short distance farther west, just beyond where Hwy. 1A merges with U.S. Hwy. 1.

Information: Ninigret NWR, c/o Rhode Island NWR Complex, P.O. Box 307, Charlestown, RI 02813; tel.: (401) 364-9124.

South Carolina

Cape Romain, containing 64,229 acres, was established in 1932 on the central coast of South Carolina. Large areas of this refuge consist of extensive, cordgrass-dominated, estuarine salt marsh habitat. Intricately meandering tidal creeks divide this wetland into numerous islands that are inundated during high tide, a twenty-mile stretch of Atlantic coastal barrier islands with areas of sand dunes behind long sandy beaches. Nearly half of the refuge is the open water of Bull's Bay, and a little less than half of Cape Romain is designated as a unit of the National Wilderness Preservation System. More than 330 bird species have been recorded here.

The refuge's centerpiece is 5,496-acre Bull's Island, part of an ancient barrier reef that is one of Cape Romain's three largest barrier islands. The island, which was named for 17th-century English settler Stephen Bull, contains several large brackish impoundments and ponds. The island's uplands support roughly 2,000 acres of maritime forest of such species as live oak, southern magnolia, loblolly pine, redbay, wax myrtle, sweetgum, yaupon and American holly, cabbage palmetto, and the low-growing saw palmetto.

In 1989, Hurricane Hugo slammed into the South Carolina coast and devastated the island's climax forest. As described by Refuge Biologist Craig Sasser:

The force of Hurricane Hugo's 100-plus-mile-per-hour winds and 30-foot storm surge can best be demonstrated by examining the devastation that was unfurled along South Carolina's coast, especially at "ground zero". . . . Bull's Island . . . was where the eye of the storm passed, exposing it to both a windward (ocean side) storm surge and a leeward (bay side) storm surge. This high energy zone denuded Bull's Island of most of its mature trees, thus removing almost all forest structure. Tree species that survived the initial assault have, to date, continued to die from massive scarring and saltwater stress. These species include mature live oaks, cabbage palmettos, and laurel oaks. Almost every mature pine on Bull's Island was destroyed upon storm impact.

For several reasons, this natural event may have forever changed the forest structure and composition on Bull's Island. Invasive species, such as Chinese tallow, exploded because of its opportunistic strategy of remaining in a semi-dormant stage until the upper canopy is removed, and then accelerating its growth and out-competing other species for available nutrients and sunlight. . . .

Additionally, the tremendous fuel-loading left in the wake of Hurricane Hugo . . . has made forest-management practices, such as prescribed fire, nearly impossible, because of the complexity of factors that must be considered before burning. . . . These extreme fuel loads can be difficult to reduce, especially with prescribed fire, because under ideal burning conditions, the fire will burn too hot, further stressing mature trees and killing younger trees. Other methods of fuel reduction, such as . . . mechanical removal, can be labor intensive.

Large concentrations of wintering waterfowl, including the tundra swan and numerous species of ducks, are attracted to the refuge's ponds and other open water, and great numbers of wintering shorebirds flock to its beaches and mudflats. Among the many birds that nest on the refuge are several thousand pairs of both brown pelicans and royal terns, and large numbers of least and sandwich terns, herons, egrets, ibises, black skimmers, and American oystercatchers. Many thousands of clapper rails inhabit the salt marshes. During the summer and autumn, large groups of the federally listed threatened wood stork come to Bull's Island. Resident wood ducks nest in trees around the ponds. Other resident wildlife includes bald eagles, ospreys, wild turkeys, white-tailed deer, raccoons, and alligators. During spring and autumn, great influxes of warblers and other neotropical migratory songbirds pass through the refuge—notably during March and April.

Loggerhead sea turtles, a federally listed threatened species, haul themselves onto the refuge's barrier island beaches in such numbers to lay their eggs, especially on Cape Island, that Cape Romain ranks as the largest nesting beach in the United States for this species outside of Florida. The endangered leatherback sea turtle has also occasionally been recorded here.

Cape Romain refuge is one of the few places in the southeastern United States that has been targeted for the reintroduction of the federally listed endangered red wolf. In 1977, the first breeding pair was released on Bull's Island. As of 1999, the Fish and Wildlife Service reported, "The Bull's Island project began the year with 5 wolves on the Island consisting of the adult breeding pair, 2 adult males, and one two-year old male." (See the St. Vincent and Alligator River refuge texts for further discussions of the red wolf recovery program.)

As for the beauty of this refuge, Craig Sasser recalls one of his most inspiring memories:

This particular evening, I was sitting on the edge of Lower Summerhouse Pond, waiting for the tide to change to close the water-control structures. As I gazed to the west, I watched the sun sinking slowly, beyond the mighty, darkly silhouetted "wings" of ancient live oaks, infused with cabbage palmettos and Spanish moss. Like a huge painting, the sky was splashed with hues of pink, amber, yellow, and orange and was mirrored across the pond's surface—only to be shimmered by black skimmers, as they passed in formation in search of one last meal, their long beaks skimming the water. The pond was alive with the silhouettes of other bird life, as herons, terns, and wood storks chased unfamiliar prey that had just been thrust into unfamiliar hunting grounds with the last pulse of tidal water.

As the amber hues faded and darkened, a sense of sadness filled me, because it signaled the closing of this spectacular portrait. But then the eastern sky began suddenly to brighten, unveiling the rising of the full moon and signifying the onset of a new beginning—that of the nocturnals. In the distance, a family of wolves celebrated with a chorus of musical howls, for their time of foraging and exploring had just begun.

The refuge is open daily during daylight hours. There is no entrance fee. The joint Cape Romain NWR-Francis Marion National Forest's Sewee Visitor and Environmental Education Center, located on the mainland, is open on Tuesdays through Sundays. This center is managed by the South Eastern Wildlife and Environmental Education (SEWEE) Association, Inc.

Visitor activities include viewing an orientation program and interpretive exhibits at the Sewee center, wildlife observation, hiking (including a one-mile trail near the Sewee center that passes by a red wolf enclosure), picnicking (a picnic area is provided on Bull's Island), shelling, boating, fishing, and limited hunting (archery hunts for deer and raccoon). Although camping is not permitted on the refuge, facilities are provided in the nearby national forest.

Even though alligators are generally afraid of people, visitors are cautioned to stay a safe distance from them and to be alert for venomous snakes, ticks, and chiggers. Insect repellent, especially during the warmer months, and sunscreen are advised.

Lodgings and meals are available in McClellanville, Georgetown, Mt. Pleasant, and Charleston.

Access to the Sewee visitor center from Charleston is north twenty miles on U.S. Hwy. 17. The refuge itself is reached only by boat. Passenger ferry service (fee; no reservations) takes visitors the three miles (30 minutes) from Moore's Landing to Bull's Island. The ferry operates on Tuesdays, Thursdays, Fridays, and Saturdays from March 1 through November; and on Saturdays only from December 1 through February; it does not operate on Thanksgiving, Christmas Eve, or Christmas. Visitors are urged to take water, picnic snacks, insect repellent, sunscreen, and comfortable hiking shoes on Bull's Island excursions. Ferry service information, telephone: tel.: (843) 881-4582.

Information: Cape Romain NWR, 5801 Hwy. 17 North, Awendaw, SC 29429; tel.: (843) 928-3264.

Carolina Sandhills, containing 45,348 acres, was established in 1939 to restore and protect an area that had previously become an ecologically degraded and severely eroded land supporting little wildlife. The refuge is located between the Atlantic Coastal Plain and the Piedmont Plateau, in the Sandhills of northeastern South Carolina. The term "Sandhills" refers to the region's gently rolling hills, which are overlain with deep layers of porous sands.

As described by the U.S. Fish and Wildlife Service, after the federal government acquired the refuge:

Efforts began immediately to restore this damaged, barren land to a healthy, rich habitat for the plants and animals that once lived here.

The longleaf pine/wiregrass ecosystem, the characteristic habitat of the refuge, once covered more than 90 million acres across the southeastern United States from Virginia to Texas. This unique ecosystem, shaped by thousands of years of natural fires that burned through every two to four years, has been reduced to less than two million acres.

Today, only scattered patches remain, with most occurring on public lands. Factors contributing to the demise of this ecosystem include aggressive fire suppression efforts, clearing for agriculture and development, and conversion to other pine types.

The refuge contains extensive areas of open longleaf-pine forest. The longleaf pine, which grows 75 to 120 feet tall, has three-per-bundle bright-green needles measuring eight to 18 inches long, and six- to ten-inch-long cones. Beneath these pines is a scattered understory of scrub oaks and various shrubs. The dominant ground cover is the clump-forming, deeply rooted wiregrass, a species of three-awn grass that grows two to three feet tall. This grass, along with an accumulation of needles, dead wood, and other organic debris, easily fuels relatively low-burning fires that prevent or curtail the growth of most understory trees without damaging the pines, thereby maintaining open, pine-dominated woodlands. In the absence of periodic fire, dense growths of scrub oaks and other hardwoods ultimately take over as the dominant species, preventing the regeneration of the pines.

Wildlife species that thrive in this open pine woodland include wild turkey, northern bobwhite, fox squirrel, and the federally listed endangered red-cockaded woodpecker. This woodpecker has a black cap and nape, a boldly striped black-and-white back, and a prominent white cheek patch, at the top of which (on adult males) is a small red swatch—the "cockade"—that is frequently difficult to see. As explained by the U.S. Fish and Wildlife Service, "The red-cockaded woodpecker makes its home in mature pine forests; more specifically, those with long-leaf pines averaging 80 to 120 years of age and loblolly pines averaging 70 to 100. While other woodpeckers bore out cavities in dead trees where the wood is rotten and soft, the red-cockaded woodpecker is the only one that excavates cavities exclusively in living pine trees."

The nesting season of this woodpeckers runs from April through June. According to the Fish and Wildlife Service, "Upon fledging, the young often remain with the parents, forming groups of . . . typically four to five members. There is only one pair of breeding birds within each group, and they normally raise only a single brood each year. The other group members, usually males from the previous breeding season, help incubate the eggs and raise the young." Carolina Sandhills refuge supports more than 140 groups of these territorial and unusually cooperative woodpeckers—the largest population in the National Wildlife Refuge System. More than 190 bird species have been recorded here.

The Fish and Wildlife Service implements a variety of management activities designed to enhance the refuge's diverse wildlife habitats. A major emphasis is on enhancing and maintaining the woodpecker's vital foraging and nesting habitat by selective thinning, prescribed burning, and other methods of timber management to maintain high-quality forest of older pines; by installing man-made nesting cavities; and by monitoring breeding success and population trends.

In addition to the pine woodlands, this refuge also contains many small creeks that flow into either Black Creek, along the eastern side of the refuge, or Lynches River, to the west. Bottomland hardwoods and shrubs border these streams. Sandhill seeps create bogs that are special habitats for such species as the pine barrens tree frog, sundew, and several kinds of pitcher-plants.

Other habitats include thirty man-made lakes and ponds that attract waterfowl and other wildlife; forest clearings; and both fallow and cultivated fields.

The refuge is open daily during daylight hours. There is no entrance fee. The refuge office/visitor station is open on weekdays, except national holidays.

Visitor activities include wildlife observation; driving the nine-mile paved auto tour road, as well as a number of gravel roads; hiking on several trails; viewing the refuge and wildlife from two observation towers; environmental educational and interpretive programs; canoeing and boating (electric motors only; boat-launching ramps on Martins and Mays lakes and Lake Bee); fishing (Martins Lake is closed to fishing); and limited hunting on parts of the refuge during the designated seasons. Although camping is not permitted on the refuge, facilities are provided at nearby Sandhills State Forest.

Visitors are cautioned to be alert for venomous snakes, ticks, and chiggers. Insect repellent is advised during the warmer months.

Lodgings and meals are available in Cheraw, Pageland, Camden, and Hartsville.

Access to the refuge from McBee is 4 miles northeast on U.S. Hwy. I; or from Cheraw, it is II miles southwest on U.S. Hwy. I.

Information: Carolina Sandhills NWR, 23734 U.S. Hwy. I, McBee, SC 29101; tel.: (843) 335-8401.

Ernest F. Hollings ACE Basin, comprising more than II,800 acres in two units toward a goal of as much as 18,000 acres, is located along the Combahee and Edisto rivers, in southern South Carolina. In 1990, the refuge's first tract of land, the 832-acre Bonny Hall Plantation and Club property that is now part of the refuge's COMBAHEE UNIT, was acquired from The Nature Conservancy.

The ACE Basin Project, of which the refuge is a part, was initiated in 1988, when Ducks Unlimited, Inc., The Nature Conservancy, the Fish and Wildlife Service, the South Carolina Department of Natural Resources, and a number of private landowners formed the ACE Basin Task Force. ACE stands for three major rivers in the basin—the Ashepoo, Combahee, and Edisto. The 350,000-acre ACE Basin is one of the largest undeveloped estuarine wetland ecosystems remaining along the U.S. Atlantic Coast. By the year 2001, more than 136,752 acres of the Basin had been brought under various forms of conservation management.

As explained by this landmark cooperative group, "The mission of the ACE Basin Project is to maintain the natural character of the Basin by promoting wise resource management on private lands and protecting strategic tracts by conservation agencies. A major goal of the protection efforts is to ensure that traditional uses such as farming, forestry, recreational and commercial fishing, and hunting will continue in the area."

Ducks Unlimited and The Nature Conservancy have worked closely with public resource agencies in acquiring many of the lands available for public access. Private landowners are offered technical help in wildlife-habitat management by task force representatives.

The Fish and Wildlife Service is performing a number of habitat-management activities on the refuge to promote wildlife diversity. Ecologically productive expanses of brackish tidal marsh and island-like hammocks, comprising more than 40 percent of the refuge, are being protected. The refuge includes areas of upland pines and bottomland hardwoods, where forest diversity is enhanced by selective thinning, prescribed burning, and the creation of clearings. Fire management helps prevent fuel overloading, reduce understory vegetation in some areas, promote nutrient cycling, and spur the sprouting of herbs and grasses for the benefit of such species as deer and wild turkeys. Several fallow fields are also treated with fire, triggering the growth of forbs and grasses valued by turkeys, bobwhite, and numerous songbirds.

Water levels within former rice-field impoundments are seasonally regulated for moist-soil management, to promote the growth of nutrient-rich foods for the benefit of waterfowl and other wildlife. As explained by the Fish and Wildlife Service, the flow of water, between a tide-influenced creek or river and a moist-soil impoundment, is regulated by means of "wooden culverts with flap gates" that "operate on tidal surge."

The historical and architectural highlight of the refuge's EDISTO UNIT is Grove Plantation House that dates from 1828. This three-story structure, which is on the National Register of Historic Places, is one of only three antebellum rice plantation mansions in the ACE Basin to survive the Civil War. The house, which is surrounded by great spreading Spanish "moss"-draped live oaks, was beautifully renovated in the mid-1990s and serves as the refuge headquarters and visitor center.

The refuge is open daily during daylight hours. There is no entrance fee. The refuge office, located on the Edisto Unit, is open on weekdays, except national holidays.

Visitor activities include wildlife observation; hiking on trails; boating, canoeing, and kayaking on the Basin's meandering tidal waterways; fishing in the tidal creeks and freshwater streams; and hunting on parts of the refuge during the designated seasons.

Even though alligators are generally afraid of people, visitors are cautioned to stay a safe distance from them and to be alert for venomous snakes, ticks, and chiggers. Insect repellent and sunscreen are advised during the warmer months.

Lodgings and meals are available in Beaufort, Edisto Island, South Point, Yemassee, Walterboro, and Charleston.

Access to the refuge headquarters (on the Edisto Unit) from U.S. Hwy. 17 at Osborn is south just over three miles on State Hwy. 174, right at a flashing light onto State Hwy. 55 (Willtown Rd.) for about two miles, and left onto State Hwy. 346 (Jehossee Island Rd.) for about two miles. The several tracts of the refuge's Combahee Unit are reached from U.S. Hwy. 17 (just west of the Combahee River) by turning northwest onto State Hwy. 33, from which trails offer hiking opportunities from a number of parking areas.

Information: Ernest F. Hollings ACE Basin NWR, 8675 Willtown Rd., Hollywood, SC 29449; tel.: (843) 889-3084.

South Dakota

Dakota Tallgrass Prairie Wildlife Management Area (WMA), established in 2001, represents a new concept in wildlife conservation, one designed to help save an ecosystem from extinction. The goal is to eventually preserve 190,000 acres of what was once the vast expanse of the northern tallgrass prairie. The refuge will accomplish protection primarily through the purchase of perpetual grassland easements from willing sellers. The lands acquired are a part of the National Wildlife Refuge System and are administered locally by national wildlife refuges and wetland management districts. The entire Dakota Tallgrass Prairie WMA encompasses more than 80 percent of the remaining northern tallgrass prairie. The WMA includes parts of 28 counties in eastern South Dakota and 4 counties in southeastern North Dakota.

Conservation on the WMA began with the first easement on June 27, 2001. As of 2008, approximately 60,000 acres of conservation easements had been purchased from willing partners. Using perpetual easements, these partners retain ownership of their land, while the prairie is permanently protected. The WMA is presently in the early stages of development, and easement acquisition is the primary focus. As more acreage is added, the emphasis will shift to prairie enhancement and restoration.

As fragmentation of remaining prairie sites continues to reduce the viability of the ecosystem, the goal of the WMA is the preservation of the few remaining large blocks of this habitat in the Dakotas. Major focus areas include the Prairie Coteau, located in northeastern South Dakota, and lands adjacent to the Sheyenne National Grasslands in southeastern North Dakota.

Tallgrass prairie is the most altered and possibly the most endangered ecosystem in North America. Today, less than four percent of the native northern tallgrass prairie remains, which means that nearly 45 million acres of northern tallgrass prairie have been destroyed. Most of the losses are due to the continuous conversion of prairie to croplands since the late 1800s. The potential for species extinction in the northern tallgrass prairie is of serious concern. Grassland-dependent bird species have shown steeper and more consistent and geographically widespread declines than any other group of North American species.

Northern tallgrass prairie is visually dominated by such grasses as big bluestem, little bluestem, Indian grass, switch grass, prairie dropseed, porcupine grass, and needle-and-thread grass. However, 90 percent of the plants on the prairie are wildflowers. Some of the better-known species include blazing stars, hoary puccoon, catnip, Maximilian sunflower, gentians, and the white lady's-slipper orchid.

This biologically diverse system supports forty species of ground-nesting, neotropical migratory birds and a dozen species of waterfowl. Neotropicals include the bobolink, grasshopper sparrow, cedar waxwing, and common yellowthroat. Common waterfowl include blue-winged teal, mallard, gadwall, and the giant Canada goose. Greater prairie chicken and sharp-tailed grouse are two resident game birds that inhabit the WMA. Of the 435 bird species that nest within the United States, 160 breed in native tallgrass prairie habitat. Even in winter, when other birds leave this harsh northern climate, the ecosystem attracts the Lapland longspur, snow bunting, and snowy owl.

More than 24 species of true tallgrass prairie mammals have been recorded within the WMA. Among these are the western harvest and meadow jumping mice, least weasel, and eastern spotted skunk. The plains pocket gopher and Franklin's ground squirrel are among the few mammals that are restricted to the tallgrass prairie.

Reptiles and amphibians include the painted turtle, garter snake, tiger salamander, and northern leopard frog. Fish such as the Topeka shiner, which depend on clear prairie streams, may not survive if this habitat continues to be lost. Numerous butterflies, including the Dakota skipper and Regal fritillary, are dependent on a multitude of prairie plants to fulfill their life cycles.

The WMA is home to more than 317 state-listed rare or endangered plant and animal species. Federally listed threatened and endangered species include the western prairie fringed orchid, American burying beetle, and the Topeka shiner.

(With special thanks to Craig Mowry, former Dakota Tallgrass Prairie Coordinator, for providing the above description.—RDB)

Information: Dakota Tallgrass Prairie Wildlife Management Area, 44401 134A St., Waubay, SD 57273; tel.: (605) 947-4521.

Sand Lake, comprising 21,498 acres, was established in 1935 to enhance and protect the ecologically significant prairie marsh ecosystem of shallow lakes, marsh, wooded lakeshore, shelterbelts, and grassland in the heart of the prairie pothole region, along the James River of northeastern South Dakota. This refuge is a vitally important major staging and nesting area—a mecca for hundreds of thousands of migratory birds, especially waterfowl.

As many as a quarter-million snow geese have been seen during autumn and up to 1.2 million during spring. Tundra swans and bald eagles pause on their migrations, with up to 100 eagles in the spring. American white pelicans gather in large concentrations. Substantial numbers of white-faced ibises, cattle egrets, and black terns nest at Sand Lake. In recent years, the refuge has been supporting the world's largest nesting colony of Franklin's gulls, totaling from 86,000 to 155,000 pairs. More than 265 bird species have been recorded here.

Sand Lake refuge has been designated as a "Wetland of International Importance" by the Convention on Wetlands of International Importance and the U.S. Department of the Interior. It is the first refuge in the prairie pothole region to be so honored.

Two low-head dams, a number of dikes and other water-control structures, and nesting islands were built during the early years of the refuge to enhance waterfowl habitat. Sand Lake, behind Columbia Dam, and Mud Lake, behind Houghton Dam, provide long expanses of open water and some wetland habitat of cattails, bulrushes, and common reed (*Phragmites*). Great numbers of waterfowl, wading birds, and shorebirds congregate to rest and feed here during the spring and autumn migrations. Some stretches of lakeshore are bordered with cottonwood trees, willows, and other woodland vegetation that attract many kinds of migratory songbirds.

Soon after the refuge was established, the Civilian Conservation Corps planted close to a half-million trees on the refuge to provide shelterbelts for wildlife against the powerful winter winds. Green ash, American elm, eastern cottonwood, and the non-native Russian olive and Siberian elm were the major species introduced onto the refuge. On some refuge lands that were previously cropland or pasture, the Fish and Wildlife Service has planted a mixture of native grasses. Areas of dense nesting cover for ducks and other wildlife have been planted with sweet clover, alfalfa, and wheatgrass.

One of this refuge's most outstanding wildlife conservation programs has been the restoration of the giant Canada goose. This magnificent subspecies, with a wingspread up to nearly six feet, was on the brink of extinction as the result of over-hunting and egg collecting during the early 20th century. In 1962, the Fish and Wildlife Service and the South Dakota Department of Game, Fish, and Parks initiated a joint restoration program. Several thousands of these geese, which have been raised from a captive flock of 200 birds that is maintained by the State of South Dakota on Sand Lake refuge, have been released into the wild and have been reestablished on suitable waterfowl habitats throughout the Dakotas.

Sand Lake refuge's habitat maintenance and enhancement activities include managing water levels to provide optimum conditions for waterfowl and other wildlife; prescribed burning; planting shrubs and seeding native grasses, grazing, haying; and cooperative farming that allows a portion of crops such as corn to be left unharvested for the benefit of wildlife.

Establishment of this refuge was made possible partly with revenues from the sale of Migratory Bird Hunting and Conservation Stamps (Duck Stamps). Ducks Unlimited, Inc. and other private organizations have assisted with important habitat enhancement projects. These projects have included the construction of water-control facilities, a nesting exclosure, and nesting islands.

The refuge is open daily during daylight hours, between early April and late September (depending on weather conditions). There is no entrance fee. The visitor center and refuge headquarters are open on weekdays, except national holidays. The visitor center may also be open on some spring weekends, depending upon the availability of volunteers.

Visitor activities include wildlife observation; viewing exhibits in the headquarters/visitor center; climbing a 100-foot tower near the visitor center for a panorama of the refuge; driving the 15-mile interpretive auto tour route; watching wildlife from an observation deck on the shore of Sand Lake; hiking a 0.75-mile trail at the refuge's Columbia Recreation Area; picnicking (a wheelchair-accessible picnic area at recreation area); fishing (at four sites); and hunting on certain parts of the refuge during the designated seasons (a wheelchair-accessible waterfowl hunting blind is provided). A pond adjacent to the visitor center/headquarters offers an opportunity for close viewing of waterfowl. Although camping is not permitted on the refuge, facilities are available at several nearby state parks.

Lodgings and meals are available in Aberdeen, Columbia, and Hecla.

Access to the refuge from Aberdeen is east seven miles on U.S. Hwy. 12 to Bath Corner, and north twenty miles on County Rd. 16.

Information: Sand Lake NWR, 39650 Sand Lake Dr., Columbia, SD 57433; tel.: (605) 885-6320.

Waubay, consisting of 4,650 acres, was established in 1935 to enhance and protect an ecologically diverse area of lakes and ponds, marshes, prairie, and deciduous forest, in northeastern South Dakota's prairie hills pothole region. The refuge's name is derived from the Lakota Indian word that appropriately means "a nesting place for birds."

Of the more than 240 species of birds that have been recorded at this refuge, more than 100 nest here. Prominent among these is the giant Canada goose. This subspecies, with a wingspan up to nearly six feet, was on the brink of extinction as the result of over-hunting and egg collecting in the early 20th century. Fortunately, it was successfully introduced on the refuge in 1937 from a donated privately owned flock.

Among other nesting birds are five species of grebes, and ducks such as blue-winged teal, mallards, gadwalls, shovelers, redheads, and lesser scaup. Waubay is the farthest south site in North America where the red-necked grebe is known to nest. In addition, there are large nesting colonies of cormorants, the American white pelican is conspicuous and common, and the ranges of a number of eastern and western songbirds overlap here.

Establishment of this refuge was made possible partly with revenues from the sale of Migratory Bird Hunting and Conservation Stamps (Duck Stamps). Ducks Unlimited, Inc. has assisted with important habitat enhancement projects.

This refuge is open daily during daylight hours. There is no entrance fee. The headquarters and visitor center are open on weekdays, except national holidays.

Visitor activities include wildlife observation, viewing exhibits and displays in the visitor center building, hiking on a loop trail (part of which is wheelchair-accessible) that includes an observation tower, picnicking at a picnic site at Hillebrand's Lake, fishing ("walk-in" ice fishing, from December to ice-out), and deer hunting on part of the refuge during the designated season. Camping is not permitted on the refuge, but facilities are provided at nearby state parks.

Lodgings and meals are available in Webster, Milbank, Watertown, and Aberdeen.

Access to the refuge from I-29 at Summit is west 11 miles on U.S. Hwy. 12, and right onto County Rd. 1 for 7 miles.

Information: Waubay NWR, 44401 134A St., Waubay, SD 57273; tel. (605) 947-4521.

Tennessee

Cross Creeks, containing 8,862 acres, was established in 1962. The refuge produces waterfowl food crops; regulates and restricts hunting, trapping, and fishing; and otherwise manages habitats for the protection of wildlife and fish populations. The refuge is located on the Cumberland River along the headwaters of the U.S. Army Corps of Engineers reservoir, Barkley Lake, in northern Tennessee.

The refuge is named for the meeting of two creeks on opposite sides of the river—North Cross and South Cross creeks. Habitats include upland oak-hickory forest, seasonally flooded bottomland hardwood forest, agricultural fields, managed moist-soil units, 16 waterfowl impoundments, and various other wetlands.

This refuge provides important wintering habitat for migratory waterfowl. Ducks of many species and Canada geese typically arrive in large numbers during mid-November and depart in late February. Peak winter waterfowl concentrations commonly range between 15,000 and 30,000 Canada geese and between 40,000 and 60,000 ducks. As refuge manager Walter Neasbitt explains:

Cross Creeks National Wildlife Refuge is one of three refuges in the southern United States where the southern James Bay population of Canada geese principally winters. Since the early 1990s, this population has been declining and by the mid-1990s had declined by almost half. Providing winter food and resting habitat for these birds is, therefore, a critically important function of this refuge.

For many years, the black duck population has also been in decline. As the human population increases its use of once-isolated sections of rivers and their wetlands, these waterfowl will have fewer and fewer places to spend the winter. While the majority of the ducks using Cross Creeks are mallards, the refuge provides a safe haven for the second largest wintering black duck concentration in the southeastern United States. Consequently, Cross Creeks Refuge plays an increasingly important role in the conservation of this species.

To ensure that the refuge provides this sufficiently productive winter waterfowl habitat, the Fish and Wildlife Service conducts several habitat management programs. Refuge staff regulate water levels in impounded water units to produce moist-soil habitat. Moist soils produce seed-bearing grasses and herbaceous plants that offer food and cover for waterfowl and other wildlife. The refuge also manages 1,200 acres of cultivated cropland under cooperative agreements with local farmers. Each year, a portion of their annual corn crop is left unharvested for the benefit of wildlife. The Fish and Wildlife Service personnel farm another 600 acres in milo, buckwheat, and winter wheat. The latter crop serves as the main source of browse for Canada geese.

Two pairs of bald eagles have nested on and around the refuge since the mid-1980s. One of these nests has fledged two or three eaglets each year since 1984. Throughout the year, bald eagles prey on fish and weakened waterfowl.

During spring, autumn, and winter migrations, shorebirds, raptors, and neotropical song birds pause on the refuge. For several weeks during the spring and autumn, the refuge wood-lands provide feeding and resting habitat for a tremendous influx of songbirds, such as warblers, grosbeaks, tanagers, and orioles. When weather conditions and seasonal management of the wa-terfowl impoundments offer exposed mudflats during spring and autumn, many species of shorebirds, such as sandpipers and dowitchers, take advantage of a brief respite here. During the winter, Cross Creeks attracts an influx of northern harriers and an occasional golden eagle. More than 250 bird species have been recorded here.

The refuge is open daily during daylight hours, from March 15 through October 31. From November 1 through March 14, the refuge's thirty-mile road network is closed to visitation, to avoid disturbance of waterfowl (groups wishing to visit the refuge may contact the refuge office to arrange for a staff-guided tour). There is no entrance fee. The visitor center is open year-round on weekdays, except national holidays.

Visitor activities include wildlife observation, viewing interpretive exhibits and programs at the visitor center, educational programs for youth groups, driving on 15 miles of the refuge's gravel roads (March 15 to October 31), hiking the one-mile Rattlesnake Trail (March 15 to October 31) and hiking and bicycling on gravel roads that are closed to motor vehicles, canoe-ing and boating on impoundments and reservoirs (March 15 to October 31; launching ramps are provided), boating year-round on the Cumberland River and bays having direct access to the river, fishing, and hunting on part of the refuge during the designated seasons. Although camp-ing is not permitted on the refuge, facilities are available at nearby Land Between the Lakes Na-tional Recreation Area and Paris Landing State Park.

Visitors are urged to be alert for venomous snakes and ticks. Insect repellent is advised dur-ing the warmer months.

Lodgings and meals are available in Dover, Paris, and Clarksville and in Paris Landing State Park.

Access to the refuge from Exit 4 on I-24 is west 37 miles on U.S. Hwy. 79 through Clarksville to Dover, left onto State Hwy. 49 just over 2 miles, and (following refuge directional signs) left for less than 1 mile to the visitor center.

Information: Cross Creeks NWR, 643 Wildlife Rd., Dover, TN 37058; tel.: (931) 232-7477.

Reelfoot, containing 10,428 acres in two units, was established in 1941. This refuge protects a significant staging and wintering area for migratory waterfowl, on the northern part of Reelfoot Lake, which occupies a stretch of former Mississippi River floodplain, in the northwest corner of Tennessee and southwest corner of Kentucky. The lake was named for a Chickasaw Indian chief, Kalopin (meaning Reelfoot), who was born with a deformed foot that caused him to walk with a staggering or reeling motion.

Reelfoot Lake was created in 1811–1812 as the result of the most violent earthquake ever recorded in North America. The New Madrid quake and aftershocks caused phenomenal shaking and shifting of the region's topography all across the central Mississippi River Valley. Powerful ground waves triggered landslides that covered and cut off rivers and streams, heaved up domes of land, opened fissures, and created sunken areas, including the extensive depression that was subsequently filled with the 25,000-acre Reelfoot Lake.

The refuge's wetland habitats attract several species of herons and other resident waterbirds and large concentrations of wintering birds, commonly totaling as many as 100,000 Canada geese, 300,000 ducks (mostly mallards), and 200 bald eagles that prey upon fish and sick or injured waterfowl. As many as seven bald eagle nests are annually active on and around Reelfoot refuge, as the result of a successful eagle "hacking" release program in the late 1980s. Hacking is a process by which eaglets are placed in artificial nests when they are about 8 weeks old and are released for their initial flight when they are 12 to 14 weeks old. When the eagles are about five years old, it is likely that they will return to nest within roughly 75 miles of their initial flight. During spring migration, the refuge's bottomland woodlands are filled with neotropical migratory songbirds, such as warblers, thrushes, tanagers, and orioles. More than 250 bird species have been recorded on the refuge.

As Devereux Butcher wrote in his 1963 book, *Exploring Our National Wildlife Refuges*:

Much of the lake inside the refuge boundaries is open water, but a great deal of it is . . . a beautiful forest of cypress. As one drifts by boat in the dim light of this forest, there is a sense of being in another world. . . . Here and there the water is paved with the big green leaves of yellow pond lily; and in spring and summer, the forest's beauty is heightened by the feathery leaves of the cypresses. Your boat drifts across open water areas where the sun is bright and warm; it winds through cypress strands of mottled sun and shade, and travels the narrow lily pad lanes.

The refuge was established under the terms of a 75-year lease agreement with the State of Tennessee. Subsequent land acquisitions expanded the refuge northward into Kentucky. The Fish and Wildlife Service carries out a number of important habitat-management activities. The water level of Reelfoot Lake is seasonally regulated to enhance its wetland habitats for the benefit of waterfowl and other wildlife. Within 250 acres of moist-soil habitats, water level management and mechanical vegetation management promote the growth of wild millet, spike rush, and other native vegetation that provide food and cover for waterbirds. Under cooperative agreements with local farmers, corn, winter wheat, and soybeans are cultivated on 900 acres of cropland. The refuge's 1,850 acres of bottomland hardwood forests are growing as marginal croplands are retired and reforested. Mature forests are being managed to promote woodland-habitat diversity for the benefit of wildlife.

The refuge is open daily during daylight hours. There is no entrance fee. The visitor center, containing a number of interpretive displays, is open daily from mid-January through mid-March; and during the rest of the year, the center is open on weekdays, except national holidays.

Visitor activities include wildlife observation; driving the 2.5-mile auto tour road, including a (wheelchair-accessible) boardwalk and wildlife observation platform in the GRASSY ISLAND

UNIT; driving an auto tour road on the LONG POINT UNIT, from mid-March to mid-November; a (wheelchair-accessible) observation platform on Long Point Unit; hiking on two trails; bicycling on refuge roads, canoeing and boating (a launching ramp is provided on the refuge's Grassy Island Unit); fishing; and hunting on parts of the refuge during the designated seasons. Daily guided bus tours to see eagles are provided in the adjacent Reelfoot Lake State Resort Park, from December 1 to mid-March. Although camping is not permitted on the refuge, facilities are available (reservations advised) in Reelfoot Lake State Resort Park: tel.: (731) 253-7756.

Among the best times for birdwatching at the refuge's Long Point observation area are January–February for the peak concentrations of wintering eagles; and mid-November to mid-March for large concentrations of waterfowl. The refuge's peak month is April for the influx of warblers and other neotropical migratory songbirds; and May–July for Mississippi kites.

Visitors are urged to be especially alert for venomous snakes; the western cottonmouth is very common throughout the refuge. Insect repellent is advised during the warmer months.

Lodgings and meals are available at adjacent Reelfoot Lake State Resort Park and in Union City and Tiptonville, Tenn., and Caruthersville, Mo.

Access to the refuge headquarters from Union City, Tenn., is northwest about 15 miles on Tenn. State Hwy. 22 and right onto Tenn. State Hwy. 157 for one mile. To access the refuge's Grassy Island Unit, proceed north 1 mile beyond the headquarters on Hwy. 157, left at Walnut Log and continue for 1.5 miles to the entrance. To access the Long Point Unit, proceed farther north on Hwy. 157, which becomes Ky. State Hwy 311, left onto Ky. State Hwy. 1282 and continue for 3 miles, following the directional sign left onto the refuge.

Information: Reelfoot NWR, 4343 Hwy. 157, Union City, TN 38261; tel.: (731) 538-2481.

Texas

Anahuac, comprising more than 34,000 acres, is located at the eastern end of Galveston Bay, in southeastern Texas. It was established in 1963 to protect and enhance important coastal prairie, small groves of trees that grow on ancient Native American shell middens, coastal marsh, and meandering bayou habitats, for the benefit of wintering waterfowl and shorebirds, neotropical migratory songbirds, and other wildlife. (See the Aransas Refuge text for description of the spectacular songbird "fallout" phenomenon that occasionally occurs along the Gulf Coast in April.)

Approximately 280 species of birds have been recorded on this refuge. During the winter, as many as 80,000 lesser snow geese feed on the refuge's moist-soil tracts and rice fields. More than two dozen species of ducks number in the thousands. Roseate spoonbills, herons, egrets, and ibises are among the array of wading birds that may be viewed on ponds, moist-soil tracts, and rice fields. Six species of rails inhabit marshy and salt-prairie habitats.

To provide habitat and food for a diversity of species, the Fish and Wildlife Service regulates water levels, plants crops, grazes livestock, carries out periodic prescribed burns, and controls exotic plants to help foster natural plant diversity.

Butterflies are also attracted to Anahuac Refuge. As naturalist Roland H. Wauer says, "A butterfly garden was established at the refuge headquarters in 2002. It is the best place on the refuge to find resident species and strays that occur in this eastern portion of Texas. Three species of special interest to butterfly enthusiasts to be expected here include Red-banded Hairstreak, and Broad-winged and Salt Marsh Skippers."

Establishment of Anahuac was made possible partly with revenues from the sale of Migratory Bird Hunting and Conservation Stamps (Duck Stamps). Ducks Unlimited, Inc. has assisted with important habitat enhancement projects. The Friends of Anahuac Refuge recently assisted the Fish and Wildlife Service in developing a two-acre butterfly garden and trail system that is adjacent to the visitor information station.

The refuge is open daily. No entrance fee is charged.

Visitor activities include wildlife and butterfly observation; driving 12 miles of gravel refuge roads (travel may be limited during wet weather); hiking on trails and roads; primitive camping; fishing (wade fishing along the shore of East Galveston Bay and freshwater fishing from the banks of, a bridge overlooking, or by boat on East Bay Bayou); and hunting on certain parts of the refuge during the designated season. A visitor contact station and an information kiosk are located at the refuge's main entrance. Two boat ramps are provided. The best birdwatching time is November through April.

Thousands of alligators inhabit the refuge. Even though these reptiles are generally afraid of people, visitors are cautioned to stay a safe distance from these sluggish-seeming but potentially fast-moving animals and to be alert for venomous snakes and fire ants. Insect repellent is recommended.

Lodgings and meals are available in High Island, Winnie, Anahuac, Baytown, and Port Arthur.

Access to the refuge from I-10 is south on State Hwy. 61 and Farm Market Rd. (FM) 562, and left onto FM 1985 to the refuge entrance; or from I-10 on State Hwy. 124 and right onto FM 1985 to the entrance.

Information: Anahuac NWR, c/o the Texas Chenier Plain NWR Complex, P.O. Box 278, Anahuac, TX 77514; tel.: (409) 267-3337.

Aransas, containing 58,983 acres, is located on the Blackjack Peninsula, between St. Charles and San Antonio bays, on the central Gulf Coast of Texas. The refuge was established in 1937 to protect salt marshes along the outer coastal fringe and the peninsula's sandy, gently undulating higher ground that in places supports oak woodland and thickets (mottes) of low-growing, wind-sculpted oak and red bay trees. Some parts of the refuge are maintained by the Fish and Wildlife Service for wildlife species requiring open meadow and grassland habitat. A few freshwater ponds occupy openings in the wooded areas.

Aransas is most famous as the primary wintering area of the endangered whooping crane—the tallest North American bird. This majestic species stands four to five feet tall and has a seven-foot wingspan. Adults have pure white plumage, black wing tips visible in flight, and a red face and crown. Juveniles have a rust-colored head and neck, and the rest of the body is patterned with rust and white plumage. The whooping crane gets its name from its high-pitched, trumpeting call, a sound that can carry for a mile or more. From late October to mid-April, Aransas is the bird's major wintering ground. Visitors can sometimes observe them from the refuge's observation tower and platforms. In the spring, they migrate northward 2,400 miles to their nesting grounds in northern Canada's Wood Buffalo National Park.

It is estimated that, until around 1860, there were approximately 1,300 to 1,400 cranes. By 1941, their population had plummeted to a mere 15 individuals. By 1949, the number had increased to 34. But by 1952, it had dropped again—to 21. As Devereux Butcher wrote in his 1963 book, *Exploring Our National Wildlife Refuges*, "When a species, such as the whooping crane, has been so drastically reduced, its continued existence becomes precarious. The crane's population could be wiped out overnight, and once gone, it would be extinct forever."

With intensive conservation efforts over the past few decades in the United States and Canada, however, the population has been gradually increasing. By 1960, there were around three dozen cranes. By 1981, there were 78. By 2000, the number had climbed to 185. While this naturally occurring, wild whooping crane population is still at risk, progress is encouraging. Aransas refuge has been instrumental in helping to rescue this great bird from the brink of extinction. (For additional information on whooping crane recovery efforts, see the Necedah and Chassahowitzka NWR texts.)

As Devereux Butcher also wrote in his refuges book, "Along the Texas coast, nature stages one of her grandest songbird shows. This occurs in April, when thrushes, buntings, tanagers, vireos, warblers, and dozens of other species are migrating. The songsters literally swarm through here. . . . At times they are so numerous that the trees and shrubs appear to be blossoming with animated flowers."

Influxes or arrival peaks of different species typically occur on different days—confirming the old saying, "birds of a feather flock together." For example, there could be great numbers of rose-breasted grosbeaks or scarlet tanagers arriving on one day, orchard or Baltimore orioles on the following day, hooded warblers on the next, and indigo or painted buntings on the day after.

One aspect of the huge influx of neotropical migratory songbirds is referred to as "fallout." This frenzied phenomenon occasionally occurs when unfavorable headwinds from the north slow down and make even more difficult the birds' energy-depleting, nonstop flight across the Gulf of Mexico. From such launching places as Mexico's Yucatan Peninsula, the exhausted birds drop into coastal wooded areas, from the Florida panhandle to Texas, including the Aransas refuge.

As Scott Weidensaul describes in his fascinating book *Living on the Wind: Across the Hemisphere with Migratory Birds* (North Point Press, 1999):

I never actually saw the birds come down, but I could hear them, a series of low whooshes overhead and around me, like fast pitches that brushed past my ear or the thrumming sound of sticks whirled through the air. An instant later, the lifeless trees were seething with dozens of birds, which cascaded, branch by branch, toward the ground, spilling out into the understory. They started eating without preamble, without stretching or relaxing or preening—feeding with a fervor usually seen only at state fairs during pie-eating contests. Over and over again, small explosions of birds would materialize out of the sky, whirring from on high, beyond the limit of vision and into the trees like bolts, until the woods were stuffed to overflowing with them.

. . . Thousands of songbirds had arrived, dropping straight down from great heights to join the melee, then rolling out in waves through the forest, enveloping me for a few, frantic moments, then passing me by even as the next surge came through. . . . No wonder they call it the Gulf Express.

Butterflies are also attracted to Aransas. As naturalist Roland H. Wauer says, "This central Gulf site offers a high diversity of butterflies, including such special interest species as Palamedes Swallowtail, which can be commonplace along wooded edges; Tropical Buckeyes, which can be abundant along the Loop Drive; both Laviana and Turk's-cap White Skippers, which can be common throughout; and Salt Marsh and Obscure Skippers, which can be fairly common along the Heron Flats Trail and near the observation tower."

Establishment of Aransas was made possible partly with revenues from the sale of Migratory Bird Hunting and Conservation Stamps (Duck Stamps). Ducks Unlimited, Inc. has helped enhance wetland habitat on the refuge.

The refuge is open daily during daylight hours. An entrance fee is charged. The visitor center, which is open daily except on Thanksgiving and Christmas, provides interpretive exhibits and programs.

Visitor activities include wildlife and butterfly observation, driving the 16-mile auto loop tour road, hiking a number of trails (including two short wheelchair-accessible paths), interpretive programs, picnicking (a small picnic area is provided), fishing, and hunting whitetail deer and feral hogs during the designated seasons. Camping is not permitted, but facilities are provided in nearby state and county parks. The 0.9-mile Hog Lake Trail includes an observation platform for viewing alligators and other wildlife and an observation tower offering a view of Mustang Lake and the possibility of seeing whooping cranes during the winter. The best birdwatching time is November through April. More than 400 bird species have been recorded here.

Even though alligators are generally afraid of people, visitors are cautioned to stay a safe distance from these sluggish-looking but potentially fast-moving reptiles, to be alert for venomous snakes, and stay on trails to reduce the chance of encountering poison ivy, ticks, and chiggers. Insect repellent is recommended.

Lodgings and meals are available in Port Lavaca and Rockport.

Access to the refuge from Rockport is north by way of State Hwy. 35 and following refuge signs, right onto Farm Market Rd. (FM) 774 for 9 miles, right onto FM 2040, and 6.5 miles to the refuge entrance; or south on State Hwy. 35 through Tivoli, left onto State Hwy. 239 and FM 774, left onto FM 2040, and 6.5 miles to the refuge entrance.

Information: Aransas NWR, P.O. Box 100, Austwell, TX 77950; tel.: (361) 286-3559.

Attwater Prairie Chicken, consisting of more than 9,200 acres, is located in an area of southeast Texas coastal tallgrass prairie. The refuge was established in 1972, with the initial 3,500 acres acquired by the World Wildlife Fund and The Nature Conservancy to protect and enhance this habitat of the rare and endangered Attwater's prairie chicken, a small, dark race of the greater prairie chicken.

Once numbering a million birds that inhabited roughly six million acres of Texas and Louisiana gulf coastal prairie, this species was brought to the brink of extinction by the destruction and fragmentation of its grasslands habitat and by over-hunting. By 1919, no birds remained in Louisiana. By the late 1930s, fewer than 9,000 existed in Texas. In the 1990s, repeated periods of unfavorable weather caused the loss of significant numbers of eggs and chicks. By 1999, the refuge's prairie chicken population had declined to a mere 18 birds. In the year 2000, there were 20.

As the Fish and Wildlife Service explains its recovery plan for the Attwater's prairie chicken:

To reach a goal of 5,000 birds in three geographically separate, viable populations, recovery efforts focus on five strategies: Habitat management on both public and private lands (involving voluntary cooperators only); public outreach to help generate support for ongoing recovery efforts; population management consisting of captive breeding and reintroduction efforts; coordination between government agencies and private interests; [and] research to provide information necessary for taking efficient steps toward recovery.

Biologists believe that the captive breeding program offers the most likely means of saving this species. In 1992, the first chicks were hatched at the Fossil Rim Wildlife Center, near Glen Rose, Tex. Since then, Texas A&M University; the Houston, Abilene, and San Antonio zoos; and Sea World of Texas have been raising birds for release into the wild.

Although much of the Attwater Prairie Chicken refuge contains virgin prairie that was never plowed or cultivated, the Fish and Wildlife Service is maintaining prairie chicken habitat where great herds of bison (buffalo) once grazed and lightning-ignited fires burned. This management program includes periodic prescribed burning to reinvigorate the grasses and control invasive, non-native, woody plants; grazing by bison and cattle; and recreating prairie by planting native grasses on former cultivated fields. In addition, the refuge cultivates small food plots for the benefit of these birds and other wildlife.

From February to mid-May, the male prairie chickens congregate and perform elaborate courtship rituals on an open area of short grass, known as a lek. With tails and neck feathers erect and wings drooping, the cocks inflate their golden neck sacs. With rapid foot-stamping, they then lower their heads, causing a deep, hollow, moaning sound as the sacs are deflated. During this frenzied "dancing," they leap about and charge toward other males.

Although March and April are the best months to possibly view the prairie chickens' courtship rituals, opportunities are limited by their low numbers. The nearby town of Eagle Lake and the refuge cohost an annual Attwater's Prairie Chicken Festival, during the second weekend in April.

As Refuge Manager Terry A. Rossignol has said:

From my perspective, the Texas coastal prairie ecosystem, which is home for the imperiled Attwater's prairie-chicken, is perhaps one of the most misunderstood ecosystems, yet is probably the most impacted habitat type in North America. By working on a large landscape scale with private landowners, to enhance coastal prairie habitat through the Coastal Prairie Conservation Initiative, which provides cost-shared incentives and protection from any future liabilities under the Endangered Species Act, I feel that the Attwater's prairie-chicken does have a chance of surviving. However, this is a goal that will only be realized through much hard work and cooperation from everyone involved.

In addition to the prairie chicken, this refuge features such other birds as whistling-ducks and roseate spoonbills, which inhabit marshes; wintering flocks of geese and sandhill cranes; crested caracaras; white-tailed hawks; and scissor-tailed flycatchers.

The refuge is open daily during daylight hours. There is no entrance fee. The visitor center is open on weekdays, except national holidays.

Visitor activities include wildlife and butterfly observation, viewing interpretive exhibits and a prairie chicken video in the visitor center, driving the five-mile auto tour road, hiking on two trails and along the tour road, and picnicking (picnic tables are provided near the visitor center). Not permitted on this refuge are camping (facilities are provided at Stephen F. Austin State Park), swimming, canoeing, fishing, or hunting.

Even though alligators are generally afraid of people, visitors are cautioned to stay a safe distance from them and to be alert for venomous snakes, ticks, and fire ants. Insect repellent is advised.

Lodgings and meals are available in Eagle Lake, Sealy, and Columbus.

Access to this refuge is from I-10 south on State Hwy. 36, right onto Farm-to-Market Rd. 3013, and ten miles to the refuge entrance.

Information: Attwater Prairie Chicken NWR, P.O. Box 519, Eagle Lake, TX 77434; tel.: (979) 234-3021.

Balcones Canyonlands, thus far comprising about 17,000 acres, was established in 1992 to conserve an ecologically important part of the limestone hills and spring-fed canyons along the eastern edge of the Edwards Plateau, which stretches across central Texas. The refuge protects the breeding habitat of two rare and endangered neotropical migratory songbirds—the golden-cheeked warbler and the black-capped vireo. Although this relatively new refuge has an active land acquisition program, the expansion of urban development and conversion of ranchland to housing subdivisions pose a grave threat to this as yet incomplete refuge.

The golden-cheeked warbler breeds only in the hills of central Texas, with its best habitat along or near the Balcones Escarpment, to the west of Austin and San Antonio. It migrates here from its wintering habitat in the wooded highlands of Honduras and Guatemala and in the state of Chiapas in southern Mexico. The males arrive around mid-March, to declare and defend their favored nesting habitat in old-growth oaks and junipers. The females arrive a few days later, choose a mate, and build a nest. Together the adults raise their young on a diet of insects gathered from the woodland canopy. In July or early August, they begin their southward migration back to the tropics.

The entire population of golden-cheeks may number as few as 5,000 to 15,000 pairs. Dr. Chuck Sexton, the wildlife biologist at Balcones Canyonlands, describes a certain irony in the conservation efforts for this species: "Although long-term land use patterns have resulted in an expansion of second-growth juniper across the central Texas landscape, old-growth stands of oak-juniper woodlands continue to be lost to land clearing, ranching, and urbanization." By 1990, declines in warbler habitat and populations were serious enough to prompt the Fish and Wildlife Service to place the species on the Endangered Species List.

The black-capped vireo breeds from central Oklahoma, southward through the Edwards Plateau and West Texas, to the state of Coahuila in northern Mexico. It migrates here from its wintering range along the west coast of Mexico, primarily from Sinaloa south to Michoacan. The males arrive at their breeding area from late-March to mid-April, and the females soon after. The male and female share in nest building, raising their young, and fending off the serious threat of nest parasitism by brown-headed cowbirds. In contrast to the warbler, vireos like a particular composition of low shrubby growths of oaks or sumac, which typically sprout up after a disturbance such as fire. Sexton's research has shown that the vireo, a rather narrow-habitat specialist, occupies habitat that occurs only on a few specific soil and rock types of central Texas.

Balcones Canyonlands is one of the botanically most diverse refuges in the entire system, with nearly 700 species of plants identified thus far. Habitats are a mosaic of woodlands, savannas, and open grasslands. Upland woods contain a mixture of oaks (plateau live, Spanish, post, scaly-bark, and others) and Ashe juniper, the loose, stringy bark of which is used by the warbler as nesting material. Other trees and shrubs include cedar elm, Texas sugarberry, Texas ash, escarpment cherry, agarita, and Texas persimmon. Pecan, American elm, American sycamore, and black willow grow along narrow riparian corridors. Several other distinctive plant communities occur around springs in moist canyon heads and along canyon rimrocks. There are remnants of the original tallgrass-prairie grasslands, dominated by little bluestem, Indiangrass, and sideoats grama. Wildflower displays in April and May and again in September and October can be spectacular. Among the refuge's wildflowers are prairie verbena, pink evening primrose, firewheels, bitterweed, Blackfoot daisy, blazing star, bluebell gentian, and carpets of bluebonnets.

In addition to the warbler and vireo, a few of the other interesting birds of this refuge are Bell's vireo, cave swallow, canyon wren, yellow-breasted chat, rufous-crowned and black-throated sparrows, and canyon towhee. Swainson's hawks dominate a diverse stream of migrant raptors passing overhead in October.

Among the mammals are an abundance of white-tailed deer, along with bobcats, gray foxes, raccoons, ringtails, eastern cottontails, fox and rock squirrels, and nine-banded armadillos. Although diamondback rattlesnakes are present, a visitor is more likely to encounter one of the swift western coachwhips or catch a glimpse of a Texas spiny lizard. Butterflies provide a display on autumn wildflowers, including the massive parade of southbound migrant monarchs heading toward their wintering grounds in Mexico.

The refuge is open daily during daylight hours. There is no entrance fee.

Visitor activities include wildlife and butterfly observation, hiking, and hunting during the designated seasons. Refuge staff and local volunteers lead various field trips and outdoor education programs throughout the year.

The Shin Oak Observation Deck is located in excellent vireo habitat on Ranch Rd. 1869, in the northern part of the refuge. Because of the sensitive habitat, no hiking trails are available in the vireo observation area. However, a well-developed trailhead with miles of hiking trails (including some into good warbler habitat) is provided at the nearby Doeskin Ranch tract, on Ranch Rd. 1174. Other trail systems are planned for the future.

Lodgings and meals are available in Lago Vista, Liberty Hill, Marble Falls, Burnet, Leander, Cedar Park, Georgetown, and Austin.

Access to the refuge's Doeskin Ranch public use area from Austin is north about 15 miles on U.S. Hwy. 183 to Cedar Park, left onto Ranch Rd. 1431 for 26 miles, and right onto Ranch Rd. 1174 for about 5 miles; or north from Austin about 25 miles on U.S. Hwy. 183 to Seward Junction, left onto State Hwy. 29 for 2.3 miles to Liberty Hill, left onto Ranch Rd. 1869 for about 10 miles, and left onto Ranch Rd. 1174 for about 2 miles.

Information: Balcones Canyonlands NWR, 10711 Burnet Rd., Suite 201, Austin, TX 78758: tel.: (512) 339-9432.

Laguna Atascosa, presently comprising 69,500 acres, is located near the southern end of the Gulf Coast of Texas, in what was formerly the Rio Grande Delta. The refuge was established in 1946 to protect and enhance the most extensive area of the former delta's natural and restored habitats—originally for the benefit of redhead ducks. More than 406 species of birds have been recorded on Laguna Atascosa—more than any other refuge in the National Wildlife Refuge System!

The refuge attracts enormous numbers of migratory waterfowl and shorebirds and provides protection for a number of rare and endangered species. One of the latter species is the aplomado falcon, the encouraging recovery efforts for which are being cooperatively aided by a nonprofit organization, The Peregrine Fund, Inc. (For further information on this falcon, see the Matagorda Island NWR text.)

A unique combination of subtropical, desert, temperate, and coastal habitats lies within the boundaries of this refuge. Some of the flora and fauna are typical of northern Mexico and are at the northern end of their range here; and many migratory bird species that breed far to the north, such as waterfowl and the sandhill crane, spend the winter here.

The refuge contains expanses of flat coastal savanna and salt flats, ridges (known locally in Spanish as lomas) covered with dense thorny shrubs, some brushland of mesquite and associated species, and places where yucca and cactus grow. To the east stretches Laguna Madre, a broad bay that is hemmed in from the open waters of the Gulf of Mexico by the long narrow barrier of Padre Island.

As agricultural land drainage and irrigation programs have greatly curtailed the quantity of water that flows into the refuge, water needed to maintain wildlife habitats is held in resacas (former Rio Grande oxbows), ponds, and the refuge's largest body of fresh water, Laguna Atascosa. Water levels are raised or lowered during the year to accommodate the needs of waterfowl and wading birds. In addition, the Fish and Wildlife Service carries out periodic prescribed burns to maintain areas of prairie grassland (savanna) habitat.

Highlights of Laguna Atascosa refuge are two rare and endangered cats—the ocelot and jaguarundi. Both species are secretive in the dense brushy habitat and are consequently seldom seen. The fur coat of the ocelot is beautifully patterned with black spots and elongated and angular bars and patches on a yellow background. Adult males measure roughly three to four feet from head to tip of their long tail and weigh 15 to 25 pounds. They prefer thick thorn-scrub habitat, in which they are well camouflaged beneath the shrubby canopy. About 30 ocelots are believed to inhabit the refuge. With U.S. estimates at fewer than 100 ocelots, Laguna Atascosa Refuge represents their last stronghold in this country.

The jaguarundi has two uniform color phases: either russet-brown or gray. It looks like a cross between a miniature mountain lion and a weasel. From head to tip of its very long tail, it measures roughly 3 to 4.5 feet, with a small head, widely spaced rounded little ears, slender body, and short legs; it weighs from around 15 to 18 pounds. It is not known if jaguarundis still inhabit the refuge, as there has been no photographic or other evidence of them since 1985.

Butterflies are also attracted to this refuge. As naturalist Roland H. Wauer says, "The new garden, behind and alongside the visitor center, attracts an abundance of butterflies. More than 150 species have been recorded at this site and along various roadsides. Among those that regularly occur are Silver-banded Hairstreak; Clytie Ministreak; Red-banded and Blue Metalmarks; Theona Checkerspot; White Peacock; Dorante's, Teleus, and Brown Longtails; and Fawn-spotted and Obscure Skippers."

Former Assistant Refuge Manager Tim Cooper, who expresses a special fondness for Laguna Atascosa Refuge, explains:

Laguna Atascosa NWR represents one of the finest areas for wildlife within the United States. Appreciating and finding wildlife in this refuge takes some practice. The vegetative cover is often very thick and the animals can be very cryptic. But patient observers will be rewarded for their efforts.

A mixture of influences from the Gulf of Mexico, the tropics, the Chihuahuan Desert, and temperate North America converge at this location. Therefore, species from these very diverse regions can often find suitable habitats here. . . . In many ways, this area represents an avian equivalent to the Serengeti Plains in East Africa, with huge concentrations of migrating and resident birds, a high diversity of species, and sweeping views. Laguna Atascosa is extremely important for migrating shorebirds, wintering piping plovers, waterfowl (especially redheads), staging peregrine falcons, and resident species. Migrations in April and May and throughout the fall bring different warblers, grosbeaks, other neotropicals, raptors, and waterfowl through the area. The refuge's total of 406 recorded bird species is, to date, unmatched in the refuge system.

Establishment of the refuge was made possible mostly with revenues from the sale of Migratory Bird Hunting and Conservation Stamps (Duck Stamps). Ducks Unlimited, Inc. has assisted with extensive habitat enhancement projects, including a large system for diverting river water to the resaca system.

The refuge is open daily during daylight hours. An entrance fee is charged. The visitor center, which is open daily from October through April and on weekends in May, provides interpretive exhibits and videos. Rangers and trained volunteers lead programs and wildlife watching tours on weekends, from November through April.

Visitor activities at Laguna Atascosa include wildlife and butterfly observation, interpretive programs, driving the 15-mile Bayside Drive loop and the 1.5-mile Lakeside Drive, hiking on several trails (one of which is a wheelchair-accessible path), bicycling, and deer hunting during the designated season. Although camping and fishing are not permitted in the refuge, they are allowed in the adjacent Adolph Thomae Jr. County Park. November through April is the best birdwatching time on the refuge.

Even though alligators are generally afraid of people, visitors are urged to stay a safe distance from these sluggish-looking but potentially fast-moving reptiles and to stay on the trails to reduce the likelihood of encountering the aggressive diamondback rattlesnake, ticks, and chiggers. Insect repellent is recommended.

Lodgings and meals are available in Harlingen and Brownsville.

Access to the refuge from Harlingen is east on Farm Market Rd. 106 to Rio Hondo, continuing east 14 miles on FM 106 to its end, and left onto Buena Vista Rd. for 3 miles to the refuge's visitor center. An entrance fee is charged.

Information: Laguna Atascosa NWR, P.O. Box 450, Rio Hondo, TX 78583; tel.: (956) 748-3607.

Lower Rio Grande Valley, currently containing 69,500 acres on 111 tracts of land and working toward a goal of 153,314 acres, was established in 1979 to protect habitat fragments and form wildlife corridors throughout the Rio Grande Delta region, in south Texas. This refuge and the Santa Ana and Laguna Atascosa national wildlife refuges (see separate texts) collectively comprise the South Texas Refuge Complex, which is expected to eventually protect nearly 288,000 acres, ten percent of the four-county area.

The subtropical, semi-arid climate and the transitions from seacoast to palm forest to upland shrubland and savanna make this one of the most biologically diverse regions in the United

States. With more than 480 species of birds, the Rio Grande Delta is truly a birding "hot spot." Some of the region's specialties include the following: least grebe; ducks (black-bellied whistling and masked); gray and white-tailed hawks; hook-billed kite; aplomado falcon; crested caracara; plain chachalaca; white-tipped dove; red-billed pigeon; green parakeet; red-crowned parrot; groove-billed ani; ferruginous pygmy-owl; common pauraque; buff-bellied hummingbird; green and ringed kingfishers; Couch's kingbird; great kiskadee; northern beardless tyran-nulet; rose-throated becard; green and brown jays; Mexican crow; clay-colored robin; long-billed thrasher; tropical parula warbler; olive sparrow; and altamira oriole.

The dense shrublands are also inhabited by two endangered cats, the ocelot and jaguarundi (see the discussion of these species in the Laguna Atascosa NWR text), as well as bobcat and puma.

Approximately half of all species of North American butterflies occur in the Rio Grande delta region. Hidalgo County alone has more lepidopteran species than the entire states of Florida and California combined.

Roughly 1,200 species of plants are found here, including six endangered species: border ayenia, Walker's manioc, Zapata bladderpod, star cactus, Johnston's frankenia, and ashy dogweed.

The Rio Grande Delta is about 80 miles wide at the Gulf of Mexico and extends inland some 95 linear miles. Before flood control dams and levees were initiated in the 1930s, flood-waters spread across the delta once or twice per year through an intricate network of oxbows (resacas) and distributary channels. Innumerable wetlands created by the seasonal ebb and flow through the resacas made ideal habitat for migratory birds. Riparian forests of Rio Grande ash, cedar elm, sugar hackberry, and soapberry thrived along these numerous watercourses, with massive Montezuma bald-cypress trees spreading out from the water's edge. Mesic river terraces supported evergreen forests of Texas ebony, anacua, brasil, coma, and Texas persimmon. The sabal palm occurred in scattered locations in the evergreen forests but predominated in the southmost area, below present-day Brownsville.

Beyond the floodwaters' reach, much of the delta was covered with exceedingly dense vegetation consisting of a great diversity of spiny shrubs, dominated by huge, often contorted honey mesquite trees. These shrublands gave way to an open coastal plain along the Gulf of Mexico, 10 to 15 miles wide and dominated by cordgrass prairies, saline meadows of sea ox-eye daisy, tidal mudflats, and shallow lagoons. Near Boca Chica, the mouth of the Rio Grande, the saline flats are interspersed with lomas, dunes of windblown clay capped with impenetrably dense, low shrubs.

During the 20th century, about 95 percent of the delta vegetation was cleared, and the land was leveled for irrigated farming. The shrub savannas and prairies that bordered the delta were converted to mesquite shrubland during the latter half of the 19th century, through overgrazing by vast herds of sheep and by other factors. More than two million people now live in the binational Rio Grande Delta region, and the human population continues to grow rapidly. From 1990 to 2000, the Hidalgo County population climbed by nearly fifty percent.

The Rio Grande wildlife corridor is a cooperative effort to conserve the rich biodiversity of this relentlessly developing region. In addition to the three national wildlife refuges, the Texas Parks and Wildlife Department manages more than 6,000 acres in state parks and wildlife management areas in the four-county area. Wildlife habitat is also protected in several county and municipal parks, as well as in a number of private preserves.

The coalition of habitat fragments into wildlife corridors is being accomplished through the restoration of native vegetation on cropland acquired by the Lower Rio Grande Valley refuge. Each year, roughly 750 acres of refuge-owned cropland are planted with more than 200,000 seedlings of some sixty species of native trees, shrubs, and cacti. Members of the public may participate in an annual event, "Rio Reforestation: Humanity for Habitat," that is held on the second Saturday in October. From 1994 to 2001, more than 5,900 volunteers have planted 90,000 seedlings on nearly 400 acres of retired farmland.

At this writing (April 2008), a new threat has arisen for this refuge (and others such, as Santa Ana, along the U.S.-Mexico border): the construction of a wall that is intended to keep out illegal immigrants. As an April 3, 2008, *New York Times* editorial said, "It will be a disaster on the ground. One example of what's at risk is the Lower Rio Grande National Wildlife Refuge. It runs in checkerboard fashion along the 200 miles of the Rio Grande. . . . When the fence is finished, most of the refuge's 95,000 acres—and the ocelots, jaguarundis and other rare species that live there—would wind up on the side of the fence closest to Mexico, virtually impossible to monitor and protect." In addition, much fragile and irreplaceable refuge habitat for numerous species of wildlife would be destroyed by construction of the wall and the related border patrol roadway along the barrier. The *Times* editorial also mentioned that on April 1 Michael Chertoff, the secretary of Homeland Security, "waived the Endangered Species Act, the Clean Water Act and other environmental protections so that the government could finish building the . . . border fence . . . without undertaking legally mandated reviews of the consequences for threatened wildlife and their habitats." Defenders of Wildlife, an environmental organization, is asking the U.S. Supreme Court to review the waiver of environmental law; and the Interior Department is raising objections to some of the border fencing.

Visitation is permitted on 40,000 acres of the Lower Rio Grande Valley refuge's Boca Chica, La Sal Vieja, La Sal del Rey, Monte Cristo, Yturria Brush, La Puerta, and Salineno tracts. The refuge is open daily during daylight hours. There is no entrance fee. In addition, the World Birding Center (WBC) headquarters and satellite offices are being established by the Texas Parks and Wildlife Department, the Parks and Wildlife Foundation of Texas, Inc., and nine municipalities. Refuge tracts adjacent to the nine WBC sites are open to the public, with the addition of hiking trails and other facilities.

Visitor activities include wildlife observation, hiking, fishing (several access sites onto the Rio Grande, Laguna Madre, and Gulf of Mexico), and hunting on limited areas during the designated (annually revised) seasons. Camping is not permitted on the refuge, but facilities are provided at the Bentsen Rio Grande Valley State Park and elsewhere in the valley.

Lodgings are available in Brownsville, Harlingen, and McAllen.

(Special appreciation is extended to Chris Best, Refuge Plant Ecologist, for providing the above information.—RDB)

Information: Lower Rio Grande Valley NWR, c/o South Texas Refuge Complex, Route 2, Box 202A, Alamo, Texas 78516; tel.: (956) 784-7500.

Matagorda Island, comprising 56,660 acres, was established in 1971 to protect and enhance ecologically important habitats on this 38-mile-long, actively accreting barrier island, on the central Texas Gulf Coast. The refuge, which is largely dominated by waist-high coastal prairie, includes brackish bay marshlands, tidal flats, ponds, stabilized dune ridges, and beautiful sandy beaches. Since 1994, the refuge has been cooperatively managed by the Fish and Wildlife Service, the Texas Parks and Wildlife Department, and the Texas General Land Office.

More than 320 species of birds have been recorded here—the majority during spring and autumn migrations. The whooping crane is among the wintering species (see the Aransas NWR text). This is also one of the Gulf Coast refuges where the spectacular neotropical migratory songbird "fallout" phenomenon occurs in April (see the Aransas text).

The Fish and Wildlife Service is focusing efforts at Matagorda Island on reintroducing the rare aplomado falcon. The adult male of this colorful species has slate-gray plumage on its back, the lower back of its head, and its narrow crown; whitish cheeks distinctively patterned with a black band from the eye to the lower back of the head and a black "side-burn" below the eye; a whitish throat and breast; a black upper belly hourglass-shaped band that broadens into the flanks; and dusty orange lower belly, thighs, and undertail coverts. Historically, this falcon ranged across the tropical coastal plains, arid grasslands, and savannas from southern Texas to southern Arizona, and southward through Mexico and Central America, to Patagonia and Tierra del Fuego in South America. During the past century, the aplomado falcon has become increasingly rare, especially in the northern part of its range.

As explained in late 2001 by the Refuge Manager, Jennifer Sanchez:

Reintroduction of northern aplomado falcons into the northern edge of their former range began in 1996, with the release of six young falcons on Matagorda Island. In coordination with the Peregrine Fund, Inc., additional aplomado falcons were released on the Island over the next three years. The first documented nesting on Matagorda Island occurred in 1999, when a pair of falcons successfully raised and fledged three young. . . . In 2001, a total of nine falcons fledged from three nests on the north end of the Island. Today, Matagorda Island is home to more than 20 falcons.

The refuge is open daily. There is no entrance fee.

Visitor activities include wildlife observation, interpretive programs, on-island shuttle service, hiking on the interpretive Lighthouse Trail, bicycling, swimming, camping at two state park campgrounds, fishing, and hunting during the designated season.

Even though alligators are generally afraid of people, visitors are cautioned to stay a safe distance from them and to be alert for several species of venomous snakes. Insect repellent and sunscreen are advised. Swimmers are warned that there are no lifeguards on the beaches, that there can be a hazardous undertow, and to be alert for sharks, stingrays, and man-o-wars.

Lodgings and meals are available at Port O'Connor.

Access to Matagorda Island is by passenger ferry service (fee) from Port O'Connor to the north dock on Thursdays, Fridays, weekends, and holidays. Charter services at Port O'Connor and other communities also offer excursions to the island.

Information: Matagorda Island State Park, P.O. Box 117, Port O'Connor, TX 77982; tel.: (361) 983-2215; and Matagorda Island NWR, P.O. Box 100, Austwell, TX 77950; tel.: (361) 286-3559.

Santa Ana, consisting of 2,088 acres, is located along a bend in the Rio Grande, in the lower Rio Grande Valley of south Texas. The refuge was established in 1943 to protect what is today the largest remnant of dense, subtropical hardwood and shrub thorn forest along the river, providing habitat for an extensive variety of fauna. A number of wetlands and ponds—remnants of former river oxbow lakes (*resacas*) and impoundments—are managed for waterfowl and other water birds. This relatively small area is a priceless ecological gem—a sample of the kind of wildlife-rich ecosystem that once covered wide areas along both sides of the river valley.

The refuge is inhabited by many species of birds and mammals that are native to Mexico and that reach the northern end of their range along the lower Rio Grande. Approximately 400 species of birds have been recorded on this internationally famous birding mecca. Among the avian highlights are the green jay, altamira oriole, great kiskadee, buff-bellied hummingbird, ringed and green kingfishers, black-bellied and fulvous whistling-ducks, and plain chachalaca. The latter species is a large brown, pheasant-like bird with long, white-tipped tail. While it is sometimes difficult to see, the chachalaca lets forth with a raucous, attention-getting call that suggests its name.

As described by refuge plant ecologist Chris Best:

Santa Ana, with over 450 species of vascular plants, is botanically diverse and has both subtropical and temperate affinities. Most of the uplands are covered with dense thickets of granjeno, lotebush, elbow-bush, guayacan, colima, allthorn, Wright's acacia, and many other mostly spiny shrubs, dominated by emergent honey mesquite and ebony trees. Taller gallery forests of sugar hackberry, cedar elm, and Rio Grande ash border the river and resaca channels, flanked by evergreen forests of anacua, Texas ebony, soap-berry, coma, brasil, and Texas persimmon. Gaps in the canopy are quickly filled by tepeguaje, one of the fastest growing trees in the world. These forests are festooned with two epiphytic bromeliads, Spanish moss and ball moss. Chile pequin bushes, the wild ancestors of cultivated chile peppers, thrive here in partial shade.

This refuge is a mecca for butterflies. As naturalist Roland H. Wauer says:

More butterflies (265 species) have been recorded within this refuge than at any other refuge or park in the United States. Although the garden, located at the visitor center, consistently produces the highest numbers, many of the trails, such as Jaguarundi Trail, can be superb. A few of the species to be expected include Giant White; Yojoa Scrub-Hairstreak; Clytie Ministreak; Rounded, Red-bordered, and Blue Metalmarks; Julia and Zebra Heliconians; White Peacock; Malachite; Mexican Bluewing; Pale-banded Crescent; Guava, Mimosa, and White-patched Skippers; and White-striped, Dorante's, Teleus, and Brown Longtails.

At this writing (April 2008), a threat has arisen for this refuge (and others such as the Lower Rio Grande Valley NWR, along the U.S.-Mexico border): the construction of a border "fence" that is intended to keep out illegal immigrants. The 18-foot-high barrier is reportedly to be constructed along a levee between the visitor center and the rest of the refuge, effectively blocking visitor access to the ecologically rich habitat.

The refuge is open daily during daylight hours. An entrance fee is charged, except on the first Sunday of each month. The visitor center is open daily, except on Thanksgiving and Christmas.

Visitor activities include wildlife and butterfly observation, driving the seven-mile Wildlife Drive, hiking on a dozen miles of trails and other routes (including a wheelchair-accessible path), interpreter-led tram tours (fee), and interpretive programs. November through April is the best time for birdwatching. Picnicking, camping, fishing, and hunting are not permitted on the refuge. Campground facilities are available at Bentsen Rio Grande State Park; information: tel.: (956) 585-1107.

Visitors are cautioned to be extremely careful along the Rio Grande and stay safely back from the unstable riverbank, as it is often undercut and can slump into the river. Visitors also should be alert for chiggers, scorpions, and Africanized bees that inhabit the refuge. Insect repellent is advised during the warmer months.

Lodgings and meals are available in Alamo, McAllen, Weslaco, Harlingen, and Brownsville.

Access to the refuge from Expressway 83 at Alamo is south by way of Farm Road 907 and left 0.3 mile on U.S. Military Highway 281 to the refuge entrance.

Information: Santa Ana National Wildlife Refuge, Route 2, Box 202A, Alamo, TX 78516; tel.: (956) 784-7500.

Utah

Bear River Migratory Bird Refuge, encompassing 73,645 acres, was established in 1928 to manage and protect a major oasis of marshes, mudflats, and open water in the desert. The refuge is located at the mouth of Bear River, on the northeastern shore of Great Salt Lake of northern Utah. It is scenically framed by the rugged Wasatch Mountains to the east and the Promontory Mountains to the west.

The refuge's wetland habitats attract impressive concentrations of migratory waterfowl, shorebirds, and other birds. Thousands of American white pelicans come to feed in the marshes while nesting on islands far across the vast expanse of Great Salt Lake. Many thousands of tundra swans stop to rest and feed here in October–November, on their southward migration from breeding grounds on the Alaskan tundra. The refuge is a mecca for numerous species of ducks. Many thousands nest here, and others pause by the tens of thousands during their spring migration to breeding areas farther north. In autumn, as many as a half-million waterfowl are attracted to the refuge's impoundments. Thousands of herons and egrets and more than three-quarters of North America's white-faced ibises nest here. Spectacular numbers of shorebirds, such as plovers, sandpipers, dowitchers, godwits, stilts, avocets, and phalaropes, either rest and feed here on their migrations or come to nest and raise their young. The wetlands draw huge flocks of red-winged and yellow-headed blackbirds. And in winter, the refuge hosts scores of bald eagles. More than 220 bird species have been recorded here.

By the late 19th century, northern Utah settlers were diverting increasingly large quantities of river water for development of their communities and farmlands between Great Salt Lake and the base of the Wasatch Mountains. By the early decades of the 20th century, the river's flow had significantly diminished. The delta marshlands, which formerly covered roughly 45,000 acres, had dwindled to a mere 2,000 to 3,000 acres. The resulting low water levels and exposed mudflats in the delta produced conditions that were favorable for a bacteria-caused disease that infects birds.

As described by Dr. Alexander Wetmore, a former Secretary of the Smithsonian Institution,

Following the reduction of water levels and the crowding of great concentrations of birds into smaller areas, losses from botulism were first noted about 1900. More and more ducks sickened as the epidemic spread over the stagnant waters of the shallow alkali flats, and in 1910 and again in 1913, upward of a million died around the mouth of Bear River.

The virulent toxin *Clostridium botulinum*, which attacks the nervous system, continued to cause catastrophic and gruesome avian mortality through the 1920s. Spurred by widespread public alarm, Congress authorized establishment of the Bear River refuge. By the early 1930s, fifty miles of dikes and water control structures were completed, so that water levels within the impounded wetland habitat could be carefully managed. Thousands of birds were treated with an antitoxin injection and released after recovery. In 1936, a toxicology laboratory was built on the refuge to carry out botulism research.

Establishment of this refuge was made possible partly with revenues from the sale of Migratory Bird Hunting and Conservation Stamps (Duck Stamps). Ducks Unlimited, Inc. has assisted with the restoration and enhancement of more than 20,000 acres of the refuge's wetland habitat and is presently working with the Fish and Wildlife Service in the enhancement of waterfowl breeding habitat on the refuge's 17,000-acre grassland unit.

As *Ducks Unlimited* senior writer Matt Young wrote in his January/February 2002 article, "Wetlands Under Siege":

While great progress has been made in conserving these critical wetlands, the Great Salt Lake marshes continue to face an uncertain future. The Wasatch Front is currently home to approximately 1.6 million people. Over the next 50 years, the population is expected to soar to more than 5 million. Such rapid growth will undoubtedly place extreme pressure on water supplies, open space, agricultural land, and wildlife habitat. . . .

In response to these threats, DU has stationed a biologist and an engineer in the area to coordinate conservation activities, partnership development, and funding acquisition. Ensuring adequate supplies of freshwater for high-value wetland habitats will also be critical in the years ahead. DU is presently seeking funding for research that would design geographic information system models that will help determine the likely impacts future water diversions would have on the Great Salt Lake marshes.

The refuge is open daily during daylight hours. There is no entrance fee. The refuge's James V. Hansen Wildlife Education Center is open daily, except on national holidays.

Visitor activities include wildlife observation; driving and bicycling on the entrance road and the 12-mile auto tour route (subject to closure by snow or high water); interpretive and educational exhibits and programs at the visitor center; viewing wildlife from a number of observation platforms; hiking a wetland trail network; limited fishing (a wheelchair-accessible fishing pier is provided); and hunting on parts of the refuge during the designated seasons. Canoeing and shallow-draft boating are not permitted, except during the approved hunting seasons. Although camping is not permitted on the refuge, facilities are available in Brigham City, Willard, and Mantua.

Insect repellent is advised during the warmer months.

Lodgings and meals are available in Brigham City.

Access to the refuge from Exit 366 (Forest Street) on I-15 at Brigham City is west about 15 miles on Forest St.

Information: Bear River Bird Migratory Refuge, 2155 W. Forest St., Brigham City, UT 84302; tel.: (435) 723-5887.

Ouray, containing 11,987 acres, was established in 1960 to protect and manage an area of floodplain wetlands, riverine habitat, and riparian cottonwood groves that contrasts with adjacent, arid, semi-desert uplands. The refuge is located along a meandering 12-mile stretch of the Green River, in northeastern Utah.

This lush area provides a major migration corridor for numerous species of migrating waterfowl, raptors, neotropical songbirds, and other birds; attracts a diversity of resident wildlife; and contains critical habitat for four endangered species of fish: the Colorado pikeminnow, razorback sucker, and humpback and bonytail chubs.

Miles upstream from the refuge, the Green River is harnessed by Flaming Gorge Dam. Even though the Yampa River's undammed tributary flow continues to function naturally, the pre-dam over-bank flooding that annually provided important revitalizing nutrients and other benefits to the floodplain ecosystem is now a rare event. As the Fish and Wildlife Service says in the July 2000 Ouray National Wildlife Refuge *Comprehensive Conservation Plan* (*CCP*), since construction of the dam, "the Green River system has changed dramatically, resulting in long-term loss and degradation of riparian habitats and . . . species dependent on them. The Refuge's riparian habitat is now critically important to protect declining fish and migratory bird species using the Green River corridor."

Most of the refuge's wetlands consist of floodplain marshes in the wetland bottoms that are dominated by cattails, bulrushes, and other emergent aquatic plants. Some of this marsh habitat was previously divided into levee- and dike-contained units. In 1997, the Fish and Wildlife Service began breaching some of the riverbank levees in an attempt to approximate a more natural, flood-renewed and nutrient-enriched wetland bottom ecosystem; to enhance the chances for survival for endangered fish; and to evaluate habitat and species responses to this "planned seasonal floodplain inundation."

The refuge also includes about fifty acres of moist-soil impoundments, in which water levels are seasonally regulated—raised during the spring and then gradually lowered through the summer to encourage the growth of emergent aquatic plants of value to waterfowl and other wildlife.

Under a cooperative agreement with a local landowner, about 150 acres of the refuge are devoted to the growing of alfalfa, barley, and sorghum or milo. Part of these nutrient-rich crops is left unharvested as a supplemental food source for the benefit of waterfowl, deer, elk, and other wildlife.

Among the several thousand waterfowl that come to Ouray Refuge's wetlands to nest and raise their young are Canada geese, mallards, green-winged and cinnamon teal, pintails, shovelers, gad-walls, wigeons, redheads, and ruddy ducks. Wading birds include great blue herons, white-faced ibises, black-necked stilts and American avocets. Raptors include the northern harriers, golden eagles, Swainson's and rough-legged hawks, peregrine falcons, a few wintering bald eagles, and great horned owls. Of the numerous neotropical migratory songbirds, there are yellow-billed cuckoo, black-headed grosbeak, lazuli bunting, and a number of flycatchers and warblers. More than 200 species of birds have been recorded on the refuge.

The Leota Bluffs are a scenic highlight of the refuge. These wind- and water-sculpted formations consist of colorfully banded sandstone and shale. A beautiful panorama of the refuge from an overlook is provided atop the bluffs.

Establishment of the refuge was made possible partly with revenues from the sale of Migratory Bird Hunting and Conservation Stamps (Duck Stamps). Among groups that have provided assistance to the refuge are local troops of the Boy Scouts of America and the Vernal Junior High Escape Club.

The refuge is open daily during daylight hours. There is no entrance fee. The headquarters/visitor center is open on weekdays, except national holidays.

Visitor activities include wildlife observation, interpretive and environmental education programs, driving the 12-mile auto tour route, viewing the refuge from an observation tower and from Leota Overlook, hiking, bicycling and horseback riding (on designated roads), fishing (only on the river), and hunting on parts of the refuge during the designated seasons. There are presently no designated hiking trails. As funding becomes available, plans call for the development of two interpretive trails, one of which is to be wheelchair-accessible.

Rafting and canoeing on the Green River are also a pleasurable way to view the refuge. Some rafting excursions begin upstream, within the spectacular, sheer-walled canyons of Dinosaur National Monument, and end in the refuge. A permit is required from the Unimtah and Ouray Indian Reservation in order to use a takeout facility at Ouray Bridge. About 2,600 acres of the southern end of the refuge are leased from the Native Americans. Although camping is not permitted on the refuge, facilities are available in Vernal and elsewhere in the general vicinity.

Insect repellent is advised during the warmer months. Visitors are cautioned that the refuge's unpaved roads become extremely slippery when wet.

Colorado River Wildlife Management Area (WMA), which is managed from Ouray refuge, was established in 1998 to protect ecologically important floodplain habitat along the Colorado, Green, and Gunnison river system in eastern Utah and western Colorado. As of late 2001, there were more than 950 acres in 13 individual properties along the Green and Colorado rivers, toward a goal of approximately 10,000 acres. As explained by the Colorado River WMA's Assistant Refuge Manager Lance Koch, "These areas are held as conservation easements with willing landowners, who agree to allow management and protection activities by refuge officials. Public use is not permitted, as the right to access the property is retained by the landowner."

Lodgings and meals are available near Ouray Refuge in Vernal and Roosevelt.

Access to the refuge from Vernal is west 14 miles on U.S. Hwy. 40 and left onto State Hwy. 88, for 13 miles.

Information: Ouray NWR, HC 69, Box 232, Randlett, UT 84063; tel.: (435) 545-2522.

Vermont

Missisquoi, containing 6,592 acres, was established in 1943 to protect extensive wetlands on most of the Missisquoi River Delta. The refuge provides important feeding, resting, and breeding habitats for migratory waterfowl, neotropical songbirds, and other wildlife. It is located near the northern end of Lake Champlain and close to the U.S.-Canada border, in northwestern Vermont.

The name *Missisquoi* is derived from an Abenaki Indian word meaning "place of flint." The river winds through extensive beds of wild rice and other wetland vegetation, such as bulrushes, rushes, sedges, wild celery, pickerelweed, and arrowhead. Although approximately 5,000 acres of the refuge contain natural marsh habitat, another 1,200 acres are managed wetlands within three diked impoundments. These pools provide a mixture of open water; nutrient-rich, emergent plants offering food and cover for waterfowl and other wildlife; and wooded and shrub-dominated swamp habitats. Water levels in the impoundments are seasonally regulated to promote the growth of such plants as wild rice and buttonbush.

The peak influx of migrating waterfowl occurs in autumn, when thousands of ring-necked ducks; hundreds of American black ducks, mallards, and green-winged teal; and lesser numbers of other species are attracted here. Autumn concentrations of waterfowl frequently peak at around 20,000 birds. The largest rookery of great blue herons on the Vermont shore of Lake Champlain is located on Shad Island, at the northern end of the refuge. More than 500 heron nests have been counted in this area.

The refuge also provides important nesting habitat for the black tern. Although nesting success may vary from year to year, since 1999 the refuge's population is reported to have comprised 94 to 100 percent of all black terns that nested in Vermont.

According to Refuge Manager Mark Sweeny, "the importance of the refuge to birds is so significant that Vermont Audubon adopted the refuge in 1986 and designated it as an Important Bird Area . . . in 1999." More than 200 bird species have been recorded here.

In addition to water management within impoundments, other habitat-management activities include the placement of nesting boxes, cones, and other structures throughout the delta to supplement natural nesting sites for such species as wood and black ducks, common goldeneyes, and hooded mergansers. Haying, mowing, and periodic prescribed burning are implemented to maintain roughly 350 acres of grassland habitat for the benefit of bobolinks and other songbirds, as well as waterfowl that seek the cover of grass for nesting. The non-native purple loosestrife and common reed (*Phragmites*) are controlled to keep these aggressive, invasive plants from crowding out native species (see the discussion of loosestrife-control techniques in the Montezuma Refuge NWR text).

About 700 acres of Missisquoi refuge consist of the ecologically outstanding Maquam Bog, which has been designated as a research natural area. It is the only pitch-pine bog community in this state and supports such other plants as highbush blueberry, cranberry, rhodora, and sphagnum moss.

Establishment of this refuge was made possible in large part with revenues from the sale of Migratory Bird Hunting and Conservation Stamps (Duck Stamps). A number of nonprofit organizations are providing important assistance to the refuge, including Ducks Unlimited, Inc., Franklin County Sportsman's Club, Friends of Missisquoi National Wildlife Refuge, and the Green Mountain and Vermont Audubon societies.

The refuge is open daily during daylight hours. There is no entrance fee. The refuge headquarters is open on weekdays, except national holidays.

Visitor activities include wildlife observation; environmental education programs; hiking on a number of trails; cross-country skiing and snowshoeing; canoeing, kayaking, and boating (boat-launching sites are at Louie's Landing and on Mac's Bend Rd.—the latter available only from September 1 through the close of the waterfowl hunting season in December); fishing (from the river bank, on the river, and on Lake Champlain); and hunting on parts of the refuge during the designated seasons. Some lakeshore parts of the refuge are closed to boating, to avoid disturbing wildlife. Camping is not permitted on the refuge, but facilities are available at a number of nearby state parks.

Insect repellent is advised during the warmer months.

Lodgings and meals are available in Swanton, Alburg, and St. Albans.

Access to the refuge from Exit 21 on I-89 is west 1 mile on State Hwy. 78 into Swanton and northwest 2 miles on Hwy. 78 (which runs through the refuge); or from Exit 42 on I-87, it is east 13 miles (through Rouses Point, N.Y., and Alburg, Vt.), and left onto State Hwy. 78.

Information: Missisquoi NWR, 29 Tabor Rd., Swanton, VT 05488; tel.: (802) 868-4781.

Virginia

Back Bay, containing more than 8,600 acres, was established in 1938. The refuge protects many islands in the northern part of Back Bay; part of a narrow, barrier island-like coastal peninsula that separates the bay from the Atlantic Ocean; and lands along the bay's western shore. It is located in the southeastern corner of Virginia.

The refuge contains a stretch of sandy ocean beach, sand dunes, maritime woodland, freshwater impoundments, brackish marshes, and cropland. A tremendous diversity of wildlife is attracted to this refuge, including large concentrations of wintering waterfowl. Especially in December and January, the refuge hosts as many as 10,000 greater snow geese and large concentrations of tundra swans, Canada geese, and many species of ducks. Large influxes of shorebirds and neotropical songbirds pause on the refuge during their spring and autumn migrations. Wood ducks, ospreys, bald eagles, and the federally listed threatened piping plover are among the many species of birds that nest here. More than 300 bird species have been recorded here.

White-tailed deer, mink, river otters, and raccoons are among the resident native mammals. Three non-natives unfortunately cause harmful impacts: nutrias, introduced from South America into the southeastern United States in the early 20th century, continually burrow into and damage refuge dikes; feral hogs uproot and destroy important marsh plants; and wild horses trample native vegetation.

The refuge's woodland trees are mostly wind-sculpted loblolly pines and live oaks. Prominent species of shrubs include wax myrtle, bayberry, highbush blueberry, black cherry, and persimmon.

The Fish and Wildlife Service carries out a number of habitat-management activities for the benefit of wildlife. Water levels within a number of impoundments (pools) are seasonally regulated with water-control structures to enhance the growth of plants that provide food for waterfowl. Periodic prescribed burning triggers nutrient cycling, curtails the invasion of woody vegetation where it is not desired, and promotes the renewal of vegetation that provides food and cover for wildlife.

Establishment of the refuge was made possible partly with revenues from the sale of Migratory Bird Hunting and Conservation Stamps (Duck Stamps). Ducks Unlimited, Inc. has helped enhance more than 1,500 acres of the refuge's wetland habitat.

The refuge is open daily during daylight hours. An entrance fee is charged during certain times of the year. The visitor contact station is open daily, except on Saturdays, from December 1 through March, and is open on Memorial Day, July 4, and Labor Day.

Visitor activities include wildlife observation; driving the entrance road to the contact station; viewing interpretive displays and a film at the contact station; hiking on two trails, two (wheelchair-accessible) boardwalk paths, two (seasonally closed) dikes, and a four-mile stretch of beach; bicycling on some interior dikes; canoeing, kayaking, and boating (only non-motorized watercraft that can be hand-carried to the bay's edge); surf- and freshwater-fishing in some areas; and hunting on part of the refuge during the designated seasons. Although camping is not permitted on the refuge, facilities are provided on adjacent False Cape State Park and in Virginia Beach. Swimming, surfing, and sunbathing are not permitted on the refuge but are popular activities at Virginia Beach.

Visitors are cautioned to be alert for venomous snakes, ticks, and chiggers. Insect repellent during the warmer months and sunscreen are advised.

Lodgings and meals are available in Virginia Beach, Chesapeake, and Norfolk.

Access to the refuge from Exit 284 on I-64 in Norfolk is east 13 miles on I-264, the Virginia Beach–Norfolk Expressway, taking the last expressway exit and proceeding south on Bird Neck Rd. for just over 3 miles; right onto General Booth Blvd. for just over 2 miles; left onto Princess Anne Rd.; at the first stoplight proceeding left onto Sandbridge Rd. for 3 miles; and right onto Sandpiper Rd. for 4 miles to the refuge entrance.

Information: Back Bay NWR, 4005 Sandpiper Rd., Virginia Beach, VA 23456; tel.: (757) 721-2412.

Chincoteague, comprising 14,032 acres, was established in 1943 to protect important habitat for the greater snow goose and other migratory birds. Most of the refuge is located on Virginia's portion of Assateague Island, a coastal barrier island in northeastern Virginia and southeastern Maryland. In an unusual boundary arrangement, most of the Chincoteague refuge lies within the southern portion of the Assateague Island National Seashore. More than 320 bird species have been recorded here.

Smaller parts of the refuge include Wildcat Marsh at the northern end of Chincoteague Island, Morris Island, and all or part of three smaller barrier islands that extend southward from the main part of the refuge. These islands are Cedar, Assawoman, and Metompkin (part of the latter is owned and managed by the Fish and Wildlife Service and the rest by The Nature Conservancy). The refuge also includes a tract of just over 400 acres on the Maryland portion of Assateague Island.

This refuge is ranked as one of the top five migratory shorebird staging areas in the United States, east of the Rocky Mountains. In 1990, the barrier islands of the eastern shore of Virginia and Maryland were designated as an International Shorebird Reserve, and this barrier island–coastal lagoon system has also been named as a World Biosphere Reserve by the United Nations' Educational, Scientific, and Cultural Organization. Shorebirds pass through the refuge by the hundreds of thousands, from mid-April to mid-June and from mid-July to mid-August.

In addition to major concentrations of wintering waterfowl and migrating shorebirds, Chincoteague refuge's habitats attract large numbers of wading birds, seabirds, migrating and nesting raptors, and neotropical migratory songbirds. Ospreys are commonly seen hunting for fish in the impoundments and marshes, and they like to nest on hunting blinds that are scattered across the open water of Chincoteague Bay and Assateague Channel. In recent years, a couple of active bald eagle nests have been located on the refuge.

Another of the refuge's raptors is the peregrine falcon. As explained by the Fish and Wildlife Service:

Chincoteague NWR is one of the prime eastern U.S. focal points for observing arctic peregrine falcons during their autumn migration. The Wash Flats impoundments and the protected north beach provide resting and feeding habitat for an estimated 875-900 peregrines . . . [that] may stop over on the island for a day to several weeks. An international banding program indicates that more than half the peregrines observed at the refuge during the fall migration originate in Greenland, with others coming from Quebec, the Northwest Territories, and the Yukon. Some of these peregrines travel as far south as southern Argentina.

The refuge habitats include sandy ocean beaches, sand dunes that support dune-grass, a shrub community that is typical of back-dunes and flats, several large stands of maritime forest, areas of brackish wetlands, and extensive areas of salt marsh. There are 2,600 acres in 14 moist-soil units, in which water levels are lowered in the spring to create mudflat environment that attracts shorebirds and to promote the growth of food plants for waterfowl later in the year when water levels are raised.

Restoration and management of the refuge's maritime forest includes efforts to curtail the spread of the southern pine beetle that harms or kills loblolly pines and to enhance the woodlands for the endangered Delmarva Peninsula fox squirrel, which was "translocated" to the refuge in the late 1960s and early 1970s. These activities include thinning, prescribed burning, and planting of native hardwoods, such as oaks, persimmon, and flowering dogwood. (See the description of the fox squirrel in the Blackwater NWR text.)

To help protect the federally listed threatened, beach-nesting piping plover, refuge biologists erect protective closures around nests, control predation, and monitor chicks from March through August.

As the Fish and Wildlife Service says of refuge wildlife:

Snow goose populations have recovered since the 1930s and 1940s when they were in trouble, resulting in the formation of the Chincoteague Refuge. The refuge's current midwinter snow goose population averages around 6,000-12,000 geese but can range as high as 50,000 for a few weeks. . . .

A heron, egret, and ibis rookery is located on several marsh islands in Chincoteague Bay. Other rookeries are located in the outer marsh fringe between Chincoteague Island and the Mainland. The eastern brown pelican also delights visitors as they often soar just above the water and just beyond the breakers in the ocean. . . .

The refuge also provides excellent nesting habitat for colonial and other beach nesting birds. Colonial species include common, least, and gull-billed terns, and black skimmers. Wilson's and piping plovers nest on beach ridges and overwash areas. . . . Raptor migration through the area occurs in September and October; this event can be spectacular, depending on the weather conditions.

Two mammals are non-natives: The sika, an Asian elk, which is much smaller than the native white-tailed deer; and the Chincoteague "ponies," which are descendants of colonial domestic horses introduced onto Assateague Island in the 17th century. The latter are wild horses that have adapted to this coastal environment.

Establishment of this refuge was made possible partly with revenues from the sale of Migratory Bird Hunting and Conservation Stamps (Duck Stamps). Ducks Unlimited, Inc. has helped enhance more than 2,200 acres of the refuge's wetland habitat.

The refuge is open daily during daylight hours. There is an entrance fee. The refuge's Herbert H. Bateman Educational and Administrative Center is open daily, except on Christmas. Near the southern end of the refuge, the National Park Service maintains the national seashore's Toms Cove Visitor Center, offers interpretive walks and programs, and manages recreational activities and facilities.

Visitor activities include wildlife observation; viewing interpretive exhibits and programs at the Bateman Center; driving the road to the Toms Cove area and, from 3 p.m. to dusk, the 3.25-mile Wildlife Loop; hiking on a half-dozen trails, one of which includes a (wheelchair-accessible) boardwalk and observation platform; bicycling; picnicking; swimming; boating (boats are permitted to land at Fishing Point, from September 1 to March 14); fishing; crabbing; shellfishing (in Toms Cove); and hunting on parts of the refuge during the designated seasons (archery and firearm deer and/or sika hunts are held when control of the herds is needed; a sika hunt area is reserved for mobility-challenged hunters). Although camping is not permitted on the refuge, facilities are available at private campgrounds on Chincoteague Island; on the National Park Service–administered portion of the national seashore, in Maryland; and at Maryland's Assateague State Park. Motor vehicles are prohibited outside of established roads, parking areas, and designated off-road vehicle (ORV) areas.

Visitors are cautioned to stay a safe distance from the Chincoteague ponies, as they are wild and unpredictable horses that can be dangerous; be careful when swimming in the ocean; and be alert for ticks, which may transmit Lyme disease. Insect repellent during the warmer months and sunscreen are advised.

Lodgings and meals are available in Chincoteague Island, New Church, and Onancock, Va., and Pocomoke and Salisbury, Md.

Access to the refuge from Pocomoke City, Md., is south eight miles on U.S. Hwy. 13, east ten miles on State Hwy. 175 to the town of Chincoteague, left onto Main St., right onto Maddox Blvd.; and just over two miles, crossing Assateague Channel onto Assateague Island. From Virginia Beach, it is north 85 miles on U.S. Hwy. 13, right onto State Hwy. 175 and proceeding as above.

Information: Chincoteague NWR, 8231 Beach Rd., Chincoteague, VA 23336; tel.: (757) 336-6122.

Eastern Shore of Virginia, containing 752 acres, was established in 1984 to enhance and protect an area of maritime forest, wax myrtle and bayberry thickets, grasslands, and freshwater and brackish ponds. The refuge is located at the southern tip of the Delmarva Peninsula, on the Eastern Shore of Virginia.

From late August through early November, enormous numbers of migrating birds, notably songbirds, raptors, swallows, and waterfowl, fly southward along the peninsula, which encompasses

Delaware and the Eastern Shore of Maryland and Virginia (Delmarva). The narrow southern end of the peninsula acts like a funnel, forcing the birds together in spectacular concentrations. At this strategic location, they often pause to await favorable wind and weather before crossing the broad mouth of Chesapeake Bay.

One species that migrates south to spend from late autumn to midwinter on the refuge is the American woodcock—a squat, comical-looking little bird, with a long beak and large eyes set high on the sides of the head. At times, scores, if not hundreds, of them, with twittering sounds and whirring wings, fly out of the woods at dusk to feed on worms in the refuge's fields. More than 300 bird species have been recorded on the refuge.

Historically, the end of the peninsula was also strategically valued for military purposes. At the start of World War II, the federal government established Fort John Custis on much of the land now within the refuge. In 1950, the fort was transferred to the U.S. Air Force and converted to the Cape Charles Air Force Station, which was closed in 1980. Four years later, the Air Force transferred 180 acres to the Fish and Wildlife Service, securing the initial tract of land for the refuge.

A number of habitat-enhancement activities are being carried out on the refuge. Most of the military buildings have been removed; vegetation has been planted that provides cover for wildlife; ponds have been created, offering freshwater wetland habitat for waterfowl, wading birds, and shorebirds; nesting platforms have been erected for ospreys; and nest boxes and other structures have been provided for wood ducks, bluebirds, and owls. Ducks Unlimited, Inc. has helped enhance some of the refuge's wetland habitat. In addition, the refuge contains habitat that is being managed for the numerous species of butterflies that inhabit or migrate through the area.

The refuge is open daily during daylight hours. There is no entrance fee. The visitor center (located on the east side of U.S. Hwy. 13, just north of the Chesapeake Bay Bridge Tunnel) is open daily from March through December and is open Fridays through Sundays in January and February.

Visitor activities include wildlife and butterfly observation, viewing interpretive exhibits and video programs at the visitor center, hiking on two trails, and limited hunting (archery deer hunting by lottery on the first day; and first-come, first-served thereafter; and shotgun by lottery) in certain parts of the refuge during the designated times. Although camping is not permitted on the refuge, facilities are available at Kiptopeke State Park; information: tel.: (757) 331-2267.

Lodgings and meals are available in area communities such as Cape Charles and Virginia Beach.

Access to the refuge from Virginia Beach is north on U.S. Hwy. 13 via the 20-mile Chesapeake Bay Bridge Tunnel (toll) and continuing north about 30 miles, and right onto County Rd.600 to the refuge entrance; or south from Salisbury, Md., about 100 miles on U.S. Hwy. 13, and left onto County Rd. 600.

Information: Eastern Shore of Virginia NWR, 5003 Hallett Circle, Cape Charles, VA 23310; tel.: (757) 331-2760.

Elizabeth Hartwell Mason Neck, containing 2,277 acres, was established in 1969 as the first national wildlife refuge specifically for the then-federally listed endangered bald eagle. The refuge is located on the southern shore of the Potomac River, 18 miles south of Washington, D.C., in northern Virginia.

The refuge's habitats include close to five miles of river shoreline, the largest freshwater marsh in northern Virginia, and mixed hardwood and pine forest. Other protectively managed lands on the 8,000-acre Mason Neck Peninsula are the adjacent Mason Neck State Park and Gunston Hall Plantation, as well as nearby Pohick Bay Regional Park. The refuge and these other areas, which are working together as the loosely allied Mason Neck Management Area, total more than 6,000 acres that are cooperatively managed for eagle protection. The Fish and Wildlife Service reports "overall numbers of eagles in the area have increased dramatically . . . with up to 50 or more birds in the winter."

Mason Neck refuge also contains one of the largest rookeries of the great blue heron in the mid-Atlantic states. It has grown tremendously, from 26 nests that were discovered in 1979, to more than 1,400 nests in 2000. Among the refuge's habitat-management activities are avoiding human disturbance of the heron rookery during the nesting season; providing nesting boxes for wood ducks, bluebirds, and bats, to supplement the supply of natural tree cavities; and promoting the growth of native food plants for the benefit of wintering waterfowl.

Among the most abundant of the many species of wintering waterfowl at Mason Neck are greater and lesser scaup, American black ducks, mallards, ring-necked ducks, common and hooded mergansers, buffleheads, ruddy ducks, Canada geese, and tundra swans. During spring and autumn migrations, large influxes of neotropical songbirds come to or through the refuge's woodlands. More than 200 species of birds have been recorded here.

Recorded human history of Mason Neck began at least as early as the 1600s, when colonial settlers began buying land along the Potomac River. In the 1750s, Gunston Hall, which is a prime example of formal mid-18th-century Georgian-style architecture, was built on Mason Neck by plantation owner George Mason (1725-92). This Virginia statesman wrote the first draft of the Virginia Declaration of Rights, which was adopted in its final form by the Virginia convention in Williamsburg on June 12, 1776. His words ("That all men are by nature equally free and independent, and have certain inherent rights . . . namely, the enjoyment of life and liberty, with the means of acquiring and possessing property, and pursueing and obtaining Happiness and Safety") were the forerunner of Thomas Jefferson's Declaration of Independence. Mason's ideas also became the model for subsequent bills of rights that were included in many other state constitutions and in the U.S. Constitution. For information on tours and events: Gunston Hall Plantation, 10709 Gunston Road, Mason Neck, VA 22079; tel.: (703) 550-9220.

During the 19th and early 20th centuries, as described by the Fish and Wildlife Service:

Logging was the principle land use of what is now refuge lands. Roads were cut and much of the mature pine and hardwood timber removed. This human disturbance and the elimination of nest trees reduced the bald eagle population.

By the 1960s, timber had grown back, but residential development posed a new threat. Local residents worked with The Nature Conservancy to protect the land. In 1969, the Fish and Wildlife Service purchased 845 acres from the Conservancy and the Mason Neck National Wildlife Refuge was established.

Ducks Unlimited, Inc. has helped enhance an area of the refuge's wetland habitat.

The refuge is open daily during daylight hours. There is no entrance fee. The refuge headquarters is open on weekdays, except national holidays.

Visitor activities include wildlife observation, hiking on two interpretive trails (one of which is wheelchair-accessible; the other with a platform overlooking Great Marsh), interpreter-led hikes and programs, bicycling on paved roads, and limited deer hunting (by lottery) on designated days. An environmental-education pavilion and adjacent fields and trails are available for organized groups by advance reservation. Although camping is not permitted on the refuge, facilities are provided at Pohick Bay Regional Park and Prince William Forest Park.

Visitors are cautioned to be alert for venomous copperhead snake, ticks, and chiggers. Insect repellent is advised during the warmer seasons.

Lodgings and meals are available in Lorton, Woodbridge, and Springfield.

Access to the refuge from Exit 163 on I-95 at Lorton is east on Lorton Rd. to U.S. Hwy. 1 (Jefferson Davis Hwy.), right onto U.S. Hwy. 1, left onto Gunston Rd. for just over 4.5 miles, and right onto High Point Rd. to the refuge's Woodmarsh Trail directional sign. To the Great Marsh Trail, continue 1.5 miles on Gunston Rd. A scenic alternative route from Washington, D.C., is south along the Potomac River on the George Washington Memorial Parkway to Mount Vernon, west on State Hwy. 235, and left onto Hwy. 1 to Gunston Rd.

Information: Elizabeth Hartwell Mason Neck NWR, c/o Potomac River NWR Complex, 7603 High Point Rd., Lorton, VA 22079; tel.: (703) 490-4979.

Great Dismal Swamp, encompassing nearly 115,000 acres, was established in 1974 to restore and manage the ecological diversity of an extensive forested wetland, in southeastern Virginia and northeastern North Carolina. In the middle of the refuge is 3,100-acre Lake Drummond, which was discovered in 1665 by North Carolina's colonial governor, William Drummond.

Great Dismal Swamp was long subjected to and greatly impacted by drainage and numerous timber harvesting activities. Twenty-six years before George Washington became the first president of the United States, he visited this swamp and then formed the Dismal Swamp Land Company, which proceeded to drain and log off part of the area. Logging the swamp's bald cypress, Atlantic white cedar, and other trees was economically so lucrative that it continued until 1976.

As the Fish and Wildlife Service explains:

The entire swamp has been logged at least once, and many areas have been burned by periodic wildfires. The Great Dismal Swamp has been drastically altered by humans over the past two centuries. Agricultural, commercial, and residential development destroyed much of the swamp, so that the remaining portion within and around the refuge represents less than half the original size of the swamp [estimated to have been between 500,000 and two million acres].

In 1973, the Union Camp Company donated just over 49,000 acres of its land to The Nature Conservancy, which transferred the property the following year to the Fish and Wildlife Service. According to Great Dismal Swamp's Refuge Manager Lloyd A. Culp, Jr. (author of the chapter "Refuges and Ecosystem Protection" in the 2000 publication *The Natural History of the Great Dismal Swamp*):

Human activity in the Great Dismal Swamp inflicted subtle but significant changes in its physical features. Beginning in the 1760s with Washington Ditch, the . . . 150 miles . . . of ditches created a drier swamp by draining surface water which, in conjunction with the logging and suppression of natural wildfires, changed the composition of the forest. Thus, a Great Dismal Swamp with a diversity of forested habitats (including large cypress and Atlantic white cedar stands) gradually changed to an area dominated by red maple trees. Only remnants of cypress and cedar stands remain.

Lloyd Culp goes on to describe a number of 21st-century management issues for the Great Dismal Swamp. For example, to promote hydrologic restoration, the Fish and Wildlife Service will continue maintaining and monitoring more than thirty water-control structures to slow the drainage of the forested wetlands. Restoration of Atlantic white cedar and bald cypress forest will continue to be a major focus, and the use of fire and other timber-management techniques will be expanded. Additional land acquisition within the refuge's authorized boundary will be accomplished, as funding becomes available, to acquire land from willing sellers, with assistance from such organizations as The Nature Conservancy and The Conservation Fund. And the protection of vital wildlife corridors for such species as the black bear, providing links between the refuge and other natural habitats, will also be encouraged.

Ducks Unlimited, Inc. has helped enhance more than 20,000 acres of the refuge's wetland habitat.

The refuge is open daily during daylight hours. There is no entrance fee. The refuge headquarters, at the western edge of the refuge, is open on weekdays, except national holidays.

Visitor activities include birdwatching, photography, hiking, bicycling, boating and canoeing (a boat-launching ramp, offering access to Lake Drummond, is provided onto the Feeder Ditch, at the eastern edge of the refuge), fishing, and deer hunting on parts of the refuge during the designated season. Although camping is not permitted on the refuge, campground facilities are available in the general vicinity.

Hiking opportunities include the nearly 0.75-mile (wheelchair-accessible) Dismal Town Boardwalk Trail, located on Washington Ditch Road, which winds through part of the swamp habitat, and a number of the refuge's unpaved roads that are also open to bicycling. The peak influx of neotropical migratory songbirds, such as numerous species of warblers, is from late April to mid-May. More than 200 bird species have been recorded here.

Visitors are cautioned to be alert for ticks, chiggers, and venomous snakes. Insect repellent is advised during the warmer months.

Lodgings and meals are available in such communities as Suffolk, Chesapeake, Norfolk, and Virginia Beach.

Access to the refuge from Suffolk is south on U.S. Hwy. 13 (Washington St.), left onto State Hwy. 642 (White Marsh Rd.) for seven miles, and left onto the Washington Ditch entrance road to the boardwalk trail. Refuge headquarters is about a mile farther south on State Hwy. 642, and left onto Desert Rd. for about two miles. The boat-launching access, on the eastern edge of the refuge, is adjacent to U.S. Hwy. 17.

Information: Great Dismal Swamp NWR, 3100 Desert Rd., Suffolk, VA 23434; tel.: (757) 986-3705.

Occoquan Bay, containing 644 acres, was established in 1998 and is on a peninsula that lies at the junction of the Potomac and Occoquan rivers, about twenty miles south of Washington, D.C., in northern Virginia. The refuge, across Occoquan Bay from Mason Neck refuge, protects a diversity of habitats including freshwater wetlands, woodlands, and one of the region's last remaining, undeveloped areas of native grassland. The unusual mix of habitats in a relatively small area provides exceptional bird watching opportunities and allows visitors to traverse a variety of habitat types within a short distance.

The refuge combines lands that were acquired when the U.S. Army's Woodbridge Research Facility was closed and 63 acres of the former Marumsco National Wildlife Refuge, which was established in 1973. The name *Occoquan* is derived from a Dogue Indian word, meaning "at the end of the water."

The refuge's meadows contain such native grasses as the eastern gamagrass, deer tongue, and bushy panic grass; and other plants including Carolina pasture and multiflora roses, oxeye daisy, goldenrods, and asters. Among the many birds that are attracted to the grasslands are northern bobwhite, bobolink, eastern meadowlark, northern harrier, eastern bluebird, indigo bunting, and field and grasshopper sparrows.

More than fifty species of butterflies have been recorded on the refuge. They include the five species of swallowtails, red-banded hairstreak, eastern tailed and spring azure blues; great spangled and variegated fritillaries; pearly crescentspot; comma; American painted lady; red admiral; buckeye; red-spotted purple; viceroy; and monarch.

As Occoquan Bay refuge is still in its developmental stage as of this writing, the area is open only on weekends (closed on Christmas and in poor weather) and visitor facilities are limited. It is anticipated that the refuge will eventually be open daily, that interpretive and other visitor use facilities, including a visitor contact station and auto tour route, will be provided.

Visitor activities include wildlife and butterfly observation, hiking on a number of gravel roads, and organized group field studies by advance arrangement. Fishing and hunting are expected to be permitted.

Visitors are cautioned to be alert for the venomous copperhead snake, ticks, and chiggers. Insect repellent is advised during the warmer months.

Lodgings and meals are available in the nearby community of Woodbridge.

Access to the refuge from U.S. Hwy. 1 in Woodbridge is east 0.7 miles on Dawson Beach Rd.

Information: Occoquan Bay NWR, c/o Potomac River NWR Complex, 14344 Jefferson Davis Hwy., Woodbridge, VA 22191; tel.: (703) 490-4979.

Washington

Columbia, containing 23,200 acres, was established in 1944 to protect and manage an ecologically important area of lakes, ponds, and irrigated croplands for the benefit of migrating and wintering waterfowl. The refuge, which also features canyons, with dark cliffs of lava flow-formed basalt, and sagebrush-grassland habitat, is located along Crab Creek, within the high desert of the Columbia Basin, in east-central Washington.

The refuge attracts large concentrations of wintering mallards and smaller numbers of Canada geese. During the peak of autumn migration, more than 100,000 waterfowl have been

Trumpeter swan family, Red Rock Lakes NWR, Montana

Mule deer buck, Crescent Lake NWR, Nebraska

American bison, Fort Niobara NWR, Nebraska

Bison herd, Fort Niobara NWR

Spring-fed pool, Ash Meadows NWR

Endangered Amargosa pupfish, Ash Meadows NWR, Nevada

Ash Meadows NWR

Amargosa pupfish research, Ash Meadows NWR, Nevada

Sheep Range, Desert NWR, Nevada. Russell D. Butcher photo

Ruby Lake NWR, Nevada

Ruby Lake NWR. Russell D. Butcher photo

Stillwater NWR, Nevada Russell D. Butcher photo

Desert NWR, Nevada

Great Bay NWR, New Hampshire

Great egret, Edwin B. Forsythe NWR, New Jersey

Eastern cottontail, Edwin B. Forsythe NWR

Great Swamp NWR, New Jersey

Great Swamp NWR

Snow geese, Bosque del Apache NWR. Russell D. Butcher photo

Bosque del Apache NWR

Blackbird flock, Bosque del Apache NWR, New Mexico

Snow geese and marsh at sunrise, Bosque del Apache NWR

Wild turkey flock, Bosque del Apache NWR, New Mexico

Greater sandhill cranes in flight, Bosque del Apache NWR

Cardinal, Elizabeth A. Morton NWR, New York

Sevilletta NWR, New Mexico

Raccoon in marsh, Montezuma NWR, New York

Great blue heron catching fish, Montezuma NWR

Wertheim NWR, New York

Royal tern nest colony, Cedar Island NWR

Brown pelican rookery, Cedar Island NWR, North Carolina

Mattamuskeet NWR, North Carolina

Nesting osprey, Pea Island NWR, North Carolina

J. Clark Salyer NWR

Northern shoveler pair, J. Clark Salyer NWR, North Dakota

J. Clark Salyer NWR

"Prairie pothole" country, Lostwood NWR

Savannah sparrow, Lostwood NWR,
North Dakota

Lostwood NWR

Little River NWR, Oklahoma

Scissor-tailed flycatcher, Sequoyah NWR, Oklahoma

River of boulders, Wichita Mountains NWR

"Kissing" blacktail prairie dogs, Wichita Mountains NWR, Oklahoma

Old growth forest, west central Oregon

Cape Meares NWR, Oregon

recorded on the refuge. Nesting waterbirds include the abundant American coot and such ducks as mallards, gadwalls, cinnamon teal, redheads, and ruddy ducks. Regarding other wildlife, the Fish and Wildlife Service says that, "The ledges, cracks, and holes that abound in the numerous basalt cliffs provide important nesting habitat for many red-tailed hawks, American kestrels, great horned owls, barn owls, and a few ravens. The cliffs are used by large colonies of cliff swallows to hold and shelter their mud nests. Great blue herons are frequently seen standing like sentinels at the top of cliffs and rock outcrops near water. Increasing numbers of sandhill cranes visit the Refuge during spring and fall migrations. Northern harriers are common, as are magpies, pheasants, California quail, and black-crowned night-herons. Long-billed curlews and American avocets . . . nest on the Refuge." More than 200 bird species have been recorded here.

The refuge also lies within the Drumheller Channels National Natural Landmark, which was designated in 1986 to recognize and interpret the "Channeled Scablands." Beginning around 100,000 years ago, continental glacial ice gradually extended southward from British Columbia across much of what is now Washington, Idaho, and Montana. This advance dammed the flow of the Clark Fork River on numerous occasions, near the Idaho-Montana border. Geologists explain that, at its maximum around 12,000 years ago, the resulting huge lake covered roughly two million acres and was nearly 2,000 feet deep. When the ice dam was breached, it is estimated that the outpouring of water was perhaps ten times the combined flow of all the rivers in the world. When this incredible flood reached the Columbia Basin, the water's immense volume, speed, and turbulence eroded deep canyons into the basaltic lava flows. In what is now the northern part of the refuge, there is a hodgepodge of canyons, cliffs, and remnants of lava flows. This portion of the Scablands is known as the Drumheller Channels. It is ranked as the most spectacular eroded area of its size in the world. As Deputy Project Leader Rob Larranaga says, "The geology of the refuge is as intriguing as the wildlife." A short detour from State Highway 17 and 26 is necessary to view these landscapes.

The human history of this part of the Columbia Basin has also brought significant changes to the landscape. As described by the Fish and Wildlife Service:

During the 1860s, cattle were brought into the area and the land was soon overgrazed. When grass conditions became too poor for cattle, sheep were introduced. By the . . . [start of the 20th] century, sheep, plus 3,000 feral (wild) horses that ranged along Crab Creek . . . , had taken a heavy toll upon the land. . . .

Early irrigation efforts in the . . . area encouraged some farmers, but failed when local water supplies proved inadequate. Serious planning to irrigate the Columbia Basin on a large scale began in 1918 and hinged on construction of a dam on the Columbia River at Grand Coulee. . . . construction of Grand Coulee Dam began in 1934. On August 10, 1951, the first irrigation water began flowing to Columbia Basin farmlands. Columbia National Wildlife Refuge was established in conjunction with the irrigation project . . . and has been actively managed since 1955.

With the availability of a reliable supply of abundant water, the project changed quickly and dramatically. The water table rose as predicted and lakes appeared in former canyons and low spots throughout the Refuge, and additional lakes and ponds were created by damming spring seepage flows. All current Refuge lakes and impoundments are the result, directly or indirectly, of irrigation water.

Around the Refuge, dryland wheat areas and many acres of sagebrush grasslands were soon converted to a wide variety of irrigated crops. Many of these crops, particularly corn, provided abundant food for ducks, geese, and sandhill cranes. The agricultural development, together with the numerous water areas, combined each year to provide ideal feeding and resting areas for thousands of migrating and wintering waterfowl.

Establishment of Columbia Refuge was made possible partly with revenues from the sale of Migratory Bird Hunting and Conservation Stamps (Duck Stamps). Ducks Unlimited, Inc. has helped enhance more than 1,100 acres of the refuge's wetland habitat.

The refuge is open daily. There is no entrance fee. The refuge office, located at 735 East Main Street, Othello, is open on weekdays, except national holidays.

Visitor activities include wildlife observation, driving the 23-mile auto tour route, hiking on several trails, bicycling on roads open to motor vehicles, canoeing and boating (gasoline-powered watercraft not permitted on Hutchinson, Shiner, Royal, and Upper and Lower Hampton lakes), primitive camping (at Soda Lake Campground and at nearby state sites), fishing, and hunting on parts of the refuge during the designated seasons. Swimming is not permitted.

Visitors are cautioned to be alert for rattlesnakes. Insect repellent and sunscreen are advised during the warmer months.

Lodgings and meals are available in Othello.

Access to the refuge from Exit 179 on I-90 at Moses Lake is southeast about 10 miles on State Hwy. 17, right about 6.5 miles on O'Sullivan Dam Rd. (State Hwy. 262), and south onto Morgan Lake Rd.; or from State Hwy. 26, it is north on Broadway Ave. (State Hwy. 24) to Othello, continuing north just under 2 miles on Broadway, bearing northwest for several miles on McManamon Rd., and right onto Morgan Lake Rd.

Information: Columbia NWR, P.O. Drawer F, Othello, WA 99344; tel.: (509) 488-2668.

Grays Harbor, consisting of 1,471 acres, was established in 1990 to protect a major staging area for awesome concentrations of shorebirds. The refuge is located on the central Pacific Coast of Washington.

The peak numbers of semipalmated plovers, western sandpipers, dunlin, dowitchers, and other shorebirds pause at the refuge, to rest and enhance their fat reserves, from late April through early May, on their way to Arctic breeding grounds. Some of these migrants fly from as far away as Argentina and travel more than 7,000 miles in each direction. Roughly 85 percent of the northbound shorebirds seen at Grays Harbor are western sandpipers, which nest and raise their young primarily along the northwestern edge of Alaska and the eastern end of Siberia. Thousands of dunlin spend the winter here.

The refuge's habitats include intertidal mudflats, salt marsh, freshwater wetlands, a grove of red alders, and uplands. Although the refuge encompasses only two percent of the Grays Harbor's intertidal zone, it draws roughly half of all the shorebirds that come to this estuary. As the Fish and Wildlife Service explains, "The Refuge mudflats are the last areas in Grays Harbor to be flooded at high tide and the first areas to be exposed as the tide recedes. This gives shorebirds extra time to feed. Shorebirds must peck and probe almost continuously to obtain a constant supply of food. The mudflats provide an abundance of invertebrates for food."

The refuge also attracts many species of waterfowl, as well as gulls, terns, bald eagles and other raptors, and songbirds. Black-tailed deer is the most prominent resident mammal.

The refuge is open daily during daylight hours. There is no entrance fee.

Visitor activities include wildlife observation; photography; and hiking the one-mile Sand-piper Trail that is reached from the end of a paved road (parking is opposite a café). Swimming, boating, fishing, and hunting are not permitted on the refuge. Camping is not allowed on the refuge, but facilities are provided nearby.

Lodgings and meals are available in Hoquiam, Aberdeen, Ocean Shores, and Olympia.

Access to the refuge from the junction of U.S. Highways 101 and 12 in Aberdeen is west 4 miles on U.S. Hwy. 101 to Hoquiam,left 1.5 miles on State Hwy. 109, left on Paulson Rd., and right on Airport Rd.

Information: Grays Harbor NWR, c/o Nisqually NWR, 100 Brown Farm Rd., Olympia, WA 98516; tel.: (360) 753-9467.

Hanford Reach National Monument/Saddle Mountain National Wildlife Refuge, comprising 195,000 acres, was established in 2000 to protect an outstanding diversity of ecological, geo-logical, and archaeological values. The monument/refuge is located along the meandering Han-ford Reach of the Columbia River, downstream from four miles below Priest Rapids Dam downstream to the city of Richland, in south-central Washington. More than 200 bird species have been recorded here.

As described by the proclamation signed by President Bill Clinton establishing the first national monument under Fish and Wildlife Service management:

The Hanford Reach National Monument is a unique and biologically diverse landscape, encompassing an array of scientific and historic objects. This magnificent area contains an irreplaceable natural and historic legacy, preserved by unusual circumstances. Maintained as a buffer area in a Federal reservation conducting nuclear weapons development and, more recently, environmental cleanup activities, with limits on development and human use for the past 50 years, the monument is now a haven for important and increasingly scarce objects of scientific and historic interest. . . . The monument is also one of the few remaining archaeologically rich areas in the western Columbia Plateau, containing well-preserved remnants of human history spanning more than 10,000 years. The monument is equally rich in geologic history, with dramatic landscapes that reveal the creative forces of tectonic, volcanic, and erosive power.

The monument is a biological treasure, embracing important riparian, aquatic, and upland shrub-steppe habitats that are rare or in decline in other areas. Within its mosaic of habitats, the monument supports a wealth of increasingly uncommon native plant and animal species. . . .

The monument includes the 51-mile long "Hanford Reach," the last free-flowing, nontidal stretch of the Columbia River. The Reach contains islands, riffles, gravel bars, oxbow ponds, and backwater sloughs that support some of the most productive spawning areas in the Northwest, where approximately 80 percent of the upper Columbia Basin's fall chinook salmon spawn.

The refuge contains five administrative units. The 57,000-acre WAHLUKE UNIT consists of riparian wetlands and shrub-steppe habitats along the east side of the Columbia River. Wahluke Lake, near the center of the unit, supports dense stands of cattails and bulrushes. The scenically spectacular, twenty-mile-long White Bluffs of the Columbia contain significant pale-ontological resources, with a tremendous diversity of fossil remains, from ancient forms of bison, camel, and rhinoceros to dragonflies. This unit is open to visitation.

The 77,000-acre FITZER/EBERHARDT ARID LANDS ECOLOGY RESERVE UNIT, located to the west of the Columbia River, contains a prominent landmark known as the Rattlesnake Hills, the highest point of which is 3,600-foot Rattlesnake Mountain. As the Fish and Wildlife Service explains, "This unit was set aside in 1967 by the U.S. Atomic Energy Commission to preserve native shrub-steppe vegetation. It once served as a buffer zone for the Department of Energy's Hanford operations. Until a wildfire in 2000 devastated native plants, especially big sagebrush, this unit harbored one of the largest remnants of shrub-steppe vegetation in the state. . . . In the wake of the fire, the Service is working to restore big sagebrush. . . . The unit still is home to a large herd of Rocky Mountain elk." Public access onto this unit is limited to approved environmental education trips and research.

The 32,000-acre SADDLE MOUNTAIN UNIT, located along State Hwy. 24 and the north bank of the Columbia River, encompasses the original Saddle Mountain National Wildlife Refuge that was established in 1971. Visitor access is not permitted onto this unit.

The 9,000-acre MCGEE RANCH/RIVERLANDS UNIT includes a former pioneer ranch that contains a number of rare plant species. It provides an important protected corridor of land between the Arid Lands Ecology Reserve Unit and the U.S. Army's Yakima Training Center and is presently closed to visitation, except for those lands north of Midway Rd., which are open for day uses. Currently, there are no visitor facilities, and access routes are primitive.

The 25,000-acre RIVER CORRIDOR UNIT, along the south and west banks of the Columbia River, includes 16 islands in the river's main channel and the Hanford Dune Field, which contains actively moving barchan sand dunes and partly stabilized, 10- to 16-foot-high transverse dunes. The Fish and Wildlife Service explains that this unit is managed by the U.S. Department of Energy. "The shoreline and islands are owned by a number of government agencies and private landowners. Access is controlled by the owners. Some islands downstream of Savage Island are open seasonally to public use. Lands on the south and west side of the river and all islands upstream of Savage Island are closed to the public."

The Wahluke Unit is open daily during daylight hours. There is no entrance fee. Currently there are no visitor use facilities.

Visitor activities on the Wahluke Unit include wildlife observation; driving the east-west State Hwy. 24 to a signed gravel road that leads south onto the unit to a scenic river overlook and to the old White Bluffs ferry landing; hiking; bicycling only on roads open to motorized vehicles; boating and fishing on the Columbia River and its backwaters (primitive boat-launching sites are available at White Bluffs Landing, Vernita Bridge, Ringold, and the ramp at the old Hanford Ferry crossing); and hunting on parts of the unit during the designated seasons.

Visitors are cautioned to be aware of certain hazards along the Hanford Reach, such as widely fluctuating river levels that are caused by flow releases from Priest Rapids Dam, swift currents, shallow-water areas, and rocky shores. Areas of the Hanford Reach Unit are within an "emergency planning zone for the Hanford Site. In the event of a siren, tune a radio to the Emergency Broadcast Station (KONA, 610 AM or 105.3 FM) or marine band radio channel 22." Federal personnel or county sheriffs may also warn visitors to leave the unit.

Lodgings and meals are available in Yakima, Sunnyside, Richland, Othello, Desert Aire, and Mattawa.

Access to Hanford Reach monument/Saddle Mountain refuge's Wahluke Unit from I-82 at Yakima is east and then north 44 miles on State Hwy. 24 to the junction of State Highways 243 and 24 just after crossing the Columbia River, continuing right on Hwy. 24 about 29 miles (through the Saddle Mountain Unit), and right onto the unit's gravel road. From I-82 at Sunnyside, it is north 17 miles on State Hwy. 241, right onto State Hwy. 24 for 13 miles to the junction of Highways 243 and 24, and right, as above. From I-182 at Richland, it is northwest 34 miles on State Hwy. 240, north 5 miles on State Hwy. 24 to the junction of Highways 243 and 24, and right onto Hwy. 24, as above.

Information: Hanford Reach National Monument/Saddle Mountain NWR, 3250 Port of Benton Blvd., Richland, WA 99352; tel.: (509) 371-1801.

Julia Butler Hansen Refuge for the Columbian White-Tailed Deer, encompassing more than 5,453 acres, was initially established in 1972 as the Columbian White-Tailed Deer National Wildlife Refuge. It was renamed in 1988 to honor the memory of the late congresswoman Julia Butler Hansen (1907–1988), who advocated the protection of this small endangered subspecies of white-tailed deer and who was instrumental in establishing the refuge. The refuge is located along the north banks of the lower Columbia River, in southwestern Washington, and also Tenasillahe Island (pronounced tenah-SIL-ahee), on the Oregon side of the river.

This species of deer was first described in 1806 by Meriwether Lewis, of the Lewis and Clark Expedition. It is one of more than thirty deer subspecies in North America, and formerly ranged from Washington's Puget Sound southward through Oregon's Willamette and Umpqua river valleys. By the 1930s, its population had declined to fewer than 150 individuals. Now this refuge manages a mosaic of pastures, wetlands, and wooded habitat for roughly 300 deer, with perhaps another 400 to 500 on private lands along the river. A small herd of Roosevelt elk, a Pacific Northwest coastal subspecies, also inhabits the refuge. Other mammals include mink, river otters, beavers, muskrats, and the abundant, non-native nutria, a large rodent introduced from South America.

The refuge's flooded pastures, marshes, and sloughs attract large concentrations of migrating and wintering waterfowl, including tundra swans, three subspecies of Canada geese (dusky, western, and lesser), and many species of ducks, such as mallard, northern pintail, American wigeon, green-winged teal, and bufflehead. Water levels within some wetland impoundments are seasonally regulated with water-control structures—either to contain water during the drier summer months or to remove excess water and control flooding during the heavier precipitation of autumn and winter. As the Fish and Wildlife Service explains:

Before the 1920s, much of the mainland and Tenasillahe Island were marshes flooded by the daily rising tides of the Columbia River.

The Wahkiakum Diking District #4 was formed in the 1920s, at which time the area between Cathlamet and Skamokawa . . . was diked and drained. The dikes converted permanent wetlands into agricultural lands which were farmed for nearly fifty years until the establishment of the refuge.

Although the dikes and fields remain today, management of the area is now focused towards managing deer and wintering waterfowl habitat.

The swans, in particular, are drawn to a favorite food, the wapato, an aquatic plant with a nutrient-rich tuber. The refuge also supports a nesting colony of great blue herons. Raptors include nesting and wintering bald eagles, nesting ospreys, northern harriers, and occasional white-tailed kites. Steller's jays, varied thrushes, chestnut-backed chickadees, and winter and Bewick's wrens are among the smaller birds that inhabit the woodland areas that contain such trees and other plants as Sitka spruce, black cottonwood, willows, red alder, Pacific dogwood, bigleaf and vine maples, salal, salmonberry, and sword fern.

In recent years, improvement of habitat for the deer and other wildlife has been a major focus of refuge management. Infestations of the non-native, invasive reed canary grass on more than seventy percent of the refuge's pastures and wetlands, along with difficulty in establishing areas of riparian woodland, have impaired suitable deer habitat. The encouraging news is that management activities "have resulted in increased deer use, an increase in shorebird and waterfowl use, as well as a large increase in breeding amphibians."

Establishment of this refuge was made possible partly with revenues from the sale of Migratory Bird Hunting and Conservation Stamps (Duck Stamps).

The refuge is open daily during daylight hours. There is no entrance fee. The refuge headquarters is often open daily, including national holidays; but wildlife viewing and refuge information are available even when the headquarters building is closed.

Visitor activities include wildlife observation; driving and bicycling on nine-mile auto tour route; hiking; canoeing, kayaking, and boating; fishing (interior sloughs on all refuge units are closed); and hunting on parts of the refuge during the designated seasons. Swimming is not permitted on the refuge. Although camping is not permitted on the refuge, facilities are available nearby. Hiking opportunities include the 3-mile Center Rd. (June through September); and Steamboat Slough and Brooks Slough roads (open all year). Hiking on Tenasillahe Island is permitted only on the encircling dike.

Part of the Columbia River Heritage Canoe Trail winds through the refuge, several boat-launching sites are provided near the refuge; and canoe and kayak rentals are available in Skamokawa. The Fish and Wildlife Service warns that, "Tidal flows, strong winds, and large wakes from ships can make boating difficult and sometimes dangerous. Deep channels separate most of the islands at high tide, but during low tides, sandbars and exposed logs may hinder boat travel or even ground your boat. Consult navigational charts and tide tables [and weather reports] before venturing out."

Lodgings and meals are available in such communities as Cathlamet, Skamokawa, and Longview.

Access to the refuge headquarters from Cathamet, Wash., is northwest about 2.2 miles on State Hwy. 4 and left onto Steamboat Slough Rd.; or, it is just east of Skamokawa on State Hwy. 4 and right onto Steamboat Slough Rd.

Information: Julia Butler Hansen Refuge for the Columbian White-tailed Deer NWR, P.O. Box 566, Cathlamet, WA 98612; tel.: (360) 795-3915.

Little Pend Oreille, containing 40,198 acres, was established in 1939 to restore and manage an ecologically diverse area of montane conifer forest and riparian and other wetland habitats for the benefit of migratory birds and other wildlife. This is the only mountainous, mixed-conifer forest refuge in the National Wildlife Refuge System within the lower 48 states. It is located on the west slope of the Selkirk Mountains, in northeastern Washington.

The name *Pend Oreille* (pronounced pondo-RAY) is French for "ear pendant." The Little Pend Oreille River originates three miles to the northeast of the refuge. It flows through the northeastern and northwestern parts of the refuge, providing important stream and adjacent alluvial riparian habitats. Tributary streams include all of the Bear Creek watershed and most of the Cedar Creek and Olson Creek watersheds. A number of lakes, beaver ponds, cattail marshes, and seeps are scattered here and there. The refuge's riparian and other deciduous trees include black cottonwood, water and paper birches, Sitka and mountain alders, quaking aspen, and Douglas maple (a subspecies of Rocky Mountain maple). In the refuge's lowest, warmest, and driest areas, the conifer forest consists mostly of ponderosa pine. The wetter mid-elevation conifer forest is dominated by Douglas-fir, grand fir, western redcedar, and western hemlock, with some areas of lodgepole and western white pines and western larch. Engelmann spruce and subalpine fir also grow on the highest ridges.

The refuge's habitats attract such wildlife as elk, moose, white-tailed and mule deer, black bears, beavers, Canada geese, wood ducks, mallards, goldeneyes, mergansers, hawks, owls, and numerous neotropical migratory songbirds. More than 190 bird species have been recorded here.

Regarding the history of this area, Little Pend Oreille Refuge's April 2000 Final *Comprehensive Conservation Plan* explains that:

Beginning in 1879 and continuing until 1931, 188 homestead claims were patented . . . [within what subsequently became the refuge]. . . . When the Depression hit in the 1930s, many homesteaders had already given up and moved from the area. The short growing season, harsh winters, and overgrazed conditions were factors that led to the Resettlement Administration classifying the land as "submarginal." In 1935, most of the homesteads were acquired through the Soil Conservation Service as public lands for rehabilitation purposes. . . .

Early management [of the refuge] focused on restoring degraded habitat conditions to improve habitat for deer, fur bearing animals, upland game birds, waterfowl, and fish. Considerable effort went into planting a variety of shrubs and grasses to benefit wildlife, managing horse and cattle grazing, and planting crops to feed deer and game birds. Management ignited [prescribed] fires and selectively cut forests to improve deer winter range.

In 1965, the Washington Department of Fish and Wildlife (known then as the Washington Department of Game) assumed management responsibility through a cooperative agreement with the Service. Although the Service provided a budget to manage the Refuge, the State had considerable latitude to manage the area primarily for game species and recreation. The State scheduled most of the Refuge for selective timber harvest on a continual rotation basis. . . .

Prompted by an internal audit by the General Accounting Office, the Service decided to resume onsite management . . . of the Little Pend Oreille National Wildlife Refuge in 1994.

Management activities now include the creation of more stands of older-aged ponderosa pines and Douglas-firs that are vitally important for some species of wildlife. The primary methods for accomplishing this goal are selective thinning and prescribed burning. The careful use of fire reduces hazardous fuel overloading where fire has long been suppressed, promotes nutrient cycling, spurs the growth of nutrient-rich plant species that benefit many species of wildlife, and results in a more natural open-grown ponderosa pine woodland ecosystem.

Riparian habitats that have been impaired by past land use practices are being restored by stabilizing stream banks, planting trees and shrubs, and creating conservation buffers to protect sensitive areas bordering fish-bearing streams and lakes. In addition, non-native invasive pest plants that pose a threat to native species are being controlled. It is expected that livestock grazing will be phased out.

Refuge Manager Lisa Langelier explains, "It will take decades to provide the large trees and other features of mature forest that are relatively uncommon on the Refuge and surrounding lands. How we manage today will help shape the future of these valleys, lakes and mountains as vital wildlife habitat."

The refuge is open daily. There is no entrance fee. The refuge headquarters is open on weekdays, except national holidays.

Visitor activities include wildlife observation; driving on designated refuge roads; hiking; mountain biking and horseback riding on established roads and designated trails; camping (only in designated camps; firewood permits are available); boating (non-motorized watercraft only); fishing (April through October); and hunting on parts of the refuge during the designated seasons.

Lodgings and meals are available in Colville and Chewelah.

Access to the refuge headquarters from I-90 in downtown Spokane is north 71 miles to Colville, right at the Main St. and Third Ave. intersection onto State Hwy. 20 for 6 miles (toward Tiger, Wash.). Just after passing White Mud Lake, turn right onto Artman-Gibson Rd. and proceed 1.7 miles to a four-way intersection. Turn left onto Kitt-Narcisse Rd. and proceed for 2.2 miles. At a Y-junction, bear right onto unpaved Bear Creek Rd. and proceed 3.3 miles to the refuge headquarters.

Information: Little Pend Oreille NWR, 1310 Bear Creek Rd., Colville, WA 99114; tel.: (509) 684-8384.

Nisqually, consisting of 2,925 acres, was established in 1974. The refuge protects and manages a diversity of wetland and other Nisqually River Delta habitats where the freshwater from the river meets the saltwater, at the southern end of Puget Sound in west-central Washington.

Encompassing one of the state's last largely undisturbed estuaries, this refuge attracts large concentrations of migratory birds to its ponds, freshwater marshes, estuarine marshes and mudflats, grassland, and riparian woodlands. The diversity of wildlife includes Canada geese, many species of ducks, western sandpipers and other shorebirds, bald eagles and ospreys, and numerous neotropical migratory songbirds. Many birds merely pause on the delta habitat to rest and feed on their way to late-spring or summer breeding grounds farther north or to wintering habitat farther south. Others gather here during the winter months and some nest on the refuge, as, for instance, a colony of great blue herons. Over 200 bird species have been recorded here.

Part of the delta's ecosystem was altered in the early 1900s, when Alson Brown constructed a dike across part of the area to block the saltwater and thereby expand his farmland. This dike continues to keep the tidal waters from reaching the freshwater wetland and grassland habitats. Refuge planners are presently evaluating the potential for restoring some of these lands to historic estuary by removing or altering parts of the dike.

The refuge's vegetation includes Douglas-firs; western redcedars; black cottonwoods; red alders; bigleaf and vine maples; common snowberry; red elderberry; and sword, deer, and bracken ferns.

Establishment of the refuge was made possible partly with revenues from the sale of Migratory Bird Hunting and Conservation Stamps (Duck Stamps). Recent habitat restoration efforts have enhanced wetlands and resulted in planting thousands of native trees and shrubs to benefit more than 200 acres of freshwater wetlands, with the help of partners such as Ducks Unlimited, Inc. and the Washington Conservation Corps.

The refuge is open daily during daylight hours. A small, per-family entrance fee is charged. The visitor center is open on Wednesdays through Sundays, except on Thanksgiving, Christmas, and New Year's Day. An education center is open by appointment. The refuge office is open on weekdays, except national holidays.

Visitor activities include wildlife observation; hiking on several trails, including a one-mile (wheelchair-accessible) boardwalk; viewing the visitor center's interpretive exhibits; canoeing, kayaking, and small boating in the area outside the Brown Farm Dike (tides and wind can be hazardous); and fishing in the area outside the Brown Farm Dike and in the designated McAllister Creek Bank Fishing Area. Camping and swimming are not permitted on the refuge. Although hunting is not permitted on the refuge, it is allowed on the state's adjacent lands.

Lodgings and meals are available in Lacey, Olympia, and Tacoma.

Access to the refuge is a half-mile (following refuge directional signs) from Exit 114 on I-5.

Information: Nisqually NWR, 100 Brown Farm Rd., Olympia, WA 98516; tel.: (360) 753-9467.

Quillayute Needles, encompassing 300 acres, was established in 1907 by President Theodore Roosevelt to provide protection for breeding seabirds off the Pacific Coast of the Olympic Peninsula, in northwestern Washington. The 125-acre Flattery Rocks and 60-acre Copalis Rock national wildlife refuges were established at the same time for the same purpose. Taken together, these three Washington Islands Refuges, extending along more than 100 miles, consist of roughly 870 coastal islands, rocks, and reefs. These bits of surf-pounded land range in size from less than an acre to 36 acres.

As described by the Fish and Wildlife Service, "Most of the islands have precipitous shorelines rising above treacherous surf. A few islands have a cap of glacial till [unsorted sediments that were deposited by glacial ice] that supports luxuriant vegetation. Most vegetated islands are dominated by salal and salmonberry shrubs, although a small number have stands of Sitka spruce." All of the islands, except Destruction Island, are within the Wilderness Islands Wilderness, a unit of the National Wilderness Preservation System.

The three refuges support more than a dozen species of marine birds, with breeding populations estimated at over 100,000 pairs. These species include Leach's and forked-tailed storm petrels; double-crested, pelagic, and Brandt's cormorants; black oystercatcher; glaucous-winged gull; common murre; pigeon guillemot; Cassin's and rhinoceros auklets; and tufted puffin. Other nesting birds include bald eagle and peregrine falcon. During spring and autumn migrations, there may be more than a million seabirds, waterfowl, and shorebirds within the Washington Islands Refuges. Harbor seals and the California and Steller sea lions haul themselves onto rocks and reefs, and sea otters inhabit surrounding kelp beds.

These islands are closed to visitation, and the Fish and Wildlife Service urges that boats be kept at least 200 yards offshore, both for safety and to avoid disturbing the nesting bird colonies and other wildlife.

Information: Quillayute Needles, Flattery Islands, and Copalis Rock National Wildlife Refuges, c/o Washington Maritime NWR Complex, 33 South Barr Rd., Port Angeles, WA 98362; tel.: (360) 457-8451.

Ridgefield, containing 5,150 acres in five units, was established in 1965 to protect and manage wintering habitat for migratory waterfowl. The refuge consists of woodlands, grasslands, lakes and ponds, and tidally influenced marshes and sloughs. It is located along the lower Columbia River, in southwestern Washington.

Prominent among wintering birds are many tundra swans; many thousands of Canada geese of seven subspecies, including dusky, cackler, western, and Taverner's; and ducks of numerous species, such as mallard, northern pintail, northern shoveler, green-winged teal, and American wigeon. The dusky Canada goose, which nests on southern Alaska's Copper River Delta, winters only along the lower Columbia River and in Oregon's Willamette River Valley. The refuge also attracts wintering bald eagles and large numbers of migrating shorebirds, and provides winter roosting habitat for sandhill cranes and colonial nesting sites for the largest rookery of great blue herons in the Pacific Northwest.

The refuge's most prominent mammal is the black-tailed deer, and the biggest nuisance is the abundant non-native nutria, a large South American rodent that burrows into and damages dikes and ditches. Other native species include coyote, red fox, river otter, beaver, muskrat, raccoon, striped skunk, and brush rabbit.

Protection of the Columbia River floodplain is the primary management goal within the refuge's Carty and Roth units. During the spring, when melting mountain snow raises the level of the river, these areas are inundated. As the U.S. Fish and Wildlife Service explains:

Basalt outcroppings on the Carty Unit form knolls above the high water level. These knolls are wooded with ash, oak and Douglas-fir trees and are covered with brilliant wildflowers in the spring. The knolls become extremely dry in summer, in contrast with the lush greenery of surrounding marshes. The Roth unit is flatter and forested with cottonwood, ash and willow. Cattle graze on parts of these units to maintain grasslands in suitable condition for wintering waterfowl, especially Canada geese.

The River "S" Unit and Bachelor Island, on the other hand, are protected from flooding by dikes around their perimeters. Crops, such as corn, barley, and native grasses, are grown to provide food for waterfowl. Pumps provide the proper amount of water to each pond and lake to foster the growth of aquatic waterfowl food plants and to create resting areas for the birds. Grasslands are grazed by cattle and are cut for hay or silage. This leaves behind the short green browse preferred by Canada geese when they arrive in the fall.

Establishment of this refuge was made possible partly with revenues from the sale of Migratory Bird Hunting and Conservation Stamps (Duck Stamps). Ducks Unlimited, Inc. has helped enhance more than 1,700 acres of the refuge's wetland habitat.

The refuge is open daily during daylight hours. There is no entrance fee. The refuge headquarters, located at 301 North Third Ave. in Ridgefield, is open on weekdays, except national holidays.

Visitor activities include wildlife observation; driving on the 4.2-mile refuge auto tour road within the River "S" Unit; boating on Lake River, Bachelor Slough, and the Columbia River (boat-launching at Ridgefield Marina); fishing; and hunting on part of the refuge during the designated season. Although camping is not permitted on the refuge, facilities are available at nearby Paradise Point State Park. Hiking opportunities include the 2-mile Oaks-to-Wetlands Wildlife Trail along the edge of the Carty Unit's floodplain wetlands and through woodlands of Douglas-fir and Oregon white oak; and a 1.5-mile seasonal trail on the River "S" Unit. The Bachelor Island, Ridgeport Dairy, and Roth units are closed to public access.

Lodgings and meals are available in Ridgefield, Woodland, Longview, and Vancouver, Wash., and Portland, Ore.

Access to the refuge from Exit 14 on I-5 is west about three miles to Ridgefield, following refuge directional signs.

Information: Ridgefield NWR, P.O. Box 457, Ridgefield, WA 98642; tel.: (360) 887-4106.

Turnbull, comprising 15,628 acres, was established in 1937 to restore and protect an ecologically diverse and ruggedly scenic area of water-sculpted basalt formations and depressions known as the Channeled Scablands (see the Columbia NWR text). The refuge is located south of Spokane, in east-central Washington.

Numerous marshes, wet meadows, sloughs, streams, small lakes, and pothole ponds attract large concentrations of migrating and nesting ducks, geese, swans, and shorebirds. Other habitats include grassland, shrub steppe, riparian woodland, groves of quaking aspens, and forested areas of ponderosa pine. More than 200 bird species have been recorded here.

This area long supported the Spokane Indians, who came here not only to hunt wildlife, but who gathered many of the native plants for food, such as bitterroot, camas, and wild onion. But as the Fish and Wildlife Service describes, the Euro-American settlers arrived in the late 19th century to develop farmlands,

and before long there was a demand for more cropland. Drainage of the lakes and marshes continued until they were almost completely gone by the early 1920s. This excellent wildlife area might have been lost forever had it not been for the failure of the lakebeds to produce crops as expected, and for the efforts of individuals who felt that the area should be returned to its natural state.

Conservationists and sportsmen encouraged the addition of this area to the rapidly growing system of National Wildlife Refuges. Their efforts bore fruit . . . when the refuge was created and named for early settler Cyrus Turnbull.

Since then, the lakes and marshes have been restored to be much the same as they were prior to settlement. The area has been preserved through long, untiring efforts of countless workers, sportsmen, naturalists, and citizens interested in wildlife conservation.

As the Service also explains, important habitat management activities are being implemented:

We are using fire as a management tool after over 60 years of fire suppression on the refuge. Past logging, grazing and suppression of fire . . . [have] created pine stands with tree densities 2 to 4 times the pre-settlement condition. Large trees greater than 24 inches (60 cm) in diameter constitute less than 10% of the stands. Greater than 75% of the refuge ponderosa pine forest exists as closed canopy, multi-storied stands with similar age and size structure. Fuel loading in refuge pine stands is 5 times greater than the average for this forest type. Conditions are ripe for catastrophic loss due to insects, disease, and [wild]fire.

Establishment of this refuge was made possible mostly with revenues from the sale of Migratory Bird Hunting and Conservation Stamps (Duck Stamps). Vital partnerships with private organizations are assisting the refuge. Ducks Unlimited, Inc. has helped enhance roughly 100 acres of the refuge's wetland habitat. The Spokane Chapter of National Audubon Society has been assisting with riparian habitat restoration and has obtained a grant to fund volunteer training workshops as part of the refuge's environmental education program. The Friends of Turnbull National Wildlife Refuge supports environmental education.

The refuge is open daily during daylight hours. There is a small entrance fee from March 1 through October. The refuge office, located at the east end of Smith Rd., is open on weekdays, except national holidays.

Visitor activities include wildlife observation; driving the 5.5-mile loop auto tour route; walking a (wheelchair-accessible) boardwalk; hiking a number of trails, including a 4.75-mile stretch of the state-managed Columbia Plateau Trail; bicycling on the auto tour road; cross-country skiing; and interpretive and environmental education programs. Camping is not permitted on the refuge, but facilities are available at nearby private campgrounds. Swimming, boating, fishing, and hunting are presently not permitted on the refuge.

Lodgings and meals are available in Cheney and Spokane.

Access to the refuge from Exit 270 (Four Lakes) on I-90 (about 11 miles southwest of downtown Spokane) is south and then southwest 6 miles on State Hwy. 904 to Cheney, and left 4 miles on Cheney Plaza Rd.

Information: Turnbull NWR, 26010 South Smith Rd., Cheney, WA 99004; tel.: (509) 235-4723.

Willapa, consisting of 14,755 acres, was established in 1937 to protect and manage important habitats for migrating and wintering waterfowl, shorebirds, and other wildlife. The refuge is located in Willapa Bay and at the northern end of Long Beach Peninsula, in southwestern Washington.

The refuge's diverse coastal habitats include areas of temperate forest with some old-growth Sitka spruces, western hemlocks, and western redcedars; and an area of dike-enclosed grassland maintained for the benefit of geese and other wildlife. In the spring, the bay's mudflats are a mecca for more than 100,000 migrating shorebirds. Willapa Bay, the second largest estuary on the Pacific Coast, has been designated as a Western Hemisphere Shorebird Reserve.

Extensive areas of eelgrass in Willapa Bay attract large concentrations of migrating and wintering brant. The bay is a key staging area for this species of goose prior to their spring flight to Arctic breeding grounds in Canada, Alaska, and Siberia. (See the Humboldt Bay NWR text.)

Marine mammals that can sometimes be observed include harbor seals, sea lions, porpoises, and migrating gray whales. Sandbars in the bay offer pupping grounds for harbor seals. Willapa Bay also attracts various species of salmon, including chum, coho, and chinook. The refuge is presently working to restore and enhance anadromous fish runs on refuge streams within the Willapa Basin. These efforts include the recent installation of fish ladders that are reopening access to two streams, so that salmon can once again reach their spawning grounds.

A major part of this refuge is Long Island, the largest estuarine island on the Pacific Coast. As described by the Fish and Wildlife Service:

Long Island's 5,460 acres contain a rare 274-acre remnant of old growth lowland coastal forest known as Cedar Grove. Some western red cedar trees in this grove have been growing for more than 900 years. The rain-drenched forests on Long Island grow rapidly and densely, with salal, huckleberry and salmonberry bushes carpeting the forest floor beneath tall western hemlock, Sitka spruce and western red cedar trees. Fallen trees, called nurse logs, provide shelter and a rich growing medium for young trees. . . .

The forests of Long Island are home to mammals such as black bear, Roosevelt elk, black-tailed deer, beaver, and river otter. The mature forests provide special niches for numerous sensitive wildlife species. The largest trees provide wide sturdy limbs suitable for the platform nests of marbled murrelets, a seabird that has lost much of its historical nesting habitat due to logging of old growth forests. Bald eagles and great blue herons also nest in large trees on the island.

More than 240 bird species have been recorded here.

The Roosevelt elk is the refuge's largest terrestrial mammal. This subspecies, which is darker and somewhat larger than the Rocky Mountain elk, ranges along the Pacific Northwest coast, from northern California northward in scattered areas along the Oregon coast, Washington's Olympic Peninsula, and Canada's Vancouver Island. These stately animals graze across the refuge's open fields and marshes, and use the shelter of forested areas for cover.

The refuge's RIEKKOLA UNIT contains managed grasslands within the diked tidelands at the southern end of the bay. This habitat offers feeding and resting habitat for wintering Canada geese, ducks, and other wildlife. The grazing of cattle during the summer helps maintain fields of short grass that is favored by the geese. The LEWIS and PORTER POINT UNITS are managed for their important freshwater marsh habitat, where water levels are manipulated to provide food for migratory waterfowl, rearing habitat for salmonids, and breeding areas for aquatic amphibians.

The refuge's LEADBETTER POINT UNIT contains beaches and sand dunes and is one of three nesting areas in Washington used by the threatened snowy plover. As the Fish and Wildlife Service explains:

These small cryptic shorebirds nest on the upper ocean beaches in small scrapes in the sand. Their well camouflaged eggs can be inadvertently stepped on by people or run over by vehicles. Incubating adults are easily frightened off the nests, allowing sand to cover the eggs or predators to destroy them. A 372-acre portion of Leadbetter Point along the ocean side is closed to ALL public entry, including foot travel, generally from March through September to protect the nesting snowy plovers.

As explained by refuge's wildlife biologist, Deborah Jaques, "Leadbetter Point is one of the only locations on the Oregon-Washington coast where snowy plovers nest successfully without the use of predator exclosures. Its remote location, natural balance of predators, and continual sand erosion and deposition make it one of the most ecologically sound plover-nesting areas on the West Coast."

A very serious problem that threatens the ecological integrity of Willapa Bay and refuge is the rapidly spreading infestation of a non-native, invasive plant, Spartina (smooth cordgrass). The Fish and Wildlife Service says:

Willapa Bay has the largest Spartina infestation of any estuary on the Pacific Coast. Spartina eliminates the value of intertidal areas for wildlife, the aquiculture industry and recreational pursuits, because it forms dense, monotypic stands of vegetation, traps sediment, and alters existing hydrologic processes.

Spartina alterniflora was introduced in 1894. In 1991, there were approximately 2,500 acres of Spartina in Willapa Bay. The infestation . . . [by late 2001, covered] between 15,000 and 18,000 acres of tidelands, and it is projected to occupy 56,000 out of the 80,000 acres of Willapa Bay if left uncontrolled. . . .

Control and eradication of Spartina is difficult, dangerous, and expensive. Large tidal fluctuations, unconsolidated mud, costly herbicides and control equipment, the rapid rate of spread for Spartina, as well as strict water quality regulations have enabled the Spartina infestation to overwhelm control efforts.

Establishment of this refuge was made possible partly with revenues from the sale of Migratory Bird Hunting and Conservation Stamps (Duck Stamps). More than 200 acres of the refuge's wetland habitat have recently been restored.

Parts of the refuge are open daily during daylight hours, with the exception of overnight camping at five designated primitive campgrounds on Long Island (campsites are available on a first-come, first-served basis). The refuge headquarters is open on weekdays, except national holidays.

Visitor activities include wildlife observation; hiking; kayaking and boating; fishing; waterfowl hunting on the refuge's Riekkola and Lewis units; archery hunting (elk, deer, bear, and grouse) on Long Island; and rifle big-game hunting on some refuge areas during the designated seasons. Hiking opportunities on Long Island include the 0.7-mile Trail of the Ancients, which visitors can reach by walking 2.5 miles on a gravel road that leads from the Long Island boat landing. Trails that can be reached by motor vehicle include a 5-mile dike on the refuge's Riekkola Unit and a network of trails, including a 1.1-mile interpretive loop, on the Leadbetter Point Unit and adjacent state park. Trails at Leadbetter Point are flooded during the rainy season (usually from October through May).

Lodgings and meals are available in Ilwaco, Seaview, Long Beach, Ocean Park, South Bend, and Raymond, Wash., and Astoria, Ore.

Access to the refuge office from the junction of State Hwy. 4 and U.S. Hwy. 101 is about five miles southwest on Hwy. 101. Prospective visitors to the Lewis and Riekkola units and to Long Island are urged to obtain directional information from the refuge office. To reach the Leadbetter Point Unit from the junction of Highways 4 and 101, drive southwest 13 miles on Hwy. 101, right onto State Hwy. 103 for 2 miles to Seaview, right and continue 11 miles on Hwy. 103 to Ocean Park, jogging right and then left on Hwy. 103 to Oysterville, jogging left and then right onto Stackpole Rd. to its end.

Information: Willapa NWR, 3888 SR 101, Ilwaco, WA 98624; tel.: (360) 484-3482.

West Virginia

Canaan Valley, presently comprising 3,292 acres toward an authorized goal of 24,000 acres, was established in 1994. It is located in the Allegheny Mountains, in northeastern West Virginia. The name *Canaan* is locally pronounced kah-NANE. The refuge protects an extraordinary freshwater mountain-valley wetland and boreal-forest ecosystem that is the result of Canaan Valley's high altitude and cool, damp climate. At 3,200 feet elevation, this is the largest high-elevation valley east of the Mississippi River.

The refuge already includes important components of the largest freshwater wetland in the central and southern Appalachians and relict boreal habitats. Continued land acquisitions will occur only from willing sellers. Management objectives of the refuge include the protection and, where appropriate, the enhancement and restoration of these ecologically rich habitats and their diversity of plant and animal communities. Nearly 600 species of plants have already been identified in the valley, and the refuge presently lists more than 160 species of birds that are known or expected to occur here.

As described by the U.S. Fish and Wildlife Service:

Canaan Valley has been described as "a little bit of Canada gone astray." The high elevation of the valley floor gives it a boreal climate, colder than that of the surrounding area. Some plants living here are usually found much farther north. Red spruce, a ridge-top species in the high elevations of West Virginia, works its way down the mountain slopes in the valley. . . . The combination of wet soils and uplands, forests, shrub lands, and open lands throughout the valley adds to the diversity of habitats. . . .

A patchwork of twenty-three wetland types, including bogs, shrub swamps and wet meadows, carpets the valley floor. At approximately 7,000 acres, this is the largest wetland complex in West Virginia. . . .

. . . ducks call, herons fly, and shorebirds probe the earth for food. . . . Mallards, black ducks, and wood ducks nest. . . . Solitary sandpipers are found wherever a small pocket of wetland exists. . . . Beavers ply the [Blackwater] river, finding dam sites from place to place. . . .

One-hundred years ago, people altered this landscape, taking out its timber. . . . the recovery of the forest has been slow. Stands of spruce, balsam fir and hemlock remind us of the boreal forest that once was the dominant cover type of the valley. . . .

Woodlands of beech, cherry, maple, etc., cover the slopes of the mountains and add color to our fall. Squirrels, ruffed grouse, turkey and bear all make their homes in these woodlands. Wood thrush, ovenbirds and woodland warblers also find their place here. The world's largest diversity of salamanders find their niche in these and other southern Appalachian woodland streams.

The refuge is open daily during daylight hours. There is no entrance fee. The refuge headquarters is open on weekdays, except national holidays. Visitor center hours fluctuate seasonally; visitors should call ahead, to obtain current hours.

Visitor activities include wildlife observation, education and interpretive programs, hiking on several trails, wildlife viewing by horseback riding and bicycling (allowed on Forest Service Rd. 80), fishing on the Blackwater River (along Timberline Rd.), and hunting on parts of the refuge during the designated seasons. Although camping is not permitted on the refuge, facilities are provided on adjacent Canaan Valley Resort State Park.

Lodgings and meals are available locally and in Davis.

Access to the refuge from U.S. Hwy. 219 at Thomas is southeast about eight miles on State Hwy. 32; or from U.S. Hwy. 33 at Harman, it is north about nine miles on State Hwy. 32.

Information: Canaan Valley NWR, HC 70, Box 200, Davis, WV 26260; tel.: (304) 866-3858.

Wisconsin

Horicon, comprising 21,417 acres, was established in 1941 to enhance and protect the northern two-thirds of the nation's largest freshwater cattail marsh, encompassing 32,000 acres, primarily for the benefit of migratory waterfowl. The refuge is located in southeastern Wisconsin.

The refuge attracts numerous species of ducks—notably the largest eastern breeding population of redhead ducks, as well as many shorebirds, marsh birds, and other wildlife. Roughly 200 tundra swans and 800 American white pelicans pause to rest and feed during autumn migration; some pelicans also nest here. Wisconsin's largest great blue heron rookery is located on the southern part of the marsh.

The refuge provides critical stopover habitat for impressive concentrations of migrating Canada geese. From September through December, up to a million of these geese, which nest in the Hudson Bay area of Canada, migrate through here on their way to wintering areas along the lower Ohio River Valley. More than 200,000 of them congregate in the area on peak days of October and November.

The southern one-third of the marsh lies within the 11,000-acre Horicon Marsh State Wildlife Area, managed by the Wisconsin Department of Natural Resources. Consequently, the entire marsh ecosystem is protected for wildlife. The wetland has been designated as a Wetland of International Importance and a Globally Important Bird Area.

As described by refuge ranger Molly Stoddard:

Horicon Marsh lies within a shallow, peat-filled lake bed, measuring 14 miles long by three-to-five miles wide that was scoured out of limestone by the Green Bay lobe of the massive Wisconsin continental glaciation, when it retreated from the region about 12,000 years ago. The so-called original vegetation of the marsh was possibly sedge meadow and/or a peat marsh. It very likely contained much greater diversity of plant life. According to early accounts, cranberry and wild rice thrived here.

The name "Horicon" is a Mohican Indian word meaning pure, clean water. . . . In 1846, settlers . . . constructed a dam on the Rock River, where it flows out of the marsh, converting the marsh into the largest man-made lake in the world at that time. . . .

Once the dam was removed in 1869, it took three years for the lake to drain back to a marsh. Already popular for waterfowl hunting, the area became famous for uncontrolled market and recreational hunting. Starting in 1883, two shooting clubs leased much of the marshlands and provided restricted, exclusive access to their members. Without laws to conserve wildlife, hunters could shoot anything they wanted, any time they wanted, in any quantity they wanted, in any way they wanted, and with any type of weapon they wanted. . . .

Market-hunted ducks were packed in wooden barrels, with marsh hay, and shipped by the hundreds by railroad to upscale restaurants and hotels in Milwaukee, Chicago, and New York. Market hunting persisted during the shooting club years and provided continuous hunting pressure on the Horicon Marsh. However, it is obvious that ducks could have been obliterated from the marsh without the clubs. These shooting clubs ironically represent a transition period between commercial exploitation and conservation. They were the first to impose their own voluntary rules on shooting seasons and techniques, to control water levels for the benefit of waterfowl, and plant duck foods, such as wild rice. And the clubs eventually contributed greatly to the fight to save and restore the marsh. In about 1920, they formed a group called the Horicon Marsh Game Protective Association, which recognized the advantage of limited entry to the marsh for the long-term conservation of waterfowl. This group later became a chapter of the Izaak Walton League of America.

Before the marsh was saved and restored for wildlife, the greatest impact struck. From 1910 to about 1918, an attempt was made by agricultural interests to dredge, ditch, and drain the wetlands—without authority and in direct violation of a ruling of the state supreme court. Their goal: to improve the land for farming. . . .

Ditching and draining the marsh permanently impacted its ecology—destroying the original marsh vegetation, promoting the invasion of weed plants, and increasing the risk of peat fires that sometimes raged for weeks at a time. The Main Ditch straightened and lowered the channel of the Rock River, which increased the speed of flow and lowered the water table by about a foot. According to the Izaak Walton League, "That huge ditch became a vampire stream, which bled white the famous Horicon Marsh." Ditching and draining "succeeded in spoiling the best ducking ground in the whole country, as there is not water enough left to run a boat, and the mud is too soft and deep to walk over." Attempts at muck farming ultimately failed because effective drainage for that activity could not be achieved.

Once only viewed as wasteland, the marsh now really was a wasteland. With low water, there was no food for waterfowl, and it was unusable for transportation, recreation, industry, or agriculture.

After a long struggle during the 1920s and 1930s, the Izaak Walton League and other protection advocates finally achieved success in urging Congress to give this ecologically significant area the protection it so richly deserved. Establishment of Horicon refuge was made possible partly with revenues from the sale of Migratory Bird Hunting and Conservation Stamps (Duck Stamps). Ducks Unlimited, Inc. has helped enhance nearly 3,000 acres of the refuge's wetland habitat. The University of Wisconsin–Stevens Point and the U.S. Geological Survey have installed monitoring devices and have been carrying out research to learn more about the marsh's water quality.

The refuge's primary management activity is the management of water levels for the benefit of waterfowl and shorebirds. Molly Stoddard says:

The presence or absence of water, water depth, and timing are all coordinated to produce various stages of marsh plant succession, upon which the birds rely. Various impoundments, subdivided off the main body of the marsh using a system of dikes and water-control structures, are managed on seasonal, annual, and multiple-year cycles. Because of changing water levels, you may notice some wetland areas of open, deep water; others with dense stands of cattails, and yet others with bare mudflats.

In addition to the refuge's more than 16,000 acres of wetlands, there are also more than 4,000 acres of forested and shrubby uplands. The refuge also contains about 3,600 acres of grasslands, which are periodically treated with prescribed burning. The use of fire helps provide improved nesting habitat for some species of ducks and shorebirds, causes ecologically important nutrient cycling, and promotes a greater natural diversity of plant life.

Yet another significant management activity is the installation of nesting platforms for ospreys, which is a state-listed threatened species in Wisconsin. As the Fish and Wildlife Service reported in 2001, "Alliant Energy donated two utility poles and provided staff and equipment to install the poles on August 14. A three-foot-wide, octagon-shaped platform was attached to the top of each pole. The platforms are 25 feet above the ground and are made of wood with chicken wire."

The refuge is open daily during daylight hours. There is no entrance fee. The visitor center is open daily in spring and autumn and on weekdays the rest of the year, except national holidays.

Visitor activities include wildlife observation (including huge numbers of waterfowl in the autumn seen from a popular roadside pullout on State Hwy. 49), interpretive and environmental programs and tours, driving the three-mile auto tour route and the three-mile Main Dike Rd. (open from April 15 to September 15), hiking on a number of trails, viewing marsh habitat from a (wheelchair-accessible) boardwalk, bicycling on the auto tour route and Main Dike Rd., cross-country skiing on trails and the auto tour route, snowshoeing, fishing, and hunting on most of the refuge during the designated seasons. Camping is not permitted on the refuge, but facilities are available nearby. April is the best month to see large concentrations of ducks, May is the best for warblers and other neotropical migratory songbirds, and October–November are the best for Canada geese. More than 265 bird species have been recorded on this refuge.

Although canoeing, kayaking, and boating are not permitted on the refuge, they are allowed on the adjacent state wildlife area, where there are six launching ramps. Canoe and kayak rentals are available in the city of Horicon.

Insect repellent is advised during the warmer months

Access to the refuge's visitor center from the intersection of U.S. Hwy. 41 and State Hwy. 49 (about 13 miles south of Fond du Lac) is west 12 miles on Hwy. 49, left 3.5 miles on County Rd. Z, and right on Headquarters Rd.; or from the intersection of U.S. Hwy. 151 and State Hwy. 49, it is east 6 miles on Hwy. 49, right 3.5 miles on County Rd. Z, and right onto Headquarters Rd.

Information: Horicon NWR, W4279 Headquarters Rd., Mayville, WI 53050; tel.: (920) 387-2658.

Necedah, containing 43,656 acres, was established in 1939 to manage numerous pools and impoundments, bogs, woodlands, and oak savanna for the benefit of a large diversity of migratory waterfowl and other wildlife, in central Wisconsin. The refuge's wetlands are a remnant of the Great Central Wisconsin Swamp—a once-extensive expanse of peat bogs, interlaced with sandy ridges. This landscape was created when the most recent continental glaciation of this region was melting and withdrawing northward, roughly 10,000 years ago. The refuge's name is derived from a Ho-chunk Indian word that means "land of yellow waters"—referring to the brownish-yellow color of waters that are stained by minerals from peat-bog soils.

Following periods of timber harvesting; various attempts to drain the wetlands; farming; wildfires; and the impact of the Great Depression of the 1930s, numerous farmsteads in this area were abandoned. Some of these lands were purchased by the federal government.

The refuge attracts large concentrations of Canada geese, ducks of many species, shorebirds, bald eagles, and numerous neotropical migratory songbirds as they pause here during their spring and autumn migrations or come to breed and raise their young. Around mid-October, the refuge's star avian attraction is the spectacular concentration of greater sandhill cranes, totaling between 2,000 and 2,500 of these four-foot-tall birds. Great numbers of them come here again in the spring and perform their awesome courtship displays. The best months for bird-watching are April through early May and late September through October. More than 220 bird species have been recorded here.

An especially significant and exciting wildlife management program on this refuge is the reintroduction of the federally listed endangered whooping crane (See the Aransas and Chassahowitzka NWR texts for further information). As Refuge Manager Larry Wargowsky explains:

A new chapter of refuge history was initiated in 1999, when Necedah National Wildlife Refuge was selected by the Whooping Crane Recovery Team (WCRT) as the site for reestablishing an eastern population of whooping cranes. The federally endangered whooping crane almost became extinct . . . with only 15 or 16 birds left in the world in 1941-1942. Today, only one migratory population exists, with fewer than 200 birds over-wintering at Aransas NWR in Texas. Any catastrophic event, such as a hurricane, oil spill, disease outbreak, could jeopardize . . . [the then-lone migratory population on Aransas refuge, in Texas.] The WCRT selection of Wisconsin for a new separate, distinct migratory population offers new security for this magnificent endangered species.

This ambitious project started in 2000 with a pilot study project using sandhill cranes, trained by foster humans to follow three small ultralight aircraft more than 1,200 miles to the Chassahowitzka NWR in Florida and return on their own to Necedah NWR in 2001. The pilot project was a success and later in 2001, a small flock of whooping cranes was trained to follow ultralights to Chassahowitzka refuge.

The project was not only successful in starting to establish a new population of whooping cranes in the eastern United States, but also instantly brought national and even international media attention to Necedah. . . .

The historic, first ultralight-led migration with only whooping cranes began on October 17, 2001, with eight whooping cranes departing Necedah NWR. One bird turned back on the first day and was recaptured and trucked the entire route, for fear it would pull out again and lead other cranes away from the ultralights. Only one fatality occurred during the entire migration, with a bird striking a powerline after a strong windstorm collapsed the temporary holding pen at night, releasing the birds. Heavy morning fog, high temperatures, and headwinds delayed the migration. However, the longest human-led migration with an endangered species ended on December 5, 2001, on day 50, when seven birds settled into their winter home on Chassahowitzka NWR. . . . Two of the cranes were killed by bobcats in Florida. In spring 2002, the remaining five birds successfully migrated northward on their own—four arriving back on Necedah Refuge on April 19, and the other on May 3. They covered the 1,200 miles in only 8 days of flying, taking a more direct route and using thermal air currents that allowed for periods of gliding. Their progress was monitored with satellite and conventional transmitters.

In the first seven years, the program has led 108 whooping cranes south. By February 2008, the total number of successfully reintroduced eastern migratory cranes in the wild had reached 76 individuals. (Adding together all whooping cranes of both the western and eastern populations, as of 2008 there are about 485 birds—340 in the wild and 145 in captivity.)

As Larry Wargowsky has said:

The success of the project continues to be due to the tremendous teamwork of the refuge's dedicated staff in conjunction with the Whooping Crane Eastern Partnership that was formed in 2000. The governmental and nonprofit partners are the Whooping Crane Recovery Team, U.S. Fish and Wildlife Service, the International Crane Foundation, Wisconsin Department of Natural Resources, The Natural Resources Foundation, Operation Migration (Canada), The Patuxent Wildlife Research Center, and the National Fish and Wildlife Foundation [plus several corporations]. This partnership has joined forces to safeguard the rarest species of crane in the world by assisting with the project's funding and support services. More than half of the funding for the project comes from private donations. The continuing project is aimed at eventually establishing 25 breeding pairs and a total of 125 individuals in this eastern population of the whooping crane, to help in the recovery of North America's tallest bird.

The wolf is another species of wildlife receiving special attention on this refuge. As explained by the Fish and Wildlife Service, Necedah refuge "provides habitat for the southernmost pack of gray wolves in Wisconsin and the United States. The gray wolf . . . was listed as federally endangered in Wisconsin in 1967, when only a handful remained. Today, wolves are on their way to recovery, with 70 packs established in the northern and central portions of the state" as of 2001.

From mid-June through early August, the annual flights of the federally listed, endangered Karner blue butterfly are a special attraction. Necedah refuge currently has the largest population of this species in the world. These colorful little butterflies, with only a one-inch wingspread, depend upon the refuge's oak-savanna habitat where their larvae feed entirely upon lupine plants and the adults thrive on the nectar of various species of wildflowers.

Establishment of Necedah refuge was made possible partly with revenues from the sale of Migratory Bird Hunting and Conservation Stamps (Duck Stamps). Ducks Unlimited, Inc. has helped enhance more than 1,100 acres of the refuge's wetland habitat.

The refuge is open daily during daylight hours. There is no entrance fee. The refuge headquarters is open on weekdays, except national holidays.

Visitor activities include wildlife and butterfly observation; viewing the refuge and wildlife from an observation tower and several decks; driving a 13-mile auto hot-spots route on township roads that run through parts of the refuge; hiking on three trails; cross-country skiing and snowshoeing on ungroomed trails (December 15 through March); non-motorized boating, kayaking, and canoeing on Goose and Sprague pools; motorized boating (permitted on the Suk-Cerney flowage); fishing in designated waters; and hunting on parts of the refuge during the designated seasons. Camping is not allowed on the refuge, but facilities are available at nearby state and county parks.

Insect repellent is advised during the warmer months.

Lodgings and meals are available in Necedah, New Lisbon, Camp Douglas, Tomah, Black River Falls, and Wisconsin Rapids.

Access to the refuge from the Exit 61 (New Lisbon) on I-94 is north 12 miles on State Hwy. 80 to the town of Necedah, left onto State Hwy. 21, and following refuge directional signs to the refuge headquarters, located at the junction of Headquarters Rd. and Grand Dike Rd. (20th St. West).

Information: Necedah NWR, W. 7996 20th St. West, Necedah, WI 54646; tel.: (608) 565-2551.

Trempealeau, comprising 6,200 acres, was established in 1936 to restore, enhance, and protect floodplain wetland habitats that attract large concentrations of migratory waterfowl and other wildlife, adjacent to the Mississippi and Trempealeau rivers along the western edge of Wisconsin. *Trempealeau* is a French word meaning "mountain with wet feet."

This refuge initially contained just over 700 acres but was expanded in 1979 to its present size, with acquisition of the former Delta Fish and Fur Farm. Approximately 80 percent of the refuge consists of marsh and open pools. The remaining acreage supports scattered areas of swampy bottomland hardwoods, shrubby and meadow habitats, and several hundred acres of gently rolling upland sand prairie.

As the Fish and Wildlife Service says:

Although now isolated from adjacent rivers by railroad dikes, Refuge wetlands were once backwaters of the Mississippi River. Hence, the remains of old river side channels and oxbows can be found in the western portion of the Refuge. Prior to 1900, the Trempealeau River entered the Mississippi from the north, forming a large delta at a point which is now at the center of the main Refuge pool. The Trempealeau River channel was later diverted to the east and barrier dikes were constructed to exclude floodwaters.

A railroad dike borders the southern edge of the refuge for six miles, between the western boundary and Trempealeau Mountain. This dike creates a barrier between the refuge's pool and the Mississippi River's main channel. No culverts exist to permit any interchange between the river and the pool; so, the refuge is protected from impacts of barge traffic and from river-level fluctuations resulting from U.S. Army Corps of Engineers water management.

Prominent among the refuge's breeding waterfowl are wood ducks, which nest in cavities of bottomland hardwood trees and several thousand of which have been known to gather on the refuge in the autumn. Other abundant nesting waterfowl include blue-winged teal, mallards, hooded mergansers, and Canada geese.

The black tern has been the focus of special research on nesting habits and factors affecting nesting success and habitat quality. About sixty pairs of them build their nests within areas of dense water lily pads and stands of bulrushes and cattails, annually producing between 100 and 150 juveniles. Tundra swans are a conspicuous migrant, with anywhere from 500 to nearly 1,000 pausing to rest and feed. A few bald eagles winter on the refuge, more than 200 of which can be observed when the ice goes out in the marsh. The best times for observing large concentrations of migrating birds on the refuge are April through mid-May and October through mid-November. More than 250 species of birds have been recorded here.

The refuge also supports white-tailed deer, approximately fifty colonies of beavers and lots of muskrats. Monarch butterflies thrive on the nectar of one of the refuge's most beautiful wildflowers, the blazing star.

One of the refuge's ecologically important management activities is prescription burning. As explained by the Fish and Wildlife Service:

Traveling through the refuge in the springtime, visitors will notice the blackened fields in several areas, where fire has occurred. Those fields may not look pleasing just after the refuge staff burns them, but in a few weeks native flowers, such as wild lupine and spiderwort, will be blooming. The grasses and flowers that are native to the refuge sand prairies have adapted [naturally] to fire. Fire restores vigor to the perennial native plants and helps the seeds of other plants to sprout. Fire also "sets back" the non-native grasses, such as brome, quack, and bluegrass, and discourages trees and shrubs from invading the prairie.

The refuge is open daily during daylight hours. There is no entrance fee. The refuge headquarters is open on weekdays, except national holidays. Public access to the refuge is commonly restricted during annual spring high water, when part of the main entrance road is inundated; usually the refuge's Marshland Rd. is then open to motor vehicles.

Visitor activities include wildlife observation; viewing the marsh from an observation deck; driving the five-mile interpretive Wildlife Drive; hiking on several trails (one of which is wheelchair-accessible); bicycling (part of the Great River State Trail, popular for bicycling, runs through the refuge); cross-country skiing and snowshoeing on un-groomed trails; canoeing, kayaking, and boating (only hand-powered watercraft or boats with electric motors; a boat-launching ramp is available); fishing; ice fishing; and hunting on parts of the refuge during the designated seasons. Around mid-October, the refuge hosts a special two-day waterfowl hunt for mobility-challenged hunters. Although camping is not permitted on the refuge, facilities are available on the adjacent Perrot State Park and elsewhere.

Insect repellent is advised during the warmer months.

Lodgings and meals are available in such communities as Winona, Minnesota and Trempealeau and Fountain City, Wisconsin.

Access to the refuge from Winona, Minn. is across the Mississippi River on Wisc. State Hwy. 54, right onto State Highways 54/35 for five miles, and right just over a mile on West Prairie Rd. to the refuge entrance. From Trempealeau, Wis., north five miles on Hwy. 35 to Centerville, left on Highways 35/54 just over three miles, and left just over a mile on West Prairie Rd.

Information. Trempealeau NWR, W28488 Refuge Rd., Trempealeau, WI 54661; tel.: (608) 539-2311.

Whittlesey Creek was established in 1999 to enhance and protect important coastal wetland and spring-fed stream habitats for migratory birds and anadromous fish at the mouth of Whittlesey Creek. The refuge, which is part of an extensive, shallow wetland complex, is located at the head of Lake Superior's Chequamegon Bay, in northern Wisconsin.

Habitats within the projected refuge boundary of 540 acres include Lake Superior coastal wetlands, sedge meadow, lowland hardwood swamp, and black spruce bog. The Fish and Wildlife Service explains that refuge habitats have been

altered substantially by human use. One hundred ten acres of sedge meadow was converted for agricultural use earlier this century and altered further for construction of a golf course. Four non-vegetated ponds were created during construction of the golf course. . . . Changes in water regime as well as past land use has changed wetland vegetation; most wet meadow acres are dominated by reed canary grass, an invasive non-native species. Some wet meadows are becoming dominated by shrubs and might re-grow to low-land swamp with black ash and cedar.

In 1949, the Army Corps of Engineers dredged 4,500 feet of Whittlesey Creek stream channel in an effort to de-water and stabilize the floodplain. . . .

Even with this significant alteration, the wetland portion of the [creek's] mouth constitutes a rare coastal wetland; and Whittlesey Creek remains a high-quality stream, with spring-fed waters that flow year-round.

A major habitat-management goal of the refuge is the restoration and protection of Whittlesey, Little Whittlesey, and Terwilliger creeks for the benefit of migrating, spawning, and rearing of anadromous coho salmon and a strain of brook trout, known as "coaster" brook trout; restoration, as much as possible, of the historical hydrological conditions of Whittlesey Creek and coastal wetlands. Other planned activities include the restoration and management of habitat for waterfowl, neotropical songbirds, and other migratory birds; the enhancement of existing constructed ponds for the benefit of wildlife; management of the refuge for compatible wildlife-dependent recreational uses; and coordination of these management activities with adjacent managers of the Wisconsin Department of Natural Resources and the U.S. Forest Service's Northern Great Lakes Visitor Center.

As the Fish and Wildlife Service explains, "The Service intends to continue its partnership with the Northern Great Lakes Visitor Center, which includes . . . having one or more Service staff at the Center and contributing to the Center's mission. This staff will oversee Refuge operations and help develop and coordinate education and interpretive programs at the Center and Refuge."

Refuge manager Pam Dryer says, "The Whittlesey Creek Refuge is a little refuge with a big impact. It has a quality coastal wetland that helps feed the huge Lake Superior, it has a significant anadromous fish population, and it protects the last remaining stretch of the large coastal wetland complex in Chequamegon Bay."

It is expected that the refuge will be open daily during daylight hours, when sufficient lands have been acquired. Priority visitor uses are planned to include wildlife observation, hiking, interpretive and conservation education programs, fishing, and hunting on part of the refuge during the designated season. The adjacent Northern Great Lakes Visitor Center is open daily, except Thanksgiving, Christmas, and New Year's Day.

Lodgings and meals are available in Ashland.

Access to the Northern Great Lakes Visitor Center is west two miles on U.S. Hwy. 2 from Ashland.

Information: Whittlesey Creek NWR, 29270 County Hwy. G, Ashland, WI 54806; tel.: (715) 685-2678.

Wyoming

National Elk Refuge, containing 24,778 acres, was established in 1912 to enhance and protect important wintering habitat for the Jackson Hole herd of Rocky Mountain elk. The refuge adjoins the southern boundary of Grand Teton National Park, in northwestern Wyoming. Elk are also called wapiti, a Shawnee Indian name for "white rump," in reference to their pale-yellowish rump.

During the unusually bitter cold and snowy winters of 1909, 1910, and 1911, thousands of elk perished for lack of adequate forage. In response to the request of many alarmed local citizens, who asked for help from both the state and federal governments, funds were provided to purchase hay for the starving animals and to acquire the initial acreage for this refuge.

From November through April, the refuge supports roughly 7,500 of these great mammals—more than half of the herd's total population. Most of them spend the summer at higher, cooler elevations in the forests and meadows of Grand Teton National Park, the southern part of Yellowstone National Park, and the Bridger-Teton National Forest. This is the longest elk herd migration in the United States (outside of Alaska). The National Elk Refuge provides vital elk wintering habitat as an integral part of the Greater Yellowstone Ecosystem. Although farms, ranches, ranchettes, and the community of Jackson occupy much of the valley's original elk-wintering range, the National Elk Refuge protects about a quarter of the historic wintering habitat.

The carrying capacity of the refuge is determined by the Fish and Wildlife Service staff, in consultation with the Wyoming Game and Fish Department. So as to not exceed the habitat's capacity to sustain these grazing and browsing animals, a regulated late autumn elk hunt is carried out on the refuge and adjacent public lands. In the past, some elk have also been transplanted from the refuge to establish small populations in other parts of the country.

The valley of Jackson Hole is magnificently framed by the jagged peaks of the Teton Mountains to the northwest and the Gros Ventre Range to the southeast. Refuge habitats include grassy meadows, marshes, ponds, aspen groves, riparian woodland along the Gros Ventre River, and scattered rock outcroppings on sagebrush-covered foothills of the Gros Ventres. The highest point on the refuge is atop 6,509-foot Miller Butte.

The Fish and Wildlife Service maintains the refuge's grassland forage with an irrigation system, seeding, and periodic prescribed burns. When the depth of snow or a hard, icy crust prevents the elk from reaching their natural forage, the refuge provides them with pelletized alfalfa hay. To assist with the cost of elk feeding, the local troop of Boy Scouts holds an annual auction (on the Jackson town square) of elk antlers that have been shed on the refuge.

Other large ungulates that usually spend the winter here include bighorn sheep, moose, mule deer, and approximately 500 bison (buffalo). Among other wildlife are trumpeter swans, Canada geese, and many species of ducks that are attracted to the refuge's ponds and marshes. The greater sage-grouse inhabits the sagebrush habitat. (See the Seedskadee NWR text for description of this grouse.) More than 170 bird species have been recorded here. November through April is the best time for viewing the elk and other wintering wildlife.

The refuge is open daily during daylight hours. There is no entrance fee. The visitor center, at 532 North Cache St., Jackson, is open daily, except on Christmas. The refuge headquarters is on Broadway St., a mile east of the Jackson town square, and is open on weekdays, except Christmas.

Visitor activities include wildlife observation; viewing wildlife from turnouts along the east side of U.S. Hwy. 26; educational programs and exhibits at the refuge's visitor center and the National Museum of Wildlife Art (located two miles north of Jackson on U.S. Hwy. 26); driving unpaved refuge roads (Flat Creek and Curtis Canyon roads are open seasonally); limited hiking; interpretive horse-drawn sleigh rides (a fee is charged and passengers must dress very warmly) from late December through March, beginning at the museum; picnicking (facilities are provided), trout fishing (some refuge waters are closed to fishing), and elk hunting on the northern half of the refuge during the designated season (a limited number of elk permits is issued under a system of weekly drawings). Camping is not permitted on the refuge, but facilities are available in Grand Teton and Yellowstone national parks and Bridger-Teton National Forest.

Lodgings and meals are available in Jackson, and Grand Teton and Yellowstone parks.

Access to the National Elk Refuge is between Jackson and Grand Teton National Park.

Information: National Elk Refuge, P.O. Box 510, Jackson, WY 83001; tel.: (307) 733-9212.

Seedskadee, consisting of 26,382 acres, was established in 1965 to enhance and protect a scenic, 36-mile stretch of the Green River, in the Green River Valley of southwestern Wyoming. The refuge consists of a mixture of cottonwoods, willows, and marsh habitat and expanses of arid, sagebrush-covered uplands. The refuge's name is derived from a Shoshone Indian word, *sisk-a-dee-agie*, which means "river of the prairie hen," for the sage-grouse that inhabits this area.

This refuge was established to help offset the loss of marsh and riparian habitats that resulted from construction of the Bureau of Reclamation's Fontenelle Dam, upstream from the refuge, and the Flaming Gorge Dam, downstream. The bureau has provided funds to acquire refuge lands and complete habitat enhancement projects. Some of the river water is diverted into adjacent wetland impoundments, to restore important marsh habitat. The water level in these wetlands is seasonally regulated by the Fish and Wildlife Service, to provide sufficient water for a large variety of wetland species such as trumpeter swans, geese, ducks, shorebirds, and rails during the spring, summer, and autumn. Adjacent to the marshy impoundments, native shrubs and grasses offer vital cover for nesting ducks.

Elsewhere along the river's former floodplain, groves of cottonwood trees and thickets of willows are dwindling because of the declining water table and lack of annual flooding. The refuge is trying to find ways to promote the growth of young cottonwoods, willows, and shrubs that provide food and shelter for such species as moose, mule deer, raptors, and songbirds.

Sagebrush uplands predominate on lands beyond the riparian bottomlands. Here the refuge is working to enhance habitat degradation caused by earlier overgrazing by livestock. Fencing is helping restore native shrubs and grasses to these areas.

One of the star attractions of the upland sagebrush areas of Seedskadee refuge is the greater sage-grouse. These large, grayish birds, which Lewis and Clark referred to as "cocks of the plains," are the size of a small turkey. The males measure about thirty inches in length. In the spring, the cocks congregate and strut about, rapidly and repeatedly performing their elaborate courtship displays.

Other prominent species of wildlife are moose, pronghorn, mule deer, prairie dogs, golden eagles, American white pelicans, trumpeter swans, Canada geese, various species of ducks and shorebirds, many neotropical migratory songbirds, and sandhill cranes. More than 225 species of birds have been recorded here.

The refuge is open daily during daylight hours. There is no entrance fee. The refuge headquarters, containing a small visitor center, is open on weekdays, except national holidays.

Visitor activities include wildlife observation; driving the refuge's three gravel tour roads; hiking; canoeing, rafting, and drift-boating on the river (four boat-launching sites are provided within the refuge, and another is upstream near Fontenelle Dam); fishing (the river supports a trophy trout fishery); and hunting (seasonal closures on parts of the refuge are sometimes implemented to decrease disturbance of sensitive species). Although camping is not permitted on the refuge, facilities are available near Fontenelle Dam.

The refuge's elevation is close to 6,500 feet. Winter visitors are advised to be well prepared for bitter cold and snowy conditions. Regardless of the season, the Fish and Wildlife Service advises visitors to bring adequate water, food, and fuel, as Seedskadee is 15 miles from the closest store and service station and 37 miles from the nearest town of Green River.

Lodgings and meals are available in Green River, Rock Springs, Kemmerer, Diamondville, LaBarge, and Farson.

Access to the refuge is west from Green River on I-80 for 6 miles to exit 83, northwest about 28 miles on State Hwy. 372, and east 2 miles to the refuge headquarters.

Information: Seedskadee NWR, P.O. Box 700, Green River, WY 82935; tel.: (307) 875-2187.

4

The Other National Wildlife Refuges

(Descriptions Arranged Alphabetically by State)

Alabama

Cahaba River was established in 2002 to manage a 7-mile stretch of Alabama's longest free-flowing river and adjacent lands for the protection of "64 rare and imperiled plant and animal species, 13 of which are nowhere else in the world." These species include the Cahaba shiner, goldline darter, round rocksnail, cylindrical lioplax snail, longleaf pine, and shoals lily (a.k.a. Cahaba lily). This refuge, presently containing about 3,000 acres, is in the early phases of land acquisition. As the F&WS says, "Development of public use programs and facilities such as hiking trails, interpretive kiosks, and fishing and hunting opportunities will play a large role in the future management of the refuge." Access from West Blockton (southeast of Tuscaloosa) is east on County Rd. 24 for about 6 miles. Information: (256) 848-7085.

Choctaw contains 4,218 acres to manage an area of bottomland hardwood forest, cypress sloughs, creeks and ponds, moist-soil impoundments, pine ridges, and croplands, in southwestern Alabama. The refuge attracts wintering waterfowl, wading birds, nesting wood ducks, alligators, and other wildlife. Access, from headquarters at 1310 College Ave., Jackson, is north on State Hwy. 69 to Coffeeville, left on U.S. Hwy. 84 for about 8 miles, right onto County Rd. 21 for about 4 miles to Barrytown, right onto County Rd. 14 to Womack Hill, and right. Information: (334) 246-3583.

Eufaula contains 11,184 acres to manage an area of impounded wetlands of Lake Eufaula and several tributary creeks along the Chatahoochee River, as well as woodland, oak savannah-grassland, and cropland. Concentrations of wintering waterfowl, wading birds, shorebirds, alligators, and other wildlife are attracted to the refuge, which is in southeastern Alabama and southwestern Georgia. Access from Eufaula is north 5 miles on U.S. Hwy. 431 to Lakeport State Park, and right onto State Hwy. 285 for 2.5 miles. Information: (334) 687-4065.

Fern Cave contains 199 acres to protect a large limestone cave that offers habitat for the threatened or endangered gray and Indiana bats and the American hart's-tongue fern. While entry to the cave is by research permit only, the refuge's upland hardwood forest is open to visitors. The refuge is 20 miles west of Scottsboro and 2 miles north of Paint Rock, in northern Alabama. Information: (256) 350-6639.

Key Cave contains 1,060 acres to protect two limestone caves that provide habitat for the endangered gray bat and Alabama cavefish. While entry to the caves is by research permit only, the refuge's grassland and hardwood forest are open to visitors. The refuge is about 5 miles southwest of Florence, in northern Alabama. Information: (256) 350-6639.

Mountain Longleaf contains 9,016 acres and was established in 2003 "to preserve some of the finest old-growth stands of mountain longleaf [*Pinus palustris*] in the United States," located along the slopes of Choccolocco Mountain (a southern outlier of the Blue Ridge Mountains), near Anniston, in northeastern Alabama. This refuge encompasses the U.S. Army's former Fort McClellan military installation.

As the F&WS explains, a hundred years of woodland fires

have maintained healthy longleaf pine forests over much of the refuge. Without recurring fire, these same forests have disappeared from much of the surrounding region. The refuge provides a unique laboratory for studying and understanding the natural composition of fire-maintained second- and old-growth longleaf pine forests. . . . Without recurring fire, many forests have developed a closed canopy of encroaching hardwoods. In the absence of sunlight on the forest floor, longleaf pine seedlings fail to germinate.

Visitor activities presently include wildlife observation and hiking within roughly 3,000 acres of the refuge. The rest is closed until the cleanup of contaminants is completed. Access from westbound I-20's Exit 199 at Heflin is north on State Hwy. 9 for 12 miles, left onto Joseph Springs Motorway, right onto Choccolocco Rd. and immediately left onto Bain's Gap Rd. to an information kiosk at this road's junction with Ridge Rd. (sections of the latter are steep and Ridge Rd. South is likely unsuitable for passenger cars); or from eastbound I-20's Exit 185 at Oxford, it is north on State Hwy. 21 for 12 miles, right into McClellan on the road to Bain's Gap Rd. Information: (256) 848-6833.

Sauta Cave contains 264 acres to protect a limestone cave that offers habitat for the endangered Indiana and gray bats. While entry to the cave is by research permit only, the refuge's hardwood forest is open to visitors. The refuge is 7 miles west of Scottsboro, in northern Alabama. Information: (256) 350-6639.

Watercress Darter contains 7 acres to protect Thomas Spring, a spring-fed pond that provides habitat for the endangered fish, the watercress darter. A second pond has been created to potentially expand the darter's habitat. The refuge, which is open to visitation, is located near Bessemer, in northern Alabama. Information: (256) 350-6639.

Alaska

Becharof contains 1.2 million acres in the upper Alaska Peninsula of southwestern Alaska. It protects an area of tundra wetlands, rolling hills, glaciers, prominent volcanic peaks, and 35-mile-long and 15-mile-wide Becharof Lake that is the nursery for the world's second largest run of salmon. The refuge's spawning streams and the lake annually produce more than 10 million adult salmon for Bristol Bay, to the north of the Alaska Peninsula. In turn, this fishery supports one of the state's largest concentrations of brown bears. The refuge's southern edge contains rugged Pacific coastal cliffs, rocky capes, deep bays, and tidal estuaries, providing habitat for thousands of seabirds, including tufted and horned puffins. The refuge's wetlands attract large numbers of waterfowl and shorebirds. Access is by small aircraft; no roads to or within the refuge. Information: (907) 246-4250.

Innoko contains 4.6 million acres in two separate units, in the central Yukon River Valley of west-central Alaska. More than half the refuge consists of vast wetlands, including river floodplain, muskeg, wetland meadows, marshes, black spruce bogs, rivers, streams, and thousands of lakes and ponds that provide habitat for as many as 100,000 ducks, geese, and other waterbirds. Mammals include moose, grizzly and black bears, gray wolf, beaver, and a wintering herd of barren ground caribou. Access is by floatplane and boat. Hunting/fishing information: (907) 524-3323. Northern unit information: (907) 656-1231. Southern unit information: (907) 524-3251.

Kanuti contains 1.6 million acres straddling the Arctic Circle, in central Alaska. It protects the Kanuti Flats, a vast river basin drained by the westward-flowing Kanuti and Koyukuk rivers, with numerous meandering streams, marshes, black spruce bogs and meadows, hundreds of lakes and ponds, and extensive white spruce-dotted taiga. The wetlands provide breeding habitat for large numbers of waterfowl, including trumpeter and tundra swans, greater white-fronted geese and many species of ducks, and abundant shorebirds. Mammals include moose, grizzly and black bears, gray wolf, beaver, and a wintering herd of barren ground caribou. More than 15 species of fish inhabit the refuge's waters. The refuge contains no roads or developments. Hunting/fishing information: (907) 524-3323. Information: (907) 456-0329.

Koyukuk contains 3.55 million acres to protect the vast lower Koyukuk River wetlands floodplain, north of this river's junction with the Yukon River, in west-central Alaska. This river meanders through 400 miles of the refuge. Beyond its banks is an intricate maze of rivers, streams, sloughs, and hundreds of lakes and ponds. Habitats include shrubby willow and alder thickets, dense forests of white spruce, paper birch, and quaking aspen; extensive black spruce bogs; and white spruce-dotted taiga. These habitats support many thousands of nesting ducks and geese, including trumpeter and tundra swans; and numerous sandhill cranes and shorebirds. Mammals include moose, grizzly and black bears, gray wolf, beaver, and a herd of barren ground caribou that commonly winters here. The 10,000-acre Nogabahara Sand Dunes are a scenic highlight. The refuge contains no roads or developments. Hunting/fishing information: (907) 524-3323. Information: (907) 656-1231.

Nowitna contains 1.56 million acres to protect the lower two-thirds of 300-mile-long Nowitna River and its vast wetlands basin and Nowitna Canyon, in central Alaska. Extensive wetlands, hundreds of lakes and ponds, and numerous rivers and streams provide breeding habitat for large numbers of ducks, geese, swans, sandhill cranes, loons, and other waterbirds. Mammals include moose, grizzly and black bears, pine marten, gray wolf, and wintering barren ground caribou. Salmon and other species of fish inhabit the refuge waters. Much of the refuge supports a boreal forest of white and black spruces and a mixture of paper birch and balsam poplar, while other areas consist of taiga and tundra. Hunting/fishing information: (907) 524-3323. Information: (907) 656-1231.

Selawik contains 2.15 million acres to protect a vast mosaic of wetland habitats, including bogs, sedge and grass meadows, 24,000 lakes and ponds, numerous rivers and streams, and the Kobuk River delta; as well as boreal woodlands of white spruce and paper birch, spruce-dotted taiga, and tundra, in northwestern Alaska. The name *Selawik* is an Inupial Eskimo word that means "place of sheefish," an anadromous species that spawns in the refuge's rivers and streams. The wetlands provide important breeding habitat for thousands of ducks, geese, and shorebirds, as well as such other birds as the tundra swan, sandhill crane, and loons. Mammals include moose, grizzly and black bears, gray wolf, and several hundred thousand barren ground caribou that migrate across the refuge in spring and autumn. Hunting/fishing information: (907) 442-3420. Information: (907) 442-3799.

Togiak contains 4.3 million acres of a vast wilderness between Kuskokwim and Bristol bays, in southwestern Alaska. The refuge includes wetlands, forests, and tundra; lakes and ponds; rivers, streams, estuaries, and lagoons; coastal cliffs and beaches; and the Ahklun and Wood River mountains, which occupy about 80 percent of the refuge. Prominent wildlife includes Pacific walrus, Steller sea lion, moose, barren ground caribou, and brown bear that feed on the enormous spawning runs of salmon. More than half of the world's population of Pacific black brant feeds on the refuge's extensive beds of eelgrass in Chagvan and Nanvak bays. Sandhill cranes nest on Nushagak Peninsula. Millions of seabirds, including horned puffins, nest on the spectacular headlands of Cape Newenham and Cape Peirce. More than a million of five salmon species spawn annually in the 1,500 miles of rivers and streams. Information: (907) 842-1063.

Yukon Flats contains 8.6 million acres to protect a vast wetland basin encompassing 300 miles of the Yukon River, in east-central Alaska. The refuge's estimated 40,000 lakes and ponds and other wetland habitat offer some of North America's preeminent breeding habitat for 1 to 2 million ducks and 10,000 to 15,000 geese annually. Waterfowl banded here have been recovered in 45 of the 50 states, most Canadian provinces, Mexico, Central and South America, and Russia. The refuge also consists of rolling hills of white spruce, paper birch, and quaking aspen boreal forest; spruce-dotted taiga; and tundra. Barren ground caribou winter in the higher parts of the refuge. Hunting/fishing information: (907) 459-7200. Information: (907) 456-0440.

Arizona

Imperial contains 25,125 acres to manage freshwater marsh and riparian habitats, moist-soil impoundments, and backwater lakes, along 28 miles of the lower Colorado River, upstream from Imperial Dam, in southwestern Arizona and southeastern California. Crops of alfalfa, wheat, barley, milo, millet, and corn are grown on about 300 acres, providing nutrient-rich food for large concentrations of wintering ducks and geese. Wetland and riparian habitat restoration activities include control of the invasive non-native salt cedar and common reed, construction of dikes, and installation of water-control structures. Roughly 14,000 acres of the refuge consist of Sonoran Desert upland and rugged mountains, inhabited by such species as desert bighorn, coyote, and bobcat. Access from Yuma is north 25 miles on U.S. Hwy. 95 and left onto Martinez Lake Rd. for 13 miles. Information: (928) 783-3371.

Leslie Canyon contains 2,768 acres to promote the recovery and protection of a number of rare species of indigenous fish and wildlife associated with a perennial stream and bordering riparian habitat of cottonwoods and willows that is surrounded by Chihuahuan Desert uplands, in southeastern Arizona. Although most of the refuge is closed to public entry, a small part is open during daylight hours; and Leslie Canyon Rd., 16 miles north of Douglas, runs through the refuge. Information: (520) 364-2104.

San Bernardino contains 2,369 acres to promote the recovery and protection of a number of rare species of indigenous fish and wildlife associated with *cienega* (marshy wetlands and springs) habitat that is surrounded by Chihuahuan Desert uplands and grassland. The refuge, which is adjacent to the U.S.-Mexico border in southeastern Arizona, is 16 miles east of Douglas by way of Geronimo Trail Rd. Information: (520) 364-2104.

Arkansas

Bald Knob contains about 15,000 acres in two units to manage feeding and resting habitat for wintering waterfowl and other wildlife, in northeastern Arkansas. The refuge consists of forested wetlands including cypress swamp, oxbow lakes, meandering Overflow Creek, bottomland hardwood forest, and fields planted with such crops as rice, milo, and millet, part of which remains unharvested for wintering waterfowl and other wildlife. Access to the refuge headquarters and Farm Unit is from State Hwy. 367 by way of Coal Chute Access Rd. in the town of Bald Knob; or from State Hwy. 64, by way of Mingo Creek Access Rd., about 5 miles east of the town of Bald Knob. Information: (870) 347-2614.

Big Lake contains 11,038 acres to manage an area of wetlands for wintering waterfowl and other wildlife, in northeastern Arkansas. The refuge's old-growth bald cypress swamp, meandering waterways, and bottomland hardwood forest surround Big Lake. Nesting boxes are maintained to offer supplemental nesting cavities for wood ducks. Flooded conditions are likely during autumn, winter, and spring. Access is by way of State Hwy. 18: either west 18 miles from I-55 at Blytheville or east 2 miles from Manila. Information: (870) 564-2429.

Cache River contains more than 56,000 acres in scattered tracts toward a goal of 175,000 acres to restore and manage an area of wetlands for large concentrations of wintering mallards and other waterfowl, in northeastern Arkansas. Exceptional cypress swamp, winding sloughs, oxbow lakes, and bottomland hardwood forest extend along Cache, White, and Bayou DeView rivers. The refuge is carrying out a program of reforesting former farmlands by planting native oaks, pecan, bald cypress, and gum trees to enhance wildlife habitat. Visitor activities include wildlife observation, boating, and seasonal hunting. Information: (870) 347-2614.

Holla Bend contains 7,055 acres to manage former river-oxbow wetlands that attract large concentrations of wintering ducks and geese, as well as nesting wood ducks, wading birds, migratory shorebirds, wintering bald and golden eagles, and numerous neotropical songbirds. The refuge is located in the Arkansas River Valley, in west-central Arkansas. Mammals include white-tailed deer, bobcats, coyotes, river otters, beavers, and an occasional black bear. Access is a mile south of Dardanelle on State Hwy. 7 and left onto State Hwy. 155 for 4 miles. Information: (501) 229-4300.

Logan Cave contains 123 acres to protect a cave inhabited by more than 20,000 of the endangered gray bat, as well as the rare grotto salamander and blind Ozark cavefish, near Dardanelle in northwestern Arkansas. The cave is open only by special permit for research. Information: (501) 229-4300.

Oakwood Unit contains 2,263 acres to manage wetland impoundments and reforest former farmlands, in southeastern Arkansas. The refuge is open only by special request for wildlife observation and photography. Information: (870) 364-3167.

Overflow is ultimately expected to contain more than 18,000 acres to protect a seasonally flooded area of bottomland hardwood forest in the Overflow Creek watershed and to manage seasonal water impoundments and croplands for wintering waterfowl and other wildlife, in southeastern Arkansas. Access from U.S. Hwy. 165 at Wilmot is west 8 miles on State Hwy. 52; or from U.S. Hwy. 425 at Hamburg, it is east 6 miles on State Hwy. 8. Information: (870) 364-3167.

Pond Creek contains 27,300 acres to protect one of the last remaining ecologically significant tracts of mature bottomland hardwood forest and meandering sloughs in the Red River Basin, between the Cossatot and Little rivers in southwestern Arkansas. These wetlands attract wintering waterfowl, nesting wood ducks, bald eagles, and wading bird rookeries. Access from Ashdown is north 15 miles on U.S. Hwy. 71 to Falls Chapel and left for 2 miles; or from State Hwy. 41 at Horatio, it is east 7 miles on Central Rd. Information: (870) 386-2700.

Wapanocca contains 5,621 acres to restore and manage historical hunt club land dating back to the Civil War, in northeastern Arkansas. The refuge consists of bottomland hardwood forest in early stages of reforestation, seasonal water impoundments, grassland, cropland, Wapanocca Lake, and a 1,200-acre cypress swamp. These habitats attract as many as 200,000 wintering waterfowl, as well as wading birds, wild turkeys, nesting wood ducks, bald eagles, and numerous neotropical songbirds. Access is north from West Memphis about 15 miles on I-55 to Exit 21 and east 1.5 miles on State Hwy. 42. Information: (870) 343-2595.

California

Antioch Dunes contains 55 acres in two separate units to restore and protect important remnants of rolling riverine sand dunes that provide critical habitat for a number of rare and endangered species of plants and insects. The refuge is located along the south bank of the San Joaquin River, just east of Antioch, in central California. Isolation of these dunes for thousands of years enabled the development of species and subspecies of plants and insects found nowhere else. One endangered subspecies is the Lange's metalmark butterfly, which in its caterpillar stage feeds only on the naked-stemmed buckwheat. The refuge's restoration program has included planting thousands of buckwheat seedlings and controlling non-native plants that threaten to crowd out the buckwheat. Because of the habitat's sensitivity, the refuge is closed to visitation. Information: (510) 792-0222.

Bitter Creek contains 14,094 acres to protect roosting and foraging habitat for the endangered California condor, in the arid foothills of the southern San Joaquin Valley, in central California. For information on the California Condor Recovery Program, see the Hopper Mountain NWR text. Although Bitter Creek refuge is closed to public entry, it is possible to view some of the refuge and possibly see a condor from State Hwy. 166 and Cerro Noroeste Rd. Information: (805) 644-5185.

Blue Ridge contains 897 acres to protect a historic California condor roosting area. For information on the California Condor Recovery Program, see the Hopper Mountain NWR text. Blue Ridge refuge is closed to visitation. Information: (805) 644-5185.

Butte Sink contains 733 acres to restore and manage wetland habitat primarily for wintering waterfowl, located within an 11,000-acre expanse of wetlands and hunt clubs. The refuge is located east of the Sacramento River, near Colusa, in north-central California. The F&WS says that this refuge "typically supports one of the greatest concentrations of waterfowl in the world on a per-acre basis, over 300,000 ducks and 100,000 geese." This refuge is closed to visitation. Information: (530) 934-2801.

Castle Rock contains nearly 14 acres to protect one of the most significant places along the Pacific Coast for large concentrations of colonial nesting seabirds. The surf-pounded rock, rising 335 feet from the sea, is located less than a half-mile offshore from Crescent City, in northwestern California. Tufted puffins, pigeon guillemots, and an estimated 75,000 common murres (California's largest breeding colony) are attracted to the rock. Harbor and elephant seals and California and Steller sea lions swim in the vicinity of the rock and haul themselves onto a beach. Although the refuge is closed to visitation, it can be viewed with the aid of a spotting scope or binoculars from an interpretive viewing area along North Pebble Beach Drive. Information: (707) 733-5406.

 Clear Lake contains 46,460 acres to protect and manage roughly 20,000 acres of open reservoir water that attracts concentrations of migratory waterfowl, in the Klamath Basin of northeastern California. Small rocky islands in the lake provide secure colonial nesting habitat for white pelicans, cormorants, and gulls. Adjacent arid uplands of sagebrush and scattered junipers provide habitat for pronghorn, mule deer and greater sage-grouse (the latter species is described in Hart Mountain and Seedskadee refuge texts). Clear Lake is one of six refuges in the Klamath Basin; and the refuge-complex headquarters and visitor center are 5 miles west on Hill Road from the town of Tulelake, Calif. Access to Clear Lake refuge is about 20 miles southeast of Tulelake on State Hwy. 139 and left onto Forest Service Rd. 136 for about 10 miles. Information: (530) 667-2231.

Coachella Valley contains 3,276 acres to restore and protect an area of vital sand dune habitat for the threatened Coachella Valley fringe-toed lizard. The refuge, which is part of the 20,114-acre Coachella Valley Preserve, is at the northern end of Coachella Valley, in the Colorado Desert of southern California. Although nearly all of the refuge is closed to public access to avoid disturbing the fragile ecosystem, there are hiking opportunities in other parts of the preserve, which is cooperatively managed by The Nature Conservancy, U.S. Bureau of Land Management, and state agencies. Access to the preserve from I-10's Ramon Rd. Exit is east about 4 miles on Ramon Rd., and left for about a mile on Thousand Palms Canyon Rd. to the visitor center. Coachella Valley Preserve information: (760) 343-2733.

Colusa contains 4,507 acres to manage seasonally flooded marsh, riparian, permanent pond, watergrass, and upland grass habitats primarily for as many as 200,000 ducks and 100,000 geese during autumn and winter, in the Sacramento Valley of north-central California. Access from I-5 just north of Williams is east 7 miles on State Hwy. 20 and right. Information: (530) 934-2801.

Delevan contains 5,797 acres to manage seasonally flooded marsh, riparian, permanent pond, watergrass, and upland grass habitats primarily for as many as 500,000 ducks and 200,000 geese during autumn and winter. Access to a wildlife-viewing pullout on the north side of Maxwell Rd. is east 4.5 miles on this road from I-5 at Maxwell. Information: (530) 934-2801.

Ellicott Slough contains 196 acres to protect vital coastal upland habitat for the endangered Santa Cruz long-toed salamander, near Monterey Bay in northern California. The refuge consists of seasonal ponds, grassland, coastal scrub, and oak woodland habitats. It is closed to visitation to avoid disturbing sensitive species, but can be viewed from San Andreas and Spring Valley roads, 4 miles west of Watsonville. Information: (510) 792-0222.

Kern contains 10,618 acres to manage wintering habitat for large concentrations of ducks and geese, replacing a small part of once-vast Central Valley wetlands, at the south end of the San Joaquin Valley of southern California. For the benefit of the waterfowl, about 5,000 acres of the refuge are flooded and managed as marsh from September through March; and 1,200 acres are devoted to growing food plants, such as millet and swamp timothy. A 6.5-mile auto tour road offers opportunities to observe wildlife. Access from State Hwy. 99's Delano Exit is west 19 miles on State Hwy. 155 (Garces Hwy.) to the T-junction with Corcoran Rd., and following directional signs to the refuge. Information: (661) 725-2767.

Marin Islands contains 339 acres on two islands and adjacent tidal mudflats to provide protection of nesting and roosting waterbirds and other wildlife. The refuge is located on the northwestern shore of San Pablo Bay, which is part of greater San Francisco Bay. West Marin Island's California buckeye trees provide the largest nesting colony of herons and egrets in northern California. Although the refuge is closed to public access, boating and kayaking are popular ways to enjoy viewing the refuge from a distance that avoids disturbing the birds. Information: (707) 562-3000.

Merced contains 8,277 acres to manage seasonal and semi-permanent wetlands and croplands for large concentrations of wintering and breeding waterfowl, lesser sandhill cranes, migrating shorebirds, and other wildlife. The refuge is near the northern end of the San Joaquin Valley, in central California. From November through February, as many as 100,000 geese of four species (Ross's, snow, greater white-fronted, and cackling Canada), thousands of ducks, and as many as 15,000 sandhill cranes are attracted to the refuge. Visitor activities include wildlife observation from a 5-mile auto tour route. Access from the city of Merced is south 8 miles on State Hwy. 59 and right onto Sandy Mush Rd. for 8 miles. Information: (209) 826-3508.

Modoc contains 7,021 acres to manage a wetland oasis for migratory waterfowl, wading birds, shorebirds, nesting white pelicans and sandhill cranes, and other wildlife, along the western edge of the Great Basin Desert, in the northeast corner of California. The refuge consists of an extensive area of bulrush-and-cattail marsh, diked ponds, and irrigated meadows, as well as riparian corridors and adjacent sagebrush uplands. Visitor activities include an opportunity to observe waterbirds on Teal Pond from an auto tour route. Access from Alturas is south on U.S. Hwy. 395 to just south of the North Fork Pit River, left onto County Rd. 56, right onto County Rd. 115, and left onto the refuge road. Information: (530) 233-3572.

Pixley contains 6,389 acres to manage and protect wetland habitat for migratory waterfowl and shorebirds, as well as arid grassland and shrub habitat for the endangered San Joaquin kit fox, Tipton kangaroo rat, and blunt-nosed lizard. The refuge is near the south end of the San Joaquin Valley, in southern California. Wetland water levels are maintained during autumn and winter especially for wintering waterfowl. From late September to mid-March, as many as 4,000 sandhill cranes gather on the refuge. Access from State Hwy. 99's County Ave. Exit is west about 5 miles on County Ave. 56 and north a mile on County Rd. 88. Information: (661) 725-2767.

Sacramento River contains about 9,000 federally owned acres; and an additional 6,675 easement acres within more than 23 units toward a goal of roughly 18,000 acres, to manage stretches of the Sacramento River's riparian habitat between Red Bluff and Princeton, in north-central California. Only the LLANO SECO and PACKER LAKE units are open to visitation. The former consists of seasonally flooded marsh, permanent pond, watergrass, and upland grass habitats; and the latter consists of a 30-acre oxbow lake. Access to the Llano Seco Unit from I-5 at Willows is east on State Hwy. 162 to about 2 miles east of Butte City and left 9 miles on Rd. Z, which jogs around the south end of the unit and becomes Seven Mile Rd. Access to the Packer Lake Unit from Princeton is north 5 miles on State Hwy. 45 and right onto a narrow dirt road to the lakeshore. Information: (530) 934-2801.

Salinas River contains 367 acres to restore and protect an ecologically important coastal dune system, a 45-acre saline pond, and salt marsh, riparian scrub, and native coastal prairie habitats, on and near the shore of Monterey Bay in northern California. As the refuge's vision statement says, "Endangered or threatened species will receive management priority, with special emphasis on the recovery of the western snowy plover," a species that nests on beach fore-dune habitat. To protect this sensitive habitat, the refuge's upper beach and coastal dunes are closed to visitation, except on the Ocean Beach Trail. The saline pond and salt marsh are closed to visitation. Access from State Hwy. 1 is by way of the Del Monte/Marina Blvd. exit and left onto an unpaved road to the refuge's parking area. Information: (510) 792-0222.

San Diego contains roughly 10,000 acres in two separate units, in southwestern California. The refuge's 7,500-acre OTAY-SWEETWATER UNIT consists of several tracts of land along and near Sweetwater River, including riparian woodland, freshwater marsh, vernal pools (inhabited by a number of endangered and rare plants and animals), native grassland, live oak woodland, and chaparral and sagebrush scrub. The 2,330-acre SOUTH SAN DIEGO BAY UNIT protects salt marsh, diked ponds, rare beds of eelgrass that are especially important to Pacific black brant, and one of southern California's largest contiguous expanses of tidal mudflats. These wetlands attract hundreds of thousands of birds—notably wintering waterfowl, migrating shorebirds, and nesting seabirds. Information about limited access onto the Otay-Sweetwater Unit and access to a bike path along the edge of the San Diego Bay Unit that is closed to visitation: (619) 669-7295.

San Joaquin River contains 6,713 acres toward an authorized goal of 12,000 acres to manage and protect important wintering habitat for the Aleutian Canada goose, near the northern end of the San Joaquin Valley, in central California. Concentrations of other wintering waterfowl and sandhill cranes are also attracted to this floodplain and riparian area, which extends along the San Joaquin River, from its junction with the Tuolumne River downstream to its junction with the Stanislaus River. Lands within the boundary are being acquired either by federal purchase or under conservation easement agreements with landowners. The refuge will not be open to visitation until completion of the refuge's planning process, but wildlife can be viewed from adjacent county roads. Access from State Hwy. 99 at Modesto is west 9 miles on State Hwy. 132. Information: (209) 826-3508

San Pablo Bay contains 13,189 acres toward a goal of about 21,000 acres to restore and protect tidally influenced wetland habitat for large concentrations of migratory waterfowl and shorebirds, wading birds, raptors such as white-tailed kite, and endangered species such as California clapper rail. The refuge consists of open bay waters, salt marsh, intertidal mudflats, seasonal wetlands, and uplands. It is located within the northern reach of San Pablo Bay, which is part of greater San Francisco Bay, in northern California. Peak numbers of waterbirds gather here from November through January.

The refuge headquarters and the North Bay Discovery Center are at Building 505 on Mare Island in Vallejo. The best overview of the refuge is at a designated pullout from the westbound lane of I-80, 3 miles east of the Vallejo city limits. Visitor activities presently occur mostly on the refuge's TOLAY CREEK UNIT, accessed from U.S. Hwy. 101, it is east about 8 miles on State Hwy. 37; or from I-80, it is west about 14 miles on State Hwy 37. Information: (707) 562-3000.

Seal Beach contains 923 acres to restore and manage rare salt marsh habitat for endangered species, migratory waterfowl and shorebirds, seabirds, and other wildlife, on the Orange County coast of southern California. A major management issue is the welfare of three endangered subspecies: the California least tern, Belding's savannah sparrow, and light-footed clapper rail that inhabits remnant cordgrass salt-marsh areas, from Ventura County southward into Mexico. The refuge overlays part of the U.S. Navy's Seal Beach Naval Weapons Station. In coordination with the Navy's natural resources protection staff, the refuge is striving to restore areas of Anaheim Bay salt marsh and to convert degraded lands to wildlife habitat. The refuge is open to visitors only through prearranged guided tours. Information: (562) 598-1024.

Sonny Bono Salton Sea contains nearly 1,800 managed acres along the southeastern shore of the Salton Sea, in southern California. The refuge consists of impounded ponds and fields of nutrient-rich crops, such as alfalfa and wheat, which are cooperatively planted by local farmers and the refuge for wintering waterfowl (notably thousands of snow and Ross's geese). An endangered subspecies, the Yuma clapper rail, inhabits the refuge's dense habitat of cattails and bulrushes. The Salton Sea's fish populations attract large numbers of white pelicans, as well as brown pelicans, cormorants, gulls, and terns. More than 380 species of birds have been recorded on this refuge.

Hiking opportunities include 1-mile Rock Hill Trail from the visitor center. Access from I-8's Forrester Rd. Exit is north on Forrester Rd. (through Westmoreland), continuing north (from the junction with Eddins Rd.) on Gentry Rd., and left onto Sinclair Rd. to the visitor center. From I-10, access is south from Indio on State Hwy. 111 to 5 miles south of Niland and right for 6 miles. Information: (760) 348-5278.

Stone Lakes contains more than 4,000 acres toward a goal of 18,000 acres to restore and manage wetland, riparian woodland, and grassland habitats, in the northern part of the Central Valley's delta of the Sacramento and San Joaquin rivers of central California. The refuge, which also has three permanent lakes, attracts thousands of migratory waterfowl, sandhill cranes, and shorebirds, during autumn and winter months. Although a relatively small part of the refuge is federally owned, a number of privately owned tracts are being managed under cooperative agreements and conservation easements. Habitat restoration is being accomplished through a variety of partnerships with volunteers, conservation groups, farming neighbors, and other land-management agencies. Access from I-5's Grobe Blvd. Exit is west at the end of the exit ramp. The refuge gate is just ahead and visitors can park near the gate. Information: (916) 775-4421.

Sutter contains 2,591 acres to restore and manage seasonally flooded marsh, permanent pond, watergrass, and upland grass habitats primarily for at least 160,000 ducks and 55,000 geese during autumn and winter months, in the Sacramento Valley of northern California. The refuge can be viewed from a public highway that runs through the area. Access from State Hwy. 45 in Colusa is east 12 miles on State Hwy. 20, then right 2.5 miles on Tarke Rd., left 2 miles on McGrath Rd., right 2.5 miles on Progress Rd., left 3.5 miles on Oswald Rd., and east through the refuge on Hughes Rd. Or from State Hwy. 99 in Yuba City, it is west 2 miles on State Hwy. 20, then left onto Washington Blvd. for 5 miles, right onto Oswald Rd. for 3.5 miles, right onto Schlag Rd. for 0.8 mile, and left onto Hughes Rd. Information: (530) 934-2801.

Tijuana Slough contains 1,072 acres to restore and manage open water, tidal salt marsh, riparian, vernal pool, coastal sand dune, and upland habitats for migratory waterfowl, shorebirds, and other wildlife. The refuge is located where the Tijuana River flows into the Pacific Ocean, a mile north of the U.S.-Mexico border, in the southwest corner of California. According to the F&WS, "San Diego County is now home to more federally listed threatened and endangered species than any other county in the continental United States." Among these are the endangered light-footed clapper rail, California least tern, and least Bell's vireo; and the threatened western snowy plover. More than 370 species of birds have been recorded here.

The refuge supports numerous research and educational programs, and the latter and the visitor center (which includes a native plant garden) are administered by the California Department of Parks. Access from I-5's Coronado Ave. Exit is west on Coronado Ave., left on Fourth Street, right on Caspian Way to a traffic circle, and left into the parking area. Information: (619) 575-2704.

Tule Lake contains 39,116 acres to manage bulrush-and-cattail marsh, open water, and cropland mainly for migrating and wintering waterfowl, within the southern part of the Klamath Basin, in northern California. Roughly 17,000 acres of the refuge are leased from local farmers and another 1,900 acres of grain and alfalfa cropland are farmed by refuge permit holders, to provide a major food source for waterfowl and other wildlife. Visitor activities include wildlife observation from a 10-mile auto tour route (a fee is charged), hiking two short trails, and canoeing a route through the marsh. Access to the visitor center from U.S. Hwy. 97 (just south of the California-Oregon state line) is east on California State Hwy. 161 (through Lower Klamath NWR), and south on Hill Rd. The west entrance of the refuge's tour road is 5 miles farther south on Hill Rd. and then left. Or from California State Hwy. 139 at the community of Tulelake, it is west 6 miles on East-West Rd. and left on Hill Rd. Information: (530) 667-2231.

Caribbean: Puerto Rico

Cabo Rojo contains 1,836 acres to restore and protect native flora and fauna—notably the endangered yellow-shouldered blackbird, a glossy black bird with yellow epaulets, which is endemic to Puerto Rico, in the Greater Antilles of the West Indies. Among many other species are the smooth-billed ani, bananaquit, black-faced and yellow-faced grassquits, troupial (a species of oriole), and Puerto Rican tody. For decades, this area of gently rolling hills, which was originally covered with mature hardwood forest, was degraded by overgrazing. The refuge's goal is to restore native trees and grasses. The refuge also includes the Cabo Rojo Salt Flats, providing key habitat for tens of thousands of migrating shorebirds annually. The refuge and visitor center are open on weekdays; and there is a 2-mile interpretive trail. Information: (787) 851-7258.

Desecheo contains 360 acres to restore and protect historic seabird colonies and natural ecosystems on Isla Desecheo, 14 miles off Puerto Rico's west coast. Much of the island's rocky terrain supports native dry forest and thorny scrub vegetation. Historically, there were vast colonies of such nesting seabirds as brown and red-footed boobies, magnificent frigatebird, sooty tern, and brown noddy. Unfortunately, as the F&WS explains, they "have virtually disappeared, which is attributed to impacts by military bombing, illegal hunting, fires, and the introduction of nest-predating rhesus monkeys." The refuge is closed to public access because of unexploded military ordnance. Information: (787) 851-7258.

Laguna Cartagena contains 1,059 acres to restore and maintain habitats of this important freshwater lagoon, near the southwest coast of Puerto Rico. Only about 10 percent of the lagoon is open water, the rest being choked with cattails, water hyacinth, and other aquatic plants. This dense growth, in a process called eutrophication, was promoted by runoff containing concentrations of agricultural fertilizers, pesticides, and sediments for many years of sugarcane cultivation and livestock grazing. In 1995, the F&WS began restoring the lagoon to a key resting and feeding area for migrating waterfowl and other waterbirds. Work has also begun toward restoring upland sugarcane and grazing lands to native forest. Information: (787) 851-7258.

Navassa Island contains roughly 300,000 acres to protect this 1,280-acre island and an extensive expanse of coral reefs, located to the west of Puerto Rico. Because of safety concerns, the refuge is not open to visitation. Information: (787) 851-7258.

Vieques contains about 17,770 acres in two units to restore and protect the western and eastern ends of the island of Vieques, located 7 miles to the east of the main island of Puerto Rico. The refuge includes beaches, coastal lagoons, mangrove wetlands, and some of the best upland subtropical dry forest in Puerto Rico. The marine environment that surrounds the island consists of outstanding shoreline coral reefs, tropical fish, and seagrass beds and is inhabited by the manatee and green, loggerhead, hawksbill, and leatherback sea turtles. Because this area was previously used as a U.S. Navy bombing range, much of the refuge will remain off limits to public access until the search for unexploded warheads is complete. The visitor center is at Vieques Office Park, Rd. 200, km 0.4. (P.O. Box 1527, Vieques, PR 00765). Information (calling ahead is recommended): (787) 851-7258.

Caribbean: U.S. Virgin Islands

Buck Island contains 45 acres to manage this island's value for migratory birds and to protect its cactus scrub habitat and rocky shores, located about a mile south of St. Thomas Island, in the U.S. Virgin Islands. As the F&WS explains, "birds rarely use the refuge because of an overwhelming abundance of black rats." Only a few red-billed tropicbirds and a colony of laughing gulls succeed in nesting here. The refuge's goal is to eliminate the non-native rodents so that the historically large seabird nesting colonies can be restored. Access is by boat from Charlotte Amalie. Information: (809) 773-4554.

Green Cay contains 14 acres to protect the largest remaining population of the endangered St. Croix ground lizard and important colonial nesting bird habitat, located near the northern shore of St. Croix Island, in the U.S. Virgin Islands. Green Cay (pronounced "kee") consists of dry forest (mostly pink cedar and orange manjack trees), cactus scrub, and rocky beaches. Birds include brown pelican, brown booby, magnificent frigatebird, white-cheeked pintail, and white-crowned pigeon. The refuge is closed to public access to avoid disturbing the St. Croix ground lizard habitat and nesting birds. Information: (809) 773-4554.

Colorado

Browns Park contains 13,455 acres to enhance and protect wet meadowland and other riparian habitat for migrating and nesting waterfowl and wintering elk and deer along the Green River, in northwestern Colorado. Prior to completion of Flaming Gorge Dam in 1964, these riparian wetlands were maintained by the river's natural annual flooding, but the dam has largely contained the floodwaters. The F&WS now diverts river water to about 1,300 acres of the refuge's marshes and meadows. Visitor activities include wildlife observation from an 11-mile auto tour route and boating (a launching ramp is provided). Access from U.S. Hwy. 40 at Maybell is northwest 60 miles on State Hwy. 318; or from U.S. Hwy. 191 in Utah, it is southeast about 30 miles on an unpaved road, connecting with State Hwy. 318. Information: (970) 365-3613.

Rocky Flats contains roughly 6,500 acres of the scenic transition zone between the western Great Plains and the Front Range of the Rocky Mountains, 16 miles northwest of Denver, Colorado. The "Flats" was a federal government nuclear weapons production facility from 1951 to 1989. In 2005, the environmental cleanup of the property was certified by the U.S. Department of Energy as complete. The refuge consists of upland shrublands, extensive grasslands (including 1,500 acres of a rare xeric tallgrass prairie), and shallow canyons with permanent or intermittent streams that dissect the prairie uplands. For Rocky Mountain elk, mule deer, black bears, mountain lions, coyotes, bald eagles and more than 200 other species of wildlife, the buffer zone around the industrial facilities was a de facto refuge for 30 to 40 years; it's now simply official.

Hiking trails and interpretive programs are being developed. The refuge is bounded on the east by Indiana St., on the north by State Hwy. 128, on the west by State Hwy. 93, and on the south by 100th Ave. Information: (303) 289-0232.

Two Ponds contains 72 acres to restore and protect an area of upland prairie and wetland habitats, including three man-made ponds and cottonwoods and willows that border irrigation canals, in Arvada, Colorado. The refuge offers a hands-on educational opportunity for area school students and other groups, emphasizing "the inherent values of wetlands and wildlife in an urban environment." The refuge is bounded on the north by West 80th Ave. and on the west by Kipling St. Information: (303) 289-0232.

Florida

Caloosahatchee contains 40 acres of mangrove and upland habitats on a cluster of eight islands in the Caloosahatchee River, adjacent to Ft. Myers and a few miles upstream from the southwestern Gulf Coast of Florida. Because the refuge is adjacent to a Florida Power & Light power plant, the outflow of warm water provides favorable wintering habitat for the endangered manatee. Egrets, herons, ospreys, and bald eagles are also attracted to the refuge. Boaters are urged to consult a navigational chart and tide schedules before attempting to visit the shallow waters around the islands and to avoid approaching the islands during nesting season. Information: (941) 472-1100.

Cedar Keys contains about 800 acres to protect 13 subtropical coastal islands, located 14 miles south of the mouth of the Suwannee River, on the upper Gulf Coast of Florida. These islands, ranging from 1 to 165 acres, support one of north Florida's largest colonial nesting rookeries for such species as white ibis, great and snowy egrets, great blue and little blue herons, and brown pelican. Other birds include magnificent frigatebirds, wintering bald eagles, and nesting ospreys. From spring through autumn, the endangered manatee inhabits the coastal waters. The refuge consists of cordgrass salt marsh and mangrove wetlands, as well as wooded hammocks on slightly higher terrain.

Visitor entry onto these islands is limited to the beaches (but not on Seahorse Key) and a short trail on Atsena Key. Although access is by boat, these islands are surrounded by shallow sand, mud, and grass flats and are relatively inaccessible, especially at low tide. Information: (352) 493-0238.

Crystal River contains 46 acres to protect undeveloped parts of Kings Bay—the headwaters of Crystal River, on the upper Gulf Coast of Florida. This refuge's primary purpose is to preserve the exceptional ecosystem of warm, spring-fed waters and rich aquatic vegetation that provide outstanding wintering habitat for roughly 250 of the endangered manatee. The refuge also includes 20 islands. Entry by boat into the designated manatee sanctuary is prohibited from November 15 through March 31. Regulations ban the harassment of manatees and require that boats be operated at idle or slow speed in posted speed zones. Information: (352) 563-2088.

Egmont Key contains a 350-acre barrier island at the mouth of Tampa Bay, on the central Gulf Coast of Florida. The refuge protects important nesting, feeding, and resting habitat for many species of colonial nesting waterbirds, such as brown pelicans, snowy egrets, great blue herons, and white ibises. Other birds include black skimmers and numerous shorebirds, gulls, and terns. The endangered manatee inhabits the waters around the island. Guided trips are offered by commercial tour companies in St. Petersburg. Information: (352) 563-2088.

Great White Heron contains 7,407 acres of land and 186,287 acres of water to protect great white herons, egrets, and other birds on three small keys located between Marathon and Key West, Florida. The refuge's many small keys consist mostly of salt marsh and mangrove wetlands, small areas of wooded hammocks on slightly higher terrain, and beaches where female threatened loggerhead and endangered green sea turtles come ashore to lay their eggs in summer. Numerous wading birds, magnificent frigatebirds, brown pelicans, shorebirds, gulls, terns, ospreys, bald eagles, migrating raptors, and white-crowned pigeons are among the refuge's more than 250 species of birds.

The waters around the keys can be accessed by boat, but entry onto the keys themselves is by special permit only, to avoid disturbing the bird colonies. Commercial guided tours and boat rentals are available. Information: (305) 872-0774.

Island Bay contains 20 acres in six separate tracts near Cape Haze, on the southwestern Gulf Coast of Florida. In 1908, President Theodore Roosevelt established this refuge to protect egrets and herons from plume hunters. The refuge encompasses parts of four keys at the mouth of Turtle Bay and two large oyster shell mounds (middens) that were created centuries ago by Calusa Indians who lived on the nearby mainland. Large numbers of wading birds, waterfowl, and shorebirds feed, roost, and nest on the refuge; and the endangered manatee inhabits the brackish waters. Boaters are urged to consult a navigational chart and tide schedules before attempting to visit the refuge and to avoid approaching the islands during the nesting season. Information: (941) 472-1100.

Key West contains 2,019 acres of water and a cluster of small mangrove keys to the west of Key West, Florida. In 1908, President Theodore Roosevelt established the refuge to protect egrets and herons from plume hunters. These islands consist of mangrove wetlands, small areas of wooded hammock on slightly higher terrain, salt ponds, and beaches where female threatened loggerhead and endangered green sea turtles come ashore to lay their eggs in summer. The refuge provides important resting, feeding, and some nesting habitat for wading birds, magnificent frigatebirds, brown pelicans, ducks, shorebirds, gulls, terns, ospreys, bald eagles, and white-crowned pigeons.

Areas of the refuge open to visitation are the beach on the northwestern half of Boca Grande Key, the western half of the beach on Woman Key, and most beaches on the Marquesas Keys. The refuge headquarters is on Big Pine Key. Access is by boat from Key West. Information: (305) 872-0774.

Lake Wales Ridge, located in central interior Florida, is the first national wildlife refuge designated primarily to preserve endangered species of flora. When completed to its authorized goal of roughly 19,000 acres in four separate units, it will provide protection for more than 30 species of rare plants. Lake Wales Ridge is a 100-mile-long, geologically ancient beach and sand dune system ranging from 4 to 10 miles wide. The ridge was formed roughly 25 million years ago, when sea levels were much higher (the East Coast is now 60 miles to the east of the ridge). Unique species have evolved here, among them scrub plum, pygmy fringe tree, short-leaved rosemary, scrub blazing star, scrub lupine, and Florida ziziphus.

The refuge is not open to visitation. For those wishing to see scrub habitat, the Fish and Wildlife Service recommends contacting The Nature Conservancy's Tiger Creek Preserve: (863) 635-7506; or Lake Wales Ridge State Forest: (941) 648-3163.

Lake Woodruff contains roughly 21,750 acres to protect the 2,200-acre spring-fed Lake Woodruff and surrounding marsh, hardwood swamp, a stretch of the upper St. John's River, and uplands, near DeLeon Springs in northeastern Florida. This area attracts more than 240 species of birds, including several species of egrets and herons, white and glossy ibises, wood storks, limpkins, nesting wood ducks, wintering waterfowl, numerous nesting ospreys, and a large pre-migratory roosting colony of swallow-tailed kites. The endangered manatee inhabits many of the refuge's 50 miles of waterways, nearly half of which are designated as manatee protection zones.

Two interpretive trails meander through wooded habitat, and dikes bordering three wetland impoundments also offer hiking opportunities. Access from I-95's Exit 88 is west 25 miles on State Hwy. 40, left on U.S. Hwy. 17 about 6 miles to DeLeon Springs, right onto Retta St. one block, left onto Grand Ave. for about 0.5 mile, and right onto Mud Lake Rd. Information: (386) 985-4673.

Matlacha Pass contains 825 acres on 23 islands in Matlacha Pass estuary and San Carlos Bay, near Ft. Myers, on the southwestern Gulf Coast of Florida. This refuge was established by President Theodore Roosevelt in 1908 to protect important nesting and roosting habitat for large concentrations of such birds as the brown pelicans, anhingas, wood storks, white ibises, magnificent frigatebirds, and many species of herons and egrets. Boaters are urged to consult a navigational chart and tide schedules before attempting to visit any of the islands and to avoid approaching the islands during the nesting season. Information: (941) 472-1100.

Passage Key contains a 30-acre coastal barrier island at the mouth of Tampa Bay, on the central Gulf Coast of Florida. The refuge, which supports one of Florida's largest nesting colonies of royal and sandwich terns, was established in 1905 by President Theodore Roosevelt. Other birds that nest, rest, and feed here include brown pelicans and black skimmers. To avoid disturbing the birds, visitor entry onto the island is not permitted. Information: (352) 563-2088.

Pine Island contains 548 acres on 17 islands clustered in Pine Island Sound estuary near Ft. Myers, on the southwestern Gulf Coast of Florida. The refuge was established by President Theodore Roosevelt in 1908 to protect important nesting and roosting habitat for large concentrations of such birds as brown pelicans, anhingas, wood storks, white ibises, magnificent frigatebirds, and many species of herons and egrets. Boaters are urged to consult a navigational chart and tide schedules before attempting to visit the refuge and avoid approaching the islands during the nesting season. Information: (941) 472-1100.

Pinellas contains several small islands totaling 403 acres near the mouth of Tampa Bay, just offshore from St. Petersburg, on the central Gulf Coast of Florida. The refuge protects important breeding and roosting habitat for such colonial nesting birds as brown pelicans, white ibises, roseate spoonbills, egrets, and herons. Tarpon Key supports one of Florida's largest pelican rookeries. To avoid disturbing the birds, visitor entry onto the islands is not permitted. Information: (352) 563-2088.

St. Johns, containing 6,160 acres, was established to protect habitat for the endangered dusky seaside sparrow, near Titusville in central interior Florida. Wildfires unfortunately burned throughout much of the sparrow's limited range, from which the population never recovered. The species is now believed to be extinct. The refuge's salt marsh habitat is being managed for herons, egrets, ibises, wood storks, and black rails ("rail tours" are offered several times annually). Although the refuge is otherwise presently open to visitation only by special permit, the F&WS is planning for expanded visitor use. Information: (321) 861-0667.

Georgia

Banks Lake contains 3,559 acres to manage this lake and adjacent marsh habitat, near Lakeland in southeastern Georgia. The refuge attracts wading birds, wood ducks, shorebirds, and sandhill cranes. The lake is popular with anglers. A fishing pier and boat-launching ramps are provided. Access from Lakeland is west 2 miles on State Hwy. 122. Information: (912) 496-7836.

Bond Swamp contains more than 6,290 acres toward a goal of about 18,000 acres to enhance and protect a stretch of bottomland hardwood swamp and adjacent upland along Ocmulgee River, about 7 miles south of Macon, in central Georgia. Meandering creeks and sloughs, oxbow lakes, and beaver swamps are scattered throughout the floodplain. Major trees include bald cypress, American sycamore, and water-tolerant oaks. The refuge attracts a wide diversity of wildlife, including wintering waterfowl, nesting wood ducks, herons, egrets, wild turkeys, bald eagles, black bears, white-tailed deer, and alligators. Some parts of the refuge may be closed to public access during periods of river flooding or to avoid disturbing nesting eagles.

Visitor activities include wildlife observation, hiking on trails, and seasonal hunting. Access from I-16's Exit 6 is south 4.2 miles on U.S. Hwy. 23 to Stone Creek parking area, on the right side of the road. Information: (478) 986-5441.

Harris Neck contains 2,824 acres to protect an extensive area of salt marsh, smaller areas of fields and grassland, mixed deciduous woods, and scattered swamplands along South Newport River, on the north-central coast of Georgia. Six man-made impoundments are managed mainly for a rookery for the endangered wood stork. Other wildlife includes brown pelicans, anhingas, ospreys, wild turkeys, ibises, egrets, herons, wintering waterfowl, white-tailed deer, and alligators. More than 15 miles of roads and trails offer access into many parts of the refuge. Access from I-95's Exit 67 is south 1 mile on U.S. Hwy. 17 and left onto Harris Neck Rd. for 7 miles. Boat access to the refuge's tidal waters is from a launching ramp at the end of Harris Neck Rd. Information: (912) 652-4415.

Wassaw contains 10,053 acres to protect Wassaw Island (actually two barrier islands), near the northern end of the Georgia coast. Habitats include extensive salt marshes, a 7-mile-long sandy beach, gently rolling sand dunes, and virgin-growth woodlands of slash pines and live oaks. The refuge supports heron and egret rookeries, and attracts numerous species of wintering waterfowl, migrating shorebirds, and nesting bald eagles. White-tailed deer and alligators are common residents. Female loggerhead sea turtles haul themselves onto the beach to lay their eggs in summer. The endangered manatee inhabits the waters in and around the refuge.

Wassaw and Pine islands (but not Flora Hammock on the latter) are open to visitation. Access is by way of a boat-launching ramp adjacent to Skidaway Island Bridge; and boat charter trips can be arranged at marinas on Skidaway Island and Isle of Hope. Information: (912) 652-4415.

Wolf Island contains 5,126 acres to protect three coastal barrier islands (4,500-acre Wolf, 600-acre Egg, and 400-acre Little Egg) and an extensive adjacent area of saltwater marsh, on the central coast of Georgia. The refuge attracts many species of wading birds, wintering waterfowl, shorebirds, gulls, terns, and brown pelicans. Wax myrtle and southern redcedar grow on Wolf Island's highest elevations—only a few feet above sea level. The rest of the island is salt marsh (dominated by salt meadow cordgrass), small wetland hammocks, and tidal creeks. The refuge's beach, marsh, and upland are closed to visitation, but adjacent areas of open water and tidal creeks are open to visitors. Boat charter trips can be arranged at marinas, such as in the town of Darien. Information: (912) 652-4415.

Hawai'i and Pacific Remote Islands Complex: Hawai'i

Hanalei contains 917 acres to manage habitat for a number of endangered Hawaiian waterbirds in scenically beautiful Hanalei Valley, near the north shore of the Island of Kaua'i, Hawai'i. Continuing a 1,200-year tradition, local farmers cultivate crops of taro within the refuge's wetlands. A system of ditches diverts water from the Hanalei River to maintain open impoundments and to irrigate the pond-fields, known as "taro patches." The open ponds, taro patches, and marshy areas provide feeding and nesting habitat for the Hawaiian duck, Hawaiian coot, Hawaiian moorhen, and Hawaiian black-necked stilt. This refuge is not open to public visitation, but an overlook pullout is provided on State Hwy. 56, just downhill from the Princeville Shopping Center. Information: (808) 828-1413.

Hule'ia contains 241 acres to protect ecologically rich, seasonally flooded bottomlands, estuary, and wooded slopes along Hule'ia River, near the southeastern shore of the Island of Kaua'i, Hawai'i. For the benefit of the same endangered waterbirds as on Hanalei NWR, the land is being managed to provide areas of open water, reestablish native vegetation, and restore some of the former taro patches. Although this refuge is not open to visitation, it can be viewed from Menehune Fishpond Overlook, which is south from Liu'e on Rice St.-Waapa Rd. (in the direction of Nawiliwili Harbor), and right onto Hulemalu Rd. for 0.6 mile to the overlook on the left. Information: (808) 828-1413.

James C. Campbell contains 164 acres in two units to manage and protect KII UNIT's man-made ponds and PUNANMANO POND UNIT's spring-fed marsh, on the north shore of the

Island of O'ahu, Hawai'i. These wetlands provide important habitat for the same endangered waterbirds as on Hanalei NWR. Other species attracted here include Pacific golden plover and wandering tattler. Visitation is only by prearranged interpretive group tours on Thursdays and Saturdays, from August 1 to February 15. Information: (808) 637-6330.

Kakaha'ia contains 44 acres to enhance and protect two ponds primarily for the endangered Hawaiian black-necked stilt and Hawaiian coot. Pintails and a number of migratory shorebirds are also attracted to the refuge, which is located on the south shore of the Island of Moloka'i, Hawai'i. One of the ponds is a historic Polynesian-Hawaiian fishpond (loko i'a) that contains marshy habitat and the other is an expanse of open water that was created in the mid-1980s. Entry onto this refuge is only by special use permit. Information: (808) 875-1582.

Kealia Pond contains 700 acres to manage and protect a brackish pond and a series of diked impoundments that provide vital wetland habitat for the endangered Hawaiian black-necked stilt and the Hawaiian coot, as well as for a number of migratory ducks and shorebirds, near the south-central shore of the Island of Maui, Hawai'i. Public entry onto the refuge is restricted from March through August to avoid disturbing the nesting birds. Access from the junction of State Hwy. 31 and 311 in Kihei is north just over 0.75 mile on State Hwy. 311 and left onto a 0.4-mile paved spur road. Information: (808) 875-1582.

Pearl Harbor contains 61 acres in two units to manage and protect man-made wetlands within the Pearl Harbor U.S. Naval Reservation, about 10 miles west of Honolulu on the Island of O'ahu, Hawai'i. These wetlands provide important habitat for the same endangered waterbirds as on Hanalei NWR. Other birds include a number of migratory ducks and shorebirds, black-crowned night-herons, and occasionally the short-eared owl. Entry onto the refuge is only by special permit for environmental education classes, guided tours during special events, and non-guided birdwatching, and wildlife photography. A wildlife observation platform is provided at the refuge's HONOULIULI UNIT, on Pearl Harbor's West Loch. Information: (808) 637-6330.

Hawai'i and Pacific Remote Islands Complex: Pacific Remote Islands

Baker Island contains 30,909 acres to protect this uninhabited, 27-foot-high, coral-topped emergent seamount island and a narrow fringing tropical coral reef, located 13 miles north of the Equator, about 1,600 nautical miles southwest of Honolulu, Hawai'i, in the mid-Pacific Ocean. The refuge provides nesting, roosting, and foraging habitat for roughly 20 species of seabirds and shorebirds. Among the seabirds are the lesser frigatebird, red-tailed tropicbird, common fairy-tern, sooty tern, three species each of boobies and noddies, and wedge-tailed and Audubon's shearwaters. The threatened green sea turtle and pods of bottlenose dolphins inhabit the waters around the island. The refuge is also home to 160 species of reef fish and many varieties of corals. The refuge is closed to visitation, except by special permit for approved research. Information: (808) 541-1201.

Hawaiian Islands contains more than 1,766 acres of emergent lands and 610,148 acres of submergent lands in the Northwestern Hawaiian Islands—a chain of small islands, atolls, and reefs that stretches across more than 1,000 miles of mid-Pacific Ocean to the northwest of the main islands of Hawai'i. In 1909, President Theodore Roosevelt established the Hawaiian Islands Reservation to offer protection for seabirds that were being slaughtered for their elegant feathers, to satisfy the demands of fashion. In 1940, the reservation was upgraded to a national wildlife refuge. In 2006, President George W. Bush established by proclamation the Northwestern Hawaiian Islands Marine National Monument—the world's largest marine protected area. The name of the 89.6-million-acre monument was subsequently changed to the Polynesian-Hawaiian name: Papahanaumokuakea.

Within this vast area, the F&WS continues to manage and protect the emergent and submergent lands and the National Oceanic and Atmospheric Administration manages the oceanic expanses. Among the colonial nesting birds are Laysan and black-footed albatrosses, bonin and Bulwer's petrels, wedge-tailed and Christmas shearwaters, red-tailed tropicbirds, three species of boobies, great and lesser frigatebirds, fairy-terns, gray-backed and sooty terns, and three species of noddies. Other prominent birds include Laysan ducks, Laysan and Nihoa finches, Nihoa millerbirds, the endangered Hawaiian monk seal, and the threatened green sea turtle. This refuge is closed to visitation, except by special permit. Information: (808) 541-1201.

Howland Island contains 32,074 acres to protect this uninhabited, 20-foot-high, coral-topped emergent seamount island and fringing coral reef, located 48 miles north of the Equator, about 1,600 nautical miles southwest of Honolulu, Hawai'i, in the mid-Pacific Ocean. It mainly provides nesting, roosting, and foraging habitat for the same bird species as on Baker Island NWR. The refuge is closed to visitation, except by special permit for approved research. Information: (808) 541-1201.

Jarvis Island contains 36,483 acres to protect this uninhabited emergent seamount island and a surrounding tropical reef, located 25 miles south of the Equator and about 1,300 nautical miles southwest of Honolulu, Hawai'i, in the mid-Pacific Ocean. It mainly provides nesting, roosting, and foraging habitat for the same bird species on Baker Island NWR. The refuge is closed to visitation, except by special permit for approved research. Information: (808) 541-1201.

Johnston Atoll contains 696 acres of land to provide protection for numerous species of nesting seabirds and the surrounding coral reef ecosystem at one of the world's most isolated atolls. This refuge is located 718 nautical miles southwest of Honolulu, Hawai'i, in the central Pacific Ocean. Roughly 70 million years ago, numerous volcanic eruptions of lava at the bottom of the sea gradually created a submarine volcano whose summit ultimately reached the ocean surface as an island. During subsequent millions of years, the mountaintop island gradually eroded and sank. As it slowly subsided, coral reef formations grew around its edges. The resulting extensive growth of corals and coralline algae now comprises a broad, submerged, platform-like, 50-square-mile reef. This atoll is inhabited by 15 species of seabirds (as many as 150,000 sooty terns breed here), five species of migratory shorebirds, 33 varieties of coral, more than 300 species of tropical fishes, and the threatened green sea turtle and wintering North Pacific humpback whales. Visitor entry is restricted to avoid disturbing the seabirds. Information: (808) 421-0011, ext. 3182.

Kingman Reef contains roughly 483,700 acres to protect more than 25,800 acres of coral reef habitat and surrounding waters to protect a large diversity of coral reef fishes, corals, and other marine life, as well as migratory seabirds, shorebirds, and the threatened green sea turtle. The refuge, which is not open to visitors, is the northernmost of the Line Islands, located about 1,000 miles south of Hawai'i in the central Pacific Ocean. Information: (808) 541-1201.

Rose Atoll contains 39,251 acres to protect a 15-acre emergent island and surrounding submerged land and water, located in the U.S. territory of American Samoa, about 2,700 nautical miles south-southwest of Hawai'i in the southwest Pacific Ocean. The refuge, which feature's one of the world's smallest atolls, protects habitat that attracts seabirds, the threatened green sea turtle and endangered hawksbill sea turtle, more than 40 varieties of coral, and 100 species of fish. Among the seabirds are red-footed booby, great and lesser frigatebirds, common fairy-tern, sooty tern, and black noddy. Because of the sensitivity of the seabird colonies and other wildlife, entry onto this refuge is by special use permit only. Information: (808) 541-1201.

Idaho

Bear Lake contains 18,085 acres to manage and protect an extensive wetland, locally known as Dingle Marsh, primarily for migrating and nesting Canada geese and ducks of many species, on mountain-framed Bear Lake in southeastern Idaho. In late September, flocks of greater sandhill cranes are frequently attracted to the refuge's grain fields on their southward migration to wintering areas in Arizona, New Mexico, and Mexico.

An auto tour road through the refuge's SALT MEADOW UNIT offers opportunities to view wildlife. Boat-launching sites are provided on the RAINBOW UNIT and at adjacent North Beach State Park, offering opportunities for canoeing and boating from September 20 to January 15. Other visitor activities include cross-country skiing, snowshoeing, and seasonal hunting on parts of the refuge. Access from the junction of U.S. Highways 30 and 89 in Montpelier is west 3 miles on U.S. Hwy. 89 and left onto unpaved Bear Lake County Airport Rd. for 5 miles. Refuge headquarters is at 370 Webster St., Montpelier. Information: (208) 847-1757.

Camas contains 10,578 acres primarily to protect wetlands that attract concentrations of migrating and nesting waterfowl, shorebirds, and other wildlife, located at the northeastern end of the arid Snake River Plains in southeastern Idaho. The refuge is a mixture of sub-irrigated meadows and bulrush marshes to open lakes and ponds, as well as upland meadows and sagebrush-and-grass. Camas Creek flows through the refuge. Nutrient-rich crops of barley, wheat, and alfalfa are grown for waterfowl and other wildlife. Sometimes as many as 50,000 trumpeter and tundra swans pause here during spring and autumn migrations. Other birds are greater sandhill cranes, white pelicans, Canada geese, a number of duck species, and usually a few wintering bald eagles. Mammals include Rocky Mountain elk, white-tailed and mule deer, pronghorns, bobcats, and beavers.

An auto tour route and a hiking trail that meanders through an area of riparian woodland offer wildlife-viewing opportunities. Other visitor activities include cross-country skiing, snowshoeing, and seasonal hunting. Access from the I-15's Hamer Exit is north on the frontage road and (at a refuge directional sign) left 2 miles. Information: (208) 662-5423.

Oxford Slough Waterfowl Production Area contains 1,878 acres to provide nesting habitat for waterfowl, notably redhead ducks, by managing bulrush marsh and scattered expanses of open water, surrounded by wet meadow, cropland, saltgrass flats, and playa, in southeastern Idaho. Much of the meadowland offers feeding habitat for geese and sandhill cranes; and irrigated cropland is cooperatively farmed so that some of the grain crop remains unharvested for wildlife. Visitor activities include wildlife observation, hiking, and seasonal hunting. Access from I-15 is southeast 12 miles on Hwy. 91, right onto County Rd. DI for 8 miles to just north of the village of Oxford, and left onto a gravel road that runs along the northern edge of the waterfowl production area to a parking area (this access road may be impassable during wet weather). Information: (208) 847-1757.

Illinois

Emiquon is a refuge-in-progress toward a goal of roughly 11,000 acres to restore and protect wetland and related habitats in the Illinois River Valley of west-central Illinois. As ultimately envisioned, the refuge will consist primarily of backwater lakes, permanent marsh, bottomland hardwood forest, and other seasonally flooded wetlands. Small parts of the refuge will include upland forest and prairie grassland, as well as some acreage retained for growing crops for waterfowl and other wildlife. Emiquon is one of three refuges (Chautauqua and Meredosia are the others) comprising the Illinois River National Wildlife and Fish Refuges, located along a 125-mile stretch of the river. Visitor activities include wildlife observation, boating, and seasonal hunting. Access from Havana is west 1 mile on U.S. Hwy. 136 and right on State Hwy. 78/79. Information: (309) 535-2290.

Meredosia contains roughly 3,400 acres toward a planned goal of around 5,200 acres, to manage and protect floodplain and adjacent uplands habitats (similar to Emiquon NWR) at the upper end of the Alton Navigational Pool, along the east bank of the Illinois River in west-central Illinois. Short trails offer the chance to view wildlife. Access from State Hwy. 104 in the town of Meredosia is north on Putnam St. to the refuge entrance, at the north edge of town. Information: (309) 535-2290.

Middle Mississippi River contains roughly 5,000 acres to manage important wetland habitat for migratory waterfowl and other wildlife, located along a stretch of the Mississippi River downstream from St. Louis, in southwestern Illinois and southeastern Missouri. This multi-unit refuge is undeveloped for visitor use, but visitor activities include wildlife observation, hiking, and seasonal hunting. Information: (618) 997-3344.

Two Rivers contains 8,501 acres in three separate units to manage important wetland habitat for migratory waterfowl and other wildlife, located along the Illinois and Mississippi rivers, in southwestern Illinois. The refuge consists of moist-soil impoundments that are flooded in time for autumn migration when thousands of ducks and geese pause to rest and feed here. Bald eagles accompany this influx of waterfowl. Under cooperative agreements, local farmers plant certain areas of the refuge with crops of corn, wheat, and soybeans—leaving a portion in the fields as a supplemental food source for wildlife. Gilbert Lake Overlook Rd. and an observation deck at the refuge headquarters offer opportunities for viewing wildlife. Access to the GILBERT LAKE OVERLOOK UNIT is west from Alton, Ill., about 20 miles on State Hwy. 100 and left onto the refuge overlook road. Information: (618) 883-2524.

Iowa

Driftless Area contains more than 600 acres in seven scattered units to manage a mixture of hardwood forest and grassland habitats for the benefit of the endangered Iowa Pleistocene snail and a threatened plant—the northern monkshood, in northeastern Iowa. Land acquisition is continuing, toward providing these species with protection sufficient to ultimately merit their removal from endangered and threatened status. Visitor activities include wildlife observation and seasonal hunting. Ecologically sensitive parts of the refuge for these species are closed to visitors. Information: (319) 873-3423.

Port Louisa contains 10,791 acres in four separate units to manage wetland, grassland, and woodland habitats along a stretch of the Mississippi River floodplain, in southeastern Iowa and western Illinois. Tens of thousands of migrating ducks and a few thousand geese pause to rest and feed here in spring and autumn. Bald eagles are most numerous from late autumn to early spring. To avoid disturbing waterfowl concentrations, the LOUISA UNIT is closed to visitors from mid-September through December and the HORSESHOE BEND UNIT is closed from mid-September through November. Visitor activities include wildlife observation, hiking, boating, and seasonal hunting. Access to the refuge headquarters, on the Louisa Unit, is 6 miles east from Wapello on Great River Rd. (County Hwy. X-61). Information: (319) 523-6982.

Union Slough contains 2,845 acres to manage an area of wetland habitat for migratory waterfowl and other wildlife along nearly 8 miles of Union Slough and Buffalo Creek, in north-central Iowa. The slough's wetlands have been enhanced with dikes, dams, and other water-control structures. Six wetland units are seasonally regulated to promote the growth of aquatic plants for ducks and geese that pause to rest and feed during spring and autumn migrations. Hundreds of migrating white pelicans frequently stop here. Some of the refuge consists of tallgrass prairie, along the eastern edge of the northern Great Plains.

Deer Meadow (with its Indian Bluff Nature Trail) toward the southern end of the refuge is open to visitors from March 1 to November 15. Vanishing Prairie Grassland near the northern end of the refuge is open to visitors from July 15 through September. Visitor activities include wildlife observation, hiking, and seasonal hunting. Access from Algona is north about 14 miles on U.S. Hwy. 169 (to the south edge of Bancroft) and right onto County Rd. A-42 for 6 miles; or from I-90 at Blue Earth, Minn., it is south about 33 miles on U.S. Hwy. 169 (to the south edge of Bancroft) and left onto County Rd. A-42 for 6 miles. Information: (515) 928-2523.

Kansas

Marais Des Cygnes contains 7,500 acres to restore and protect an area of bottomland hardwood forest along the Marais des Cygnes River, near the Missouri state line in eastern Kansas. The French name, meaning "Marsh of the Swans," apparently came from the historical use of the area by trumpeter swans. In addition to the river and adjacent woodlands, refuge habitats include floodplain ponds, small farm and mine ponds, upland oak-hickory forest, tracts of native tallgrass prairie, and former farm fields. Seasonal flooding occurs on about a quarter of the refuge. Waterfowl, shorebirds, raptors, and neotropical songbirds are among the many migratory birds attracted here. Resident birds include wild turkeys and bobwhite quail. More than 300 bird species have been recorded on this refuge.

Visitor activities include wildlife observation, hiking, canoeing and boating (no launching facilities), and seasonal hunting. Access from Pleasanton is north 5 miles on U.S. Hwy. 69 and right onto State Hwy. 52 for a mile. Information: (913) 352-8956.

Louisiana

Bayou Cocodrie contains 13,168 acres to enhance and protect important habitat for nesting wood ducks, wintering waterfowl, wading birds, neotropical songbirds, and other wildlife, along this area of the lower Mississippi River Valley of east-central Louisiana. Roughly a quarter of the refuge is wetland where seasonal rains fill basins and where beavers build dams that create ponds, attracting large concentrations of wintering ducks and other waterbirds. More than three-quarters of the refuge consists of bald cypress swamp and a relatively pristine remnant of bottomland hardwood forest.

Visitor activities include wildlife observation from roads and trails, pre-arranged interpretive tours and interpretive programs, and seasonal hunting on parts of the refuge. Access to the refuge contact station is south from Ferriday by way of State Hwy. 15, and right onto Poole Rd. for about 3.5 miles. Information: (318) 336-7119.

Bayou Sauvage contains 22,770 acres to manage an area of freshwater and brackish marshes and swamps, bayous, lagoons, and canals, within the city of New Orleans, Louisiana. This largest urban wildlife refuge in the United States was established to provide wetland habitat for tens of thousands of wintering waterfowl and other waterbirds, such as the brown pelican. More than 265 bird species have been recorded here. The American alligator is abundant.

In 2005, Hurricane Katrina damaged or destroyed a number of refuge facilities. Some of them have been or will be repaired or rebuilt. Flooding from the hurricane pushed salt water into some freshwater habitat, and the F&WS expects these areas will gradually recover. Many trees were destroyed, and a program of tree-planting is helping with restoration. Access from I-10 is south on U.S. Hwy. 11; or by way of U.S. Hwy. 90, just northeast of downtown New Orleans. Information: (504) 646-7555.

Bayou Teche contains 9,028 acres in a number of separate units, toward a goal of roughly 27,000 acres, primarily for the protection of the threatened Louisiana black bear. The refuge is near Franklin, in southeast coastal Louisiana. Other wildlife includes wintering waterfowl, wading birds, bald eagles, numerous species of neotropical songbirds, white-tailed deer, bobcats, river otters, and alligators. The refuge consists of bottomland hardwood forest and cypress swamp. The refuge is expected to offer interpretive programs and opportunities for wildlife-oriented recreation. The refuge's office is presently adjacent to State Hwy. 182 about 2 miles southeast of the town of Franklin. Information: (985) 853-1078.

Big Branch Marsh contains roughly 15,000 acres to manage an area of freshwater and salt marshes, bayous, cypress sloughs, cypress-and-hardwood hammocks, low ridges of pine woodland, and sandy beaches. The refuge is near the town of Lacombe on the shore of Lake Pontchartrain, across from New Orleans, Louisiana. Concentrations of wintering waterfowl, nesting wood ducks, numerous wading birds, shorebirds, and neotropical songbirds are attracted to the refuge. The endangered red-cockaded woodpecker inhabits the refuge (see details on this species in the Carolina Sandhills NWR text).

Visitor activities include interpretive tours and educational programs. In 2005, some facilities damaged by Hurricane Katrina have since been repaired or rebuilt, including the Boardwalk. Thousands of trees were destroyed, but a tree-planting program is helping with restoration. Access from I-12 is south on State Hwy. 434 to Lacombe, then left onto U.S. Hwy. 190 for 2.5 miles, right onto Transmitter Rd., right onto Bayou Paquet Rd., and left onto Boy Scout Rd. Information: (985) 892-1441.

Black Bayou Lake contains 4,200 acres to protect habitat for wintering waterfowl, wading birds, shorebirds, and nesting wood ducks. The refuge is located north of Monroe in northeastern Louisiana. The refuge includes 2,000-acre Black Bayou Lake with impressive bald cypress and tupelo trees, as well as bottomland cypress-and-hardwood forest and mixed pine-and-hardwood uplands. The visitor center, in a restored planter's house, is at the 40-acre Black Bayou Lake Environmental Education Center, which also includes a wildlife-observation deck, boat-launching facility, arboretum, 3-acre demonstration prairie, and nature trail. Access from Monroe is north about 4 miles on U.S. Hwy. 165 and right onto Richland Place. Information: (318) 387-1114.

Bogue Chitto contains 37,000 acres to enhance and protect an important remnant of the Pearl River's pristine cypress-and-mixed hardwood bottomland forest, extending along both sides of the Louisiana-Mississippi border, about 40 miles northeast of New Orleans, Louisiana. More than 50 miles of waterways, including oxbow lakes and sloughs, wind throughout the refuge. Water levels fluctuate widely and most of the refuge is at times inundated. This area provides habitat for wintering waterfowl, nesting wood ducks, and numerous neotropical songbirds. Self-guiding canoe routes offer opportunities to explore the refuge, with favorable water levels being most likely from January through spring.

Visitor activities include wildlife observation, canoeing and shallow-draft boating, and seasonal hunting. Commercial outfitters provide canoes and guides for one-day or multi-day excursions. Access to the Louisiana side of the refuge from the I-59 Pearl River Turnaround Exit 11 is west to the Holmes Bayou Trail or east to a fishing area; access to the Mississippi side from I-59 at Picayune is on State Hwy. 43 to Walkiah Bluff Water Park or Dumas Wise Rd. Information: (985) 882-2000.

Breton contains 18,273 acres encompassing a chain of sandy barrier islands, curving eastward from Louisiana's Mississippi River Delta toward the coast of Mississippi. In 1904, President Theodore Roosevelt established this as the nation's second wildlife refuge, to protect the largest breeding colonies of brown pelicans and terns in the United States. Other birds include magnificent frigatebirds and black skimmers.

The 2005 storm season heavily damaged this refuge. In June, tropical storm Arlene overwashed the islands, destroying many pelican eggs; and then an oil spill polluted nesting habitat, coating many young pelicans with oil. Later, the refuge took a direct hit from Hurricane Katrina, causing major erosion and impacting large areas of beaches, marshes, and vegetation that helps stabilize the islands and offers nesting habitat for the pelicans. Visitor use of the refuge is limited mostly to spring through autumn; seabird nesting colonies are posted as closed to public entry during the nesting season. Information: (985) 882-2000.

Cat Island contains 9,623 acres toward a goal of more than 36,000 acres to restore and manage bottomland hardwood forest wetlands near the Mississippi River, about 30 miles northwest of Baton Rouge, in southeastern Louisiana. The refuge lies along the southernmost stretch of the river without levees and is inundated usually from January to June by up to 15 feet of water. Among the wildlife are swallow-tailed kites, wood storks, wood ducks, wild turkeys, large numbers of neotropical songbirds, white-tailed deer, bobcats, river otters, the endangered

Louisiana black bear, and alligators. Of the refuge's exceptional old-growth cypresses, the F&WS says, "Many of the bald cypress trees are estimated to be anywhere from 500 to 1,000 years old. In fact, the Grand National Champion bald cypress, which is also the largest tree of any species east of . . . [California's] Sierra Nevada . . . , is located within the . . . [refuge] boundary."

Visitor activities include wildlife observation, hiking, and seasonal hunting. Access from St. Francisville is north on U.S. Hwy. 61, left onto State Hwy. 66 for 1.5 miles, left onto Solitude Rd. for 3.5 miles, and right at a refuge directional sign. Information. (601) 442-6696.

D'Arbonne contains 17,421 acres to manage the meandering course of D'Arbonne Bayou, adjacent cypress swamp, numerous sloughs, creeks, oxbow lakes and ponds, seasonally flooded bottomland hardwood forest, and upland pine and hardwood forest. This refuge is located on the western edge of the lower Mississippi River's alluvial valley, in northeastern Louisiana. A tract of former farmland, known as the Beanfield, is being managed as a moist-soil impoundment area for wintering waterfowl, wading birds, and shorebirds. Other wildlife includes nesting wood ducks, wild turkeys, roadrunners (at the northeastern end of their range), the endangered red-cockaded woodpecker, white-tailed deer, and a few alligators (near the northern end of their range).

Visitor activities include canoeing and boating on 15 miles of the bayou, viewing wildlife on the Beanfield from an observation platform, and seasonal hunting. Access from either I-20's Mill Street exit or U.S. Route 80 in Monroe is just over 12 miles on State Hwy. 143. Information: (318) 726-4222.

Grand Cote contains 6,000 acres to enhance and protect remnants of original bottomland hardwood forest, cypress sloughs, reforested former farming lands, moist-soil impoundments, and croplands for concentrations of wintering waterfowl (notably pintails). The refuge is located southeast of Alexandria, in central Louisiana. In Cajun-French (Acadian), *grand cote*, means "big hill," in reference to a prominent bluff. Other wildlife includes wading birds, shorebirds, numerous species of neotropical songbirds, and alligators. Visitor activities include wildlife observation and hiking. Access from Marksville is 7 miles northwest on State Hwy. 1, then in Fifth Ward Community left onto State Hwy. 1194 for about 4 miles. Information: (318) 253-4238.

Handy Brake contains 466 acres to restore a small tract of land originally consisting of mixed bottomland hardwood forest that was cleared for agriculture, near Bastrom, in northeastern Louisiana. An observation platform offers visitors a view of waterfowl and wading birds on a 300-acre area of shallow lake wetland habitat. Access from the courthouse square in Bastrom is east 1.1 miles on U.S. Hwy. 165, left at the third stoplight for 6.4 miles on Parish Rd. 830-4 (Cooper Lake Rd.), and right at a refuge sign. Information: (318) 726-4222.

Lake Ophelia contains roughly 15,000 acres to manage and protect wetlands for waterfowl and to restore an area of bottomland hardwood forest that is laced with meandering waterways and a cypress-bordered oxbow lake that was formerly a bend in the Red River, in central Louisiana. Wildlife includes tens of thousands of wintering waterfowl, wading birds, nesting wood ducks, and alligators. Visitor activities include wildlife observation, hiking, boating on the lake, and seasonal hunting. Access from Marksville is northeast 25 miles on State Hwy. 452. Information: (318) 253-4238.

Mandalay contains 4,212 acres to protect extensive freshwater marshes located within the western Terrebonne Parish wetland complex, in south-central Louisiana. Other habitats include cypress swamp, ponds, and many canals. The refuge, which is bisected by the Gulf Coast Intracoastal Waterway, attracts large concentrations of wintering waterfowl, wading birds, bald eagles, and alligators. Visitor activities include wildlife observation, boating, and seasonal hunting. Access to the refuge is by boat from Cannon's Landing, on Southdown-Mandalay Rd. (parallel to State Hwy. 182), about 5 miles west of Houma. Information: (985) 853-1078.

Red River contains roughly 6,000 acres toward a goal of about 50,000 acres to restore bottomland hardwood forest on nonproductive farmland along a 120-mile stretch of this river, between the Arkansas state line and Colfax, Louisiana. Established in 2002, the refuge will also be managed to attract wintering waterfowl and migrating shorebirds. As the F&WS explains, "The refuge is the product of a carbon sequestration project that will offset the environmental impacts of fossil fuel emissions." Restoration of this forestland is projected to remove 240 tons of carbon from the atmosphere annually. The Service's partners that are making this refuge possible include The Conservation Fund, Entergy Corporation, Friends of the Red River, and Environmental Synergy, Inc. Visitor activities will include wildlife observation, hiking, environmental education programs, and seasonal hunting. Information: (318) 726-4222.

Sabine contains 124,511 acres to enhance and protect an extensive expanse of impounded freshwater marsh, estuarine coastal marsh, bayous, lakes, ponds, low ridges, and wooded islands, in the southwestern corner of Louisiana. This largest Gulf Coast national wildlife refuge provides habitat for thousands of wintering and migratory birds—notably snow geese and white pelicans. Other birds include the roseate spoonbill and several species of herons and egrets. Sabine is one of the Gulf Coast refuges where the spectacular neotropical songbird "fallout" phenomenon occurs in April (see Aransas NWR text). More than 25,000 American alligators inhabit the refuge, which also provides important nursery habitat for estuarine-dependent marine animals, such as shrimp and many varieties of fin fish.

The refuge is presently closed to visitor uses, such as wildlife observation, hiking, and seasonal hunting, because of severe damage by Hurricane Rita in 2005. The visitor center, offices, and maintenance shops were damaged beyond repair; and marshes and canals were severely impacted. Damaged bridges, piers, observation platforms, and boardwalks will be repaired before the refuge reopens. Access from I-10 at Sulphur is south 27 miles on State Hwy. 27. Information: (337) 558-5574 or 558-5631.

Shell Keys contains 78 acres to protect low-lying barrier island habitat in the Gulf of Mexico, south of New Iberia, Louisiana. In 1907, President Theodore Roosevelt established the refuge to protect brown pelicans, black skimmers, laughing gulls, and royal and sandwich terns. The refuge originally consisted of several islands, but in recent years only one fragile islet remains. Comprised almost entirely of tiny shell fragments and supporting virtually no vegetation, it builds or erodes and is often over-washed with passing storms. Visitation is restricted because of the refuge's remoteness. Information: (985) 882-2000.

Upper Ouachita contains more than 40,000 acres to enhance and protect an area of bottomland hardwood forest along 18 miles of the Ouachita River, extending south from the Arkansas border, in northeastern Louisiana. The refuge includes numerous bayous, sloughs, and creeks, as well as an area of pine-covered uplands. The separate MOLLICY UNIT was added to the refuge so that a bottomland forest area that was formerly cleared for agriculture can be restored. Much of the refuge's bottomland is flooded by shallow backwaters from the rising level of the river, which usually peaks in March and April. Wildlife includes migrating waterfowl, wading birds, wild turkeys, neotropical songbirds, white-tailed deer, and a few alligators.

Visitor activities include wildlife observation, canoeing and boating (two boat-launching ramps are provided), and seasonal hunting. Access from Monroe is north on U.S. Hwy. 165, left onto State Hwy. 2 to Sterlington, right onto State Hwy. 143 to Haile, and right onto Haile Baptist Church and Hooker Hole roads for 4 miles. Information: (318) 726-4222.

Maine

Aroostook contains 4,700 acres in several scattered tracts to restore and protect wildlife habitats on what was formerly part of the Loring Air Force Base, in northeastern Maine. The refuge includes wetlands, lakes, and ponds that attract migratory waterfowl, such as wood ducks, black ducks, and hooded mergansers. Forested uplands provide nesting habitat for numerous species of neotropical songbirds, such as thrushes and warblers. Four-hundred acres of grassland offer nesting habitat for upland sandpipers and bobolinks; and in spring, woodcocks perform their aerial courtship displays over these open areas. Mammals include moose, black bear, mink, marten, and fisher. About 6 miles of trails offer opportunities for wildlife observation, hiking, and cross-country skiing. Access from U.S. Hwy. 1 at Caribou is east on State Hwy. 89 and left on Loring Commerce Rd. for about 2 miles to the visitor contact station. Information: (207) 328-4634.

Maryland

Martin contains 5,157 acres of lower Chesapeake Bay tidal marshlands along parts of a 6-mile-long archipelago, in southeastern Maryland and northeastern Virginia. The refuge's main part consists of 4,423 acres on Smith Island, 11 miles west of Crisfield, Md. Large concentrations of migratory waterfowl, and nesting marsh birds, wading birds, shorebirds, gulls, and terns are attracted to the refuge. More than 1,500 tundra swans, 4,000 Canada geese, and 10,000 ducks (such as black, pintail, surf scoter, and red-breasted merganser) commonly winter on the refuge; and glossy ibis and several species of herons and egrets nest in rookeries. Spring Island boasts "the largest colony of brown pelicans in the Maryland portion of Chesapeake Bay." The refuge provides nesting platforms for ospreys, creating "the largest concentration of nesting ospreys in the region"; and the refuge's several nesting towers have proven successful for pairs of the endangered peregrine falcon.

To avoid disturbing nesting and wintering wildlife, this refuge is not open to visitation. A small visitor center is located at Middleton House, in the town of Ewell, on the non-refuge part of Smith Island. Information: (410) 228-2677.

Susquehanna was established to protect part of the Susquehanna Flats in what was exceptional habitat in the 1930s for large concentrations of diving ducks—notably canvasback, at the mouth of the Susquehanna River, in northeastern Maryland. Erosion has subsequently reduced the habitat to less than half an acre. The Fish and Wildlife Service says the refuge "possesses little or no value to wildlife." It is closed to visitation. Information: (410) 228-2677.

Massachusetts

Assabet River contains 2,230 acres in two tracts to manage an area of freshwater wetlands, pine-and-hardwood forest, cedar swamp and bog wetlands, vernal pools, shrubland, and open fields for migratory and resident wildlife. The refuge is located along the Assabet River, on the U.S. Army's former Fort Devens training annex, near Sudbury, in eastern Massachusetts. Visitor activities include wildlife observation, hiking on trails, and seasonal hunting. At this writing, a visitor center is being planned. Access to the refuge's main parking area from the Sudbury Town Center is west 3 miles on Hudson Rd. Information: (978) 443-4661.

Mashpee contains 335 federally owned acres within an authorized boundary of 5,871 acres to manage an area of salt marshes, pine barrens, cedar swamps, cranberry bogs, and a vernal pool for migratory and resident wildlife, near Mashpee, in southeastern Massachusetts. Migratory waterfowl, shorebirds, neotropical songbirds, and nesting ospreys are attracted here. The Fish and Wildlife Service explains that a unique partnership of federal, state, and private landowners jointly manages this Cape Cod refuge. Several of the partners are planning a refuge nature trail. Access is east on State Hwy. 28 and east on State Hwy. 151; at the rotary, continue on Great Neck Rd. south to Jehu Pond Conservation Area. Information: (978) 443-4661.

Massasoit contains 196 acres in two tracts to protect an area of pitch pine-scrub oak habitat and coastal Crooked Pond, located near the community of Plymouth, in southeastern Massachusetts. The refuge's primary mission is to provide habitat for the endangered Plymouth redbelly turtle and "Work cooperatively with partners to protect . . . [the] turtles through land-acquisition, cooperative management, research, and education." The refuge is presently closed to visitation to avoid disturbing the turtles. Unfortunately, trespassing by hikers, bikers, horseback riders, and ATVs threatens the refuge's habitat. Information: (978) 443-4661.

Nantucket contains 24 acres for migratory birds and other wildlife, located at the tip of Great Point on the northern end of Nantucket Island, in southeastern Massachusetts. The threatened piping plover and other shorebirds inhabit the beach, where gray and harbor seals often haul themselves out to rest. The refuge is presently managed by the Trustees of Reservations, owner of an adjacent wildlife sanctuary. Information about this organization's natural history tours on the refuge: (508) 228-6799. Refuge information: (978) 443-4661.

Nomans Land Island contains 628 acres to protect wetland and early successional upland habitats for migratory birds that rest, feed and/or nest on the island. The F&WS explains that "The refuge is considered the most important site in . . . Massachusetts for peregrine falcon during their fall migration." Because the island was previously a U.S. Navy bombing range, there is still the danger of unexploded ordnance. Consequently, the refuge is closed to visitation. Information: (978) 443-4661.

Oxbow contains 1,647 acres in several tracts, which were formerly part of Fort Devens Military Reservation, to enhance and protect important areas of oxbow wetlands, floodplain woodlands, freshwater marshes, and upland habitat along the Nashua River. The refuge, which is about 40 miles northwest of Boston, in eastern Massachusetts, attracts wood ducks and other waterfowl, wading birds, ruffed grouse, and numerous neotropical songbirds. In the spring, woodcocks perform their aerial courtship displays over the refuge's fields.

Visitor activities include wildlife observation; canoeing (a canoe-launching site is located near the parking area); hiking, cross-country skiing, and snowshoeing on 7 miles of trail; and seasonal hunting on parts of the refuge. Access from I-495 is west 3 miles on State Hwy. 117, right 3 miles on State Hwy. 110, and left on Still River Depot Rd. Information: (978) 443-4661.

Thacher Island contains 22 acres to protect shrub, grass, and rocky shoreline habitats for colonial nesting birds and other wildlife at the northern end of this island, located just off Cape Ann, in northeastern Massachusetts. The refuge attracts large concentrations of great black-backed and herring gulls, as well as a few glossy ibises. Under a memorandum of agreement, the town of Rockport provides oversight, protection, and periodic interpretive tours as conditions allow. Information: (978) 465-5753.

Michigan

Harbor Island consists of a 695-acre U-shaped island in Lake Huron's Potaganissing Bay, in northeastern Michigan. The island supports a variety of deciduous trees on higher ground, white cedars and balsam firs on lower areas, and fringes of marsh habitat along the sheltered bay. Wildlife includes a number of ducks, including scoters, mallards, black ducks, goldeneyes, and red-breasted mergansers; black terns; great blue herons; bald eagles; ospreys; ruffed grouse; numerous resident and neotropical songbirds; black bears; white-tailed deer; coyotes; red foxes; beavers; and snowshoe hares. Access to Harbor Island is by private boat. Information: (906) 586-9851.

Huron Islands contains 147 acres to protect a cluster of eight small islands located in Lake Superior, 3 miles north of the northern shore of Michigan's Upper Peninsula and about 18 miles east of the Keewenaw Peninsula. In 1905, President Theodore Roosevelt established this refuge, which protects sparse vegetation of pines, birches, and shrubs and large expanses of exposed granite. Bald eagles and nesting colonies of gulls are attracted to Cattle and Rock islands. Only West Huron Island is open to visitation. Information: (906) 586-9851.

Michigan Islands contains 623 acres to protect eight islands that attract migratory birds and other wildlife. Gull, Pismire, Shoe, and Hat islands in the Beaver Island group, are located in northern Lake Michigan, about 15 miles south of the southern shore of Michigan's Upper Peninsula; Scarecrow and Thunder Bay islands are in Lake Huron, about 2.5 miles east of North Point, in northeastern Michigan's Lower Peninsula; and Big and Little Charity islands are situated in Lake Huron's Saginaw Bay, about 10 miles east of the community of Au Gres. Among the refuge's wildlife are cormorants, Caspian terns, and ring-billed and herring gulls. Bald eagles are attracted to Big Charity Island. The refuge is closed to visitation to avoid disturbing colonial bird-nesting activity. Information on the Lake Michigan islands: (906) 586-9851; and on the Lake Huron islands: (989) 777-5930.

Whitefish Point contains 30 acres to protect a strategic point of land for major concentrations of migrating birds during spring and autumn, located at the northeastern tip of Michigan's Upper Peninsula. Adjacent to the refuge is the Whitefish Point Bird Observatory, a nonprofit organization that is "dedicated to the study and conservation of migrating birds in the Great Lakes region." As described by the observatory, "Whitefish Point is a phenomenal concentration spot for migrating raptors, waterbirds, and song birds." Access from Paradise is north 11 miles on Whitefish Point Rd. Information: (906) 586-9851.

Minnesota

Big Stone contains 11,520 acres to protect an area of tallgrass prairie, marsh, swamp, and woodland habitats along more than 11 miles of the upper Minnesota River valley, in west-central Minnesota. Roughly 4,200 acres of the refuge's wetlands were created when the U.S. Army Corps of Engineers built a dam. The reservoir's wetlands attract large numbers of migrating waterfowl, shorebirds, and other wildlife. About 850 acres of the refuge consist of low-lying, seasonally flooded woodland, where wood ducks and hooded mergansers use nesting cavities in old-growth trees. Roughly 4,000 acres are planted with crops for wildlife or have been restored to grasslands. The refuge also includes a scenic area of reddish granite outcropping canyon formations.

Visitor activities include wildlife observation, canoeing (from mid-April through September), hiking, cross-country skiing, snowshoeing, and seasonal hunting. The 0.75-mile Outcrop Prairie Interpretive Trail offers opportunities to see wildlife, prairie flora, rock outcroppings, and river meanders. Access from U.S. Hwy. 12 at Ortonville is southeast 2 miles on U.S. Hwy. 75 and right onto the refuge road. Information: (320) 273-2191.

Crane Meadows contains about 2,000 acres in scattered tracts, toward an authorized boundary of 13,540 acres, to restore and protect tallgrass prairie, oak savanna, and wetland habitats for the benefit of migratory waterfowl and other wildlife. The refuge, which is located about 30 miles north of St. Cloud in central Minnesota, attracts one of the largest nesting populations of greater sandhill cranes in Minnesota. The 3.5-mile Platte River Trail offers opportunities for wildlife observation, hiking, cross-country skiing, and snowshoeing. Access from Little Falls is south about 2 miles on State Hwy. 10 and a left-lane exit onto County Hwy. 35 east for about 4.5 miles to the Platte River Bridge, after which it is left to refuge headquarters. Information: (320) 632-1575.

Glacial Ridge contains nearly 2,500 acres toward a goal of 37,756 acres, "advancing the largest tallgrass prairie and wetland restoration project in U.S. history," located near Mentor, in northwestern Minnesota. This refuge, which was established in 2004, is being aided by a long list of partners, such as The Nature Conservancy, Ducks Unlimited, Pheasants Forever, the Minnesota Waterfowlers Association, and the Minnesota Department of Natural Resources.

The F&WS explains that "Over the last 30 years, much of the proposed refuge area has been drained or converted for agricultural purposes. The refuge seeks to restore up to 12,000 acres of wetlands and 14,000 acres of tallgrass prairie upland habitat. . . . The Nature Conservancy owns 24,140 acres . . . that will eventually make up the refuge. The remaining acres are owned by private landowners and/or by the State of Minnesota." A major mission of the refuge is to bring about the return of the greater prairie chicken to these lands.

Visitor activities presently include wildlife observation, interpretive programs, and seasonal hunting; and anticipated future facilities include hiking and cross-country skiing trails, observation platforms, and a visitor center. Access from U.S. Hwy. 2 at Mentor is west for 6 miles. Information: (218) 687-2229.

Hamden Slough contains 3,150 acres toward a goal of nearly 6,000 acres, in the transition zone between rolling hardwood forest and flat tallgrass prairie, near Audubon, in northwestern Minnesota. The refuge's main mission is to restore and manage roughly 3,000 acres of shallow wetlands and 2,250 acres of upland grassland. Habitat restoration projects during the past few years, including 112-acre Bisson Lake, have already yielded dramatic increases in populations of waterfowl, shorebirds, and prairie songbirds. Visitor activities include wildlife observation and hiking. Access to the refuge's southern end is north from U.S. Hwy. 10 on County Hwy. 13 to downtown Audubon, east and then north 1.5 miles on County Rd. 104, and 0.25 mile northwest on Township Rd. 440. Access to the refuge's northern part (to view prairie wetland habitat) is north from Calloway on U.S. Hwy. 59, left on County Hwy. 14, and left on County Hwy. 13. Information: (218) 847-4431.

Mille Lacs, at one-half acre, is the smallest refuge in the NWR System. It consists of two small rock islands, Hennepin and Spirit, for colonial nesting common terns, ring-billed and herring gulls, and cormorants. The refuge is located in the southern part of Mille Lacs Lake, in east-central Minnesota. Other birds pause here during migration, including Caspian and black terns, white pelicans, and common loons. The islands can be reached from a number of boat landings on the lake's south shore (along State Hwy. 27 between U.S. Hwy. 169 and the town of Isle). During the nesting season, visitors are urged to avoid disturbing the colonies by remaining well offshore. Information: (218) 768-2402.

Rice Lake contains 18,281 acres in two units to enhance and protect ecologically important habitat for many thousands of migratory waterfowl (notably ring-necked ducks) and an abundance of other wildlife, in east-central Minnesota. The refuge consists of the shallow, 4,500-acre wild-rice-producing Rice Lake and two smaller lakes; surrounding areas of freshwater marsh, white-cedar swamp, tamarack-and-black-spruce bogs; a stretch of meandering Rice River; and some grasslands remaining from prior farming. The area straddles a transition zone between coniferous forest to the north and deciduous forest to the south. Over 270 species of birds have been recorded here.

Wild rice is a tall variety of native grass that thrives in mucky soils of shallow lakes and marshes. In September, local Ojibwe Indians continue their traditional methods of harvesting the lake's crop. No machines are used, to ensure that sufficient grains remain for wildlife and to naturally reseed the lake. Wildlife includes Canada geese, wood ducks, sandhill cranes, sharp-tailed and ruffed grouse, black bears, and white-tailed deer. Large concentrations of waterfowl are attracted here in September and October.

Visitor activities include wildlife observation from the 9.5-mile auto tour road and a number of trails, cross-country skiing, and seasonal hunting. Access to the refuge's main unit from McGregor is east about 2 miles on State Hwy. 210 and right on State Hwy. 65 for 5 miles. Information: (218) 768-2402.

Mississippi

Coldwater River contains 2,069 acres to manage an area of abandoned farmland near Crowder, in northwestern Mississippi. During the winter and spring, nearly all of the refuge is inundated by the Coldwater and Tallahatchie rivers. Some of the seasonally flooded land is being restored to bottomland hardwood forest and cypress swamp. The refuge includes 25 former catfish ponds, the water levels of which are being regulated for waterfowl, shorebirds, and other wildlife. Large concentrations of wintering greater white-fronted geese, mallards, and green-winged teal are attracted to the wetlands, and nesting boxes are provided for wood ducks. Other birds include bald and golden eagles, peregrine falcons, and wood storks.

Visitor access is limited to wildlife observation from the Panola-Quitman Floodway Levee Rd. Access from Charleston is north 2 miles on State Hwy. 35, left on Puducah Wells Rd., and right onto the levee road. Information: (662) 226-8286.

Dahomey contains 9,691 acres to manage an area of bottomland hardwood forest and meandering bayous near the Mississippi River, in northwestern Mississippi. Roughly 1,600 acres of the refuge consist of abandoned, seasonally flooded farmland that is being restored to hardwood forest and cypress swamp. A small population of the endangered Louisiana black bear has been reestablished on the refuge. Nesting boxes are provided for wood ducks, and wintering waterfowl and migratory shorebirds are attracted to the wetlands.

Visitor activities include wildlife observation from an auto tour route (conditions permitting) and from a public road that runs through the refuge, and seasonal hunting. Access from Cleveland is south on State Hwy. 61 and right at Boyle on State Hwy. 446 for 6 miles. Information: (662) 742-9331.

Grand Bay contains 9,510 acres toward a goal of 32,000 acres to protect one of the largest expanses of undisturbed pine savanna habitat in the Gulf Coastal Plain region, in southeastern Mississippi and southwestern Alabama. The refuge's savanna and pine woodlands are intermingled with evergreen bays and stands of cypress, freshwater marsh, and brackish estuarine marsh. The latter is essential nursery habitat for more than 80 species of shellfish and finfish. Wildlife includes concentrations of wintering waterfowl, mink, and alligators. One of the refuge's goals is to provide suitable habitat for the establishment of a second breeding flock of the endangered Mississippi sandhill crane (see the Mississippi Sandhill Crane NWR text).

Entry onto the refuge is limited, but available by boat and from the Mississippi side. Visitor activities include wildlife observation, environmental education programs, and boating. Access from I-10's Exit 75 is south 0.25 mile on Franklin Creek Rd., crossing U.S. Hwy. 90 onto Pecan Rd. for a mile to a very active railroad crossing, and bearing right onto Bayou Heron Rd. for about a mile. Information: (228) 475-0765.

Holt Collier was established in 2004 to restore and manage bottomland hardwood forest and other habitats for such wildlife as waterfowl, wading birds (including roseate spoonbills, egrets, ibises, and wood storks), shorebirds, raptors (including Mississippi kites), and neotropical songbirds. This refuge is located southeast of Greenville, in west-central Mississippi. It contains 2,033 acres (including 633 acres that were donated as "mitigation" lands by the U.S. Army Corps of Engineers).

Holt Collier was born to an African-American slave family. He became famous throughout the region as "a legendary bear hunter and sportsman." In 1902, President Theodore Roosevelt accompanied him near Onward, Miss., on a bear hunt that became famous for spawning the creation of America's favorite toy, the "Teddy Bear."

As the F&WS explains, "Approximately 1,000 acres of marginal agricultural lands have already been reforested with native bottomland tree species. . . . As additional lands are purchased, much of it will be reforested . . . to help provide essential habitat for the endangered Louisiana black bear." Limited visitor activities presently include wildlife observation, hiking, and seasonal hunting. The Holt Collier Environmental Education and Interpretation Center is being planned. Access from Greenville is east on U.S. Hwy. 82 to just east of Leland, right onto U.S. Hwy. 61, left onto Avon Darlove Rd. to Darlove. Information: (662) 839-2638.

Mathews Brake contains 2,418 acres to restore and protect an area of bottomland hardwood forest and an oxbow lake adjacent to the Yazoo River, in west-central Mississippi. These habitats attract concentrations of wintering waterfowl (as many as 30,000 ducks), as well as nesting wood ducks, wild turkeys, numerous species of neotropical songbirds, white-tailed deer, bobcats, river otters, beavers, and alligators.

Visitor activities include wildlife observation, limited hiking, boating on the oxbow lake (a boat-launching ramp is provided), and seasonal hunting. Access from Greenwood is south 9 miles on U.S. Hwy. 49, right at Sidon; after crossing railroad tracks, left at the second street for about 5 miles; about 100 yards beyond a bridge, left for about 0.5 mile, and right onto a gravel road. Information: (662) 839-2638.

Morgan Brake contains 7,381 acres to enhance and protect an area of bottomland hardwood forest, sloughs, cypress-tupelo brakes, ponds, and agricultural fields, in west-central Mississippi. These habitats attract large concentrations of waterfowl (more than 100,000 ducks), and such other wildlife as nesting wood ducks, wild turkeys, numerous species of neotropical songbirds, white-tailed deer, bobcats, river otters, beavers, and alligators. The refuge includes a mile-long segment of loess bluffs (compacted wind-blown soil deposits that have eroded vertically) with a unique array of trees and understory plants.

Visitor activities include wildlife observation from roads in and adjacent to the refuge, hiking, and seasonal hunting. Access from Tchula is north about 2 miles on U.S. Hwy. 49E and right onto Providence Rd. for 2 miles. Information: (662) 839-2638.

Panther Swamp contains 38,601 acres to manage an area of bottomland hardwood forest, cypress-tupelo brakes, bayous, and sloughs along the Yazoo River, in west-central Mississippi. These habitats attract large concentrations of wintering waterfowl, and such other wildlife as nesting wood ducks, wild turkeys, numerous neotropical songbirds, white-tailed deer, bobcats, river otters, beavers, and alligators. Visitor activities include wildlife observation from designated roads, hiking on roads and levees, canoeing and boating (launching ramps are provided onto Lake George and Deep Bayou) and seasonal hunting. Access from Yazoo City is north 2 miles on U.S. 49W, left onto River Rd. for about 6 miles, and right at Gumbo Acres. Information: (662) 839-2638.

St. Catherine Creek contains 24,442 acres to manage seasonally flooded bottomland hardwood forest, cypress swamp, sloughs, and other wetland areas, along old St. Catherine Creek and the Mississippi River, near Natchez in southwestern Mississippi. Wildlife includes large concentrations of wintering waterfowl, nesting wood ducks, wading birds, shorebirds, wild turkeys, numerous neotropical songbirds, white-tailed deer, bobcats, river otters, beavers, and alligators. Cypress and several species of oaks are being planted on lands that were previously cleared for agriculture. Management plans include the construction of water-control structures, so that seasonal backwater flooding can be regulated for waterfowl and other wildlife. Under cooperative agreements, other lands are devoted to the production of crops, whereby farmers leave a portion unharvested for waterfowl and other wildlife.

Visitor activities include wildlife observation, hiking (an interpretive trail is located near headquarters), canoeing and boating; and seasonal hunting. Access from Natchez is south 10 miles on U.S. Hwy. 61, right onto York Rd. for 2 miles, and left onto Pintail Lane. Information: (601) 442-6696.

Tallahatchie contains 4,200 acres to manage an area of abandoned farmland, meandering cypress-bordered bayous, and scattered small tracts of forest, in northwestern Mississippi. Some of the seasonally flooded land that was previously cleared for agriculture is being restored to bottomland hardwood forest. Water levels of moist-soil impoundments are regulated for wintering waterfowl, wading birds, and shorebirds. Visitor activities include wildlife observation, boating, and seasonal hunting. Access from Grenada is west on State Hwy. 8 through Holcomb. Just west of its junction with State Hwy. 35, Hwy. 8 borders and then runs through the refuge. Information: (662) 226-8286.

Theodore Roosevelt contains 6,600 acres in scattered Farmers Home Administration tracts that are being exchanged for a single tract of land, located near Onward, in west-central Mississippi. This refuge, which was established in 2004 to restore and protect bottomland hardwood forest and other habitats for such wildlife as waterfowl, wading birds, raptors, neotropical songbirds, and the endangered Louisiana black bear. Visitor activities will include wildlife observation, hiking, and seasonal hunting. Information: (662) 839-2638.

Yazoo contains 12,941 acres to restore and protect an area of bottomland hardwood forest, cypress-tupelo brakes, bayous, sloughs, marsh, lakes and ponds, and impoundments, located near the Mississippi River in west-central Mississippi. As many as 50,000 wintering geese and 100,000 wintering ducks are attracted to the refuge's wetlands. Other wildlife includes the endangered Louisiana black bear, numerous species of neotropical songbirds, and alligators. More than 250 species of birds have been recorded here. The refuge is reforesting lands that were previously cleared for agriculture. Some impoundments are seasonally regulated to produce moist-soil plants for waterfowl and shorebirds; while green-tree reservoirs are flooded for wintering waterfowl. Nesting boxes are provided for wood ducks. Under cooperative agreements, farmers leave a portion of their crops unharvested for waterfowl and other wildlife.

Visitor activities include wildlife observation from designated refuge roads, hiking on dikes and levees, and seasonal hunting. Access from Greenville is south 22 miles on State Hwy. 1 and left onto the refuge road for 3 miles. Information: (662) 839-2638.

Missouri

Big Muddy National Fish and Wildlife Refuge contains more than 10,000 acres in eight locations, toward an authorized goal of restoring and managing some 60,000 acres of floodplain habitat along the Missouri River, from its confluence with the Kansas River to the Mississippi River, near St. Louis, Missouri.

The largest, most accessible units include the 2,050-acre OVERTON BOTTOMS UNIT, a few miles west of Columbia, consisting of old fields, dense young-growth woodland, and a narrow riverbank stretch of old-growth cottonwoods, accessed from I-70's Exit 111, north 100 yards, and right onto Hwy. 98 for 2 miles to the unit's 4 miles of gravel refuge roads and a boat ramp; and the 1,871-acre JAMESON ISLAND UNIT, a few miles northwest of Booneville, consisting of mostly dense young-growth woodland and featuring the 1-mile Lewis and Clark Discovery Trail, accessed from I-70's State Hwy. 41 Exit, north to Main St. in Arrow Rock, left uphill and around behind the Lyceum Theater, and (following a refuge directional sign) 0.25 mile to the refuge parking area.

Across the river from the latter area is the 2,013-acre LISBON BOTTOM UNIT consisting of mostly young-growth woodland, accessed from I-70's State Hwy. 87 exit, northwest through Booneville, left onto Hwy. K 4 miles to Lisbon, and left (at the church) about 1.5 miles to the refuge parking area. Refuge headquarters is at 4200 New Haven Rd., in Columbia. Information: (573) 876-1826.

Clarence Cannon contains 3,751 acres to manage an area of wetland impoundments, bottomland forest, grassland, and cultivated fields for migratory waterfowl, wading birds, shorebirds and other wildlife. The refuge is located in the Mississippi floodplain of eastern Missouri. Habitat management includes the regulation of water levels in moist-soil impoundments for migrating waterfowl, and in green-tree impoundments containing bottomland forest with large trees containing nesting cavities used by wood ducks and other wildlife. Prominent among the 230 species of birds recorded here are the large concentrations of Canada and snow geese and many species of ducks during migrations, as well as shorebirds, bald eagles, and numerous neotropical songbirds.

Visitor activities include wildlife observation, driving refuge roads, and hiking. Access from I-70 at St. Peters is north 35 miles on State Hwy. 79 to Annada and right a mile on County Rd. 206. Information: (573) 847-2333.

Great River contains 9,800 acres to manage and protect an area of wetland habitat for migratory waterfowl and other wildlife, along the Mississippi River floodplain, in northeastern Missouri and western Illinois. Challenging visitor activities on the Fox Island and Long Island divisions of the refuge include boating, hiking, and seasonal hunting. Nearby Bear Creek and Canton Chute recreation areas, in Canton, offer boat-launching facilities. Information: (573) 847-2333.

Ozark Cavefish contains 40 acres to protect Turnback Creek cave spring, the outlet of an underground stream inhabited by a population of the endangered blind cavefish, in southwestern Missouri. The refuge is closed to visitation. Information: (573) 222-3589.

Pilot Knob contains 90 acres to protect critical roosting habitat in abandoned iron ore mine shafts, for the endangered Indiana bat, as well as for the little brown and long-eared bats, in southeastern Missouri. The refuge is closed to visitation. Information: (573) 222-3589.

Swan Lake contains 10,795 acres to manage an area of wetland and grassland habitats for migratory waterfowl and other wildlife, in north-central Missouri. As the F&WS says, "this refuge has one of the largest concentrations of Canada geese in North America and is now the primary wintering area for the Eastern Prairie Population." As many as 100,000 to 200,000 geese are attracted here at one time, with up to 75,000 wintering on the refuge. In addition, the refuge attracts more than 100,000 ducks of many species during autumn migration; and up to 150,000 snow geese, 1,000 to 2,000 white pelicans, and 125 bald eagles. In addition to moist-soil impoundments, other managed wetlands, open water, grassland, and crops cultivated to offer supplemental food for wildlife, the refuge includes a 1,000-acre old-growth riparian woodland research natural area.

Visitor activities include wildlife observation from refuge roads, from a loop trail, and from an observation tower just east of the visitor center; and seasonal hunting (including a special primitive-weapons deer hunt). Access from Macon is west 40 miles on U.S. Hwy. 36, left 7 miles on State Hwy. 139 to Sumner, and south a mile on Swan Lake Dr. Information: (660) 856-3323.

Montana

Black Coulee contains 1,494 acres to manage an area of predominantly upland grassland and a small reservoir for migratory waterfowl and shorebirds, sharp-tailed grouse, and other wildlife, located about 38 miles northwest of Bowdoin NWR, in northeastern Montana. Access from Harlem is north and northeast about 24 miles on a paved road, and then right 5 miles on a gravel road. Information: (406) 654-2863.

Bowdoin contains 15,552 acres to enhance and protect an area of lakes, ponds, marshes, shelterbelts, and prairie grassland for migratory birds, near Malta, in northeastern Montana. The refuge attracts large concentrations of migratory waterfowl and shorebirds, with as many as 1,000 tundra swans and 30,000 ducks and geese pausing to rest and feed in the autumn. White pelicans, Caspian terns, ring-billed and California gulls, great blue herons, and cormorants nest on islands in 5,459-acre Lake Bowdoin. Such birds as grebes, bitterns, and rails nest in areas of cattail and bulrush marshes. In early spring, sharp-tailed grouse perform their elaborate courtship displays on the grassland dancing grounds, known as leks.

Visitor activities include wildlife observation from the 15-mile auto tour road, canoeing and boating (a boat-launching ramp is provided near headquarters), and seasonal hunting on parts of the refuge. Access is a mile east of Malta on U.S. Hwy. 2, and right at a refuge directional sign onto County Rd. 2 for about 6 miles. Information: (406) 654-2863.

Creedman Coulee contains 2,728 acres to manage a small area of open water, marsh, sagebrush coulee, and grassland habitats for migratory birds, near the U.S.-Canada border crossing at Port of Willow Creek, in north-central Montana. Wildlife species are similar to those on Bowdoin

NWR. The refuge's privately owned lands are managed by the F&WS under conservation easement agreements. Consequently, permission is required from local landowners for visitor entry. Access from U.S. Hwy. 2 at Havre is north about 30 miles on State Hwy. 233. Information: (406) 654-2863.

Hailstone contains 1,988 acres to manage wetlands and surrounding shortgrass prairie for migratory waterfowl and other wildlife, located about 35 miles northwest of Billings, in south-central Montana. Three-hundred acre Hailstone Lake and its mudflats attract such birds as wigeons, shovelers, grebes, avocets, and phalaropes. In the summer months, Franklin's gulls are attracted to the lake. The prairie is inhabited by such species as pronghorns, coyotes, black-tailed prairie dogs, and burrowing owls. Visitor activities include wildlife observation, hiking, and seasonal hunting. Access from I-90 at Columbus is north nearly 25 miles on County Rd. 306 to Rapelje, right 4 miles on Rapelje-Molt Rd., and left 1.5 miles on Hailstone Basin Rd. Information: (406) 538-8706.

Halfbreed Lake contains 4,318 acres to manage three extensive areas of wetland habitat joined by Cedar Creek that are a mecca—when there is sufficient water—for large numbers of migrating waterfowl and shorebirds, and a few summering Canada geese. The refuge is located about 30 miles northwest of Billings, near Hailstone NWR, in south-central Montana. Visitor activities include wildlife observation and hiking. Access from I-90 at Columbus is north nearly 25 miles on County Rd. 306 to Rapelje, right 7 miles on Rapelje-Molt Rd., and right 1 mile. Information: (406) 538-8706.

Hewitt Lake contains 1,680 acres to manage a small area of former river oxbow ponds, marsh, and grassland for migratory birds, about 7 miles north of Bowdoin NWR, in northeastern Montana. The refuge's privately owned lands are managed by the F&WS under conservation easement agreements. Consequently, permission is required from local landowners for visitor entry. Access from U.S. Hwy. 2 at Saco is north 5 miles on County Rd. 243, and left 3 miles on a gravel road. Information: (406) 654-2863.

Lake Mason contains 11,204 acres in three contiguous units to manage a lake and areas of shortgrass prairie—the "premier migratory bird area in central Montana." The LAKE UNIT contains 1,288-acre Lake Mason, which, in wet years, attracts large concentrations of migratory Canada geese, ducks, and shorebirds in the spring and autumn. Most of the surrounding prairie habitat supports pronghorns, coyotes, badgers, and black-tailed prairie dogs. Visitor activities include wildlife observation, canoeing and non-motorized boating (a primitive boat-launching site is available), and seasonal hunting. Access from I-90 at Billings is north 49 miles on U.S. Hwy 87 to Roundup, left 6.5 miles on Golf Course Rd., and right 3 miles.

The WILLOW CREEK UNIT contains shortgrass prairie; and the NORTH UNIT contains shortgrass prairie—covered ridgetops and flats, and alluvial draws of sagebrush and grassland. These habitats support such species as pronghorns, golden eagles, sage-grouse, upland sandpipers, long-billed curlews, and chestnut-collared longspurs.

Visitor activities on the latter two units include wildlife observation, hiking, and seasonal hunting. Access to the North Unit from Roundup is north 11.8 miles on U.S. Hwy. 87, left

6.9 miles on Snowy Mountain Rd., right 7.2 miles on Graves Rd., and left 2.2 miles. Information: (406) 538-8706.

Lake Thibadeau contains 4,040 acres to manage ponds, marsh, and grassland for migratory birds, north of Havre and 15 miles southeast of Creedman Coulee NWR, in north-central Montana. Nearly all of this refuge consists of privately owned lands that are managed by the Fish and Wildlife Service under conservation easement agreements with local landowners. The refuge is closed to visitor entry. Information: (406) 654-2863.

Lamesteer contains 800 acres to manage wetland habitat in northeastern Montana. The F&WS has acquired only the water rights with which to manage the impounded waters of a 110-acre marsh for migratory waterfowl and other wildlife. The refuge consists of privately owned lands that are managed under conservation easement agreements with local landowners. The refuge is closed to visitor entry. Information: (406) 789-2305.

Lost Trail contains 9,325 acres to manage migratory bird habitats on a former cattle and horse ranch in Pleasant Valley, in northwestern Montana. This scenically beautiful montane-valley refuge includes 160-acre Dahl Lake, sub-irrigated wet meadows of largely reed canary grass, a mosaic of upland prairie grassland, and surrounding forested lower mountain slopes. Visitor activities include wildlife observation, hiking, and seasonal hunting. Access from Kalispell is west 21 miles on U.S. Hwy. 2, right at Marion onto Pleasant Valley Rd., and bearing right in 1.3 miles at the road fork. This road turns into a dirt road at the northern end of Bitterroot Lake and (at 5 miles from Marion) crosses Haskill Pass, continuing for about 8 miles to the refuge and another 7 miles to headquarters. Information: (406) 858-2216.

Ninepipe and **Pablo** both contain roughly 2,000 acres to manage an irrigation reservoir's open water and marsh habitat, between Missoula and Kalispell, in the Flathead Valley of northwestern Montana. The wetlands provide feeding, resting, and nesting areas for such species as Canada geese, mallards, teal, pintails, shovelers, wigeons, ruddy ducks, and other waterbirds. The largest concentrations of waterfowl are attracted to the refuges during spring and autumn migrations. The refuges are located on Tribal Trust Lands of the Confederated Salish and Kootenai Tribes, within the Flathead Indian Reservation.

Since the F&WS has acquired the rights relating only to the management of wildlife and its habitat, these are easement refuges, under an agreement with the Bureau of Indian Affairs-Flathead Irrigation Project and the tribes. Access to Ninepipe is from I-90's Exit 96 (8 miles west of Missoula), north about 40 miles on U.S. Hwy. 93 (or south from Polson about 20 miles), and onto a short unpaved road that ends at the refuge boundary and a wildlife-viewing area. Visitor activities on these refuges include wildlife observation and hiking. Access to Pablo from I-90 is north about 65 miles on U.S. Hwy. 93; or south from Polson about 3 miles. Information: (406) 644-2211.

Rocky Mountain Front Conservation Area was approved in 2005 allowing the F&WS to implement a program for managing wildlife habitats on private lands along the eastern edge of the Rocky Mountains, known as the Rocky Mountain Front, in north-central Montana. The plan calls for management under perpetual conservation easement agreements with willing landowners, toward a goal of 170,000 acres, between Birch Creek and the South Fork of the Dearborn River. The project, which will not include any federal fee title acquisition, will allow the conservation of "high quality wildlife habitat," while maintaining "the historic ranching heritage" of this region.

As the F&WS explains, "The purpose of the project is to create and maintain a significant, intact block of important wildlife habitat between existing protected areas, including State Wildlife Management Areas, The Nature Conservancy's Pine Butte Swamp Preserve and the Boone & Crockett Club's Theodore Roosevelt Memorial Ranch." The area contains riparian corridors, wetlands, and uplands for such wildlife as waterfowl (including trumpeter swans), raptors, and grizzly bears. Information: (406) 727-7400.

Swan River contains 1,568 acres to manage an area of river floodplain, including a series of oxbow sloughs, located in mountain-framed Swan Valley, southeast of Kalispell in northwestern Montana. The largest part of the floodplain supports reed canary grass, with smaller areas of coniferous forest and cottonwoods bordering Swan River. The refuge provides habitat for such birds as tundra swans, mallards, common goldeneyes, cinnamon teal, wood ducks, black terns, great blue herons, and ruffed grouse. Among the mammals are Rocky Mountain elk, moose, white-tailed deer, black bears, bobcats, river otters, and beavers.

Visitor activities include wildlife observation from viewing platforms, canoeing and boating, hiking on Bog Rd. (a route not maintained for vehicles), and seasonal hunting Access from Kalispell is south 8 miles on U.S. Hwy. 93, left for about 5 miles on State Hwy. 82, right onto State Hwy. 35 for about 2 miles, and left onto State Hwy. 83 for 23 miles; or from I-90's Exit 109 (6 miles east of Missoula), it is east 32 miles on State Hwy. 200 and left onto State Hwy. 83 for 72 miles. Information: (406) 644-2211.

UL Bend contains 58,400 acres to manage part of the central area of the north shore of Fort Peck Lake, on the Missouri River, in central Montana. The refuge is bounded by the U-turn of the reservoir to the south and by the more accessible Charles M. Russell NWR to the east and west. It supports a population of sage-grouse and large herds of wintering pronghorns. Roughly 20,000 acres are within the National Wilderness Preservation System. Information: (406) 538-8706.

War Horse contains 3,192 acres in three tracts to manage habitat for migratory birds and other wildlife, located about 30 miles south of the western end of the Charles M. Russell NWR, in central Montana. Two units contain a natural shallow basin that normally fills with water during spring, when they attract concentrations of waterfowl and shorebirds. The surrounding arid uplands are predominantly covered with sagebrush and inhabited by sage-grouse and pronghorns. The third unit consists of a state-owned agricultural irrigation reservoir, where open water and mudflats attract concentrations of waterfowl and shorebirds; and where canoeing and boating are permitted.

Visitor activities on all three units include wildlife observation, hiking, and seasonal hunting. Access to the first two units is north a few miles from State Hwy. 200 at the community of Teigen; and to the third unit, it is south from State Hwy. 200 near Winnett just over 7 miles on State Hwy. 244, and right onto Yellow Water Rd. (a gravel road) for 6 miles. Information: 9406) 538-8707.

Nebraska

Boyer Chute contains more than 2,500 acres toward a goal of 9,000 acres to manage a 2.5-mile stretch of bottomland habitat along a chute (river channel) that parallels the main course of the Missouri River, on the eastern edge of Nebraska.

In the 1930s, Boyer Chute was one of numerous braided channels that were cut off from the Missouri, when the U.S. Army Corps of Engineers built a wall and dikes across the upstream end of this channel. Even though culverts were installed to allow some river water to enter the chute, accumulating sediments eventually blocked most of the flow. Since 1994, the Boyer Chute Restoration Project completed channel excavation, and native prairie and floodplain woodland restoration. The F&WS says that "The chute is once again a functioning part of the Missouri River." This is also an inspiring place where visitors may see how a formerly altered and degraded environment can be successfully restored.

Visitor activities include wildlife observation from 2 miles of road, hiking on two interpretive trails, and seasonal hunting on part of the refuge. Access from Omaha is north 8 miles on U.S. Route 75 and east 3 miles from Calhoun. Information: (712) 642-4121.

Crescent Lake contains 45,995 acres to manage an area of scattered lakes, ponds, and marshes set amid a vast expanse of grass-covered, gently rolling sandhills, in the Nebraska panhandle. The refuge's open water, cattail and bulrush marshes, lushly vegetated meadows, and arid shortgrass prairie attract large concentrations of migrating and nesting Canada geese and ducks, such as blue-winged teal, mallards, gadwalls, shovelers, and pintails. Migratory shorebirds, such as avocets, phalaropes, and curlews, pause here in spring and autumn or nest and raise their young. More than 275 species of birds have been recorded here. Prairie grasslands are inhabited by such species as pronghorn, deer, and sharp-tailed grouse, the latter performing their elaborate courtship displays in April.

Visitor activities include wildlife observation from an auto tour route, hiking, and seasonal hunting. Access from Oshkosh is north on West Second St. for 28 miles, following refuge directional signs on a route that can become muddy and difficult to drive. Information: (308) 762-4893.

North Platte contains 2,909 acres in four separate units to manage Lake Minatare, Winters Creek Lake, and Lake Alice, just north of Scottsbluff; and Stateline Island in the North Platte River, near the town of Henry, at the western end of the Nebraska panhandle. These areas provide habitat for as many as 200,000 ducks and geese, as well as sandhill cranes, and numerous shorebirds that pause to rest and feed during migrations. Visitor activities, which are seasonally restricted, include wildlife observation and hiking. Access to Lake Minatare and Winters Creek from Minatare is north 7 miles on Stonegate Rd.; to Lake Alice is north from Scottsbluff 10 miles on Sugar Factory Rd.; and to Stateline Island from U.S. Hwy. 26 at Henry is south 1 mile. Information: (308) 635-7851.

Nevada

Anaho Island protects important colonial nesting bird habitat, near the east shore of 25-mile-long Pyramid Lake, in northwestern Nevada. Because of the lake's fluctuating water levels, the rocky island's size has varied from 247 acres, when the refuge was established in 1913, to 750 acres in the 1960s and around 525 acres more recently. The most notable species here is the white pelican—the second largest breeding colony in North America (Chase Lake NWR in North Dakota supports the largest). In 2000, more than 16,000 adults and 4,800 juveniles were recorded on the island; and more recently, 8,000 to 10,000 pelicans have been recorded.

Because of the importance of avoiding any human disturbance, the refuge is closed to visitation. Boaters are urged to remain well offshore. Other species include cormorants, great blue herons, black-crowned night-herons, and California gulls. The island contains unusual rock formations known as "tufa"—calcium carbonate that has precipitated out from hot springs as the much larger pluvial Lake Lahontan receded.

From I-80 at Reno/Sparks, access to Pyramid Lake, which lies within the Pyramid Lake Paiute Indian Reservation, is 33 miles north on Pyramid Lake Hwy. (State Hwy. 445) to a viewing place along the road. Information: (775) 423-5128.

Fallon contains 17,902 acres to protect an area of wetlands that attracts waterfowl and other waterbirds, where a branch of the Carson River ends here in the Carson Sink of Lahontan Valley, in west-central Nevada. Other parts of the refuge include flat to gently rolling desert-shrub playa, and a system of both active and stable sand dunes. In years of high Carson River water flows, the refuge attracts concentrations of migratory waterfowl and shorebirds. Because of recent drought conditions in this part of the Great Basin Desert, there has been little active management on this refuge, which is near Stillwater NWR.

Access from Fallon is 15 miles north on Indian Lakes Rd. However, roads are primitive (a four-wheel-drive vehicle is advised); and visitors are urged to stop at the Stillwater/Fallon NWR headquarters at 1000 Auction Rd., in Fallon, to obtain a map and directions; or call ahead for information: (775) 423-6452.

Moapa Valley contains 117 acres to restore and protect thermal spring-fed stream channel habitat that is vital for an endangered small fish species, the Moapa dace. The refuge is located within the headwaters of Moapa Valley's Muddy River watershed, in the Mojave Desert about 60 miles northeast of Las Vegas and 9 miles west of Glendale, in southern Nevada. Although the refuge is presently closed to visitation, visitor facilities may eventually include an interpretive trail and environmental education programs when restoration work is completed—assuming that funding and staffing become available. Information: (702) 879-6110.

Pahranagat contains 5,382 acres to manage a Mojave Desert oasis of lakes and marshes along a 10-mile stretch of Pahranagat Valley, about 90 miles northeast of Las Vegas, in southern Nevada. The name *Pahranagat* is derived from a Paiute Indian expression, "valley of shining waters." The waters that sustain this wetland habitat for concentrations of waterfowl and other waterbirds come from large thermal springs to the north of the refuge. The F&WS manages four primary water impoundments: North Marsh, Upper Pahranagat Lake, Middle Marsh, and Lower Pahranagat Lake. The refuge also includes areas of riparian cottonwood and willows, open fields, and Mojave Desert/Great Basin Desert scrub habitat.

Visitor activities include wildlife observation on an auto tour route, hiking on refuge roads and a 2.5-mile trail, canoeing and boating (small non-motorized and electric-powered), and seasonal hunting on parts of the refuge. Access from Las Vegas is northeast 22 miles on I-15 to Exit 64 and north about 68 miles on U.S. Hwy. 93. Information: (775) 725-3417.

New Hampshire

John Hay contains 164 acres as part of the management and protection of the former 876-acre Hay Estate, on the east shore of Lake Sunapee, in southwestern New Hampshire. The refuge consists of the summer home and associated landscaped gardens, known as The Fells, of American diplomat and writer John M. Hay (1838-1905). Under an agreement with the F&WS, the nonprofit Friends of the John Hay National Wildlife Refuge manages 62 acres of the refuge and buildings, and operates the refuge's environmental education center, which provides guided interpretive walks (a fee is charged), workshops and classes, exhibits, and special events. Trails are available for hiking. Access from State Hwy. 103 at Newberry is north 2.2 miles on State Hwy. 103A and left onto the entrance road. Information: (603) 763-4789.

Wapack contains 1,672 acres to protect a scenic area on 2,290-foot North Pack Monadnock Mountain, in south-central New Hampshire. The refuge lands were donated by Dr. Laurence K. Marshall, with deed restrictions that prohibit consumptive wildlife uses, motor vehicles, and tree cutting, to maintain the land for "wilderness" and "wildlife refuge" purposes. The area consists of a mixture of coniferous and deciduous forest, with a few open, grassy "balds" and granite outcroppings around the summit. The latter affords an excellent vantage from which to observe hawk migrations. The refuge provides nesting habitat for numerous species of neotropical songbirds, along with such other birds as ruffed grouse and pileated woodpeckers. Mammals include white-tailed deer, black bears, bobcats, gray foxes, fishers, and mink.

Visitor activities include wildlife observation, hiking (including the refuge's 3-mile section of 30-mile Wapack Trail), cross-country skiing and snowshoeing. Access to Wapack Trail is

Hart Mountain NWR, Oregon

Petroglyphs, Hart Mountain NWR, Oregon

Malheur NWR, Oregon

Oregon Islands NWR

William L. Finley NWR, Oregon

John Heinz NWR at Tinicum, Pennsylvania

Harlequin ducks, Sachuest Point NWR, Rhode Island

Short-eared owl, Lacreek NWR, South Dakota

Wintering trumpeter swans, Lacreek NWR

Sand Lake NWR, South Dakota

Reelfoot NWR, Tennessee

Black-bellied whistling duck, Laguna Atascosa NWR, Texas

Laguna Atascosa NWR

Ocelot with radio collar, Laguna Atascosa NWR

Black-shouldered kite feeding nestlings, Laguna Atascosa NWR

Green jay, Santa Ana NWR, Texas

Plain Chachalaca, Santa Ana NWR

Bear River NWR, Utah

Black-crowned night-heron, Fish Springs NWR, Utah

Fish Springs NWR

Fish Springs NWR

Canada geese, Fish Springs NWR, Utah

Fish Springs NWR

Missisquoi NWR, Vermont

Geese at sunset, Chincoteague NWR

Chincoteague NWR, Virginia

Mason Neck NWR, Virginia

Columbia NWR, Washington

Gray's Harbor NWR, Washington

Saddle Mountain NWR, Washington

Protection Island NWR, Washington

Umatilla NWR, Washington

Horicon NWR, Wisconsin

Beaver dam and pond, Canaan Valley, West Virginia

Horicon NWR

Necedah NWR, Wisconsin

Ultralight-led cranes, Necedah NWR. U.S. Fish and Wildlife Service Photo

Whooping cranes, Necedah NWR. U.S. Fish and Wildlife Service photo

Necedah NWR

National Elk Refuge, Wyoming

Bull elk at National Elk Refuge

Wintering trumpeter swans, National Elk Refuge

Sleigh ride for elk viewing, National Elk Refuge

Indian paintbrush, Seedskadee NWR, Wyoming

Trumpeter Swans

most easily reached from the Miller State Park parking area, located off State Hwy. 101, to the southeast of Peterborough. Information: (603) 431-7511.

New Jersey

Supawna Meadows contains 2,856 acres to manage tidally influenced wetlands for migrating, wintering, and nesting waterfowl, wading birds, shorebirds, and other wildlife, located on the east bank of the Delaware River, in southwestern New Jersey. Large concentrations of wintering ducks include mallards, northern pintails, and black ducks. The refuge provides nesting boxes for wood ducks. Ospreys and bald eagles also nest here. Large influxes of neotropical songbirds pause in the refuge's upland habitat during migrations. Visitor activities include wildlife observation, hiking, and seasonal hunting on parts of the refuge. Access from I-295's Exit 1 (off the east end of the Delaware Memorial Bridge) is east on State Hwy. 49, right onto Fort Mott Rd. for about 1.5 miles, and left onto Lighthouse Rd. and following directional signs. Information: (856) 935-1487.

New Mexico

Bitter Lake contains 24,551 acres in three units to manage varied habitats for migratory waterfowl and other wildlife, in the Pecos River Valley of southeastern New Mexico. As many as 10,000 wintering lesser sandhill cranes and at least 20,000 geese (snow, Canada, and Ross's), along with several thousand ducks are attracted here. Habitats include playa lakes and marsh, colorful gypsum sinkholes and springs, streams, a stretch of the Pecos River, shrubby riparian bottomland, managed impoundments and cropland, rolling desert uplands, sand dunes, and an area of erosion-sculpted reddish bluffs. The Capitan Mountains rise to the west.

The refuge lies within a major environmental transition between the Chihuahuan Desert, extending northward from Mexico, and the shortgrass prairie at the western edge of the southern Great Plains. It is also situated where the ranges and migration routes of some eastern birds overlap with many western species. Springs and sinkholes provide vital habitat for such rare fish species as the Pecos pupfish, greenthroat darter, and endangered Pecos gambusia.

Visitor activities on the MIDDLE UNIT include wildlife observation from an 8-mile auto tour route, hiking on two trails, and seasonal hunting. The NORTH UNIT is within the National Wilderness Preservation System and the SOUTH UNIT is closed to visitation. Access to the Middle Unit from Roswell is east about 3 miles on U.S. Hwy. 380 (Second St.), left onto Red Bridge Rd. (at a refuge sign), and follow refuge signs for about 8 miles. Information: (575) 622-6755.

Grulla contains 3,236 acres to manage habitat for lesser sandhill cranes and other migratory birds, near the Texas state line in eastern New Mexico. Grulla (pronounced GRU-ya) is the Spanish word for "crane." Roughly two-thirds of the refuge is a playa, called Salt Lake, while most of the rest is shortgrass prairie. Although the lake is commonly dry for a year or more, during periods of sufficient precipitation, a body of water attracts concentrations of cranes and waterfowl. Visitor activities include wildlife observation from a trail that leads to the top of a hill. Access from Portales is southeast about 25 miles on State Hwy. 88. Information: (806) 946-3341.

Maxwell contains 3,698 acres to manage an area of scattered lakes and grassland at the mountain-bordered western edge of the Great Plains, in northeastern New Mexico. Thousands of Canada geese and ducks, along with lesser sandhill cranes and bald eagles, winter on the refuge. Migratory white pelicans pause here on their late-summer/early-autumn migration. More than 340 species of birds have been recorded here. Visitor activities include wildlife observation from 7 miles of refuge roads, hiking two trails, and shallow-draft boating on Lake 13. Access from I-25's Maxwell exit is north 0.8 mile on State Hwy. 445, and left onto State Hwy. 505 for 2.5 miles. Information: (575) 375-2331.

San Andres contains 57,215 acres to enhance and protect important habitat of the desert bighorn sheep, mule deer, mountain lions, and other wildlife inhabiting the southern part of the canyon-carved San Andres Mountains, in the Chihuahuan Desert of southern New Mexico. The refuge is within the White Sands Missile Range and is closed to visitation. Information: (575) 382-5047.

New York

Amagansett contains 36 acres to protect a unique area of double-dune Atlantic Ocean barrier beach, located in the Town of East Hampton, on the south fork of eastern Long Island, New York. The refuge's habitats, which consist of beach, dunes, seabeach amaranth, and intertidal cranberry bogs and swales, attract a large variety of migratory shorebirds, raptors, and songbirds, including wintering Ipswich sparrows. Although the beach is open to visitation, the rest of the refuge is open only by special use permit. Access from State Hwy. 27 in the town of Amagansett is south on Atlantic Ave. Information: (631) 286-0485.

Conscience Point contains 60 acres to manage and protect an area of mature oak-beech forest, shrub, maritime grassland, and both freshwater and salt marshes, located on the northern shore of Long Island, near North Sea, New York. The refuge's wetlands attract concentrations of waterfowl—notably wintering black ducks, as well as wading birds and shorebirds. During the spring, numerous species of neotropical songbirds nest here or pause on their way to breeding areas farther north. Nesting platforms are provided for ospreys. Entry onto this refuge is only by special use permit. Information: (631) 286-0485.

Elizabeth A. Morton contains 187 acres to protect an area of sand-and-pebble beaches, steeply eroded bluffs, upland deciduous woodlands, freshwater and brackish ponds, kettle holes, fields, salt marsh, and a lagoon. The refuge encompasses Jessups Neck, a narrow peninsula extending between Noyack and Little Peconic bays, on the north shore of Long-Island's south fork, just west of Sag Harbor, New York. Among the refuge's wildlife are several endangered and threatened species, including piping plovers; roseate, common, and least terns; ospreys; peregrine falcons; and Kemp's ridley and loggerhead sea turtles. Wading birds and shorebirds are common during the warmer months, and sea ducks are common in winter.

The refuge's peninsula is closed to visitation during the April through August nesting season of plovers and terns. Visitor activities include wildlife observation from two trails and environmental education programs. Access from Exit 9 on State Hwy. 27 is north on North Sea Rd., right onto Noyack Rd. for 5 miles, and left onto the refuge road. Information: (631) 286-0485.

Lido Beach Wildlife Management Area protects 22 acres of estuarine salt marsh and adjacent shrub-thicket habitat for wintering waterfowl, wading birds, shorebirds, and other wildlife. It is located on the Hempstead Bay side of Long Beach—a coastal barrier island on the south shore of Long Island, New York. Habitat management includes restoring tidal wetlands, controlling invasive species, and providing nesting platforms for ospreys. Hempstead Bay is considered "significant coastal habitat" by the F&WS's Northeast Estuary Program, which has suggested that the entire bay merits designation as a national wildlife refuge. Information: (631) 286-0485.

Sayville contains 126 acres to protect an area of pitch pine-oak woodland and scattered fields that attract neotropical songbirds. The refuge is located in West Sayville, about 4 miles inland from the north shore of Great South Bay, in south-central Long Island, New York. This area supports one of only a dozen known populations (and the most prolific) of an endangered plant, the sandplain gerardia. Entry onto the refuge is only by special use permit. Information: (631) 286-0485.

Seatuck contains 196 acres to protect an area of pine barren, grassland, and salt marsh habitats, located on the north shore of Great South Bay, in south-central Long Island, New York. The name *seatuck* is derived from a Native American word meaning the mouth of a tidal river or creek. The refuge's wetlands attract wading birds, shorebirds, and many species of waterfowl—notably wintering black ducks and Atlantic brant. During the spring, numerous species of neotropical songbirds nest here or pause on their way to breeding areas farther north. Nesting platforms are provided for ospreys. Entry onto the refuge is only by special use permit. Information: (631) 286-0485.

Target Rock contains 80 acres to manage and protect an area of wooded uplands, a brackish pond, several vernal pools, and a half-mile of rocky beach, located at the east end of Lloyd Neck Peninsula, along Huntington Bay on the north shore of Long Island, New York. As the F&WS says, "The chestnut oak/mountain laurel association and oak hardwood forest offer good food and cover for migrating neotropical songbirds. The sand ridge areas have juniper trees which provide habitat for olive-sided hairstreak butterflies. The prickly pear cactus which is a New

York State protected species is found in the sand ridge areas of the beach. Excellent marine invertebrate populations in the offshore, beach and pond habitats provide foraging for piping plovers, [other] shorebirds, wintering waterfowl and fish species."

Visitor activities include wildlife observation, hiking, and environmental education programs. To avoid disturbing nesting activities of bank swallows and the threatened plover, the shore area in the vicinity of 14-foot-high Target Rock is closed to visitation from April 1 through August. Access from State Hwy. 110 in Huntington is west 0.25 mile on State Hwy. 25A, right onto West Neck Rd., and continuing to the end of Lloyd Harbor Rd. Information: (631) 286-0485.

Wertheim contains 2,550 acres to protect one of the last remaining undeveloped estuary systems and the largest contiguous wetland on Long Island, New York. The refuge is located on the island's central south shore, near the town of Shirley. Roughly half of the refuge consists of marine bay, tidal river, freshwater streams, hardwood swamp, and both freshwater and salt marshes. Forested uplands include pitch pine, mixed pine-and-oak, and oak woodlands. During the winter, large concentrations of waterfowl—notably black ducks—are attracted here; while nesting waterfowl include Canada geese, black and wood ducks, gadwalls, and green-winged teal. Nesting platforms for ospreys and nesting boxes for wood ducks are provided. During the spring, large influxes of neotropical songbirds nest on or pass through the refuge. Over 280 species of birds have been recorded here.

Visitor activities include wildlife observation, hiking, environmental education programs, canoeing on Carmans River, which is a state-designated wild and scenic river. Access from the junction of County Hwy. 46 (William Floyd Parkway) and State Hwy. 27A in Shirley is west 0.6 mile on County Hwy. 80W and left onto Smith Rd. for 0.25 mile. Information: (631) 286-0485.

North Carolina

Cedar Island contains 14,482 acres to protect extensive expanses of largely undisturbed black needlerush and cordgrass salt marsh for wading birds, migratory shorebirds, thousands of wintering waterfowl, and other wildlife. The refuge is located at the confluence of Pamlico and Core sounds, on the central coast of North Carolina. Other wildlife includes brown pelicans, black skimmers, black rails, ospreys, gulls, terns, influxes of numerous species of neotropical songbirds that migrate through here during spring and autumn, white-tailed deer, black bears, mink, and river otters; and the alligator is near the northern end of its range on the refuge. More than 270 species of birds have been recorded here.

Visitor activities include wildlife observation; canoeing, kayaking, and boating (two launching ramps are provided); hiking and bicycling; and horseback riding on undeveloped trails. Access from Beaufort is about 40 miles northeast on U.S. Hwy. 70 and State Hwy. 12. Information: (252) 926-4021.

Currituck contains 4,100 acres in five main tracts to protect sandy beaches, grassy dunes, inter-dunal wetlands, more than 1,200 acres of needlerush and cordgrass brackish marsh and freshwater cattail marsh, with scattered ponds, shrubby thickets, and 700 acres of live oak-and-loblolly pine maritime forest. The refuge, which attracts large concentrations of wintering waterfowl, wading birds, and shorebirds, is located on the Outer Banks between Currituck Sound and the Atlantic Ocean, in northeastern North Carolina. Refuge staff and summer interns closely monitor the nesting activities of the endangered piping plover and threatened loggerhead sea turtle—an especially challenging task, given the volume of vehicular traffic on the Outer Banks beaches.

Visitor activities include wildlife observation, hiking, and seasonal waterfowl hunting from specified blind sites (by drawing). Access to the refuge's Monkey Island and Swan Island units is on foot from near the north end of State Hwy. 12, by four-wheel-drive vehicle (only on the beach), or by small boat across Currituck Sound. Information: (252) 429-3100.

Swanquarter contains 16,411 acres to protect an extensive expanse of needlerush, sawgrass, and cordgrass salt marshes, located along the shore of Pamlico Sound, on the central coast of North Carolina. The roughly 13,000 acres of brackish wetlands attract large concentrations of wintering waterfowl, wading birds, and shorebirds. About 3,000 acres of the refuge consists of hardwood swamp and small stands of loblolly pine. Other wildlife includes nesting ospreys and influxes of numerous species of neotropical songbirds that pause here during migrations.

Visitor activities include wildlife observation; hiking on two trails; canoeing, kayaking, and boating; and seasonal hunting on part of the refuge. Access from the town of Swan Quarter is west 4 miles on U.S. Hwy. 264 and left for 2 miles; or by small boat. Information: (252) 926-4021.

North Dakota

Appert Lake contains about 640 acres to manage habitat for migratory waterfowl and other wildlife, located about 25 miles southeast of Bismarck, in south-central North Dakota. The refuge consists of a 118-acre impoundment of marsh and open water that attracts concentrations of migrating ducks such as mallards, wigeons, pintails, and gadwalls. Surrounding grassy upland is inhabited by sharp-tailed grouse and the non-native gray partridge and ring-necked pheasant. White-tailed deer is the most prominent mammal. Because this refuge is managed under a conservation easement agreement with the private landowner, it is closed to visitation. Information: (701) 387-4397.

Ardoch contains 2,696 acres to manage a wetland that is a mecca for migratory waterfowl and other wildlife, located in the Red River Valley, about 25 miles northwest of Grand Forks, in northeastern North Dakota. Impounded 1,000-acre Lake Ardoch is bordered mostly by cattail-and-bulrush marsh and attracts the giant Canada goose, which nests here, and such ducks as mallards, blue-winged teal, and gadwalls; as well as bitterns, avocets, and phalaropes. Because this refuge is managed under conservation easement agreements with private landowners, it is closed to visitation. Information: (701) 662-8611.

Bone Hill contains 640 acres to manage an area of natural marsh, reservoir, and surrounding pasture and agricultural lands for migratory birds, located a few miles south of Jamestown, in southeastern North Dakota. Because this refuge is managed under conservation easement agreements with private landowners, it is closed to visitation. Information: (701) 647-2866.

Brumba contains 1,977 acres to manage wetland habitat for migratory waterfowl and other wildlife, north of the former town of Church's Ferry, in northeastern North Dakota. Because this refuge is managed under conservation easement agreements with private landowners, it is closed to visitation. Brumba is close to two other refuges: Snyder to the south and Rock Lake to the north. Information: (701) 662-8611.

Buffalo Lake contains 1,563 acres to manage a 660-acre reservoir for migratory waterfowl and other wildlife, within the headwaters of the Sheyenne River, about 25 miles south of Rugby, in north-central North Dakota. Because all of this refuge, except 23 acres, is managed under conservation easement agreements with private landowners, entry for wildlife observation and hiking is only with landowner permission. Access from U.S. Hwy. 2 at Rugby is south 25 miles on State Hwy. 3, left onto State Hwy. 19 for about 5 miles, and right about 1 mile. Information: (701) 768-2548.

Camp Lake contains 755 acres in two units with two lakes that attract a few waterfowl, located near Butte, in north-central North Dakota. The F&WS says that "Habitat values are very low" and that "both units should be dropped from refuge status." Visitor entry onto this easement refuge is not permitted. Information: (701) 442-5474.

Canfield Lake contains 313 acres to protect wetland habitat for migrating waterfowl, located about 25 miles north of Bismarck, in north-central North Dakota. Because most of this refuge is managed under a conservation easement agreement with a private landowner, it is closed to visitation. Information: (701) 387-4397.

Chase Lake contains 4,385 acres to manage a vast expanse of wetland habitat that is a major breeding, resting, and feeding area for waterfowl and other waterbirds. The refuge, which was established in 1908 by President Theodore Roosevelt, consists of a 2,057-acre alkaline lake and surrounding grassland within the gently rolling, lake-dotted Missouri Coteau region, northwest of Medina, in central North Dakota.

Prominent among the refuge's wildlife is North America's largest breeding colony of the white pelican. In recent years, from 17,000 to 20,000 of these birds have been congregating on the lake's two nesting islands (when not inundated by high water) and a shoreline peninsula. The peak of their breeding season runs from mid-April through July. Other nesting waterbirds include the giant Canada goose, various ducks, and the endangered piping plover. Tundra swans and sandhill cranes are among numerous migrating birds that pause here to rest and feed. The refuge's prairie grassland provides nesting habitat for such species as sharp-tailed grouse, upland plover, and bobolink. White-tailed deer, coyotes, and red foxes are among the mammals.

Visitor activities include wildlife observation from refuge roads, hiking, and seasonal deer hunting. Access from I-94's Exit 230 at Medina is north 10 miles on State Hwy. 30/County Rd. 68, left for 7 miles, and left about a mile to Chase Lake Pass, from which is the best overview of the refuge. Information: (701) 752-4218.

Cottonwood Lake contains 1,013 acres to maintain a lake as resting and staging habitat for migrating waterfowl, shorebirds, and other wildlife, located near Minot, in north-central North Dakota. Several thousand mallards commonly pause to rest and feed here during migrations. This refuge is managed under a conservation easement agreement with a private landowner. Seasonal hunting is permitted, but wildlife observation and hiking are at the landowner's discretion. Information: (701) 768-2548.

Dakota Lake contains 2,799 acres to manage wetland habitat along the James River that attracts migratory waterfowl, shorebirds, and other wildlife, near Ludden, (just 4 miles north of Sand Lake NWR, S. Dak.), in southeastern North Dakota. The refuge includes the river channel, some bordering riparian habitat, the reservoir behind Dakota Lake Dam, and agricultural fields. Because the refuge is managed under conservation easement agreements with private landowners, it is closed to visitation. Information: (701) 647-2866.

Florence Lake contains 1,888 acres to manage a 132-acre lake and wetland, nearly 1,000 acres of virgin mixed-grass prairie, and cropland for migratory waterfowl and other wildlife, near Wing, in central North Dakota. Visitor activities include wildlife observation and hiking. Access from I-94 at Sterling is north 30 miles on State Hwy. 14, then (following refuge directional signs) left onto a gravel road for 3 miles, right on a gravel road for a mile, and right for a mile. The latter mile is unimproved prairie trail that is impassible when wet. Information: (701) 387-4397.

Halfway Lake contains 160 acres to protect wetland and upland prairie grassland breeding habitat for migratory waterfowl and other wildlife, near Medina, in southeastern North Dakota. Under the terms of a conservation easement agreement with the private landowner, only seasonal hunting and trapping are permitted here. Access from I-94's Exit 230 at Medina is south about 2 miles on State Hwy. 30 (the refuge is on the east side of this highway). Information: (701) 285-3341.

Hiddenwood contains 675 acres of a lake and adjacent land, located a few miles north of Lake Sakakawea, within the Fort Berthold Indian Reservation, southwest of Minot, in west-central North Dakota. This popular boating and fishing lake does attract some migrating waterfowl that pause here to rest and feed during spring and autumn migrations. The F&WS says that "Habitat and wildlife values are quite low with the exception of an excellent strip of shrub and tree riparian habitat around the lake." The refuge's 580 acres of cropland are being managed for wildlife under a conservation easement agreement with the private landowner. Information: (701) 442-5474.

Hobart Lake contains 2,077 acres to protect wetland habitat for concentrations of Canada geese, ducks, and a few tundra swans, located east of Jamestown, in southeastern North Dakota. Under a conservation easement agreement with the private landowner, only seasonal hunting and trapping are permitted here. Access is from several easy-to-find places from I-94, which cuts through the refuge between Exits 283 and 288. Information: (701) 285-3341.

Hutchinson Lake contains 479 acres to maintain an area of wetland habitat on part of Hutchinson Lake that attracts migrating waterfowl to rest and feed here during spring and autumn migrations, located east of Bismarck, in central North Dakota. Because this refuge is managed under a conservation easement agreement with the local landowner, visitor entry is only with the landowner's permission. Information: (701) 387-4397.

Johnson Lake contains 2,008 acres to manage wetland habitat for the benefit of migratory waterfowl and other wildlife, southeast of Devils Lake, in east-central North Dakota. Under the terms of a conservation easement agreement, only seasonal hunting and trapping are permitted. Information: (701) 285-3341.

Kelly's Slough contains 1,269 acres to manage wetland and upland habitats for migratory waterfowl and other wildlife, 8 miles west of Grand Forks, in northeastern North Dakota. During migrations, thousands of ducks, geese, and shorebirds pause here to rest and feed. Nesting waterfowl include the giant Canada goose and such ducks as mallards, blue-winged teal, pintails, and gadwalls. Visitor activities include wildlife observation from three hiking trails and two observation platforms, and seasonal hunting. Access from I-29 in Grand Forks is west 7.5 miles on U.S. Hwy. 2 and right onto an unpaved road for just over 3 miles to a parking area and overlook. Information: (701) 662-8611.

Lake Alice contains 12,156 acres to manage wetland habitat primarily for nesting and migrating waterfowl, located near the former town of Church's Ferry, northwest of Devils Lake, in north-central North Dakota. Large concentrations of snow geese pause to rest and feed here during migrations. An important nesting species is the giant Canada goose, for which artificial nesting sites have been provided. White-tailed deer is the most prominent mammal. Visitor activities include wildlife observation from an auto tour road, hiking, and seasonal hunting. Access from U.S. Hwy. 2 in Devils Lake is north 17 miles on State Hwy. 20, left onto County Rd. 10 for 7 miles, right for 1 mile, and left for 2 miles. Information: (701) 662-8611.

Lake George contains 3,119 acres to manage two lakes, wetland habitat, and adjacent upland grassland, located southwest of Medina, in south-central North Dakota. During autumn migration, several thousand Canada geese and several hundred snow geese and ducks pause here to rest and feed. Sharp-tailed grouse and white-tailed deer, and numerous grassland songbirds inhabit the uplands. Because most of the refuge is managed under conservation easement agreements with private landowners, this refuge is closed to visitation. Information: (701) 387-4397.

Lake Ilo contains 4,033 acres to manage wetland and open-water habitat of this prairie-encircled lake, the adjacent 145-acre marshy Lee Paul Slough, and a score of scattered smaller wetlands, north of Dickinson, in west-central North Dakota. During migrations, large concentrations of waterfowl (as many as 100,000) and shorebirds are attracted to the 990-acre reservoir behind Lake Ilo Dam. Just over half of the refuge consists of gently rolling uplands of grassland. About 50 acres of croplands are planted under cooperative agreements with local farmers, by which part of the crop is left unharvested for waterfowl, pheasants, and deer.

Visitor activities include wildlife observation from refuge roads, hiking on a number of trails (including an interpretive trail), and boating (a launching ramp is provided). Access from I-94 at Richardton is north 34 miles on State Hwy. 8, and left on State Hwy. 200 to a mile west of Dunn Center; or from I-94 at Dickinson, it is north 32 miles on State Hwy. 22, and right onto State Hwy. 200 for 5.5 miles. Information: (701) 548-8110.

Lake Nettie contains 3,325 acres to manage a semi-saline lake, a freshwater marsh, a stretch of Turtle Creek, and adjacent uplands, located 5 miles east of Lake Audubon NWR, in central North Dakota. The refuge attracts concentrations of waterfowl, sandhill cranes, and shorebirds, especially during migrations. To enhance some of the lake's wetland habitat, nesting islands have been created. Visitor activities include wildlife observation from several public roads along the edge of the refuge, hiking, and seasonal hunting. Access from the town of Turtle Lake is north 8 miles on State Hwy. 41 and left onto State Hwy. 8 for 4 miles. Information: (701) 442-5474.

Lake Otis contains 320 acres to manage a prairie-surrounded cluster of small wetlands, located a few miles northeast of Lake Audubon NWR, in central North Dakota. The marsh habitat attracts concentrations of waterfowl and other waterbirds, especially during migrations. Because this refuge is managed under a conservation easement agreement with the private landowner, visitor entry is not permitted. Information: (701) 442-5474.

Lake Patricia contains 800 acres to manage an area of impounded wetland and some adjacent grassland for migratory waterfowl and other wildlife, located southwest of Bismarck, in central North Dakota. The majority of this refuge being cooperatively managed by the North Dakota Game and Fish Department. Visitor activities include wildlife observation from adjacent State Hwy. 21 and two unpaved county roads, hiking on trails, and seasonal hunting. Access from Flasher is 1.5 miles east on State Hwy. 21. Information: (701) 548-8110.

Lake Zahl contains 3,739 acres to maintain wetland and upland prairie habitats for migratory waterfowl and other wildlife, north of Williston, in northwestern North Dakota. The refuge's 1,500 acres of wetlands are managed as staging and resting areas for as many as 10,000 snow geese and 40,000 ducks of many species. The giant Canada goose and many ducks also nest here. Whooping cranes, bald eagles, peregrine falcons, and a variety of shorebirds are also attracted to the refuge. Visitor activities include wildlife observation, hiking, and seasonal hunting. Access from Williston is north 12 miles on U.S. Hwy. 85/2, north 16 miles on U.S. Hwy. 85, and left onto State Hwy. 50. Information: (701) 385-3214.

Lambs Lake contains 1,206 acres to maintain an area of wetland habitat for migratory waterfowl and other wildlife, west of Grand Forks, in east-central North Dakota. This refuge is managed under conservation easement agreements with the private landowners, and visitor entry is permitted only with landowner permission; or it can be viewed from a public road. Access from U.S. Hwy. 2 at the town of Michigan is south 6 miles on State Hwy. 35 and left onto an unpaved county road for a mile. Information: (701) 662-8611.

Little Goose contains 288 acres to maintain an area of wetland habitat for migratory waterfowl and other wildlife, southeast of Devils Lake, in east-central North Dakota. Because this refuge is managed under a conservation easement agreement with a private landowner, visitor entry is not permitted, although it can be viewed from an unpaved county road, 5 miles south of U.S. Hwy. 2 at Niagara. Information: (701) 662-8611.

Long Lake contains 22,498 acres to manage marsh and open water of this shallow 16,000-acre lake and surrounding prairie grassland, ravines, small areas of trees and shrubs, and cultivated fields for migrating and nesting waterfowl and other wildlife, located a few miles southeast of Bismarck, in central North Dakota. The refuge's most abundant nesting ducks include mallards, pintails, blue-winged teal, and gadwalls. Among the birds that rest and feed here during migrations are thousands of sandhill cranes; many species of ducks; and Canada, snow, and greater white-fronted geese. The refuge's grassland provides nesting habitat for such species as sharp-tailed grouse and upland sandpipers.

Visitor activities include wildlife observation, hiking, boating (25 hp motors or less), and seasonal hunting. Access from I-94 at Sterling is south 9 miles on U.S. Hwy. 83, left onto 102nd Ave. SE for 3 miles, and right onto 353rd St. SE. for a mile; or from U.S. Hwy. 12 at Selby, it is north 83 miles on U.S. Hwy. 83 and right onto 128th Ave. SE for just over a mile. Information: (701) 387-4397.

Lords Lake contains 1,915 acres to maintain a shallow wetland adjacent to the Turtle Mountains, near Bottineau, in north-central North Dakota. This refuge provides resting and feeding habitat for thousands of lesser snow geese, as well as tundra swans and numerous ducks, especially during September and October. Depending on precipitation, the lake level fluctuates widely, and may even dry up.

The refuge is managed under conservation easement agreements with private landowners. Seasonal hunting is permitted, but other visitor uses, such as wildlife observation and hiking, are at the discretion of the landowners. Opportunities for wildlife observation are possible from adjacent county roads. Access from Bottineau is east about 12 miles on State Hwy. 5 and right onto a township road for about a mile; or from State Hwy. 3 at Dunseith, it is west about 6 miles on State Hwy. 5 and left for about a mile. Information: (701) 768-2548.

Lost Lake contains 960 acres to maintain a 200-acre alkali lake, a few miles southeast of Lake Sakakawea, in central North Dakota. The open areas of water attract concentrations of Canada geese and other waterfowl, especially during migrations. Encircling the lake is gently rolling prairie grassland, through which meanders Painted Woods Creek. This refuge is managed under a conservation easement agreement with a private landowner. Visitor entry is permitted only with permission of the landowner and the refuge. Information: (701) 442-5474.

Maple River contains 1,120 acres to manage a stretch of this river's main channel, which includes a small dam that floods an adjacent 90-acre marsh, a second dam that holds water on an 82-acre marsh as the river's flow declines following spring runoff, riparian fringes along the riverbanks, and cultivated fields, near Ellendale, in southeastern North Dakota. The refuge attracts migrating waterfowl and shorebirds during migrations, as well as nesting marsh and waterbirds. While a small part of the refuge is open for such visitor activities as wildlife observation and seasonal hunting, the rest is managed under a conservation easement agreement and is closed to visitation. Access from Ellendale is east 4.5 miles on State Hwy. 11, left for 5 miles, and right for a mile on county and township roads. Information: (701) 647-2866.

McLean contains 824 acres to protect wetland habitat of a small marshy reservoir, Lake Susie, within the Fort Berthold Indian Reservation, in west-central North Dakota. The refuge's wetland attracts concentrations of waterfowl, especially during migrations; and Canada geese have been successfully re-established here. Roughly half the refuge is managed under a conservation easement agreement with the North Dakota State Land Department. Visitor activities include wildlife observation and hiking. Access from Roseglen is west 4.5 miles on State Hwy. 37, right for 4 miles, and left for 0.5 mile. Information: (701) 442-5474.

Pleasant Lake contains 897 acres to maintain wetland habitat for migratory waterfowl and other wildlife, east of Rugby, in north-central North Dakota. This refuge is managed under a conservation easement agreement with a private landowner, and visitor entry is only with landowner permission; or the refuge can be viewed from U.S. Hwy. 2 between Knox and Rugby. Information: (701) 662-8611.

Pretty Rock contains 800 acres to maintain marsh wetland habitat around the shore of a lake that attracts migratory and nesting waterfowl and other wildlife, near New Leipzig, in southwestern North Dakota. Because this refuge is managed under a conservation easement agreement with a private landowner, visitor entry is not permitted. Information: (701) 548-8110.

Rabb Lake contains 260 acres to maintain a 102-acre lake and surrounding densely wooded upland, on the U.S.-Canada border north of Dunseith, in north-central North Dakota. The refuge and North Dakota Game and Fish Department's adjacent wildlife management area provide resting and feeding habitat mainly for migratory diving ducks—notably canvasbacks. Ruffed grouse and white-tailed deer are among the many species of wildlife inhabiting upland areas of quaking aspen and green ash. This refuge is managed under conservation easement agreements with a private landowner and the state. Although seasonal hunting is permitted, other visitor activities are at the discretion of the landowners. Information: (701) 768-2548.

Rock Lake contains 5,506 acres to maintain wetland habitat for migratory waterfowl and other wildlife, east of Dunseith, in north-central North Dakota. This refuge is managed under conservation easement agreements with private landowners, and visitor entry is only with landowner permission. The refuge can be viewed from State Hwy. 5 at the town of Rocklake and from an unpaved county road to the north of Rocklake. Rock Lake is close to two other refuges to the south: Brumba and Snyder. Information: (701) 662-8611.

Rose Lake contains 836 acres to maintain an area of wetland habitat for migratory waterfowl and other wildlife, east of Devils Lake, in east-central North Dakota. This refuge is managed under a conservation easement agreement with a private landowner, and visitor entry is only with the landowner's permission. Or the refuge can be viewed from an unpaved county road about 3.5 miles north of the western arm of Stump Lake. Access from U.S. Hwy. 2 at Lakota is 2 miles south on State Hwy. 1, right onto a gravel road for 5 miles, left for a mile, and right for a mile. Information: (701) 662-8611.

School Section Lake contains 297 acres to maintain wetland habitat mainly for migratory waterfowl, on and around this 305-acre reservoir in the headwaters of Indian Creek, near Rolla and the U.S.-Canada border, in north-central North Dakota. Ruffed grouse and white-tailed deer are among many species of wildlife inhabiting the surrounding wooded uplands of quaking aspen and green ash. This refuge is managed under conservation easement agreements with a private landowner and the state. Visitor entry is at the discretion of the landowners for wildlife observation and hiking, but is closed to hunting. Information: (701) 768-2548.

Shell Lake contains 1,835 acres to manage wetland and upland prairie habitats for migratory birds and other wildlife, west of Minot, in northwestern North Dakota. The refuge's wetlands are maintained as staging and resting areas for as many as 5,000 migrating sandhill cranes, 1,000 snow geese, and 5,000 ducks of many species, some of which also nest here. Other migratory birds attracted to this refuge are whooping cranes, bald eagles, peregrine falcons, and various shorebirds

About a third of the refuge is managed under conservation easement agreements with private landowners. Because of the combination of federally and privately owned lands, visitor entry is not permitted. Whooping crane roosting areas can be seen from the refuge boundary—a viewing area that is accessed from a prairie trail on the adjacent Moen Waterfowl Production Area. Information about the latter: (701) 848-2722. Access from U.S. Hwy. 2 at Blaisdell is south 12 miles on an unpaved road, and then right and right again for a half mile. Information: (701) 385-4046.

Sheyenne Lake contains 797 acres to maintain wetland and open-water habitats of this lake for concentrations of migratory waterfowl, especially during migrations, south of Anamoose, in central North Dakota. This refuge, which is managed under an agreement with the U.S. Bureau of Reclamation (BOR), is surrounded by 36,000 acres of additional BOR-owned lands that are managed as a wildlife management area by the North Dakota Game and Fish Department. Visitor activities include wildlife observation, hiking, and seasonal hunting. Access from U.S. Hwy. 52 at Anamoose is south about 10 miles on State Hwy. 14. Information: (701) 442-5474.

Sibley Lake contains 1,077 acres to maintain wetland habitat for migratory waterfowl, south of Lakota, in east-central North Dakota. This refuge is managed under conservation easement agreements with private landowners. Visitor entry is only with landowner permission. Access from U.S. Hwy. 2 at Lakota is south a few miles on State Hwy. 1. Information: (701) 285-3341.

Silver Lake contains 3,347 acres to maintain wetland habitat for migratory waterfowl and other wildlife, south of the former town of Church's Ferry, in northeastern North Dakota. Because this refuge is managed under conservation easement agreements with private landowners, visitor entry is only with landowner permission. Access is west 2 miles from Church's Ferry on U.S. Hwy. 2 and left onto U.S. Hwy. 281 for just over 2 miles. Information: (701) 662-8611.

Slade contains 3,000 acres mainly to manage 900 acres of wetlands habitat for migratory and nesting waterfowl, near Dawson, in south-central North Dakota. The refuge consists of five lakes, many marshes, and 15 pothole wetland areas that attract large numbers of migrating Canada and snow geese that pause here during autumn migration. Beginning in 1924, a wildlife conservationist and former Northern Pacific Railroad executive, George T. Slade, committed to purchasing, enhancing, and maintaining this area's wetlands as a private hunting reserve. In 1940, he donated the reserve to the F&WS. In 1968, the refuge, the Northern Prairie Wildlife Research Center, and the state Game and Fish Department jointly undertook a propagation project to reestablish a breeding population of the giant Canada goose—a subspecies that had been brought from the brink of extinction across the northern Great Plains. Many pairs now nest here. Other species include white pelicans and shorebirds.

Visitor activities include wildlife observation, hiking, and seasonal hunting. Access from I-94 at Dawson is just a short way south on State Hwy. 3. Information: (701) 387-4397.

Snyder Lake contains 1,550 acres to maintain wetland habitat for migratory waterfowl and other wildlife, south of Rocklake, in northeastern North Dakota. This refuge is managed under conservation easement agreements with private landowners. Although visitor entry is only with landowner permission, the refuge can be viewed from the east side of U.S. Hwy. 281. Snyder Lake is close to two other refuges to the north: Brumba and Rock Lake. Access from State Hwy. 5 at the town of Rocklake, Snyder Lake refuge is south 7 miles on U.S. Hwy. 281. Information: (701) 662-8611.

Springwater contains 640 acres primarily to manage an 8-acre impoundment created by a dam on Clear Creek, near Linton, in south-central North Dakota. Although most of the refuge's wetland no longer exists, the refuge consists of a mixture of grassland, coulee (ravine), and riparian habitats. This refuge is managed under a conservation easement agreement with a private landowner. Visitor entry is only with landowner permission. Information: (701) 387-4397.

Stewart Lake contains 2,230 acres to maintain marsh wetlands around the shores of this lake that attracts migrating and nesting waterfowl and other wildlife, between Amidon and Bowman, in southwestern North Dakota. More than two-thirds of this remote refuge is managed under conservation easement agreements with private landowners. Visitor activities include wildlife observation and hiking; but hunting and trapping are not permitted. Access is south 8 miles from Amidon. Information: (701) 548-8110.

Stoney Slough contains 2,000 acres to maintain wetland habitat for migratory waterfowl and shorebirds, southwest of Valley City, in east-central North Dakota. Among the more prominent species are snow and white-fronted geese, tundra swans, and various dabbling ducks that pause here to rest and feed during migrations. Part of the area consists of upland prairie. Much of this refuge is managed under conservation easement agreements with private landowners. Visitor activities include wildlife observation, hiking, and seasonal hunting. Access from I-94's Exit 276 is south for 12 miles on State Route 1 and left for 3 miles. Information: (701) 285-3341.

Storm Lake contains 686 acres with a perpetual right to maintain a reservoir for water conservation, for drought relief, and for migratory waterfowl and other wildlife, near Milner, in southeastern North Dakota. The wetland habitat is especially important for western and pied-billed grebes and diving ducks. This refuge is managed under a conservation easement agreement with a private landowner, and visitor entry is only with landowner permission. Hunting is not permitted. Information: (701) 724-3598.

Stump Lake contains 27 acres to manage wetland habitat on two islands and two shore peninsulas primarily for nesting and migrating waterfowl, at Stump Lake's western arm, southwest of Lakota, in east-central North Dakota. Stump Lake is actually a semi-permanent brackish wetland, with large beds of sago pondweed. Colonial nesting birds that are attracted here include white pelicans, ring-billed gulls, and cormorants. At times, there are more than 5,000 tundra swans on the refuge, along with snow and Canada geese, and numerous ducks, including as many as 25,000 canvasbacks. Visitor entry is not permitted. Information: (701) 662-8611.

Sunburst Lake contains 328 acres to maintain a 27-acre impoundment that provides wetland habitat for migrating and nesting waterfowl, southwest of Sterling, in south-central North Dakota. This refuge is managed under a conservation easement agreement with a private landowner, and visitor entry is only with landowner permission. The adjacent 580-acre Schiermeister Waterfowl Production Area (WPA) provides habitat for such species as white-tailed deer and the non-native ring-necked pheasant. Visitor activities on the WPA include wildlife observation, hiking, and seasonal hunting. Access to the WPA from I-94 at Sterling is south 32 miles on U.S. Hwy. 83 and right onto an unpaved road for 12 miles. Information: (701) 387-4397.

Tomahawk contains 440 acres to maintain an area of wetland habitat for migratory waterfowl, notably large numbers of Canada geese and diving ducks during migrations, northwest of Valley City, in east-central North Dakota. This refuge is managed under a conservation easement agreement with a private landowner, and visitor entry is only with landowner permission. Information: (701) 285-3341.

White Lake contains 1,040 acres to manage marsh wetlands habitat around the shores of a lake that attracts migrating and nesting waterfowl and other wildlife, just east of Amidon, in southwestern North Dakota. Visitor entry is allowed only by special permit, which can be obtained at Lake Ilo NWR headquarters. Information: (701) 548-8110.

Wild Rice Lake contains 778 acres, southeast of Milnor, in southeastern North Dakota. The F&WS says this easement refuge "is no longer providing waterfowl values due to a lack of permanent water, with the loss of water control structures." Consequently it is the agency's "desire to eventually divest" this refuge from the National Wildlife Refuge System. Information: (701) 724-3598.

Willow Lake contains 2,621 acres to maintain this 1,200-acre lake in the headwaters of Willow Creek, north of Dunseith and 3 miles south of the U.S.-Canada border, in north-central North Dakota. The lake level fluctuates widely, depending on precipitation and runoff. Many species of ducks and other waterfowl are attracted to Willow Lake, especially during autumn migration. This refuge is managed under conservation easement agreements with private landowners. Seasonal hunting is permitted, but wildlife observation and hiking are at the discretion of the landowners. Access from Dunseith is west 3 miles on State Hwy. 5 and right onto an improved gravel township road for 7 miles. Information: (701) 768-2548.

Wintering River contains 239 acres to maintain a shallow 86-acre marsh created by a dike and other water-control structures, east of Minot, in north-central North Dakota. The wetland is dominated (even choked) by dense growths of cattails, bulrushes, and bog rush. Several thousand mallards and smaller concentrations of other migratory waterfowl pause here to rest and feed, especially during autumn migration. The wetland's water level fluctuates widely, depending on precipitation and runoff. White-tailed deer and the non-native ring-necked pheasant also inhabit the area. This refuge is managed under conservation easement agreements with private landowners. Seasonal hunting is permitted, but other visitor activities are at the discretion of the landowners. Information: (701) 768-2548.

Wood Lake contains 280 acres to maintain marsh habitat for migratory waterfowl and other wildlife, on the Devils Lake Sioux Indian Reservation, in east-central North Dakota. This refuge is managed under a conservation easement agreement. Visitor entry is only with landowner permission. Access is 1.5 miles west of Tokio. Information: (701) 662-8611.

Ohio

Cedar Point contains 2,445 acres to manage marsh habitat where the southwestern end of Lake Erie meets Maumee Bay, near Toledo, in northwestern Ohio. This former private hunt club consists of three extensive, impounded pools that support growths of cattails, bulrushes, and other emergent vegetation, attracting herons, egrets, bald eagles, a small colony of black terns, and large concentrations of many species of migrating ducks. Except for seasonal bank fishing along the shore of a pond reached from Yondota Rd., visitor entry is allowed only by special permit. Information: (419) 898-0014.

West Sister Island contains 77 acres to protect the largest rookery of great blue herons and great egrets in the Great Lakes region, located 9 miles offshore near the western end of Lake Erie, in northwestern Ohio. Other nesting species include black-crowned night-herons and cormorants.

To avoid disturbing the rookeries, visitor entry is only by special permit. Information: (419) 898-0014.

Oklahoma

Deep Fork contains more than 9,000 acres toward a goal of about 18,000 acres to restore and manage bottomland hardwood forest along Deep Fork River and adjacent native tallgrass prairie, south and west of Okmulgee, in east-central Oklahoma. Among the refuge's wildlife are wintering waterfowl, nesting wood ducks, numerous neotropical songbirds, white-tailed deer, bobcats, and beavers. Areas of bottomland previously cleared for grazing or pecan orchards are being replanted with native hardwoods. Visitor activities include wildlife observation, hiking, canoeing and boating, and seasonal hunting. Access from Tulsa is south about 35 miles on U.S. Hwy. 75 to Okmulgee; or from I-40, it is north 14 miles to Okmulgee. A Fish and Wildlife Service map indicates the location of refuge properties. Information: (918) 756-0815.

Little River contains more than 13,000 acres to protect an area of oak-hickory bottomland hardwood forest and bald cypress swamp with meandering creeks, sloughs, and former river oxbows, along the north side of Little River, in the southeastern corner of Oklahoma. The refuge encompasses the largest remaining area of this habitat in the state. Among the refuge's wildlife are wintering mallards, nesting wood ducks, herons, egrets, wild turkeys, Mississippi kites, numerous species of neotropical songbirds, beavers, and alligators. Visitor activities include wildlife observation, driving on 10 miles of primitive roads (some of which are flooded during high water), hiking, canoeing and boating, and seasonal hunting. For detailed directions, visitors are urged to stop at the refuge headquarters, at 635 South Park Dr., in Broken Bow. Information: (580) 584-6211.

Optima contains 4,333 acres primarily to protect prairie grassland habitat for migratory birds and other wildlife, located east of Guymon, in the Oklahoma Panhandle. The refuge is about equally divided between shortgrass prairie and a tallgrass vegetative type known as sandsage-bluestem prairie. Among the more than 250 species of birds that nest or migrate through here are scissor-tailed flycatchers, Mississippi kites, wild turkeys, bobwhite and scaled quail, and the non-native ring-necked pheasant. Visitor activities include wildlife observation and seasonal hunting. Access to three entry places and parking areas are about 1.2 miles northwest from Hardesty on State Hwy. 3 and 0.6 mile west on gravel Z Rd.; about 2.4 miles due west from Hardesty on a paved county road that becomes gravel; or about 2 miles north from State Hwy. 3, just east of Hardesty. Information: (580) 664-2205.

Ozark Plateau contains about 3,000 acres within a complex of nine small, forested tracts that consist of numerous caves, west of Sallisaw, in east-central Oklahoma. The refuge was established to protect several species of endangered bats, the threatened blind Ozark cavefish, and other species of concern that are endemic to the Ozarks, including a cave crayfish found in only one cave. Because of the sensitive nature of these species, the refuge is closed to visitation, except by special permit for scientific research. Information: (918) 773-5251.

Tishomingo contains 16,464 acres to manage a diversity of south-central Oklahoma habitats, including hardwood forest; wild-plum thickets; riparian woodland; crops of corn, milo, and winter wheat that are cultivated for wintering waterfowl; a number of ponds; the meandering course of the Washita River; and the broad expanse of Cumberland Pool—the northern arm of Lake Texoma behind Denison Dam. Among the more than 250 species of birds attracted to this refuge are tens of thousands of wintering ducks and geese, nesting wood ducks, herons, egrets, white pelicans, wintering bald eagles, shorebirds, and numerous species of neotropical songbirds.

Visitor activities include wildlife observation from 15 miles of refuge roads and from an observation platform, hiking throughout the refuge (including the 1-mile Craven Nature Trail), canoeing and boating (March 1 through September), and seasonal hunting. Access from I-35 at Ardmore is east on State Hwy. 199 to Tishomingo, east on State Hwy. 78 to the east end of town, right onto Refuge Rd. for 3 miles. Information: (580) 371-2402.

Washita contains 8,200 acres to manage an area around and upstream from Foss Reservoir, northwest of Clinton, in west-central Oklahoma. The refuge consists of gently rolling prairie-grassland hills, brushy ravines, bottomlands, scattered riparian woodland and marsh along the tributary creeks, and the meandering course of the Washita River, which merges into the upper end of the U.S. Bureau of Reclamation reservoir. Under cooperative agreements, 2,100 acres of cropland are planted with wheat and milo, part of which is left unharvested for waterfowl. Wildlife includes tens of thousands of wintering geese and ducks, white pelicans, shorebirds, Mississippi kites, bald eagles, sandhill cranes (as many as several thousand pause here in early November), numerous species of neotropical songbirds, scissor-tailed flycatchers, roadrunners, white-tailed deer, beavers, and prairie dogs.

Visitor activities include wildlife observation, hiking, canoeing and boating, and seasonal hunting. Access from Butler is west 5 miles on State Hwy. 33, and right for a mile and left 0.5 mile. Information: (580) 664-2205.

Oregon

Ankeny contains 2,796 acres to manage areas of wetland, riparian forest, native wet prairie, and croplands, near the junction of the Santiam and Willamette rivers, in the Willamette Valley of western Oregon. Notable among the many species of wildlife attracted to Ankeny (pronounced ANN-kennee) are the large concentrations of the dusky Canada goose, a dark-plumaged subspecies that remains here from autumn through spring and then breeds on southern Alaska's Copper River Delta. Other birds include tundra swans, bald eagles, peregrine falcons, and multitudes of migratory ducks and shorebirds.

Visitor activities include wildlife viewing from roads adjacent to the refuge (observation platforms next to Ankeny Hill and Buena Vista Rds.) and from wildlife viewing blinds along a 0.5-mile boardwalk (the trailhead is reached from Wintel Rd.). Access from I-5's Exit 243 is west about 0.25 mile on Ankeny Hill Rd., and at an intersection turn right and continue 1.5 miles to a viewing area and kiosk. Information: (541) 757-7236.

Bandon Marsh contains more than 800 acres in two units to protect the largest remaining area of tidal salt marsh in the Coquille River estuary, located in Bandon, on the southern coast of Oregon. The salt marsh provides habitat for waterfowl, wading birds, and large concentrations of shorebirds during migrations. Visitor activities in the BANDON MARSH UNIT include wildlife observation from a boardwalk and viewing deck (a parking area is adjacent to Riverside Dr.), canoeing and kayaking (a launching ramp is provided at Ballard's Beach State Park), and seasonal hunting. Access from U.S. 101 is west into Bandon and right onto Riverside Dr. Information: (541) 867-4550.

Baskett Slough contains 2,492 acres to provide wintering habitat for the dusky Canada goose (see the Ankeny NWR text) and other waterfowl, located a few miles west of Salem, in the Willamette Valley of western Oregon. The refuge consists of shallow wetlands, rolling hills covered with Oregon white oaks, upland prairie, and croplands. Visitor activities include wildlife observation from a number of public roads that cross or border the refuge (a viewing place is provided adjacent to State Hwy. 22), hiking the Baskett Butte Trail through oak savanna and upland prairie (parking is located off Colville Rd. and an observation platform is provide atop the butte). Access from I-5's Exit 253 is west 10 miles on State Hwy. 22 to the junction with State Hwy. 99W , and continuing on State Hwy. 22 about 2 miles to a parking area and kiosk on the right. Information: (541) 757-7236.

Bear Valley contains 4,200 acres to manage and protect an area of mature conifer forest (mostly of ponderosa pines, white firs, Douglas-firs, and incense cedars) that attracts several hundred wintering bald eagles that roost here at night. The refuge is located at the western edge of the Klamath Basin, in south-central Oregon. Although this refuge is not open to visitation, except walk-in deer hunting before November 1, there are outstanding opportunities to witness the eagles' fly-outs at dawn, from December through mid-March. Access from Klamath Falls to the eagle-viewing area is southwest about 13 miles on U.S. Hwy. 97, west (right) across railroad tracks, immediately bear left on an unpaved roads, and continue about 0.5 mile. Information: (530) 667-2231.

Cold Springs contains 3,116 acres to protect habitat for migratory waterfowl and other wildlife, located near the Columbia River, in the high desert of northeastern Oregon. In 1909, President Theodore Roosevelt established this area as the Cold Springs Reservation for nesting birds. The refuge overlays a U.S. Bureau of Reclamation irrigation reservoir, the water level of which fluctuates seasonally, shrinking from about 1,500 acres to as little as 200 acres by late summer. As many as 5,000 to 6,000 ducks and nearly 1,000 geese, as well as large numbers of migrating shorebirds are attracted here. A nesting colony of great blue herons occupies cottonwoods and willows bordering the reservoir; and mule deer are among the resident mammals of this oasis. The refuge's upland high-desert of sagebrush and bitterbrush is inhabited by such species as California quail, bobcats, coyotes, and badgers.

Visitor activities include wildlife observation, hiking, canoeing and boating (non-motorized and electric-powered), and seasonal hunting. Access from U.S. Hwy. 395 at Hermiston is east 6 miles, first on Highland Hills Rd. and then Loop Rd. Information: (509) 545-8588.

Lewis and Clark contains 41,034 acres to protect approximately 20 estuarine islands that consist of 8,000 acres of tidal wetlands amid a maze of sloughs and other waterways, adjacent to wave-tossed open water of the Columbia River estuary, in northwestern Oregon. This area remains essentially as the Lewis and Clark Expedition must have seen it when they canoed toward the mouth of the river on November 7, 1805; and again as they began their eastward return trip, following the estuary's south shore on March 23, 1806, following their rain-sodden winter at nearby Fort Clatsop. The islands consist mostly of marsh, with smaller areas of upland pasture, sand flats, and tidal swamp. Tens of thousands of ducks, thousands of Canada geese, and hundreds of tundra swans spend the winter here. Shorebirds, wading birds, gulls, terns, and bald eagles are attracted to the refuge.

Visitor activities include wildlife observation, seasonal hunting, and sea kayaking and canoeing (part of the Columbia River Heritage Canoe Trail runs through the refuge). Philip N. Jones's *Canoe and Kayak Routes of Northwest Oregon* suggests several routes through the refuge's confusing waterways. Access is from boating-launching sites adjacent to Oregon State Hwy. 30 and Washington State Hwy. 4. Information: (360) 795-3915.

McKay Creek contains 1,837 acres to manage riparian habitat of cottonwoods, willows, and other vegetation along the shore of a U.S. Bureau of Reclamation irrigation reservoir, near Pendleton, in the high desert of northeastern Oregon. The reservoir fluctuates widely from 1,300 acres of open water in late spring to an average of only 250 acres by late summer. Large concentrations of migrating and wintering waterfowl (mostly mallards and Canada geese) are attracted here. Among other wildlife are bald and golden eagles, mule deer, bobcats, coyotes, and badgers. Visitor activities include wildlife observation from the refuge's gravel road along the reservoir's west shore and from a county road along the east shore, hiking, boating (launching ramps are provided), and seasonal hunting. Access from Pendleton is south about 8 miles on U.S. Hwy. 395 and left onto the refuge's gravel road. Information: (509) 545-8588.

Nestucca Bay contains 730 acres toward an authorized goal of 3,436 acres to manage vital wintering habitat for six Canada goose subspecies, including the only coastal population of the dusky Canada goose and the world's small population of Semidi Islands Aleutian cackling goose. This refuge is located just south of Pacific City, on the northern coast of Oregon.

The cackling goose numbers have increased from 790 individuals in 1975 to 118,000 in 2006 by the eradication of a non-native predator where these geese breed in Alaska, bringing about its removal from the endangered species list. Among other wildlife are ducks, wading birds, shorebirds, brown pelicans, bald eagles, peregrine falcons, and neotropical songbirds. Pasture management for the geese is made possible by cooperative agreements with local dairy operators. Habitats also include salt marsh, riparian wetlands, forested uplands, and the southernmost coastal sphagnum bog on the Pacific Coast. The bay and its rivers support spawning migrations of several species of anadromous fish.

The refuge has been closed to visitation; but beginning in 2008, construction of an overlook at Cannery Hill is expected to provide a paved path from parking areas to an elevated observation deck offering visitors a panorama of the refuge. Access is south of Pacific City, just west of U.S. Hwy. 101. Information: (541) 867-4550.

Siletz Bay contains 519 acres toward a goal of 1,906 acres to restore and protect salt and brackish marsh, tidal sloughs and mudflats, and coniferous and deciduous forest, located just south of Lincoln City, on the northern coast of Oregon. Among the wildlife are wintering waterfowl, brown pelicans, wading birds, shorebirds, bald eagles, peregrine falcons, neotropical songbirds, Roosevelt elk, black-tailed deer, and river otters. The bay and its river support spawning migrations of several species of anadromous fish. The refuge can be viewed from U.S. Hwy. 101, which runs through the refuge, and from State Hwy. 229, which branches east along the Siletz River. Information: (541) 867-4550.

Tualatin River contains more than 1,200 acres toward a goal of 3,058 acres to restore and manage remnants of floodplain habitat along this meandering river, near Sherwood, about 15 miles south of downtown Portland, Ore. Habitats include emergent freshwater wetlands, creeks, ponds, grasslands, and riparian and upland woodlands. Wildlife includes three subspecies of Canada goose (western, dusky, and cackling), tundra swans, various ducks, bald eagles, and peregrine falcons. A major mission of the refuge is the implementation of what the F&WS describes as "a dynamic wetland restoration program." A variety of "restoration projects will provide valuable habitat for migratory waterfowl, shorebirds, marsh birds, neotropical migratory birds, amphibians, reptiles, resident and anadromous fish, and . . . resident mammal species."

Although the refuge is presently closed to visitation, several county roads offer opportunities to view the area and the refuge can be seen from State Hwy. 99W, between Metzger and Tigard. The refuge plans to provide interpretive hiking trails, wildlife observation structures, and environmental education programs. Information: (503) 590-5811.

Umatilla contains 25,347 acres in five units to mitigate the inundation of wetland habitat that resulted from construction of John Day Dam on the Columbia River. The refuge, located in northern Oregon and southern Washington, manages a 20-mile stretch of the river's islands and backwater sloughs, riparian woodlands, croplands, and adjacent high-desert uplands. Wintering waterfowl are attracted here, including 100,000 to 400,000 ducks of many species and tens of thousands of Canada geese. The islands offer breeding habitat for Canada geese, terns, and colonies of great blue herons and cormorants. Notable among Umatilla's shorebirds is the long-billed curlew, which performs its amazing aerial courtship of whirring wings and diving acrobatics in March.

Visitor activities include wildlife observation from the McCORMACK UNIT's 5-mile auto tour route, in Oregon; hiking; canoeing, kayaking, and boating (launching ramps are provided); and seasonal hunting. Access to the McCormack Unit from I-84's Exit 168 is east on U.S. Hwy. 730, and north to the main entrance; and to the Boardman Unit, it is from I-84's

Exit 164 at Boardman. In Washington, the Whitcomb, Ridge, and Paterson units are reached from State Hwy. 14. Information: (509) 545-8588.

Upper Klamath contains 14,966 acres in two units to manage cattail and bulrush wetland habitat and bordering areas of cottonwoods, willows, and aspens, along the northwest end of Upper Klamath Lake, within the Klamath Basin of south-central Oregon. The wetlands attract large concentrations of nesting and migrating waterfowl, colonial-nesting white pelicans and herons, and other waterbirds.

Visitor activities include wildlife observation, canoeing and boating (two launching sites are provided), and seasonal hunting. The 9.5-mile Upper Klamath Canoe Trail, located partly on the refuge and partly in Winema National Forest, offers an excellent opportunity to view the marsh and open water of Upper Klamath's Pelican Bay (a canoe-trail leaflet is available). This is one of six national wildlife refuges in the basin, for which the visitor center/headquarters is located 5 miles west on Hill Rd. from the community of Tulelake, California. Access to the canoe trail is northwest 26 miles on State Hwy. 140 and right onto Rocky Point Rd. to a boat launch. Information: (530) 667-2231.

Rhode Island

Block Island contains 102 acres in five units to manage and protect strategically important migratory bird habitat, at the north end of Block Island, about 12 miles south of the mainland coast of Rhode Island. As the F&WS says, "Block Island is internationally famous among birders for its spectacular fall songbird migration. . . . Thousands of Neotropical migrants, representing 70 species, have been documented." As many as 40 species of shorebirds pass through here from mid-summer to early autumn; and more than 250 species of birds have been recorded here. Visitor activities include wildlife observation and hiking. Access to the island is by all-year ferry from Point Judith, R.I., and New London, Conn.; seasonally from Newport and Narragansett, R.I., and Montauk, N.Y.; and by air from the Westerly, R.I., airport. Information: (401) 364-9124.

Sachuest Point contains 242 acres to restore and manage upland shrub habitat on a prominent headland and an adjacent area of salt marsh, located on the largest island in Narragansett Bay, in southeastern Rhode Island. Among the wildlife attracted here are migrant raptors, influxes of neotropical songbirds, and "typically thousands" of migrating tree swallows that pause on the headland before continuing on their migration. Black ducks, scaups, eiders, and scoters, plus large concentrations of wintering harlequin ducks are among the many waterfowl on the waters around the point.

Visitor activities include wildlife observation, hiking on three trails that lead to observation platforms, and interpreter-led walks. Access from U.S. Hwy. 1 is east 8.5 miles on State Hwy. 138, crossing Newport (toll) Bridge, east 0.6 mile on Miantonomi and continuing east 1.2

miles on Green End Ave., right onto Paradise Ave. for 1.3 miles, left onto Hanging Rock Rd. for 0.3 mile, and right onto Sachuest Point Rd. for 1.5 miles. Information: (401) 364-9124.

Trustom Pond contains 787 acres to protect a 160-acre brackish pond and surrounding wetland, forested freshwater wetlands, shrubland, grasslands, and a narrow stretch of barrier beach, near South Kingstown, on the south shore of Rhode Island. Prominent among the grassland-nesting birds are bobolink and meadowlark. More than 260 species of birds have been recorded here, including large concentrations of neotropical songbirds in April and May. Moonstone Beach, which provides vital nesting habitat for the threatened piping plover and (state-listed) threatened least tern, is closed to visitation above the mean high-tide line from April 1 to mid-September to avoid disturbing these species. Visitor activities include wildlife observation, hiking on trails leading to observation platforms, and seasonal hunting. Access from U.S. Hwy. 1's Moonstone Beach exit is south 1 mile, right onto Matunuck Schoolhouse Rd. for 0.7 mile, and left. Information: (401) 364-9124.

South Carolina

Pinckney Island contains 4,073 acres to protect a cluster of low-lying islands, located just west of Hilton Head Island, near the southern end of coastal South Carolina. About two-thirds of the refuge consists of salt marsh and meandering tidal creeks; and the rest is a mixture of woodland, shrubland, fields, grassland, and freshwater ponds. Concentrations of wading birds, shorebirds, wintering waterfowl, nesting ospreys, and numerous neotropical songbirds are attracted here. White-tailed deer and alligators are common residents. Visitor activities include wildlife observation, hiking and bicycling 14 miles of trails, boating (a launching ramp is provided), and seasonal deer hunting when population management is needed. Access from I-95's Exit 8 at Hardeeville is east 18 miles on U.S. Hwy. 278 and left at the refuge sign. Information: (912) 652-4415.

Santee contains 15,095 acres to manage diverse wildlife habitats along the north shore of Lake Marion, the reservoir behind Santee Dam on the Santee River, in south-central South Carolina. Periodically flooded bottomland hardwood forest, croplands cultivated by farmers with corn, wheat, millet, and soybeans (a portion of which is left unharvested for wildlife), seasonally regulated impoundments, and open-water expanses attract wintering waterfowl and bald eagles, influxes of neotropical songbirds, and resident wild turkeys, white-tailed deer, and alligators. Nesting boxes are provided for wood ducks.

Visitor activities include wildlife observation, driving the CUDDO UNIT's auto tour route, hiking several trails, viewing the visitor center's interpretive displays on the BLUFF UNIT, and seasonal hunting. More than 295 species of birds have been recorded here. Access from I-95's Exit 102 is 0.25 mile, following directional signs. From Santee, it is north on U.S. Hwy. 15/301 or from Summerton, it is south 8 miles on U.S. Hwy. 15/301. Information: (803) 478-2217.

Savannah contains 28,168 acres to manage an area of bottomland hardwood forest, freshwater marshes, and tidal creeks and rivers, along the Savannah River, just upstream from the city of Savannah, in southeastern South Carolina and northeastern Georgia. The water levels of freshwater impoundments are regulated for migratory waterfowl. Roughly half of the refuge consists of periodically flooded bottomland forest with such trees as bald and pond cypresses. Among the refuge's wildlife are concentrations of wading birds and wintering waterfowl, nesting wood ducks, bald eagles, ospreys, white-tailed deer, bobcats, river otters, and alligators.

Visitor activities include wildlife observation from a 4-mile auto tour route, hiking on trails, and seasonal hunting. Access from I-95's Exit 5 at Hardeeville, S.C., is south 6 miles on U.S. Hwy. 17, and right onto State Hwy. 170. Or in Georgia, from I-95's Exit 109, it is south on State Hwy. 21, east on State Hwy. 30, north of State Hwy. 25 through Port Wentworth, east across the Savannah River, and onto the refuge on S.C. Hwy. 170. Information: (912) 652-4415.

Tybee contains 100 acres to manage habitat for wintering waterfowl, wading birds, shorebirds, gulls, terns, and other wildlife, located at the mouth of the Savannah River, along the southern end of coastal South Carolina. The nucleus of the refuge is Oyster Bed Island, which has been created by sediments dredged up from the river bottom by the U.S. Army Corps of Engineers for river and harbor improvements. Some parts of the refuge are covered with dense vegetation, which attracts many species of birds. The refuge is closed to visitation. Information: (912) 652-4415.

Waccamaw contains 7,400 acres toward an authorized goal of nearly 50,000 acres of floodplain swamp along the Great and Little Pee Dee rivers and the Waccamaw River, in northeastern South Carolina. Habitats include black-water forested wetlands, tidal forested wetlands, and tidal marshes. Among the wildlife attracted here are concentrations of wintering waterfowl, shorebirds, migrant raptors, and neotropical songbirds. This is the northernmost nesting area of the swallow-tailed kite. The refuge's 4,600-acre Bull Island is the largest tract acquired so far. It is accessible by boat, and visitor activities include wildlife observation and seasonal hunting. Information: (843) 527-8069.

South Dakota

Bear Butte is a 566-acre easement refuge, located near Sturgis in south-central South Dakota that is managed as a state park by the South Dakota Game, Fish & Parks Department. Information: (605) 685-6508.

Karl E. Mundt contains 780 acres to protect one of the last stretches of essentially natural Missouri River bottomland, located just downstream from the U.S. Army Corps of Engineers' Fort Randall Dam, in southeastern South Dakota. Bald eagles gather here in winter in cottonwood trees bordering the river, with peak numbers in December and January—the largest concentration of wintering bald eagles in the lower 48 states. To avoid disturbing these majestic birds, the refuge is closed to visitation. However, an eagle observation place, on adjacent Corps of Engineers land, provides an outstanding viewing opportunity. Other wildlife attracted to this refuge includes large concentrations of migratory waterfowl, white pelicans, wild turkeys, bobwhite quail, the non-native ring-necked pheasant, white-tailed and mule deer, bobcats, and coyotes. Access to the eagle-viewing area is just west of Pickstown on U.S. Hwy. 281. Information: (605) 487-7603.

Lacreek contains 16,500 acres to manage spring-fed wetlands—an expanse of sub-irrigated meadow, located adjacent to shortgrass prairie uplands and sandhills in Lake Creek Valley, at the northern edge of the Nebraska Sandhills, in southwestern South Dakota. Roughly 5,400 acres of marsh wetlands and open water encompass eleven water impoundments, water levels of which are regulated for ducks, geese, swans, shorebirds, and other wildlife. During spring migration, the influx of waterfowl totals nearly 12,000 birds, while in autumn their numbers exceed 20,000. More than 270 species of birds have been recorded here. Other wildlife includes wintering sharp-tailed grouse and resident ring-necked pheasants, white-tailed and mule deer, and a few pronghorn.

Visitor activities include wildlife observation from a 4-mile auto tour route, hiking, and seasonal hunting on parts of the refuge. Access from the junction of U.S. Hwy. 18 and State Hwy. 73 in Martin is southeast 13 miles on the latter route and then following refuge signs. Information: (605) 685-6508.

Lake Andes contains 5,638 acres to manage shallow prairie lake and adjacent grassland habitats, primarily for breeding waterfowl and other waterbirds, in southeastern South Dakota. Of the refuge's acreage, 4,700 are managed under conservation easement agreements with private landowners. As Lake Andes depends on precipitation and natural runoff, its level fluctuates widely. Roughly once every two decades, the lake dries up completely. Under the terms of an easement agreement with the state, the F&WS manages the lake with dikes that divide the body of water into three units, within which water levels are regulated (subject to the constraints of an impermanent water supply) for waterfowl. The Owen's Bay marsh unit, which is fed mostly from an artesian well, allows far more consistently reliable water management. In addition to breeding ducks, the refuge attracts bald eagles, black terns, Franklin's gulls, grebes, bobolinks, ring-necked pheasants, white-tailed deer, and beavers.

Visitor activities include wildlife observation from a platform and an interpretive loop trail, and seasonal hunting. Access from Ravinia is north 2 miles and west 1 mile. Information: (605) 487-7603.

Tennessee

Chickasaw contains 23,856 acres toward a goal of just over 55,000 acres to restore and protect a stretch of the meandering Mississippi River floodplain, at the western edge of Tennessee.

Large concentrations of wintering waterfowl commonly reach as many as 20,000 to 40,000 ducks (mainly mallards) and sometimes up to 4,000 Canada geese. More than 19,000 acres of the refuge consist of seasonally flooded bottomland hardwood forest, where the refuge's emphasis is on reestablishing and maintaining this habitat. Water levels within moist-soil impoundments are seasonally regulated for wading birds, migrating shorebirds, and wintering waterfowl.

Visitor activities include wildlife observation; hiking; canoeing and boating on oxbow lakes, sloughs, and small rivers (launching ramps are provided); and seasonal hunting. Access from the only stoplight on U.S. Hwy. 51 in Ripley is north on Edith Central Rd.; at the 4-way stop, the name changes to Edith Nankipoo Rd. Continue north and then left at a refuge directional sign onto Hobe Webb Rd. Information: (731) 635-7621.

Hatchie contains 11,556 acres to manage seasonally flooded bottomland hardwood forest, marshes, sloughs, creeks, oxbow and other lakes, upland forest, and cropland along a meandering stretch of the Hatchie River, in southwestern Tennessee. Concentrations of as many as 40,000 wintering ducks (notably mallards) are attracted to the refuge. Water levels within moist-soil impoundments are seasonally regulated for wading birds, migrating shorebirds, and wintering waterfowl. Other wildlife includes wild turkeys, numerous neotropical songbirds, white-tailed deer, bobcats, coyotes, and river otters.

Visitor activities include wildlife observation, hiking, canoeing and boating (launching ramps are provided), a sport-fishing program for physically challenged visitors, and seasonal hunting. Access to the refuge's Oneal Lake area from I-40's Exit 56 is south 4 miles on State Hwy. 76 and left onto the entrance road; or to the eastern part of the refuge, from I-40's Exit 52, it is southeast 12 miles on State Hwy. 179 and left onto Hillville Rd. for 5 miles. Between Exits 52 and 56, I-40 cuts through the western part of the refuge. Information: (731) 772-0501.

Lake Isom contains 1,850 acres to manage wintering and nesting habitats of open water, moist-soil impoundments, forested wetlands, and croplands for migratory birds and other wildlife. The refuge is located in northwestern Tennessee. Concentrations of wintering waterfowl commonly total as many as 10,000 Canada geese and 30,000 ducks. Visitor activities from March 15 to October 15 include wildlife observation, hiking, canoeing and boating, and seasonal hunting on part of the refuge. Access from Union City is west and southwest about 23 miles on State Hwy. 22 to Samburg, continuing southwest on Route 22 to the spillway, and left onto the first paved road for about 2.5 miles. Information: (731) 538-2481.

Lower Hatchie contains 7,707 acres toward a goal of just over 15,400 acres to restore and protect more than 4,000 acres of seasonally flooded bottomland hardwood forest, along the lower meandering stretch of the Hatchie River, adjoining the Mississippi River, in southwestern Tennessee. Large concentrations of wintering waterfowl, as well as wading birds, shorebirds, bald eagles, and neotropical songbirds, are attracted to the refuge. Visitor activities include wildlife observation, hiking, canoeing and boating (two launching ramps are provided), and seasonal hunting. Access to the refuge headquarters from U.S. Hwy. 51 at Henning is west about 19 miles on State Hwy. 87. Information: (731) 635-7621.

Tennessee contains 51,358 acres in three units to manage forest wetland and other habitats for migratory birds around three parts of Kennedy Lake, a Tennessee Valley Authority reservoir behind Kentucky Dam on the Tennessee River, in northern Tennessee. During the winter months, as many as 30,000 Canada geese and as many as 300,000 ducks (notably mallards) are attracted to the refuge. More than 90 bald eagles also winter here. Nesting boxes have been provided for wood ducks and hooded mergansers. During migrations, influxes of numerous species of neotropical songbirds pass through the refuges forests. Wild turkeys and bobwhite quail are among the resident birds.

Visitor activities include wildlife observation, hiking, canoeing and boating (launching ramps are provided), and seasonal hunting on parts of the refuge. Access to the BIG SANDY UNIT (the largest) from U.S. Hwy. 79 at Paris (refuge headquarters is at 3006 Dinkins Lane) is southeast 14 miles on Alt. State Hwy. 69 to Big Sandy and left onto Lick Creek Rd. for 12 miles. Information: (731) 642-2091.

Texas

Big Boggy contains 4,526 acres to manage an area of coastal prairie, salt marsh, and two large saltwater lakes, located on the upper Gulf Coast, about 7 miles south of Wadsworth, in southeastern Texas. The refuge provides wintering habitat for roughly 20,000 geese (mostly lesser snows) and as many as 10,000 ducks of many species. Dressing Point Island supports one of the most important bird rookeries on the Texas coast for roseate spoonbills, white ibises, snowy egrets, and brown pelicans. Big Boggy is closed to visitation, except for special tours and seasonal waterfowl hunting on part of the refuge. Information: (979) 849-6062.

Brazoria contains 43,388 acres to manage an area of coastal prairie, freshwater and salt marshes, salt flats, mudflats, ponds, and several saltwater lakes for concentrations of wintering waterfowl, shorebirds, wading birds, and other wildlife such as alligators. As many as 50,000 geese (predominantly lesser snows) along with thousands of wading birds and shorebirds, are attracted to the refuge in December and January. This is also one of the Gulf Coast refuges where the spectacular neotropical migratory songbird "fallout" phenomenon occurs in April (see Aransas NWR text). The refuge is located on the upper Gulf Coast between Galveston and Freeport, in southeastern Texas. More than 300 species of birds have been recorded here.

Visitor activities include wildlife observation from a 7.5-mile auto tour route and from observation platforms; hiking; canoeing, kayaking, and boating on Salt Lake (a launching ramp is provided); and seasonal waterfowl hunting on part of the refuge. Access from Houston is south on State Hwy. 288 to Lake Jackson, left onto Farm Market Rd. 2004 for about 5 miles, and right onto FM Rd. 523 for 5.5 miles. Information: (979) 849-6062.

Buffalo Lake contains 7,664 acres to manage a reservoir and adjacent marsh and cultivated lands, located southwest of Amarillo in the Texas Panhandle. Subsequent to the refuge's establishment, diversion of Tierra Blanca Creek for agricultural irrigation dried up the refuge waters. Consequently, what was formerly an important wetland habitat now supports mostly arid-land wildlife. Heavy rainfall occasionally fills the lakebed, attracting waterfowl and shorebirds. Visitor activities include wildlife observation, driving a 4.5-mile auto tour route, and hiking on two trails. Access from Canyon is west on U.S. Hwy. 60 to Umbarger and left onto Farm Market Rd. 168 for 2 miles. Information: (806) 499-3382.

Caddo Lake contains 7,172 acres to manage an area of forested wetlands, including cypress swamps surrounding Caddo Lake and along Harrison Bayou, located on parts of the U.S. Army's Longhorn Army Ammunition Plant, 3 miles west of the Louisiana state line, in northeastern Texas. As described by a Notice in the Oct. 19, 2000, *Federal Register*, "The refuge is designed to protect one of the highest quality old-growth bottomland hardwood forests in the southeastern United States." This wetland habitat, which includes exceptional areas of bald cypress swamp, attracts migratory and resident waterfowl, white pelicans, bald eagles, and neotropical songbirds. Areas of loblolly and shortleaf pines are inhabited by such species as wild turkeys and white-tailed deer.

The refuge is faced with several threats: large expanses of the lake are rapidly being infested with the world's most aggressive invasive aquatic plant, the giant salvinia, from South America; millions of gallons of water that flow into and maintain the level of the lake may be diverted elsewhere; and refuge lands may be transferred for an industrial development. Information: (580) 584-6211.

Hagerman contains 11,320 acres in two units to manage an area of marsh, prairie, woodland, ponds, and cultivated fields around Big Mineral Arm of Lake Texoma, located 75 miles north of Dallas, Texas. This reservoir, which was created by the U.S. Army Corps of Engineers' Denison Dam on the Red River, attracts concentrations of wintering and migrating Canada and snow geese and ducks. In September and April, thousands of migrating white pelicans rest and feed on the refuge; and in autumn, large flocks of scissor-tailed flycatchers stop on their way to wintering areas in Mexico and Central America. More than 315 species of birds have been recorded here.

Visitor activities include wildlife observation from a 4-mile auto tour route, hiking on the 1-mile Crow Hill Trail, boating from April through September (a launching ramp is provided), and seasonal hunting. Access from U.S. Hwy. 75's Sherman/Farm Market 1417 exit is north on FM Rd. 1417 to a refuge sign, and left 6 miles; or from I-35, it is east on U.S. Hwy. 82 and following refuge directional signs. Information: (903) 786-2826.

Little Sandy contains 3,802 acres to protect bottomland hardwood forest and oxbow lakes for wintering waterfowl, nesting wood ducks, wading birds, wild turkeys, numerous neotropical songbirds, white-tailed deer, alligators, and other wildlife. The refuge is located along the Sabine River, north of Tyler in northeastern Texas. The F&WS says that "The Refuge contains some of the highest quality old-growth bottomland hardwood forest remaining in the State of Texas." Because this refuge is managed under a conservation easement agreement with a private hunting and fishing club, visitation is allowed only on tours arranged with special permission from the club. Information: (580) 584-6211.

McFaddin contains 57,000 acres to manage mostly freshwater and intermediate marsh habitats on the upper Gulf Coast, near the southeastern corner of Texas. This refuge attracts tens of thousands of wintering snow geese and over two-dozen species of ducks. More than 270 species of birds have been identified here, and this is one of the Texas coastal refuges where the spectacular neotropical migratory songbird "fallout" phenomenon can occur in April (see Aransas NWR). The refuge also supports one of the largest populations of alligators in Texas.

Visitor activities include wildlife observation from 8 miles of refuge roads, hiking on a short trail near the refuge headquarters and on a strand of beach, canoeing and shallow-draft boating (launching ramps are provided), and seasonal hunting. Access from Port Arthur is south 15 miles on State Hwy. 87 to Sabine Pass and west (right) 12 miles on that route. Information: (409) 971-2909.

Moody contains 3,517 acres to maintain coastal marsh and prairie habitats for wintering waterfowl, shorebirds wading birds, and other waterbirds, located on Galveston Bay, in southeastern Texas. The 714-acre Lake Surprise, a shallow body of water that annually attracts large concentrations of lesser scaup and other diving ducks, is a centerpiece of this refuge. Alligators inhabit freshwater marsh habitat. Because the refuge is managed under a conservation easement agreement with a waterfowl hunting club, it is closed to public entry. Information: (409) 267-3337.

Muleshoe contains 5,809 acres to manage a number of shallow lakes that attract wintering waterfowl and thousands of lesser sandhill cranes (largest numbers are generally in late November and early December and late January and early February). The refuge is located northwest of Lubbock, in the South Plains of West Texas. Spring-fed Paul's Lake nearly always contains water, but Goose and White lakes are frequently dry, since they are dependent on runoff from sufficient rainfall in this arid region. Shortgrass and mid-grass plains habitat, with areas of scattered mesquite trees, surround the lakes. At least 316 species of birds have been recorded here.

Visitor activities include wildlife observation from the auto tour route and hiking on two trails. Access from Lubbock is northwest on U.S. Hwy. 84, left at Littlefield for 19 miles on State Hwy. 54, and right onto State Hwy. for 5 miles; or from Clovis, N.M., it is southeast on U.S. Hwy. 84, right at the town of Muleshoe and south 20 miles on State Hwy. 214. Information: (806) 946-3341.

Neches River was designated in 2007 to encompass up to 25,000 acres along a 38-mile stretch of the upper Neches River, consisting of some of the ecologically finest remaining bottomland hardwood forest in Texas. This area is roughly 100 miles southeast of Dallas, near Neches, in eastern Texas. With donation of the initial acre of land, the refuge was officially established. However, the City of Dallas has plans to build a dam creating 30,000-acre Fastrill Reservoir that would inundate and destroy the very habitat that the F&WS has rated as "Priority 1" for protection. The Texas Water Development Board and the city have filed lawsuits to block the refuge.

If it is allowed to reach its full potential, the refuge would provide protection of habitat for a diversity of wildlife, including migratory waterfowl and neotropical songbirds. It would also offer such visitor activities as wildlife observation, hiking, canoeing, environmental education programs, and seasonal hunting. The future of this refuge appears to be in doubt. Information: (505) 248-6911.

San Bernard contains 27,414 acres to manage coastal prairie, freshwater marsh and ponds, coastal salt marsh, many saltwater lakes and ponds, and a colonial water bird rookery. Tens of thousands of wintering lesser snow geese and ducks of many species, shorebirds, wading birds, and other wildlife are attracted here. This is one of the Gulf Coast refuges where the spectacular neotropical migratory songbird "fallout" phenomenon can occur in April (see Aransas NWR). More than 300 species of birds have been recorded here. Alligators inhabit freshwater areas. Visitor activities include wildlife observation from a 3-mile auto tour route, hiking on three trails, and seasonal waterfowl hunting on parts of the refuge. Access from Houston is south on State Hwy. 288 to Lake Jackson, right for 13 miles. Information: (979) 849-6062.

Texas Point contains 8,900 acres to manage estuarine, coastal salt marsh, and intermediate marsh habitats; and some wooded upland, located along the upper Gulf Coast, in the southeast corner of Texas. This refuge attracts as many as 100,000 wintering ducks of more than two-dozen species. It is also one of the Gulf Coast refuges where the spectacular neotropical migratory songbird "fallout" phenomenon can occur in April (see Aransas NWR). More than 270 species of birds have been recorded here. Alligators are abundant in freshwater habitat. Visitor activities include wildlife observation, hiking, shallow-draft boating (for a fee, there is a launching facility at a private dock near the east end of the refuge), and seasonal waterfowl hunting. Access from Port Arthur is south 15 miles on State Hwy. 87 to Sabine Pass and the adjacent refuge entrance. Information: (409) 971-2909.

Trinity River contains more than 18,000 acres to manage an area of mixed hardwood and bottomland hardwood forests, and cypress swamp with numerous bayous and oxbow lakes along the Trinity River floodplain, in southeastern Texas. Among the wildlife attracted to this refuge are concentrations of wintering waterfowl, rookeries of colonial water birds, nesting wood ducks, numerous species of neotropical songbirds, and alligators. Visitor activities include wildlife observation, environmental education programs, hiking, canoeing and boating, and seasonal hunting. Access to the refuge headquarters, at 1351 N. Main St., in Liberty, is 0.9 mile north of U.S. Hwy. 90. Information: (936) 336-9786.

Utah

Fish Springs contains 17,992 acres to protect a 10,000-acre marsh, the water for which comes almost entirely from a complex of warm, saline, artesian springs, located in the midst of an arid expanse of the Great Basin Desert, in west-central Utah. Some of the ponds of this lush oasis support a population of the Utah chub, a native fish that typically grows to eight inches or less. The marsh habitat attracts many thousands of migrating waterfowl (peak numbers are generally around mid-April and late September), including tundra swans, Canada geese, and many species of ducks. Among other wildlife are great blue herons, snowy egrets, white-faced ibises, mule deer, bobcats, and coyotes. More than 270 species of birds have been recorded here.

Visitor activities include wildlife observation from an 11-mile auto tour route; hiking; and canoeing, kayaking, and boating (gasoline motors not permitted) between mid-July and mid-May. Access from I-80's Exit 99 is south about 42 miles on State Hwy. 36 and right 63 miles on unpaved Old Pony Express and Stage Route; or from Delta, it is northeast 16 miles on U.S. Hwy. 6, left onto State Hwy. 174 for about 41 miles to the end of pavement, continuing straight for about 15 miles to the intersection with Pony Express Route, and left for about 7 miles. Information: (435) 831-5353.

Virginia

Featherstone contains 325 acres to manage and protect an area of tidal marsh and riparian hardwood forest along the Potomac River and one side of the mouth of Neabsco Creek, near Woodbridge, in northern Virginia. These habitats attract waterfowl, ospreys, and numerous species of neotropical songbirds. The refuge is presently not open to visitation, but if a suitable access onto the refuge can be negotiated, a hiking trail will likely be provided. Information: (703) 490-4979.

Fisherman Island contains 1,850 acres to protect a vital barrier-island stopover area for numerous migrating birds and butterflies, as well as nesting habitat for such species as brown pelicans, glossy ibises, black ducks, skimmers, ospreys, and royal and sandwich terns. The refuge is located just south of Cape Charles, at the mouth of Chesapeake Bay, in southeastern Virginia. While all other Virginia barrier islands are shrinking in size, Fisherman Island has been growing. The Chesapeake Bay Bridge-Tunnel runs across the island. Access to the refuge is only by prearranged tour from October through March. Information: (757) 331-2760.

James River contains 4,200 acres to protect an area of mostly wooded habitat along the James River, primarily for the long-term benefit of the thousands of bald eagles that roost along this stretch of the river—one of the largest summer roosting areas east of the Mississippi River. The refuge is located about 30 miles southeast of Richmond, in east-central Virginia. Other wildlife includes many species of ducks, Canada geese, herons, ospreys, numerous neotropical songbirds, white-tailed deer, red foxes, and beavers. Visitor activities are presently limited to seasonal hunting, but future plans are expected to include hiking trails and conservation education programs. Information: (804) 333-1470.

Nansemond contains 423 acres to protect an area of tidal marsh and the Nansemond River estuary, a tributary of the James River, just west of Norfolk, in southeastern Virginia. Because this refuge lies within a U.S. military facility, it is closed to visitation. Information: (757) 986-3705.

Plum Tree Island contains 3,501 acres to protect wetland habitat for waterfowl, shorebirds, and other wildlife. The refuge is closed to visitation because of unexploded ordnance on this former military bombing range. Information: (757) 721-2412.

Presquile contains 1,329 acres to manage and protect an island in the James River, a few miles downstream from Richmond, in east-central Virginia. Roughly half the island consists of seasonally flooded bottomland hardwood forest and swamp, and the rest is tidally influenced marsh and upland fields. About 300 acres of upland are being converted to native grassland to provide winter forage for Canada geese and nesting cover for bobwhite quail. Bald eagles and ospreys nest here; and nesting boxes are provided for wood ducks. Concentrations of wintering ducks of many species and Canada and snow geese are attracted to adjacent waters. Visitor activities include wildlife observation, hiking a 0.75-mile trail, and seasonal hunting (canoeing to the island is discouraged because of strong river currents). Information about the refuge and access: (804) 333-1470.

Rappahannock River Valley contains more than 7,700 acres toward a goal of 20,000 acres to enhance and protect tidal marsh, woodland, and former agricultural fields, located along the tidal portion of this major Chesapeake Bay tributary, in eastern Virginia. Tens of thousands of wintering and migrating waterfowl, notably as many as 30,000 Canada geese and ducks of many species, feed and rest along the river's open waters and adjacent wetlands and fields of this area. Hundreds of bald eagles roost and feed along the river and its tidal creeks; and as many as 80 active bald eagle nests that produced over a hundred young were recorded on the refuge in 2001. Other wildlife includes numerous neotropical songbirds, white-tailed deer, red foxes, river otters, and beavers.

Visitor activities on the Wilna tract include wildlife observation, hiking on a trail (others are planned), conservation education programs (by advance reservation), canoeing and kayaking on 35-acre Wilna Pond, and seasonal hunting. Four other tracts of the refuge are open only by reservation. Information about the refuge and access: (804) 333-1470.

Wallops Island contains 3,737 acres to enhance and protect parts of this coastal barrier island, located in the northeast corner of the Eastern Shore of Virginia. Roughly half of the island consists of salt marsh, through which numerous tidal creeks meander and two man-made channels intersect. Wildlife attracted to the wetland habitat includes wintering snow geese and such nesting ducks as black ducks, gadwalls, and blue-winged teal. Among other wildlife are ospreys, herons, egrets, shorebirds, and white-tailed deer. Because this refuge is under special management with the National Aeronautical and Space Administration (NASA), it is closed to visitation. Information: (757) 336-6122.

Washington

Conboy Lake contains 6,532 acres to restore and manage this lake for migrating and wintering waterfowl and other wildlife, located at the southeastern foot of 12,276-foot Mount Adams, in south-central Washington. From February to April, concentrations of tundra swans, Canada geese, and many species of ducks, along with bald eagles, are attracted here. The refuge is one of only three places in this state where sandhill cranes nest. Blue and ruffed grouse and wild turkeys are among the resident birds. The scenic valley in which Conboy Lake is situated consists of meadows, deciduous woodland, and coniferous forest.

Visitor activities include wildlife observation, driving public roads that run through the refuge, hiking a 2-mile loop trail, and seasonal hunting on parts of the refuge. Access from State Hwy. 14 at Underwood (in the Columbia River Gorge) is north 21 miles on State Hwy. 141 and right 9 miles. Information: (509) 364-3410.

Copalis Rock contains 60 acres and was established by President Theodore Roosevelt in 1907 to provide protection for nesting seabirds, along the coast of the Olympic Peninsula, in northwestern Washington. This refuge is managed jointly with two others, Flattery Rocks and Quillayute Needles; and all three are within the Washington Islands Wilderness that encompasses more than 800 islands, rocks, and reefs dotted along 100 miles of Pacific Coast, from Cape Flattery south to Copalis Beach. Among the thousands of nesting seabirds are murres, puffins, auklets, and petrels. Migrating waterfowl and shorebirds are also abundant. Marine mammals include harbor and fur seals, northern and California sea lions, and sea otters. The islands are closed to visitation to avoid disturbing the nesting birdlife. Boaters are urged to stay well away from the islands (at least 200 yards). (See Quillayute Needles NWR for further details.) Information: (360) 457-8451.

Dungeness contains 772 acres to protect the 5.5-mile-long Dungeness Spit with its sand and gravel beaches and adjacent sheltered tideflats and bay, extending from the northeast shore of the Olympic Peninsula into the Strait of Juan de Fuca, in northwestern Washington. Waterfowl and shorebirds are attracted here. Visitor activities include wildlife observation, hiking a 0.4-mile trail that leads up a bluff to an overlook, hiking the 4.5-mile beach to the lighthouse, boating (refuge waters are open to boating, clamming, and crabbing from May 15 through September; no-wake zone), and tours of the historic New Dungeness Lighthouse. Access from Sequim is west 5 miles on U.S. Hwy. 101 and right onto Kitchen-Dick Rd. for 3 miles. Information: (360) 457-8451.

Flattery Rocks contains 125 acres and was established by President Theodore Roosevelt in 1907 to provide protection for nesting seabirds, along the coast of the Olympic Peninsula, in northwestern Washington. (See Quillayute Needles NWR and Copalis Rock NWR for further details.) Information: (360) 457-8451.

Franz Lake contains 553 acres to protect an area of tidal wetland for wintering tundra swans and other waterfowl, located along the north bank of the Columbia River, within the Columbia River Gorge, in southwestern Washington. The refuge is closed to visitation, but can be seen from an interpretive overlook near Milepost 32 on State Hwy. 14, about 30 miles east of Vancouver or 14 miles west of Stevenson. Information: (509) 427-5208.

McNary contains 3,294 acres in three divisions to provide mitigation for wildlife habitat, near the junction of the Snake and Columbia Rivers, which was inundated by the reservoir created behind McNary Dam, about 30 miles downstream on the Columbia River. The refuge attracts concentrations of tundra swans, Canada geese, and ducks of many species. MCNARY DIVI-SION consists of a narrow area of wetland habitat with ponds and a slough, adjacent to the community of Burbank.

Visitor activities include wildlife observation, viewing interpretive displays at the environmental education center, hiking a 1-mile loop trail, and seasonal hunting on parts of the refuge. STRAWBERRY ISLAND DIVISION, containing an island in the Snake River, is closed to entry from Oct. 1 through June; and HANFORD ISLAND DIVISION, containing seven islands in the Columbia River, is closed during spring and summer to avoid disturbing nesting birds. Access to the refuge headquarters from I-82 at Pasco is south a mile on U.S. Hwy. 395 and east on Maple St. Information: (509) 545-8588.

Pierce contains 337 acres to manage and protect a small but important area of wetland, a chum salmon-spawning stream, grassland, and forested habitats that attract Canada geese, ducks of many species, bald eagles, and other wildlife. The refuge is located adjacent to Beacon Rock State Park, on the north bank of the Columbia River, within the Columbia River Gorge, in southern Washington. Although the refuge is closed to visitation, it can be seen from the state park, which is reached by way of State Hwy. 14, about 35 miles east of Vancouver or 9 miles west of Stevenson. Information: (509) 427-5208.

Protection Island contains 364 acres to protect a major seabird nesting island at the mouth of Discovery Bay, off the northeast shore of the Olympic Peninsula, in northwestern Washington. The refuge supports more than 70 percent of all seabirds that nest in Puget Sound, including an estimated 12,000 pairs of the burrow-nesting rhinoceros auklet. Other birds include pelagic cormorants, pigeon guillemots, and tufted puffins. Waterfowl, such as brant, Canada geese, three species of scoters, harlequin ducks, and long-tailed ducks, are attracted to the waters around the island. A few hundred harbor seals haul themselves onto the island's rocky beaches. The refuge is closed to visitation to avoid disturbing the wildlife. Boaters are urged to stay well away from the island (at least 200 yards). Commercial tours are available. Information: (360) 457-8451.

San Juan Islands contains 448 acres to protect more than 80 islands, rocks, and reefs that provide habitat for nesting seabird colonies, scattered throughout the San Juan Islands, at the northern end of Puget Sound, in northwestern Washington. Most of the islands are within the National Wilderness Preservation System. Seabirds include cormorants, pigeon guillemots, and rhinoceros auklets. Loons, grebes, and ducks of many species are attracted to the waters around the islands; and bald eagles nest and winter on and around the refuge. Harbor seals commonly haul themselves onto beaches and rocks. Harbor porpoises and orcas (the killer "whale" that is a large member of the dolphin family) inhabit Puget Sound.

The refuge is closed to visitation, except for Turn Island (near Friday Harbor) and Matia Island (northwest of Orcas Island), where moorage buoys and docks are available and where state parks offer primitive picnicking and camping sites. Hiking on Matia is permitted only on a 1-mile wilderness trail. Information: (360) 457-8451.

Steigerwald Lake contains 974 acres to provide partial mitigation for construction of a second powerhouse at Bonneville Dam. The refuge is located on the north bank of the Columbia River, at the western end of the Columbia River Gorge, in southwestern Washington. Several thousand wintering Canada geese can be seen here, along with ducks of several species. Bald eagles are attracted by annual spawning runs of coho and Chinook salmon and steelhead. The refuge is closed to visitation, but the Columbia River Dike Trail, which starts in Steamboat Landing State Park, offers opportunities for wildlife observation and hiking. The refuge is located just east of Washougal and about 15 miles east of Vancouver. Information: (509) 427-5208.

Toppenish contains 1,978 acres to manage wetland habitat of marshes and ponds along Toppenish Creek for migrating, nesting, and wintering waterfowl and other wildlife. The refuge is located within the Yakima Indian Reservation, in the Yakima River Valley of south-central Washington. Large concentrations of Canada geese and numerous species of ducks pause here during migrations. Trumpeter swans, geese, and many thousands of ducks winter on the refuge, along with bald eagles. Visitor activities include wildlife observation, hiking a 1-mile loop trail, and seasonal hunting on parts of the refuge. Access from I-84's Exit 104 is northeast about 57 miles on U.S. Hwy. 97; or from State Hwy. 22 at Toppenish, it is about 6 miles southwest on U.S. Hwy. 97. Information: (509) 545-8588.

West Virginia

Ohio River Islands contains 3,221 acres along 362 miles of the Ohio River. The refuge presently includes all or part of 21 islands and three mainland tracts in northwestern West Virginia; two islands just downriver from Pittsburgh, Pennsylvania; and two islands in northern Kentucky. Over a dozen other islands and up to 100 embayment wetlands within the refuge's authorized boundary may ultimately add more than 8,000 acres to the refuge between Pittsburgh and Cincinnati, Ohio. The refuge's mission is to restore and manage ecologically valuable river floodplain hardwood forest habitat for many species of wildlife.

Visitor activities include observation of waterfowl and other wildlife; driving a signed 1.5-mile auto tour route and hiking an interpretive trail on Middle Island; canoeing and boating (including a self-guiding tour route around Muskingum Island, near Parkersburg, W. Va.); and seasonal hunting. Access to Middle Island is by bridge from near St. Marys, W. Va. Information: (304) 422-0752.

Wisconsin

Fox River contains 1,001 acres to enhance and manage an area known as the Fox River Sandhill Crane Marsh and adjacent upland grassland, savanna, and wooded habitats, located north of Portage, in southeastern Wisconsin. This refuge is an important staging and breeding ground for the greater sandhill crane. Other prominent wildlife includes Canada geese, mallards, blue-winged teal, great blue herons, wild turkeys, white-tailed deer, and mink. The refuge is closed to visitation, except for seasonal deer hunting. Access from State Hwy. 23 at Montello is southwest 6 miles on County Rd. F, which runs along the refuge's eastern boundary. Information: (920) 387-2658.

Gravel Island contains 27 acres on 4-acre Gravel Island and 23-acre Spider Island, located in Lake Michigan, off the end of Door Peninsula, in northeastern Wisconsin. To avoid disturbing nesting herring and ring-billed gulls, cormorants, great blue herons, black-crowned night-herons, mallards, black ducks, and common mergansers, the refuge is closed to visitation. Information: (920) 387-2658.

Green Bay contains 2-acre Hog Island, located in Lake Michigan, off the eastern shore of Washington Island, in northeastern Wisconsin. To avoid disturbing nesting herring gulls and waterfowl such as mallards, the refuge is closed to visitation. Information: (920) 387-2658.

Wyoming

Bamforth contains 1,116 acres in three tracts to protect an occasionally flooded playa (salt flat), located about 6 miles northwest of Laramie, in southeastern Wyoming. When there is water, this refuge is transformed to a small mecca for waterfowl and shorebirds. Pronghorn and coyotes are among the mammals inhabiting the surrounding arid habitat. The refuge is closed to visitation. Information: (970) 723-8202.

Cokeville Meadows contains 7,677 acres toward a goal of 27,000 acres to enhance and manage wetland and upland habitats along a 20-mile stretch of the Bear River floodplain, just south of Cokeville, in the southwest corner of Wyoming. The refuge consists of ponds, deep-water marshes, wet-meadow impoundments, irrigated cropland, riparian woodland, and arid uplands of sagebrush and grasses. Among the wildlife attracted here are nesting Canada geese, numerous species of nesting and migrating ducks (notably redheads), great blue herons, colonies of snowy egrets and white-faced ibises, many shorebirds, and nesting greater sandhill cranes and greater sage-grouse. Prominent mammals include pronghorn, mule deer, and wintering elk.

Although the refuge is presently closed to visitation, it is expected that visitor activities will include wildlife observation, hiking, environmental education programs, and seasonal hunting. Access from Cokeville is south on State Hwy. 30, which is adjacent to the refuge's eastern acquisition boundary. Information: (307) 875-2187.

Hutton Lake contains 1,968 acres to manage a cluster of five lakes and related bulrush marsh, with adjacent wet meadows and arid grassland, located south of Laramie, in southeastern

Wyoming. In the spring, these habitats attract as many as 20,000 migratory ducks (notably red-heads and canvasbacks). More than 275 bird species have been recorded here. Visitor activities include wildlife observation from refuge roads that lead to all the lakes. Access from I-80 at Laramie is south 0.5 mile on U.S. Hwy. 287, right onto Fort Sanderson Dr. to the Monolith Concrete Plant, right and across railroad tracks, then left 7 miles on Sand Creek Rd., and right at a refuge directional sign. Information: (970) 723-8202.

Mortenson Lake contains 1,776 acres to manage four areas of wetland habitat for the benefit of the last known breeding population of Wyoming toad. The range of this endangered sub-species is limited to the Laramie plains in southeastern Wyoming. A captive breeding program was implemented over the past few years. According to the F&WS, "Toad releases at Morten-son have occurred since 1995 with numbers ranging between 500 and 6,600 individuals re-leased. Annual surveys of the toads are conducted every spring and fall, and have produced up to 295 juveniles and 27 adults." As of this writing, continuing efforts still hold out the hope that this vulnerable amphibian can be saved from extinction. The refuge is closed to visitation. Information: (970) 723-8202.

Pathfinder contains 16,807 acres to manage habitat for waterfowl and other waterbirds, over-laying four parts of Pathfinder Reservoir, which is 50 miles southwest of Casper, in east-central Wyoming. The wetlands offer resting, feeding, and nesting areas for concentrations of migratory Canada geese and ducks of many species. Adjacent semi-desert is inhabited by such species as sage-grouse, mule deer, pronghorn, bobcats, and coyotes. Visitor activities include wildlife observation and seasonal hunting. Access from Casper is southwest about 50 miles on State Hwy. 220, left onto Buzzard Rd., which passes near the upper end of the reservoir's Sweetwater Arm. Dirt roads branch from this road to the lakeshore and from Pathfinder Rd., which leads to the dam. Information: (970) 723-8202.

5

Friends and Other Refuge Support Organizations

Alabama

Friends of Bon Secour NWR
12295 State Highway 180
Gulf Shores, AL 36542
(334) 540-7720

Friends of Cahaba River NWR
P.O. Box 323
West Blocton, AL 35184
(256) 848-7085

Wheeler Wildlife Refuge Association
P.O. Box 239
Decatur, AL 35602
(256) 544-5930

Alaska

Alaska Natural History Association
401 West First Avenue
Anchorage, AK 99501
(907) 274-8440

Friends of Alaska National Wildlife Refuges
2440 E. Tudor Rd., PMB 283
Anchorage, AK 99507

Friends of the Kenai NWR
P.O. Box 1449
Soldotna, AK 99669
(907) 562-5451

Arizona

Friends of Buenos Aires NWR
P.O. Box 65855
Tucson, AZ 85728
(800) 714-4365

Friends of Cabeza Prieta
P.O. Box 64940
Tucson, AZ 85728
(520) 387-6483

Arkansas

Friends of Felsenthal NWR
P.O. Box 1157
Crossett, AR 71635
(870) 226-6679

California

Dunes Center
P.O. Box 339
Guadalupe, CA 93435
(805) 343-2455

Friends of [the proposed] Alameda NWR
2530 San Pablo Ave., Suite G
Berkeley, CA 94702
(510) 653-9441

Friends of Havasu
P.O. Box 3009
Needles, CA 92363
(760) 326-3853

Friends of Modoc NWR
P.O. Box 1610
Alturas, CA 96101
(530) 233-3572

Friends of San Pablo Bay NWR
7715 Lakeville Hwy.
Petaluma, CA 94954
(707) 769-4200

Friends of Seal Beach NWR
P.O. Box 815
Seal Beach, CA 90740
(562) 430-8495 or 598-1024

Friends of the Dunes (re: Humboldt Bay
   NWR)
P.O. Box 186
Arcata, CA 95518
(707) 444-1397

Friends of the Sacramento Valley Wildlife
   Refuges
P.O. Box 5227
Chico, CA 95927
(530) 898-8468

Friends of the San Diego Refuges
c/o Tijuana Slough NWR
301 Caspian Way
Imperial Beach, CA 91932
(619) 575-2704

Klamath Basin Wildlife Association
Route 1, Box 74
Tulelake, CA 96134
(530) 667-2231

Sacramento Valley Wildlife Association
752 County Road 99W
Willows, CA 95988
(530) 934-2801

Salton Sea Wildlife Association
906 West Sinclair Road
Calipatria, CA 92233
(760) 348-5278

San Francisco Bay Wildlife Society
P.O. Box 524
Newark, CA 94560
(510) 792-0222

Stone Lakes NWR Association
2233 Watt Avenue, Suite 230
Sacramento, CA 95825
(209) 953-8840

Colorado

Friends of San Luis Valley NWR
9383 El Rancho Lane
Alamosa, CO 81101
(719) 587-7211

Rocky Mountain Arsenal Wildlife Society
c/o RMA NWR, Building 111
Commerce City, CO 80022
(303) 289-0820

Two Ponds Preservation Foundation
7692 Garrison Court
Arvada, CO 80002
(303) 423-8085

Connecticut

Friends of Outer Island
P.O. Box 305
Branford, CT 06405

Delaware

Friends of Bombay Hook
2591 Whitehall Neck Road
Smyrna, DE 19977
(302) 653-6872

Friends of Prime Hook NWR
RD 3, Box 195
Milton, DE 19968
(302) 684-8419

Florida

"Ding" Darling Wildlife Society
c/o J. N. "Ding" Darling NWR
1 Wildlife Drive
Sanibel, FL 33957
(941) 472-1100

Friends and Volunteers of the Refuges
    (Florida Keys)
P.O. Box 431840
Big Pine Key, FL 33043
(305) 872-0645

Friends of Lake Woodruff NWR
2045 Mud Lake Rd.
DeLeon Springs, FL 32130
(386) 985-4673

Friends of the Carr Refuge
P.O. Box 510988
Melbourne Beach, FL 32951
(407) 676-1701

Friends of the Chassahowitzka NWR
    Complex
1502 Southeast Kings Bay Drive
Crystal River, FL 34429
(352) 563-2088

Friends of the Florida Panther Refuge
3860 Tollgate Boulevard, Suite 300
Naples, FL 34114
(941) 947-3567

Friends of the Loxahatchee Refuge
P.O. Box 6777
Delray Beach, FL 33482
(561) 734-8303

Hobe Sound Nature Center, Inc.
P.O. Box 214
Hobe Sound, FL 33475
(561) 546-2067

Loxahatchee Natural History Association
P.O. Box 2737
Delray Beach, FL 33447
(561) 338-5190

Merritt Island Wildlife Association
c/o Merritt Island NWR
P.O. Box 6504
Titusville, FL 32782
(407) 861-0667

Pelican Island Preservation Society
P.O. Box 781903
Sebastian, FL 32978
(561) 663-9750

St. Marks Refuge Association
c/o St. Marks NWR
P.O. Box 368
St. Marks, FL 32355
(850) 386-9212

Georgia

Okefenokee Wildlife League
c/o Okefenokee NWR
Route 2, Box 3330
Folkston, GA 31537
(912) 496-7836

Hawai'i

1000 Friends of Kauai
P.O. Box 698
Kilauea, HI 96754
(808) 828-2166

Friends of Midway Atoll NWR
1048 Edison Avenue
New York, NY 10465
(800) 371-0772

Kilauea Point Natural History Association
c/o Kilauea Point NWR
P.O. Box 1128
Kilauea, HI 96754
(808) 828-1413

Idaho

Friends of Deer Flat Wildlife Refuge
13751 Upper Embankment Rd.
Nampa, ID 83686
(208) 468-0402

Friends of Kootenai NWR
P.O. Box 1101
Bonners Ferry, ID 83805

Illinois

Friends of Crab Orchard
8588 Route 148
Marion, IL 62918
(618) 997-3344

Friends of Illinois River
700 East Adams
Springfield, IL 62701
(217) 525-7980

Friends of the Cache River Watershed (re:
    Cypress Creek NWR)
1220 Old Highway 51N
Anna, IL 62906
(618) 833-5343

Indiana

Muscatatuck Wildlife Society
c/o Muscatatuck NWR
12987 East U.S. Highway 50
Seymour, IN 47274
(812) 579-5127

PRIDE (re: Patoka River NWR)
540 Oriole Drive
Evansville, IN 47715
(812) 476-3248

Iowa

Friends of Boyer Chute & DeSoto NWRs
1434 – 316 Lane
Missouri Valley, IA 51555
(712) 642-4121

Friends of the Prairie Learning Center
c/o Neal Smith NWR
P.O. Box 399
Prairie City, IA 50228
(515) 787-5705

Friends of Union Slough NWR
1710 - 360th Street
Titonka, IA 50480
(515) 928-2523

Midwest Interpretive Association
c/o Desoto NWR
1434-316th Lane
Missouri Valley, IA 51555
(712) 642-2772

Kansas

Friends of Quivira NWR
2458 Coolidge
Wichita, KS 67204
(316) 838-4062

Kentucky

Friends of Clarks River NWR
P.O. Box 89
Benton, KY 42025
(270) 527-5770

Louisiana

Friends of Black Bayou, Inc.
P.O. Box 9241
Monroe, LA 71211
(318) 387-5906

Friends of Cat Island NWR, Inc.
P.O. Box 1926
St. Francisville, LA 70775
(225) 635-4753

Friends of Louisiana Wildlife Refuges, Inc.
P.O. Box 890
Lacombe, LA 70445
(504) 646-7555

Red River Refuge Alliance
P.O. Box 52506
Shreveport, LA 71135

Tensas River Refuge Association
Route 2, Box 295
Tallulah, LA 71282
(318) 574-2664

Maine

Friends of Aroostook NWR
P.O. Box 121
Caribou, ME 04736
(207) 498-3639

Friends of Maine Seabird Islands
P.O. Box 232
Rockport, ME 04856
(207) 236-6970

Friends of Moosehorn
103 Headquarters Rd., Unit 10
Baring, ME 04694
(207) 454-7161

Friends of Rachel Carson NWR
P.O. Box 7427
Ocean Park, ME 04063
(207) 646-9226

Friends of Sunkhaze Meadows NWR
1033 South Main Street
Old Town, ME 04468
(207) 827-6138

Maryland

Friends of Blackwater NWR, Inc.
5123 Brook Road
Woolford, MD 21613
(410) 221-1874

Friends of Eastern Neck, Inc.
21170 Green Lane
Rock Hall, MD 21661
(410) 639-7085

Friends of Patuxent Wildlife Research
Center
c/o Patuxent Wildlife Research Center
10901 Scarlet Tanager Loop
Laurel, MD 20708
(301) 262-1010

Massachusetts

Friends of Great Meadows NWR
63 Lexington Road
Concord, MA 01742
(617) 248-8468

Friends of Mashpee NWR
P.O. Box 1283
Mashpee, MA 02649
(508) 495-1702

Friends of Monomoy NWR
c/o Monomoy NWR
Wikis Way
Chatham, MA 02633
(617) 720-6333

Friends of Oxbow NWR
P.O. Box 646
Bolton, MA 01740
(978) 779-2259

Friends of Parker River NWR
P.O. Box 184
Newburyport, MA 01950
(978) 749-9647

Michigan

Friends of Shiawassee NWR
P.O. Box 20129
Saginaw, MI 48602
(517) 790-3178

Seney Natural History Association
c/o Seney NWR
HCR #2, Box 1
Seney, MI 49883
(906) 586-9851

Minnesota

Big Stone Natural History Association
902 South Seventh Street
Milbank, SD 57252
(605) 432-6158

Friends of Rice Lake Refuge
36289 State Hwy. 65
McGregor, MN 55760
(218) 768-2402

Friends of Rydell Refuge Association
Route 3, Box 75A
Erskine, MN 56535
(218) 574-2622

Friends of Sherburne NWR
c/o Sherburne NWR
17076-293rd Avenue
Zimmerman, MN 55398
(612) 389-1696

Friends of the Minnesota Valley
c/o Minnesota Valley NWR Visitor Center
3815 East Eightieth Street
Bloomington, MN 55426
(612) 858-0706

Friends of the Prairie Wetlands Learning
  Center
c/o Fergus Falls WMD
P.O. Box 23
Fergus Falls, MN 56537
(218) 826-6515

Tamarac Interpretive Association
35704 County Highway 26
Rochert, MN 56578
(218) 847-2641

Mississippi

Friends of Dahomey NWR, Inc.
123 South Court Street
Cleveland, MS 38732
(601) 843-6100

Friends of Noxubee Refuge
2970 Bluff Lake Rd.
Brooksville, MS 39739
(662) 323-5548

St. Catherine Creek Refuge Association,
  Inc.
P.O. Box 1027
Natchez, MS 39121
(601) 442-0585

Missouri

Friends of Big Muddy
P.O. Box 58
Columbia, MO 65205
(573) 445-0086

Friends of Squaw Creek NWR
9718 East Fifty-Third Street
Raytown, MO 64133
(816) 353-9024

Midwest Interpretive Association
c/o Mingo NWR
RR I, Box I03
Puxico, MO 63960
(314) 222-3589

Montana

Glacier Natural History Association
c/o National Bison Range
P.O. Box 428
West Glacier, MT 59936
(406) 888-5756

Nebraska

Fort Niobrara Natural History Association
839 West B Street
Valentine, NE 6920I
(402) 376-590I or 3789

Nevada

Friends of Sheldon Refuge
P.O. Box 3I07
Winnemucca, NV 89445
(775) 623-3376

Order of the Antelope
P.O. Box 6I3
Lakeview, OR 97630
(54I) 947-3I47

New Hampshire

Friends of Great Bay NWR
336 Nimble Hill Road
Newington, NH 0380I
(603) 523-1136

Friends of John Hay NWR
P.O. Box 276
Newbury, NH 03255
(603) 763-4789

Friends of Pondicherry (re: Silvio O. Conte
    NWR)
Owl's Head Highway, Box 157A
Jefferson, NH 03583
(603) 586-4598

Friends of Umbagog
3 Silk Farm Road
Concord, NH 03301
(603) 224-9909, ext. 317

Friends of Wapack
P.O. Box 115
Peterborough, NH 03468
(603) 878-4251

New Jersey

Friends of Forsythe NWR
P.O. Box 355
Oceanville, NJ 08231
(609) 641-4671

Friends of Great Swamp NWR
c/o Great Swamp NWR
152 Pleasant Plains Road
Basking Ridge, NJ 07920
(973) 635-1083

New Mexico

Friends of Bitter Lake NWR
P.O. Box 7
Roswell, NM 88202
(505) 622-6755

Friends of Bosque del Apache NWR
P.O. Box 340
San Antonio, NM 87832
(505) 835-1828

New York

Friends of Iroquois NWR
c/o Iroquois NWR
1101 Casey Road
Basom, NY 14013
(716) 948-9154

Friends of Montezuma NWR
c/o Montezuma NWR
3395 Route 5 & 20E
Seneca Falls, NY 13148
(315) 568-5987

Friends of Wertheim
P.O. Box 376
Brookhaven, NY 11719
(516) 286-5897

North Carolina

Coastal Wildlife Society (re: Alligator River
  and Pea Island NWRs)
P.O. Box 1808
Manteo, NC 27954
(252) 473-1131, ext. 230

Friends of Pee Dee NWR
8138 Cedarbrook Drive
Charlotte, NC 28215
(800) 476-8220

Partnership for the Sounds
P.O. Box 55
Columbia, NC 27925
(252) 796-1000

Red Wolf Coalition
P.O. Box 2318
Kill Devil Hills, NC 27948
(252) 441-3946

North Dakota

Chase Lake Foundation (re: Chase Lake
  NWR)
3156 Fifty-Fifth Avenue SE
Medina, ND 58467
(701) 486-3228

Sullys Hill Wildlife Refuge Society
P.O. Box 286
Ft. Totten, ND 58335
(701) 766-4573

Theodore Roosevelt Nature and History
  Association (re: Sullys Hill NGP and
  Upper Souris NWR)
P.O. Box 167
Medora, ND 58745
(701) 623-4884

Ohio

Ottawa NWR Association
P.O. Box 254
Oak Harbor, OH 43449
(419) 836-8411

Oklahoma

Association of the Friends of the Wichitas
  (re: Wichita Mountains WR)
P.O. Box 7402
Lawton, OK 73506
(580) 537-5488

Friends of Tishomingo Refuge
P.O. Box 144
Tishomingo, OK 73460
(580) 371-9248

Great Salt Plains Association (re: Salt
  Plains NWR)
111 South Grand
Cherokee, OK 73728
(580) 596-3053

Oregon

Friends of Haystack Rock
P.O. Box 1222
Cannon Beach, OR 97110

Friends of Sheldon Refuge (re: Sheldon
    and Hart Mountain NWRs)
P.O. Box 3107
Winnemucca, NV 89445
(775) 623-3376

Friends of the Tualatin River NWR
P.O. Box 1306
Sherwood, OR 97140
(503) 625-1205

Malheur Refuge Association
c/o Malheur NWR
HC 72, Box 245
Princeton, OR 97721
(541) 493-2612

Order of the Antelope
P.O. Box 613
Lakeview, OR 97630
(541) 947-3147

Pennsylvania

Friends of Heinz Wildlife Refuge at Tinicum
2 International Plaza, Suite 104
Philadelphia, PA 19113
(610) 534-0698

Rhode Island

Friends of the NWRs of Rhode Island
P.O. Box 553
Charlestown, RI 02813
(401) 364-9124

South Carolina

SEWEE Association, Inc. (re: Cape Ro-
    main NWR)
P.O. Box 1131
Mt. Pleasant, SC 29465
(843) 884-7539

Friends of Santee NWR
2125 Ft. Watson Rd.
Summerton, SC 29148
(803) 478-2217

South Dakota

Friends of the Prairie
P.O. Box 446
Milbank, SD 57252
(605) 432-9229

Tennessee

Friends of Hatchie Refuge
4172 Highway 76
South Brownsville, TN 38012
(731) 772-0501, ext. 25

Friends of Reelfoot NWR (also re: Lake
Isom NWR)
Room 129, Federal Building
Dyersville, TN 38024
(731) 287-0650

Texas

Friends of Anahuac Refuge
111 Welch, Apartment B
Houston, TX 77006
(409) 267-3080

Friends of Aransas and Matagorda Island
NWRs
P.O. Box 74
Aransas, TX 77950
(361) 286-3559

Friends of Balcones
c/o Balcones Canyonlands NWR
10711 Burnett Road, Ste 201
Austin, TX 78758
(515) 339-9432

Friends of Brazoria NWR
P.O. Box 505
Lake Jackson, TX 77566
(409) 297-7726

Friends of Hagerman NWR
P.O. Box 178
Sherman, TX 75091
(903) 786-2826

Friends of Laguna Atascosa NWR
P.O. Box 465
Rio Hondo, TX 78583
(956) 428-4897

Friends of the Wildlife Corridor (re: Lower
Rio Grande Valley NWR)
Route 2, Box 204
Alamo, TX 78516
(956) 783-6117

Friends of Trinity River Refuge
P.O. Box 12
Liberty, TX 77575
(936) 336-9847

Valley Nature Center (re: Santa Ana
NWR)
P.O. Box 8125
Weslaco, TX 78599
(956) 969-2475

Utah

Friends of the Bear River Bird Refuge
58 South 950 West
Brigham City, UT 84302
(435) 734-9464

Vermont

Friends of Missisquoi NWR
371 N. River Street
Swanton, VT 05488
(802) 868-4781

Virginia

Chincoteague Natural History Association
   (also re: Eastern Shore of Virginia
   NWR)
c/o Chincoteague NWR
P.O. Box 917
Chincoteague, VA 23336
(757) 336-3696

Friends of Back Bay
2232 Sandpiper Road
Virginia Beach, VA 23456
(757) 721-5011

Friends of Potomac River Refuges
14344 Jefferson Davis Hwy.
Woodbridge, VA 22191
(703) 490-4979

Great Dismal Swamp Coalition, Inc.
P.O. Box 847
Suffolk, VA 23439
(757) 986-3705

Rappahannock Wildlife Refuge Friends
P.O. Box 1565
Warsaw, VA 22572
(804) 566-6851

Washington

Friends of Little Pend Oreille NWR
Box 215
Colville, WA 99114
(509) 684-8384

Friends of Mid-Columbia River Wildlife
   Refuges
311 Lake Rd.
Burbank, WA 99323
(509) 543-8322

Friends of Nisqually Refuge
100 Brown Farm Rd.
Olympia, WA 98516
(360) 753-9467

Friends of Ridgefield NWR
c/o Ridgefield NWR
Ridgefield, WA 98642
(360) 887-4106

Friends of Turnbull NWR
P.O. Box 294
Cheney, WA 99004
(509) 328-0621

Friends of Willapa NWR
P.O. Box 627
Ocean Park, WA 98640
(360) 665-6859

West Virginia

Friends of the 500th (re: Canaan Valley NWR)
P.O. Box 422
Davis, WV 26260
(304) 866-4114

Wisconsin

Friends of Necedah NWR
1830 County
Clarkdale, WI 54613
(608) 564-7104

Friends of the Upper Mississippi River
  Refuges
West 5094 Highland Place
La Crosse, WI 54601
(608) 787-0853

Midwest Interpretive Association
c/o Horicon NWR
West 4279 Headquarters Road
Mayville, WI 53050
(414) 387-2658

Upper Mississippi River Interpretive
  Association
555 Lester Avenue
Onalaska, WI 54650
(608) 783-8403

Wyoming

National Museum of Wildlife Art
c/o National Elk Refuge
P.O. Box 6825
Jackson, WY 83002
(307) 733-5771

National Organizations

Boone and Crockett Club
250 Station Drive
Missoula, MT 59801
(406) 542-1888
www.boone-crockett.org

Defenders of Wildlife
1101 14th Street, NW, Suite 1400
Washington, DC 20005
(877) 682-9400
www.defenders.org

Ducks Unlimited, Inc.
One Waterfowl Way
Memphis, TN 38120
(901) 758-3825
www.ducks.org

National Audubon Society
700 Broadway
New York, NY 10003
(212) 979-3000
www.audubon.org

National Park Trust
415 Second Street, NE
Washington, DC 20002
(202) 548-0500
www.parktrust.org

National Wildlife Refuge Association
1901 Pennsylvania Avenue, NW, #407
Washington, DC 20006
(202) 333-9075
www.refugenet.org

The Nature Conservancy
4245 North Fairfax Drive, Suite 100
Arlington, VA 22203
(800) 628-6860
www.tnc.org

Wildlife Forever
2700 Freeway Boulevard, Suite 1000
Brooklyn Center, MN 55430
(763) 253-0222
www.wildlifeforever.org

Appendix: References and Further Reading

Alsop, Fred J. *Birds of North America: Eastern Region* (Smithsonian Handbooks). New York: DK Publishing, Inc., 2001.

——. *Birds of North America: Western Region* (Smithsonian Handbooks). New York: DK Publishing, Inc., 2001.

Amos, William H. *Assateague Island: A Guide to Assateague Island National Seashore, Maryland and Virginia.* National Park Handbook 106. Washington, D.C.: U.S. Department of the Interior, 1980.

Armstrong, Robert H. *Guide to the Birds of Alaska* (Fourth Edition). Portland, Oregon: Alaska Northwest Books/Graphic Arts Center Publishing Company, 1998.

Beasley, Conger, Jr. *Wichita Mountains Wildlife Refuge.* Albuquerque, New Mexico: Southwest Natural and Cultural Heritage Association, 1997.

Behler, John L. *The Audubon Society Field Guide to North American Reptiles & Amphibians.* New York: Alfred A. Knopf, Inc., 1979.

Brown, David E. *Arizona Game Birds.* Tucson, Arizona: University of Arizona Press, 1993.

Bull, John, and John Farrand, Jr. *National Audubon Society Field Guide to North American Birds: Eastern Region* (revised edition). New York: Alfred A. Knopf, Inc., 2000.

Burt, William Henry. *A Field Guide to the Mammals: North America North of Mexico* (Peterson Field Guides, third edition). Boston: Houghton Mifflin Company, 1980.

Butcher, Devereux. *Exploring Our National Wildlife Refuges.* Boston: Houghton Mifflin Company, 1963.

Butcher, Russell D. *The Desert.* New York: The Viking Press, 1976.

Cahalane, Victor H. *Mammals of North America.* New York: The Macmillan Company, 1947.

Carson, Rachel. *Silent Spring.* Boston: Houghton Mifflin Company, 1962.

Cartright, Paul Russell. *Lewis and Clark: Pioneering Naturalists.* Urbana, Illinois: University of Illinois Press, 1969.

Cerulean, Susan, and Ann Morrow. *Florida Wildlife Viewing Guide.* Helena, Montana: Falcon Publishing Company, 1993.

Chadwick, Douglas H. "Sanctuary: U.S. National Wildlife Refuges," *National Geographic,* Vol. 190, No. 4. Washington, D.C.: The National Geographic Society, October 1996.

Collingwood, G.H., Warren D. Brush, and revised and edited by Devereux Butcher. *Knowing Your Trees.* Washington, D.C.: The American Forestry Association (renamed American Forests), 1978.

Crisler, Lois. *Arctic Wild.* New York: Harper & Row, Publishers, 1958.

Curson, Jon, David Quinn, and David Beadle. *Warblers of the Americas: An Identification Guide.* Boston: Houghton Mifflin Company, 1994.

Darling, Jay N. "Ding." "The Story of the Wildlife Refuge Program," *National Parks Magazine,* Vol. 28, Nos. 116 and 117. Washington, D.C.: National Parks Association, January-March and April-June 1954.

Day, Albert M. *North American Waterfowl.* New York: Stackpole and Heck, Inc., 1949.

Dolin, Eric Jay, and Bob Dumaine. *The Duck Stamp Story.* Iola, Wisconsin: Krause Publications, 2000.

Dolin, Eric Jay. Photographs by John and Karen Hollingsworth. *Smithsonian Book of National Wildlife Refuges.* Washington: Smithsonian Books, 2003.

Dunn, Jon L., and Kimball L. Garrett. *A Field Guide to Warblers of North America* (Peterson Field Guides). Boston: Houghton Mifflin Company, 1997.

Dykinga, Jack W. (photographs), and Charles Bowden. *The Sonoran Desert.* New York: Harry N. Abrams, Inc., 1992.

Furtman, Michael. *Duck Country: A Celebration of America's Favorite Waterfowl.* Memphis, Tennessee: Ducks Unlimited, Inc., 2001.

Gabrielson, Ira N. *Wildlife Conservation.* New York: The Macmillan Company, 1941.

———. *Wildlife Refuges.* New York: The Macmillan Company, 1943.

Gilmore, Jackie. *Wildlife Legacy: The National Elk Refuge.* Moose, Wyoming: Backwaters Publications, 1993.

Gilmore, Jene C. *Art for Conservation: The Federal Duck Stamps.* Barre, Vermont: Barre Publishers, 1971.

Gooders, John, and Trevor Boyer. *Ducks of North America and the Northern Hemisphere.* New York: Facts on File, Inc., 1986.

Graetz, Rick and Susie. *Montana's Charles M. Russell National Wildlife Refuge.* Helena, Montana: Northern Rockies Publishing Company, 1999.

Graham, Frank. *The Audubon Ark.* New York: Alfred A. Knopf, 1990; Austin, Texas: University of Texas Press, 1992.

Grove, Noel. *Wild Lands for Wildlife: America's National Refuges.* Washington, D.C.: National Geographic Society, 1984.

Gurlach, Duane (ed.). *The Wildlife Series: Deer.* Mechanicsburg, Pennsylvania: Stackpole Books, 1994.

Handy, E.S. Craighill, and Elizabeth Green Handy. *Native Planters in Old Hawaii: Their Life, Lore, and Environment.* Honolulu, Hawai'i: Bishop Museum Press, 1991.

Harrison, Peter. *Seabirds of the World: A Photographic Guide.* Princeton, New Jersey: Princeton University Press, 1987.

Hawkins, A.S., R.C. Hanson, H.K. Nelson, and H.M. Reeves (eds.). *Flyways: Pioneering Waterfowl Management in North America.* Washington, D.C.: U.S. Department of the Interior, Fish & Wildlife Service, 1984.

Hedin, Robert, and Gary Holthaus (eds.). *Alaska: Reflections on Land and Spirit.* Tucson, Arizona: The University of Arizona Press, 1989.

Hollingsworth, John and Karen. *Seasons of the Wild: A Journey Through Our National Wildlife Refuges.* Bellevue, Colorado: Worm Press, 1994.

Hornaday, William T. *Our Vanishing Wildlife.* New York: New York Zoological Society, 1913.

———. *Thirty Years War for Wildlife.* New York: Scribners, 1931.

Hunter, Celia, and Ginny Wood. *Alaska National Interest Lands.* Anchorage: Alaska: *Alaska Geographic,* Vol. 8, No. 4, The Alaska Geographic Society, 1981.

Hymon, Steve. "Bringing Up Coral" (endangered coral reef ecosystems), *National Parks,* Vol. 75, No. 9-10. Washington, D.C.: National Parks Conservation Association, September-October 2001.

Jewell, Susan. *Exploring Wild South Florida.* Sarasota, Florida: Pineapple Press, 1997.

Jones, Stephen R. *The Last Prairie: A Sandhill Journal.* Camden, Maine: Ragged Mountain Press, 2000.

Kortright, F. H., *The Ducks, Geese, and Swans of North America.* Washington, D.C.: American Wildlife Institute, 1942.

Landau, Diana (ed.). *Wolf: Spirit of the Wild.* Berkeley, California: The Nature Company, 1993.

Laycock, George. *The Sign of the Flying Goose.* New York: The Natural History Press, 1965; Garden City, New York: Anchor Natural History Books, 1973.

LeMaster, Richard. *The Great Gallery of Ducks and Other Waterfowl.* Mechanicsburg, Pennsylvania: Stackpole Books, 1985.

Linduska, Joseph P. (ed.). *Waterfowl Tomorrow.* Washington, D.C.: U.S. Department of the Interior, Fish and Wildlife Service, 1964.

Maass, David (art) and Michael McIntosh (text). *Wildfowl of North America.* St. Paul, Minnesota: Brown & Bigelow, Inc., 1999.

Madson, John. *Where the Sky Began: Land of the Tallgrass Prairie.* Ames, Iowa: Iowa State University Press, 1982.

Mathiessen, Peter. *Wildlife in America.* New York: The Viking Press, 1987.

Maurer, Stephen G. *Bosque del Apache National Wildlife Refuge.* Albuquerque, New Mexico: Southwest Natural and Cultural Heritage Association, 1994.

McAlister, Wayne H. and Martha K. *Aransas: A Naturalist's Guide.* Austin, Texas: University of Texas Press, 1995.

———. *Matagorda Island: A Naturalist's Guide.* Austin, Texas: University of Texas Press, 1993.

McManus, Reed. "Where the Caribou Roam" (Arctic National Wildlife Refuge), *Sierra,* Vol. 85, No. 4. San Francisco, California: Sierra Club, July/August 2000.

Miller, Debbie S., Roger Kaye, and L.J. Campbell. *Arctic National Wildlife Refuge.* Anchorage, Alaska: *Alaska Geographic,* Vol. 20, No. 3, The Alaska Geographic Society, 1993.

Murie, Olaus J. *The Elk of North America.* Washington, D.C.: Wildlife Management Institute, 1951.

Murphy, Robert. *Wild Sanctuaries: Our National Wildlife Refuges—A Heritage Restored.* New York: E.P. Dutton & Co., 1968.

National Audubon Society. *Audubon Guide to the National Wildlife Refuges* (9 regional guides by various authors). New York: St. Martin's Griffin, 2000.

National Geographic. *Field Guide to the Birds of North America* (Third Edition). Washington, D.C.: National Geographic Society, 1999.

Niemeyer, Lucien (photographs) and George W. Folkerts (text). *Okefenokee.* Jackson, Mississippi: University Press of Mississippi, 2002.

O'Neill, David, and Elizabeth A. Domingue. *Paddling Okefenokee National Wildlife Refuge.* Helena, Montana: Falcon Publishing, Inc., 1998.

Opler, Paul. *A Field Guide to Western Butterflies* (Peterson Field Guides, second edition). Boston: Houghton Mifflin Company, 1999.

Parton, William ("Web"). *Wing Shooter's Guide to Arizona.* Gallatin Gateway, Montana: Wilderness Adventures Press, 1996.

Pasquier, Roger F. *Watching Birds: An Introduction to Ornithology.* Boston: Houghton Mifflin Company, 1977.

Perry, John, and Jane Greverus. *Sierra Club Guide to the Natural Areas of Florida.* San Francisco, California: Sierra Club Books, 1992.

Peterson, Roger Tory. *A Field Guide to the Birds of Eastern and Central North America* (Fourth Edition). Boston: Houghton Mifflin Company, 1980.

———. *A Field Guide to Western Birds* (Third Edition). Boston: Houghton Mifflin Company, 1990.

Pratt, H. Douglas, Phillip L. Bruner, and Delwyn G. Berrett. *A Field Guide to the Birds of Hawaii and the Tropical Pacific.* Princeton, New Jersey: Princeton University Press, 1987.

Pyle, Robert Michael. *National Audubon Society Field Guide to North American Butterflies.* New York: Alfred A. Knopf, Inc., 1998.

Raffaele, Herbert A. *A Guide to the Birds of Puerto Rico and the Virgin Islands.* Princeton, New Jersey: Princeton University Press, 1989.

Rauzon, Mark J. *Isles of Refuge: Wildlife and History of the Northwestern Hawaiian Islands.* Honolulu, Hawai'i: University of Hawai'i Press, 2001.

Reed, Nathaniel P., and Dennis Drabelle. *The United States Fish & Wildlife Service.* Boulder, Colorado: Westview Press, 1984.

Riley, Laura and William. *Guide to the National Wildlife Refuges.* New York: Macmillan, Inc., 1979, revised 1992.

Ross-Macdonald, Malcolm (ed.) *The World Wildlife Guide.* New York: The Viking Press, 1971.

Sherwonit, Bill. "Nanuuq of the North" (threats to polar bears), *National Parks,* Vol. 75, No. 9-10. Washington, D.C.: National Parks Conservation Association, September-October 2001.

Sibley, David Allen. *The Sibley Guide to Birds.* New York: Alfred A. Knopf, Inc., 2000.

———. *The Sibley Guide to Bird Life and Behavior.* New York: Alfred A. Knopf, Inc., 2001.

Simmerman, Nancy Lange. *Alaska's Parklands: The Complete Guide.* Seattle, Washington: The Mountaineers, 1983.

Smith, Bruce L., and Russell L. Robbins. *Migrations and Management of the Jackson Elk Herd.* Washington, D.C.: U.S. Department of the Interior, National Biological Survey, 1994.

Svingen, Dan, and Kas Dumroese. *A Birder's Guide to Idaho.* Colorado Springs, Colorado: American Birding Association, Inc., 1997.

Taylor, Kenny. *Puffins.* Stillwater, Minnesota: Voyageur Press, 1999.

Teale, Edwin Way. *North with the Spring.* New York: Dodd, Mead & Company, 1951.

Terborgh, John. *Where Have All the Birds Gone? Essays on the Biology and Conservation of Birds That Migrate to the American Tropics.* Princeton, New Jersey: Princeton University Press, 1989.

Toweill, Dale E., and Valerius Geist. *Return of Royalty: Wild Sheep of North America.* Missoula, Montana: Boone and Crockett Club, 2001.

Trefethen, James B. *An American Crusade for Wildlife.* Alexandria, Virginia: Boone and Crockett Club, 1975, 1985.

Trimble, Stephen. *The Sagebrush Ocean: A Natural History of the Great Basin.* Reno and Las Vegas, Nevada: University of Nevada Press, 1989.

Tuck, Kari. *Klamath Basin National Wildlife Refuges.* Tulelake, California: The Klamath Basin Wildlife Association, 1997.

Udvardy, Miklos D.F. *National Audubon Society Field Guide to North American Birds: Western Region* (revised edition by John Farrand, Jr.). New York: Alfred A. Knopf, Inc., 2000.

Van Meter, Victoria Brook. *The Florida Panther.* Miami, Florida: Florida Power & Light Company, 1988.

Wall, Dennis. *Western National Wildlife Refuges: Thirty-Six Ecological Havens from California to Texas.* Santa Fe, New Mexico: Museum of New Mexico Press, 1996.

Weidensaul, Scott. *Duck Stamps: In the Service of Conservation.* New York: Gallery Books, 1989.

———. *Living on the Wind: Across the Hemisphere with Migratory Birds.* New York: North Point Press, of Farrar, Straus and Giroux, 1999.

———. *The Raptor Almanac.* New York: The Lyons Press, 2000.

Whitaker, John O., Jr. *National Audubon Society Field Guide to North American Mammals* (revised edition). New York: Alfred A. Knopf, Inc., 2001.

White, E.B. *The Trumpet of the Swan.* New York: HarperCollins Publishers, 1970.

White, Mel. *Guide to Birdwatching Sites* (2 volumes: Eastern U.S. and Western U.S.). Washington, D.C.: National Geographic Society, 1999.

Williamson, Sheri L. *Hummingbirds of North America* (Peterson Field Guides). Boston: Houghton Mifflin Company, 2001.

NWR System Index: National Wildlife Refuges

General Index

Other Books by Russell D. Butcher

Maine Paradise
New Mexico: Gift of the Earth
The Desert
Exploring Our National Parks and Monuments (Ninth Edition)
Exploring Our National Historic Parks and Sites
Guide to National Parks (regional guides)
Field Guide to Acadia National Park, Maine

About the Author

Russell D. Butcher is a lifelong conservationist who has worked for such organizations as Save-the-Redwoods League, National Audubon Society, and National Parks Conservation Association. He has written numerous articles and editorials for publications including *National Parks, Audubon, American Forests, Down East,* and the *New York Times.* His books include *Maine Paradise,* a portrait of Mount Desert Island and Acadia National Park in Maine; *The Desert,* with text and photographs highlighting the American West's desert regions; *New Mexico: Gift of the Earth,* with text and photographs featuring many of the state's natural and cultural assets; *Exploring Our National Historic Parks and Sites;* and the ninth edition of his parents' long-popular *Exploring Our National Parks and Monuments* (written by Devereux and Mary Butcher). Russ has traveled extensively throughout the United States and Europe, visiting numerous national parks and wildlife refuges. He and his wife, Karen, live in Tucson, Arizona.